The Double Face of Janus
and Other Essays in the History
of Medicine

OWSEI TEMKIN

The Double Face of Janus

and Other Essays
in the History of
Medicine

THE JOHNS HOPKINS UNIVERSITY PRESS

Baltimore and London

The Johns Hopkins University Press, Baltimore, Maryland 21218
The Johns Hopkins Press Ltd., London
Library of Congress Catalog Card Number 76–47380
ISBN 0–8018–1859–1
Library of Congress Cataloging in Publication data will be found on the last printed page of this book.

To the Memory of
My Parents

Contents

V
BASIC MEDICAL SCIENCES AND BIOLOGY

VI
HEALTH AND DISEASE

VII
SURGERY AND DRUG THERAPY

Preface

An anonymous reviewer recently wrote: "It is a bold historian who experiences no qualms when his old papers reappear in book form." Since the initiative for bringing out a selection of my papers was taken by friends, including my publisher, I feel that they share with me the burden of considering some of my essays worth reprinting. But qualms particularly my own arose over the selection of the material. Suggestions made to me pointed in various directions, so that the decision had to be my responsibility.

The old saying that writings have their own fate denies the author the right to arrogate to himself the final judgment over the worth, or lack of it, of what he once said. The judgments of others certainly are neither uniform nor final. If then there is no appeal to absolute authority, the author may serve himself and the reader best by allowing subjectivity to expose itself frankly.

Thus, I tried to remember the circumstances in which my essays originated and under which they were written. In doing so, I found reasons (not always stated) for choosing this one or discarding that, I repeatedly felt a need to comment on my present attitude, and I discovered (or became conscious of) links between disparate essays. In short, reviewing my essays autobiographically gave me the hope that an autobiographical introduction to the collection might give unity to the topical diversity of the essays themselves.

A publication of collected essays by their author is intrinsically an immodest undertaking that is accentuated but hardly compounded by adding autobiography. I have kept the biographical element more or less in line with what is pertinent for the volume, and I have tried, to the best of my ability, to be accurate. But memory, the treasury of all autobiography, also lays traps of which I have become only too conscious where documents could be consulted.

But all scruples were outweighed by what seemed to be obvious advantages: the possibility of commenting on essays that have been omitted and sometimes also on those selected. This pertains, above all, to my German work, of which only a small fraction is included, and to my writings on teaching and research in medical history. The introduction also gives at least some hints of my present opinion where it has changed considerably.

The choice of "The double face of Janus" as the title of the Introduction, and thus of the whole book, was prompted by the use of this allegory by my teacher, Henry E. Sigerist, during my early, formative years. Some historians of medicine will deny its symbolic relevance for their development, and the denial, if it comes from those who are not physicians by training, will be understandable. It may also be objected that the Janus head of medical history was meant to refer only to the discipline and not to its disciples as well. If so, the allegory would have been applicable to all history—for the uses of history are manifold—and would thereby have lost its specific force.

The essays have been grouped according to topics, and they have been numbered continuously. Apart from those translated from the German, the essays appear with a minimum of corrections, mostly related to obvious misprints, with cross references to the present collection, and with very few changes. To bring the essays up to date would have meant rewriting them, a hopeless undertaking that would never have seen the light of day.

I wish to thank all those who stimulated and encouraged me in preparing this volume, above all the late Richard H. Shryock, who planted the idea, and Mr. Jack Goellner, director of the Johns Hopkins University Press, who while waiting patiently did not allow me to forget it. I am grateful to my wife, C. Lilian Temkin, who not only prepared the English translations of the German essays (which we then went over together) but helped me with stylistic improvement of the introductory essay.

Bibliographical note: Essays and page numbers in brackets in footnotes refer to essays and pages in this volume.

I

Introduction

1

The Double Face
of Janus

WHEN MATRICULATING at the University of Leipzig, Germany, in the spring of 1922, I was asked to state my field of study. "Medicine and philosophy," I said. My reply was not acceptable; only one school *(Fakultät)* could be chosen, and so I declared for medicine. It would satisfy my interest in science, particularly human biology, while eventually enabling me to make a living in a useful manner. As a native of Russia (Minsk) I was stateless, for my family, apprehensive of a pogrom, had emigrated to Germany in 1905, and after the revolution of 1917 we had lost our Russian citizenship. As an alien, I could not count on becoming a teacher at a Gymnasium or a university, and there was no other possibility of supporting myself in philosophy or in history, which had also attracted me since boyhood.

I was fascinated by the preclinical subjects and devoted myself to them with abandon, allowing only my old friend, philosophy, to share in my zeal. As a boy of about fourteen, I had come across the popular writings of Ernst Haeckel, the propagator of Darwinism and of monism. Stirred by them, I had mapped out a program for reading the main works of all the major philosophers. Manhood would be the time for action, yet action must proceed from solid knowledge of primary causes and moral principles. I proceeded forthwith to the pre-Socratics and finished with Schopenhauer's *Welt als Wille und Vorstellung* when I was already in medical school. However little I understood of what I was reading, my determined plodding at least familiarized me with the names of philosophers, with philosophical problems and terminology.

The German universities prided themselves on the principle of *Lernfreiheit,* the student's liberty to seek instruction in any part of the university. I took advantage of this freedom and attended courses in the school of arts and sciences *(philosophische Fakultät):* among others, on Hegel's philosophy of history, on Kant's *Critique of Judgment,* on Leibniz's short philosophical writings offered by Hans Driesch, the erstwhile zoologist and leading vitalist, and on the origin of the literary public in the eighteenth century, given by the Anglicist, Herbert Schöffler. Schöffler's seminar was an exercise in intellectual and social history from which I was to benefit greatly. Hearing Driesch, when vitalism still enjoyed some degree of respectability, was not without importance for my own activity.

It had occurred to me that there might be a life-force, separate from, yet analogous to, the other forces of nature, with its own biological fields. Eager as I was to define the range of this force and to give it mathematical expression, I tried hard to master existing knowledge in physics and in biology beyond the requirements for a medical student. Physiology was of particular interest to me, and I actually considered switching from medicine to pure science. Fortunately, my mother dissuaded me from taking this step.

An anecdote tells of Sidgwick, the English professor of philosophy, exclaiming over the dissertation of a pupil (McTaggart): "I can see that this is nonsense, but what I want to know is whether it is the right kind of nonsense."[1] Had I been acquainted with the work of Bichat and other "vitalistic materialists"[2] of the early nineteenth century and with Helmholtz's anti-vitalistic reasoning that led him to the law of the conservation of energy,[3] the idea of vital force as an addition to the known forces of physics might not have held me in its grip. Yet it was the kind of idea that made me enlarge my scientific knowledge, made me happy with my work and one of the most industrious students.

I was awakened from my dream when a philosopher friend[4] pointed out to me that, being a *Ganzheit* (a whole), the organism could not be reduced to forces analogous to those of physics and chemistry. The immediate effect of the exorcism of materialistic vitalism by holism was largely negative; gone was my wish to become a physiologist. I had now entered upon my clinical years, and I had a short-lived vision of becoming a country doctor (for which I was eminently unsuited). In the meantime I supplemented my clinical studies by writing a "logic of medicine," an analysis of the constitutive concepts of medicine, such as health, disease, diagnosis, prognosis, and healing. The manuscript of this work must still rest somewhere in the depths of my files. I have not had the courage to dig it out and to confront my youthful self. But the interest in the basic concepts of medicine has never quite left me. After periods of suspended animation it has come to full life again in articles on the ideas of health, disease, infection, specificity, and in sidelong glances in articles on other subjects.[5] There was, however, a change from a logical analysis to a historical one.

---

[1]George E. Moore, "An autobiography," in *The Philosophy of G. E. Moore,* ed. by Paul Arthur Schilpp (Evanston and Chicago: Northwestern University, 1942), p. 21.

[2]For the meaning of "vitalistic materialism," see Essay 25, p. 341, in this volume.

[3]The sum total of energy is not diminished by the death of an organism, i.e., by the disappearance of the alleged vital force.

[4]Norbert Elias, who at that time was leading a Socratic existence in Heidelberg. He later turned to sociology, and I have benefited from his work, *Ueber den Prozess der Zivilisation* (2nd ed., 2 vols., Bonn and Munich: Francke, 1969), which deserves greater attention from cultural historians than it has received. My friendship with Norbert Elias, as well as with Rudolf Schönheimer, the famous biochemist, originated in our common membership in "Blau-Weiss," a Jewish branch of the youth movement. The weekly excursions and long hiking trips during vacation time awakened in me, the city boy, a feeling for nature as a majestic power, terrible in her wrath, yet when peaceful soothing the wounds inflicted by human society, and a susceptibility for the lure of campfires, folk song, and guitar playing.

[5]See Essays 29–33 in this volume.

In the fall of 1925, I began to attend the course on the history of medicine offered by Henry E. Sigerist, who had arrived from Switzerland early that year.[6] What led me to take this course, which was elective, as were most courses in German universities? I knew that Sigerist had been called to succeed Karl Sudhoff; I believed that it behooved a physician to have a knowledge of the history of his profession; I probably also felt that my inquiry into medical thought might benefit from historical illumination. Mere curiosity may also have come into play. At any rate, I remember the entrance of a middle-sized man, balding though not yet old, wearing a well-tailored suit without the customary white laboratory coat of the medical professor. He reached the lecturer's stand with a few long, rapid strides, opened the folder containing his notes, and looking at us earnestly he began to speak clearly, fluently, and in full mastery of his material.

The lecture room was not crowded, the audience dwindled somewhat with the passing weeks, as is the way with academic audiences, and I cannot claim a sudden revelation of my true vocation. Yet I realized that the history of medicine had something to offer me. Sigerist had spoken about the Hippocratic concept of disease; I wished to explore this further and asked him whether I might make it the subject of my dissertation for the M.D. degree. He readily consented; a small desk in the Institute was assigned to me, two piles of books, many in Latin, were placed on it to start with, and I had become Sigerist's pupil.

In his course, which extended over two semesters, Sigerist covered the whole history of medicine. In principle it was a lengthy outline course, indicating the direction we should take and preventing our being engulfed by the enormous mass of material that the past contained. Although every teacher will present a different outline, such courses share a strong traditional element because of their function to trace the steps leading to the present situation. Hippocrates, Galen, Paracelsus, Vesalius, Paré, Harvey, Haller, Hunter, Morgagni, Bichat, Laennec, Morton and Jackson, Claude Bernard, Virchow, Pasteur, Lister are names that occur almost regularly because they demarcate the development of Western medicine.

Their traditional element may be responsible for the low opinion in which outline courses are often held, it being alleged that their content can just as well be found in textbooks. But I think this is true only of bad or mediocre courses. The importance of the outline course lies in its nature as a guide for beginners, where gestures and voice can modulate emphasis, omissions and additions can adapt the material to the occasion, and the personal point of view permeates the whole more convincingly than a book whose author does not confront his audience and cannot gauge whether it follows him or not. Outline courses should be entrusted to the most experienced teachers because of the forceful impact they can, and should, have. For as

---

[6]I have commented on Sigerist as a medical historiographer in two articles which appeared in *Bull. Hist. Med* 31 (1957): 296–99 and 32 (1958): 485–99. The following remarks see him in the different perspective of my reminiscences of the Leipzig Institute.

Henry Adams said: "A teacher affects eternity; he can never tell where his influence stops."[7] Sigerist's was a good course and, although I have come to see many things differently, it was he who first made me see a mental picture of medicine, i.e., it was he who changed the past into history.[8] I still believe that to do this is one of the foremost tasks of a professor of the history of medicine, because it gives unity to the conglomerate of skills, scientific disciplines, and aims called medicine.

The Institute for the History of Medicine (*Institut für Geschichte der Medizin*) at the University of Leipzig owed its organization and its rise to a unique center of teaching and research to Karl Sudhoff (1853–1938), who had also established the *Archiv für Geschichte der Medizin* (now *Sudhoffs Archiv: Zeitschrift für Wissenschaftsgeschichte*) and a monograph series (*Studien zur Geschichte der Medizin*), who had guided a large number of medical and dental students through their doctoral dissertations, and who ruled the German society for the history of medicine with an iron hand. After his retirement in 1925 he kept an office in the Institute, and the resounding step of this powerful personality, powerful in physique as well as in character, informed us of his arrival. Although I knew Sudhoff well, I was his pupil only by descent, since he had been Sigerist's teacher.[9]

When Sigerist succeeded Sudhoff he was not yet a famous man, and the call to the Leipzig chair expressed the preference of the governmental administration for the young, liberal Swiss, rather than that of the faculty. Sigerist's coming to Leipzig and the first four years of his directorship of the Institute coincided with the few good years of the Weimar republic. The immediate sequelae of World War I, together with the inflation and the threats of political coups, had been overcome, Germany's political situation was steadily improving, economic life (fed by American loans) was booming, and cultural life was flourishing. On the surface at least things looked good and the future promising.

In "Reminiscences of my activity in Leipzig," Sigerist told the story of his call, of his achievements in terms of lectures, seminars, colloquia, publications, student participation, and relationship to the authorities, and interpreted the meaning the directorship had had for him.[10] Being probably the only one still alive who participated in these activities almost from their beginning, and because of the importance of these years for my own de-

---

[7]*The Education of Henry Adams*, ch. 20 (New York: The Modern Library, 1931), p. 300.

[8]I have here tried as consistently as possible to differentiate between the past, i.e., everything that happened; history, i.e., the past organized into a tale; and historiography, i.e., research into, and description and explanation of, the past, rendering it into history or correcting former historical accounts. Cf. Jacques Barzun, *Clio and the Doctors* (Chicago: University of Chicago Press, 1974), p. 1, ftn.

[9]A series of papers on Sudhoff (including one by me on "Karl Sudhoff, the rediscoverer of Paracelsus"), read on the occasion of his eightieth birthday, appeared in *Bull. Hist. Med.* 2 (1934): 1–25.

[10]"Erinnerungen an meine Leipziger Tätigkeit," *Wissenschaftliche Zeitschrift der Karl-Marx-Universität Leipzig* 5 (1955–56), Mathematisch-Naturwissenschaftliche Reihe, fasc. 1–2, pp. 17–21. For excerpts from this article in English, see *Autobiographical Writings of Henry E. Sigerist,* ed. by Nora Sigerist Beeson (Montreal: McGill University Press, 1966), pp. 62–63.

velopment, I add a few personal impressions that are to supplement what Sigerist and others have written.

By temperament and historical outlook, Sigerist and Sudhoff had little in common. The fact of their remaining on good terms is a testimonial to the mutual bond between teacher and pupil, to Sigerist's tact and, possibly, Sudhoff's resignation to the new order of things. "Geheimrat" Sudhoff was authoritative toward others, unsparing of himself, and dedicated to his work. He belonged to the positivistic era of historical research. The two volumes on the genuineness of the Paracelsian writings, which the then country practitioner published in the 'nineties, the edition of the medical and scientific works of Paracelsus, and a host of articles and monographs testify to his main strength: archival research.

It may well be asked what bearing this kind of research had on the science and practice of medicine, and the question is all the more pertinent because medical history was generally considered the physician's domain. A few classicists, medievalists, and oriental scholars busied themselves with the edition of texts, and much of Sudhoff's work and that of his contemporaries could have been done by them. But the dividing line between scholars cultivating the humanities and physicians as scientists was not quite as sharply drawn as it is today. Many European doctors, perhaps even a majority, possessed a good classical education which remained dear to their hearts and which had familiarized them with the reading of sources. A knowledge of medical literature was a traditional requirement of academic research, and radically new departures had not yet broadened the gulf between "recent" and "old" to the extent of making all but the publications of the last decade seem antiquated.

Thus many physicians considered themselves well equipped for historical work, while the number of professionals, i.e., those who made their living as professors of medical history, was very small: Neuburger, Sigerist, Sticker, Sudhoff, and perhaps Singer and Szumowski, are the only names that come to my mind. Many countries had medico-historical societies, an international society was organized with the main purpose of holding biennial congresses, and there existed a number of journals. Altogether, however, occupation with the history of medicine was something of a valuable decoration and a hobby, though the standard of the work done was usually higher than could be expected of practicing physicians today.

With Sigerist, a new spirit began to emanate from the Leipzig Institute. Sigerist was singularly free from the awe-inspiring characteristics of many German professors. His lack of prejudice, the absence of any attempts to impose his views upon others, an unquestioning welcome for all who showed interest and good will, little regard for restrictive bureaucratic rules, generosity in supplementing the budget, a hospitality ever ready to unite the members of the Institute at parties,[11] these all engendered a

---

[11]Some of these parties took place in the Institute and lasted far into the night, causing great chagrin to our landlord, the director of the mineralogical institute, on the floor above. Sigerist

feeling of ease and eagerness to partake of the intellectual fare that the Institute offered. Now as before, the Institute supplied the facilities for historical work. But in addition to being an instrument for research, it became a community where a spirit of tolerance, of broad culture, and of good fellowship attracted young people for whom history and philosophy were a means of satisfying their curiosity and of deepening their understanding of the science and art of healing.

It was not Sigerist's way to criticize the student's efforts. Apart from the lecture courses, teaching and training consisted mainly in offering opportunities to come, to study, to hear what the others (including Sigerist himself, of course) had to say, and to offer one's own product for discussion. This spirit of *laissez-faire* was stimulating to the point of headiness, and it was not without its dangers. At an age when self-confidence and venturesomeness easily get the upper hand, the student was thrown upon his own resources of self-criticism.

Sigerist was young with the young. In early 1927, he published an appeal to medical youth in which he proclaimed the end of the epoch of materialistic medicine, self-satisfied, intoxicated by its "progress," and blind to the human being. The knowledge of that epoch was to be acquired, but only as a springboard. "Leave behind the handbooks, those tombstones of a past age, the *Zentralblätter*, those dung-water pits *(Jauchengruben)* of the human spirit; away and off to the new tasks."

These were strong words, written in a moment of Paracelsian exhilaration;[12] they caused much shaking of heads and wagging of tongues and, together with the parties at the Institute, gave Sigerist the reputation of an *enfant terrible*. They also reflected the romantic mood so manifest in the German youth movement. The new medicine was to build on the old medicine, before its debasement, and the way leading to it was "the way which Hippocrates and Paracelsus had once walked, which leads through love to man."

Much of what was said and written in the Institute in those early years was not free from romanticism. It may even be seen in the emblem that Sigerist devised: a triangle over which a capital Greek omega was stretched out, topped by a circle. "The triangle," Sigerist explained, "symbolized the program of the Institute; the alliance of medicine, history, and philosophy.... The thought to be expressed was: If medicine, conscious of its historical situation and pervaded by philosophy, stands in the sign of the spirit [omega], then a path opens up to a better and more perfect medicine,

---

also organized a costume ball for the very staid association of the professors of the Leipzig University. It was on this occasion that I met Clarice Lilian Shelley of Newport, Mon., England, who was working on her M.A. thesis in German. We were married on July 15, 1932, about a month before we left Germany.
[12]"Worte an die medizinische Jugend," *Deutsche medizinische Wochenschrift* 53 (1927): 261 (Praemedicus, 1927, No. 3). There existed *Zentralblätter* for many specialties, abstracting and reviewing the current literature. Sigerist complained that the article had appeared without his having been shown proof. My reason for dwelling on this article will become clear later, when I touch on the reaction to Sigerist's socio-political opinions.

indicated by the circle."[13] This emblem appeared not only on the yearbook of the Institute but also on the stationery and even on the cigarettes that were specially manufactured for us and could be bought from the *Institutsgehilfe,* the decent, faithful, and obliging Mr. Robert Richter.

In those days, the intellectual climate was strongly influenced by Johann Daniel Achelis, a physiologist and friend of the sociologist Hans Freyer. After a brief tenure as *Assistent* at the Institute, Achelis returned to physiology but remained associated with the Sigerist group. Tall, blond, blue-eyed, possessed of great personal charm and very popular among the students, Achelis too was a profound student of Paracelsus, whose works he knew intimately and whose basic concepts he tried to interpret in a manner and spirit quite different from that of Sudhoff. Fascinating as Achelis's interpretation of Paracelsus was, I must confess that much of it was too esoteric for my understanding. Paracelsus has remained for me something of a seducer, beckoning me to follow into his world of parable, faith, experience, and intuition, only to leave me to a lonely return to the more sober medicine and science of Galenists and Aristotelians on the one hand and non-Hermetic innovators on the other.

Nevertheless, elusive though Paracelsus has proved to me, his motto: "alterius non sit qui suus esse potest" (he who can be his own [master] should not belong to another) on the Hirschvogel portrait of 1538 impressed me deeply. It was much quoted in my youthful days, when Jules Benda's *La trahison des clercs* was a moral guide to many of us. Now, when there is an eagerness to "identify" with one or another issue of the day, Paracelsus's motto is as discarded as is Benda's accusation of those scholars who refuse to study matters *sub specie aeternitatis.*

Sigerist gave the Institute its own organ of publication, a yearbook under the name of *Kyklos,* of which four volumes appeared. In the preface to the first volume he formulated his view of the current task of the history of medicine:

The history of medicine has entered upon a decisive phase. Summoned to cooperation by the living healing art, it will have to show whether it is able to follow this summons, whether it is able to participate in the solution of the great problems which today occupy the physicians' world. But the history of medicine has a Janushead. One face looks to the future with the eyes of the physician, the other one is turned backward. With the eyes of the historian it tries to light up the darkness of the past. Here too the history of medicine will have to prove itself. Here too it will have to show whether the rebirth of spirit which today we experience in all spheres has passed it by, whether in purely positivistic fashion it wishes to add facts to facts, or whether it is capable of interpreting the past, of enlivening it, and of rendering it fruitful for a better future.[14]

[13]Sigerist, "Erinnerungen an meine Leipziger Tätigkeit" (see above, ftn. 10), p. 20.
[14]*Kyklos: Jahrbuch des Instituts für Geschichte der Medizin an der Universität Leipzig,* 4 vols. (Leipzig: Georg Thieme, 1928–32), 1: 5. The *Kyklos* period I am here commenting on is represented by vols. 1–3; vol. 4 contains, beside my long article on Hippocratism, only a brief preface and a report on the activities of the Institute during the two academic years 1929–31. —After completion of the present essay, I noticed that the quoted passage appears as a motto

The dissociation from historical positivism, the belief in a partnership of medicine and historiography, and the self-identification of the medical historian with the physician, all this remained true for Sigerist's future work. But the feeling of "a decisive phase," of a "summons" of medical history, and of a "rebirth of the spirit," belong to the *Kyklos* period, as does the unfinished project of translating the Hippocratic works as part of a program "to make Hippocrates and Paracelsus fruitful for the present," and the article on "Culture and disease."[15]

There was much more give and take in the early years of the Institute, with Sigerist sometimes in the role of a communal spokesman. The last-named article was colored by the influence of Achelis, especially the interpretation of the plague as marking the beginning and end of the Middle Ages in more than a chronological sense.

Paul Diepgen, temperamentally and in his outlook the very opposite of Sigerist, was a severe, yet convention-bound, critic of the spirit of the *Kyklos* period. Although we indignantly rejected his charges, I have come to realize that the insinuation of "romanticism" was not entirely undeserved.[16] But whereas Diepgen, mindful of the romantic period of German medicine in the early nineteenth century, used the term as an accusation, especially aimed at Achelis, if I am not mistaken, I cannot see an immanent pejorative sense in it. "Romantic" does no more than designate a certain temperament, a mood, a philosophy, be it of an individual or of an epoch. As is the case with other labels, such as "positivistic," "idealistic," or "materialistic," "romantic" too is praised or blamed according to our like or dislike of it and according to the consequences that we impute to it. Romanticism, I think, becomes dangerous only when it substitutes sentiment for rational thought and when its love for the mysterious obstructs analysis. Achelis did not escape the danger. His presence in the Institute was highly stimulating during the 'twenties. Then traditional German nationalism, illusions about the supremacy of the state and about unquestioning acceptance of the authority of "great" men as a power to overcome intellectual and moral dissolution, and willingness to compromise with the evil in Hitler and his henchmen had by 1933 become strong enough to make him accept a position in the new Nazi government, at least temporarily. Later he became professor of physiology in Heidelberg. I understand that in 1945, as *Rektor* of the university, he handed over its keys to the American forces.

---

to the *Historia universal de la medicina,* ed. by Pedro Laín Entralgo (Barcelona: Salvat Editores, 1972–75).

[15]*Kyklos* 1: 165, and "Kultur und Krankheit," *ibid.,* pp. 60–63.

[16]Diepgen, by-passed as Sudhoff's successor and practicing gynecology at Freiburg, attacked Sigerist's approach in his review of the first volume of *Kyklos* (*Deutsche medizinische Wochenschrift* 54 [1928]: 975) and the philosophizing tendencies at the Institute (especially mine) in the review of vol. 2 (*ibid.* 55 [1929]: 1775 f.). Although Diepgen did not mention the *Kyklos* in his article on "Alte und neue Romantik" (Old and new romanticism), which appeared in *Klinische Wochenschrift* 11 (1932): 28–34 (reprinted in his *Gesammelte Aufsätze,* ed. by W. Artelt. E. Heischkel, J. Schuster [Stuttgart: Enke, 1938], pp. 224–42), I have little doubt that his criticism included the neo-romantic tendencies in Leipzig.

Not everything done in the Institute until 1929 was tinged by this youthful spirit. Sigerist himself was an experienced philologist; he had worked on early medieval medical manuscripts under Sudhoff and considered early medieval medicine his field of predilection. Many a candidate for the doctoral degree was put to work on a Latin text, and I too received my introduction to Latin paleography from him. In the summer of 1926 he read with me, the only participant in the course, Hippocrates's *On Ancient Medicine,* and since my Greek was as yet woefully weak, he tactfully did the translating. Thus the philologist in Sigerist kept alive the tradition of positivistic research.

His two outstanding papers of that period, on "Sebastian-Apollo" and on "Harvey's position in the intellectual history of Europe," both reflect his strong and genuine love of art.[17] "Sebastian-Apollo" was based on an iconographic study, and assigning Harvey's work to the Baroque meant assigning it to an artistic style. I mention these papers because they climaxed, so to speak, the Leipzig historiography of the *Kyklos* period.

Imperceptibly at first, the mood at the Institute changed after 1929. Work did not slacken; on the contrary, activity was at a peak. Walter Pagel worked at the Institute from April to September 1930, and Erwin H.Ackerknecht was writing his dissertation on the medical reform movement of 1848.[18] But events were taking place, some personal in nature and some national, that affected all of us.

To revert to my own affairs: In the summer of 1927 I passed my *Staatsexamen* and began my year's internship at the university hospital, receiving my license to practise medicine in 1928. In 1927 I also finished my doctoral dissertation and obtained my degree. Dr. Erich Ebstein, the medical director of the old people's home of the city of Leipzig and an enthusiastic historian, offered me the residency which was to become free at the end of my internship, and we anticipated a happy cooperation in medical care and in historical research. But the municipal authorities rejected my application with the curt remark that my services were not needed. No reasons were given; my lack of citizenship may well have been decisive. What was I to do? In my uncertainty I took the risk of following my inclination, working in the Institute on a voluntary basis and waiting for a miracle. It came sooner than expected. The Institute was granted a second assistantship as of September 1, 1928, and the Saxon government was willing to let me have it. Thereupon, my application for citizenship was soon granted. Now I was a man with civic rights, with a passport that allowed me to travel, and an academic career ahead of me.

My rejection by the city magistrate of Leipzig had turned out to be one of

---

[17]"Sebastian-Apollo," *Archiv für Geschichte der Medizin* 19 (1927): 301–17, and "William Harvey's Stellung in der europäischen Geistesgeschichte," *Archiv für Kulturgeschichte* 19 (1928): 158–68 (English trans. in Henry E. Sigerist, *On the History of Medicine,* ed. by Felix Marti-Ibañez [New York: MD Publications, 1960], pp. 184–92.
[18]"Beiträge zur Geschichte der Medizinalreform von 1848," *Sudhoffs Archiv* 25 (1932): 61–109 and 113–83.

the most fortunate events in my life. Curiously enough, my fate became connected with a somewhat parallel event in Sigerist's life. A large institute for the history of medicine and science was to be established in Berlin, and Sigerist counted on becoming its director. He had gone abroad for a vacation and I was looking after the affairs of the Leipzig Institute, when a note from Diepgen informed Sigerist that he, Diepgen, had received the call to Berlin. It was my embarrassing duty to forward this news to Sigerist, knowing that it would hurt him deeply and make him unhappy. Since then I have often wondered what would have happened had the call come to him. He might have devoted his full energies to the organization of this new institute, only to be forced out by the Nazi regime in 1933.

At any rate, Sigerist became restless, and the Leipzig Institute now seemed confining. At that time he was engaged in the writing of two of his main books: *Einführung in die Medizin* (translated as *Man and Medicine*) and *Grosse Ärzte (The Great Doctors)*. These books, which appeared in early 1931 and 1932, proved extremely successful and made him famous. In them, Sigerist had found his strength. Not a romantic by temperament, he turned away from an orientation that was not fundamentally his own and that was hard to maintain in the face of the drab realities of those days: depression, mounting unemployment, and the steady rise of National Socialism.

In the winter of 1931–32, Sigerist went to the United States, where The Johns Hopkins University had invited him as visiting professor. In Baltimore, he was offered the chair of the history of medicine and the directorship of the Institute of the History of Medicine at The Johns Hopkins University. After his return to Leipzig, he accepted the offer. Before his departure, he lectured on American medicine to overflowing audiences. These lectures were delivered with the greatest enthusiasm and did not admit of any flaw in American medicine. They were integrated into a book, the preface of which, dated Leipzig, May 1932, ended with the words: "I begin this book in Europe, although or rather because my future field of work will be in America. I wished to write it as a spectator before myself becoming a part of American medicine."[19]

While in Baltimore, Sigerist had negotiated my call to Johns Hopkins. He left Germany in the early summer of 1932, and my wife[20] and I followed in August. After a vacation in England we embarked for New York in September, and I did not visit Germany again until 1959.

II. WORK IN LEIPZIG

I was about eighteen years old when our German teacher made us write an essay on "How I became what I am" *(Wie ich wurde was ich bin)*. We probably did not appreciate the implied compliment of being persons worth writing about. Fortunately my present task is less formidable, since I have merely to account for my development as a medical historian.

[19]*Amerika und die Medizin* (Leipzig: Thieme, 1933), p. 11.
[20]See above, ftn. 11.

I am inclined to divide my work during my Leipzig period into two phases. Although most of my German essays belong to the first, from 1927–30, it was only in the second, from 1930–32, that history became my real objective. This second phase counted but one major essay, the "History of Hippocratism in late antiquity,"[21] but the beginnings of my intensive occupation with Galen and post-Galenic Greek medicine also belong to it, as does my plan to write a history of epilepsy. The cleavage between the two phases was real enough, and my interpretation of the work of the first phase will explain the shift in motives that induced the change.

In the early years I wrote on what happened to interest me at the moment, and occasionally the impetus came from outside. Thus my very first publication, "On the history of syphilis and morality,"[22] was a paper for Sigerist's seminar on "civilization and disease," offered in the summer of 1927, when I started my internship that eventually included the venereal disease ward for women. Nor would I have worked on "Zimmermann's philosophy of the physician"[23] had it not been for the wish of a Swiss medical journal to commemorate the two hundredth birthday of that Swiss physician.

In rereading the essays of this phase, I am surprised to discover, at least *in nuce,* so many of the ideas which I thought had come to me much later. At the same time, I am shocked at the youthful unconcern for my questioable adequacy to approach fundamental problems. The combined length of these essays, excessive Greek quotations, and the all but untranslatable phraseology of some of them have made it inadvisable to resuscitate the bulk of them in English. Instead, I shall attempt to summarize what appears to me essential now, disregarding original motives and chronological order.

The collection of Greek medical writings ascribed to Hippocrates is generally believed the work of many authors mostly around 400 B.C., a few much later. Yet behind the diversity of knowledge, speculation, and practices, these writers must have shared assumptions that enabled their readers to understand them and offered a basis for debate for physicians and for communication with their patients. A systematic context (not a system) existed in the concepts supplied by pre-Socratic natural philosophy, the emphasis on prognosis, and the integration of observational data into the alleged nature of the patient or of the disease. Humoral pathology went together well with a predilection for the anatomy of blood vessels and with dietetic therapy that approached the patient as a whole. There existed tendencies in other directions: localistic pathology (especially in surgical works) and diagnosis of diseases as entities. But the common features were

---

[21]"Geschichte des Hippokratismus im ausgehenden Altertum," *Kyklos* 4 (1932): 1–80, of which ch. 2 is included as Essay 11 of this volume. The German titles of the articles included in this article will be found in footnotes to the translations.

[22]Essay 32 in this volume.

[23]Essay 16 in this volume.

outstanding enough to give to Hippocratic medicine its own physiognomy.[24]

Greek medicine did not begin with Hippocrates, though in its earlier stage it probably lacked the theoretical comprehensiveness that distinguished the Hippocratic writings. Together with medicine in ancient Mesopotamia and Egypt, it was of the archaic type, beyond illiterate prehistory yet without the rationalization that eliminated magic and fostered physiological and pathological speculation.[25] But "archaic medicine" was not homogeneous. Apart from differences in positive knowledge, its forms differed structurally. In the Egyptian papyri, for instance, prognosis was implied in the verdict whether the physician would, or would not, treat the case, whereas in Mesopotamia the formula *ibalut* (he will recover) formed a link between general omens and medical prognostication.[26]

Although Hippocratic medicine remained an ideal for later Greeks and for medical men of modern times, it remained structurally different even when imitation was attempted. Thus "the English Hippocrates," Thomas Sydenham, concentrated on studying the natural history of disease entities, whereas the Hippocratic *Epidemics* stressed individual factors. Both the Hippocratic author and Sydenham were clinical observers, yet their observations served different goals, each using the conceptual framework that his time offered.[27] For Sydenham this meant classification of diseases as species, a principle of order in a causally determined universe.[28]

If Harvey and Sydenham illustrate an alignment of medical science and clinical medicine to contemporary style and thought, Molière reveals an alienation of medicine (the Paris faculty) from the public. His physicians were ridiculous because they were opinionated, tradition-bound pedants, full of humanistic learning yet ignorant of the working of the human machine and helpless in the face of disease. For Molière and his audience this kind of medicine had lost meaning.[29]

[24]For this section see my doctoral dissertation, "Der systematische Zusammenhang im Corpus Hippocraticum" (The systematic context in the Hippocratic corpus), *Kyklos* 1 (1928): 9–43. Pedro Laín Entralgo, who has given generous support to the intention of this dissertation (*La medicina hippocratica* [Madrid: Revista de Occidente, 1970], p. 43, ftn. 1), has also rightly pointed out the undue emphasis placed there on the humoral theory.

[25]In view of R. Joly, *Le niveau de la science hippocratique* (Paris: Les belles lettres, 1966), I now refrain from calling Hippocratic medicine scientific. But medicine as a whole has only become rigorously scientific in recent decades, and even then often more in intent than in fact.

[26]See "Beiträge zur archaischen Medizin" (Contributions to archaic medicine), *Kyklos* 3 (1930): 90–135.

[27]Cf. "Die Krankheitsauffassung von Hippokrates und Sydenham in ihren 'Epidemien'" (The concept of disease of Hippocrates and Sydenham in their "Epidemics"), *Archiv für Geschichte der Medizin* 20 (1928): 326–52. This article somewhat underestimated the nosological tendencies in the Hippocratic works.

[28]Cf. "Thomas Sydenham und der Naturbegriff des 17. Jahrhunderts" (Thomas Sydenham and the concept of nature of the seventeenth century), *Neuburger Festschrift* (Vienna, 1928), pp. 1–9. In the days of Hippocrates, i.e., prior to the Stoics, the world was not yet seen as causally determined throughout.

[29]Cf. the chapter on "Molière und der Sinn der Medizin im 17. Jahrhundert" (Molière and the meaning of medicine in the seventeenth century), in "Studien zum 'Sinn'-Begriff in der Medizin" (cited in ftn. 32) and my later article on "The meaning of medicine in historical perspective" (Essay 2 in this volume). It has been rightly remarked that the physicians Molière ridicules were not of the medieval type, as contended in my article of 1929.

"Meaning" in medicine is not restricted to its changing significance for particular periods. A physician who has examined a patient complaining about black spots before his eyes may say, "these spots mean nothing; they are just particles floating in the vitreous body of the eye." In this case, "mean nothing" is equivalent to saying that the condition is harmless and that nothing need be done about it. Generally speaking, a medical consultation results in an accumulation of data that have significance from the point of view of the patient's health or disease, his treatment, his recovery, invalidism, or death. They enter into the patient's medical record, where the events of his life have their particular medical meaning, and where the language is that of the sphere of medicine.

Patients' records have been a part of medical literature since the days of the Hippocratic *Epidemics*. If the records of different periods are compared, they show remarkable differences in content as well as in structure, for they mirror the medicine of their day. The lack of temperature and blood pressure readings, of X-ray pictures, of indications of the presence or absence of protein and sugar in the urine, and similar entries, is to be expected before the nineteenth century. Beyond such differences in positive knowledge, there is also in earlier times an absence of clear distinction between subjective complaints and objective data. In the Hippocratic writings we are sometimes even unable to make a diagnosis, because the data recorded, which were meaningful for the Hippocratic physician intent on evaluating crises in disease, do not fit into our diagnostic categories. Facts obtain meaning when they become part of an understandable context analogous to words in a sentence.[30]

There is still another kind of meaning connected with medicine, viz. the meaning of disease in a person's life. Disease can mean unemployment and economic ruin, it can mean relief from responsibility, it can mean punishment for sin or a warning to mend one's ways. The interpretations vary from mundane to metaphysical and religious, and this is true not only of individual disease but also of epidemics, where communities, nations, or mankind are the patients. In the late fifteenth century, epidemic syphilis was regarded as divine retribution for man's blasphemous way of life. For Rudolf Virchow, 350 years later, epidemics were signposts of disturbances in a nation's development.

As the meaning of individual disease is to be found in the person's biography, so the meaning of epidemics is to be found in history. The biographer will distinguish between the significance attached to illness by the subject of his biography and that attached to it by himself. The historian will distinguish between the meaning given to the epidemic by contemporaries (for the black death of 1348, see the introduction to Boccaccio's *Decameron*) and the significance he attaches to it (for instance, the black death as an upheaval in the economic and cultural life of the Middle Ages).

Before bacteriology and immunology gave methods for the causal

---

[30]Cf. the chapter on "Krankengeschichte und Sinnsphäre der Medizin" (Medical record and medicine's sphere of meaning), in the article cited in ftn. 32.

analysis of infectious processes, epidemiology was not much more than a historical description of epidemics. Even this had become possible only after specifically different diseases had been delineated from the amorphous notion of pestilence. With the rise of scientific studies, the causal explanation of the mechanism of infection paid scant attention to biographical and historical circumstances under which infections had occurred. The rise of psychoanalysis and the popularity of a book like Thomas Mann's *Magic Mountain* were signs of the resurgent interest in the meaning of individual disease. Historical perspective was bound to reflect interest in the meaning of epidemic diseases.[31]

The various forms of meaning in medicine were chapters of a very long essay, "Studies on the concept of 'meaning' in medicine."[32] Its aim was to bring into relief the character of medicine as a sphere in human life, as a special, historically bound aspect of meaning in human affairs. The article was criticized by Diepgen, rightly I think, as regards its philosophical discursiveness.[33] But I think that over the faults of presentation the criticism missed the main points that I have here tried to bring out more sharply. I still think them worth making in view of attempts to reduce medicine to the application of biology or other sciences. In particular, to define medicine as applied biology is to reaffirm the limitation of its sphere to biology, to deny that health and disease involve man as a cultural being. Even in saying that medicine uses biology (and other sciences), it should not be overlooked that healing, together with hunting, agriculture, and animal husbandry, is much older than our biological science. Concepts of health and disease existed before Aristotle established Western biology. Notions of healthy and diseased conditions of the body entered into the Aristotelian teleological idea of living beings, so that to some extent medicine has found in biology what it put into it.

Altogether, to be historically comprehensive, medicine cannot be defined as a science or the application of any science or sciences. Medicine is healing (and prevention) based on such knowledge as is deemed requisite. Such knowledge may be theological, magic, empirical, rationally speculative, or scientific. The fact that medicine in our days is largely based on science does not make other forms less medical—though it may convince us that they are less effective. My personal association with the culture of the West does not allow me to give to other forms the same value as to Western medicine. But that is no reason for denying a plurality, of which Hippocratic medicine and Western medicine since the Renaissance are instances. A

---

[31]Cf. the chapter on "Epidemiologie und Geschichte der Medizin" (Epidemiology and the history of medicine) in the article cited in ftn. 32. The chapter, however, pays scant attention to the meaning of individual disease.

[32]"Studien zum 'Sinn'-Begriff in der Medizin" (Studies on the concept of meaning in medicine), *Kyklos* 2 (1929): 21–105.

[33]Diepgen's review appeared in *Deutsche medizinische Wochenschrift* 55 (1929): 1775 f. The first chapter, "Kritisch-logische Voruntersuchungen" (Critical and logical preliminaries), which I have not discussed here, could profitably have been omitted, and some of the theoretical discussions introducing the other chapters should have been shortened.

fruitful comparative study of medicine must take this assumption as a working hypothesis. I came to advocate comparative study much later,[34] but I like to look back upon my "Contributions to archaic medicine"[35] as an early anticipation.

The 'twenties were a time of eager discussion of historicism and of historical relativism as one of its possible consequences. Historical relativism had not yet fallen into general disrepute. Ranke's saying that "before God all generations have equal rights" was frequently cited.[36] In the history of medicine, historicism was largely a reaction against neglect of what was not considered a step toward present-day knowledge.

How closely my work of that phase skirted on relativism is evident from statements such as "that truths can only be measured in their temporal context" and "the Enlightenment... lacked the necessary relativity for such a yardstick."[37] How far relativism could go in those days evinces from an episode which I relate to the best of my memory.

In the winter of 1926–27, Sigerist conducted a seminar on "the miracle." At one of the sessions, a medical student read a paper on the stigmatization of St. Francis, which he tried to explain in terms of pathological physiology. But a professor from the philosophical faculty who also participated made short shrift of this explanation. All our knowledge of St. Francis, he argued, rested on contemporary sources, to which erythrocytes, capillary blood vessels, and so on were totally foreign. For them, the stigmatization was the supreme manifestation of the closeness to Christ that St. Francis had achieved; it was a part of the true miracle, the successful *imitatio Christi.* To go behind our sources and to isolate the stigmatization as an independent reality to be explained in scientific terms was a methodological blunder, an anachronistic use of modern concepts.

Apart from illustrating the influence of historicism, the story points to the dilemma of the history of medicine and of science. As medieval historians we should possibly accept the argument.[38] But can we do so as histo-

[34]See Essay 7 in this volume. For current ideas on comparative studies in medical history, see Paul U. Unschuld, "Professionalisierung im Bereich der Medizin: Entwurf zu einer historisch-anthropologischen Studie," *Saeculum* 25 (1974): 251–76.

[35]See ftn. 26.

[36]Leopold von Ranke, *Ueber die Epochen der neueren Geschichte: Vorträge dem Könige Maximilian von Bayern im Herbst 1854 zu Berchtesgaden gehalten,* ed. by Alfred Dove (Leipzig: Drucker and Humblot, 1888), p. 6: "aber vor Gott erscheinen alle Generationen der Menschheit als gleichberechtigt." Cf. Friedrich Meinecke, "Deutung eines Rankewortes," in *Werke,* ed. by Hans Herzfeld et al. (Stuttgart: Kochler, 1959), 4: 117–39. On "historicism" see the article by Maurice Mandelbaum in *The Encyclopedia of Philosophy* (New York: Macmillan and The Free Press, 1967), 4: 22–25, and Essay 6 in this volume.

[37]See below, pp. 241 f.

[38]I am here referring to the seminar discussion only, leaving its relationship to the true history of St. Francis quite open. I have used a somewhat similar argument in pointing out that the discussion about Mohammed's alleged epilepsy rested on using religious texts as if they were clinical notes and allowed a separation of medical symptoms from religious beliefs. (Cf. my *Falling Sickness* [see ftn. 49 below], 2nd ed., p. 153). I hope that my recent occupation with Mohammed has not tinged my reconstruction of the debate that took place in Leipzig so long before.

rians of medical science? Scientifically speaking, the story of St. Francis claims a case of stigmatization, and the period of its occurrence, the thirteenth century, is important only because of specific psychological circumstances. The intrusion of modern concepts, the attempt at least to ascertain what really (scientifically speaking) happened, cannot be warded off a priori, even if the case were adjudged unproven because the nature of the evidence did not allow us to tell whether the stigmata occurred or were only imagined. To yield would, in the final analysis, mean the end of all communication between the ages and a surrender of the invariance of scientific laws.

This, I think, was vaguely felt by the medical participants in the seminar. But so great was the fascination of historicism for us medical historians, who had not yet been exposed to its subtler manifestations, that we were thrilled by this unfamiliar way of seeing things, without as yet realizing the inherent antinomy between history and science.

However exciting they were, discussions on historical relativism did not weigh heavily on me. Instead, in the course of time, I began to contemplate my suspension between philosophy and history with increasing unease. I hesitated to devote myself fully to the philosophy of medicine, for I did not believe my abilities could live up to my ideals of philosophical originality and creativeness. Yet I could hardly call myself a historian. My general knowledge might be reasonably good, but nowhere did it go deep enough to stand independently, without the support of the ideas it helped to analyze. For instance, I had written about the structure of Hippocratic medicine, but was I prepared to write a good history of Hippocratic medicine in all its medical details as well as its manifold ramifications in ancient Greek civilization?

This kind of question was lingering in my mind, when an answer came through a lecture on the Hippocratic problem given by Ludwig Edelstein on January 15, 1930. I had heard of this young classical scholar who was working on Hippocrates, and who had remarked that the historians of medicine knew nothing about Hippocrates. Yet I at least had read the entire Littré edition of the Hippocratic works and was curious to hear and to meet the man who could so belittle us! Edelstein spoke for two hours, without notes, slowly, but without hesitation or any slip of the tongue, without rhetorical embellishments or emotional appeal, with the simple forcefulness of logic based on interpretive mastery of every single Hippocratic work and close familiarity with Greek civilization. The Hippocratic physician, the meaning of Hippocratic prognosis, Hippocrates himself, and the history of the collection ascribed to him, all emerged from this lecture in an entirely new light.[39]

All of us, including some well-known classicists, listened spellbound. In

---

[39]The lecture gave the gist of chs. 2–4 of Edelstein's *Peri Aeron und die Sammlung der hippokratischen Schriften*, of which chs. 2 and 3, in English translation, are included in *Ancient Medicine: Selected Papers of Ludwig Edelstein*, ed. by Owsei Temkin and C. Lilian Temkin (Baltimore: The Johns Hopkins Press, 1967).

spite of the objections I raised to views that flatly contradicted my own opinions (or perhaps just because of the lusty initial debate), the evening was the beginning of a friendship that lasted until Edelstein's death in 1965, a friendship to which I owe much.

Edelstein's dedication to classical history and philosophy was too great to leave much sympathy for my efforts on behalf of medicine. But his lecture and subsequent conversations with him convinced me that interest in medicine could not substitute for sound historical scholarship, which was not to be acquired by ranging over the whole past. Exploration of one period in depth was needed, even if only to make one aware of the craftsmanship necessary for dealing with other periods.

An attraction to what is obscure and slightly exotic in the past made me turn to the period between the death of Galen (about A.D. 200) and the end of the school of medicine in Alexandria (around A.D. 700). This was the time when Hippocrates and Galen rose to uncontested authority, and when the reading and interpretation of their works constituted the teaching of medical science, while encyclopedias served the needs of the practitioner. What was done in Alexandria during this time by men for whom we had some names without personalities behind them was not well known, yet it was important because it bequeathed Greek medicine to the world of Islam. Besides Greek and Latin, working in this period also required a knowledge of Arabic, into which I was initiated by Hans Heinrich Schaeder, then professor in Leipzig. I concentrated on "The history of Hippocratism in late antiquity," the title of my *Habilitationsschrift,* a dissertation with which I became *Privatdozent* in the history of medicine at Leipzig, the first since Theodor Puschmann in 1873.[40]

Four chapters of narrative text described the attitude to Hippocrates and the use made of his teachings in the West[41] as well as in the Eastern Roman Empire. An appendix on "The canonization of Hippocrates and Galen" discussed the men who helped to regulate the study of Hippocratic and Galenic writings in Alexandria. This appendix utilized a considerable amount of manuscript material gathered in part in Paris.[42] I had thus lived up to the tradition of Sudhoff and Sigerist, which expected familiarity with archival work from a historian of medicine.

Rightly or wrongly, I now could look the medico-historical Janus straight in the eye of his backward-looking face. But what about the other face? The

[40]"Geschichte des Hippokratismus im ausgehenden Altertum," *Kyklos* 4 (1932): 1–80. The long introduction in vol. 1 of his *Alexander von Tralles* (2 vols., Vienna: Braumüller, 1878–79) served Puschmann as his *Habilitationsschrift.* Thus, by coincidence, we had both been attracted by the same period.

[41]See Essay 11 in this volume, which is the English translation of chapter 2. It has recently been supplemented by Fridolf Kudlien, "The third century A.D. —a blank spot in the history of medicine?" in *Medicine, Science, and Culture: Historical Essays in Honor of Owsei Temkin,* ed. by Lloyd G. Stevenson and Robert P. Multhauf (Baltimore: The Johns Hopkins Press, 1968), pp. 25–34.

[42]The material discussed in the appendix may still be of interest to scholars of ancient and Arabic medicine. In the assumption that these scholars hardly need a translation, while others would profit little from it, I have omitted it here.

history of Hippocratism in late antiquity, even if it were good history, could hardly be considered a contribution to "the solution of the great problems which occupy the world of the physician today." As a historian I felt committed to scholarship rather than to a profession. My professional commitment was to medicine, for which I had been trained, and the feeling of obligation to medicine never left me throughout my career as an active member of a medical faculty.

In 1931 I solved the problem by deciding to undertake a work on the history of epilepsy. This disease had received attention in an unbroken tradition since the days of Hippocrates. Nevertheless, it was still badly understood and historical clarification might be of some help to neurologists. Moreover, the rich popular and cultural lore surrounding epilepsy lent its history a cultural aspect as well. My investigation would give me an opportunity to apply a more rigorous historical methodology to the history of a disease than was usual. The book might, therefore, turn out to be both methodically useful and historically instructive.

The second phase of my work in Leipzig, which had begun in 1930 with my concentration on late antiquity, thus ended in the summer of 1932 with two projects: continuation of the study of late Alexandrian medicine and the history of epilepsy. These two projects, together with the inherent dichotomy of interests which they represented, I carried with me to Baltimore, where my wife and I arrived on September 29, 1932.

III. BALTIMORE: 1932–1947

The Institute of the History of Medicine of The Johns Hopkins University School of Medicine occupies the top floor of the library named in honor of William H. Welch (1850–1934). Dr. Welch had been appointed professor of pathology five years before the opening of the Johns Hopkins Hospital (1889) and nine years before the opening of the School of Medicine (1893), of which he was also to be the first dean. Throughout his long connection with the medical institutions, Dr. Welch was a guiding spirit, instrumental also in establishing the School of Hygiene and Public Health.[43] The organization of an Institute of the History of Medicine was the last of his creations. As a young man he had gone to Germany for his training as a pathologist;[44] later, he had studied bacteriology there, and when the time came to make plans and to purchase books for the new venture, he went to Germany again, particularly to Leipzig, to consult Sudhoff and Sigerist.[45] The very name "Institute" for the department was probably imported from Germany, where it denotes a place housing the

---

[43]Thomas B. Turner, *Heritage of Excellence* (Baltimore: The Johns Hopkins Press, 1974), p. 281, has summarized Welch's influence at Hopkins.

[44]See Essay 18 in this volume.

[45]Simon Flexner and James Thomas Flexner, *William Henry Welch and the Heroic Age of American Medicine* (New York: Viking, 1941), pp. 425 f.

physical facilities (library, working rooms, laboratories, etc.) provided for the study of a discipline.

I met Dr. Welch in 1927, possibly already in June, during his sojourn in Leipzig,[46] certainly in September in Bad Homburg at a meeting of the German society for the history of medicine. I saw him again in later years at the Institute (in 1928 and 1931). One day he casually asked me whether I had ever thought of going to America. I now assume that he was sounding me out, but my thoughts were preempted by enticing work; Sigerist, to whom I mentioned the question, could not enlighten me as to its meaning; I felt confused and do not even remember my answer.

As it turned out, I did come to the United States; my office was next to that of Dr. Welch, and I believe that the cordiality with which my wife and I were accepted as welcome newcomers was enhanced by my previous acquaintance with Dr. Welch, as well as with Colonel Fielding H. Garrison, the head of the Welch Library, whom I had met at a congress in Budapest, in 1929.

Being newly married, my wife and I had no old home to break up, and we immediately looked on Baltimore as our home. Germany had not yet fallen into the hands of Hitler, there were no nightmares to haunt us, and we thought of summer vacations in Europe, when I might even lecture in Leipzig during the summer semester. This was not to be. In January of the following year (1933) Hitler came to power; I was deprived of my status as *Privatdozent,* and in 1934 also of my German citizenship; until our American naturalization in May 1938, foreign travel had once more become impossible.

Of all American universities, Johns Hopkins was closest to the German academic pattern. The medical school as part of the university, full-time for the professors, research as an integral part of professorial duties, well-equipped laboratories and libraries, and the residency system, none of these were inventions of the founders of Johns Hopkins, whose genius showed itself in adapting the imports to American traditions. The School of Medicine remained a school, i.e., it had a curriculum of four years of study with a prescribed schedule of courses with examinations; it expected its students neither to switch to other schools nor to attend courses in other parts of the university, and the student could anticipate being taught what he was required to know.

But the main difference between the German university and the American lay in the milieu in which each of them operated. Johns Hopkins professors might have a sense of dignity and of mission resembling that of their German colleagues. Yet American democratic habits, which permeated all spheres of life, and the utilitarian spirit of the country did not encourage the formation of an academic caste imposing its ideals of culture and learning upon the nation. Even had they wished it, American profes-

---

[46]See *Kyklos* 1 (1928): 169; also Henry E. Sigerist, *American Medicine* (New York: Norton, 1934), p. xi, and the Welch diaries in the William H. Welch Library.

sors could not become "mandarins."[47] Characteristically enough, members of the medical faculty called themselves "doctor" rather than "professor," for a successful physician was more highly valued than a good professor.

I had left Germany as a very minor "mandarin," and my pigtail had not yet had time to grow long and heavy. The lack of stifling authoritative formality between senior and junior members of the faculty and between instructors and students appealed to me. Though the students of medicine might actually know less in humanistic subjects than their European counterparts, I appreciated their openness to all that was new to them, their eagerness to learn, and the absence of a blasé, know-it-all attitude. The faculty was free from the blind nationalism and stubborn, unreasoning opposition to academic or social reforms that marked so many professors of the Weimar period. But it emulated the positive side of the German professor: his dedication to research and disdain for shoddy and unmethodical work. There was little criticism of purely positivistic research, and neither Sigerist nor I was anxious to import it. Sigerist arrived full of plans for a three-volume *catalogue raisonné* of early medieval Latin manuscripts, to which he devoted several summers of research in European libraries. His project dovetailed with my own plans for a history of the late school of Alexandria. When the political storm in Germany began to blow in full force, we were happy to be able to continue free research.

My move from Leipzig to Baltimore did not interrupt my work. I took up my teaching at the point where I had left it. Since we had to announce our courses for the year 1932–33 long before our arrival, I chose a seminar on Galen's *Ars medica* which I had conducted in Leipzig. This choice showed my ignorance, for the seminar presupposed a knowledge of Greek. Surprisingly enough, however, it actually did take place, and there was even a medical student among the few participants, the others being members of the faculty. During the ten years from 1932 to 1942, my old projects and two major new ones kept me fully occupied. I continued to read Galen and collect material on the Alexandrians.[48] By 1943 I had finished my history of epilepsy,[49] the draft of a translation of Soranus's *Gynecology* was now complete, and I had written a lengthy history of surgery, which, however, was never published.

A publisher had expressed interest in a book on the history of surgery, and Sigerist urged me to undertake the task. The outcome was not a very happy one. The publisher, as I came to realize, was thinking of a book stressing the romantic side of surgery. In spite of what I have said about the romantic spirit of the early days in Leipzig, writing a romance of surgery was neither in my power nor did it conform to my ideas of scholarship, and the book satisfied neither publisher nor author. We agreed to cancel the

[47]I borrow this expression from Fritz K. Ringer, *The Decline of the German Mandarins: The German Academic Community, 1890–1933* (Cambridge, Mass.: Harvard University Press, 1969).

[48]Essay 12 in this volume is an example.

[49]*The Falling Sickness: A History of Epilepsy from the Greeks to the Beginnings of Modern Neurology* (Baltimore: The Johns Hopkins Press, 1945). A revised edition appeared in 1971.

contract, and the war, the desire for a respite from surgical subjects, and new interests kept me from revising the manuscript along more professional lines. Nevertheless, the time spent on it was not entirely wasted; I published some of my results in the form of articles.[50]

While my work was not interrupted by my immigration, it underwent changes, some of which were obvious, others more subtle and not always manifest to myself at the time.

The most obvious change was that of language, which meant, in the first place, acquiring greater fluency in English. I gratefully remember the forbearance with which colleagues and students tolerated mistakes in grammar and pronunciation. But for an intellectual worker, the assimilation of a language means assimilation of the way of thinking of which the language is the form. It implies both how to think and what to think about. As a professional linguist, my wife, who corrected (and still corrects) my literary products, soon told me that to write acceptable English I had to think in English, which involved an educational process. The lack of strict definitions of words and the ease with which new words can be formed make German an ideal philosophical language. These qualities, however, easily protect vagueness and lack of clarity hiding behind an array of words that give a false impression of depth. My assimilation to English became concomitantly a critical review of much German writing, including some of my own.[51]

I also soon noticed that my new environment was not very receptive to philosophizing. Before World War II, scientific medicine in America felt itself to be the solver of problems without itself being problematic. There was, of course, the splitting into specialties, but this the unifying historical synthesis was expected to palliate. The atmosphere suited me, and the "refractory period" regarding philosophical analysis in which I still found myself was probably lengthened by it.

In the early 'thirties, medical history in the United States, as elsewhere, was cultivated by physicians. Many of them belonged to the generation of Osler's pupils. Osler had died in 1919, but his influence was alive among those who acknowledged him as their direct or indirect teacher. Philadelphia, with E. B. Krumbhaar, Esmond Long, R. F. Packard, David Riesman, Victor Robinson, was the center. The *Annals of Medical History* and *Medical Life* were edited there, and the American Association for the History of Medicine, founded by Krumbhaar, met annually in nearby Atlantic City.[52] There were George W. Corner (from 1923–40 in Rochester, N.Y.), Walter Steiner (Hartford, Connecticut), Harvey Cushing, Henry Viets, and Ben-

[50]See Essays 33–35 in this volume.

[51]For instance, my essay on "Sydenham und der Naturbegriff des 17. Jahrhunderts" (see above ftn. 28) proved untranslatable. The translation of "Zur Geschichte von Moral und Syphilis" (Essay 32 in this volume) required considerable editorial changes to smooth the style and to mitigate major inconsistencies in citation.

[52]Prior to its incorporation (in 1958), the Association's name was the American Association of the History of Medicine. For its early history, see E. B. Krumbhaar, "Notes on the early days of the American Association of the History of Medicine," *Bull. Hist. Med.* 23 (1949): 577–82.

jamin Spector (Boston), John Fulton (Yale), Ralph Major and Logan Clendening (Kansas City), Wyndham Blanton (Richmond, Virginia), William Middleton (Madison, Wisconsin), and Chauncey Leake and Sanford Larkey (San Francisco). And there was the Baltimore group with Welch, Garrison, John Rathbone Oliver, and Harry Friedenwald. Of the few men not engaged in one or another form of medical work, W. B. McDaniel, 2nd, from Philadelphia, and Richard H. Shryock (from 1925–38 at Duke, then in Philadelphia until 1949) deserve particular mention.

Most of these men, as well as others not mentioned here,[53] used to meet in Atlantic City, and the medical orientation of the Association was underlined by the coordination of these meetings with those of the Association of American Physicians. Until its reorganization in 1938, largely on Sigerist's initiative, the meetings of the historical association were modest affairs: half a day of presentation of papers followed by the dispensation of the most potent cocktails I have ever tasted in my life, and by a dinner session. The gatherings were small and cordial, most participants being old friends.

Medical historiography in the United States included general histories of medicine, histories of medicine in the United States, of medical specialties, of diseases, with bio-bibliography much in vogue. Publications were intended for a medical public whose education in the humanities was still relatively high compared to what it has become since World War II, but whose interest in the social sciences had not yet been awakened. Side by side with considerable learning and excellent writing, particularly on the part of those mentioned above, there also existed much rehashing, neglect of original sources, and an outlook that isolated the development of medicine from the surrounding intellectual and social life.

The pedagogic aims and methods were those of Osler: to root the medical student in a knowledge of his predecessors, and to enrich him with the master minds of the past. Historical digressions as part of scientific and clinical instruction, references to original articles and recommendation of classics served this purpose and constituted the valuable positive side of the Oslerian method. A few men, with Welch foremost among them, had a broader vision. In a speech of 1929, as newly appointed professor of the history of medicine, Welch said: "We are so absorbed in tremendous additions to our medical knowledge, in the great discoveries in the biological field, that the cultural aspect, the humanizing aspect, is often lost sight of. We should remember the great advantage to all society, not merely to the individual patient, to be derived from this aspect. All that will be brought to the front, will be cultivated with this kind of cultural interest which I claim for the history of medicine. I think this will permeate the whole study [of medicine]."[54]

[53]Krumbhaar, *ibid.*, and Arturo Castiglioni, *A History of Medicine*, trans. and ed. by E. B. Krumbhaar (2nd ed. New York: Knopf, 1958), pp. 1112–15, list most of the medical historians active around 1932.

[54]Quoted from Flexner and Flexner, *op. cit.* (above, ftn. 45), p. 437. Welch was also ahead of many people in suggesting "that there should be workers specifically interested in the ideas, the concepts of medicine" (*ibid.*, p. 520, ftn. 17). See also below, ftn. 84.

His visit to Leipzig and the prospect of a similar institute in Berlin obviously had roused in Dr. Welch great expectations for the new venture at Johns Hopkins. Sigerist too, on his arrival in Baltimore, was full of optimism. He confidently predicted the establishment of departments of medical history in many medical schools within five years. But these sanguine expectations were to be disappointed. Not a single fulltime department had been added by 1937. For many years, therefore, the Johns Hopkins Institute played a role that was unique because of what was done there, as well as of what was not done elsewhere.[55]

The Institute became a central home for medical history, where a fulltime staff did active research, offered courses to the medical students, and lectures and seminars in the "Graduate Weeks," when participants gathered from all over the country for a week of hospitality and painless training. The Institute also offered visitors a place to work for periods of varying length. All these activities, especially the research work of the staff and Fellows (I mention only Erwin H. Ackerknecht, Ludwig Edelstein, Sanford V. Larkey [who succeeded Garrison], Genevieve Miller, and E. I. Drabkin), needed an outlet, which was provided by the *Bulletin of the Institute of the History of Medicine,* that began to appear in 1933. Staff and Fellows, moreover, were joined from time to time by scholars who served as Noguchi Lecturers (Arturo Castiglioni, Edward Hume, Gregory Zilboorg, J. M. D. Olmsted, and Heinrich Zimmern).

The Institute usually sent a contingent to the meetings of the American Association for the History of Medicine. After the reorganization in 1938, the *Bulletin,* which had been the organ of the Institute, became in addition the organ of the Association and changed its name to *Bulletin of the History of Medicine.* With Sigerist in a dominant position, the Institute served as an unofficial office for the Association.

Until 1957, it is true, all of the courses in the Institute were elective. Nevertheless, this was something of a deviation from Osler, who had fostered the infusion of history into medical teaching, while doubting the value of formal courses.[56] I believe that this negative side of the Oslerian method was justified as long as the horizon of the courses was not much

[55]See the volumes of the *Bull. Hist. Med.* from 1933–47, where Sigerist chronicled events under "Medico-historical activities" and in the successive annual reports of the activities of the Institute. Here, as in the case of the Leipzig Institute, I only mention what was or became important to my own work.

[56]William Osler, "A note on the teaching of the history of medicine," *The British Medical Journal,* July 12, 1902, p. 93: "In the present crowded state of the curriculum it does not seem desirable to add the 'History of Medicine' as a compulsory subject. An attractive course will catch the good men and do them good, but much more valuable is it to train insensibly the mind of the student into the habit of looking at things from the historical standpoint, which can be done by individual teachers who themselves appreciate the truth of Fuller's remark: 'History maketh a young man old, without either wrinkles or grey hair. . . .'." At the beginning of the article, Osler states that since the opening of the Johns Hopkins Hospital, John S. Billings "has given an annual course, attendance upon which is optional." Though Osler did not condemn an optional course, he obviously considered his own method preferable. Apparently Billings's course was not an attractive one. In his dedicatory address, "The binding influence of a library on a subdivided profession," presented at the opening of the Welch

different from what Osler offered in so attractive a manner. Fundamentally, the dispute over the Oslerian method is a dispute over *what* should be taught. Formal courses must justify themselves by presenting medicine as developing within cultural, intellectual, and social surroundings of which a professor of medicine will rarely have adequate knowledge, and which he would find difficult to fit into his clinical teaching.

I doubt that the courses at the Institute caused a weakening of the historical infusion in other departments. Yet I believe that the channeling of historical articles away from the *Bulletin of the Johns Hopkins Hospital* (now *Johns Hopkins Medical Journal*) to the *Bulletin of the History of Medicine* and the transfer of the meetings of the Johns Hopkins Medical History Club from the Hospital (where Osler had founded it in 1890) to the Institute tended to isolate the history of medicine, to make it appear an activity which, by its methods and by its interests, was separated from scientific and clinical medicine. As early as 1929, at the inauguration of the Institute, Harvey Cushing had wondered whether the new foundation would "merely mean still another group of specialists having their own societies, organs of publication, separate places of meeting, separate congresses, national and international, and who will also incline to hold aloof from the army of doctors, made and in the making?"[57] This was an early warning to which I shall have to come back when dealing with its implications for myself.

Until the end of World War II, however, these matters did not concern me much. I was engaged in my research and teaching, and when Sigerist was away for any length of time I had to look after the affairs of the Institute. I saw much of Sanford Larkey and, after 1941, of Erwin H. Ackerknecht, who brought along his refreshing and stimulating interest in primitive medicine. I attended the meetings of the History of Ideas Club where, among others, I met Arthur O. Lovejoy, Gilbert Chinard, Kemp Malone, George Boas, Harold Cherniss, Paul Dumont, and Ernst Feise.

From his arrival in Baltimore in 1934, Ludwig Edelstein had an office next to mine, and there was a daily exchange of ideas on ancient medicine. He allowed himself to be persuaded to join Drs. Nicholson J. Eastman, Alan F. Guttmacher, and me in translating the gynecological work of Soranus (who flourished about A.D. 120). Our group met in my office once or twice a week, when I presented a tentative translation from the Greek (after my wife had helped to smooth the English). The translation underwent minute critical review, in which Edelstein proved particularly helpful. As a classicist, he watched over the correct interpretation of the Greek text, resisting attempts to deviate in the interest of what appeared to make better medical sense, but often turned out to be misapprehension. I am afraid

Library (*Bulletin of The Johns Hopkins Hospital* 46 [1930]: 29–42), Harvey Cushing remarked that the course given by Billings was "slimly attended" and "came . . . to be replaced by something far more palatable to the students—the Oslerian method of slowly but surely arousing an historical appetite by the proper touch in each exercise upon the historical bearings of the subject under discussion."

[57]Cushing, *op. cit.* (above, ftn. 56), p. 38.

that for Edelstein these sessions were an unmitigated chore, which he accepted out of a sense of duty and friendship. Our group, augmented at times by transient participants, met for about seven years, and we had completed our task, when the intervention of the war compelled me to postpone the final revisions as well as the introduction and appendices on ancient names and materia medica.[58]

Some time after the entry of the United States into the war, I became associated with the Division of Medicial Sciences of the National Research Council. One of the main tasks that fell upon my colleague, Dr. Elizabeth Ramsey, and me was the preparation of reports on current research concerning the therapy of certain diseases important in the war effort. This work was outside the scope of medical history proper, yet it has taught me a lesson of great value. It has impressed upon me the difference between the confusing present and the past, which presents itself to the historian as through a screen. The present: a multiplicity of conflicting experiences, experiments, and views of persons of different temperament, training, and attainment. The past: a paucity or abundance of documents, depending on chance as much as on intention and already moulded into history by legend, tradition, or previous research. I came to realize that the application of historical methods, excellent and necessary as over-all rules, does not assure certainty, any more than the rules of evidence and a jury's unanimous vote exclude error. This may be a truism, but a truism in theory only; in practice, many a historian will take his Bible oath on having established beyond mere probability "how it really was," to quote Ranke once more.

The end of the war marked an end as well as a new beginning for my work, and in no small measure this was so because of a personal reorientation. I became impatient with the self-imposed abnegation of issues transcending strict historical investigation. I felt the need to assert my own position toward the history of medicine, rather than merely to work within it. Thus I came to write my "Essay on the usefulness of medical history for medicine."[59] Little did I foresee that circumstances would make this article the beginning of a long preoccupation.

The need for intellectual self-assertion was closely connected with what I felt to be a change in my personal situation. Diverse as our reasons may have been, Sigerist and I had both left philosophy behind when we came to Baltimore. But a new star had arisen in the Institute: sociology. Sigerist became engaged in the debates over health insurance and interested in Soviet Russia, which, to him, represented socialized medicine as an idea.[60] I appreciated the importance of historical sociology for medicine, but I neither felt called upon to involve myself in debates over the best scheme

---

[58]The translation appeared in 1956 under the title: *Soranus' Gynecology* (Baltimore: The Johns Hopkins Press).

[59]Essay 4 in this volume.

[60]For Sigerist's sociological development, see Erwin H. Ackerknecht's introduction to *A Bibliography of the Writings of Henry E. Sigerist,* ed. by Genevieve Miller (Montreal: McGill University Press, 1966), pp. 4–6.

for medical care, nor could I see Soviet Russia with Sigerist's eyes. The dissociation in our beliefs led me further away from medical sociology than might have been the case in the absence of ideological disagreement.

But with all this I could not, and cannot, forget that the Sigerist, whose socio-political ideas shocked so many and caused enmity even among his colleagues at Johns Hopkins,[61] had been an *enfant terrible* as far back as 1927, when politics were not involved, and the author of a book as enthusiastic about American medicine as he now was about medicine in Russia. If both admirers and opponents had lent less resonance to his *outré* views, he might have become less entrenched in them and for a shorter time.[62]

Even under the best of circumstances, ideological differences form a poor cement to keep people together. Because of my lengthy absences from Baltimore during the war, I necessarily had less contact with the day to day concerns and activities of the Institute. Moreover, in his initial enthusiasm, Sigerist had predicted that I would occupy a chair in some other place within a short time. But more than twelve years had passed, and I was still around.

At any rate, I felt a certain coolness mounting in Sigerist's attitude toward me. Whether imagined or real, this coolness made me stop thinking of myself as the permanent co-worker of any chief, protected from external disturbances. I had to take stock and define my position.

When Sigerist left Baltimore in the summer of 1947, I knew that an association of twenty-one years had come to an end. I saw my old teacher and chief once more, in Pura in 1956, and I think we were both genuinely glad to meet again.

IV. BALTIMORE: SINCE 1947

One morning in early 1914, on my way to school, I reflected sadly on our times, which seemed so dull, so lacking in promise of stirring events. Not for us the Napoleons, the great wars and revolutions! Our lives were destined to be spent in drab monotony. This was a few months before the outbreak of World War I, and the feeling of the boy on that day conjures up to me a world long past, when peace was considered the normal state of the world, progress a reality, and science and medicine destined to make the life of all mankind better and happier.

We no longer take peace and stability for granted and we have lost our faith in progress as a function of the passage of the years. Science appears

---

[61]See Thomas B. Turner, *op. cit.* (above, ftn. 43), pp. 376–80. Sigerist himself often and angrily repudiated the legend of his forced resignation. At the dinner in his honor in the great hall of the Welch Medical Library shortly before his departure, Dr. Alan M. Chesney, the dean of the medical faculty, represented the School of Medicine.

[62]In his *Landmarks in the History of Hygiene* (London: Oxford University Press, 1956), p. 56, Sigerist stated that being "back in Europe I am no longer in favor of health insurance and I think better solutions should be found." It should not be overlooked that health insurance, so shocking in 1947, is now discussed with little animosity.

as a huge and complicated machinery that can be used for good or evil, and even medicine is ambivalent. Since World War II medicine has expanded into a "health industry," and the physician is a member of one of the "health professions." Improved modes of living, advances in public health and in the ability to prevent and to cure diseases have changed their relative prevalence, prolonged life expectancy, and mitigated much suffering. Hence the "right to health" has been claimed ever more loudly. But the advances have also accentuated the miseries of old age and contributed to the malnutrition of growing populations. They have not stopped the general malaise manifested in drug addiction, in violent protests, in senseless crime, and in the need for psychiatric help. Not so long ago, the history of medicine and the history of science were conceived as a march of progress culminating in the present state of superior medical and scientific knowledge. Such historiography is now under frequent attack, corresponding, I think, to the self-questioning medicine and science have undergone since World War II.

The self-questioning mood made philosophy more acceptable. During the war, Edelstein gave a course that drew an astoundingly large audience of medical students. Most obvious is the upsurge of sociology. To cite the names of Sigerist and Shryock is sufficient reminder of the existence of historical sociology and sociological historiography in medicine prior to the war. Nevertheless, the appointment in 1949 of Richard H. Shryock as Sigerist's successor at the Johns Hopkins Institute is symptomatic for the post-war upsurge.

Shryock was a general (American) historian, specializing in the history of medicine, to which he brought a sociological approach. He was, moreover, interested in the sociology of medicine, which he was expected to cultivate.[63] Shorn of political overtones, medical sociology was very welcome at Johns Hopkins. Because of insufficient funding its expansion on a large scale was not possible. But it remained one of Shryock's major personal concerns, while his teaching of the history of medicine was done chiefly in the School of Arts and Sciences, where he held an appointment in the department of history.

Shryock was anxious to expand in the direction of the history of science,[64] and Henry Guerlac, then Alexandre Koyré, were attracted as visiting lecturers. Budgetary considerations thwarted the realization of these plans, and the history of science came to Hopkins later, independently of the Institute. Lack of resources, after several years, also put an end to the fellowships that Shryock had inaugurated at the Institute. While they

---

[63]*The Johns Hopkins Circular: President's Report November 1949*, p. 47: "... the [medical] Faculty confidently looks forward to a blending of the activities of the Institute, particularly in the field of the relation of medicine to society."

[64]In his report on the activities of the Institute in 1949–50, *Bull. Hist. Med.* 24 (1950): 586–89, Shryock wrote (p. 586): "The Institute plans to extend the scope of its interests to include the history of science in general as well as that of medicine in particular." The annual reports, begun by Sigerist (see above, ftn. 55), were continued by Shryock and then by me. They are a source for the Institute's history until 1968.

lasted, these fellowships accommodated a number of younger scholars who already possessed their Ph.D. degree or were about to receive it (there was only one doctor of medicine among them).

The interest in the history of science was in step with the times. Not very long after the war, the history and philosophy of science began to acquire a strong foothold in American colleges and universities, far beyond the number of academic positions available to the history of medicine. Science loomed large in the post-war consciousness of the American people. So did medicine, but medical progress was attributed to medical science, so that to most people the history of medicine seemed to merge with the history of science, as its partner or as one of its subdivisions. The revolutionary changes in physics, and the explosion of the atom bombs in 1945, invited scientists, especially physicists, to meditate on the philosophical foundations of science and its economic and social consequences, and to consider how it had all come about. Yet strong as the interest of scientists was, the history of science did not remain wedded to them. It is not easy to say where science ends; for George Sarton, the founder of *Isis* and the enthusiastic leader and teacher of the history of science in the United States, it was practically synonymous with all positive knowledge, advancing on many sides through the individual sciences. Though it comprised all the individual sciences, the history of science was not the mere sum of their sundry histories. It had an individuality of its own and could be taught as an autonomous historical subject. The young historians of science were trained as historians; they thought of themselves as such, and the range and depth of their scientific knowledge varied considerably.

The developments I have sketched so summarily have influenced my thoughts and my activities. In the first place, they revived my interest in philosophy. Until Sigerist's departure in the summer of 1947, I enjoyed a period of relative ease between war work and new assignments to come. I began working on a new project, successor to my research on the history of epilepsy, which had come to an end with the publication of *The Falling Sickness.*

The first installment of the new project was an article on "The philosophical background of Magendie's physiology."[65] It was to initiate an analysis of the relationship between physiology and philosophy in the nineteenth century, and this article was followed by several more installments.[66] The project marked the reawakening of my interest in philosophy; at the same time, it brought me back to physiology. The problems that had stirred me so deeply in my early student days now occupied me once more. There was even a relationship to an early experience, a course in anatomy in which the lecturer had talked about Cuvier and others outstanding in the romantic-idealistic period of anatomy. Enthusiasm rather than clarity marked his talk; it was the kind of lecture that makes the

[65]Essay 24 in this volume.
[66]Essays 25–28 in this volume.

student scent something exciting without illuminating him, and thus spurs him on to investigate the matter himself.

The article on Magendie had focused on the relationship of matter and life on the one hand, and on body and mind on the other. The latter theme led me to phrenology, and both themes were taken up in my Garrison lecture on "Basic science, medicine, and the romantic era."[67]

When this lecture was delivered, my original project had already been diverted. Physiology of the early nineteenth century was dominated by the concept of irritability, which had to be dealt with. Within the framework of my project I need not have gone further back than Albrecht von Haller, who had accepted the term from Glisson, had given the notion an experimental turn, initiated a debate and, however innocently, had laid the groundwork for making irritability the key to a philosophy of medicine. Haller and his debate had occupied me before, when I had re-edited the English translation of his *Dissertation on the Sensible and Irritable Parts of Animals*[68] and had guided Genevieve Miller's Master's essay on his debate with Robert Whytt.[69] Yet my work on the history of epilepsy had made me suspect that the history of irritability antedated Glisson. At first I thought of interrupting my project by a lengthy essay, or a small book, on the history of irritability. But the more I dug, the more the subject grew, and the more complex it became. Irritability and its precursor, irritation, were concepts that had their origin in psychology and pathology and had stayed alive in these two disciplines. "Stimulus" and "response," activating irritability and describing the subsequent action, were notions that went far beyond biology. Again, it was not satisfactory to deal with irritability and irritation as concepts without asking what actual forms of behavior they represented at varying times.

For better or for worse my old project had been channeled into a new one, the writing of a history of irritability. A few installments appeared,[70] and when I was invited to deliver three Hideyo Noguchi lectures at the Johns Hopkins School of Medicine in 1969, I gratefully seized the opportunity to crystallize my thoughts. The lectures were delivered under the title, "On the History of Anger, Irritation, and Irritability," but I have not published them, hoping to expand them in a much more comprehensive book. These projects and my continuing occupation with Galen and the Alexandrian school (about which I will speak later) satisfied my personal need for combining history, philosophy, and a medically or scientifically provocative problem. But was this personal solution adequate for dealing objectively with the Janus head of medical history? Was it good enough to

[67]Essay 26 in this volume. My article on "Gall and the phrenological movement," *Bull. Hist. Med.* 21 (1947): 275–321, has been omitted because of its length.

[68]Baltimore: The Johns Hopkins Press, 1936 (reprinted from *Bull. Hist. Med.* 4 [1936]: 651–99).

[69]Genevieve Miller, "Albrecht von Haller's Controversy with Robert Whytt" (M.A. Essay, The Johns Hopkins University, 1939).

[70]Essays 22, 23, 36 in this volume, and cf. my "Scientific medicine and historical research" *Perspectives in Biology and Medicine* 3 (1959): 82–83.

form a policy for the history of medicine? Could it be recommended to all who wished to become full-time medical historians?

In 1947 I was far from asking such questions with the clarity they now seem to me to possess. Nor was there any need for me to go beyond my essay on the usefulness of medical history for medicine, where I had met Cushing's disquieting question by stating: "For the physician who has made history his life task, it means that he must not allow himself to be wholly absorbed by the historical interest itself. While at work he must be unhampered by any considerations foreign to the subject he is investigating. But he must also be able to account for the pragmatic value of the subjects he chooses. In method he will be a historian, but in aim a physician."[71] The essay did not deny others, who were not physicians, the right to cultivate medical history; it merely ignored them. Nor did it tell the physician-historian what to do if he failed to be attracted by a subject of pragmatic value. The essay had been satisfied with the bland assurance that: "If the historian and the profession alike are convinced of its usefulness, the history of medicine will play its part in the future development of medicine."[72]

Developments after Sigerist's departure did not permit acquiescence with bland assurances and turned my essay into the beginning of a long preoccupation. Ackerknecht was now the head of the new department of the history of medicine at the University of Wisconsin; Edelstein had left the Institute in the same year as Sigerist, so that Genevieve Miller and I constituted the entire full-time staff. Because the American Association for the History of Medicine had relied heavily on Sigerist's guidance and help, his office had to be kept functioning until the Association was able to stand on its own feet. Until mid-1948, Genevieve Miller edited the *Bulletin of the History of Medicine;* then she also left, and I inherited the editorship. Shryock's arrival relieved me of my temporary administrative responsibilities. But in our division of labor, the teaching of medical students and of house staffs fell to me, and I retained the editorship of the *Bulletin.* Since the latter was also the organ of the Association, I remained involved in the Association's life. From 1948 on, the development of medical history became an official concern of mine and the editorial policy of the *Bulletin* a responsibility beyond assuring the life of a journal.

There had been no intention on the part of the *Bulletin* to compete with the *Annals of Medical History* and with *Medical Life.* But, whatever the reasons, these two journals stopped publication, the former in 1942, the latter in 1938. For several years, until the appearance of the *Journal of the History of Medicine and Allied Sciences* in 1946, the *Bulletin* was the only major medico-historical journal in the United States, and this fact, together with the acceptance of all papers presented at meetings of the Association, swelled its size and allowed the appearance of material of doubtful historical workmanship. Reduction of the size to financially bearable limits was an unavoidable necessity which I was resolved to use in the interest of raising

[71]See below, p. 92.
[72]*Ibid.*

the editorial standard. It was easy to resolve upon such a course, yet more difficult to implement it. Articles by physicians were prone to be among the methodologically weak contributions, yet too strict a policy would have estranged the medical profession. Without its backing the history of clinical medicine, surgery, and obstetrics would fall into neglect, and medical history might also lose in influence upon medical men. The standard had to be raised slowly enough to allow acclimatization of the readers and to exert an educational function which, I trusted, would be helped by the teaching at new departments of medical history. Yale organized such a department in 1951, and there was hope that other places would follow, or provide competent instruction in some form.

Of course, this required the availability of instructors. New blood was urgently needed, and after succeeding Shryock as director of the Johns Hopkins Institute in 1958, I applied for a training grant, which the National Institutes of Health awarded in a most gratifying manner.[73] The training program was activated in 1960; it was facilitated by the new teaching schedule for medical history at the Johns Hopkins School of Medicine, whereby the course, already made required in 1957, was considerably extended. Parallel with it, a course of lectures on the history of public health became required at the School of Hygiene and Public Health. For our trainees these courses provided a broad initial orientation and an opportunity to gain some teaching experience when they had advanced sufficiently.

The articles I wrote on medical historiography between 1946 and 1968, the year of my retirement from administrative and editorial work, have to be understood against this background. Shryock had drawn a simple consequence from a simple and generally recognized fact. It was a fact that modern society, in all its workings, was so intimately connected with science and medicine that without them it would cease to be what it is. Therefore, medicine and science had a rightful place in general historiography. Shryock pleaded for their integration into the teaching and the textbooks of history. In my opinion, his argument is so convincing that I fail to understand on what grounds, other than traditionalism and lack of familiarity with these subjects, historians can close their minds to it. In this specific connection it was also reasonable to speak of the history of medicine and science in one breath.

In my function as an academic teacher I tried to contribute my share to the promotion of the history of medicine at large by admitting scholars in nonmedical fields to our training program. My main task, however, was to look after the specific interests of medical history within medicine and medical schools, with the aim of broadening the medical perspective through closer contact with the humanities, the history of science, and sociology.[74]

---

[73]Yale received a training grant simultaneously with Johns Hopkins.

[74]For further details see my paper, "Who should teach the history of medicine?" *Education in the History of Medicine,* ed. by John B. Blake (New York: Hafner, 1968), which was presented two years before my retirement from the directorship of the Johns Hopkins Institute.

But my function as editor had to go beyond this. The *Bulletin* had no right, I felt, to restrict itself to medical authors and medical readers. The more the history of medicine attracted others, including historians of science, the greater the influx of good papers from nonmedical sources became. A parallel process occurred within the American Association for the History of Medicine. It had developed into a truly national society, meeting every year in a different city. From representing physicians interested in medical history, it has come to represent a profession *sui generis* as well.

The professionalization of medical historiography is connected with the general expansion of medicine. This expansion renders parochial the "iatrocentric" orientation[75] of what used to be the history of the science, art, and profession of healing. Medical historiography is now becoming the history of a much broader, scientific, professional, social, technical, and economic complex. The rising profession is united in its historical interests, but its members vary greatly in their relation to medicine. There will be those for whom historiography will be an integral part of medicine. The existence of this first group remains very important, because from it are likely to come the historians of those subjects, like clinical medicine, where a substantive, technical knowledge that can hardly be acquired from books alone is essential. Others, in the manner of Shryock, without personal involvement in medicine, will take it as a social phenomenon that concerns us all, or, as historians of science, will cultivate the basic medical sciences. A last group (I may cite Edelstein as an example) may view medicine as an institution within a particular period.[76]

Professionalization puts the subject in the hands of those who derive a living from cultivating it, who form a community that promotes their interests, especially in the universities, who apply the standards to which they have been trained, who increasingly communicate among themselves, and who fractionize their competence into ever narrower areas. Professionalization can help to fulfill more objectively a general function of all historiography, viz., to serve as critic of its subject, as an objective evaluation of the present in the light of the past. But professionalization also has its dangers, especially in the history of medicine, where it may lead to the alienation of the medical professions. More generally speaking, communication among the members can become communication for the members, the sense of stability may engender preoccupation with the rules of the game and proper methods, to the point where it becomes tactless to ask whether the game is worth playing at all.

Once medical historians have varied aims, the statue of Janus can be removed from their meeting hall. Perhaps it was my personal preoccupation that put it there in the first place; be that as it may, having retired from administrative, editorial, and teaching duties, I can now continue my re-

---

[75]See George Rosen, "Levels of integration in medical historiography: a review," *Journal of the History of Medicine and Allied Sciences* 4 (1949): 460–67.

[76]This rough categorization does not exclude that physicians are found in all groups and nonmedical persons in the first.

search without thinking that I must carry the old god's head on my shoulders.

I have already mentioned my work on the history of irritability, and it remains to speak of my work on Galen and the Alexandrians. Here too my project underwent changes. The importance of Alexandria lay in its contribution to the systematization of medicine around Galen and Hippocrates, i.e., the formation of medical scholasticism. Hence I decided to make the formation of scholasticism my main theme, dropping the concentration on, and limitation to, Alexandria and taking Byzantium and the assimilation of Greek medicine in the Arabic world within my orbit. Helped by a grant from the American Philosophical Society, I was able in 1956 to survey a considerable number of manuscripts in European libraries and to gain an impression of the kind of Graeco-Latin material that could be counted on. Participation in a symposium at Dumbarton Oaks gave me an opportunity to take Byzantium as my vantage point.[77]

Because of his dominating position in scholastic medicine, Galen was the basis from which research had to start. Again and again I was led back to him.[78] When Cornell University invited me to deliver the Messenger lectures in 1970, I chose as my title *Galenism: Rise and Decline of a Medical Philosophy*. In these lectures, which in modified form have appeared as a book,[79] I could summarize what I had done so far.

Working on Galen, I have been increasingly impressed by the difficulty of evaluating his ideas, spread as they are over scores of writings, while remaining ignorant of the author's true character and temperament, of the life he led, and of the reception he and his work were given during his lifetime. Analogous questions had already arisen in my mind when I tried to account for the elusiveness of Paracelsus. In writing that "our conviction of man's essential unity seems to stimulate us to the attempt at systematizing the thoughts and acts of historical personalities," and by citing Paracelsus as an example of the dubiousness of such attempts, I actually assailed the bias I had shared.[80] And I was assailing the same bias when I began asking myself whether Galen's ideas progressively evolved or whether, throughout his life, they remained labile, responding to the challenges of the day.[81]

This turn to the personal is not a reversal to the biographical vogue that prevailed in medical history, when, in a somewhat naive Carlylean fashion, ideas were deemed to emanate from the hero's brain as by spontaneous generation. My work on the history of irritability, begun as the history of a physiological concept, also led me to human feelings, to the experience of

[77]Essay 14 in this volume.

[78]Essays 9, 10, 23 in this volume. I have omitted my translations from Galen's *Anatomical Administrations* in view of Charles Singer's translation of the whole work.

[79]*Galenism: Rise and Decline of a Medical Philosophy* (Ithaca, N.Y.: Cornell University Press, 1973).

[80]Essay 15, ftn. 37, in this volume.

[81]See "On Galen's pneumatology" (Essay 9 in this volume). This article and the one on Paracelsus's elusiveness (Essay 15 in this volume) were written at about the same time.

anger and irritation in people of various times. To put it more generally: abstractions such as the Zeitgeist, economic and social factors, all have their place in historiography; it would be plain foolishness to disregard them. But they create nothing unless operating in living persons, be they single individuals or groups. Living persons are people living in a present of harmonizing and conflicting desires, demands, and decisions, considered by them as right or wrong, wise or foolish, profitable or harmful, good or bad, noble or shameful.

To say this is not to proclaim the metaphysical principle of the freedom of the will as against the metaphysical principle of causal necessity. When we consider what we should do, we live in the present; a reminder that our wishes and demands are causally determined carries little weight, because it will not stop us from deliberating, debating, and directing. On the other hand, an appeal to values is equally meaningless in scientific analysis. The two different approaches often exist regardless of our metaphysics.[82] In historiography the matter is rather complex. Up to a point, we can explore the past as a set of events to be explained psychologically, sociologically, even biologically, i.e., by means of the science of our preference. But we can also bring the past back to life, change it into a present, and enter into it. Particularly, we do this whenever we look for "great men" to model ourselves after (e.g., the role Osler's life is still playing in Anglo-Saxon medical education), or for situations that might help us to decide on a course of action (e.g., current debates over the Hippocratic oath, or the Flexner report of 1910).

The study of history that stresses man and his values is one of the humanistic disciplines. Looking back on my work, I realize that it has increasingly tended toward the humanistic pole of historiography. I use the word "humanistic" not without hesitation, for under the doubtful name of "humanistic medicine," there has arisen a miscellany oriented toward humanistic tradition, human value, humane attitude, and, sometimes, anything that is not natural science. The rise of "humanistic medicine" is understandable as a counterpoise to medical science when it forgets that cases are individuals.[83] I should like to hope that it will also become a stimulus for better, and regenerated, humanistic education of the future physician, rather than a surrogate for the advancing elimination of the humanities from the future doctor's schooling. Humanistic, in the sense in which I take it, refers to the humanist tradition in philosophy, history, and

---

[82]This distinction of the world of facts, i.e., things done, and the world of things to be done is no more than a reflection of the dichotomy underlying Kant's distinction of "pure" and "practical" reason, and the many modifications down to Martin Buber's distinction of "it" and "thou," and P. F. Strawson's analytical approach in "Freedom and resentment," *Proceedings of the British Academy* 48(1962):187–212. Metaphysics begins when we attempt to find a basis for reconciling or justifying them.

[83]Jacques Barzun, "The education of candidates for medical school," *Bulletin of the New York Academy of Medicine* 49 (1973): 253–57, has rightly remarked (p. 256, ftn. 1) "that the stimulation of the medical student's imagination, which many people today wish were more active and humane, will not be easy to arouse if his teachers tell him continually that he is a machine, a physicochemical arrangement of prefabricated, predetermined parts which work like a computer tied to a pump and a stove."

literature. It is oriented toward man and his values,[84] but it remains a discipline, a matter of the brain. Its study in schools of medicine is needed to complement the scientific education, biological and sociological, that deals with man statistically. But humaneness, resting on compassion, involves the heart and should pervade all medical teaching, rather than be relegated to special lectures, seminars, or departments.[85]

Having joined the happy ranks of those out of public affairs, free to plow the ancestral acres with my oxen, as Horace has it,[86] I need no longer concern myself with the pragmatic worth of humanistic historiography, be it for medicine or for anything else. Some years ago I even thought of devoting the years of my retirement to a study of the great historians, notably those of antiquity, to learn what induced them to look upon the past as they did, and what picture of man guided their work and resulted from it. Yet in 1968, when retirement came, I was too busy bringing out the revised edition of *The Falling Sickness,* preparing the Hideyo Noguchi lectures and then the Messenger lectures and, generally speaking, trying to save my earlier projects. Thus the contemplation of the historians was postponed, and I realize that as long as I have creative powers left I shall probably not stray far from medical historiography.

Indeed, why turn to new fields to study the moral nature of man?[87] We can behold truth only in the form of samples, and if the historiography of medicine is to comprise "all that is historical in medicine, as well as all that is medical in history,"[88] it constitutes a sample of considerable size. It is also a good sample, I believe. Hippocrates, Galen, Avicenna, Averroes, Maimonides, Paracelsus, Rabelais, Haller, Virchow, Claude Bernard, and Freud were among the intellectual leaders of mankind. Physicians have been both praised and ridiculed in novels and on the stage. Health and disease have been subjects of religious and philosophical meditation, and as metaphors they are to be found in politics, science, and literature. The human body in the glory of health and in the wretchedness of sickness has been depicted in art. Man has speculated over the meaning of his disease for himself and for his community. Medicine is not only a science and an art; it is also a mode of looking at man with compassionate objectivity. Why turn elsewhere to contemplate man's moral nature?

[84]I believe that Dr. Welch, speaking about the humanizing influence of history (see above), wished to offer a counterweight to the detached presentation of medical science. He wished to place science and scientists in the world of human values that decides whether science should or should not be part of its culture.

[85]Compassion is not the same as sentimentality, the outpouring of emotion without rational restraint. Compassion presumes awareness of a common bond, yet it is more than a purely theoretical acknowledgment of the brotherhood of man. Brothers do not necessarily love one another.

[86]*Epodes* 2. 1–4: Beatus ille qui procul negotiis,
Ut prisca gens mortalium,
Paterna rura bobus exercet suis
Solutus omni faenore.

[87]Moral is here taken in the sense of man as an evaluating being; it should not be confused with moralizing.

[88]I offered this definition in "Who should teach the history of medicine?" (see above, ftn. 74), p. 55.

II

The Historical Approach
to Medicine

2

The Meaning of Medicine
in Historical Perspective*

IT IS A GREAT privilege for me to be allowed to participate in these ceremonies. Of course , every great medical library establishes a connection with the past. Even the books acquired while they are new turn into
old books and thus into links between the generations. For this very reason,
it is but natural to give the history of medicine a home in a medical library,
where it is close to its tools. But this library need not await old age. It will
house historical treasures already admired the world over. And it will be
the future task of the medical historian to use them so that the past will
help to instruct the present.

The more closely we study the past of medicine, the more we find every
generation beset by its own beliefs and uncertainties. If we wish to know
what meaning of medicine prevailed in a former period, the old sources
will give a variety of answers which often are conflicting, just as modern
views are. Out of the variety we shall select for discussion a few historical
documents, events, and opinions that seem relevant for problems beset-
ting Western medicine today. And we shall begin with the best-known
medical document, the so-called Oath of Hippocrates.[1]

Medicine is here referred to as an art or craft (*technē*) to be learned from
a teacher who, among other things, hands down precepts and gives oral
instruction. Apart from regulating the relationship to the teacher and to
prospective students, the Oath defines the attitude of the physician toward
his patients and their families in a series of specific pledges: a regimen
beneficial to the patient, no dispensing of poisons or abortifacients, absten-
tion from operations with the knife and from acts detrimental to the
household visited, silence about things seen or heard that should not be
revealed. There is no concern for society at large, nor is there any insistence on adding to medical knowledge. The patient's welfare is the main
object. In Western civilization, ever since the Hippocratic Oath was
adopted, the practicing physician has acknowledged the treatment of the
patients entrusted to him as his personal responsibility.

It may not always have been so. The medical works of older civilizations
speak a rather impersonal language. The large number of prescriptions in

---

*From *Bibliotheca Medica: Physician for Tomorrow. Dedication of the Countway Library of Medicine,
May 26 and 27, 1965*. Edited by David McCord (Boston: Harvard Medical School, 1966),
pp. 30–45.
[1]For text, translation, and interpretation see Ludwig Edelstein, *The Hippocratic Oath* (Baltimore: The Johns Hopkins Press, 1943) (Supplements to the *Bulletin of the History of Medicine*,
no. 1).

Egyptian and Mesopotamian texts indicates that the physician, up to a point, could try a variety of remedies. But on the whole, the physician appears as the dispenser of predetermined modes of practice, rather than as the individual healer of his patients. Even in ancient Greece individualized medicine, such as we are wont to connect with the name of Hippocrates, may have arisen relatively late, perhaps in the fifth century, when philosophy and the Sophists fostered curiosity as well as independence of thought and thus induced the physician to speculate about the patient's condition and to explain it to him.[2]

The Hippocratic physician was expected to take care of his patients as best he could. He wrote about the nature of medicine, and of disease, and about the possibilities of therapy. His profession was appreciated by the state, which hired public physicians.[3] Medicine meant much to a society which valued health and bodily beauty highly.[4] But society did not prescribe to the physician how to act, nor did society surround his profession with a protective halo.

In the third century B.C., when scientific anatomy made its appearance, a preoccupation with medicine as a super-individual entity came to the fore. This preoccupation manifested itself in the rise of sects whose arguments show a greater concern with the philosophical and scientific foundations of medicine than with actual treatment, which was not necessarily affected at all.

Herophilus, and Galen after him, defined medicine as "knowledge of what is healthy, diseased, and neutral."[5] This definition leaves undecided how and for whose benefit such knowledge was to be applied. The objective motive of the physician-scientist's research was to further the good of all men, including generations still unborn.[6] Subjectively he might be guided by the desire to know, by "scientific curiosity" as we would say.

To this ambivalence of possible motivations, society has reacted ambivalently too, promoting research yet expressing fears lest the urge for knowl-

[2]See Owsei Temkin, "Greek medicine as science and craft," *Isis* (1953), *44*:213–25 [Essay 8 in this volume.]

[3]In Rome, usefulness is conceded to medicine by Cicero, *De officiis* 1, c. 42; usefulness for the state is implied in Quintilian, *Institutio oratoria*, VII, 38; see Ludwig Edelstein, "The professional ethics of the Greek physician," *Bull. Hist. Med.* (1956), *30*:391–419 (p. 417, note 48).

[4]On the connection of health and beauty see C. M. Bowra, *The Greek Experience* (Cleveland and New York: The World Publishing Company, 1958, © 1957), p. 93 ff.

[5]Galen, *Ars Medica*, c. 1, ed. Kühn, vol. 1, p. 307, defines medicine as *epistēmē* of what is healthy, diseased, and neutral, and the same definition is ascribed to Herophilus in Pseudo-Galen, *Introductio seu medicus*, c. 6, vol. 14, p. 688. The *Definitiones medicae*, vol. 19, p. 351, however, make Herophilus use *technē* instead of *epistēmē*. The use of the definition by Herophilus is very likely, but not certain; see Owsei Temkin, "Studies on late Alexandrian medicine, I," *Bull. Inst. Hist. Med.* (1935), *3*:405–30 (pp. 418–19) [Essay 12 in this volume.]

[6]This motive is stressed by the dogmatists of the early first century A.D., in their defense of the vivisection of criminals which they report as having been performed by Herophilus and Erasistratus: "Nor is it, as most people say, cruel that in the execution of criminals, and but a few of them, we should seek remedies for *innocent people of all future ages*," (Celsus, *De medicina*, Proemium, 26. Translation by W. G. Spencer, Loeb Classical Library [Cambridge, Mass.: Harvard University Press, 1935], vol. 1, p. 15, italics mine.) The difference in the ethics of healer and scientist is stressed by Edelstein, "The professional ethics."

edge overcome the humaneness of the healer. The degree to which research has been aided has varied with the structure of society. In antiquity,
the munificence of kings like the Ptolemies and of a few individuals contrasted with the indifference of the public at large. In the late Roman
Empire, when provisions were made for professors of medicine, research
was on its way to book learning. Suspicion of the scientist, on the other
hand, depended partly on the prevailing mode of research and partly on
popular imagination molded by the sensibilities and morals of the times. In
antiquity, when medical research was sporadic, the fear that the unscrupu-
lous physician misuse his knowledge of poisons was probably greater than
the fear that the scientist might use man's body for research.[7]

In between the physician as healer and the physician-scientist, antiquity
also knew of the physician as a public benefactor concerned about the
health of a community. A public decree, allegedly issued in recognition of
the merits of Hippocrates, praised him for having sent his pupils to various
places in Greece to teach the inhabitants how to save themselves from the
plague which had invaded the country from the lands of the barbarians.
The decree commended Hippocrates for having ungrudgingly published
his medical writings so as to increase the number of physicians who could
bring salvation, and for withholding his help from the Persians, the
enemies of the Greeks.[8] This decree was part of a novelistic literature
written around Hippocrates in the later centuries of antiquity.

At this time, then, the physician as a healer, but not as a citizen, found his
meaning[9] in the care of the individual patient, be he friend of foe.[10] The
public-minded physician, as a citizen, applied his knowledge for the good
of a city or even of a whole nation. The physician-scientist referred to the
welfare of mankind. There neither was, nor is there, necessarily complete
harmony between these three aspects, although they all show a common
aim: health.

From health as the aim of medicine we turn to its object: man. There
seems to have been widespread agreement from antiquity through the
Middle Ages and Renaissance and far into modern times that professional
medicine dealt with man's body. With his soul medicine dealt only in so far
as behavior was associated with somatic conditions. The physician was the

[7]On the attitude towards research in antiquity see Ludwig Edelstein, "Motives and incentives for science in antiquity," *Scientific Change*, ed. A. C. Crombie (New York: Basic Books,
1963), pp. 15–41.
[8]E. Littré, *Oeuvres complètes d' Hippocrate*, t. 9 (Paris: Baillière, 1861), pp. 400–2, also pp.
312–21. For physicians actually honored by decrees see Louis Cohn-Haft, *The Public Physicians
of Ancient Greece*, Northampton, Mass.: Department of History of Smith College, 1956 (Smith
College Studies in History, vol. 42).
[9]"Meaning" here does not refer to personal motives which, as Edelstein, "The professional
ethics," p. 409, has shown, differed greatly. When Galen, *That the Best Physician also is a
Philosopher*, c. 2 (see Edelstein, *ibid.*, pp. 406 and 408, note 31) speaks of medicine as a
philanthropic art and refers to people who practice medicine for money rather than "for the
sake of good service done to men," he counts on general recognition of medicine as beneficial,
leaving it open for what special reasons approval is given.
[10]Expressed clearly by Scribonius Largus; see Edelstein, "The professional ethics," p. 409.

natural philosopher, the *physicus,* while the philosopher or the priest was the physician of the soul. In antiquity, as Edelstein has shown, philosophers, intent upon the moral guidance of man, used to point to the power of the physician to whom free men entrusted their bodily welfare.[11] In the Middle Ages, the preoccupation with the body gave the physician the reputation of being a materialist or even an atheist. On the other hand, so long as society believed that good and evil were of the soul, not of the body, the physician was not burdened by a concern for the crimes and sins of man; society assured medicine moral neutrality. As late as the seventeenth century, Thomas Sydenham defended his treatise on venereal disease by saying that he was dealing with this disease, "not with the view of making men's minds more immoral, but for the sake of making their bodies sounder. This is the business of the physician."[12]

Philosophy was the tool by the aid of which medicine tried to find the true causes of health and disease. In the association with natural philosophy we discern the desire to incorporate medicine into the totality of human knowledge. Yet the art of healing rested on age-old experience stored in the works of the authorities, and this had to be learned. Therefore, medicine represented not only philosophy, it also represented learning. In the Renaissance, when regaining the knowledge of the ancients seemed an important task, physicians such as Fracastoro, Linacre, and Fuchs were among the leading humanists. The people were imbued with respect for learning as well as for rank, bestowed upon the doctor of medicine by the Universities in ceremonies which were impressive and costly.

Orthodox medicine, therefore, meant the proper form for dealing with sickness; it did not always mean love and trust. Moreover, changing criteria of what constituted true knowledge also changed the character of medical science. To the iconoclast Paracelsus, the "Luther of the physicians," the scholar-physician decked in his academic regalia was a meaningless sham, intent on exploiting the ignorant. Experience ought to be gathered from Nature, not from books. The new anatomy of Vesalius with its realistic pictures, multiplied by the printing press, propagated a new sense of what was fact. Physiological experiment fitted into the new philosophy of the seventeenth century, which insisted on experimental proof rather than on authority and rank. Indeed, Descartes, the great visionary of a mechanistic biology, looked on medicine as the prime beneficiary of the new science.[13]

But we must distinguish between the growth of the medical sciences and

[11]Ludwig Edelstein, "The relation of ancient philosophy to medicine," *Bull. Hist. Med.* (1952), 26:299–316. Plato, *Republic,* 342 D ff. speaks of the physician as "a ruler of bodies." According to Democritus, fragment 31, "Medicine heals diseases of the body, wisdom frees the soul from passions." (Kathleen Freeman, *Ancilla to the Pre-Socratic Philosophers* [Cambridge, Mass.: Harvard University Press, 1948], p. 99). For later formulations of medicine and philosophy as sisters, and of medicine as the philosophy of the body and philosophy as medicine of the soul, see Owsei Temkin, "Studies on late Alexandrian medicine, I.," p. 418 [p. 187].

[12]*The Works of Thomas Sydenham,* transl. R. G. Latham, vol. 2 (London: Sydenham Society, 1850), p. 33.

[13]R. Descartes, "Discours de la méthode," *Oeuvres de Descartes,* publiées par C. Adam et P. Tannery, VI (Paris: Cerf, 1902), p. 62.

their meaning for practical medicine. Prior to the late nineteenth century the progress of the new sciences did relatively little to enhance the ability to cure disease. In retrospect, some of us are prepared to go so far as to condemn the older medicine altogether, claiming that it did more harm than good. Possible exaggerations aside: can medicine really be meaningful to society if it is unable to prevent and to cure disease?

This is not a new question. Around 400 B.C., a Hippocratic physician defended the existence of the medical art against those who attributed recoveries to mere luck.[14] On the whole, however, radical skepticism seems to have been rare in antiquity, in spite of criticism by Plato, Pliny, Martial, and others who hit certain forms of medicine and the human weaknesses of physicians rather than the possibility of therapy.

Even such a bitter critic as Petrarch, in the fourteenth century, disclaimed contempt for medicine and physicians *per se* and directed his invective against contemporary manifestations. "The ancient physicians were wont to cure silently," Petrarch wrote; "you kill while you are pleading, disputing, and shouting all together. . . . While you forge syllogisms, people die who, without you, could have lived. How often have I vainly said: cure, heal! Leave eloquence to those whose proper business it is; it cannot be yours."[15]

Of the great critics of medicine, Molière, three hundred years after Petrarch, came nearest to denying medicine all positive meaning. In *Le malade imaginaire*, M. Béralde confesses his disbelief in medicine. To his mind, there is nothing more ridiculous than a man who undertakes to cure another. If left to herself, Nature will rid herself of the disorder; only our impatience does not allow her to do it. As a result, "almost all men die of their remedies and not of their diseases." The physicians fool themselves or others when they promise to cure, and when they pretend to help Nature and to prolong life they just tell us the tall story *(le roman)* of medicine.[16] Some physicians give themselves away naïvely. Dr. Diafoirus is annoyed with persons of quality, for "when they happen to be sick they are absolutely insistent that their physicians cure them." Toinette, tongue in cheek, commiserates with Dr. Diafoirus about such impertinence. "This is by no means the purpose of your attending them; you are only there to receive your stipend and to give them medicines: it is up to them to recover if they can!"[17]

Obviously, the physicians whom Molière ridiculed were not of an advanced type. They were anachronisms upholding medieval forms in a world where such forms were becoming meaningless.[18] The coming generation of doctors with their new science were to take their rightful place, in

[14]Hippocrates, *On the Art.*

[15]Francesco Petrarca, *Invective contra medicum,* ed. Pier Giorgio Ricci (Rome: Edizioni di Storia e Letteratura, 1950) (Storia e Letteratura, 32), p. 80.

[16]Molière, *Le malade imaginaire,* Act III, Scene 3.

[17]*Ibid.,* Act II, Scene 5.

[18]There are some expressions in *Le malade imaginaire* which hint at Molière's possible belief in the new mechanical science; see Owsei Temkin, "Studien zum 'Sinn'-Begriff in der Medizin," *Kyklos,* 1929, 2:21–105 (see p. 74).

the age of Enlightenment. The eighteenth century was not the first to see medicine in an enlightening role. Some of the most telling attacks against magic and superstition are to be found in the Hippocratic collection. Even during the Middle Ages orthodox medicine adhered to the idea of mania and melancholy as natural diseases. In the sixteenth century, a physician, Wier, took the lead against the persecution of witches. Not all doctors were enlightened in the sense commonly given to this word, and Paracelsus and Van Helmont would be hard to fit into this category. But medicine, with its concern for the science and welfare of the body, easily adapted itself to the new era, and physicians like Tissot were instrumental in propagating enlightened views among the public. Medical enlightenment meant reform of daily hygiene and rejection of superstitious practices. It also meant lessening of the social prejudices against surgery as a lower branch of the healing art.

From the Enlightenment the doctor emerged as a civic leader but not necessarily as a more potent healer. Less than two hundred years after Molière's death, a movement arose within the profession, echoing his arguments against medicine. The therapeutic nihilists of the mid-nineteenth century insisted that medicine was quite unable to cure diseases and that the patients would be better off if placed under hygienic conditions and left to the healing power of nature. Contemporary medicine was said to be unable to cure diseases, because it had no understanding of the biological processes involved. However, whereas Molière had used this argument to ridicule the doctors, the therapeutic nihilists postulated a moratorium on curative medicine until such time as a new foundation for a promising therapy had been laid. Nobody could foretell how long the completion of the new foundation would take, and until then medicine should find its meaning in research.

Therapeutic nihilism was a revolution against the prevailing pharmacological treatment in internal medicine. It marked the turn from traditional forms of healing to what we call scientific medicine. It strengthened the idea that the life of a medical man can be meaningful removed from any treatment of the sick, if it is devoted to science; and it helped to undermine the notion that medicine was the domain of physicians only.[19]

Therapeutic nihilism met with strong resistance on the part of clinicians. Primarily an academic movement, it found little favor in the United States, where medical sects blossomed more than ever before. The resistance suggests that medicine can be felt to be meaningful even when unable to prevent and to cure disease.[20] Molière and the nihilists had demanded all or nothing: either cure or resign! As if the physician who prescribed

[19]I have dealt with these aspects of therapeutic nihilism in "Historical aspects of drug therapy," in *Drugs in Our Society*, ed. by Paul Talalay (Baltimore: Johns Hopkins Press, 1964), pp. 3–16, where literature on the subject is cited.

[20]This does not, of course, deny the existence of a vested interest reluctant to admit the inability to cure.

quinine in the mistaken belief that he was preventing infection with malaria or radically curing it, did not benefit his patient![21] Hippocratic wisdom merely admonished "to help or at least to do no harm."[22] Seen over the ages, medicine is a social institution, a response, in other than purely spiritual forms, to the need for aiding the sick and protecting the healthy. Radical cure is an ideal that may or may not be realized.

If we contrast Claude Bernard and Oliver Wendell Holmes, we obtain an impression of how differently medicine could be envisaged a hundred years ago. Claude Bernard's *Introduction to the Study of Experimental Medicine* put its faith in the future. Eventually, exploration of the mechanism of disease would give the insight necessary for curative intervention. At the moment, such insight was only beginning. On the other hand, in 1867 Oliver Wendell Holmes delivered an introductory lecture, on "Scholastic and Bedside Teaching," which reads like a criticism of Claude Bernard's attitude. Chemistry, anatomy, and physiology are sciences, of benefit to medicine, but the physician needs only what is practical in them. On the curative side, medicine is mainly an art, and the student should be reminded "that a physician's business is to avert disease, to heal the sick, to prolong life, and to diminish suffering."[23]

Yet, like many of his contemporaries, Holmes was an outspoken skeptic where the traditional *materia medica* was concerned. His distrust in exuberant promises of science was balanced by faith in the prevention and treatment of disease by providing the individual and the community with wholesome physical, mental, and social conditions. The meaning that Holmes gave to medicine has to be seen against the background of the great public health movement of the mid-nineteenth century. As described by Ackerknecht,[24] it was a movement directed toward improving man's life through the betterment of his environment. Partly, this environment was physical, but partly it was man-made, i.e., social. The medical reformer easily became a social, and even a political, reformer.

Medicine, it was claimed, was anthropology, the basic science of man. At the same time, it was the basis of the social sciences. The physician, acquainted with human misery, was best qualified to be the advocate of suffering humanity. Medicine ought to be more than a way to alleviate individual suffering. Through its science and its disciples, medicine was to lead mankind towards a brighter future.

The movement represented an alliance between medicine and public

[21]It must not be overlooked that the standards of what constitutes real "cure" (a very complex notion) have differed greatly.

[22]Hippocrates, *Epidemics* I, xi, translation by W. H. S. Jones, Loeb Classical Library (New York: Putnam, 1923), vol. I, p. 165.

[23]Oliver Wendell Holmes, *Medical Essays 1842–1882* (Boston and New York: Houghton, Mifflin and Company, 1891), pp. 273–311 (see p. 274).

[24]For the following see: Erwin H. Ackerknecht, *Rudolf Virchow: Doctor, Statesman, Anthropologist* (Madison: University of Wisconsin Press, 1953); idem, "Hygiene in France, 1815–1848," *Bull. Hist. Med.* (1948) 22:117–55; idem, "Beiträge zur Geschichte der Medizinalreform von 1848," *Arch. Gesch. Med.* (1932) 25:61–109 and 115–83.

health. Gradually, over the centuries, public health had become the business of physicians, as well as of administrators. Alliance with public health through its concern with the community broadened the outlook of the physician. The radical form which this movement took with Virchow in the revolutionary period of 1848 subsided afterwards. But the idea has survived into our own days and is reflected in the aim of the World Health Organization to provide health as "a state of complete physical, mental, and social well-being and not merely the absence of disease or infirmity."[25]

With the advent of bacteriology, scientific medicine entered the phase of curative confidence.[26] The first big step came with the rise of antiseptic surgery, a little less than a hundred years ago. The second step was to follow in our own century. All this is too well known to need elaboration, nor is it necessary to dwell on the preventive powers which medical science has given to modern medicine. But before touching on scientific medicine as we know it today, I would like to quote from a booklet on "The Medical Profession," published in Berlin in 1870, when modern scientific medicine was in its infancy.

Around 1800, we are told, medicine was subjective, the physician acted through his personality rather than through his science. He was closer to his patients, he had to be a psychologist, he was not only a family doctor, but a friend of the family as well. Now (in 1870) things were different. Medicine had become factual and objective. Never mind the personality of the doctor; he must know how to examine and to understand the patient as an object. Medicine had grown so much that its profession was split into its various branches.

Thereby, of course, the ground is removed from under the congenial ways of the family doctors. Thereby the personal relationship is being relaxed, for physicians are changed and selected according to the disease. Thereby a certain considerateness, demanded by the intimate association, is lost on the part of the physician and on the part of the public too. A small step further, and the profession shifts its center of gravity and finds it in gain.[27]

To us, 1870 means the days of the horse and buggy doctor; to the German whose country was then leading the medical sciences, 1870 meant the arrival of scientific medicine.

A little later, Germany introduced compulsory health insurance. This initiated a train of events which was deeply to affect the meaning of medicine in modern society.[28] To make medical care available to the popu-

[25]*Chronicle of the World Health Organization* (1947) *1*:29.
[26]Richard H. Shryock, *The Development of Modern Medicine* (New York: Knopf, 1947), especially p. 336 ff.
[27]Robert Volz, *Der ärztliche Beruf* (Berlin: C. G. Lüderitz'sche Verlagsbuchhandlung, A. Charisius, 1870), p. 34. The author, now little remembered, was born (1806) and died (1882) in Karlsruhe where he served as a high-ranking public health administrator. (Gurlt-Hirsch, *Biographisches Lexikon der hervorragenden Aerzte aller Zeiten und Völker*, vol. 6 [Vienna and Leipzig: Urban und Schwarzenberg, 1888], p. 151).
[28]Henry E. Sigerist, "From Bismarck to Beveridge," *Bull. Hist. Med.* (1943), *13*:365–88.

lation is a demand at least as old as the Greek institution of the public physician. The demand was strengthened at the time of the public health movement of the mid-nineteenth century. But what to Bismarck appeared as politically desirable social legislation began to merge with a "consumer" demand when people became convinced that medicine could cure them and prolong their lives. The demand became louder and it spread more widely the more medicine developed into a large structure of disciplines, both medical and paramedical, with a vastly increased diagnostic and therapeutic instrumentarium and with hospitals which have long ceased to be merely the refuge of the needy. As medicine progressed so did the cost of medical care. Could medical progress be considered meaningful unless its fruits were in the reach of all? We know what powerful factors in the economic and political life of nations the answers to this question have become.

The very name "medicine" seems no longer sufficient. We speak of the health professions, of the health sciences, of the health field, terms which indicate our groping towards a new common denominator. What *the* meaning of this medicine will be, we do not yet see clearly. We perceive many goals and challenges, some of which we have glimpsed in their historical formation. We are passing through a time in which many of the old standards clash. The very effectiveness of Western medicine has contributed to economically dangerous over-population, to increased life expectancy with consequent invalidism, to such efficient health protection in wartime as to make large-scale wars possible. On the other hand, a new utopia looms on the horizon, where medicine is to free man from feelings of sin, to eradicate crime together with all other diseases, and to award perfect health and an endlessly expanding life span; in other words: a mirage of happiness.[29]

In fact then as well as in imagination, medicine has become so powerful a factor in human life with its choice of good and bad, that the conscious quest for its meaning forces itself upon us. In saying that we cannot yet see the future meaning of medicine, I merely claim for our time what probably was true at all times. The historian can try to perceive unity within the conflicting aims and possibilities of the past. Yet for a living generation, meaning has to be *imparted*.[30] The historian may be able to elucidate the past in order to give perspective to the present, but to elucidate the future remains the task of the prophet.

[29]René Dubos, *Mirage of Health,* reprinted in Anchor Books (Garden City, New York: Doubleday and Company, 1961), p. 230, stresses the utopian nature of imagining a static paradise on earth with a life free from all danger.

[30]Fundamentally, "the" meaning of medicine, even for past periods, remains an ideological construct. Whether it is seen as a mere abstraction or as a reality of the order of Platonic ideas and of Hegel's *objectiver Geist,* will depend upon the historian's metaphysical bias.

3

Medicine
and the Problem of Moral
Responsibility*

1

WHILE I WAS pondering over a suitable subject for tonight's presentation, Mephistopheles must have stood close behind me. For reasons best known to him he made me constantly think of that scene in
Goethe's Faust where he gives advice to Faust's pupil about academic
studies. His speech is full of libels and deceit, especially when he discusses
medicine, a profession which he seems to favor beyond all others. Why
should the Devil like medicine? Perhaps, I told myself, because he hopes to
get hold of the doctor, to make him an atheist and blind towards man's
moral responsibilities. Is it not true that the physician is not expected to
censure his patients for the sins or virtues that may have caused sickness?
The doctor is supposed to cure the disease, saintliness or vice are either
beside the point or merely indirect factors. At any rate, I decided to take
this idea for my theme and to investigate the relationship between medicine
and moral responsibility a little further.

Even a superficial glimpse at the history of medicine suggests that the
attitudes towards responsibility for disease have varied. Theologians,
philosophers and common people very often have been inclined to view
sickness primarily from a moralistic point of view. Nor have physicians
always excluded this point of view from their approach to the sick. You will
permit me to concentrate upon the physicians' side of the picture and you
will excuse me if I try to sketch a few typical attitudes rather than follow
their development in a detailed and strictly chronological account.

If we were to pursue our thought along purely speculative lines, we
should probably expect the concept of disease as guilt, or more specifically
as sin, to antedate any other. But the language of the oldest medical texts
from Mesopotamia and Egypt is not clear on this point. In the Assyrian and
Babylonian medical tablets various diseases are treated by drugs and the
recital of incantations. Charms and incantations are indicative of a moral
concept of disease, though perhaps in the primitive form of a mere ritualistic trespass. If gods, spirits or demons are invoked to relieve the disease,
these or similar powers are assumed to have caused it or at least permitted

*Bull. Hist. Med., 1949, vol. 23, pp. 1–20.
Paper read before the History of Ideas Club, The Johns Hopkins University, on January 8,
1948.

it. Somehow and somewhere, the sick individual must have exposed himself to these influences by breaking a law or overlooking a taboo. But I wonder whose practices the so-called medical texts from Mesopotamia reflect. The letter of the physician Arad-Nanā[1] and the medical paragraphs of the Hamurabi Code speak a very worldly language. Their tone is more consonant with the Edwin Smith surgical papyrus which originated in Egypt around 2800 B.C. and presents a series of surgical cases where the disorder (mostly injuries) is described and treated rationally. Incantations only occur exceptionally. But the form of the Egyptian papyri which set forth typical cases rather than a coherent medical theory, makes it hard to tell what the physicians thought.

I find myself unable to decide what attitude was first assumed by physicians. The whole question is intimately connected with the early relationship of priestcraft and medicine, a question on which we possess little evidence. Here perhaps, as so often, it will be wiser not to argue from hypothetical origins but to analyze a mature situation. Such a situation existed in ancient Greece at the time of the Hippocratic physicians, that is about 400 B.C. In the so-called Hippocratic collection, or at least in some of its writings, we find the very clear statement that the gods do not cause disease, and that purifications and similar rites have no place in medicine. All diseases are natural, and their treatment consists in prescribing a detailed regimen with special emphasis upon right food, proper drugs and, if necessary, surgical manipulation. In fractures, dislocations and wounds the latter of course stand in the foreground.

There is no doubt that the Hippocratic attitude constitutes a fundamental element in medical philosophy. Even today a majority of doctors and laymen will probably agree that it represents just that attitude which is to be expected from a medical man. But upon closer scrutiny it reveals implications and complexities which can lead to divergent interpretations. The formula "disease is a natural process" is as yet undefined regarding the relationship of "nature" to human life and the extent of the concept of "disease."

In the first place the question arises as to how the patient's life and his disease are connected. There is, above all, the loose link to which we give the name of "accident." Here we are immediately reminded of broken arms and legs, dislocated joints, and wounds, disorders which belong to the domain of surgery. Indeed it is in the surgical books from the Egyptian Papyrus Smith down to our own textbooks of surgery that we find this idea most clearly pronounced. Now when we consider the occurrence of a disease as an "accident" we imply that the ordinary life of the individual and the cause of the disease had no inner connection, or at least, that no such connection can or need be established.

Of more far-reaching commitment is the view according to which disease

---

[1]Cf. Ch. Johnston, "The epistolary literature of the Assyrians and Babylonians," *Journal of the American Oriental Society*, 1897, vol. 18, p. 162 f.

comes as "fate," not inevitable perhaps, but at least outside the individual's power and responsibility. Significantly enough, such an explanation is offered in both Hippocratic works which deny the divine character of certain diseases and claim that all diseases are equally divine because, as we should add, they are all ruled by the laws of divine nature. In one of these works, which deals with epilepsy, the author states that "its origin is hereditary, like that of other diseases."[2] In the other one it is national custom which causes many Scythians to become sterile. Since the wealthy among them practically live on horseback, they develop diseases of the joints which they treat by bleeding from a vein behind the ear, and this, in turn, causes impotence. The poor do not develop the disease because they do not ride. The author uses this as an argument against the belief of the Scythians that sterility is a punishment by a god. In that case, the incidence ought to be reversed, since the rich have better means of placating the gods than the poor.[3]

Neither heredity nor national custom can be blamed upon the patient who is in the physician's care. Epidemics and endemic diseases can also be included in this group of diseases brought on by fate. According to the Hippocratics, they are engendered by polluted air or by the climatic and geographical constitution of a country. And since the condition of the air, the character of the seasons, winds and soil were believed to be influenced by the sun and moon, by the constellations of the stars and the course of the planets, epidemics fitted particularly well into the astrological picture of the middle ages and the renaissance. Astrology has always been accused of fatalism. The astrological explanation of epidemics meant their removal from the scene of human activity. We must not be diverted by the fanciful and demonistic side of astrology from recognizing the essential element of this astrological explanation. Paracelsus, in the sixteenth century, numbered the "ens astrale" among the five principal entities that were involved in man's health and disease. By the "ens astrale" Paracelsus did not mean the alleged direct influence of individual stars or constellations. To him it symbolized the fact that human health is subject to the great revolutions of the universe, to the changes of seasons, to special conditions which might exist in the history of heaven and earth and rule over the coming and going of epidemics.[4] In less offensive form, these views were still dominant less than a hundred years ago. The great *Handbook of Geographical and Historical Pathology* by August Hirsch, the second edition of which appeared in the early eighties when the old epidemiology was being revolutionized by the discoveries of bacteriology, still discussed telluric phenomena like winds, rainfall, and condition of the soil in their association with epidemic diseases. With a renewed change of emphasis and a very much advanced knowledge, our own time also accepts the subjection of the individual to

---

[2]"On the sacred disease"; *The genuine works of Hippocrates*, transl. Francis Adams, 2 volumes in one, New York, W. Wood, 1892, II, p. 338.

[3]"On airs, waters, and places," ch. 22; *ibid.*, I, p. 178 f.

[4]Cf. J. D. Achelis, *Paracelsus, Volumen Paramirum*, Jena, Diederichs, 1928, p. 6.

factors like heredity, social necessities and epidemics as outside of his control.

As long as diseases are considered as accident or fate, the problem of individual responsibility is avoided. However, I cannot think of any period in the history of medicine that succeeded in relegating all diseases to either of these two categories, least of all the period of ancient medicine. According to the Greek physicians who were followed by the Romans, the Arabs and occidental doctors, sickness, to a large part was the result of dietary mistakes. The Hippocratic author who distinguishes two kinds of fevers says of the first kind that it befalls everybody and is called pestilence. "The other one," he adds, "which is due to unwholesome diet, arises individually in those who live an unwholesome manner of life."[5] But the manner of life is within the power of the individual, at least of the man who does not have to earn a living and can follow the dictates of his physician. If he becomes sick, he has himself to blame for it. The whole abundant development of ancient dietetic medicine with its stress on personal hygiene is, as Dr. Edelstein has shown,[6] intimately connected with the insistence on the side of the physicians that disease can and must be prevented, and the willingness of the laity, on the other hand, to acknowledge health as one of the highest, if not the highest, good. Here is the point where the ancient physician became a moralist and assumed the right to criticize people for their way of life. But we must immediately add that crime and punishment were of the same category. The crime consisted in having neglected the rules of health; disease or painful treatment were the punishment.[7] It is even doubtful whether such censorship can rightly be called moral. As long as man is accountable for his health to himself alone, he can harm himself but hardly inculpate himself thereby. An immoderate eater may concede that he acts unwisely, but he will probably resent being called a sinner.

2

The physician entered the medieval world as the advocate of the body.[8] There is a curious passage in Psellus' *Dialogue on the Operation of Daemons,* a work written in the 11th century and fundamental for medieval demonology. One of the persons of this dialogue tells how the monk Marcus explained to him the symptoms caused by the assault of subterranean demons.

"But Marcus," said I, "physicians persuade us to be of another way of thinking, for they assert that such affections are not produced by daemons, but are occasioned by

[5]"On winds," ch. 6; E. Littré, *Oeuvres complètes d'Hippocrate,* t. 6, Paris, 1849, p. 96–98.
[6]Ludwig Edelstein, "Antike Diätetik," *Die Antike,* 1931, vol. 7, pp. 255–270; Emma J. Edelstein and Ludwig Edelstein, *Asclepius,* vol. 2, Baltimore, The Johns Hopkins Press, 1945, p. 123.
[7]The idea of painful treatment as punishment is to be found in Plato's "Gorgias." 479a.
[8]There is a passage in the so-called "Anonymus Londinensis" which stresses the chief concern of medicine with the body. Cf. W. H. S. Jones, *The medical writings of Anonymus Londinensis,* Cambridge University Press, 1947, p. 83. On the other hand, Dr. Edelstein, in a

an excess or deficiency of humours, or by a disordered state of the animal spirits, and accordingly they endeavour to cure them by medicine or dietetical regimen, but not by incantations or purifications." Marcus replied: "It is not at all surprising if physicians make such an assertion, for they understand nothing but what is perceived by the senses, their whole attention being devoted to the body."[9]

I do not quote this passage in order to prove that during the middle ages physicians were reputed to explain possession as disease, i.e., a natural process. Rather I wish to illustrate the new light in which this explanation makes the physician appear. He knows of the body only, and is ignorant of the spiritual order in which disease, as a natural process at least, has no place. On the contrary, it has now become possible to reverse the position and to suggest that even disease of the body is but a manifestation of the spiritual and moral world. I do not know how far back these attempts go, they seem to have grown out of the theological interpretation of the Bible, particularly the miraculous cures of Christ. With Origenes and the early Fathers of the Church it has become customary to read a general religious truth into these cures, quite beyond their isolated historical occurrence. The widest possible meaning could be given to the passage of chapter 5 of St. John, which tells of Christ meeting a man whom he had cured from an old sickness and telling him: "Behold, thou art made whole: sin no more, lest a worse thing come unto thee"[10] At the 4th Lateran Council of 1215, Pope Innocence III ordained that the physician was bound to insist that his patients confess. This decree which threatened the disobedient physician with excommunication was, as Diepgen has shown, influenced by the concept of disease as originating from sin.[11] Confession was necessary not only because of the eventuality of a fatal outcome, but because the patient might recover when his sin was removed. Nor was the sin the only possible spiritual cause of disease. According to the theologians, disease might have been sent for any of the following reasons: To enhance the merits of the just through their patience, to safeguard virtue from pride, to correct the sinner, to proclaim God's glory through miraculous cures and, finally, as the beginning of eternal punishment as in the case of Herod. This concept did not remain uncontradicted; it was also contended that God's judgment in sending disease was unfathomable.[12] But the list proves that all and every disease could conceivably be interpreted as a corporeal manifestation of the relationship between God and man and this meant of man's spiritual and moral life. Disease could be the fate of the just and of the sinner as an

---

personal communication has reminded me that a spiritual element is inherent in the tradition of the Hippocratic "Oath" and the relationship of ancient medicine to the cult of Asclepius.

[9]*Psellus' dialogue on the operation of daemons,* translated into English by Marcus Collisson, Sydney, Tegg, 1843, p. 35.

[10]Cf. Paul Diepgen, *Die Theologie und der ärztliche Stand,* Berlin-Grunewald, Rothschild, 1922, p. 52.

[11]*Ibid.*

[12]*Ibid.,* footnote 290.

individual or as a group, but fate of a higher order than heredity, national custom or polluted air.

It is obvious that physician and patient alike were now confronted with a situation different from that of pagan antiquity. Was the patient morally bound to lead a healthy life and to call the physician in case of sickness? The answers varied according to the prevailing degree of asceticism. Yet there was a side which gave a very emphatic "yes" to these questions. The body was the dwelling of the soul and man, therefore, was in duty bound to take care of it. Besides, did not the Bible say: "Honor a physician with the honor due unto him?"[13] In this light, man's obligation to health assumed a new moral character. Sickness was to be prevented, not because health was good in itself, as the ancients said, but because man was accountable to God for his body.

In spite of martyrs and saints, I do not believe that medieval men clung less to life than people of other epochs. But the lust for life needed a rationalization which would bring it into harmony with the prevailing religious and metaphysical outlook. This rationalization found its proper form by elevating health from a natural good to a moral duty. It would be altogether erroneous to assume that the religious spirit of the middle ages always acted as an impediment upon medicine. But there is no denying that the physician was confronted with a dilemma. Should he reckon with the sinner or saint in his patient? No uniform answer was given; the attitudes changed with circumstances and individuals, and a few examples can only serve to illustrate the variety.

To take confession first: It was an obvious thing that a man had to confess before his death. Whether the physicians always considered it *their* duty to insist upon confession is doubtful, and whether they expected recovery from it is highly questionable.[14] However, the problem of confession occupied the physician's mind too, as evinces from the following advice which a Salernitan author of the late 12th century gives to the doctor who is summoned to a sick-bed:

> Thus when you approach his [i.e., the patient's] house and before you go near him, inquire whether he has laid open his conscience to a priest. If he has not done so, he should either do it or promise to do it. For if mention is made of it after the patient has been seen and the signs of the disease considered, he will begin to despair over his recovery because he will believe that you too despair of it.[15]

Plague and leprosy were two of the great scourges of medieval Europe. The plague was God's whip, but its victims were not ashamed before man; the lepers, on the other hand, were loved by God but hated by men. If their disease was recognized, their fate became a sad one, for they were segre-

---

[13]Ecclesiasticus, ch. 38. Cf. also Diepgen, *op. cit.*, pp. 7 ff. and 12 ff.
[14]Cf. Diepgen, *op. cit.*, p. 48 ff.
[15]"De adventu medici ad aegrotum," S. De Renzi, *Collectio Salernitana*, Vol. 2, Napoli, 1853, p. 74.

gated from the community of their fellow citizens. Guy de Chauliac, the French surgeon of the 14th century, tells the physician how to proceed in his examination of suspected lepers:

In the first place, invoking the help of God, he must comfort them with the thought that this disease means salvation of the soul and that they must not hesitate to tell the truth. For if they are found to be lepers, their souls are already in purgatory, and if the world hates them, not so does God who loved Lazarus the leper more than the others. If, however, they are not found to be lepers, they will be left in peace. Then he should make him swear to answer the questions truthfully.[16]

Here the physician conformed to the religious view and used it as a means of recognizing the case.

At the end of the 15th century, Europe became acquainted with a new disease, syphilis. The physicians knew that syphilis was a natural process like any other disease of the body. Yet by 1520 it was becoming clear that in the majority of cases it was due to a venereal infection and, therefore, to an act of sin. Should the physician reckon with the moral responsibility of his patient? I cite two answers that were given, one positive and one negative. For the understanding of the first answer it has to be remarked that in the 16th century the most widely used treatment of syphilis consisted in an intensive application of mercury pushed to the degree of more or less severe mercurial poisoning and causing great suffering, sometimes even the death of the patient. In 1527 Jean de Béthencourt published a work on syphilis under the significant title of "A new lent of penitence." He writes concerning the disease:

It never yields but under the influence of a medication which imposes upon the body the chastisement of its impurity and upon the soul the punishment of its sins.[17]

How different was the answer given in 1673 by Thomas Sydenham, the greatest English physician, when he had to justify writing on the treatment of venereal disease.

As a preliminary, however, I must remark that I have met with many persons who, either from the praiseworthy desire of terrifying the unchaste by the fear of future trouble, or for the sake of claiming credit for continence on their own part, have not hesitated to argue that the cure of the *venereal disease* should not be taught. With such I disagree. If we reject all cases of affliction which the improvidence of human beings has brought upon themselves, there will be but little room left for the exercise of mutual love and charity. God alone punishes. We, as we best can, must relieve. Neither must we be too curious in respect to causes and motives, nor too vexatious in our censorship.

Hence I will state what I have observed and tried in the disease in question; and

---

[16]*Ars chirurgica,* Venetiis apud Iuntas, 1546, fol. 58 v.

[17]J. de Béthencourt, *Nouveau carême de pénitence,* transl. A. Fournier, Paris, 1871, p. 55. Cf. also O. Temkin, "Zur Geschichte von 'Moral und Syphilis,'" *Arch. Gesch. Med.,* 1927, vol. 19, pp. 331–348 [Essay 32].

that not with the view of making men's minds more immoral, but for the sake of making their bodies sounder. This is the business of the physician.[18]

Sydenham was no atheist. He had fought in Cromwell's army and we can credit him with puritan leanings. Although he was not the first to express views like the above, his statement, because of its clarity and the authority of his name, carries additional weight. If the physician was accused of being ignorant of the spiritual world, he might reply that his exclusive concern for the body was not a result of ignorance, but of a charity which dispensed to friend and foe, which connected the ancient idea of philanthropy towards sick and poor[19] with the Christian ideal of neighborly love as exemplified by the good Samaritan.

3

It will have become clear that the problem of moral responsibility for disease as presented to the physician is connected with the ethical responsibility of the physician towards his patient. Without entering upon a discussion of medical ethics[20] I should like to pursue a more general line of thought. So far it has appeared that society again and again felt the need for the existence of a profession which would view the lives of their fellow men without regard to right and wrong. To be sure, there were limits and safeguards, not only religious ones, but civil ones as well. The medieval surgeon, for instance, was bound to bring injuries to the attention of the magistrates so that crime might not remain undetected.[21] Similar laws exist today. But within the legal limits, as we have seen, the physician was neither compelled nor expected to act as a moral inquisitor. This does not present any particular problems as far an antiquity is concerned. In the first place, ethics and nature were not opposed to each other. To many ancient philosophers and physicians health constituted a life led in accordance with divine nature and the physician's sole concern with health still remained within the boundaries of the divine. Nor must it be forgotten, that most ancient physicians were traveling craftsmen, sometimes even slaves. Greek and Roman patricians might entrust their bodies to the physician's skillful supervision, but it is not likely that they would allow the socially inferior to meddle with whatever conscience they possessed. The physician, in his turn, was little interested in the morals and social institutions of the foreign

[18]*The works of Thomas Sydenham*, transl. R. G. Latham, vol. 2, London, The Sydenham Society, 1850, p. 32 f.

[19]Cf. Edelstein, *Asclepius, loc. cit.*, p. 175.

[20]I am very conscious of the fact that a comprehensive discussion of "medicine and the problem of moral responsibility" would have to include medical ethics. However, a thorough analysis of this aspect would have gone beyond the scope of the present paper.

[21]For the surgeons of medieval Paris, e.g. cf. the documents quoted by E. Nicaise, *Chirurgie de Maître Henri de Mondeville*, Paris, Félix Alcan, 1893, p. lxiii. Cf. also I. Fischer, *Ärztliche Standespflichten und Standesfragen*, Wien-Leipzig, Braumüller, 1912.

city in which he happened to exercise his trade.[22] This explains the rather remarkable fact that we find hardly any traces of interest in public health in ancient medical literature. Public health was the responsibility of city magistrates and emperors who employed public physicians of whose functions, incidentally, we know very little.[23]

But in the middle ages, the situation was vastly changed. As a Christian, the physician was a member of the spiritual community that embraced all. As a doctor of medicine, he was even a member of the university which resolved religious, metaphysical and legal issues. How, then, could the physician exempt himself from the interest in the soul? In principle, at least, I think that the question was decided on the basis of a hierarchy of knowledge. The doctor, the "physicus," was a philosopher in the realm of nature. Natural philosophy was a legitimate, but not the highest branch of knowledge. Supremacy went to theology. "In as far as the soul is more precious than the body, in so far the priest must be held in higher respect than the physician of the body."[24] Not being a theologian, the physician need not possess the higher knowledge. But as a consequence he must refrain from interfering where somatic disease ceases and moral guilt begins.

During the middle ages this arrangement seems to have worked to some degree. Most physicians accepted the situation as a matter of course. Others accepted it grudgingly or derisively, but I do not know of any major rebellion. After the breakdown of the medieval hierarchy the situation did not change much. Even the Cartesian philosophy which exerted a very great influence upon medical science was not favorable towards removing the barrier between the mechanical machine, i.e., the body, and the moral liberty of the soul. It did away with the ancient and medieval theory of a natural soul that resided in the liver and regulated our appetites, and a vital soul in the heart that accounted for such emotions as anger and wrath. It left the rational soul as the only soul and thereby it deepened rather than bridged the gulf between disease and moral responsibility. The Cartesian view, where strictly applied, could not conceive of a psychological causation of disease, nor could it even admit a disease of the mind. I mention these implications of Cartesianism, since, avowedly or—more often—by implication, this philosophy was not confined to the 17th century, but can be found among scientists of the 19th and even the 20th century.

However, the relationship between medicine and moral responsibility is not only dependent on philosophical views. As already indicated it is also determined by the social position of the doctor. As long as the organization of society was predominantly feudalistic or aristocratic, the physician, to

[22]There are, however, interesting exceptions to this rule, for instance Soranus' explanation of the frequency of rickets in Rome (*Sorani Gynaeciorum libri IV*, ed. I. Ilberg, Lipsiae et Berolini, Teubner, 1927, p. 85).

[23]Cf. Owsei Temkin in: *Social medicine, its derivations and objectives*. The New York Academy of Medicine institute on social medicine, 1947. Ed. by Iago Galdston. New York, Commonwealth Fund, 1949, p. 5.

[24]Cf. Diepgen, *op. cit.*, p. 9.

some extent, was still in the position of his ancient colleague who was merely required to render certain services. Medicine fulfills a social function. Medicine and society, therefore, must meet on a common field so as to speak the same language. In scientific and technical knowledge the physician will be much superior to his patient. But fundamentally both must agree on what should be considered disease and health, otherwise they can hardly get together. But as long as the doctor did not belong to those strata of society that expressed accepted standards, his views were determined by the tradition of his profession and the varying circumstances in which he found himself. As an example I should like to mention a peculiar type of literature that was popular among medical authors up to the 17th century, viz., the allegorical and moral interpretation of the parts, functions and diseases of the human body. We find this topic treated in the *Monstrorum Historia* of the physician and zoologist Ulysses Aldrovandi. The particular section starts with a paragraph on "The mystical meaning of the parts of the human body" and ends with a paragraph "On morals derived from human diseases." Aldrovandi remarks:

. . . Just as the pulse is diligently examined by the physicians, that the affections of the heart may be known, so the moral physicians—the prince or a dynast, of course—must sometimes examine the pulses of the subjects carefully enough to recognize the dispositions of their hearts and to draw back from the wrong course those that are functioning badly. Or indeed the name of moral physician may be assigned to the confessor who must observe the pulses of the penitents with great industry, that he may be able to understand the intimate dispositions of their hearts. Therefore, the chief afflictions which ruin the human body must now be examined in as far namely as they submit to the moral doctrine. Beginning therefore with the diseases of the head, we shall first consider patchy loss of hair which arises when acrid humors erode the roots of the hairs. The head is the Prince and the hairs are the people subject to his power. Thus, when the hairs, i.e., the subjects, are infected by bad humors, namely by the bad example of the princes, then they immediately fall into decay and become loose. General baldness too is produced by falling hair and may connote loss of virtues produced by the violence of sin. Just as a youth whom baldness befalls can again acquire hair, while an old man is freed from baldness with difficulty or not at all, in like manner the youth, bald of his lost virtues, is through the power of penitence again decorated with the hairs of virtue. An old man attains this with difficulty, since the faults of old people seem to be incorrigible. For in the proverbs we have this sentence: "Train up a child in the way he should go; and when he is old, he will not depart from it.[25]

In this recital medicine is used purely allegorically. Medicine is still of the body. Not the medical man, but the priest and above all the prince is the moral physician who watches over diseases in the state and takes appropriate measures to root them out. If anything, then, it is indicative of the autocratic regime of the Italian states in which its author lived.

[25]Ulysses Aldrovandi, *Monstrorum historia,* Bononiae, 1642, p. 256. For an interesting moral interpretation of the plague cf. C.-E. A. Winslow and M. L. Duran-Reynals, "Jacme d'Agramont and the first of the plague tractates," *Bull. Hist. Med.,* 1948, vol. 22, p. 761 ff.

In the late 17th and then in the 18th century, concomitant with the rise of Enlightenment, the physicians, who were mostly members of the middle classes, moved into social conditions where they and their fellow citizens could claim to set the tone. It could hardly fail that the morality of their own class would now also express itself in their views of moral responsibility for disease. The physicians were notoriously protagonists in the fight for enlightenment which abolished not only demons, witches and occult powers of nature, but also tended to introduce a new moral tone wherever it became independent from aristocratic predominance. The doctors had been traditionally unbelievers in the demons which had frightened medieval man.[26] But they became early crusaders against the vices by which people were in danger of destroying themselves. Benjamin Rush's fight against alcoholism may serve as an example of what is meant. In his *Inquiry into the Effects of Ardent Spirits upon the Humon Body and Mind,* he designated drunkenness as a disease and described its natural history.

It belongs to the history of drunkenness to remark that, its paroxysms occur, like the paroxysms of many diseases, at certain periods, and after longer or shorter intervals. They often begin with annual, and gradually increase in their frequency until they appear in quarterly, monthly, weekly, and quotidian or daily periods. Finally they afford scarcely any marks of remission either during the day or the night. There was a citizen of Philadelphia many years ago in whom drunkenness appeared in this protracted form. In speaking of him to one of his neighbours, I said, "does he not *sometimes* get drunk?" "You mean" said his neighbour, "is he not *sometimes* sober?"[27]

Yet the disease, alcoholism, is itself a vice. Not only does it lead to criminal actions, but by destroying his health the drunkard ranges with the suicide.

Yes—thou poor degraded creature, who art daily lifting the poisoned bowl to thy lips—cease to avoid the unhallowed ground in which the self-murderer is interred, and wonder no longer that the sun should shine, and the rain fall, and the grass look green upon his grave. Thou art perpetrating gradually, by the use of ardent spirits, what he has effected suddenly by opium—or a halter. Considering how many circumstances from surprise, or derangement, may palliate his guilt, or that (unlike yours) it was not preceded and accompanied by any other crime, it is probably his condemnation will be less than yours at the day of judgment.[28]

By necessity, therefore, the treatment which Rush has to offer is both moral and physical. It is also characteristic that he feels the necessity to justify treating such a disease and that his apology is very similar to that of Sydenham a hundred years before:

[26]Cf. A. Franz, *Die kirchlichen Benediktionen im Mittelalter,* vol. 2, Freiburg i. Br., 1909, p. 525 ff.

[27]Benjamin Rush, *An inquiry into the effects of ardent spirits upon the human body and mind,* fourth edition, Philadelphia, n. d., p. 9.

[28]*Ibid.,* p. 16 f.

I am aware that the efforts of science and humanity, in applying their resources to the cure of a disease, induced by an act of vice, will meet with a cold reception from many people. But let such people remember, the subjects of our remedies, are their fellow creatures, and that the miseries brought upon human nature, by its crimes, are as much the objects of divine compassion, (which we are bound to imitate) as the distresses which are brought upon men, by the crimes of other people, or which they bring upon themselves, by ignorance or accidents.[29]

Rousseau likewise made himself felt. At the turn of the century, for instance, Thomas Beddoes published a book with the significant title: *Hygeia, or Essays Moral and Medical, on the Causes Affecting the Personal State of Our Middling and Affluent Classes* in which "the vulture of fashion," too much reading of novels, etc., are made accountable for all manners of conditions which we now should call neurotic.

The characteristic element of these examples can be seen in the belief that many diseases have their origin in an immoral or misguided inclination of the free individual. It is, therefore, not enough to treat the consequences of vice, ignorance and wrong upbringing. In some cases the treatment itself must include moral correction. But beyond this, the physician must combat conditions that make these diseases possible. Whatever his attitude towards the suffering patient may be, the physician as a responsible member of society cannot remain silent where the lives of others are threatened. He must educate, he must enlighten and he must interest himself in public health.

Dr. Sigerist has analyzed the rise of the public health movement since the 18th century and the various forms it assumed.[30] It is not in the scope of this paper to dwell on its history as such. Only the factors connecting it with the moral responsibility for disease have to be elucidated. And I see three such factors. First, the expansion from the patient's responsibility to the responsibility of statesmen, educators, churchmen and other social, political and religious functionaries. This recognition of responsibility had probably never been lacking; but it had formerly been restrained by the knowledge that the initiative had to come from above. Even in the 18th century, a man like Johann Peter Frank expected the Government to enforce health regulations down to minute details. But now, and this is the second factor, social conditions had matured to such a degree that the doctor could no longer stand aside. The third factor which emerged very slowly was an increasing body of facts which made an active intervention look promising.

In an early part of this paper I mentioned disease as fate. But fate in

[29]*Ibid.*, p. 39 f. Percival, in 1803, wrote: "Yet whoever reflects on the variety of diseases to which the human body is incident, will find that a considerable part of them are derived from immoderate passions, and vicious indulgencies. Sloth, intemperance, and irregular desires are the great sources of those evils, which contract the duration, and imbitter the enjoyment of life. But humanity, whilst she bewails the vices of mankind, incites us to alleviate the miseries which flow from them" (Thomas Percival, *Medical ethics*, Manchester, 1803, p. 24).

[30]Henry E. Sigerist, *Medicine and human welfare*, New Haven, Yale University Press, 1941, p. 78 ff.

medicine is relative since it depends on our actual ability of prevention and treatment. With regard to epidemic diseases this ability was slight in antiquity and the middle ages in spite of the endeavors of town physicians and magistrates. Not because of lack of good will but largely because of insufficient scientific knowledge. As soon as the mechanism of the transmission of a disease became sufficiently known to allow intervention, fate gave way to responsibility. The history of the gradual conquest of epidemic diseases is too well known to require repetition. The point which deserves mentioning is the changed attitude which medicine developed towards these responsibilities. A hundred years ago, Rudolf Virchow wrote: "Epidemics resemble great warnings from which a statesman in the grand style can read that a disturbance has taken place in the development of his people, a disturbance which not even a carefree policy may longer overlook."[31] These words are somewhat reminiscent of Aldrovandi's medical allegories, but for Virchow and his contemporaries they conveyed anything but an allegorical meaning. If the statesman continued to overlook the warnings, then political pressure had to be exerted to make him change his policy. From the end of the 18th century, the responsibility for disease has become an ever larger part in national as well as international political life.

The suppression of epidemics through special measures like vaccination and general sanitary improvements produced such dramatic results that these diseases, by the middle of the 19th century, were much more strongly connected with the idea of human responsibility than those showing a sporadic incidence. To be sure, there were occupational diseases and industrial hazards against which workers had to be protected. There was also a group of diseases that might be prevented by proper physical and mental education. Yet in between there remained the large group of diseases for which neither the patient nor any social conditions could be held responsible, which crossed the life of the individual as mere accidents. In 1847 Virchow made the following interesting remark. Speaking about teleology in pathology, he maintained that at best this approach could be applied to the healing processes.

But if one wishes to extend this method to the entire morbid processes, then one logically arrives at the point where one establishes diseases as consequences of original sin or as punishments of a personal grudging deity, just as one looked for the purpose of the world in the glorification of a god who took pleasure in it. There just is no purpose to be discovered in somebody's developing a tumor. This is, as we use to say, an *accident,* an aimless event by which in the animal body the orderly course of a series of phenomena is stimulated, the visible result of which is the tumor. Pathogenesis, therefore, can have no other task but to acquaint itself with that accident and to explore the laws according to which the subsequent phenomena take their course.[32]

---

[31]Rudolph Virchow, *Gesammelte Abhandlungen aus dem Gebiete der öffentlichen Medicin und der Seuchenlehre,* Bd. 1, Berlin, 1879, p. 22. Cf. also Erwin H. Ackerknecht, "Hygiene in France, 1815–1848," *Bull. Hist. Med.,* 1948, vol. 22, p. 141 f.
[32]Rudolf Virchow, "Ueber die Reform der pathologischen und therapeutischen

Virchow is such an outstanding figure in medical science of the 19th century that I cannot resist the temptation of dwelling upon the unique integration of scientific, medical and political thought which he represented. Virchow is the founder of cellular pathology, that is the theory which envisages disease as being seated in the cells. In politics, Virchow was a liberal and Hirschfeld has pointed out how his liberal opinions found their analogy in his pathological theories.[33] According to Virchow, the human body and the body politic have the same pattern. The cells are the elements of the body; if the cells are healthy, the body too is healthy, whereas disease can be resolved into a diseased state of cells. Similarly, the citizens represent the elements upon whose good or bad behavior the fate of the state rests. In addition, however, Virchow's liberal views extended in two other directions. As a German liberal he stood in opposition to the autocratic government of the princes and later of Bismarck. This led him and many other German physicians in 1848 to make medical reform a part of the program for general political reform.[34] But as a liberal of the mid-19th century, Virchow was also inclined to see the world and human life as a free interplay of forces. He formulated disease as life under changed circumstances, but in the individual sphere these changed circumstances were accidental. There is a certain parallelism between such a view in pathology and in general biology where Darwin made new species develop out of accidental changes furthered or suppressed by natural selection.

However this may be, disease as accident was, and is, a very fruitful point from which to view and investigate the mechanism of disease. It reached its climax at the heroic period of bacteriology. Many early bacteriologists accepted a very simple formula: When man and germ happen to meet, disease will result. Once the mode of infection was known, individuals could be taught how to protect themselves and others effectively. If they failed to act accordingly, they certainly could be blamed.[35] Yet there was no inner connection between irresponsible behavior and subsequent disease. The latter took its course regardless of all human conflicts. The physician, therefore, need not let morals enter into his treatment. This view prevailed, a fortiori, with regard to diseases which were not transmissible by infection or heredity.

Anschauungen durch die mikroskopischen Untersuchungen," *Virchows Archiv*, 1847, Bd. 1, p. 230 (italics mine).

[33]Ernst Hirschfeld, "Virchow," *Kyklos*, 1929, vol. 2, p. 115.

[34]Cf. Erwin H. Ackerknecht, "Beiträge zur Geschichte der Medizinalreform von 1848," *Arch. Gesch. Med.*, 1932, vol. 25, pp. 61–109 and 113–183.

[35]It is remarkable, how slowly the idea of the social responsibility of the sick person towards others developed. Before the nineteenth century instances are rare where the patient himself is expected to avoid the transmission of his illness. The community might place restrictions upon him to which he had to submit, but these restrictions were mainly a matter of public law, not necessarily supported by the patient's own conscience. Only from about the middle of the last century on does the recognition spread that prevention of the "accident" or "fate" of disease in others may be the responsibility of the patient himself. I have touched upon this point in "Zur Geschichte von 'Moral and Syphilis'" (cf. above note 17) where I have shown that the emphasis upon the patient's social responsibility leads to an interpretation of disease as crime.

Only towards the close of the last century did a reaction set in. This reaction started from the field of mental diseases, particularly of hysteria and neurosis. The prevailing view considered neurosis either as an epiphenomenon of somatic disease—or it was not accepted as a disease at all, but as moral weakness or depravation. Fundamentally this was still the Cartesian position. But the treatment of these diseases did not prove very successful. Here again I need not detail the rise of the psychological technics which under the name of psychosomatic medicine today extend far into general medicine, nor is it my task to comment upon their medical significance. Yet, from the historical perspective of our discussion, the following point must not be overlooked. Diseases are not always accidents; even diseases that express themselves somatically may, under certain circumstances, owe their origin to psychological conflicts which the individual has been unable to solve. Perhaps I can cite no more telling example than what Dr. Flanders Dunbar has named "accidentitis." There seem to be persons to whom accidents happen frequently because they have developed an accident habit. Their personality pattern, moreover, is stated by Dr. Dunbar to match that of criminals.[36] If even accidents may not always be mere accidents, then it is obvious that diseases that are open to psychological analysis of this kind do not happen by chance, but are a part of the patient's reaction towards the conflicts of his life. In other words, they have motives and to lay bare these motives is a legitimate task of medicine.

But it is equally obvious that somewhere and somehow the question then remains whether there is meaning in calling these motives good and bad because dependent on the individual's choice, or whether they are but the interplay of natural urges and drives. If the latter view is accepted, then indeed crime itself is nothing but a disease, a natural process.

4

Perhaps we had better stop now for a moment and reconsider the course of our discussion. Our main theme so far was the responsibility for disease. We started from the view that the physician is not supposed to play the moral judge of his patient. We tried to find the various historical forms in which this idea manifested itself as well as the trends in a different direction. Only at the end did our discussion culminate in the general problem, whether moral responsibility in itself might be a natural phenomenon and lack of responsibility a mere pathological abnormality. We had now best summarize what we have found by briefly considering this general problem.

Wherever a separate medical profession exists its very existence expresses the belief on the part of society that disease may have natural causes and be susceptible to natural cures. For where all disease is conceived as

---

[36]Flanders Dunbar, *Mind and body,* New York, Random House, 1947, p. 102.

originating in sin or guilt, secular medicine has no place. The physician is, so to speak, the social appointee of the natural side of man. As an empiricist the physician notes the relationship between environmental and physiological factors on the one hand and man's character on the other. Thus Hippocrates described the people who lived in cities exposed to different winds according to their somatic as well as psychic behavior. In cities lying to the east, for instance, "the persons of the inhabitants are, for the most part, well colored and blooming, unless some disease counteract. The inhabitants have clear voices, and in temper and intellect are superior to those which are exposed to the north . . ."[37] The physician also notes the influence of diseases and drugs upon man's behavior. He has to push his analysis as far as he can and he easily arrives at the metaphysical generalization that man's soul is wholly dependent upon his body. Galen, the last of the great physicians of antiquity, was led to write a book, the title of which indicates its thesis: "That the Faculties of the Soul Follow the Temperament of the Body." In a roundabout way he suggests that the soul has no existence separate from the body and that in reality it is nothing but the mixture, the temperament, of the body. This alone, to his mind, will explain the different behavior of small children, the mental effects of drunkenness and fever and the phenomena of madness. From such premises he then draws the following consequence: "Neither are all men born enemies of justice nor are they all its friends, since they become such as they are because of the temperament of their bodies." And if the question is raised, how one may rightly dispense praise or blame, hate or love since men are good or bad not by themselves but by the temperament which they receive from other causes, the answer is quite simple: "Because, so we shall answer, we all have the faculty to prefer, search and love the good and to turn away from evil and to hate and flee it without, in addition, considering whether it is innate or not."[38] Evidently Galen avoids the last consequence of complete relativity of good and evil only by a pragmatic appeal to the reality of life. But just as Galen for more than 1000 years became the greatest medical authority, so he also embodied a tradition in the medical attitude towards crime, which again and again came to the fore. In 1496, for instance, the Leipzig professor and doctor of medicine, Martin Pollich von Mellerstadt, disputed the question whether medicine could cure all mortal sins. I give here an English rendering of the following paragraphs from their awkward Latin original.

The instruments of the voluntary disorders, which the theologians call mortal sins, have their beginning in the psychic spirit in the brain that moves all parts of the body proportionally to what is wished and desired as is demonstrated by the sinews of the chest in apoplectic persons.

---

[37]"On airs, waters, places," ch. 5; Adams' translation, *loc. cit.*, I, p. 160.
[38]Galen, *Scripta minora*, vol. II, ex recognitione Iwani Mueller, Lipsiae, Teubner, 1891, p. 73.

Such accidents, therefore, formally fall under the consideration of the physician, in so far as they express the complexion of the body, for whose motions the soul is said to become naturally altered. Granted, then, that the laws may rectify things of this kind according to custom and liberty of will, nevertheless the physician modifies them according to nature . . .[39]

Small wonder then that the physician had the reputation of being an atheist, a "Nulla fidian" as the doctor called himself in William Bullein's *Dialogue Against the Fever Pestilence*.[40] Certainly, as Kocher has pointed out in the recent study of "The Physician as Atheist in Elizabethan England,"[41] this reputation was exaggerated. But the radicalism of a few tinged the good name of the many. In following centuries this attitude became ever more widespread and occasionally gave rise to popular movements. I have had an opportunity of studying the so-called phrenological movement initiated in the early 19th century by the doctors Gall and Spurzheim.[42] According to these neurologists the psychic faculties, including good and bad drives, are innate functions of certain regions of the brain. Pushed to its extreme consequences, phrenology had to consider all criminals as sick persons since they were deplorable victims of an abnormal disposition. But as yet the religious forces in the authors themselves were strong enough to give the doctrine a turn away from a denial of moral responsibility. Altogether it can be said that as long as society, through religion or a customary morality, preserves the belief that intellect and will have laws of their own too, it exempts these laws from being incorporated into physiology and pathology. Only when these reservations yield does nature become all comprehensive and so do the concepts of health and disease. They then only need an extension into the field of society since morality involves the relationship of human beings. Some such concept seems to me expressed in a recent formula which defines health as "a state of complete physical, mental, and social well-being and not merely the absence of disease or infirmity."[43] I do not think that I read too much into this formula if I believe that it tends to include moral values and to identify health with happiness.

The physician must believe in the value of health, for this is implicit in his own professional integrity. Society expects of him the rôle of defending and extending the claims of health. But is the pursuit of happiness itself wholly a medical matter? Our life has many values and those physicians who have lost their own health in the exercise of their profession remind us that happiness can sometimes be achieved at the sacrifice of health.

[39]Karl Sudhoff, *Aus der Frühgeschichte der Syphilis,* Leipzig, Barth, 1912, p. 44 f. (Studien zur Geschichte der Medizin, Heft 9).

[40]William Bullein, *A dialogue against the fever pestilence,* ed. Mark W. Bullen and A. H. Bullen, London, Early English Text Society, 1888 (reprinted 1931), p. 14.

[41]Paul H. Kocher in *The Huntington Library Quarterly,* 1947, vol. 10, pp. 229–249.

[42]Owsei Temkin, "Gall and the phrenological movement," *Bull. Hist. Med.,* 1947, vol. 21, pp. 275–321.

[43]"Constitution of the World Health Organization," *Chronicle of the World Health Organization,* 1947, vol. 1, p. 29.

The metaphysical question as to the existence and nature of moral responsibility is not a medical one. It is for this very reason that the physician can avoid becoming a moralist in practising his art. But if health is defined so broadly as to include morality, then the danger exists that the physician will also be burdened with all the duties of the medieval priest. This would indeed be the medieval position in reverse, and I wonder whether it would prove acceptable to medicine and society.

4

An Essay on the Usefulness of Medical History for Medicine*

*"By despising all that has preceded us, we
teach others to despise ourselves. Where there is
no established scale nor rooted faith in
excellence, all superiority—our own as well as
that of others—soon comes to the ground."*
—William Hazlitt, *On Reading New Books*

IT IS OBVIOUS that the history of culture includes the history of medicine. But it is not equally obvious that the history of medicine should be cultivated by physicians as a branch of medicine. Indeed, a good prima facie case can be made against any such claims. Medicine, it may be argued, is a progressive science which has to look forward to further improvements rather than backward to stages now superseded. The history of medicine may interest the historian, it may occupy the leisure hours of the physician, but it teaches nothing new and is, therefore, useless.

But the fact remains that for more than 2000 years physicians have studied medical history.[1] It seems promising, therefore, to inquire into the

*Bull. Hist. Med., 1946, vol. 19, pp. 9–47.

The thoughts expressed in the following pages had been accumulating in my mind for many years before I decided on writing this essay. I am, therefore, not able to cite all the publications to which I may be indebted, not to thank all those to whom I owe some stimulating suggestions. I should, however, like to thank Dr. Henry E. Sigerist and my present and former colleagues, especially Dr. Ludwig Edelstein and Dr. Erwin Ackerknecht, for the benefit I derived from frequent conversations on topics related to this essay. At the same time I wish to state that responsibility for the views here expressed rests on me alone.

[1] I wish to emphasize that this essay is not intended as an outline of the history of medical historiography. This subject has been dealt with by Paul Diepgen and his school in the following publications:

a. Paul Diepgen. Zur Geschichte der Historiographie der Medizin. *Abhandlungen aus dem Gebiete der mittleren und neueren Geschichte und ihrer Hilfswissenschaften. Eine Festgabe zum siebzigsten Geburtstag Geh. Rat Prof. Dr. Heinrich Finke gewidmet von Schülern und Verehrern des In- und Auslandes.* Aschendorffsche Verlagsbuchhandlung, Münster i. W., 1925, pp. 442–465. This article is a general introductory outline with main emphasis on Le Clerc and Freind. It does not go beyond the early 18th century.

b. Edith Heischkel. *Die Medizingeschichtschreibung von ihren Anfängen bis zum Beginn des 16. Jahrhunderts.* Berlin, Emil Eberling, 1938 [Abhandlungen zur Geschichte der Medizin und der Naturwissenschaften. Heft 28]. This is a detailed study of the period indicated by the title. The 18th century and 19th century (for Germany) have been covered by:

c. Paul Diepgen. Albrecht Haller und die Geschichte der Medizin. *Historische Studien und Skizzen zu Natur- und Heilwissenschaft. Festgabe Georg Sticker zum siebzigsten Geburtstage dargeboten.* Berlin, Julius Springer, 1930, pp. 100–111.

purposes which have motivated their historical researches in the past and present. Such an inquiry will show whether these purposes still have a medical meaning, and will reveal the possible usefulness of history for medicine. Consequently, the main part of the present essay will be devoted to a sketch of the uses to which the various forms of medicial history have been put up to the present day. To this, a few remarks will be added on the special needs of our time for medical history.

I

Before the true forms of history can be discussed, it is necessary to deal with its most archaic form: mythology. Mythology is the antipode of history. But since nobody thinks or acts without some picture of the past, we are all apt to accept a historical myth where we cannot rely on historical knowledge. Where history is lacking, mythology takes its place and those who disdain history are among the foremost victims of mythology.

1

According to legend, Asclepius, the healing god of the Greeks, learned his art from the centaur Cheiron and bequeathed it to the physicians, the "sons of Asclepius." In ancient Egypt, the Gods themselves were credited with the authorship of the sacred medical texts.[2] Indian surgeons, in support of their claim that surgery was the oldest of all the branches of medicine, referred to the divine Ashvins who had reunited the head and trunk of the decapitated god Yajna.[3]

In all these myths there is a desire to trace the origin of medicine back to the gods and a very remote past. What is old is sacred, and what the gods invented is above human criticism. Man may have misused the invention and may have spoiled it, but in itself it is good and pure. "Honour a physician with the honour due unto him for the uses which ye may have of him: for the Lord hath created him," says Jesus the son of Sirach,[4] meaning that medicine is not mere human arrogance, but God's own creation and therefore honorable and just. To the mythological way of thinking the whole development of medicine may appear as a fall from original greatness. This is particularly the case with the reformer who intends to bring to

    d.   Edith Heischkel. *Die Medizinhistoriographie im XVIII. Jahrhundert.* Leiden, E. J. Brill, 1931.

    e.   Hans von Seemen. *Zur Kenntnis der Medizinhistorie in der deutschen Romantik.* Zürich-Leipzig-Berlin, Orell Füssli, 1926 [Beiträge zur Geschichte der Medizin. Heft III.].

    f.   Edith Heischkel. Die deutsche Medizingeschichtschreibung in der ersten Hälfte des 19. Jahrhunderts. *Klinische Wochenschrift,* vol. 12, 1933, pp. 714–717.

    g.   Paul Diepgen. Das Schicksal der deutschen Medizingeschichte im Zeitalter der Naturwissenschaften und ihre Aufgaben in der Gegenwart. *Deutsche Medizinische Wochenschrift,* vol. 60, 1934, pp. 66–70.

[2]Cf. J. H. Breasted, *The Edwin Smith Surgical Papyrus,* vol. 1, The University of Chicago Press, 1930, p. 5.

[3]Cf. *An English translation of the Sushruta Samhita,* edited and published by Kaviraj Kunja Lal Bhishagratna, vol. 1, Calcutta, 1907, p. 6 f.

[4]Ecclesiasticus, ch. 38.

69

light again the old and essential truth. Thus Paracelsus opens the defense of his own life and work with the following myth: "Whereas God suffered the spirit of medicine to emerge in its fundamentals through Apollo, through Machaon, Podalirius and Hippocrates, and suffered the light of nature to work without a darkened spirit, exceeding wonderful great works, great *Magnalia,* great *Miracula,* were performed through the Mysteries, Elixirs, Arcana and Essences of nature, and medicine was marvellously conceived in a few pious men, as was told above. Whereas, however, the Evil One with his corn cockles and his weeds suffers nothing to grow for us in an undefiled wheatfield, medicine has been darkened by the first spirit of nature and has fallen among the anti-physicians and has become so entangled with persons and sophistries, that no one has been able to advance as far in the works as Machaon and Hippocrates did."[5]

Thus the myth serves as justification, whether of the profession as a whole or of a special doctrine, by sanctifying its origin. With the decline of the religious form of mythological thinking, imagination in a more rationalistic garb takes over the same function. A theory of the origin of medicine is now advanced which sounds plausible, and is yet based on belief rather than on fact. The earliest rationalistic myth of this kind is to be found in the book "On Ancient Medicine" of the Hippocratic collection. Its author wants to prove that none of the newfangled philosophical systems of his time can be considered as a reliable basis for medicine. Instead he claims that "medicine has long had all its means to hand, and has discovered both a principle and a method, through which the discoveries made during a long period are many and excellent, while full discovery will be made, if the inquirer be competent, conduct his researches with knowledge of the discoveries already made, and make them his starting-point."[6] In order to progress the physician has but to follow in the footsteps of ancient medicine. The essence of this ancient medicine is explained in a myth concerning its origin. In some remote past, man lived on the same crude food as animals. The severe suffering which he had to endure from this diet led him to prepare such food as we eat now. The next step in the same direction led to the discovery of medicine. "Experimenting with food they boiled or baked, after mixing, many other things, combining the strong and uncompounded with the weaker components so as to adapt all to the constitution and power of man, thinking that from foods which, being too strong, the human constitution cannot assimilate when eaten, will come pain, disease, and death, while from such as can be assimilated will come nourishment, growth and health. To this discovery and research what juster or more appropriate name could be given than medicine, seeing that it has been discovered with a view to the health, saving and nourishment of

[5]Seven Defensiones, translated by C. Lilian Temkin, in: *Four treatises of Theophrastus von Hohenheim, called Paracelsus,* ed. Henry E. Sigerist, Baltimore, The Johns Hopkins Press, 1941, p. 10.

[6]*Hippocrates,* with an English translation by W. H. S. Jones, vol. 1, 1923, p. 15 [The Loeb Classical Library].

man, in the place of that mode of living from which came the pain, disease and death?"[7] This is the way in which medicine was discovered and this is the right way in which it should proceed. Of course, the author of this book had no real historical evidence by which to support his thesis and had, therefore, to rely on plausible arguments. Among others he adduced the example of the barbarians in order to prove the condition of the premedical state of humanity. "At any rate even at the present day such as do not use medical science, barbarians and some Greeks, live as do those in health, just as they please, and would neither forgo nor restrict the satisfaction of any of their desires."[8] Without putting undue strain on the imagination, it is possible to draw a parallel between this passage and the modern attempts to reconstruct the origins of medicine from analogies with the so-called primitives. Indeed, primitive medicine plays its rôle in our histories of medicine just because we do not know much more about the beginning of medicine than the Hippocratic author did.[9] Yet we are loathe to admit our ignorance and to await the discovery of more telling historical material than we possess today before embarking upon a tale of the origins. We claim that useful drugs were discovered by a process of trial and error because our belief in the experimental method tempts us to assume its existence wherever useful things are found.[10] Lucas-Championnière fought for the decompression therapy of intracranial diseases, and accordingly credited prehistoric man with an unconscious insight into the curative value of trephining.[11]

There also exists mythology in reverse, where the evil of the present is imputed to the survival of an older past. This form of historical invention is more closely attached to the "enlightened" frame of mind, and finds its ancient model in the most enlightened work of the Hippocratic collection, the book "On the Sacred Disease." The author contends that epilepsy, the sacred disease, is as natural as any other disease and curable by the same natural means. He combats popular superstition and the magicians who impute the cause of the disease to the gods and treat it by magic rites. To hit this concept at its very root he discredits its origin. "My own view is that those who first attributed a sacred character to this malady were like the magicians, purifiers, charlatans and quacks of our own day, men who claim great piety and superior knowledge."[12] It was along similar lines of thought that many "enlightened" myths were invented before as well as after the 18th century. Today too, this kind of myth plays its rôle when the prehis-

---

[7]*Op. cit.*, p. 19 f.

[8]*Op. cit.*, p. 21, where, however, I have replaced Jones' translation of "foreigners" by the more literal "barbarians."

[9]This remark in no way reflects upon the serious study of medicine among primitive peoples, a discipline in its own right.

[10]Cf. E. H. Ackerknecht, Problems of primitive medicine, *Bull. Hist. Med.*, vol. 11, 1942, pp. 503–521, especially pp. 504 and 512 f.

[11]Lucas-Championnière, *Trépanation néolithique, trépanation pré-Colombienne, trépanation des Kabyles, trépanation traditionnelle* (Les origines de la trépanation décompressive), Paris, G. Steinheil, 1912.

[12]Cf. above, note 6, vol. 2, p. 141.

toric practice of medicine is uncritically attributed to some forerunners of present-day medicine men and shamans and when it is maintained that diseases were attributed to ghosts and demons and other superstitions of primitive and folk medicine. The philosophical achievement of modern science will stand out all the more clearly if it can be contrasted with the murky background from which it had to rise. And some modern psychologists, desiring to explain conscience as the natural outgrowth of mere human relations have indulged in tales of a mythological "Ur-father" and an "Ur-horde."[13]

The criterion of a myth in the sense indicated is not whether eventually it will prove true or false. A historical theory tries to make a coherent picture out of a set of historical data, and it stands and falls with its supporting facts. A myth, on the other hand, steps in where sufficient historical data are lacking. Its function is to support a living faith without or even against historical evidence. Therein lies its strength and its weakness, its use and abuse.

2

When philosophy conquered mythology, medicine too became imbued with the spirit of speculation. The Hippocratic physicians speculated on the structure of the body, the functions of the organs and the causes of disease. In the realm of medicine, therefore, they had the same approach as had the pre-Socratic philosophers concerning the universe.

Speculation tends to culminate in opinions which never quite sever their bond with the individuality of the thinker. This is most clearly seen in the history of philosophy which presents itself as a series of systems. The same is true of medicine as long as medical thought remains speculative. It is, therefore, not surprising that the first history of medicine which we possess is a collection of the opinions of the physicians who lived in the era of Hippocrates. Nor is it surprising that this collection was prepared by Menon, a pupil of the philosopher Aristotle, for Aristotle was accustomed to cite and analyze the opinions of his predecessors so that by agreement or refutation he might elucidate his own position. In other words, the doxographical method proves vital wherever philosophy or science tries to reach truth by dialectic argument.

Throughout Antiquity, and even far into modern times, the dialectic method remained alive and doxography its necessary partner. Even where a simple description might be expected, controversy often took its place. Soranus (about 120 A.D.), the author of a textbook on gynecology, opens the chapter "On the flux of women" with the following words: "According to the ancients, as Alexander Philalethes says in the first book on Women's Diseases, the flux is 'an increased flow of blood through the uterus over a protracted period.' But according to Demetrius the Herophilean, it is 'a flow of fluid matter through the uterus over a protracted period' since the

13Cf. S. Freud, *Das Unbehagen in der Kultur,* Wien, 1930.

flux may not be sanguineous only, but different at different times. In our opinion, however, it is a chronic rheum of the uterus where the secreted fluid is perceptibly increased. According to Asclepiades and some others there are two different kinds of flux (for one kind is red, the other is watery and white), whereas according to Demetrius the differences lie in color and action" [14] and so on. Such a procedure is essentially scholastic, and indeed medieval scholasticism which quotes authorities pro and con, uses this method extensively in medical as well as in other writings. In order to reach an opinion of his own, the schoolman cites the opinions of others. And it is the opinion that counts and a claim to observed fact rather than the observation itself. Doxography does not represent a record of what previous generations have already known, but what they have opined and pretended to know.

Opinions count and are worth while debating as long as they are alive. Or vice versa: as long as opinions are still discussed they *are* alive, and their authors still treated like contemporaries. In the above quoted passage, Soranus names Alexander Philalethes, Demetrius the Herophilean and Asclepiades without giving their dates. He may or may not have presupposed such knowledge on the side of his readers, for somehow this is irrelevant to his purpose. On the contrary, full historical understanding of a person sees him as a child of his time and thereby distances him from the present. We probably know much more about the real Hippocrates and Galen than did the Middle Ages or even the 18th century. Yet for the eighteenth century, the opinions of these men were still matters of vital concern, whereas for us they have become matters of "historical" interest. Cabanis, at the outbreak of the French revolution, wrote a book "On the Degree of Certitude in Medicine" [15] which is one great eulogy of Hippocrates. If such a book were written at all in our time, it would scarcely be based on the dicta of Hippocrates.

The importance of doxography was greatly enhanced by the development of medical sects from the 3rd century B.C. on. From then on there had to be included not only the opinions of individuals but, in addition, the basic tenets of the sect to which the individual belonged. The dogmatists believed in the value of anatomical and physiological research for the understanding and proper treatment of disease. Their opponents, the empiricists, denied the possibility of ever finding the obscure causes of disease and instead placed their confidence in experience. Then, at the beginning of the present era, a third sect, that of the methodists, arose who were satisfied with grouping diseases into one of the three conditions of status strictus, status laxus or status mixtus. The fight between the sects lasted far into late Antiquity and the medical author had to declare his adherence or opposition to the sects. Thus Celsus in the preface of his work "On

---

[14]*Sorani Gynaeciorum libri IV*, ed. I. Ilberg, Lipsiae et Berolini, 1927, p. 122 [Corpus Medicorum Graecorum IV].

[15]P. J. G. Cabanis, *Du degré de certitude de la médecine*, nouvelle édition, Paris, 1803; cf. p. 6 where Cabanis states that the book ought to have appeared in 1789.

Medicine" gave a historical sketch of the development of medicine up to his own time. The emphasis of this preface was laid on the dogmas of the three sects and their main representatives and its aim was the clarification of Celsus' own attitude. The views which he finds nearest the truth "are neither wholly in accord with one opinion or another, nor exceedingly at variance with both, but hold a sort of intermediate place between divers sentiments, a thing which may be observed in most controversies when men seek impartially for truth, as in the present case."[16]

The skilful historical form which Celsus gives to his exposition should not cloud the fact that doxography of the sects is as little bound to historical understanding or even exact chronology as is doxography of individual opinions. In the little book "On Sects for the Beginners," Galen outlines the sects and his own relationship to them with scanty reference to dates and historical circumstances. The decision which the tyro has to make is one between living issues.

Not very long after Galen the opinions of the sects become largely a matter of the past. With the ascent of Galenism, medicine appears much more unified than before. If Galen is blamed for the tyranny his ideas exercised for over one thousand years he might as well be praised for the cosmopolitan character of scholastic medicine. It is first the opposition to and then the destruction of the Galenic system which again split medicine into sects. Just as with Luther the unity of the Catholic Church is decisively broken, so with Paracelsus—the "Lutherus medicorum"—the unity of Galenism is destroyed. Now the split runs between Galenists on the one hand and Chemists on the other. A hundred years later, under the impact of new discoveries and the Cartesian philosophy, Galenism succumbs altogether. In its place there arise many systems, beginning with Iatrophysics and Iatrochemistry and ending (temporarily at least) with Homeopathy. The controversial spirit of eighteenth century medicine is almost as strong as that permeating Galen's works. The doctors who clash at the bedside of the patient have often been pictured. Yet they are no mere garrulous and quarrelsome characters. Rather their behavior represents the state of medicine in which thinking and practice were still dependent on philosophical differences, and that means on conviction by argument. To know the various systems of the time was a matter of necessary orientation for the doctor. And the task of presenting the leading ideas of these systems was one of the duties which the contemporary historians took upon themselves.

The usefulness of doxography up to the early 19th century seems clear. But with the advancing century medicine approached the positive sciences. Opinion and dialectic argument inside medicine have been replaced by scientific theory and experimental or statistical proof. Once again medicine appears cosmopolitan and unified. In the present situation, therefore,

[16]Celsus, *De medicina*, with an English translation by W. G. Spencer, vol. 1, 1935, p. 25 [The Loeb Classical Library]. In the passage quoted Celsus refers to the dogmatists and empiricists since he rejects the methodists altogether.

doxography does not have the same function as in former times. Its function now is to give an account of those philosophical and social ideas which struggle over the development which medicine as a whole ought to take. The necessity of knowing and, therefore, presenting these opinions will be shown in a different connection when the reasons for entrusting medical history with this task will also be stated.

3

Easy bridges lead from the mere exposition of opinions and theories to other forms of historical endeavors, notably biography and bibliography. Interest in the teachings of individual physicians attracts attention to their lives and the greater the authority of a name, the greater the desire to know something about the man. The value of a doctrine seems enhanced if its author appears worthy of admiration, and the falsity of a heresy is even more obvious if traced back to a good-for-nothing. The great name of Hippocrates has stimulated biographical attempts since the times of Antiquity. The discrepancy between the scanty authentic data and the fame of "the father of medicine" led to many legendary embellishments and novelistic fancies. An alleged correspondence with Hippocrates as the central figure depicted him not only as a great physician and philosopher, but as a Greek national hero who refused to serve the king of Persia, the enemy of his nation. This legend probably goes back to a time when Greece, no longer really free, was yet jealous of its former greatness and when panhellenic sentiments, in retrospect, were attributed to the great men of the 5th century B.C.[17] However this may be, this story is the early example of a motive that has become very strong in modern times. In the Renaissance, medical history appeared by preference as a collection of medical biographies,[18] and the rising nationalism of the Italians, French and Germans took pride in an account of their famous physicians. This tendency, of course, is still very much alive, and has developed its good as well as bad sides: good, because it has stimulated detailed research into the national past and brought back to memory many a worthy name; bad, because it has sometimes provoked nationalistic arguments and ridiculous exaggerations. Claims for priorities, for instance some of those regarding the discovery of the circulation of the blood, have been advanced with a verve transcending the desire for historical justice. The merits of Paracelsus were exaggerated out of all proportion by some historians who considered him the protagonist of "German medicine." The latter example is all the more remarkable, since former centuries had tried to belittle Paracelsus as the hated instigator of inconvenient and absurd novelties. This remarkable Renaissance figure, astrologer, alchemist and mystic, and, at the same time, prophet of a new medical science, had been decried as a sorcerer, drunkard

---

[17]Cf. L. Edelstein, Hippocrates, in: Pauly-Wissowa, *Real-Encyclopädie d. classischen Altertumswissenschaft*, Supplementband VI, 1935, col. 1301 f.
[18]Cf. Heischkel (above note 1,b).

and wayfarer by his own contemporaries.[19] For the medical orthodoxy of the 16th and 17th centuries and the following period of Enlightenment he personified all that was bad and ridiculous in hermetic medicine.

Legends and anecdotes which so often blur the truthfulness of a biography accentuate rather than disguise an essential fact: all medical biographies deal with the lives of "great doctors." It has only to be added that greatness lies in the perspective. Hippocrates, rightly or wrongly, has been acclaimed as the founder of rational medicine, the keen observer and humane physician. His biographer may enthusiastically uphold this picture or he may critically reduce it to its true proportions. In either event, the biography centers around this real or pretended greatness. Paracelsus is the great heresiarch admired or condemned for his cosmic view of man and disease. John Hunter is the great surgeon scientist whom curiosity and the zeal for factual knowledge drive to body snatching and experimentation with his own health. Ephraim McDowell is the pioneer who successfully performs an operation which others before him did not dare to attempt. Even some obscure old "Doc Thompson"[20] may become the hero of a biography because of his modest unselfish devotion to the needs of the community or as the deterrent example of a drab routinier. In all of these cases there is one condition which must be fulfilled. The life of the man must appear as an outstanding example, be it of individual stature or of a general condition. He will be great because through him the lives of many others were endowed with meaning.

No doubt, there are many things that will find their place in a comprehensive biography. A modern historian will stress the forces, social, economic, traditional and perhaps even hereditary, which shaped the man and urged him to his work. Vesalius lived at a time that was ripe for the overthrow of Galenic animal anatomy. Before him, Leonardo da Vinci had portrayed the structure of the human body as it can be seen in reality. Contemporaneously with Vesalius, Canano had engaged upon a similar work. Undoubtedly human anatomy would have been discovered even if Vesalius had never lived. Antiseptic surgery too, would probably have been invented without Lister, for its principles were inherent in Pasteur's work and Lemaire had actually anticipated some theoretical and practical possibilities of carbolic acid.[21] But the fact remains that the reform of anatomy is due to Vesalius, and antiseptic surgery to Lister. It is their work and the particular individual form they gave to it that opened the way and influenced the subsequent development. "Many are called but few are chosen" holds good of medical discoveries and inventions too. The individual factor

---

[19]Cf. W. Artelt, Paracelsus im Urteil d. Medizinhistorik, *Fortschritte d. Medizin,* vol. 50, 1932, pp. 929–933.

[20]Cf. G. Miller, The study of American medical history, *Bull. Hist. Med.,* vol. 17, 1945, p. 3 f.

[21]Cf. H. A. Kelly, Jules Lemaire: the first to recognize the true nature of wound infection and inflammation, and the first to use carbolic acid in medicine and surgery, *J.A.M.A.,* vol. 36, 1901, pp. 1083–1088.

remains, after all social, economic and other circumstances have been duly considered and it is just this factor which forms the core of a biography.

The function of the biography then is to set an example, to invite admiration and, thereby, imitation. Of his own autobiography Samuel Gross said: "Possibly some good may grow out of such a labor, by stimulating the ambition of those who may come after me to work for the advancement of science and the amelioration of human suffering. The devotion which I have shown to my profession may, perhaps, exert a salutary influence upon the conduct of young physicians, and thus serve to inspire them with a desire to excel in good deeds." [22] In this way, medical biography is useful as an instrument of education. Through the account of their lives, the great masters survive as teachers of the following generations.

4

The writings of a great physician are a part of his life work and their titles and contents find a natural place in his biography. Moreover, if opinions are considered authoritative because of the author from whose pen they hail, then questions of authenticity become important too. Ancient and medieval professors of medicine, therefore, used to argue the genuineness of the work they set out to read and explain to their students.

But to list and analyze the works of a few outstanding physicians is not the only, perhaps not even the most essential part of medical bibliography. Probably in Antiquity, certainly among the Arabs, and ever more frequently from the Renaissance on, the works of all famous physicians are catalogued. This can take different forms. Ibn Abi Useibia (13th century) appended his bibliographic lists to the lives of the men he discussed. Here the biographic information still stood in the foreground. Van der Linden (1609–1664) followed an alphabetical arrangement by authors' names, with the accent on the writings rather than on the lives. Albrecht von Haller too used the bio-bibliographic method, choosing a chronological arrangement. Yet his various "Bibliothecae" cover different branches of science and medicine: the "Bibliotheca Botanica," "Anatomica," "Chirurgica," and "Bibliotheca Medicinae Practicae" each being independent from the other. Finally, the biographic interest may be completely overshadowed by an interest in the contents. Now as before, many bibliographies are arranged according to subjects or devoted to one subject only.

These, in brief, are some types of medical bibliography to which various transitional forms and modifications could be added. But leaving aside questions of method and technique, there is a common aim inherent in all bibliographical work, viz.: to facilitate the access to medical literature. And since it is presumed that even old medical books contain many pertinent and valuable observations, experiences and experiments, their titles are collected and their contents scrutinized.

[22]*Autobiography of Samuel D. Gross*, vol. 1, Philadelphia, George Barrie, 1887, p. 1.

It is axiomatic that every good piece of research, whether clinical or experimental, ought to include a perusal of the literature. How far back this search should go will, first of all, depend on the subject treated. The development of new physical, chemical and other scientific methods has in itself excluded much of the older literature. Nobody will search medieval authors for data on aviation medicine. Studies on the electroencephalogram in epileptics will not find material in the Hippocratic work "On the Sacred Disease." In clinical investigations matters are somewhat different. Even when a new morbid entity is described which formerly had not been recognized as such, the older authors are sometimes found to have described symptoms of the disease though they had not been aware of its nosologic individuality. Virchow, for instance, in his first publication on leukemia could refer to Hippocrates and Haller.[23] Newly recommended cures and remedies, unless they are complicated synthetic products, also happen to have a surprisingly long past. When iodine was used in cases of goiter, it was noticed with interest that the Salernitan surgeons had used it in the form of ashes of seaweed and sea sponge.[24] When the malaria therapy of general paralysis gained approval, it was pointed out that Hippocrates had known that convulsions yielded to quartan fever.[25] Even penicillin has been suspected of an old ancestor in the "moss" growing on the skulls of executed persons as described by the Paracelsist Crollius in the 17th century.[26]

As far as positive facts are concerned, there is no strict boundary line between the older literature and the recent one, between a dead past and a living present. The great French historian of medicine, Charles Daremberg, remarked that the history of medicine was the archive of medicine which contained the records of all medical experiences, discoveries and theories from the early beginnings to the present day. Medicine, based as it was on the experiences and observations of many generations could not do without its archive. According to Daremberg the history of medicine comprises medicine in its entirety, it is the sum total of our medical knowledge, including the truth and error of all times.[27]

Opinions may be divided on the question just how promising the reading of older literature may be for the practitioner and research worker. Up to the middle of the 17th century, medicine of the schools was inclined to hold the ancient authors in higher regard than the more recent ones. With the rise of the mechanistic systems of iatrophysicists and iatrochemists in

---

[23]R. Virchow, Weisses Blut, in: *Gesammelte Abhandlungen zur wissenschaftlichen Medicin,* Frankfurt a. M., 1856, pp. 149–153.

[24]Cf. G. W. Corner, On early Salernitan surgery and especially the "Bamberg Surgery," *Bull. Hist. Med.,* vol. 5, 1937, p. 17 f. Dr. Corner wisely warns us not to consider this necessarily as a result of rational therapy.

[25]Cf. F. H. Garrison, *An introduction to the history of medicine,* 4th ed., Philadelphia, Saunders, 1929, p. 738.

[26]Cf. A. G. Cranch, Early use of Penicillin (?), *J. A. M. A.,* vol. 123, 1943, p. 990.

[27]Cf. C. Daremberg, *Histoire des sciences médicales,* t. premier, Paris, 1870, pp. XIV ff. and 7 ff.

the second half of that century, the moderns began to express their different scientific approach by a disregard of the Galenic physiology. Nevertheless, even a hundred years later, Albrecht von Haller showed in the most impressive way how erudition and progressive scientific work could be combined. His tremendous literary knowledge was integrated into his "Elementa Physiologiae" which are a veritable storehouse of information where each predecessor receives his due. Magendie who was in the habit of making his own experiments first and consulting the literature afterwards, repeatedly "found the whole discovery in Haller" and "cursed more than once this wretched book where everything was to be found."[28] In clinical medicine, the tradition remained unbroken into the 19th century. For Sydenham, the Hippocratic "Epidemics" were the work which he himself tried to emulate. Baglivi, the most radical of the Iatrophysicists, turned to Hippocrates as soon as he left the laboratory and approached the bedside of the patient. To van Swieten and most of the other "enlightened" physicians of the 18th century, Hippocrates, Aretaeus, Caelius Aurelianus were colleagues who had to be consulted. Greek and Latin authors were still read and interpreted in the medical faculties of the universities in the early 19th century. For his doctoral degree Laënnec submitted a thesis on the doctrine of Hippocrates "relative to practical medicine."[29]

This changed with the generation of physiologists, pathologists and clinicians who came to the fore around the middle of the last century. Claude Bernard did not withhold his admiration and respect from "the great men who preceded us and to whom we owe the discoveries that are the basis of the present sciences."[30] However, experimental science—and medicine was to become an experimental science—must advance by revolution and "by the absorption of the old truths into a new scientific form."[31] To claim admiration and respect for the predecessors and, at the same time to recognize their work only in so far as it could be absorbed by present day science, this meant to make them mere historical figures. The many single truths which could be distilled from their works had to be fused into more general truths. "The names of the promoters of science gradually disappear in this fusion, and the more science advances the more it takes on an impersonal form *and detaches itself from the past.*"[32] It is easy to see that a barrier arose between the experimental scientist and the dead past which was admired from a distance only.

Claude Bernard hardly intended to deny the possibility of learning from older authors. "It is important to bear in mind ... that what we call experimental medicine is not at all a new medical theory. It is the medicine of all the world and of all times in as far as it contains solid acquisitions and good

---

[28]J. M. D. Olmsted, *François Magendie,* New York, Schuman's, 1944, p. 149.

[29]R.-T.-H. Laennec, *Propositions sur la doctrine d'Hippocrate relativement à la médecine-pratique,* Diss. Paris, 1804.

[30]Claude Bernard, *Introduction à l'étude de la médecine expérimentale,* Paris, 1865, p. 73.

[31]*Op. cit.,* p. 72.

[32]*Op. cit.,* p. 75 (italics are mine).

observations."[33] But Claude Bernard's approach—and that of many modern medical men—to the older literature is different from the approach up to a 100 years ago. He recognizes only that which fits into the present mode of scientific thought and can be assimilated into it. And therein lies his limitation. He inclines to make present-day science the sole judge over the "solid acquisitions and good observations" of the past. The temptation is very great to dismiss lightly or to laugh off those alleged observations that do not fit into the present picture. There is a scientific reverence for facts but also a scientists' prejudice against facts. Scientific thought would be chaotic without integrating theory. And in spite of all admonitions, we tend to exclude or overlook alleged facts which cannot easily be integrated into our prevailing theories. This tendency is all the greater if we are confronted with a work written at a time when controlled experiments and statistical evaluations were practically unknown. We are not readily prepared to admit that even the most fantastic statement may contain some truth. It is much more easily ridiculed than tested. Hence it comes that old observations and cures are usually appreciated only after we have rediscovered them in our own way. The beneficial action of seaweed in goiter and the therapeutic possibilities of the "moss" had little meaning as long as our attention was not directed to them by modern discoveries.

Old books cannot be read like articles in modern periodicals and yield but little information if glanced over in a casual way. They have to be approached with an open mind and just therein lies their usefulness. In trying to do them justice we educate outselves and cultivate that truly scientific objectivity that is more often presumed than possessed. They help us to see beyond the limits of a prevailing theory and may even sometimes reward us with a new comprehension of an old truth.

5

The knowledge of old medical books and of their contents does not yet give a historical picture of the past. Only when the lives of great doctors, influential opinions and theories, and factual knowledge are so arranged as to appear as links in a process do we have "historical perspective." The point of view from which the arrangement is made lies in the historian himself and changes with the time in which he lives. Medical history has been interpreted differently because different approaches have led to different evaluations of the historical material under different perspectives.

Of all possible arrangements the chronological might appear the simplest and most objective. A narrative of all the important events in their sequence from the beginning is easy to follow and would seem independent of the personal predilection of the historian. Gurlt's monumental "History of Surgery"[34] surveys the entire surgical literature of Antiquity, the Middle Ages and the Renaissance. The bulk of this work consists in a detailed

[33]*Op. cit.*, p. 363.
[34]E. Gurlt, *Geschichte der Chirurgie und ihrer Ausübung*, 3 vols., Berlin, 1898.

analysis of the contents of surgical writings of these periods. The work is almost invaluable for the study of what was thought, known and done by older surgeons. But even here the time sequence is not the only decisive factor. The distinction of periods in itself introduces accents which point to a development rather than a mere sequence in time. These accents are furthermore strengthened by grouping the authors according to countries and by including characterizations of the state of surgery at certain times and among certain peoples. The summary at the end of the work which discusses the achievements in the various fields of surgery follows a selective principle. Many things are excluded which were mentioned in the main part, and the emphasis is on those which seem to fall into the line of progress or stand apart from it.

Chronology is a frame for the arrangement of historical material, but does not yet provide sufficient guidance for the selection of the material. Everything important should be included; but this still leaves the question open as to what is important. Here the nature of medicine itself suggests an answer. As a physician, the historian has certain views of what is true and false in medicine. He compares and evaluates truth and error and, being a historian, he traces the origins and developments of both. Thus Celsus, in his historical introduction, gives a history of the sects and mentions the sequence of the physicians whose doctrines were still influential in his own days. At the same time, this approach contains a strong polemical element since the historian appears as a judge of the past. Possibly, he is a laudator temporis acti and finds that error rather than truth has increased. But if he believes that new discoveries and inventions have broadened medical knowledge in the course of the centuries, he will be guided by the idea of progress. This idea was not unknown in Antiquity (Celsus) and the Middle Ages (Guy de Chauliac), but it came fully to the fore at the dawn of the eighteenth century. The battle between the ancients and the moderns was fought, and the work of Vesalius, Harvey and others established progress, at least in anatomy and physiology. "I shall not stop to point out here all the uses which can be made of the History of Medicine; the title alone makes sufficiently known what one has to expect." With these words Daniel Le Clerc referred to his "History of medicine in which are seen the origin and progress of this art from century to century, the sects which are arisen in it, the names of the physicians, their discoveries, their opinions and the most remarkable circumstances of their lives."[35] This work, which initiated modern medical historiography, was completed for Antiquity only. But the mentioning of progress from century to century and of discoveries is suggestive of the new trend. Moreover, the emphasis on the *use* to be made of the work places it among the pragmatic histories of medicine which try to instruct the medical reader and teach him a useful lesson.[36]

[35]Daniel Le Clerc, *Histoire de la médecine, où l'on voit l'origine et les progrès de cet art, de siècle en siècle; les sectes, qui s'y sont formées; les noms des médecins, leurs découvertes, leurs opinions, et les circonstances les plus remarquables de leur vie*, nouvelle édition, La Haye, 1729.
[36]Cf. Diepgen (above, note 1a).

Pragmatism was the outstanding feature of medical history during the 18th century and came to a height with Kurt Sprengel's "Versuch einer pragmatischen Geschichte der Arzneykunde" which began to appear in 1792. In the 19th century pragmatism fell into disrepute. Yet it is pragmatism which justifies medical historiography under the perspective of progress, a perspective that cannot be dismissed altogether.

The impact of two world wars has made it doubtful whether mankind is becoming happier, wiser and morally better. But as long as medicine is not measured by these absolute values, progress towards its own limited goal is certain. The means for the prevention, alleviation and cure of disease are more numerous and more effective than heretofore. This fact gives such a firm vantage ground that today perhaps more than ever medical history is being written from the point of view of progress. Pushed to the extreme, this takes the form of emphasizing and praising everything that agrees with modern medical science and dismissing or even decrying everything that is or seems to be different. The Egyptian Edwin Smith Papyrus has been admired as an early document of true medical science to the disparagement of other medical papyri. Galen has been severely blamed for having assumed the existence of pores in the septum of the heart, only to satisfy his theory. But Harvey whose theory postulated the existence of capillaries has been lauded for his fearless logic. His physiological work has been purged of Aristotelian categories to make him appear a modern laboratory man pure and simple. The Middle Ages have been dismissed because they showed little progress, or ridiculed because of their superstitions, and the question has not seriously been raised *why* men thought so differently from us.

In this extreme form, the idea of progress shows very clearly its relationship to the time of Enlightenment when praise as well as blame and ridicule were weapons in the struggle of science against orthodoxy and superstition. Where this aim still exists today, the form too has preserved its usefulness. The doctor who combats superstitious treatments will point out that they are rooted in ignorance. When narrow minded prejudice hampers the freedom of experimental research, history will be used as a weapon adducing the instances in which experiments paved the way for progress. Enlightenment as a period has passed, but the need for enlightening is still with us and so is its historical helpmate. Only where the need for enlightening has gone has the radical form of progress history also lost its meaning. It may be amusing to dwell on the stupidity of the Middle Ages, but in historical works written for physicians this is now hardly enlightening. If medicine, today, is much further advanced and more solidly established than in former times, this is generally speaking not our personal merit.

But pragmatic history written from the point of view of progress, does not exhaust its usefulness with its enlightening function. Its interest in discoveries and inventions provides a convenient introduction to the treatment of any scientific theme. And in the form of an introduction it is widely used today. Of course, science can be taught in a systematic form without regard to its historical development. The truth of any scientific statement rests on its proof and not on the man who first pronounced it. Scientific terms can be explained by mere definition without reference to their original meaning. But the historical introduction which shows how the present state of knowledge was reached step by step, has many advantages. In the first place, the appearance of arbitrariness is thereby avoided. By current definition "healing by first intention" is defined as the healing of a wound without intervention of granulations. History explains that the term goes back to Galen who believed that nature's first intention in repairing any severance of tissues was to glue them together directly without intervention of any new substance. But he added that only in a very few tissues, especially the muscular, were nature and the physician able to follow this "first intention."[37] Secondly, by listing the progressive discoveries in any field, the reader is quickly introduced to the level on which the author wishes to discuss the subject. And if, at the same time, the principal mistakes made in the past are mentioned and disproved, much of the ground is already covered before the first chapter starts, and the position taken by the author has become clear. A treatise on antimalarial drugs, for instance, might start out with the introduction of the cinchona bark in the 17th century and the uncertainties of its use before the isolation of quinine by Pelletier and Caventou in 1820. Then the great expectations placed in this drug in the late 19th century, the various treatment schemes, and the doubtful results obtained during the first World War might be discussed. Even with these few data it could be made clear that this particular drug was not the ideal solution and why the search for other antimalarials has continued. Thus the stage would be set for more recent researches.[38] In the third place, a purely systematic arrangement often gives the impression that everything is known about the subject and forms a logical whole. This danger can be avoided by the historical method which lays bare the various roots from which particular questions and their solutions arise. It is not so easy to define the concept of filariasis. To say that it is a disease caused by filariae may give the impression that it is an entity all the symptoms of which are caused by the presence of this parasite. Yet there exist many forms of filariasis and the dependence on filariae alone is not equally well established for all of them. Misunderstanding may be avoided if the reader is told how in the 19th century a number of different syndromes (elephantiasis, chyluria, etc.) were found associated with filarial infections, and how they were then united under the common denominator "filariasis" by a theory which did not remain undisputed.[39]

But these examples are really superfluous because the whole of medical

[37]Cf. Galen, Ars medica, ch 29 f., in: *Claudii Galeni Opera omnia*, ed. C. G. Kühn, t. 1, Lipsiae, 1821, p. 385 ff.

[38]Cf. O. Temkin and E. M. Ramsey, *Antimalarial drugs, general outline*, National Research Council, Division of Medical Sciences, Office of Medical Information, Washington, 1944.

[39]Cf. O. Temkin, *A report on the medicinal treatment of Filariasis Bancrofti*, National Research Council, Division of Medical Sciences, Office of Medical Information, Washington, 1945, p. 3.

literature is full of longer or shorter historical accounts of the progress made through the ages. All this goes to show that the usefulness of pragmatic historiography in medicine is not a mere presumption. It is a reality and a form of thought often cultivated even by those who do not consciously admit the usefulness of history in medicine.

6

Given that pragmatic history is practical in the intention, then no part of medical historiography has a greater pragmatic value than the history of diseases. Here indeed, the historical method constitutes a direct approach to medical problems. The science of medicine deals with man's nature in health and disease. The history of medicine deals with this science as seen in man's thought, actions and institutions. But the history of diseases forms a connecting link, for it contributes to the study of a pathological phenomenon. Historical pathology is at once a part of history and of the science of pathology.

The usefulness of historical pathology is best demonstrated by the epidemic diseases, for epidemics come and go—that is to say, they have histories. As a matter of fact, epidemic diseases more than others have attracted the attention of medical historians. In the late Middle Ages and the 16th and 17th centuries the term "historia morbi" had various shades of meaning.[40] In the first place, it designated what we now call a case history, an account of the illness of an individual. But it also meant the description of a disease as an entity. This latter meaning prevailed with Thomas Sydenham who formulated a program of how the history of diseases should be studied. "In the first place, it is necessary that all diseases be reduced to definite and certain *species,* and that, with the same care which we see exhibited by botanists in their phytologies."[41] But the species of diseases can only be recognized by long observation over many years and epidemic diseases in particular, which may prevail at certain times and be absent at others, require this protracted observation period. Only by comparing many epidemics is it possible to establish the constant features of the underlying disease. On the other hand, Sydenham was aware that if many outbreaks of the same epidemic disease were compared with one another, they all showed certain modifications. The change in the behavior of epidemics he attributed to the "constitution" of the year. This implied that the "historia morbi," as the natural description of a disease, included the history of the disease as it manifested itself through the course of time. Thus the history of disease gradually acquired a truly historical connotation in addition to the older meaning. The 18th century saw many monographs on epidemics in certain places and in certain years. The empirical

[40]For this and the following, cf. O. Temkin, Studien zum "Sinn" -Begriff in der Medizin, *Kyklos,* Bd. 2, 1929, pp. 50 ff. and 89 ff.
[41]*The works of Thomas Sydenham,* transl. etc. by R. G. Latham, London, Sydenham Society, vol. 1, 1848, p. 13. For the following also cf. Galdston, *op cit.* (below, note 47).

material on which a more comprehensive historical view could be based was thereby considerably increased. At the turn of the century the great histories of epidemic diseases began to appear: Noah Webster's "Brief History of Epidemic and Pestilential Diseases" in 1799, Ozanam's "Histoire médicale générale et particulière des maladies épidémiques contagieuses et épizootiques" in 1817 and 1818. They were continued and crowned by the works of Hecker, Haeser and Hirsch in the following decades. Haeser's "Geschichte der epidemischen Krankheiten" in the third volume of his history of medicine (3rd ed. 1882) and Hirsch's "Handbuch der historisch-geographischen Pathologie" (2nd ed. 1881–86) were published at the beginning of the bacteriological era and represented the terminal points of the older historical pathology. They are antiquated in many respects but as yet unsurpassed for their comprehensiveness.

These historical studies were conceived as pertinent contributions to the knowledge of epidemic diseases. It was believed that they would make it possible to recognize the laws behind the variety of phenomena. Such a belief was well founded in the concept of the "constitution" as the determining factor in the appearance of epidemics. According to Sydenham, the matter stood as follows: "There are different constitutions in different years. They originate neither in their heat nor their cold, their wet nor their drought; but they depend upon certain hidden and inexplicable changes within the bowels of the earth. By the effluvia from these the atmosphere becomes contaminate, and the bodies of men are predisposed and determined, as the case may be, to this or that complaint. This continues during the influence of this or that constitution, which, after the cycle of a few years, gives ground, and makes way for another."[42] Epidemiology, therefore, consisted of the clinical description of the diseases as well as the preceding and concomitant telluric and cosmic events such as climatic changes, earthquakes, volcanic eruptions, etc. Traces of this concept which originated long before Sydenham were still to be found in Haeser's and Hirsch's works. Young Haeser, writing under the stimulus of German romanticism, had even been optimistic enough to believe that historical pathology (chiefly of epidemic diseases) would help to establish the mysterious and supreme laws which determined all evolution. "There are two apparently opposite trends that nevertheless combine to a single end, from which science may expect its next advance—the investigation of disease in its greatest and most spiritual terms, in epidemics and their forms through the centuries; and the exploration of the most minute material changes of morbid life through the microscope. Historical pathology will preserve us from forgetting the old θειον [i. e., the Divine]; with forceful admonitions it will remind us that life is not grasped with the hands alone nor seen only with the eyes. Microscopic pathology will always remind us that one thing above all is essential if firm ground is to be gained:

[42]*Op. cit.,* p. 33f.

the exploration of the most minute material life processes. May it only not forget that a world of secrets lies hidden behind the microscopic slide never to be reached by the eye of the investigator." [43]

These words were written in 1839, the year in which Schwann established the cellular theory of the animal organism. Indeed, historical pathology and microscopic pathology went hand in hand during the following decades and Virchow, the founder of cellular pathology, was no mean historian himself. Until the rise of the bacteriological era there was little doubt that the historical approach was a legitimate method in the study of epidemic diseases. With the advance of bacteriology at the end of the 19th century, historical studies seemed to lose in importance. Epidemic diseases were seen as infectious diseases caused by specific agents. The biology of the latter and the mode of infection rather than any nebulous "constitution" accounted for the outbreak of an epidemic. The virulence of bacteria and the conditions of immunity in the population explained strength, length and periodicity of the outbreaks. In the initial enthusiasm it was sometimes overlooked that the experimental method cannot altogether replace knowledge of the historical manifestations of epidemics. A theory is complete only when it leaves no questions unanswered and when no unknown "x-factor" remains. But the history of epidemics forces us to assume such a factor, e.g., when we ask why there were pandemics of bubonic plague in 1894 and of influenza in 1918. [44] Such problems are challenges to the modern epidemiologist and their solution would advance his science. History will no longer claim to explain the mechanism of disease, but historical pathology is a great reservoir whence scientific questions arise. Why did leprosy begin to decline at the end of the Middle Ages? Was it because the strict rules of isolation checked its spread, or because the "black death" had exterminated the inmates of many leprosaria? [45] And why did the plague itself retreat from Europe at the beginning of the 18th century? Was it because of a change in the rodent population? Why is there no description of small-pox to be found in the Hippocratic collection? Did this disease pass unrecorded in the books which have come down to us or did it not exist then? Why, on the other hand, was syphilis called a new disease at the end of the 15th century? Had it always existed in Europe without being recognized as a specific entity, or had it really been imported by the crew of Columbus to flare up as a violent epidemic for several decades? How was malaria overcome in the Mississippi valley? Was this due to some drug, some special sanitary measure, or to a combination of many factors including the staunch spirit of the pioneers who would not yield the ground they

---

[43]H. Haeser, *Historisch-pathologische Untersuchungen,* erster Theil, Dresden u. Leipzig, 1839, p. X f.

[44] Cf. C.-E. A. Winslow, *The conquest of epidemic disease,* Princeton University Press, 1943, p. 233.

[45]Cf. H. E. Sigerist, Der Aussatz auf den Hawaiischen Inseln, *Verhandlungen der Schweizer. Naturforschenden Gesellschaft,* Thun, 1932, pp. 452–453.

had occupied?[46] It is obvious that the answers to these and many similar questions have a bearing on almost all aspects of modern epidemiology.

For some time at least, the rise of bacteriology imposed restrictions upon the study of epidemic diseases.[47] Since these diseases were identified with infections, diseases which are not transmitted by microorganisms fell outside the scope of the epidemiologist. This group included some purely somatic illnesses like scurvy, ergotism, etc., and above all mental illnesses like mass neuroses. Besides, the search for the mechanism diverted many epidemiologists from the interdependence of epidemic disease and culture. The historical pathologists of a hundred years ago had not separated the somatic, mental and cultural aspects. Hecker's essays on the psychic epidemics of the Middle Ages, dancing mania, tarantism, etc., have remained classics. And Virchow, with a political aim in view, wrote in the revolutionary year of 1848: "History has shown more than once how the fate of the greatest empires was determined by the state of health of the nations or of the armies, and it is no longer doubtful that the history of epidemic diseases must form an inseparable part of the cultural history of mankind. Epidemics resemble great warnings from which a statesman in the grand style can read that a disturbance has taken place in the development of his people, a disturbance which not even a carefree policy may longer overlook."[48]

The psychic epidemics of the past supply a large material for the study of abnormal human behavior. Here indeed, history reveals forms of disease which may not be observable at present. In the late Middle Ages, thousands of men and women roamed over some districts, dancing and leaping until they collapsed in a state of utter exhaustion. In this form, the dancing mania does not exist among the civilized nations of today. Such strange behavior must have had its causes in the social and cultural conditions of those past centuries. Elucidation of these causes would broaden our understanding of the possible reactions of man to the milieu in which he lives. Again, we know that as late as the 17th century, cases of possession occurred frequently and were still regarded as a religious phenomenon. In the clinic of Charcot, some sixty years ago, they were considered an atavistic form of hysteria, and seem now to have become relatively rare. No theory of hysteria can be considered valid which does not account for all its forms, past and present. It was for this reason that Charcot and his pupils studied the past, not from mere historical curiosity, but as clinicians who wished to define the disease entity of "grande-hystérie."[49] But to be of value, histori-

---

[46]Cf. E. H. Ackerknecht, *Malaria in the Upper Mississippi Valley 1760–1900,* The Johns Hopkins Press, 1945 [Supplements to the Bull. Hist. Med. no. 4].

[47]Cf. Temkin (above, note 40), p. 96 ff. Cf. also I. Galdston, Humanism and public health, *Bull. Hist. Med.,* vol. 8, 1940, pp. 1032–1039, and The epidemic constitution in historic perspective, *Bull. New York Acad. Med.,* vol. 18, 1942, pp. 606–619.

[48]R. Virchow, *Gesammelte Abhandlungen aus dem Gebiete der öffentlichen Medicin und der Seuchenlehre,* 1. Bd., Berlin, 1879, p. 22.

[49]Cf. O. Temkin, *The falling sickness,* Baltimore, The Johns Hopkins Press, 1945, p. 321.

cal studies in these domains must broaden out into the political, social, economic and cultural conditions of the time. They must aim at understanding the medical phenomenon against its own background and not merely in the light of present day concepts.

Epidemics, whether somatic or psychic, are but paradigms for the general theme of "Civilization and Disease."[50] Since man never lives outside some form of civilization, all his diseases are influenced by it to some degree. On the other hand, his diseases in turn influence civilization. It is obvious that the general historian has to count with this factor. No history of the Middle Ages can by-pass the epidemic of the "black death" which is supposed to have killed one-fourth of Europe's population in the 14th century.[51] But to the physician this factor means that the study of historical pathology may better qualify him to recognize, prevent and cure some of the ills which beset our own culture.

7

From the 18th century on, the pragmatic history of medicine was guided by the idea of progress; yet although this idea remained inherent, the scope of pragmatic history broadened in other directions. Daniel Le Clerc had already said: "This history must enter into the spirit of each century and of each author, report faithfully the thoughts of all, leave to everybody what is his."[52] On the one hand, the pragmatists of the 18th century saw the history of medicine as a process dependent on political, geographic and social conditions as well as personal achievements. But on the other hand, they rationalized the causal connections in the fashion of Enlightenment.[53] Towards the end of the century, Sprengel defined pragmatic history as follows: "History is pragmatic if it makes us wise. And it does make us wise if it stimulates us to reflexions about the step by step development of human reason, to a better understanding of medical doctrines, to the utilization of attempts at fathoming truth even though they were in vain, and to a correction of our own system."[54] The causes of the development, according to Sprengel, could only be found in the history of the culture of the human mind, and the dominating philosophical systems above all gave the key to an understanding of medical opinions. The history of science, external circumstances, and the lives of the physicians should not be neglected, but basically they were of secondary importance. The emphasis on philosophy is to be expected from the contemporaries of Kant, Fichte, Schelling and Hegel. Besides, the history of medicine is not understandable without a knowledge of the history of philosophy. Just as Galen depended on Plato

<hr>

[50]Cf. H. E. Sigerist, *Civilization and disease,* Ithaca, N. Y., Cornell University Press, 1943.
[51]Cf. J. F. C. Hecker, *The epidemics of the Middle Ages,* transl. B. G. Babington, London, The Sydenham Society, 1844, p. 30.
[52]Le Clerc, *op. cit.* (above, note 35), preface ** 2 v.
[53]Cf. Diepgen, *op cit.* (above, note 1c).
[54]K. Sprengel, *Versuch einer pragmatischen Geschichte der Arzneykunde,* erster Theil, dritte umgearbeitete Auflage, Halle, 1821, p. 4.

and Aristotle, so the iatrophysicists and iatrochemists—the forerunners of the modern physiologist—depended upon the mechanistic philosophy of Descartes. The close ties between medicine and philosophy were loosened during the 19th century and physicians became increasingly prejudiced against philosophy. It was then that the history of medicine preserved a knowledge of fundamental human thought for the student of medicine and it still does so today.

Nevertheless, Sprengel and his immediate successors tended to overemphasize philosophy to the neglect of other factors. These shortcomings have gradually been corrected by the medical historians of the last 150 years. With a deepened understanding of the history of religion, the cult of Asclepius and other healing miracles ceased to be explained as frauds imposed on the credulous by the priests. An appreciation of the history of art showed the significance of Leonardo da Vinci, Stephan of Calcar and other artist-scientists. The discovery of ancient Egyptian papyri and of Babylonian medical texts put the early history of medicine on a firm ground. Archaeological studies revealed many details of the every day life of the peoples and thereby opened a new vista into the history of hygiene and medical customs. The history of science was cultivated more vigorously than before and, in turn, shed much light on the neighboring disciplines of medicine. In recent years particularly, the sociological approach has made possible many new interpretations of the past as well as of the present. The Hippocratic physicians are now seen in their historical reality as craftsmen who had to compete among themselves and against the distrust of laymen.[55] The rise of surgery from the Middle Ages is intimately bound to the rise of those classes which valued trade and practical usefulness more than a metaphysical insight into an ordered and static universe. We are aware how in our own days modes of practice are changing and new branches of medicine developing under the stress of industrialization, war, modifications in the composition of age groups, shifting economic conditions, etc. And here again the situation resembles that regarding philosophy. Medical history itself has become broader in outlook and richer in content. At the same time, by connecting the development of medicine with political history, history of religion, fine arts and science, archaeology, sociology and economics, the history of medicine keeps its students in touch with the humanities and social sciences. The history of medicine, therefore, represents the humanities and social sciences in medicine and especially in medical education.

This educational value of medical history was very clearly recognized by the historians of the last century. In 1889 Theodor Puschmann, professor of the history of medicine at the University of Vienna, made a plea for the encouragement of medico-historical studies. His plea was provoked by the almost complete neglect of history by the leading medical men and institu-

---

[55]Cf. L. Edelstein, Περὶ ἀέρων *und die Sammlung der hippokratischen Schriften,* Berlin, Weidmann, 1931.

tions of the time, a neglect which bordered on contempt. This state of affairs induced Puschmann to make the following point:

> The use of historical studies manifests itself in three ways: First, they complete general education; then, they form the foundation of professional knowledge and fortify it; and finally, they further the education and ennobling of the character.
>
> When the history of medicine and of the sciences is seen as a part of the general history of culture and is thus presented, when the teacher follows its relation to the other arts and sciences, and, vice versa, calls attention to the influence of the latter on natural science and medicine, when he considers at once political events and social conditions, and gives to the whole the characteristic aura of the age, his lectures will complement and broaden the education of the students in every way.[56]

Participation in the general culture of the time through a many-sided understanding of the evolution of medicine, this was perhaps the highest point which the pragmatic history of medicine reached. It was free from immediate utilitarian purpose and yet it was still a part of the pragmatic program. For even here, medical history was seen from the point of view of usefulness—if not for the progress of medical science directly, then at least for the general education and culture of the physician and the prestige and intellectual alertness of the profession.

When Puschmann complained about the lack of interest in medical history, he was probably unaware of the very lively interest that was developing in this country. In the same year of 1889, William Osler assumed his duties at the newly opened Johns Hopkins Hospital and immediately began to impart his own historical interest to his students and associates. The Johns Hopkins Medical History Club was organized and the beginning was made of what has become a tradition. Osler was not a professional historian; nevertheless medical history was not a mere hobby to him, for it was not separated from his main work. Osler neither edited ancient texts nor did he make any startling historical discoveries. He and his pupils often were satisfied with discussing men and books already well known. Yet medical history was a living part of Osler's work as a clinician and a teacher. If the biography of a great doctor makes him a teacher of later generations, then the life of William Osler teaches how medical history can become an integral part of a physician's work.

The tradition which Osler helped to plant and William H. Welch to cultivate became a strong moving force for the establishment of a medical library connected with an institute of the history of medicine, By 1929, when the William H. Welch Medical Library of The Johns Hopkins University was dedicated and the chair of the History of Medicine inaugurated, medicine was no longer the unified science and art it had been throughout the greater part of the 19th century. The many specialties had developed rapidly and had begun to lead an independent life. Harvey Cushing, one of

---

[56]T. Puschmann, Die Bedeutung der Geschichte für die Medicin und die Naturwissenschaften, *Deutsche med. Wchnschr.*, vol. 15, 1889, p. 817.

the main speakers at the dedication exercises, summed up the situation in these words:

> More and more the preclinical chairs in most of our schools have come to be occupied by men whose scientific interests may be quite unrelated to anything that obviously has to do with Medicine, some of whom, indeed, confess to a feeling that by engaging in problems that have an evident bearing on the healing art they lose caste among their fellows. They have come to have their own societies, separate journals of publication, a scientific lingo foreign to other ears, and are rarely seen in meetings of medical practitioners with whom they have wholly lost contact.[57]

To counterbalance this state of affairs was one of the reasons for establishing a centralized medical library permeated by the spirit of historical teaching and research. It was felt that the history of medicine would not only strengthen the humanistic side of medicine but would, moreover, form a synthesis for the many branches of medicine.[58] This feeling was shared by many men in this country and Europe alike. The history of medicine extends over the whole breadth of medicine and through its whole past. From the vantage point of history, medicine can be seen as a whole. And if this viewpoint is imparted to students and doctors, then they too will keep it a whole. To understand medicine as a whole and to preserve it as a whole, this has become one of its useful tasks in an age of specialization.

But the same process which during the last sixty years was preparing a new task for the history of medicine also threatened to engulf it. While most medical scientists were indifferent to historical studies, others outside the profession had become interested in the historical aspects of medicine. If it was true that medical history had branched out into many fields of the humanities, it was equally true that scholars in these fields had turned towards medical works. For the Egyptologist, a medical papyrus was an interesting document of Egyptian literature, language and culture. Ebers and Breasted, to name but the editors of the two most important medical papyri, were not physicians. Greek and Latin medical authors had formerly been cultivated chiefly by doctors. Now classical scholars in increasing number turned to the works of Hippocrates, Galen, Soranus, Celsus and others. Before World War II, new standard editions of Greek and Latin medical books were being published and there were very few doctors among the editors. The list could easily be enlarged by many examples from other periods up to the interpretation of the modern history of medicine.[59] It is easily understandable that usefulness for medicine was not the main goal of these scholars. And medical men themselves began to lose sight of the pragmatic value. The better trained they were in historical disciplines, the more they became attracted by the interest in the subject

[57]H. Cushing, The binding influence of a library on a subdividing profession, *Bull. Johns Hopkins Hospital*, vol. 46, 1930, p. 35.
[58]Cf. *Bull. Johns Hopkins Hospital*, vol. 46, no. 1, 1930.
[59]Cf. R. H. Shryock, *The development of modern medicine*, Philadelphia, University of Pennsylvania Press, 1936.

matter itself. No doubt, the older pragmatists too had devoted themselves to detailed philological and historical investigations. Yet they had felt it necessary to justify their work as ultimately useful to medicine. Now the possible usefulness was by no means forgotten but it assumed a secondary place. A characteristic illustration may be given by the fate of Pagel's "Ein-führung in die Geschichte der Medicin." Julius Pagel published this work in 1898 and in the first chapter he gave one of the most comprehensive outlines of the pragmatic point of view. After his death, the book was revised by Karl Sudhoff and in the last edition of 1922 this chapter does not appear.

In Germany above all, the history of medicine became an independent discipline. Its aim was the understanding of the past for the sake of histori-cal knowledge. It did not matter whether the knowledge gained could in any way be directly related to present day medical problems, nor whether the workers in the field were physicians. The only thing that mattered was the soundness of the method used and the reliability of the results. The history of medicine tended to become a branch of the history of civilization, rather than of medicine.

It is not the task of the present essay to discuss the usefulness of medical history at large. Disease and its cure have always played a great rôle in the history of human civilization, and the general historian, the sociologist and the modern statesman are aware of this. It would be neither possible nor desirable to make medical history the exclusive domain of the physician. But it has to be admitted that from the medical point of view this develop-ment includes the danger that the history of medicine may become an aloof specialty. This danger was expressed by Harvey Cushing in 1929 in his dedicatory address when he said: "Will this foundation merely mean still another group of specialists having their own societies, organs of publica-tion, separate places of meeting, separate congresses, national and interna-tional, and who will also incline to hold aloof from the army of doctors made and in the making?"[60]

This question is a serious challenge to the medical historian and the medical profession. For the physician who has made history his life task, it means that he must not allow himself to be wholly absorbed by the histori-cal interest itself. While at work he must be unhampered by any considera-tions foreign to the subject he is investigating. But he must also be able to account for the pragmatic value of the subjects he chooses. In method he will be a historian but in aim a physician. For the medical profession it means that the history of medicine must not be starved by lack of sympathy for thorough historical method. If the historian and the profession alike are convinced of its usefulness, the history of medicine will play its part in the future development of medicine.

[60]H. Cushing, *op. cit.* (above, note 57), p. 38.

II

The author of the Hippocratic book "On Ancient Medicine" argued that medicine, having existed as of old, did not have to be based on newly invented theories. All that mattered was to follow in the path of the old medicine in such a way as to satisfy the needs of the present. A similar case can be made for medical history. The history of medicine has developed many forms, each of them useful now as before. All that remains is to show that in our own time a situation has arisen which makes medical history not merely a useful, but a needed subject in medicine, and imposes some special duties on the historian of medicine.

1

It is common knowledge that in the 19th century the classics dominated all higher education, whereas today heavy emphasis is placed on science. This change may be ascribed to two closely allied causes. In the first place, the social and political development of most countries has democratized the basis of education. Not so long ago, the difference between "the educated" and "the uneducated" was one of quality, the educated having acquired knowledge of things (above all of classical languages) which lay outside the scope of the majority of the people. Today, the difference tends to become one of degree, the educated knowing more of the things which are considered to be of practical value and, therefore, desirable for all. In addition, many educators and scientists have pleaded for a replacement of dead learning by instruction in physics, chemistry and biology. However this may be, the fact remains that the change took place and that it affected premedical education too. It is fair to state that a generation of physicians has grown up who know no Greek, and little Latin, and who have not always replaced the knowledge of the classical languages by a better knowledge of the living ones. Generally speaking this process seems to be the same everywhere in the world.

Whether the ascendancy of scientific over philological training has been altogether desirable is a moot question not to be decided here. But even if deemed necessary, the decline of philological education constitutes a loss. It has often been pointed out that without a knowledge of Greek and Latin, the medical student cannot even understand the meaning of the terms he uses. This is undoubtedly true and may also explain some of the solecisms in medical writing.[61] But the essential loss is to be found at a deeper level and involves more than the decline of the classics. It is connected with the function of philology in its broadest sense. Philology is the study of language, and language is the medium through which "meaning" is conveyed in words from person to person. Philology, therefore, is the study of the means by which we can understand or make ourselves understood. Since

---

[61] For examples cf. M. Fishbein, *Medical writing,* Chicago, Press of the American Medical Association, 1938.

93

there exist many languages, philology has many provinces. But whether we study our native tongue or try to master a foreign language, the goal remains the same, viz., to understand what we hear or read and to make ourselves understood. Everybody becomes a student of philology in early childhood when he learns to speak, and the formal studies in school help to deepen and broaden our philological education. Fundamentally, philological education is not bound to the learning of foreign languages, and can be achieved in the mother tongue as is evidenced by the ancient Greeks and by many modern poets besides Shakespeare who knew little Latin and less Greek. The advantage of making the classics the training ground of this education lies in the fact that these languages are dead and belong to a culture which in historical perspective can be seen as a whole. They necessitate a careful and accurate study, sentences have to be analyzed and the meaning of each word closely evaluated. Even sixty years ago, probably few students of medicine could read Hippocrates and Celsus without the help of grammar and dictionary. But they knew what language meant and how books should be read and written. It is hard to escape the impression that this ability has declined since the days of Osler.

This diagnosis, if correct, has some direct bearing on medicine. In an address on "Books and Men" in 1901, Osler drew attention to the ever increasing number of books, and the difficulty of coping with it.[62] Since then, the number has increased tremendously, and it has become a commonplace to say that even a specialist cannot keep abreast of the literature in his own field. For this reason, information through abstracts and survey reviews has become increasingly important. But the need has also grown for the individual doctor to see the main points essential for his own work in books and articles. If his literary ability, both receptive and expressive, is lowered, this will result in the rise of a group of literary specialists who will read for the others and tell them what they should know. This in turn will result in a shrinking of the horizon of the medical investigator and may gradually reduce him to the level of a narrow technician.

What is true of medical publications holds good to an even higher degree with regard to literature that is not technical. To read philosophical, historical and poetical works profitably is in itself an art that has to be cultivated. Good books need good readers. There will hardly be any doubt that the physician should be a highly cultured person. But some doubt may be expressed whether the decline of philological education will leave him a favorable chance.

The knowledge of Greek has gone with the snows of yesteryear and Latin is in a fair way of following. There is no point in bewailing what at present has to be accepted as a fact. Perhaps the future will bring a revival of classical studies, as the past has often done before. Latin and Greek have had an eventful history and have proved adaptable to many conditions.

---

[62]W. Osler, *Aequanimitas, with other addresses to medical students, nurses and practitioners of medicine,* Philadelphia, P. Blakiston's Son and Co., 1904, p. 220 f.

Some day they may also find their place in a democratized society; or possibly, their educational function will be taken over by modern languages or even by an intensified study of the vernacular. These are broad issues which will not be decided by the exigencies of medicine alone. Therefore, the question arises as to how medicine can satisfy its own needs and preserve or enhance the literary ability of the physician.

In his above mentioned address, Osler made a remark which may be taken as a hint for a solution. "There should be in connection with every library a corps of instructors in the art of reading, who would, as a labour of love, teach the young idea how to read."[63] Now books are the tools of the medical historian, and the extraction of their meaning his main work. He is in frequent commerce with the classical books of medicine, and what better texts could be chosen for a study of medical reading than the classics of all times?[64] Not so very long ago, some of the old universities required their medical students to interpret a passage from Hippocrates, Celsus or some other ancient authority. This was a survival from the Middle Ages, when interpretation of the authors constituted the better part of medical instruction. Today, medicine is taught by interpreting nature, not books. But the art of interpreting classical works, ancient or modern, and in the vernacular of course, should not be lost. Much history and, perhaps, physiology too could be learned from a careful analysis of Harvey's "De motu cordis" in an English translation. No word and no thought should remain unexplained, a difficult yet very fruitful task. The student will acquire a better understanding of the foundation of experimental physiology, his attention will be drawn to the interplay of Aristotelian and modern ideas, and above all, he will be impressed by how much a little book may have to tell, quite apart from its "results."

If it is agreed that the knowledge of medical literature is useful and that, moreover, the history of medicine should be the connecting link with the humanities, then it is certainly up to the medical historian to teach how access to both is to be gained.

2

Medical history represents the humanities as far as they affect medicine or are affected by it. This implies mainly history itself and the historical aspects of language, sociology and philosophy. No more need be said about history itself, and language has just been dealt with. Sociology and philosophy, however, deserve some further comments.

Looking back into the history of medicine, one sees that in most periods physicians had to reckon with the social conditions under which they worked. In Greek and Roman antiquity, the prevention and treatment of internal diseases rested largely on a strict personal regimen. Dietetic medicine in the broadest sense dictated to the citizen what he should eat

[63]*Op. cit.*, p. 221.
[64]H. E. Sigerist, Classics of medicine, *Bull. Hist. Med.*, vol. 16, 1944, pp. 1–12.

and drink, how he should work and sleep and what exercise he should take. However, the physician was aware that only a rich man of leisure could regulate his mode of life according to the dictates of his medical attendant. The poor man who had to work for his living could not afford the luxury of adapting his life to his health.[65] During the Middle Ages and the Renaissance, princes and great noblemen had their body physicians among whom the tradition of dietetic medicine remained alive. Poor people went to a leech, a barber or to some old woman. In the cities which employed town physicians conditions were somewhat more even, but in the country the peasants were dependent on home remedies or itinerant quacks. The fact that books like the "Thesaurus pauperum" were written, that the "School of Salerno" was translated into the vernacular, and medical advice propagated through many popular writings attests some awareness at least of prevailing social factors. From the 18th century on, when Ramazzini published the first comprehensive monograph on occupational diseases and Tissot wrote his "Advice to People in General with Respect to their Health," through the 19th century to our own times, the complexity of social relations in medicine has increased, until now it draws attention from many sides.[66] The surroundings of the individual patient, the "milieu" from which he comes and the conditions under which he lives, mark his disease and the chances of his recovery. The prevention or eradication of certain illnesses, e.g., venereal diseases, rests preeminently on social possibilities. The treatment that a patient receives is not independent of his ability to pay for it. The density and wealth of the population influence the number of doctors and hospitals available and, in turn, influence the mode of practice. These are but a few instances of social and economic aspects that have become increasingly important, and of paramount interest. They have led to political debates inside and outside the profession about the desirability of individual practice, health insurance and state medicine. As a result, there is a mounting trend to demand instruction in medical sociology, economics and ethics.[67] For it is rightly felt that knowledge in this field has become as important as knowledge of the traditional scientific branches of medicine.

Medical sociology and economics can be studied on the basis of existing conditions. Surveys of the cost of medical care, of hospital facilities, of the medical needs in rural districts, etc., are made in great numbers. Information is compiled on the forms of health insurance in various states and countries. The existing facilities for medical education and research are examined with a view to the future needs for an intensified attack upon disease. All this can be done, and often is being done, with little regard to the way in which existing conditions have developed. Yet if the historical aspect is neglected, present conditions will not be *understood,* just as the structure of the adult body will not be *understood* without embryology, the

---

[65]Cf. L. Edelstein, Antike Diätetik, *Die Antike,* vol. 7, 1931, pp. 255–270.
[66]Cf. H. E. Sigerist, *Medicine and human welfare,* New Haven, Yale University Press, 1941.
[67]Cf. *J. A. M. A.,* vol. 129, 1945, p. 464.

history of its development. The "Goodenough Report"[68] which in 1944 was brought out under the auspices of the British government, may be cited as an example of what is meant. This report surveys the organization of medical schools in Great Britain and contains recommendations for future reforms. Far-reaching as many of its proposals are, they are not marked by any bias in favor of medical history.[69] But in its survey of the medical schools of the University of London, and in many other instances as well, sections on the historical development had to be inserted in order to make the present situation understandable.

It does not follow that medical sociology and economics have to be entrusted to the historian of medicine. But on the other hand, the historian cannot be excluded. It is very likely that all clinical disciplines and some of the basic sciences too, will be increasingly imbued with social thought. This in turn will mean that teachers, investigators and practitioners will have to acquire the habit of thinking along historical lines. The history of medicine is not and cannot be taught by the few men who have made it their specialty. Nobody is able to know the entire past of medicine in all its details. Historical teaching must be diffused through the instructors of all branches and specialties. For the so-called professional historian remains the task of teaching the main lines of the development of medicine as a whole in relation to all humanistic disciplines and of imparting a sound knowledge of historical methods to his students. Whatever else he may do as a teacher or scholar will largely depend on special circumstances and his personal inclinations. His position will be similar to that of the pathologist who is not the only one to teach or investigate pathological problems.

Now this holds true too of medical sociology and economics. If medicine is to be understood as a whole, then certainly its social and economic development, up to the present, forms a very essential part of the history of medicine. Consequently, the historian of medicine will be able to show how social and economic problems should be approached historically. Everything else will then be up to those who have to cope with these questions in their clinical or scientific work or who make them their special task.

Medical sociology and economics as a special discipline are as yet in a state of emergence. Thus it is understandable, that in some cases they are directly combined with medical history, since there exists a certain mutual affinity. But such a union does not appear necessary. What seems needed is that this new discipline should not be left without a historical basis—a basis which the medical historian will have to supply.

3

Medical sociology and economics as discussed in the preceding section have their position inside medicine. They are assumed to further the aims

[68]Ministry of Health, Department of Health for Scotland, *Report of the Inter-Departmental Committee on Medical Schools,* London, His Majesty's Stationery Office, 1944.
[69]It seems as if University College Hospital Medical School alone emphasized the need for historical instruction; cf. *op. cit.,* p. 299 ff.

of medicine by unveiling the social conditions that breed disease, and the ways and means that bring medical care to the widest possible stratum of society. There exists, however, a broader aspect from which medicine and its aims as a whole are seen against the background of society. Here the question arises as to what part medicine plays and should play in our civilization. To raise this question means to look at medicine not only from the point of view of history and sociology, but of philosophy as well.

It may be doubted whether this is a question which a medical man should raise at all. By joining the medical profession he has made the prevention, cure and alleviation of disease his avowed goal. " 'Tis no idle challenge which we physicians throw out to the world when we claim that our mission is of the highest and of the noblest kind, not alone in curing disease but in educating the people in the laws of health, and in preventing the spread of plagues and pestilences; nor can it be gainsaid that of late years our record as a body has been more encouraging in its practical results than those of the other learned professions. Not that we all live up to the highest ideals, far from it—we are only men. But we have ideals, which mean much, and they are realizable, which means more." [70] These words of Osler, spoken in 1894, mean that the doctor at least can march ahead in the knowledge of doing good. The creed which they express is certainly still alive, and has given medical men a stronger moral support than many other scientists possess today. The question of the social implications of scientific discoveries, especially in physics and chemistry, has become a very acute one, and has reached the level of popular debate. But the physician seems to be secure in the use of his researches; they serve the advance of health and are, therefore, eo ipso good. Even in wartime the doctor has the satisfaction of saving the life of friend and foe—though it should perhaps not be quite forgotten that without the advances made by modern medicine, modern warfare with its huge accumulations of men threatened by epidemic disease would also scarcely be possible.

The firm self assurance of medicine rests on the assumption that life and good health are values. It may be justified to consider these assumptions as natural, since they seem to have their roots in the biological nature of animal and man. But in the historical realm of human culture, these assumptions no longer appear as self-evident. During the Middle Ages life was but a preparation for eternity, and the health of the body of no intrinsic value. Martyrs and saints sacrificed both willingly in order to save their immortal souls. Such at least was the religious and philosophical outlook even if the every day behavior of most people did not live up to it. With Bacon and Descartes the 17th century strikes a different note. From early youth it was Descartes' aim to acquire knowledge of things "useful for life." [71] Having worked out his new philosophical method, he decided to communicate it to the world in order to further the welfare of mankind and to make them masters over nature. For this is desirable "especially for

---

[70] W. Osler, Teaching and thinking, *op. cit.* (above, note 62), p. 125.

[71] R. Descartes, Discours de la méthode, *Oeuvres de Descartes,* publiées par C. Adam et P. Tannery, VI, Paris, 1902, p. 4.

the conservation of health which is, without doubt, the primary good and the basis of all the other goods of this life; for even the mind depends so much on the temperament and the disposition of the organs of the body that if it is possible to find some means of making men generally wiser and abler than they have been heretofore, I think it must be sought in medicine." [72]

Descartes expressed an idea which has grown since his time until today it threatens to transcend into the realm of religion. Descartes valued health because everything in our life, even the state of our mind, depended on it. Yet he still recognized an immortal life of the soul. With the unchecked rise of materialistic utilitarianism, the welfare of the body is becoming an absolute value. If man no longer believes in the immortality of his soul, he yearns to make his body immortal.[73] There exists a *belief* in health as there existed a belief in values of the spirit. Naturally then the physician becomes the apostle of this faith. He must be more than the expert in matters of health and the medical adviser of the nation. He must be permeated with the "*belief* in the importance of health and the prevention of disease." [74]

This may be the vision of an emerging trend rather than of a prevailing condition. Nor is it up to the doctor to belittle the importance of health. But even for the physician it is permissible to point out that the value which health represents has to compete with other values in our life. To believe in health is one thing, to forget that there are things (like freedom, search for truth and dignity of existence) for which health may be worth sacrificing, is quite another. It can hardly be denied that in our time values are unsettled and that man is faced with the necessity of making personal decisions where tradition and habit often used to decide for him. What place the preservation of health should have in our scale of values rests on a decision which no educated person, and the doctor least of all, can evade facing consciously and thoughtfully.

Decisions must be made, they cannot be taught. The history of medicine even in its widest and most philosophical sense cannot teach what should be done. But it can help to understand the present so that the future can be faced more clearly. If we compare our own medical thought with that of Antiquity or the Middle Ages, we get to know ourselves by the contrasts and similarities we discover. This is perhaps one of the greatest rewards which the study of an old culture has to offer. We are faced with a system of medicine that differs from ours not in positive knowledge only, but in social conditions, philosophical thought and ethical aim as well. For instance, if one compares the Hippocratic Oath with modern codes of medical ethics, one sees that some of the postulates of the Oath are obsolete, while others survive. We no longer treat our teachers like our own parents, nor do we foreswear operative surgery. But we still abstain from revealing the patient's secrets and from assisting him to kill himself or his progeny. On the

[72]*Op. cit.,* p. 62.
[73]Cf. A. E. Clark-Kennedy, *The art of medicine in relation to the progress of thought,* New York, Macmillan, p. 45.
[74]Goodenough report (above, note 68), p. 25 (italics are mine).

other hand, we have an ethical attitude towards the fellow members of our profession and the welfare of the community at large—features which began to develop only in the medieval faculties and surgeons' guilds. Thus we become aware of the differences which separate us from the past and, thereby, we realize our peculiarity. And by inquiring into the development that led to the present state we discover the forces that have shaped us and the trends that may reach into the future. So much the history of medicine can do to render its student conscious of the situation in which he lives. Moreover, by acquainting him with philosophical thought, it can show him the intellectual instrument that may help him reach his own decisions.

Medicine and the preservation of health have assumed an importance as hardly ever before. This means that the physician too has to shoulder responsibilities more far-reaching than before. This rôle of leadership requires an education to which the history of medicine has something substantial to contribute. Its last aim was expressed by Oliver Wendell Holmes when he spoke of the danger faced by the "practical man."

There are, of course, in every calling, those who go about the work of the day before them, doing it according to the rules of their craft, and asking no questions of the past or of the future, or of the aim and end to which their special labor is contributing. These often consider and call themselves *practical men.* They pull the oars of society, and have no leisure to watch the currents running this or that way; let theorists and philosophers attend to them. In the mean time, however, these currents are carrying the practical men, too, and all their work may be thrown away, and worse than thrown away, if they do not take knowledge of them and get out of the wrong ones and into the right ones as soon as they may. Sir Edward Parry and his party were going straight towards the pole in one of their arctic expeditions, travelling at the rate of ten miles a day. But the ice over which they travelled was drifting straight towards the equator, at the rate of *twelve* miles a day, and yet no man among them would have known that he was travelling two miles a day backward unless he had lifted his eyes from the track in which he was plodding. It is not only going backward that the plain practical workman is liable to, if he will not look up and look around; he may go forward to ends he little dreams of. It is a simple business for a mason to build up a niche in a wall; but what if, a hundred years afterwards when the wall is torn down, the skeleton of a murdered man drop out of the niche? It was a plain practical piece of carpentry for a Jewish artisan to fit two pieces of timber together according to the legal pattern in the time of Pontius Pilate; he asked no questions, perhaps, but we know what burden the cross bore on the morrow! And so, with subtler tools than trowels or axes, the statesman who works in policy without principle, the theologian who works in forms without a soul, the physician who, calling himself a practical man, refuses to recognize the larger laws which govern his changing practice, may all find that they have been building truth into the wall, and hanging humanity upon the cross.[75]

This was said in 1860, more than eight-five years ago. Today there is still no more forceful way of expressing the usefulness—and need—of medical history for medicine.

[75]O. W. Holmes, Currents and counter-currents in medical science, *Medical essays,* 1842–1882, Boston and New York, Houghton, Mifflin and Co., 1891, pp. 175–177.

5

On the Interrelationship
of the History and the Philosophy
of Medicine*

ANYBODY WISHING to speak about the philosophy of medicine will, at the outset, encounter two difficulties: the vagueness of the term and the prejudice against the subject itself. To some degree, the two difficulties are related to each other. With the spread of positivism in the nineteenth century, philosophy became synonymous with speculations that lead nowhere. Today, too, this attitude is often met with among scientists, physicians, and historians, let alone so-called practical men. We may admit that the prejudice does not altogether lack a foundation. Undisciplined philosophical thinking can camouflage more easily than can undisciplined reasoning in the sciences or history where results carry their own evidence.

The careless manner in which the word "philosophy" is bandied about is an additional sign of the slight importance attached to it. Not infrequently the same person who disparages philosophy will also use the word where no philosophy is really involved. Thus we hear of a philosophy of this or that where no more is implied than a theory, opinion, or belief. To some extent this carelessness is in line with the general disregard for the meaning and weight of words. We read of the symptomatology of a case or of its methodology where the author has merely recorded the symptoms of a case or indicated the method he used. And indeed, if it is possible to speak of pathology in the stomach, then there is nothing remarkable in speaking of a philosophy of appendectomy.

Yet it cannot be doubted that all through its history medicine has received philosophical attention in a more than casual manner. Some of the great classics of medicine embody a true philosophy: several of the treatises that go by the name of Hippocrates, some chapters in Sydenham, Claude Bernard's *Introduction to Experimental Medicine*. We feel that, in a manner not always easily defined, these books deal with the fundamentals of medicine and are of a philosophical nature. Curiously enough, their influence has been greater than that of many writings which carry the name of philosophy of medicine or otherwise make their philosophical aim explicit. Thus it would seem that philosophy of medicine can be seen in a twofold way: as a broad line of thought that goes beyond scientific, clinical, or technical details, without claiming a philosophical title; or as the consciously

*Bull. Hist. Med., 1956, vol. 30, pp. 241–251.

Read at the twenty-eighth annual meeting of the American Association of the History of Medicine, Detroit, May 13, 1955. (Revised.)

philosophical treatment of medicine. Let us now discuss the interrelationship between the history of medicine and this general philosophical approach first, and turn to philosophy in the stricter sense afterwards.

If we look for a combination of unprofessional philosophy with medical history, we may easily think of William Osler. He referred to himself as "a plain man whose life has never been worried by any philosophy higher than that of the shepherd in *As You Like It*."[1] There is no doubt that Osler was well acquainted with the tenets of quite a number of philosophers, even if their thoughts never bothered him. His imperviousness to full dress philosophy was countered by his belief that "every man has a philosophy of life in thought, in word, or in deed, worked out in himself unconsciously."[2] Osler himself not only possessed such a philosophy, but I venture to think that the force with which he expressed his "way of life," largely accounts for his influence in the Anglo-Saxon world. He told others what they should think and feel, and the history of medicine was a powerful medium for his teaching. Osler received inspiration from old books and thus he told the budding physicians to read the journals and the old books and to leave the new books to the old men.[3] When looking at his *Evolution of Modern Medicine* or his other historical writings, my admiration for his wide culture is mingled with the feeling that the past largely reflects his own individuality, that he does not expect us to learn from historical investigation in the same sense in which he would expect a physician to learn from scientific research. "It is one of the values of lectures on the history of medicine," he writes, "to keep alive the good influences of great men even after their positive teaching is antiquated. Let no man be so foolish as to think that he has exhausted any subject for his generation."[4] Having heard these words, who will dare to admit to such foolishness, even if Osler had not bolstered his warning with examples of the influence of Virchow, Lister, and Ehrlich? Osler's "way of life" included the history of medicine. And since Osler viewed himself as a humanist, his understanding of medical history was humanistic too. The humanist sees history as made by men, and Osler certainly saw medical history as made by men, above all by the great physicians. But his biographical approach was not without a theoretical foundation. He defined history as "the biography of the mind of man" and thought that "its educational value is in direct proportion to the completeness of our study of the individuals through whom this mind has been manifested."[5] This note, even though Osler may not sound it often, should not be entirely missed. It does not make Osler a Hegelian (even though he

---

[1] William Osler, *A Way of Life*, reprinted Baltimore, Remington, 1923, p. 3.

[2] *Ibid.*, p. 1. On Osler's relation to philosophy, especially to William James and Pragmatism, cf. Ludwig Edelstein, "William Osler's Philosophy," *Bull. Hist. Med.* 1946, 20: 270–293.

[3] William Osler, "Internal Medicine as a Vocation," *Aequanimitas; with Other Addresses to Medical Students, Nurses and Practitioners of Medicine*, Philadelphia, P. Blakiston, 1904, p. 149 f.

[4] William Osler, *The Evolution of Modern Medicine*, New Haven, Yale University Press, 1921, p. 219.

[5] *Ibid.*

mentions Hegel in this connection), but it shows that the history of medicine to him had a substratum underlying its biographical diversities. History taken as the revelation of the human mind can also be approached in a different way. It should be possible to write a history of medicine that traces the development of medical thought with relatively little concern for bibliographical details or priorities of inventions and discoveries, but with emphasis "on the connection between general civilization and medicine and on the development of medical thinking."[6] These words constitute the program with which Max Neuburger prefaced his *History of Medicine.* At first sight, Osler's *Evolution of Modern Medicine* and Neuburger's *History of Medicine* seem as different as the two authors themselves. Neuburger was not a man of ringing imperatives; he was a quiet scholar who tested the old medical systems for their philosophical content. Moreover, his aim to follow the connection between general civilization and medicine continued a tradition of medical historiography that went back to the days of Daniel LeClerc. Correlating the development of medicine with philosophical systems would have been nothing new. But Neuburger's effort went in a different direction. He tried to find the common philosophical denominator for the medicine of a period and other manifestations of its cultural life. As an example we may quote his work on the healing power of nature[7] in which he showed how belief or disbelief in this power was connected with philosophical doctrines on the one hand and principles of medical practice on the other. It is not merely the wish to honor the memory of a great medical historian who died just two months ago that makes me pay tribute to Max Neuburger in this discussion of the interrelationship of the history and philosophy of medicine.

Whoever pursues the history of medicine in a philosophical vein will tend towards Osler or Neuburger. The direction will depend on whether he considers history as a medium of expressing his philosophical beliefs or as the body of material incorporating the philosophical beliefs of past generations. The two attitudes are not exclusive; they may both be present, though to different degrees.

So far we have spoken of looking at medicine and its history in a philosophical vein. Prudence would advise us to stop here. But then we would not do justice to our subject which includes the philosophy of medicine, *sensu strictiori.* What does this mean? In 1947, Professor Szumowski read a paper before the International Congress of the History of Science with the title "The Philosophy of Medicine, Its History, Essence, Designation, and Definition."[8] This paper contains an interesting account

---

[6]Max Neuburger, *Geschichte der Medicin,* 2 vols., Stuttgart, Ferdinand Enke, 1906–1910; vol. 1, p. v.

[7]Max Neuburger, *Die Lehre von der Heilkraft der Natur im Wandel der Zeiten,* Stuttgart, Ferdinand Enke, 1926.

[8]W. Szumowski, "La philosophie de la médecine, son histoire, son essence, sa dénomination et sa définition," *Arch. Internat. d'Hist. des Sci.* 1949, 2: 1097–1139.

of the history of the philosophy of medicine and is a valuable guide to the publications in the field. This is Professor Szumowski's definition:

The philosophy of medicine is a science which considers medicine as a whole. It studies its position in humanity, in society, in the state and in the medical schools. It embraces at a glance the whole of the history of medicine. It reveals the more general problems of the philosophy of biology. It analyzes the methodological form of medical thought, mentioning and explaining the errors in logic which are committed in medicine. It extracts from psychology and metapsychics the knowledge and the ideas which are of importance in the totality of medicine. It touches upon medical "praxeology," discusses the chief values in medicine, formulates ethical principles and medical deontology. And, finally, it discusses medical aesthetics.[9]

Though this seems to me an overly generous definition, I shall not try to improve on it. Instead, I suggest that, in analogy to general philosophy, the philosophy of medicine should present us with a medical logic, medical ethics, and medical metaphysics. This will lead us on to somewhat firmer ground, at least as far as logic and ethics are concerned. Medical logic is a subdivision of general logic; it is a chapter in methodology, dealing with the concepts that constitute medicine, their meaning as well as correct use. Medical ethics is a part of general ethics. Just as the latter teaches what is good and bad, medical ethics, presumably, should teach what is good and bad in medical situations.

We have facilitated our task by omitting, for the time being, medical metaphysics. Even so, the definitions we gave are merely formalistic. In essence they say that philosophy of medicine teaches the principles of right thinking and acting in medicine. What relationship does this have to the history of medicine which deals with what has been done and thought in medicine? In answer we may quote a passage from Thomas Aquinas: "The purpose of philosophy is not to know what men have thought, but what is the truth of things."[10] If we apply this general statement to our particular problem, it means that philosophy and history of medicine pursue different aims and that their connection cannot be an intrinsic one. As a matter of convenience, the putting together of medical history, philosophy, sociology, and literature may be justified from the administrative point of view of a medical school. Moreover, they often need one another's help, as we hope to show later in the case of history and philosophy. But before establishing good neighborly relations, we must bring the differences into focus, which we may do by reference to medical logic on which we possess several books,

[9]*Op. cit.*, p. 1138.
[10]*De Caelo et Mundo* (Bk. 1, lectio 22): "Studium philosophiae non est ad hoc quod sciatur quid homines senserint, sed qualiter se habeat veritas rerum."—Quoted from *Aristotles' De anima, in the Version of William of Moerbeke and the Commentary of St. Thomas Aquinas*, translated by K. Foster and S. Humphries with an introduction by Ivo Thomas, London, Routledge and Kegan Paul, 1951, p. 20.—As any textbook of historical methodology will show, the relationship of history and philosophy in general has long been an object of discussion. However, the problematic nature of a philosophy of medicine and the specialized task of medical history have made it appear to me more profitable to refrain from simply placing the present discussion within the general framework.

Blane's *Elements of Medical Logick* which first appeared in 1819, and Oester-len's[11] and Bieganski's[12] works of the same title. None of these is a historical book nor does history play a pre-eminent part in the first two named, except by way of illustration. It was Blane's intention "to expound the physiology, pathology, and therapeutics of the medical mind," because he deemed it necessary that physicians "discipline their minds, by a knowledge of the laws of evidence, and the rules of investigation."[13] Oesterlen, who came some thirty years later, stood on the shoulders of John Stuart Mill's *Logic,* and Bieganski, the German translation of whose book appeared in 1909, stood under the influence of experimental medicine. But in spite of the diversity due to the different situations under which the books were written, the underlying aim was the same: to establish correct thinking in medicine. The past yields examples of fallacies and illustrates the ways of progress. But even in citing examples from past experience, we must have a standard of fallacy and progress. The same is true of medical ethics. At first, this may sound surprising. Is it not true that medical ethics of our day largely rests on the Oath of Hippocrates, on Percival's code, and other historical documents? Should we then not benefit by their study? We certainly shall benefit in as far as our understanding of present-day medical ethics is concerned. One may even go further and claim that it is impossible to reach any understanding without a study of the historical development. Yet, understanding of the way things have come about is not the same as judging them correct and right. Historical understanding is one thing, philosophical judgment another.

The point has been made that the difference in character between history and philosophy has been confused by medical historians.[14] Allegedly, history and philosophy are sciences in their own right.[15] I believe that this implies an oversimplification of the issue, since on the authority of outstanding philosophers we must at least admit that philosophy may not be a science at all. It is for this reason that the two are separate and yet interrelated. Philosophy is not identical with any science and yet related to all of them. Where, then, does the relationship to the history of medicine lie?

Let us suppose that we wish to define the notion of health. How shall we go about it? To find a definition of some validity we first look up the word "health" in a dictionary and find: "soundness of body and figuratively of mind," etc. Obviously we must now look up the meaning of "sound," and we read: "free from disease or defects or blemishes or corruption or

[11]F. Oesterlen, *Medical Logic,* translated and edited by G. Whitley, London, Sydenham Society, 1855.
[12]W. Bieganski, *Medizinische Logik,* autorisierte Übersetzung nach der zweiten Original-Auflage von Dr. A. Fabian. Würzburg, Curt Kabitzsch, 1909. The book originally appeared in Polish.
[13]Gilbert Blane, *Elements of Medical Logick,* second edition, London, Thomas and George Underwood, 1821, pp. 15 and 14.
[14]Cf. A. W. Kneucker, *Richtlinien einer Philosophie der Medizin,* Wien, Maudrich, 1949, pp. iii, 17.
[15]Kneucker, *op. cit.,* pp. iv, 18 and *passim* speaks of "exakte wissenschaftliche Philosophie" and the transfer of its laws to medicine.

heresy." In other words, health is freedom from disease. And what is disease? "A serious derangement of health." We should not blame the dictionary for such tautology since dictionaries are meant to give nominal definitions only. Besides, the dictionary introduced a somewhat puzzling distinction which we should not overlook. It referred to health as "soundness of body" and *"figuratively* of mind." Does this mean that a body only can be healthy or diseased whereas, strictly speaking, these terms do not apply to the mind? Surely we not only speak of mental disease, we even insist that a mentally diseased person should be regarded on the same plane as, say, other sick human beings. There is then a discrepancy between the explanation of the dictionary and our own current view. Who is right? The decision will rest on what is meant by body and mind. If we conceive of the mind as a spiritual entity, entirely independent of a physical body, we may indeed wonder how it could become diseased. There existed a school of psychiatry that doubted the possibility of mental disease and therefore considered psychiatric disorders as fundamentally due to somatic disturbances. The opposing school explained mental diseases in moral or religious terms because the mind lives in the sphere of good and evil, of saintliness and sin.[16] It is true that Juvenal once said: "mens sana in corpore sano esto"—but did he think of the mind in the same purely spiritual way as did Descartes, who accentuated the difference more than anybody else had done before?

Thus, instead of resolving the argument, we have introduced historical considerations. What did these historical data contribute toward a possible clarification of the issue? They put it on a much broader basis. We found that the dictionary, echoing older views, was at variance with our idea of health which we took for granted. Now we no longer take it for granted; we have become aware of a philosophical problem. Without this awareness, our starting point would have been one-sided. I do not say that the historical way is the only one by which to reach this awareness. But it is, perhaps, the shortest. It is in this sense that we can quote Goethe's famous dictum, "dass die Geschichte der Wissenschaft die Wissenschaft selbst sei." To this he added: "One cannot clearly recognize one's own possessions until one knows how to recognize what others possessed before."[17]

There is yet another point we have to consider. Our students are taught medicine at our schools. What do we mean thereby? We mean that they are taught a certain number of facts, theories, methods, and skills which are considered valid and useful for preventing and treating disease. It is si-

---

[16]On the difference between the "somatologists" and "psychologists" cf. S. Cornfeld in Neuburger-Pagel's *Handbuch der Geschichte der Medizin*, vol. 3, Jena, Gustav Fischer, 1905, pp. 675–681, and Gregory Zilboorg, *A History of Medical Psychology*, New York, W. W. Norton, 1941, pp. 434 ff. and 464 ff.

[17]Zur Farbenlehre. Didaktischer Theil, Vorwort (*Goethes Werke*, vol. 33, Stuttgart, Cotta, 1881, p. 7). One might also cite here Fuller's dictum, "That history maketh a young man to be old without either wrinkles or grey hairs; privileging him with the experience of age without either the infirmities or inconveniences thereof," which Osler quoted in his preface to Max Neuburger, *History of Medicine*, translated by Ernest Playfair, vol. 1, London, Oxford University Press, 1910, p. vii. (Dr. W. W. Francis kindly informs me that Dr. Osler was quoting from the preface of Thos. Fuller's *History of the Holy War*, 1639.)

lently assumed that we impart the accumulated knowledge of the ages, that is, what has proved endurable and sound in the work of former genera- tions. I sometimes wonder at the assurance with which this assumption is made. On whom do those who are not interested in historical work rely when they take it for granted that everything worth while preserving has entered into modern texts? Do they rely on medical historians? Flattering as this would be, I can hardly believe that such great trust is placed in us. Do they rely on the working of progress, taking it for granted that in the process of time mistakes were constantly eliminated while truth was built on truth? I cannot quite share such confidence. The medical work of Cotton Mather that has recently been brought into relief by Beall and Shryock shows how generations may condemn what will later appear a step in the right direction. Nevertheless, it would be foolish to exaggerate the addition to practical knowledge that might accrue from historical studies. But I do deny that our students are taught medicine in the fullness of the word. Medicine deals with man, and the picture of man they receive is a partial one.

The above consideration makes us aware of a whole field of medical philosophy that we have not mentioned yet, namely medical anthropology. By this is not meant medicine of the so-called primitive tribes, but the way in which a physician looks at man.[18] Now, the medical anthropology of Hippocrates, Paracelsus, and William Osler, to take three representative figures, was not the same. The Paracelsian picture of man as a microcosm to be judged by cosmic analogies was not shared by the Greek physician or the doctor of the late nineteenth century. Nor did either of them have the firmly rooted conviction that the physician was merely God's instrument. Though for Hippocrates too nature was divine, she was not the all-powerful creator of Heaven and Earth. And the leading physicians of the time of Osler were too much imbued with the idea of man-made progress to share the religious humility of Paracelsus and Ambroise Paré.

Such fundamental differences are not subject to the filtering process of scientific progress, since they are not products of accumulating knowledge and refinement of methods. They belong in the same category as artistic styles and great philosophical thoughts. They are not just moments in an historical development, but remain as possibilities of experiencing and comprehending the world.

It may be objected that such a comprehensive view of medicine, based on the memory of whatever medical ideas existed in the world, is irrelevant. Even a philosophy of medicine should be a guide for us, not an abstract survey of logical or ethical possibilities. To give an example: any definition of medicine that starts out with "medicine is a science . . ." is incomplete, for there were and are nations that based their practice of medicine on tra- ditional procedures. It might even be wrong to say that medicine is the relationship between a physician and his patient, because such a relation-

[18]See e.g. Luis S. Granjel, "Introducción a la Antropología Médica," *Imprensa Médica*, Lisboa, 1953 (reprint).

ship is not necessarily present where a medicine man performs his rites over a sick person in the presence of the tribe. Nevertheless, we do not intend to go back to the days of unscientific medicine and we do not wish to give up the patient-physician relationship. Why, then, should we not start from where we stand? I do not presume to say what should or should not be taught in our schools. In my own limited experience the attempt at gaining an insight into the medical past, just where it appears strange, has helped me most toward understanding our present position. I view the current trend to concentrate on what is close to us with some alarm. "English *Humores* are not Hungarian, nor the Neapolitan Prussian, wherefore must thou go where they are; and the more thou seekest them out and the more thou learnest of them, the greater is thine understanding in thy native land." [19] What Paracelsus here said of the study of disease in foreign lands holds equally well of the medical study of man at different times.

Altogether we must not forget that philosophy of medicine, just as history of medicine, is not the exclusive property of the medical profession. We can therefore not decree where philosophical or historical inquiries should begin or end. And here we come to the final question regarding the interconnection of the two. The physician, general historian, or sociologist who writes medical history will have a point of view based upon the present status, aspirations, and functions of medicine. How, then, will a philosopher write medical history? The nature of his vocation makes it impossible for him to start out with a definite picture of what medicine is, since he wants to find out what it ought to be. As it so happens, the oldest history of medicine was written by Menon upon the request of his teacher, Aristotle. As far as its fragmentary remains allow us to judge, it constituted an outline of the various medical systems known to Menon. Such a collection probably was to serve Aristotle's usual procedure when philosophizing on a subject. He reviewed what others had thought not for historical purposes, but to utilize it for his own doctrine, and thus arrive at the truth. A modern philosopher would not be able to approach his task in the simple manner of Menon. In order to know what others had thought he would have to turn historian in the technical sense of the word. To quote Goethe again:

One will only really understand how a person thinks about a definite point when one knows the general constitution of his mind. This is true if we are desirous of apprehending exactly the opinions concerning scientific matters, whether of simple individuals or of whole schools or centuries. For this reason the history of the sciences is intimately bound up with the history of philosophy, but equally so with the history of the lives and characters of individuals and of peoples.[20]

[19]"Seven Defensiones," translated by C. Lilian Temkin in *Four Treatises of Theophrastus von Hohenheim, Called Paracelsus*, edited by Henry E. Sigerist, Baltimore, Johns Hopkins Press, 1941, p. 27.
[20]Materialien zur Geschichte der Farbenlehre. Erste Abtheilung, Betrachtungen über Farbenlehre und Farbenbehandlung der Alten (*op. cit.* vol. 35, p. 10).

Old books yield their meaning only if read in the context of their time. And the context of the time would primarily mean the picture of man, health, and disease which that time possessed.

But there would be more to it. Our philosopher's task would be more difficult than that of the ordinary historian. Professionally doubtful of all ready-made explanations, he would have to be wary of the many conceptual helps which we constantly use such as "influence," "advance," "social, economic, and political forces," "climate of opinion." Decidedly, we need not envy our philosopher-historian. Not only would he have to watch his step where most of us tread lightly, he would also have to penetrate into metaphysical depths which most of us avoid.

There comes to my mind a passage which I read in a very thorough work on medical ethics written a half a century ago: "... We shall look upon death as the gravest result of disease or of a drug. It is true, death is not always considered the worst evil. But even though we would otherwise agree with the poet that 'life is not the greatest of all good things,' for the medical profession there can be only one rule, that life is the supreme good, death the worst evil."[21]

We shall easily agree with our colleague who wrote this passage. But our philosopher will have to ponder about the remarkable fact that men have set up in their midst a profession charged with an idea of supreme good and evil that is admittedly not the common idea. How is this possible? Where the foundation of medical ethics, just as the foundation of medical logic merges into the metaphysical question of the whence and why of medicine, I must confess my uncertainty whether we are still in the realm of history. Perhaps it is better to leave this question to the philosopher who, today more than ever, is eager to explain our existence, and to await his answer.

[21]Albert Moll, *Ärztliche Ethik. Die Pflichten des Arztes in allen Beziehungen seiner Thätigkeit,* Stuttgart, Ferdinand Enke, 1902, p. 235.

6

The Historiography of Ideas
in Medicine*

I

IT HAS BECOME acceptable among historians of science to profess a predilection for the historiography of ideas, and even to claim that the history of science is a history of ideas. At first glance, there seems to be justification for this claim. The scientist, and this includes the medical scientist, is concerned with facts and with theories. He asks whether they are true or not. By contrast, the historian of science is concerned with the thoughts that refer to facts and theories, be they true or not. Or, as it has been phrased, the scientist studies nature, while the historian of science studies the scientist's mind.

In its exclusiveness, however, the claim is not tenable. The history of science studies not only ideas; it also studies the lives of men and of books; it studies institutions and many other matters that are not in themselves ideas. This is even more true of the history of medicine, which goes beyond the history of its basic and clinical sciences and deals with great physicians, hospitals, medical colleges, diseases and epidemics, quacks, drugs, and surgical operations, and with the peoples' thoughts on health, disease, and cure.

The historiography of medical ideas is but one aspect of the history of medicine. This aspect is not easily separated from others, for 'idea' is itself a vague term. About fifteen years ago, George Boas remarked that 'by last count' the word idea had 'some forty-two distinct meanings'.[1] Such terms as 'idea', 'concept', 'notion', 'thought' are often used synonymously. Since thought existed in early medicine, and since men were interested in others' thoughts then as well as now, there was already a historiography of ideas. The nature of the interest taken in ideas has changed and so have the historical categories under which they are conceived. But the changes have not necessarily destroyed what went before; older forms of studying ideas are still alive and cannot be omitted from an account of the historiography of ideas in recent decades.

We have to go back at least to Aristotle and his pupil Menon, fragments of whose doxographic work have come down to us.[2] From them we learn

---

*From Modern Methods in the History of Medicine, edited by Edwin Clarke, London: The Athlone Press of the University of London, 1971, pp. 1–21.

[1] G. Boas, 'Some problems of intellectual history', Boas et al., Studies in intellectual history, pp. 3–21 (see p. 3), Baltimore: The John Hopkins Press, 1953.

[2] W. H. S. Jones, The medical writings of Anonymus Londinensis, Cambridge: University Press, 1947.

what ancient Greek physicians thought about the causes of disease. Probably the collection was meant to serve Aristotle in evaluating these opinions for the truth they contained. At any rate, this purpose is manifest in the famous preface of Celsus to the first book of his *De medicina*.[3] A short outline of the history of medicine from its mythological beginnings to Celsus' own days is followed by a detailed exposition and discussion of the tenets of the three medical sects: dogmatists, empiricists, and methodists. The treatment is not only chronological but also shows the clash of opinions, as well as Celsus's own judgement.

The ancient beginnings survived in the great textbooks of the history of medicine from Daniel Le Clerc[4] on. We take it for granted that the old—and the not so old—systems of medicine and the theories of individual physicians down to Paul Ehrlich should be expounded, though no longer as live issues, but as thoughts of former generations. With books like *The growth of medical thought*,[5] where ideas are presented in distilled form, so to speak, we become aware of the long way we have travelled from very old beginnings. Some of the changes undergone and problems encountered on this way will be the subject of the following pages.

II

What Antiquity initiated for medical systems and comprehensive theories it also initiated for opinions on particular topics. The works of Soranus and of Galen are replete with critical remarks on what other physicians thought. Through the scholastic tradition this continued into the seventeenth and eighteenth centuries, when authors would discuss the different hypotheses of the function of the gall bladder, or the nature of hereditary disease.[6] Here, then, was a place for the display of learning, of critical acumen, and of observational evidence. Albrecht von Haller (1708–77) showed a remarkable blend of all three. The following brief passage from his *Elementa physiologiae* exemplifies what many a modern medical scientist may be content to require of a history of ideas. It appears in the chapter dealing with the refraction of light by the lens of the eye.

I do not know whether or not Kepler was the first to discover the refractive nature of the crystalline lens and whether Felix Plater took it from him. This was

---

[3]Celsus, *De medicina*, prooemium 10; Spencer's translation, vol. 1, p. 7 (Loeb Classical Library, 1935).

[4]D. Le Clerc, *Histoire de la médecine, où l'on voit l'origine et les progrès de cet art, de siècle en siècle; les sectes, qui s'y sont formées; les noms des médecins, leurs découvertes, leurs opinions, et les circonstances les plus remarquables de leur vie,* nouvelle édition, The Hague, 1729.

[5]L. S. King, *The growth of medical thought,* Chicago: University of Chicago Press, 1963. Books like H. Schipperges, *Ideologie und Historiographie des Arabismus,* Wiesbaden: Franz Steiner Verlag, 1961 (*Sudhoffs Arch. Gesch. Med. Naturw.* Beiheft 1), refer to the evaluation of the thought of a particular period.

[6]F. Glisson, *Anatomia hepatis,* c. 18: Fallopii sententia examinatur, Amsterdam: J. a, Ravensteyn, 1659; D. de Meara, *Pathologia haereditaria generalis, sive de morbis haereditariis,* c. 3: Fernelianae opinionis confutatio, Amsterdam: G. Schagen, 1666.

Scheiner's source, and Aemilius Parisanus defended this nature of the lens as something new. But already at Vesalius' time there were [persons] who placed the organ of vision in the retina, and he himself demonstrates, though obscurely, that he does not believe it to be in the lens. For the Ancients took the lens for the organ of vision, which is easily refuted, since when the lens is destroyed by the extraction of a cataract, vision survives and is not much poorer.[7]

In this example it is the scientific and practical validity of the ideas that matters. Characteristically, Haller, in the analytical index to the volume, labelled the paragraph containing the passage quoted 'Inventores', i.e., 'discoverers' of the refractive power of the lens. Haller wrote from an 'iatrocentric' point of view, to use a felicitous phrase of George Rosen's,[8] and he did not credit the ideas with a life of their own. Life was given to them by the Romantic movement around the turn of the eighteenth to the nineteenth century. What emerged, particularly in Germany, was a historiography of ideas in medicine still iatrocentric but conscious of dealing with more than scientific assertions.

III

The names of Herder, Goethe, Fichte, Schelling, and Hegel represent an intellectual movement with a strong feeling for the individuality of nations and periods, for development in organic life and in history through inner, 'genetic', forces, a feeling underpinned by an idealistic metaphysics in which 'the idea' and 'ideas' united nature and mind. 'The idea', wrote Hegel, 'is the adequate concept, that which is objectively true, or the true as such.'[9] And again commenting on contemporary works dealing with the history of art, of law, or of religion, he told his students: 'in our time this manner of conceptual history *(Begriffsgeschichte)* has been more developed and has been brought to greater prominence.... For like Mercury, the guide of souls, the idea is in truth the guide of nations and of the world, and it is the mind *(Geist)*, his rational and necessary will, which has led, and leads, the events of the world.'[10] Scientists (K. E. v. Baer) now spoke of species as 'thoughts of creation'[11] and historians (Ranke) thought of states as 'Ideas of God'.[12]

[7]A. v. Haller, *Elementa physiologiae corporis humani*, t. 5, p. 468, Lausanne: Grasset, 1763. With regard to Haller's *Bibliothecae*, P. Diepgen, 'Albrecht Haller und die Geschichte der Medizin', *Historische Studien und Skizzen zur Natur und Heilwissenschaft, Festgabe Georg Sticker zum siebzigsten Geburtstage dargeboten*, p. 102, Berlin: J. Springer, 1930, writes: 'Er sieht auch in den ältesten Quellen noch etwas durchaus Gegenwärtiges, mit dem er sich wie mit der modernen Literatur auseinandersetzt.' Diepgen rightly points out the broader view Haller took of medical history as a whole.

[8]G. Rosen, 'Levels of integration in medical historiography: a review', *J. Hist. Med.* 1949, *4*, 460–7 (see p. 465).

[9]G. W. F. Hegel, *Wissenschaft der Logik* 11, 3 in *Sämtliche Werke*, vol. 5, p. 236, ed. H. Glockner, 20 vols., Stuttgart: F. Frommann, 1927–30.

[10]*Vorlesungen über die Philosophie der Geschichte*, Einleitung, b. dd, *ibid.*, vol. 11, p. 33.

[11]O. Temkin, 'German concepts of ontogeny and history around 1800', *Bull. Hist. Med.* 1950, *24*, 227–46 (see p. 245) [Essay 27, p. 388].

[12]P. Geyl, *Debates with historians*, p. 14, New York: Meridian Books, 1958.

As an example of how history of ideas in medicine could be approached around 1840, we cite C. A. Wunderlich (1815–77). Himself an outstanding clinical scientist, he was yet consciously connected with the romantic view of history. Wunderlich rejected as antiquarianism the show of erudition which examined remote problems of remote periods. Physicians needed a confrontation with the relatively recent past, with which they were still engaged in a debate. On the other hand, he encouraged a kind of historical study which, he thought, was being neglected. 'Individual doctrines, specialties, therapeutic methods, should be subjected to historical investigation.'[13] By showing the genesis of certain theories, medical maxims, and assumptions, thoughtlessly accepted, their hollowness could be demonstrated. 'History of this persuasion', he wrote, 'will be little concerned with finding out the peculiarities of famous men and strange times; rather it will trace the origin of the ideas *(Ursprung der Ideen)* that govern the thought of today. It will reveal how science was formed. The illusory in theory and practice is bound to melt before it, and room can be made for a more thoughtful view of things.'[14] In the same year, 1842, Wunderlich began the publication of an article on fever. The first part of this article discussed opinions on fever from Hippocrates to his own days, whereas the rest was devoted to his scientific research. Wunderlich's method was relatively simple. The older medical literature was scanned for hypotheses and theories, and for observations and experiments supporting them. The findings were critically connected so that the reader came to understand the present situation in this particular area, as well as the mistakes that were made and should be avoided. Ideas of the past were not simply accepted or rejected but were scrutinized for the viable elements that had entered into the progressive development of the understanding of fever. In the introduction to his essay, Wunderlich set forth his philosophical views.[15] Ideas develop, in analogy to the formation of ever-higher species and the development of their foetuses. In all of them the modified surviving characteristics of more primitive stages can be recognized.

In France, the historiography of ideas in the person of J. E. Dezeimeris took a no less aggressive turn than in Germany. If Wunderlich is an example of the historiographer of medical concepts, Dezeimeris in the twenties and thirties represents the historiographer of medical ideologies. This term would, of course, already apply to Celsus and his successors, and Dezeimeris actually takes up the history of some ancient sects, especially methodism. But he is concerned less with the details of the sect as it once existed than with its 'spirit', i.e., the essence of its doctrines, in which he

---

[13]O. Temkin and C. L. Temkin, 'Wunderlich *versus* Haeser: a controversy over medical history', *Bull. Hist. Med.* 1958, *32*, 97–104 (see p. 101).

[14]*Ibid.*, p. 102.

[15]O. Temkin, 'Wunderlich, Schelling and the history of medicine', *Gesnerus* 1966, *23*, 188 [Essay 17, p. 246]. On the general theme of German medical historiography of the period see E. Heischkel, 'Die deutsche Medizingeschichtsschreibung in der ersten Hälfte des 19. Jahrhunderts', *Klin. Wschr.* 1933, *12*, 714–17.

finds the early formulation of physiological medicine as taught in his days by Broussais.[16] Speaking of medical doctrines in general, he says: 'To go back to the origin of these great thoughts, which form the basis of medicine, in order to obtain a bird's eye view of the developments they have undergone through the work of the centuries, this perhaps is, of all exercises of the intellect, the most apt to enlarge it and to bring order to its concepts.'[17] Thus to Dezeimeris, the internal history of medicine becomes predominantly a history of medical themes. He distinguishes the internal history *(l'histoire intrinsèque)*, which is the art and science of medicine in its development, from the external history *(l'histoire extrinsèque)*, which comprises all things external to medicine which have influenced its course. Both are needed, though they must not be confused. 'To write only the internal history would mean writing the complete history of the science, but a history without life, a body without soul. To limit oneself to the external history would mean not to say even the first word about the real history of the science. . . .'[18]

The metaphors of 'internal' and 'external' have found a strong echo in our own days in the sociology of knowledge,[19] and we shall have to come back to them. For Dezeimeris' intellectual disciple, Bouchut, 'nothing is truly useful', as far as history is concerned, 'but the history of the ideas by which men are guided. . . . To enumerate the doctrines, indicate their principles and the transformations which they have undergone in the course of the centuries, to relate the lives and the works of their principal exponents, this is the aim of my teaching and of this book.'[20] Yet in spite of these words, Bouchut's book was more and less than the twentieth century would expect of a history of ideas. As the title indicated, it was also a history of medicine with much information about the lives and works of the authors mentioned and many comments on the truth or falsity of their opinions.

The ways represented by Wunderlich on the one hand and by Dezeimeris and Bouchut on the other were neither mutually exclusive nor restricted to national boundaries. *Anatomisme* was one of the doctrines whose history Bouchut sketched,[21] and Rudolf Virchow's famous ẽssay on *Morgagni und der anatomische Gedanke* would find its place within this category. Virchow's essay is remarkable because in his person were united a scientist who contributed greatly to the advance of anatomical thinking and a historian who was able to trace the abstract idea of anatomical thought.

Among the French contributions to the historiography of ideas rather than of ideologies there might be cited passages from the works of Claude

---

[16]J. E. Dezeimeris, *Lettres sur l'histoire de la médecine*, pp. 200ff, Paris: chez l'auteur, 1838.
[17]*Ibid.*, p. 200.
[18]*Ibid.*, pp. 85f.
[19]W. Stark, *The sociology of knowledge*, p. 213 (heading), Glencoe, Illinois: The Free Press, 1958; 'Intrinsic and extrinsic study of the history of ideas.' The fact that Dezeimeris stressed the difference between internal and external history does not imply that he invented it.
[20]E. Bouchut, *Histoire de la médecine et des doctrines médicales*, p. iv, Paris: Germer Baillière, 1864.
[21]*Ibid.*, p. 7.

Bernard and Genil-Perrin's book on the history of the idea of degeneracy.[22] Genil-Perrin's work shows how far, in some cases, this historiography had advanced shortly before the outbreak of World War I. He looks for the mother ideas *(notions mère)* of degeneracy in ancient cosmogonies and in the works of Greek philosophers. Though mainly concerned with psychiatry, he does not stop there but also touches on manifestations of the idea in forensic medicine, anthropology, artistic life, and social thought. Genil-Perrin illustrates the impossibility of dividing the historiography of ideas into a succession of clear-cut stages. More frequently we are dealing with new emphases and tendencies rather than with new creations.

IV

Until World War I, medical historiography by and large was in the hands of medical men: scientists, clinicians, practitioners. There were a few who could completely devote themselves to the subject, but their number was extremely small. New methods of historiography were slow to enter into the horizon of medical historians, and the names of Dilthey and Max Weber were hardly encountered in their writings. On the other hand, interest in medicine was almost non-existent among general historians, with the exception of philologists whose work was largely limited to the edition of texts.

Since World War I, a change has taken place, slowly at first, but accelerating after World War II. The number of those actively interested in problems of medical history but without ties to medical practice or science has increased. This, in turn, has facilitated detachment from an exclusively iatrocentric interest in medical ideas. More than before, ideas have been examined within the framework of the times and circumstances of their flowering.[23]

Henry E. Sigerist's essay of 1928 on William Harvey may serve as an example of the trend.[24] The very title is significant; the essay tries to assign Harvey's place in the intellectual history of Europe rather than in the history of medicine. Historians frequently had investigated Galen's opinions on the movement of the heart and those of Harvey's predecessors who had challenged Galen's anatomy and had insisted on the necessity of a pulmonary pathway. There were discussions of Harvey's originality, even his dependence on Aristotelian philosophy had been analysed in detail by

---

[22]G. Genil-Perrin, *Histoire des origines et de l'évolution de l'idée de dégénérescence en médecine*, Paris: A. Le Clerc, 1913.

[23]These statements need qualifications. The political, cultural, and philosophical background of medical history was by no means neglected by medical historians at least as far back as K. Sprengel. Moreover, the generation of J. Pagel and K. Sudhoff, and that of C. Daremberg before them, was engaged in much historical work that had little bearing upon medical problems of its own days. My remarks are aimed at the historiography of ideas only.

[24]H. E. Sigerist, 'William Harveys Stellung in der europäischen Geistesgeschichte', *Arch. Kultur.* 1928, *19*, 158–68. (English translation in *Henry E. Sigerist, On the history of medicine*, pp. 184–92, ed. F. Marti-Ibañez, New York: MD Publications, 1960.)

Curtis,[25] though for a long time his book did not receive the attention it deserved. Without in the least challenging the greatness of Harvey's work, Sigerist characterized it as a phenomenon of the 'baroque'. As baroque art had introduced movement into the static art of the Renaissance, as Galileo had worked out the principles of dynamics in physics, so Harvey had made anatomy dynamic and had employed not only experiment but also a quantitative method.

Sigerist made due acknowledgement to the historian of art, Heinrich Wölfflin.[26] The history of art is especially prone to show the harmony of thought and expression during any given period.[27] There is not only an artistic style, there is also a style of thinking. It may not be inappropriate to designate as 'stylistic' the attempt to lift ideas out of their medical isolation, to place them in a contemporary context side by side with kindred ideas from other disciplines or spheres of life.

The heuristic value of such an approach is obvious and has not been exhausted yet. Problems easily suggest themselves. For instance, psychiatry in the second half of the nineteenth century was much preoccupied with the idea of degeneracy, to which Morel had devoted a classical work.[28] The impact of Morel's ideas can be traced, and has been traced, not only on medicine and anthropology but on literature as well, and so has his dependence on other medical philosophers, notably Buchez.[29] One may also remember that Morel's book appeared in 1857, the year in which Baudelaire published his *Fleurs du mal*. There seems to be good reason to study in detail Morel's work within the framework of the general idea of decadence, especially in France.[30] Morel wished to effect a prophylaxis of

[25]J. G. Curtis, *Harvey's views on the use of the circulation of the blood*, New York: Columbia University Press, 1915.

[26]H. Wölfflin, *Principles of art history, the problem of the development of style in later art*, transl. M. D. Hottinger, Dover Publications, n.d. Edith Heischkel-Artelt, 'The concept of baroque medicine in the development of medical historiography', Ithaca: 26.VIII.–2.IX.1962, *Actes du Dixième Congrès International d'Histoire des Sciences*, 2, 913–16, has challenged the concept of baroque medicine altogether.

[27]As outstanding examples related to medicine I mention: R. Klibansky, E. Panofsky, F. Saxl, *Saturn and melancholy: studies in the history of natural philosophy, religion and art*, New York: Basic Books, 1964, and W. S. Heckscher, *Rembrandt's anatomy of Dr. Nicolaas Tulp*, Washington Square: New York University Press, 1958.

[28]B. A. Morel, *Traité des dégénérescences physiques, intellectuelles et morales de l'espèce humaine et des causes qui produisent ces variétés maladives*, Paris: Baillière, 1857.

[29]Apart from the work by Genil-Perrin (note 22, above), see E. A. Ackerknecht, *A short history of psychiatry*, ch. 7, pp. 47ff, transl. S. Wolff, New York-London: Hafner Publishing Company, 1959; P. Burgener, *Die Einflüsse des zeitgenössischen Denkens in Morel's Begriff der 'dégénérescence'*, Zürich: Juris, 1964 (Zürcher medizingeschichtliche Abhandlungen, neue Reihe, No. 16); W. Leibbrand und A. Wettley, *Der Wahnsinn, Geschichte der abendländischen Psychopathologie*, pp. 524ff, Freiburg-Munich: K. Alber, 1961 (Orbis academicus); A. Wettley, 'Entartung und Erbsünde, der Einfluss des medizinischen Entartungbegriffs auf den literarischen Naturalismus', *Hochland*, Munich 1959, *51*, 348–58; A. Wettley, 'Zur Problemgeschichte der "dégénérescence"', *Sudhoffs Arch. Gesch. Med. Naturw.* 1959, *43*, 193–212.

[30]K. W. Swart, *The sense of decadence in nineteenth century France*, The Hague: Nijhoff, 1964, and A. E. Carter, *The idea of decadence in French literature, 1830–1900*, University of Toronto Press, 1958, to which cf. C. E. Rosenberg's review in *Bull. Hist. Med.* 1961, *35*, 483–4. Swart, p. 115, cites evidence for Baudelaire's having considered society decadent rather than the art dealing with it.

degeneration in society by means of public health measures,[31] a proposal which suggests the question how close theoreticians of public health in the mid-century came to the notion of degeneration.

The stylistic approach has its dangers. It is not easy, on the basis of analogies, to decide whether one is dealing with ramifications of the same idea or with superficial similarities without a real interconnection. To continue with the preceding example: although, in pathology, the notion of degeneration was old, the role it played in Virchow's cellular pathology is, nevertheless, noteworthy. Is it mere chance that this coincided with the elaboration of Morel's ideas?[32] Here we are faced with the more troublesome question of what constitutes real interconnection of ideas, or the unity of an idea expressed by different persons in different fields. The search for the common denominator is threatened by the danger of attributing mysterious powers to the spirit of a period or of a century, an unconscious relapse into Hegelian metaphysics.

Such dangers form a shortcoming of any stylistic approach that does not

[31] Morel, *op. cit.* (note 28, above), p. 78: 'Nous devons prouver, quelle que soit la difficulté de la situation, que la médecine, bien loin d'être frappée d'impuissance comme le prétendent quelques-uns de ses détracteurs, peut encore, malgré la prédominance des cas incurables, devenir pour la société un précieux moyen de salut. Elle seule peut bien apprécier la nature des causes qui produisent les dégénérescences dans l'espèce humaine, à elle seule appartient l'indication positive des remèdes à employer. Sa prétention n'est pas de se poser comme une force médicatrice exclusive; elle convie à cette œuvre de régénération ceux auxquels sont confiés le bien-être et les destinées des populations, et qui possèdent les moyens de réaliser les projets d'amélioration que la science médicale soumet à leur examen.' p. 691: '... [la société] doit faire de la *prophylaxie préservatrice* en essayant de modifier les conditions intellectuelles, physiques et morales de ceux qui, à des titres divers, ont été séparés du reste des hommes; elle doit, avant de les renvoyer dans le milieu social, les armer pour ainsi dire contre eux-mêmes afin d'atténuer le nombre des récidives.' The book concludes with the words (p. 693): 'Amélioration intellectuelle, physique et morale de l'homme, ou, si l'on préfère, sa Régénération.' Morel (p. 693) refers to a treatise on physical and moral hygiene where the principles of the use of regenerative conditions will be set out in detail. See also p. 586. The appeal to administrative authority is clear from these words (p. 77): "Si donc les causes de tant de misères peuvent céder en grande partie devant l'action favorable que seule l'autorité administrative peut exercer d'une manière utile, nous sommes en droit de réclamer son intervention.'

[32] E. H. Ackerknecht, *Rudolf Virchow: doctor, statesman, anthropologist,* p. 205, Madison: University of Wisconsin Press, 1953, asks whether Virchow, the anthropologist, in attributing deviations from a parent race to a pathological process, was succumbing 'to the same trend that in his time made the new "degeneration" concept of the psychiatrist-anthropologist Morel ... so universally popular?' Wettley, 'Zur Problemgeschichte der "dégénérescence"', *op. cit.* (above, note 29), p. 198 refers to pathology but leaves the question of a common ground open, whereas Leibbrand and Wettley, *op. cit.* (above, note 29), deny a relationship in view of Morel's 'new' departure. While it is true that Morel developed the notion of degeneracy from a theological point of view, characteristic for him and for his friends (see Burgener, *op. cit.,* above, note 29), it was not his theology that impressed those after him. The old idea of degeneration neither originated with him nor was it bound to the particular form he gave to it, interesting and important though the latter was. See also below, note 49. I find that the article 'Dégénérescence' in the *Dictionnaire encyclopédique des sciences médicales,* ed. A. Dechambre, vol. 26, pp. 212–54, Paris: G. Masson-P. Asselin, 1882, actually treats the anthropological aspects (E. Dally) as well as the anatomical-pathological (Ch. Robin), with a common introduction for both on pp. 212f. G. Hertel, *Der Begriff der Degeneration bei Virchow,* Diss. Munich, 1959, became available to me only after the completion of the present article.

proceed to an examination of the psychological and social influences connecting ideas or allowing them to exert an impact upon the human mind.

v

The problem of influences on or by ideas has much occupied philosophers of history, such as Arthur O. Lovejoy and George Boas.[33] Lovejoy pointed out that ideas need not be emotionally neutral, that they can represent moods of thoughts and metaphysical pathos. By way of a medical example, we may offer the proposition that man and animals are alike. Apart from all theoretical discussions of the proposition, people will be found to tend towards either a positive or negative attitude. Some are likely to welcome any demonstration of the effect of drugs on animals as suggestive for man, whereas others will be sceptical from the very beginning. In individual thinkers, it may be extremely difficult to account for such intellectual predispositions. In addition, there is the much broader issue of how far ideas are linked logically, and how far irrational factors, be they psychological or social, account for their origin, their spread, their modification, and their decline.

Here again, as in the case of the stylistic approach, William Harvey's ideas offer a convenient example. Few issues have been discussed with equal intellectual vigour in recent years, and even after the appearance, in 1967, of Walter Pagel's monumental work,[34] the debate still continues.

Harvey attempted to demonstrate the absurdity of the Galenic scheme of heart and blood. Logically, this demonstration culminated in the famous estimate, in chapter 9 of *De motu cordis,* of the quantity of blood expelled by the left ventricle with each systole and in half a minute, a quantity which could not be accommodated by the body unless there existed a circular motion of all the blood. This is a classical instance of a new idea clashing directly with an older set of ideas by proving the latter impossible. Ideas here are chained logically, and it would be scientifically most satisfactory if the modifications of ideas could be ascribed to logical or observational mistakes demanding new observation, experiment, and hypotheses. We would remain in the realm of ideas, and it would agree with the habit of scientists to present their own work in this manner.

Only a prejudice in favour of irrationalism will deny that logic can ever be the power linking ideas.[35] But it is certainly justified to ask whether the

[33]A. O. Lovejoy, *The great chain of being,* pp. 3–23, New York: Harper, 1960 [reprint]; Lovejoy, 'Reflections on the history of ideas', *J. Hist. Ideas* 1940, *1*, 3–23; 'The historiography of ideas', reprinted in A. O. Lovejoy, *Essays in the history of ideas,* pp. 1–13, Baltimore: The Johns Hopkins Press, 1948. For G. Boas see above, note 1, and 'The history of philosophy', in Y. H. Krikorian (ed.), *Naturalism and the human spirit,* pp. 133–53, New York: Columbia University Press, 1944.

[34]W. Pagel, *William Harvey's biological ideas: selected aspects and historical background,* New York: Hafner, 1967. This book gives a very comprehensive panorama of influences that made themselves felt in Harvey's time. W. Pagel's *Das medizinische Weltbild des Paracelsus,* Wiesbaden: F. Steiner, 1962, should also be mentioned here.

[35]Lovejoy, 'Reflectons on the history of ideas', *op. cit.* (above, note 33), pp. 16ff.

logical connection really caused the origin, the change, or the disappearance of the idea in question. Attention has been drawn to the difference
between the actual process leading to scientific results and the final presentation of his work by the scientist. Usually, no account is offered of sudden
insights, or of the disorder in which thoughts and observations may have
followed one another, and much is omitted as irrelevant.[36] If this holds true
for the modern scientist, there is good reason for wondering how Harvey
arrived at his theory. He is said to have started on the way by puzzling over
the function of the veinous valves.[37] This means that we have to consider
Harvey as a person, not merely as a disembodied mind. How far consideration may go is indicated by a recent controversy over the political associations in Harvey's work. In 1628, when *De motu cordis* appeared, Harvey was
physician to King Charles I. In this book, the heart is compared to the sun
and to the monarch, and on the biological side its formation is said to
precede that of all other organs. Later, in his *De generatione* (1651), Harvey
gave primacy to the blood over the heart. By then the monarchy had been
replaced by the Commonwealth. Had Harvey's shift from heart to blood
been influenced by the change of the political regime?[38] Did politics enter,
as they did in the case of Rudolf Virchow, where a connection between
democratic republican ideas (which placed political virtue and vice in the
citizen) and cellular pathology (which placed health and disease in the cell)
is plainly evident?[39]

Influences are notoriously difficult to establish. How far is our behaviour
dictated by the ideas we profess?[40] In a book on the healing power of
nature, Max Neuburger reviewed the opinions for and against the idea of
nature as the healer of disease.[41] Theoretically speaking, those who believed in the idea ought to have followed an expectant course in therapy,
whereas the therapeutic activists should have come from among the
mechanists, who denied nature any benevolent or malevolent intention.
But, as Erwin H. Ackerknecht has shown, this was far from always being
the case.[42]

Attempts at finding influences of a psychological nature in specific cases

---

[36]A. R. Feinstein, *Clinical judgment,* p. 1, Baltimore: Williams and Wilkins, 1967.

[37]Pagel, *op. cit.,* 1967 (above, note 34), p. 209, discusses this as part of the general problem of
what makes a genius of former times arrive at his discovery.

[38]This is the thesis propounded by C. Hill, 'William Harvey and the idea of monarchy,'
Past and Present, 1964, 27, 54–72, and rejected by G. Whitteridge, 'William Harvey, a royalist
and no parliamentarian', ibid. 1965, 30, 104–9. Commenting on this controversy, continued in later issues of *Past and Present,* C. Webster, 'Harvey's De generatione: its origins and
relevance to the theory of circulation', *Brit. J. Hist. Sci.* 1967, 3, 262–74, has pointed out
(p. 274 n. 64) that if *De generatione* was composed in 1638 (as Webster argues with good
reason), the political explanation would hardly be tenable.

[39]E. Hirschfeld, 'Virchow', *Kyklos* (Leipzig) 1929, 2, 106–16.

[40]E. H. Ackerknecht, 'A plea for a "behavorist" approach in writing the history of medicine',
J. Hist. Med. 1967, 22, 211–14.

[41]M. Neuburger, *Die Lehre von der Heilkraft der Natur im Wandel der Zeiten,* Stuttgart: F. Enke,
1926.

[42]E. H. Ackerknecht, 'Aspects of the history of therapeutics', *Bull. Hist. Med.* 1962, 36,
389–419 (see pp. 412 ff).

go together with some kind of belief in what influences man. To a large measure we rely on the everyday psychology by which we judge men and their actions, or we indulge in speculations based on a psychological theory. These are notoriously uncertain criteria for past ages. For many years Lucien Febvre has insisted on the necessity of explaining man's mentality within the effective life and the general beliefs of his time.[43] Trevor-Roper quite recently has made it clear how absurd it would be to expect a contemporary of the European witch craze to harbour the thoughts of an intellectual of the nineteenth century. Neither Johan Weyer nor any of those opposing the almost indiscriminate persecution of witches had the outlook of a modern psychiatrist, even though they may have judged many of the accused mentally ill.[44]

Recognition of influences which, at a given time, act on more than one individual is implicit in such expressions as *Zeitgeist* or 'intellectual climate'. More recently, sociologists of science have cited in evidence for social causation the multiple appearance of the same discovery, 'multiples' in the language of Robert Merton.[45] The independent discovery of inhalation anaesthesia by Crawford W. Long in Georgia and by Wells, Morton and Jackson in New England in the early 1840's is a well-known medical example. Though discoveries are not necessarily ideas,[46] both are spoken of as being 'in the air', or 'ripe for their time', expressions which bear witness to our readiness to see in ideas not merely individual strokes of genius. Thus, in Germany, a turn from idealistic speculative thinking to positivistic research with a materialistic bias is noticeable in medicine during the decade preceding the revolution of 1848, a period of political, economic and social unrest. Or, to turn to the impact of ideas on social events, the philosophical movement of *idéologie* seems to have been a catalyst for changes in clinical medicine towards the end of the French Revolution.[47]

Another factor to be taken into account is the adequacy (or lack thereof) of an idea in relation to what it is to describe, explain, or postulate. In medicine this means above all the adequacy of an idea in relation to the existing public health situation. Broussais' idea of the ubiquity of gastroenteritis is more clearly understood if the prevalence of typhoid fever and dysentery during the Napoleonic wars is remembered.[48] Similarly, the idea

[43]L. Febvre, *Combats pour l'histoire*, seconde édition, pp. 206–20 ('Histoire et psychologie') and pp. 221–38 ('La sensibilité et l'histoire'), Paris: A. Colin, 1965.

[44]H. R. Trevor-Roper, *Religion, the reformation, and social change*, pp. 99ff, 146ff, 172, 192, London: Macmillan, 1967. In this connection see also G. Rosen, *Madness in society: chapters in the historical sociology of mental illness*, especially the introduction, pp. 1–18: 'Psychopathology in the social process', London: Routledge & Kegan Paul, 1968.

[45]R. K. Merton, 'Singletons and multiples in scientific discovery: a chapter in the sociology of science', *Proc. Amer. Phil. Soc.* 1961, *105*, 470–86.

[46]I have, therefore, left out of historical consideration 'ideas' as inspirations or working hypotheses, a use common with Claude Bernard.

[47]G. Rosen, 'The philosophy of ideology and the emergence of modern medicine in France', *Bull. Hist. Med.* 1946, *20*, 328–39.

[48]E. H. Ackerknecht, *Medicine at the Paris Hospital 1794–1848*, p. 69, Baltimore: The Johns Hopkins Press, 1967.

of degeneracy appears less arbitrary if account is taken of the state of public health in French cities[49] around 1850, the fact that general paralysis was prevalent yet its specific nature not yet recognized, and that the laws of heredity were still unknown.

The interaction of ideas, diseases, and social developments falls under the general heading of the interplay of internal and external factors in medicine to which Richard H. Shryock has devoted much attention.[50] One illustration may suffice here. The surgeon who has to suture wounds, to set fractures, to open abscesses, remove tumours, naturally has to consider anatomical structures and anatomical changes. By means of percussion and auscultation the surgical point of view was extended to internal medicine. This could happen around 1800, because of the rise of the surgeon to influential professional status during the eighteenth century, obviously an external factor.[51]

Further studies in the mutual relationship between medical ideas and external events, paying particular attention to the possible mechanisms, social and psychological, by which the two sides influenced each other, would be desirable. The objection that we all carry our unconscious biases with us need frighten us no more than it frightens the natural scientist. Our task and that of our critics, present and future, is to assure as much objectivity as possible. If we are told that objectivity is altogether a chimera, we ought to remember that this dictum is no more than a variety of the radical scepticism which defeats itself by maintaining as true that truth cannot be found.

The above remarks may not be out of place here, in order to ward off the accusation that the historiography of ideas leads to historical relativism.[52] If medical ideas are treated merely as phenomena or products of their time, their medical truth too might appear to be restricted to their respective periods. Hippocrates' idea of disease, it will be argued, was different from our idea, but it was as true for his time as ours is for us, the two ideas having no connecting bond. Obviously this would run counter to the search for scientific truth. But the danger does not lie in searching for the historical meaning and circumstances of the development of ideas and their 'otherness' from us. On the contrary, by comprehending what the Hippocratics

[49]The article by Dr Bertulus, 'Considérations sur les causes de la dégénération physique et morale du peuple des grandes villes, et sur les moyens d'y remédier', *Gazette médicale de Paris* 1847, pp. 799–803 and 819–24, which appeared ten years before Morel's book, is significant; cf. above, note 31 and the respective text.

[50]R. H. Shryock, 'The interplay of social and internal factors in modern medicine: an historical analysis', reprinted in R. H. Shryock, *Medicine in America, historical essays*, pp. 307–32, Baltimore: The Johns Hopkins Press, 1966; cf. also O. Temkin, 'Scientific medicine and historical research', *Perspect. Biol. Med.* 1959, *3*, 70–85.

[51]Shryock, *op. cit.* (above, note 50), pp. 321f and O. Temkin, 'The role of surgery in the rise of modern medical thought', *Bull. Hist. Med.* 1951, 25, 248–59 [Essay 33].

[52]Lovejoy, 'Reflections on the history of ideas', *op. cit.* (above, note 33), p. 17, has discussed the problem of historical relativism as posed by K. Mannheim's sociological philosophy. See also Maurice Mandelbaum, *The problem of historical knowledge* [reprinted with a new preface in] Harper Torch books, 1967.

meant by disease we are bound to broaden our understanding of the concept of disease. The danger lies in the assumption that cultures, periods, or social classes are closed, self-centred entities, an assumption which, in the final analysis, would make historical studies senseless. Moreover, there exist themes in the history of medicine, e.g., empiricism, which recur at different times,[53] and where the style of the period merely seems to affect their formulation. Many medical ideas live through the ages and not only in their particular age. Dezeimeris and Bouchut here come into their own. There is considerable educational value in demonstrating to medical students how old ideas have survived in modern dress, provided that forced analogies are avoided. The need of the body for regulation of its temperature has been recognized since ancient times. But this does not yet allow us to equate Galen's vital pneuma with oxygen.

VI

The philosopher, Scott Buchanan, thirty years ago, said of contemporary medicine that it had 'a record maximum of knowledge and a minimum of understanding, to say nothing of practical and philosophical wisdom'.[54] If this was the situation in 1938, it is no longer so, for today medicine is eagerly inquiring into its own concepts. Even a cursory look at a current bibliography of medical history conveys the impression that in recent years the history of 'concepts' has come to demand a good deal of attention. Since intellectual comprehension is through concepts, they and their history extend over everything that is observed, thought, and done in medicine. *Concepts of medicine, La formation du concept de réflexe aux XVIIe et XVIIIe siècles, Entwicklungsgeschichte des Krankheitsbegriffes, The concept of insanity in the United State* are titles of some books which carry the word 'concept'.[55] Others, like *The historical development of physiological thought,*[56] largely deal with the history of concepts, while still others, like *The meaning of poison,* use a different word.[57] The number of articles falling into this category is large and their variety is very great. The history of the idea of disease and of concepts related to neurology and psychiatry seems to predominate, but

[53]E. H. Ackerknecht, 'Recurrent themes in medical thought', *Scient. Mon.* (N.Y.) 1949, *69,* 80–3.

[54]S. Buchanan, *The doctrine of signatures, a defense of theory in medicine,* p. x, London: Kegan Paul, Trench, Trubner, 1938. The content of this book might be paraphrased as 'the idea of medicine'.

[55]B. Lusk, *Concepts of medicine,* Oxford: Pergamon Press, 1961; G. Canguilhem, *La formation du concept de réflexe au XVIIe et XVIIIe siècles,* Paris: Presses universitaires de France, 1955; E. Berghoff, *Entwicklungsgeschichte des Krankheitsbegriffes,* 2nd ed., Vienna: Maudrich, 1947; N. Dain, *Concepts of insanity in the United States, 1789–1865,* New Brunswick, N.J.: Rutgers University Press, 1964.

[56]C. McC. Brooks and P. F. Cranefield (eds.), *The historical development of physiological thought,* New York: Hafner, 1959.

[57]L. G. Stevenson, *The meaning of poison,* Lawrence: The University of Kansas Press, 1959 (Logan Clendening lectures on the history and philosophy of medicine, seventh series). Other titles that might be mentioned are W. Riese, *La pensée causale en médecine,* Paris: Presses universitaires de France, 1950, and *La pensée morale en médecine, ibid.,* 1954.

even the concept of such a circumscribed pathological entity as 'chronic glomerulonephritis' has found its historical investigator.[58]

The impression is hard to avoid that the history of concepts has become fashionable since World War II. In many cases, the word 'concept' (or 'idea') is inserted in a title which formerly might have done without it or which might have used such terms as 'doctrine' instead.[59] But fashion or not, the trend expresses an interest in meaning rather than in material realities. In order to find an explanation for this phenomenon, we must consider a variety of aims involved.

When we write the history of a concept, such as inflammation, we may follow the genetic approach into our own times. Or we may deal with a concept with which we no longer operate, for instance, 'temperament', which hardly plays a major role in medicine today. Incidentally, this will remind us of the need for distinguishing the history of concepts from the semantic history of words. The Greeks used the word *krasis*, the Latins *temperatio* or *temperamentum,* and the Arabs *mizāj* for the same concept, yet all these words also have a history of their own. To say that the concept behind the words matters rather than the vicissitudes of the words is a truism, which, however, should not make us overlook the importance of knowing the words in which concepts appear in different languages. To get at the root of a concept, reliance on the etymology of a word in any one particular language can be very misleading. 'Physician' is derived from *physicus* and refers to the natural philosopher, whereas the French *médecin,* derived from *medicus,* refers to the healer. The concept of the physician obviously is not exhausted by either derivation alone.

But the development of a concept may appear determined not by necessity but by choice among a number of possibilities. The critic may then question whether what is presently current is necessarily the best, or he may try to determine the historical point at which an idea took a decisive turn. This leads directly to the historical analysis of a concept, where the aim is to lay bare the ingredients that have entered into our medical thinking, though we may not be aware of them.

What do we mean when we say that a person has been 'infected'?[60] Does it denote a mere 'chance' encounter of our body with pathogenic micro-organisms? Is it an 'invasion' on their part? Is it a 'struggle' between the body and the micro-organisms? Is it simply a special kind of 'poisoning' as Virchow claimed?[61] We may not be conscious of these or similar images,

---

[58]*Current work in the history of medicine* 1967, 55, 215 (no. 413).

[59]For instance, see Neuburger, *Die Lehre von der Heilkraft der Natur im Wandel der Zeiten* (above, note 41). Formerly, the term 'Anschauungen' was very popular in the German literature.

[60]I have dealt with this question rather imperfectly in 'An historical analysis of the concept of infection', in *Studies in intellectual history,* pp. 123–47, Baltimore: The Johns Hopkins Press, 1953 (a book by several authors sponsored by the Johns Hopkins History of Ideas Club in honour of A. O. Lovejoy) [Essay 31].

[61]R. Virchow, *The freedom of science in the modern state,* 2nd ed., p. 31, London: J. Murray, 1878.

which does not prove that they are not operating at some level of our mind. The full meaning of a concept can be grasped as little without its history as the adult body can be understood without its ontogeny and phylogeny.

Now when we speak of 'our' mind, the meaning of this expression is not self-evident. In the case of physicians and scientists, medical books, journals, case histories, lectures, dealings with patients, procedures of medical societies, letters to friends, and other documents will show the concept as it is consciously formulated, or unthinkingly used. If 'our' mind refers to a broader group, possibly a whole nation or a generation, the coverage will have to be broader too. 'Our' concept of the physician's task is not defined by doctors only, but by the layman as well. The less scientific a concept is, the more must the opinion of non-scientists be explored. That goes for the current use of concepts, as well as for their use in the past. Great philosopher as Plato was, his writings do not suffice to tell the historian what the Athenian people of his time thought insanity to be. In the historical analysis of medical concepts the inclusion of evidence for their *modus operandi* is particularly important.

The suspicion arises that to some extent, our situation is similar to that of Dezeimeris, Wunderlich, and Virchow. They were writing history of ideas at a time when medicine was undergoing decisive changes in its outlook, a time when points of view (*Standpunkte,* to use a term of Virchow's) were to be chosen.

With all else in our life medicine shares very rapid changes of its external and internal conditions. What has been happening within the last decades is so well known as to make elaboration unnecessary. While the ever-accumulating knowledge of disease and of the means of its prevention and cure have rendered the knowledge of earlier times insignificant, this very accumulation has posed new problems. Computer methods, to be useful in the diagnosis of disease, require clarity about the relationship of disease and its symptoms. Where classification of disease poses difficulties, as it does in psychiatry, the question arises as to the nature of that which is to be classified.[62] In both cases the concept of disease, and thereby the history of the concept, comes under discussion.

Health, the counterpart of disease, needs equal clarification if health is not merely to be the absence of disease. If we are to promote health, we must know what we mean to promote. In psychiatry the existence of differing schools of thought has stimulated the discussion of the ideas that gave rise to them. In fields where scientific progress has been most rapid it has sometimes been accompanied by the introduction of psychological terminology into the description of supposedly strictly chemical and physical processes. The use of metaphors is nothing new; scales have long been called 'sensitive'. But when human behaviour is to be explained in terms of

[62]M. M. Katz *et al.* (eds.), [Proceedings of a conference held in Washington, D.C., November 1965 on] *The role and methodology of classification in psychiatry and psychopathology,* p. 24, U.S. Department of Health, Education and Welfare, Public Health Service, National Institute of Mental Health, Chevy Chase, Md. [1968].

machines, it matters with what properties the machines have been endowed, and we need to know what the terms are supposed to mean.[63]

When dealing with the history of ideas, man's intellect is in its true milieu where thought meets thought. This makes the history of ideas an exciting enterprise. Beyond this, asking why others thought as they did challenges us to ask why we think as we do. For this question there is great need in medicine, whose progress now affects peoples everywhere for better or, sometimes, for worse. Because as a whole the situation is unprecedented, guidance is expected from insight into how we happen to be where we are, not only in our knowledge and our institutions but also in our thinking. Just because we are so greatly concerned with what we think, the explicit historiography of ideas is but a small part of the concern with ideas in almost all historical approaches to medicine today. As in other disciplines, the historiography of ideas is an aspect rather than a branch of the history of medicine.

[63] All this is closely connected with a general, philosophical, interest in 'meaning', for which see G. H. R. Parkinson (ed.), *The Theory of Meaning*, Oxford University Press, 1968.

7

Comparative Study in the
History of Medicine*

EXPERIMENTING

DURING THE SECOND semester of the past academic year, a large part of our seminar was devoted to the history of Arabic, Indian, and Chinese medicine. This was in the nature of an experiment, especially in view of the fact that none of the participants (including myself) possessed any competent knowledge in the languages, cultures, or even the medical literatures of Indian and Chinese civilizations. We chose the concept of "health" as our tentative theme, and we invited experts in the fields of Arabic, Sanskrit, and Chinese studies to conduct initial seminars on the idea of the good life, before we ourselves launched upon a somewhat sketchy reading of medical authors (in translation, of course) in the respective three civilizations.

The seminar was kept within the framework just described. But the seminar might never have taken place without a number of motives which made it an experiment within a much broader setting. Developments in general historiography, various personal encounters (some remembered,[1] others probably forgotten), requests from our students, and last, but not least, the memory of my own teacher, Henry E. Sigerist, increasingly made me realize that the traditional Western approach to the history of medicine is too narrow a basis for the historical comprehension of medicine as it is developing in our era. This had led me to the writing of "A proposal for the comparative study of medical history," which, however, is published only now. One of the reasons for the delay was my feeling that the proposal was of limited value as long as it was not bolstered by some actual experience. Another reason was my fear lest the article be mistaken for a program to which our Institute should and would henceforth devote itself. The presence of a Fellow with many years of medical experience in Ethiopia and an interest in the confrontation of different historical forms of medicine en-

*From "The Johns Hopkins Institute of the History of Medicine: Report of its activities during the academic year, 1967-68," *Bull. Hist. Med.*, 1968, vol. 42, pp. 362-371.

[1] After lecturing on the history of the concept of disease, I was once asked how ancient Chinese medicine fitted into the picture I had presented. The question not only pointed to my neglect of Chinese and Indian material, it also made me realize my inability to give a satisfactory answer or a good reason for my omission. I might also mention here the interest of my former co-worker, Dr. Gerald J. Gruman, in "universal history," and plans which Dr. Iago Galdston, years ago, mentioned to me regarding a symposium on "medicine and culture" (subsequently organized by Dr. Galdston and Dr. F. N. L. Poynter at the Wellcome Museum, London; see the report by F. Guerra in *Clio Medica*, February 1967, 2: 71-73). Whatever bearing these and other stimuli may have had on my thoughts, the responsibility for this article is my own.

couraged the planning of the seminar along the lines sketched above. This, in turn, has proved a rewarding practical test for the general thesis. As to the possible misunderstanding, my retirement from the directorship of the Institute, July 1, 1968, should make it clear that I am reporting on what was thought and done, particularly during the last academic year, leaving it to others to judge the merits and future possibilities. Our invited speakers were not concerned with the general thesis, which was only presented at the end of the seminar for discussion by this year's membership.

Readers acquainted with the two volumes of Henry E. Sigerist's History of Medicine[2] will be aware that my critique of traditional medical historiography echoes ideas which led him to envisage his own new departure. In nevertheless publishing my critique, I wished to establish a theoretical basis for a proposed program of study. What Dr. Sigerist tried to erect as an edifice, so to speak, is here proposed as a way of study for many persons. I am fully aware that the way suggested by me may not be the best. Even the very limited experience gained by our seminar has led me to corrections and additions which will be discussed in an epicrisis.

A PROPOSAL

1

Western tradition has given medical history an emphasis on the development from ancient Greece to modern civilization. This tradition has its roots in the religious exclusiveness of the Judaeo-Christian faith, in a historiography which found its oldest sources in the Bible and in Homer, in the humanistic regard for Greek intellectual culture and Roman civilization, and in the rise of Western power which went together with Western science and technology. The discovery of archeological, hieroglyphic, and cuneiform material in the nineteenth century led to the opening of an older medical past, and a better acquaintance with Chinese and Sanskrit sources suggested the exploration of medicine in the Far East. But the point of view has not shifted considerably. As embodied in textbooks and many outline courses, "the" history of medicine starts with prehistoric remains and the medical practices of so-called "primitives." Then it confronts medicine of the ancient civilizations of Mesopotamia and Egypt, possibly adding India and China. With Graeco-Roman antiquity the mainstream of the development is reached; it passes through the Middle Ages and, with a major or minor excursion into Arabic and Persian medicine, to the Renaissance. The time from the Renaissance to the early twentieth century is reserved almost exclusively to the events in Europe and North America.

It cannot be claimed that this structure is in the mind of all Western historians of medicine.[3] Arrangements may differ, and other areas which I have not mentioned may be included. We have specialists (though' their

---

[2]Henry E. Sigerist, *A History of Medicine*, 2 vols., New York: Oxford University Press, 1951 and 1961.
[3]See especially my comments, above, about Henry E. Sigerist's *History of Medicine*.

number is very small) in Egyptian, Mesopotamian, Indian, Chinese, Jewish, Arabic, and Persian medicine. There also is a great variety of approaches: biographical, technical, cultural, philosophical, and social—all of which may disregard the structure I have outlined. Some historians doubt continuity, leave alone linear progress, in the history of medicine. Nevertheless, I believe that where the attempt is made to see "the" history of medicine,[4] the structure I sketched above still prevails—and for good reason. It is both possible and, for Western needs, advantageous to trace scientific medicine[5] in its development from the Greeks. The possibility of doing so has been exemplified often enough, and the advantage lies in making understandable medical terminology and the historical ingredients of many medical concepts used today, the development of medical ethics and education, and the branching of the various medical disciplines. Nevertheless, a number of factors without and within the West are weakening modern man's sense of belonging to this tradition; these factors have, at the same time, been working toward a broadening of medical historiography.

2

Until not so long ago, the teaching, practice, and growth of scientific medicine were domiciled in the West and Japan. This is no longer the case. Western medicine is increasingly changing into global medicine, if not to the extinction of older systems, then at least in alliance or in competition with them.

Though adopted and cultivated by non-Western countries, to them Western medicine constitutes a foreign import.[6] It did not grow on native soil; it has few, if any, ties with the great indigenous systems of medicine, such as the Yunani (Pakistan), Ayurvedic (India), and traditional Chinese systems. The metamorphosis of Western medicine into global medicine is taking place at a time of unprecedented strengthening of political power and national consciousness in many non-Western countries. Nationalism leans heavily on historiography, which describes and shapes the individuality of the nation. Under the impact of these developments medical historiography has been vitalized in areas which formerly were given a more or less "exotic" status. Understandably enough, many historians of

---

[4]"The" history of medicine is a conceptual artifact, an attempt to search for and present a sequence of events that will make understandable a present set of conditions. In this limited sense, presentation of "the" history of a subject is both possible and advantageous, though it leaves a vast number of phenomena to other forms of historical comprehension. "The" history of medicine does not mean all history of medicine, or medical history in general. I hope to elaborate this thesis elsewhere.

[5]Following a widespread assumption, in speaking of "scientific medicine" I here mean medicine based on modern experimental and statistical methods and adopting all advances in the physical and biological sciences. Scientific medicine in this sense had its programmatic beginnings hardly more than 150 years ago. But see below, note 10.

[6]In this connection, I wish to draw attention to the article by George Basalla, "The spread of Western science," *Science*, May 5, 1967, vol. 156, pp. 611–622, which shows the complexities of the process of adaptation.

medicine in non-Western countries concentrate on their own medical past. The history of Western medicine seems of interest to them mainly at the point where it meets their own ancient systems. To some medical historians of the East, scientific medicine appears as a system on a par with other, indigenous, systems, so that a kind of comparative history of medicine is cultivated, sometimes not without a note of resentment against the West.[7] In China, the relationship of traditional Chinese medicine and Western medicine seems to be subject to Communist policy with consequent shifts in historical emphasis.[8]

In course of time, objective methods of historical research may prevail everywhere over the wish to bring one's own nation's medical past to general attention. But even then non-Western historians will hardly accept the traditional Western picture of the development of medicine. For instance, from the Indian point of view, ancient Greek medicine may appear as an impressive counterpart to India's classical past and relevant because of its influence on the development of "scientific" medicine. The Middle Ages and a good deal of Renaissance medicine, on the other hand, may be of little interest.

3

It would be one-sided to attribute the weakening of the Western tradition of medical historiography only to developments outside the West. Historical events since World War II have been leading to an ever-increasing broadening of the perspective under which the West sees its own past. We are realizing that the other empires and civilizations which existed side by side with Rome, the Christian Middle Ages, and the European and American national states, are part of the world's past, and not just outsiders leading a peripheral existence. This is all the more important since we have come to realize that medicine is not identical with the medical sciences but comprises all that is expected and done with regard to health and disease within a society.[9] Thus we are better prepared to take a broad view in space and in time, and not to measure past ages only by scientific and technical achievements.

The traditional structure to which I referred in the beginning was worked out by physicians who could read classical Greek and follow the later Latin medical literature. In other words, the traditional outlook was represented by generations steeped in this tradition. The present genera-

[7]See, for instance, *Theories and Philosophies of Medicine*, with Particular Reference to Greco-Arab Medicine, Ayurveda and Traditional Chinese Medicine. Literary Research Department, Institute of History of Medicine and Medical Research, Hamdard Buildings, Delhi-6, 1962. It does not appear realistic to me to treat scientific medicine as merely one among several possibilities.

[8]Ralph C. Croizier, *Traditional Medicine in Modern China*, Science, Nationalism, and the Tensions of Cultural Change, Cambridge, Mass.: Harvard Univ. Press, 1968.

[9]For formulations, see Sigerist, *op. cit.*, vol. 1, ch. 1; George Rosen, "The new history of medicine," *J. Hist. Med. & Allied Sc.*, 1951, 6: 516–522; Richard H. Shryock, *Medicine in America*, Historical Essays, Baltimore: The Johns Hopkins Press, 1966, p. xiii.

tion is no longer in this position. The medical historian who can do research in classical medicine and its historical setting is fast approaching the status of the "specialist" in Arabic medicine. The number of those able to read Latin with some ease is dwindling. A great number of us in the United States and, I suspect, in other Western countries too, have no longer a working relationship to the sources from which our medicine sprang.

The linguistic barrier that impedes our access to these sources is complemented by the uneasy feeling that the content of those sources may be medically and scientifically barren for us. In literature, art, and philosophy, the situation is different. But in medicine it is asked what even the Hippocratic writings have to teach us. Their scientific theories died long ago—if indeed they have any claim to being called scientific at all.[10] As far as therapeutics is concerned, it is strongly at odds with the chemical therapy of today. Finally, as regards clinical observation, the occasional finding of a pearl hardly justifies prolonged study. Remarkable as the Greek achievements were for their times, to many they seem now of "merely historical" interest. Therefore, it is argued or supposed, their study can be safely left to classicists who can also instruct the modern physician in the grammatical and semantic ties with Greek and Latin, who can delineate the historical setting of the Hippocratic Oath and of ancient medical ethics, and who can elucidate the other features which, as said before, induce us to uphold the Western tradition of medical historiography. The case made for (or should we say against?) Graeco-Roman medicine holds true, *a fortiori,* for the Middle Ages and can be made to include a good part of medical history of subsequent centuries, depending on the critic's orientation.

Apart from the merits of this argument, we can hardly deny that explicitly or by implication it prevails among the majority of our contemporaries, even among many of those who have strong historical interests. Such interests among physicians, as well as others, are now mainly cultural, intellectual, or sociological, rather than scientific or medical in the substantive sense. This is one of the reasons why the professional historian of medicine more and more is thought of as a historian, rather than as a medical man.

In short, what we asserted of non-Western countries is also becoming true in the West. Our own remote medical past, which preceded the growth of modern scientific medicine, becomes sequestered and confronts us as something to be proud of yet best left to the care of philologists and historians, including professional medical historians. As in the history of science, so in the history of medicine too, many young scholars concentrate on the developments during the last 150 years, with only a superficial acquaintance with what went before.

[10]See, for instance, R. Joly, *Le niveau de la science hippocratique,* Paris: Les Belles Lettres, 1966. What is and what is not scientific largely depends on one's definition of the term. In defining the term as above, note 5, I merely accept customary modern parlance for practical reasons, without excluding a broader and much older meaning.

4

We may wish that the progress of scientific medicine on a worldwide scale were not accompanied by a threatening fragmentation into national histories from which only the most recent decades are exempted. We may doubt (and I for one do doubt) whether any good history will result from a widespread ignorance of what went before, or parallel with, the events in one particular sphere. Yet bewailing current practices and trends will not do, nor, on the other hand, will a dismissal of the work of the specialists. We need more, rather than fewer, contributions by Accadian, Egyptian, Greek, Arabic, Persian, Sanskrit, and Chinese scholars; by paleopathologists, archeologists, medievalists, Renaissance men; by sociologically, economically, demographically oriented historians, and all the others to whom I apologize for not naming their particular discipline. These contributions are necessary in order to provide new material and to enlarge our knowledge. But the increase in historians of medicine specializing in particular fields will satisfy our need as little as will the reliance on dilettantism impatiently grasping for the whole. What is also needed is the attempt to overcome parochialism, be it that of a period, a culture, a nation, or a language and, without sacrificing truthfulness and thoroughness even in details, to see one's own work in proportion to the whole. If world health is a common concern, history focused upon global medicine is a legitimate aim. Once we have this aim, ways will suggest themselves; and it is the possibility of one such way for Western historians of medicine that I would like to explore here.

5

To approach the matter pragmatically, let us think of a young American physician who wishes to study the history of medicine, possessing neither particular qualifications, nor an overriding interest, in any of the traditional areas. Let us, however, assume that he has curiosity for what is happening in medicine and to medicine on a worldwide scale, how medicine is affected by and, in turn, affects the life and outlook of various peoples. He might be willing to follow a way different from the usual one. Obviously, it is not possible to learn Sanskrit, Arabic, Chinese, and Swahili, all at once within a few years. But it should be possible to undergo a training in the general history and the medical history of the nations which these languages suggest, as far as translations make this possible. It should be a comparative approach, conceivably with two aspects of comparison; the periods of pre-"scientific" medicine in each culture (including the West) and then the meeting with "scientific" medicine. It should not be inspired by missionary zeal intent on bringing scientific medicine to other nations. Rather the orientation should be towards an understanding of medicine as an eventual product of manysided endeavors.

Obviously, such an attempt will need retrenchment, as well as extension. The student will have to study traditional Western medicine, not only because it is a part of the entire picture, but also because it produced the scientific medicine which now confronts the others. But I could think that less emphasis would be placed on the remote history of the basic medical sciences and on biobibliographical details. The student will hardly be expected to know much Latin; even the traditional requirement of French and German might judiciously be replaced by some knowledge of languages less accessible through translations. On the other hand, history of disease and of public health, and of the economic, intellectual, religious, and social background of Western medicine will require much more attention than they often receive today. To these changes in the prevailing approaches will have to be added an intensive study of the political, cultural, and social history of a number of non-Western countries, with historical seminars in their medical literature as far as it has been translated. All these bookish studies should be supplemented, if possible, by travel in at least a few areas, so that the student may be confronted with different ways of thinking and feeling about health and disease.

For simplicity's sake I presupposed our student to be a young American physician. I am not sure whether the candidate has to be a physician, although I would think it preferable. In principle, my suggestions may also be valid for other than Americans, though the approaches would naturally have to differ. Even the student's age is not a matter of regulation, for I am thinking here primarily of a student in the broad sense of the word, rather than merely of a registrant in a university.

Whatever merits the above suggestions may have, two points need stressing. The program must not be allowed to favor superficiality. As I see it, one of the drawbacks may lie in too heavy demands upon the student. Not only must he study the history of the medicine of several civilizations, he must study their medicine in the broad sense of the meaning that health and disease have for them and the approaches they have developed. To take one example, study of the history of Indian medicine would not be limited to the reading of some medical classics; rather it would be the history of health and disease and of medical theory and practice in India.[11] To take another example: Scientific medicine is not only medicine tuned to the steady development of physics, chemistry, and biology; it is also marked by belonging to a society whose members take a consumer's view of medicine and demand the solution of medical problems.[12] Such a program of study will not be superficial if it yields a clearer and better founded picture of the historical components of medicine in the world of today than exists in the minds of most of us. To obtain such a picture, a great deal of exertion on the part of the student will be required, for he will have to learn something for which qualified teachers hardly as yet exist. Academically

[11]For Egypt and Mesopotamia, an example of such treatment has been set in vol. 1 of Sigerist's *History*.

[12]See Owsei Temkin, "The meaning of medicine in historical perspective," in David McCord (editor), *Bibliotheca Medica: Physician for Tomorrow*, Boston: Harvard Medical School, 1966, pp. 30–45 [Essay 2].

speaking, this means that he will have to take courses in various departments and will have no single teacher to guide him toward a synthesis. This leads to the second point: Naturally the program, wherever it may be tried, will have to be experimental. Any candidate it may attract will have to fill in the gaps in what I have sketched so imperfectly.

To avoid misunderstanding: by no means is this proposal meant to replace current activities in the history of medicine. It seeks rather to reemphasize the need for integration in the history of medicine and to clarify one possible approach to it. The aim is not new. Even the men who established the traditional picture of Western medicine dealt with what at their time seemed to represent the world. Of what was outside the West they could know little, and the little they knew must have appeared relatively unimportant to them. Yet, *tempora mutantur, nos et mutamur in illis.*[13]

EPICRISIS

The above paragraphs have been presented as originally written, with only minor modifications. Our seminar has now provided us with some experiences which have a bearing on the general proposal.[14] Our acquaintance with the historical forms of Arabic, Indian, and Chinese civilization has been enriched by the sessions conducted by our guest speakers. Moreover, we have learned from our own reports on the general history and classical literature (including medical literature) of those cultures and through our reading of medical classics in translation. But since the existence of Arabic, Indian, and Chinese medicine is no discovery of ours, the same positive results would have been reached in any course that was not limited to Western medicine. Indeed, as far as India and China are concerned, we might be said merely to have made up for previous neglect.[15]

Other matters have had a more direct bearing on the program. In the first place, the difficulties in using translations were very obvious. No translation is reliable when individual words are concerned, where the choice may be due to the translator's justifiable effort to write idiomatic English. To look for concepts behind such words may be chasing after phantoms. This difficulty—and that of comprehension in general—is particularly great in the beginning of a work. Often the reading of the whole book is necessary for a better understanding of particular passages. Two consequences follow therefrom. Selections from larger works will not serve to penetrate thoughts which are quite different from ours. Besides, whereas

---

[13]Times change, and we change with them." I end on this Latin adage as a personal reaffirmation of my Western heritage.

[14]The matter was discussed with the participants of our seminar to whom I am grateful for their comments, see above p. 127.

[15]The history of Arabic medicine has never been omitted from our curriculum; here the seminar extended and intensified previous information. But a few comments only had been devoted to ancient Indian medicine. Our limitation to three non-Western forms of medicine should not be construed as a disparagement of others, e.g., African, to mention but one example.

the constant participation of expert scholars may not be possible, such scholars should be available for consultation when the need arises.

We progressed more easily with Arabic medicine than with Indian and Chinese. The obvious reasons were greater linguistic independence and the relative closeness of the Arabic sources to the ancient Greek tradition. The latter gave us an immediate frame for comparison. Even in the more distant areas of India and China, such comparisons easily suggested themselves. This also indicates an important amendment to what was said above. The student should take one civilization as his base and study it thoroughly, including the language. This will give him something against which he can compare. In one province at least it will make him independent from others' opinions and, above all, the discipline inherent in such study will caution him against becoming a widely read dilettante without depth anywhere. The advantage of combining in one department students with different bases need hardly be pointed out. We were greatly helped by the comments on Ethiopian medicine which one of our Fellows was able to offer.

Our own experience was much too brief and too limited to allow a definite judgment as to the value of the general proposal. But it seems to have proven two points. It has corroborated the desirability of experimental approaches, of which ours was but one. And it has shown that even apart from broad schemes, the trial can be rewarding in itself.

III

Medicine: Ancient
and Medieval

8

Greek Medicine
as Science and Craft*

F ASKED to give a sketch of the development of Greek medicine that could count on general acceptance, I should offer the following outline: Little is known of Greek medicine before the fifth century b.c.; the earliest medical writings that have come down to us are represented by the so-called works of Hippocrates, although this collection is not the work of one man. Its individual books originated approximately between 450 and 350 b.c. They deal with internal diseases, surgery, and gynecology; they offer rational physiological as well as pathological theories often at discord with one another; clinical observations, with emphasis on the prognostic significance of signs, are found side by side with a schematic cataloguing of diseases. Surgical therapy of dislocations and fractures is often quite modern, the materia medica well developed, but where internal diseases are concerned, the dietetic treatment stands in the foreground. The medical literature of the subsequent 400 years is lost; events during this period have to be reconstructed from fragmentary remains and the accounts of later authors. Yet during this period, some decisive changes took place in Alexandria and Rome. The great scientist physicians of Alexandria in the early third century b.c., notably Herophilus and Erasistratus, consolidated the dogmatic school with its stress on research and theory of disease. But the dogmatic school was rivalled by the new empirical sect that banished the search for hidden causes and referred the physician to experience (his own and that of others), supplemented by analogical reasoning in unprecedented cases. After Greek medicine had established a foothold in Rome, it again gave rise to a new sect fitting the new environment. The methodists opposed the dogmatists' scientific theories as well as the empiricists' trust in experience. Instead, they stressed what is common in diseases, laxity and tenseness of the body as a whole or its parts and periods in their course, and advocated a methodical treatment by astringents and laxatives, and a metasyncritic cycle in chronic conditions.

The split into sects is brought to a certain standstill towards the turn of the first to the second Christian centuries. The available literature is more abundant: the herbal of Dioscorides, some works of Rufus of Ephesus and of the methodist Soranus; the book of Aretaeus the Cappadocian may also hail from this time. Then, of course, with the second century a.d., the wealth of the Galenic writings allows us an insight into the medical condi-

*Isis (History of Science Society), 1953, vol. 44, pp. 213–225.
Paper (modified) read at the joint session of the American Historical Association and the History of Science Society at Washington, D.C., 28 December 1952.

tions of this last scientifically creative century. Galen himself appears as a careful anatomist, although monkeys and other animals are the sole material for his dissections. His pretended physiology of man is a synthesis of animal anatomy and experiment, and speculation, and it is constructed from a rigidly teleological point of view. As a pathologist he is the self-confessed heir of Hippocrates whom he interprets as the author of the system of the four humors, blood, phlegm, yellow and black bile, embodying pairs of the contrasting qualities warm-cold and moist-dry. Galen's therapy although rich in dietetic and pharmacological detail is yet dogmatically systematized to correspond to his humoral pathology. With Galen ancient medicine has reached its turning point. What follows is on the one hand, encyclopedias and shorter treatises serving practical purposes, and on the other, commentaries explaining the classical authors, which means Hippocrates and Galen, for the use of the schools. In this encyclopedic and scholastic form, Greek medicine is bequeathed to the peoples of the East.

As it stands, the sketch might have the approval of many scholars not only of today, but even of fifty years ago, since it has carefully avoided any controversial points. Its chief weakness is its almost exclusive attention to Greek medicine as it found literary expression. True, the books are by far the main sources on which we have to rely, but did Greek medicine as a whole really follow the development mirrored by the books? Is it not conceivable that as a craft Greek medicine remained unchanged during the thousand years our sketch encompassed? In short, what is the relationship between science and craft in Greek medicine?

A tendency to distinguish two types of medical practitioners is discernible in Hippocratic times, for we find designations for medical men which hint at some difference of status.[1] Aristotle flatly claims that "'physician' means both the ordinary practitioner, and the master of the craft, and thirdly, the man who has studied medicine as part of his general education."[2] This statement is not surprising if taken as an evaluation. We need only think of the interest in medical matters evinced from pre-Socratic philosophers down to laymen like Celsus to recognize Aristotle's third type of physician. Likewise, the physician Diocles of Carystus who, as Werner Jaeger[3] has shown, was associated with Aristotle and indebted to his philosophy, obviously appeared as a master of his craft who could explain what he did, if compared with the ordinary practitioners.

But Aristotle's terminology does not necessarily indicate a distinction between two social classes of professional physicians. Here we may refer to a passage in Plato's *Laws* which has received attention.[4] Plato contrasts the

---

[1] See chs. 1 and 7 of *On Ancient Medicine* and the edition by A.-J. Festugière, *Hippocrate; L'ancienne médecine,* Paris, C. Klincksieck, p. 27 f., notes 6 and 7.

[2] Aristotle, *Politics* III, 6; 1282 a (translation by H. Rackham, Loeb Classical Library, p. 227).

[3] Werner Jaeger, *Diokles von Karystos,* Die griechische Medizin und die Schule des Aristoteles, Berlin, De Gruyter, 1938.

[4] Plato, *Laws,* IV; 720 (translation by R. G. Bury, Loeb Classical Library, vol. 1, pp. 307–309), also IX; 857, C-D; Werner Jaeger, *Paideia,* 3 vols., New York, 1939–44; see vol. 3, p. 215; Ludwig Edelstein, The Rôle of Eryximachus in Plato's Symposium, *Transactions of the American*

free-born doctor who deals chiefly with "the ailments of free men" with those practitioners, often slaves themselves, who find their patients among the slaves. Slave doctors are, of course, a known institution throughout antiquity. Since highly educated persons could become slaves, there is no reason to assume that physicians belonging to this social class were *eo ipso* of inferior skill or knowledge. Varro states that farmers near a city or near large estates "prefer to have in their neighborhood men whose services they can call upon under a yearly contract—physicians, fullers, and smiths—rather than to have such men of their own on the farm; for sometimes the death of one artisan wipes out the profit of a farm."[5] The "medicus" on the farm obviously would be a slave; the one hired from the neighborhood might be slave or free. In either event the social difference would hardly be decisive for any difference in quality.[6] Nor was it altogether decisive for Plato, according to whom those who deal with the ailments of free men do so "by investigating them from the commencement and according to the course of nature," while the others "whether they be free-born or slaves, acquire their art under the direction of their masters, by observation and practice and not by the study of nature—which is the way in which the free-born doctors have learnt the art themselves and in which they instruct their own disciples."[7] Whatever else Plato may have in mind here, one of the distinctions he establishes is the study from nature by one type of physician, and learning by rote by another. It is possible that illiteracy was also found among the latter type. On the whole, however, the great number of medical books written in antiquity hints at an equally great number of physician authors as well as a large reading public.[8] When Galen says that "the majority of those nowadays pursuing medicine or philosophy cannot even read well,"[9] the association of physicians with philosophers is consoling and indicates that the statement must not be taken too literally. It is somewhat reminiscent of the remark supposedly made by the head of the medical school of Harvard when President Eliot proposed written examinations for the M.D. degree: "I had to tell him that he knew nothing about the quality of Harvard medical students. More than half of them can barely write."[10]

Let us then say that there were two types of medical men in antiquity

---

Philological Association, 1945, vol. 76, p. 99; O. Temkin, in *Social Medicine, Its Derivations and Objectives,* ed. Iago Galdston, New York, Commonwealth Fund, 1949, p. 4 f.; and T. A. Sinclair, Class Distinction in Medical Practice: a Piece of Ancient Evidence, *Bull. Hist. Med.,* 1951, vol. 25, p. 386 ff.

[5]Varro, *On Agriculture,* I, 16, 4 (translation by W. D. Hooper, revised by H. B. Ash, Loeb Classical Library, p. 221; adapted).

[6]Joseph Schumacher, *Die naturphilosophischen Grundlagen der Medizin in der griechischen Antike,* Berlin, De Gruyter, 1940, p. 238.

[7]See above, footnote 4.

[8]I. E. Drabkin, On Medical Education in Greece and Rome, *Bull. Hist. Med.;* 1944, vol. 15, p. 350.

[9]Galen, De libris propriis, *Scripta minora,* vol. 2, ed. I. Mueller, Lipsiae, Teubner, 1891, p. 91.

[10]Quoted from Esther Lucile Brown, *Physicians and Medical Care,* New York, Russell Sage Foundation, 1937, p. 17.

and, for convenience's sake, let us designate them as physician and leech. After all, our term physician is derived from physicus, the student of nature, and the name seems appropriate for those who study diseases according to nature, as Plato says. We shall, however, beware of thinking of physician and leech as two exclusive classes. We must admit the possibility of a large intermediary group, just as we must admit the possibility of the existence of good leeches and bad physicians. Our distinction is made with an eye on the nature of the physician's science and the leech's craft.

Now it has to be said that our knowledge of the content of Greek medical science has not changed considerably during the last thirty years. That is to say, the comparison between our knowledge and that of the Greeks in anatomy, physiology, pathology, and materia medica was made rather thoroughly by the older medical historians, and we have added details only. Nor can there be any doubt that many modern scientific methods, taken as such, were known to Greek physicians. Heidel has shown this very well for the Hippocratic collection.[11] Cohen's and Drabkin's source book[12] demonstrates it for the whole period. I would even go so far as to say that some ancient works contain valuable and still unexploited information from the modern point of view. Thus I doubt whether we possess a description of the muscular system of the Barbary ape which, in fullness of detail, can compare with that in Galen's "Anatomical Administrations."

Nevertheless, we are no longer able to speak of Greek medical science with the assurance of previous generations. This uncertainty is not due so much to considerations of content as of form and purpose. Obviously, Greek medicine was somehow different from modern medicine. We can name the disciplines and their methods which make modern medicine scientific, but can we do the same for antiquity? The answer to this question depends very much on our judgment of the Hippocratic writings. Even at the end of Greek civilization they were still classical textbooks. To deny their scientific nature means to deny that Greek medicine had a scientific orientation throughout its history.

The hostility of many Hippocratic works to magic has always been considered a factor in favor of their scientific spirit. The rationalism of the treatise *On the Sacred Disease* with its condemnation of supernatural explanations is shared by many of the other works. And since the appearance of Edelstein's *Asclepius*[13] we have also obtained a better understanding of the relationship of this rationalism to religion. There is neither competition nor enmity between the god and the physician. On the contrary, the Asclepieion takes care of many cases with which the physician cannot cope. Although it is probable that Asclepius, before becoming a healing god, was

[11]William Arthur Heidel, *Hippocratic Medicine, Its Spirit and Method*, New York, Columbia University Press, 1941.

[12]M. R. Cohen and I. E. Drabkin, *A Source Book in Greek Science*, New York, McGraw-Hill, 1948.

[13]Emma J. Edelstein and Ludwig Edelstein, *Asclepius*, a Collection and Interpretation of the Testimonies, 2 vols., Baltimore, The Johns Hopkins Press, 1945. See especially vol. 2, pp. 53 ff., 139, 169.

the patron saint of the medical men, this relationship did not affect the lay character of Greek medicine.

Rationalism is a necessary but insufficient condition of science. In the quest for an additional feature, a passage in Plato's *Phaedrus* defining the method of Hippocrates himself has long offered a ready answer. Socrates asks: "Now do you think that one can acquire any appreciable knowledge of the nature of the soul without knowing the nature of the whole?" And Phaedrus replies: "If Hippocrates the Asclepiad is to be trusted, one cannot know the nature of the body, either, except by this method."[14] "This method" refers to "knowing the nature of the whole." And if by "the whole" is meant the universe, then Hippocrates thought that the understanding of the body presupposed an understanding of surrounding nature. All that remained was to identify this method in those Hippocratic writings in which it was used in order to find both science and the genuine works of Hippocrates.[15] It is an example of very much depending on very little, viz. the interpretation of the words "the whole." If the words "the whole" are understood differently, we arrive at a meaning, embodied in Jowett's translation, where Phaedrus' answer reads: "Hippocrates the Asclepiad says that the nature even of the body can only be understood as a whole."[16] The interpretation of this passage is a matter of dispute,[17] but the tendency to regard genuine Hippocratic science as interested in a study of the surrounding universe was, and still is, predominant. According to Nestle,[18] the physician's practical preoccupation with prognostic signs impressed upon him the idea of the regularity of nature and led to an investigation of causal relationships. Hippocrates, in particular, assumed that man must be considered as under the influence of surrounding nature, and elaborated this view theoretically and as applied to individual and mass diseases. Having rejected all speculative elements, medicine became an independent science and conceived of itself "as a superpersonal, spiritual unit, a work of many individuals and generations in a process of continuous change, correction, and perfection."[19] Medicine shared the method of

[14]Plato, *Phaedrus*, 270 C (translation by H. N. Fowler, Loeb Classical Library, p. 549, adapted).

[15]Attempts in this direction go back at least as far as Galen; see W. H. S. Jones, *Philosophy and Medicine in Ancient Greece*, with an Edition of Peri archaies iatrikes, Baltimore, The Johns Hopkins Press, 1946, p. 16 ff. (*Supplements to the Bulletin of the History of Medicine*, no. 8).

[16]*The Works of Plato*, selected and edited by Irwin Edman, Modern Library, p. 317. The interpretation of "the whole" as referring to the body has been given in detail by Ludwig Edelstein, *Peri aeron und die Sammlung der hippokratischen Schriften*, Berlin, Weidmann, 1931 (*Problemata*, Heft 4), pp. 118–135.

[17]Karl Deichgräber, *Die Epidemien und das Corpus Hippocraticum*, Berlin, Akademie der Wissenschaften, 1933, p. 151, in argumentation against Edelstein has tried to uphold "the whole" as meaning the universe. For a very detailed discussion of the Phaedrus passage see P. Kucharski, La 'Méthode d'Hippocrate' dans le Phèdre, *Revue des Études Grecques*, 1939, t. 52, pp. 301–357. Edelstein has maintained his interpretation against Deichgräber and others in the article "Hippocrates," Pauly-Wissowa, *Real-Encyclopädie, etc.*, Supplementbd. VI, 1935, col. 1318 ff.

[18]Wilhelm Nestle, Hippocratica, *Hermes*, 1938, vol. 73, pp. 1–38.

[19]*Ibid.*, p. 38.

strict etiological research with history, and the spiritual father of this method was the philosopher Democritus.[20]

In this view, etiological research appears as the essentially scientific element of Hippocratic medicine. The counterpart to this form of scientific medicine is represented by the treatise *On Ancient Medicine.* The book has interested historians of Greek culture, because its author starts out with a sophistic theory of the origin of civilization.[21] Man raised himself from a brutish condition when, by trial and error, he learned to prepare food more suitable to himself. Likewise by trial and error he learned that sick people needed a diet different from that of the healthy. Thus medicine arose and with it the only promising method for further medical research. All attempts to base medicine on empty hypotheses as used in talk about heaven and the regions below are futile.

Some forty years ago, Diels[22] called the author a positivist and pointed out that he paid attention to individual cases rather than general laws. This is not quite correct. In the first part of the treatise, its author argues from a therapeutic point of view and sees the perfection of medicine in an ever-increasing approximation of treatment to the manifold reactions of the human body.[23] In the last part, however, he interprets these reactions as founded in the quality of humors and the structure of organs.[24] He seems to think that by reasoning backwards from ascertained therapeutic facts, a science of nature will be possible. For this reason Gomperz,[25] as Littré before him, believed to have found here the truly Hippocratic method alluded to by Plato.[26]

The attack upon mere hypotheses and the high value set upon trial and error in the first part, have made the treatise appear a kind of "Introduction to experimental medicine." And since today the experimental approach in science enjoys aristocratic privileges, so to speak, it is not surprising that attention has focussed upon *Ancient Medicine* which in the course of a few years has been the subject of three monographs.[27]

---

[20]*Ibid.,* p. 31. The role of Democritus (next to Empedocles) for the etiological research of Greek physicians has been stressed by Hans Diller, *Wanderarzt und Aitiologe,* Leipzig, 1934 (*Philologus,* Supplementband 26, Heft 3); while Max Pohlenz, *Hippokrates und die Begründung der wissenschaftlichen Medizin,* Berlin, De Gruyter, 1938, pp. 26 and 62, tries to make Democritus dependent upon the physicians. See also Diller's review of Pohlenz in *Gnomon,* 1942, vol. 18, pp. 65–88.

[21]For details see Felix Heinimann, *Nomos und Physis,* Basel, Reinhardt, 1945 (*Schweizerische Beiträge zur Altertumswissenschaft,* H. 1).

[22]H. Diels, Über einen neuen Versuch, die Echtheit einiger Hippokratischen Schriften nachzuweisen, *Sitzungsberichte d. königl. Preussischen Akademie d. Wissensch.* Philos.-hist. Classe, 1910, vol. 53, p. 1141, footnote 1.

[23]See ch. 9 and Walter Müri, in *Hermes,* 1936, vol. 71, p. 468, and Jones, *op. cit.,* p. 73. Edelstein, Empirie und Skepsis in der Lehre der griechischen Empirikerschule, *Quellen und Studien zur Geschichte der Naturwissenschaften und der Medizin,* 1933, Bd. 3, Heft 4, p. 49, refers this to the individual reactions of each case.

[24]See ch. 19 and, especially, chs. 22–24.

[25]Theodor Gomperz, Die hippokratische Frage und der Ausgangspunkt ihrer Lösung, reprinted in *Hellenika,* 2. Bd., Leipzig, 1912, pp. 324–354; see p. 325.

[26]*Ibid.,* p. 330, where Gomperz asserts his belief that Plato, in the *Phaedrus,* when speaking of Hippocrates, had in mind the author of *Ancient Medicine.*

[27]Festugière, *op. cit.* (see above note 1), W. H. S. Jones, *Philosophy and Medicine in Ancient*

These two examples show the difficulty of identifying Greek medicine with any of the forms of modern scientific medicine. They will also have prepared us for Edelstein's attempt at separating medicine and science in ancient Greece. Edelstein proceeded from an analysis of the role of prognosis in Hippocratic medicine. In his opinion this role has to be understood from the social position of the physician as a craftsman not backed by a degree or license.[28] Apart from its psychological significance,[29] correct prognosis was the means of acquiring a reputation and of warding off suspicion in fatal cases.[30] The interest and knowledge of the physician were practical, not scientific.[31] If he talked[32] and wrote about the nature of man, of health and disease, he borrowed his concepts from contemporary, i.e., pre-Socratic, philosophy, and this relationship between medicine and philosophy remained basically unchanged.[33] Medicine was the practical art, acquired by apprenticeship and practiced "in accordance with traditional views and usages."[34] The sects were philosophical in character. The dogmatists were adherents of Aristotle and the Stoics, the empiricists followed the Academy in their denial that nature was understandable, the methodists accepted the scepticism of Pyrrho.[35] The dogmatists were connected with Aristotelian thought and thus it was in developing Aristotle's arguments that the Alexandrian physicians turned to the study of human anatomy.[36] But at no time before Galen did Greek medicine incorporate dissection and experimentation as indispensable parts; even Galen did not consider all his anatomical and physiological research essential for the physician *qua* professional healer.[37]

Edelstein's views as recently summarized[38] have a profound bearing upon the whole relationship between Greek medicine and culture. We have now two almost diametrically opposed views. On the one hand, Greek physicians are considered as the great scientific teachers, to whom even the

---

Greece (see above, note 15), and Hermann Wanner, *Studien zu Peri archaies iatrikes*, Diss. Zürich, Zürich, 1939.

[28]Edelstein, *Peri aeron* etc., chs. 2 and 3.

[29]*Ibid.*, p. 65 f.

[30]*Ibid.*, pp. 81 and 88.

[31]*Ibid.*, p. 93.

[32]*Ibid.*, p. 104 f.

[33]L. Edelstein, The Relation of Ancient Philosophy to Medicine, *Bull. Hist. Med.*, 1952, vol. 26, pp. 299–316, especially p. 304, where it is said (with reference to Aristotle, *De respiratione* 480 b 26 ff. and *De sensu*, 436 a 19 ff.): "physicians concerned with biology and physiology ... took their departure from philosophy, just as truly systematic natural philosophy ended in a consideration of the principles of life, of health and disease, and of the constituents of the body."

[34]*Ibid.*, p. 301; see also Edelstein, *Peri aeron*, p. 92 f.

[35]Edelstein, Empirie und Skepsis, *op. cit.*, see also his article "Methodiker" in Pauly-Wissowa, *Real-Encyclopädie*, Supplementbd. VI, 1935, col. 367 ff.

[36]Edelstein, Die Geschichte der Sektion in der Antike, *Quellen u. Studien zur Geschichte d. Naturwissenschaften und der Medizin*, Bd. 3, Heft 2, Berlin, 1932, see p. 95 ff.; see also The Development of Greek Anatomy, *Bull. Hist. Med.*, 1935, vol. 3, pp. 235–248.

[37]Edelstein, The Relation of Ancient Philosophy to Medicine, *loc. cit.*, p. 304. G. Lebouque, Une anatomie antique du coeur humain, *Revue des Études Grecques*, 1944, t. 77, p. 7–40, believes that Philistion dissected human bodies and refers to the Hippocratic *On the Heart* which he thinks renders a lecture by Philistion.

[38]In Edelstein's last quoted article, *Bull. Hist. Med.*, 1952, vol. 26, pp. 299–316.

philosophers are greatly indebted and whom they quote from the time of Plato. This claim is denied by Edelstein who thinks that scientifically the doctors were the recipients and that the philosophers quoted them mainly as an example. People were willing to subject their bodies to the orders of the doctor, unpleasant as these orders often were. They should be willing to accept the commands of the philosophers who treated their souls.

I believe that Edelstein's work has provided a new basis for our understanding of Greek medicine and that its fruitfulness is demonstrated not least by the questions it permits the historian of medicine to ask. One of them is concerned with a closer scrutiny of the practitioner's role in this development. We shall attempt to draw a rough picture of ancient leechcraft and then ask ourselves for the possible factors that promised to make the leech a better practitioner by turning him philosopher.

Immediately we find ourselves embarrassed by the scanty information about ancient leechcraft. Jones[39] proposed to think of it in the likeness of a medieval guild, which refers to the master-apprentice relationship rather than to any social organization about which we know next to nothing. The question then before us is: what kind of medicine did the master teach and the apprentice learn? Or to simplify even further: what did the leech treat and how did he treat it?

In the *Republic*, Plato says: "A carpenter, when he is sick expects his physician to give him a drug which will operate as an emetic on the disease, or to get rid of it by purging or the use of cautery or the knife."[40] Plato quotes this carpenter as an example of a patient who cannot afford complicated treatment. His physician may well be a leech and since drugs are mentioned, we may look for our answer to an herbal, perhaps the *Materia medica* of Dioscorides of the first century A.D. It is a large herbal, but then we want to get a picture of a good leech, not necessarily an ignorant one.[41] Opening the book at random and leaving out some botanical and pharmaceutical details we read that the caper-plant "disturbes the belly, is good for the stomach and causes thirst, but is easier on the stomach when eaten cooked than raw. Its fruit makes the spleen shrink . . . it also moves the urine and causes bloody discharge, helps in sciatica and paralysis . . . and against ruptures and convulsions, likewise it moves the menses and purges away phlegm, and stops tooth ache. . . . The dry bark of the root is suitable for the aforesaid (conditions), and cleanses all chronic, dirty, and indurated sores. With barley meal it is used as a poultice in those suffering from the spleen, if chewed it helps the tooth ache, finely ground and mixed with vinegar it wipes off leprous spots and vitiligo."[42]

---

[39]W. H. S. Jones, *The Medical Writings of Anonymus Londinensis*, Cambridge, University Press, 1947, p. 161.

[40]*Republic*, book III, ch. 15; 406 D (P. Shorey's translation, Loeb Classical Library, vol. 1, p. 275).

[41]I have purposely chosen a late and sophisticated work, just because I want to show that even here one can still imagine the existence of a core of practical knowledge relatively little affected by the course of time except for the broadened coverage of drugs.

[42]Dioscorides, *Materia medica*, II, 173; ed. M. Wellmann, vol. 1, Berlin, Weidmann, 1907, p. 241.

Most of this is immediately understandable. The drug is useful in a number of complaints, most of them symptoms or syndromes with which we too are acquainted. Of others, especially the "leprous spots and vitiligo" we are not quite sure, but we can assume that the Greek leech had learned to diagnose them. The reference to shrinking of the spleen indicates that he knew where the spleen is and how to palpate it. In view of the prevalence of malarial fevers this is not surprising. Most of the symptoms mentioned like sores, paralysis, tooth ache, can easily be described without reference to complicated or theoretical concepts. We meet with more serious difficulties when reading about "sufferers from the spleen," which may refer to a disease entity, and "purging away phlegm," where we are confronted with a concept of humoral pathology. Disregarding the latter example for a moment, and generalizing somewhat broadly, we may say that the leech was acquainted with some disease entities and a large number of symptoms. The diseases are indicated by names like peripneumonia, pleurisy, phthisis, phrenitis, epilepsy, melancholy, many of which seem of popular origin.[43] We meet them in the Hippocratic collection as well as in later works. The leech can recognize diseases and symptoms and has remedies for them, partly drugs, partly simple dietetic measures; possibly he has also learned to take into consideration the strength, age, and sex of his patient. He treats internal as well as surgical complaints, relying on some anatomical knowledge, and an accumulated store of manual skills. This knowledge is passed on from teacher to pupil; it can be increased by contact with other physicians or by accidental observations.

Nothing prevents us from imagining Greek leechcraft being thus practiced at all times of Greek history with the addition of little else. But we must also realize that there are medical limitations to this type of practice. The limitations are those of any technique without theory. The leech may know very much, but his knowledge will always consist of a certain number of skills. Beyond this number he cannot go, that is to say he cannot deal with what is unfamiliar to him and he cannot individualize his treatment. And while he may go in quest of new recipes and manipulations, he has no principle of research. Now we have had an indication that the leech was not quite without the help of some theoretical concepts; for we heard Dioscorides recommend the caper-plant as purging phlegm. Similar concepts, related to theory and yet not dependent on special theories, existed much earlier as we learn from the case histories in the first book of the so-called Hippocratic *Epidemics*. In the description of symptoms in individual patients, terms occur which are used like sense data although they transcend the realm of mere description. For instance, discharges are described as "thin, bilious, biting, scanty, black."[44] etc., or as "uncocted as it were."[45] The reader is supposed to know what marks them as "bilious" or "uncocted." But the former term also refers to a humor and the latter involves

[43]Henry E. Sigerist, *Antike Heilkunde,* München, Heimeran, 1927, p. 20.
[44]Hippocrates, *Epidemics I,* case 14 (translation, adapted, by W. H. S. Jones, Loeb Classical Library, vol. 1, p. 211).
[45]*Ibid.,* case 2 (p. 191).

the analogy between the process of digestion and cooking. If it is said that a woman having a sore throat showed a persistent "acrid, smarting and salt flux,"[46] this means a matter sensibly defined by these attributes, but it also refers to this matter as flowing. Besides, the reader is expected to have some anatomical knowledge, and be able to understand the note that a patient "at first suffered in the cardia and the right hypochondrium."[47] Similar concepts are used in other Hippocratic writings in the manner of a terminology common among all medical men at that time.[48] It is quite possible that one or the other term is of relatively late origin;[49] nevertheless it seems likely to me that some of them at least belong to a previous archaic stage. Just as some names of diseases, they may even reflect popular usage. This assumption would explain how the author of *Epidemics I* can describe the "flux" in the woman with the sore throat, how the author of *Ancient Medicine* can speak of fluxes "that turn to the throat,"[50] and how Herodotus can relate the measures the Lybians take to protect their children from a phlegm "flowing down" from the head[51]—and how all three can count on immediate understanding. Such an assumption would relieve us of unproductive attempts at tracing medical comments in Greek writers to the few medical books that happened to come down to us.

With this broad picture in mind of a leechcraft as the core of the healing art providing a certain uniformity of practice, we ask why some leeches became physicians. In antiquity, medicine was a profession, philosophy was not—unless the philosopher became a teacher. This means that the philosopher might belong to any profession, and the intellectual adventure of pre-Socratic philosophy may have attracted leeches among others. The Hippocratic author who argued that all diseases, including the sacred disease, were natural and that magic had no place in their cause or treatment

---

[46]*Ibid.*, case 5 (p. 197).

[47]*Ibid.*, case 4 (p. 193). L. von Brunn, Hippokrates und die meteorologische Medizin, *Gesnerus*, 1946, vol. 3, pp. 151–173, and 1947, vol. 4, pp. 1–18 and 65–85 has shown how supposedly empirical data of the *Epidemics* are imbued with theoretical notions, and how the firm belief in a definite order leads the Hippocratic author to doubtful generalizations. In the first book of the *Epidemics* to which I have confined myself (for reasons stated below, n. 73) the evidence is not as striking as in the third book. Schumacher, *op. cit.*, has given a very detailed interpretation of Hippocratic and pre-Hippocratic medicine in concepts of natural philosophy.

[48]Deichgräber, *Die Epidemien* etc., pp. 40–51, sketches the physiological and etiological system of the author of the *Epidemics*. While it is quite possible that the author consciously held these tenets, he did not deem it necessary to explain his system and obviously counted on the understanding of his readers. The close relationship with *Prognostics* has also been noted by Deichgräber; *Prognostics* speaks a similar language and also takes understanding for granted.

[49]Plato, in the *Republic*, III, 14; 405 D refers to a medical neologism. He blames people who because of slothful living are full of winds and fluxes and thus "compel the clever Asclepiads to give to diseases the names of gases (physai) and catarrhs." To which is added the comment that these are indeed "new and absurd disease names." From this passage it evinces that "flux" was in common usage, whereas to label diseases "gases" (physai) or "catarrh" was considered new.

[50]*On Ancient Medicine*, ch. 19.

[51]Herodotus, IV, 187; the description as "flowing down" must not be identified with Plato's criticism of catarrh as a disease name.

may well have been a leech stimulated by Democritus as Diller thinks.[52] The competitive character of Greek medicine certainly induced many leeches to borrow from the philosophers in order to construct medical theories and systems which could form the content of speeches to impress patients and whole audiences.[53] After Plato and Aristotle had declared a mere craftsman inferior to the master who could give reasons for what he did,[54] social ambition was strong enough to make a leech appear in the philosopher's dress. All these possibilities have to be conceded. But it does not follow that philosophy and science were mere epiphenomena to true leechcraft. I believe that there were medical reasons combined with social incentives that induced the leech to become a physician and that made it imperative, later on, for every physician to belong to a medical sect. These reasons I find in the rise of dietetic medicine which Edelstein has so well described,[55] and the individualization of Greek life.[56]

The rise of the dietetic physician who regulates the whole life of his patient seems to fall within the fifth century. The ancients themselves thought so;[57] Plato ascribes his emergence to Herodicus of Selymbria,[58] who from a gymnastic trainer turned into a physician. Without limiting ourselves to a single name, we can yet see a connection between the gymnast who builds up the athlete and the physician who protects the health of man and cures him by similarly regulating food and drink, work, rest, and sleep.[59] The dietetic physician who believes he knows "how to cause in men by regimen moist or dry, hot or cold," believes himself able to cure even the sacred disease[60] once he has learned from its course and causes the right moment at which to interfere with the propitious and inimical factors. Dietetic medicine is mainly concerned with the treatment of internal diseases, those which affect the whole man. There are physicians who identify medicine with dietetic medicine. It is a curious thing that the author of *Ancient Medicine* who tries to explain the development of medicine, makes no references to pharmacology and surgery at all. Asclepiades who, in the first century B.C., laid down a doctrine which was eventually to lead to the methodist sect "dispensed with the use of [medicaments] for the most part,"

---

[52]Hans Diller, *Wanderarzt und Aitiologe*, p. 111 ff.
[53]See above, n. 32.
[54]Plato, *Gorgias*, 465 ff., Aristotle, *Metaphysics* I, 2.
[55]Ludwig Edelstein, Antike Diätetik, *Die Antike*, 1931, vol. 7, pp. 255–270; and his description of the dietetic physician in *Peri aeron* etc. and, *ibid.*, p. 114, the comments on individualization.
[56]Max Neuburger, *History of Medicine*, translated by Ernest Playfair, vol. 1, London, 1910, p. 133, says of the Hippocratic physician that he found his goal in the sick individual "as Socrates individualised abstractions, as Thucydides placed personality in the foreground."
[57]Menon begins his account of dietetic etiologies of disease with Euryphon (Jones, *The Medical Writings of Anonymus Londinensis*, p. 32).
[58]Plato, *Republic*, III, 14, 406 E.
[59]On the competition between physician and gymnast see Ludwig Englert, *Untersuchungen zu Galens Schrift Thrasybulos*, Leipzig, Barth, 1929 (*Studien z. Geschichte d. Medizin*, Heft 18).
[60]Hippocrates, *On the Sacred Disease*, last chapter (translation by Jones, Loeb Classical Library, vol. 2, p. 183).

as we are informed.[61] On the other hand, many dogmatists and the empiricists set great store by drugs. These examples suffice to show that dietetics was the great dynamic element within Greek medicine. In the dietetic treatment of diseases radical differences are sometimes noticeable; the methodists, in particular, vary widely from the other two sects. And among the dogmatists and empiricists, individual differences appear which cannot merely be laid down to difference in training and experience, but in which theory plays a guiding role. Greek medicine became split into sects not over preferences for one or the other drug or one or the other surgical technique, but over different explanations of diseases[62] or the very need for such explanations.[63]

As we remarked before, theory is a guide to the unknown[64] and allows individualization in treatment. Now there is no more individualized form of therapy than the minute regulation of a man's life in all its details.[65] And in the fifth century B.C. Greek life became increasingly individualistic,[66] especially with the advent of the sophistic movement when the flow of medical literature too set in. Plato's free doctor treats his patients by "learning himself from the sufferers and imparting instruction to them ... and gives no prescription until he has gained the patient's consent"[67] etc. Plato's remark is corroborated by the following beginning of a Hippocratic work: "He who wishes to interrogate properly concerning treatment and answer him who interrogates and also object properly, must ponder the following things":[68] whereupon follows a long list of theoretical questions.

Once the expansion of medicine beyond the limits of a craft had become a necessity, this expansion could follow different directions. Systems could be built in which anatomy, crude as it was, formed a cornerstone, or where the older semi-popular concepts of humors were elaborated, or qualities emphasized. In all these attempts, the contact with philosophy was close;

[61]Celsus, *De medicina*, V, preface (translation by W. G. Spencer, Loeb Classical Library, vol. 2, p. 3).

[62]This accounts largely for the many sects among the dogmatists. As to the different explanation and treatment of disease by dogmatists see Caelius Aurelianus' (i.e., Soranus') criticism in his works on acute and chronic diseases and the so-called Anonymus Parisinus, edited by R. Fuchs, *Rheinisches Museum für Philologie*, 1894, N.F., vol. 49, pp. 532–558 and 1895, vol. 50, pp. 576–599.

[63]Even before the advent of the empiricists, Diocles claimed that one should not listen to people who believe that they must state a cause for everything. This he thinks is often quite unnecessary for practice and one should rather put one's trust in things well known from long experience (Werner Jaeger, *Diokles von Karystos*, p. 37 f.). But this criticism does not prevent Diocles from being a dogmatist.

[64]It is significant that to the empiricists the reference to mere experience became problematic in cases where the physician was confronted with a new kind of disease.

[65]I find it very difficult to imagine the complicated hygienic prescriptions for healthy persons as emanating from leechcraft. According to Adolf Palm, *Studien zur Hippokratischen Schrift Peri Diaites*, Diss. Tübingen, 1933, p. 38 f., the first zoological system in Greece developed among the physicians of the late fifth century B.C. when they endeavored to study the dietetic significance of different animals.

[66]On the individualization of Greek life and the concomitant release of intellectual energy, see E. R. Dodds, *The Greeks and the Irrational*, Berkeley, 1951.

[67]See above, footnote 4.

[68]*On Diseases, I*, ch. 1; ed. Littré (*Oeuvres complètes d'Hippocrate*), vol. 6, p. 140.

they were to lead to the science of the dogmatist school, of Galen, and, subsequently, to the modern medical sciences of anatomy, physiology, and pathology. This line of development is understandable to us, above all where anatomical reasoning in surgical cases occurs.[69] But we can even understand how an individual case might be diagnosed in terms of deranged humors and then treated correspondingly,[70] though we no longer believe in the theory of humors. Peculiarly enough, we experience greater difficulties with some of the clinical writings of the Hippocratic collection where we would expect an immediate contact. When we read the individual case histories of the first book of *Epidemics* we are at some loss to determine the purpose of their composition. Instinctively we try to "diagnose" these cases, i.e., to identify them with one or the other disease entity we are familiar with. But even when we succeed, we realize that a diagnosis of this kind was not the author's aim. It has been suggested with some degree of probability, that the book has a prognostic character.[71] From these illustrative case histories, the reader is to learn how to evaluate the appearance and disappearance of symptoms in their significance to the outcome of the disease and moreover how to recognize the right "moment" for therapeutic interference.[72] But whatever the underlying motive may have been,[73] I believe that in their form these case histories offer an explanation of Plato's saying that the free doctor treated diseases "by investigating them from the commencement and according to the course of nature." The origin, course, and outcome of sickness in the individual are under observation and the symptoms are evaluated in relation to one another. That means that the physician can learn from the comparison of many case histories, but must judge for himself in each case and cannot rely on routine as his helper may do.

The individual approach to disease as documented in these case histories has so often been stressed that it needs no further elaboration. But it is worth pointing out that here, more clearly than ever before, disease is·

[69]The surgical works of the Hippocratic collection have thus remained the most modern ones; see Owsei Temkin, The Role of Surgery in the Rise of Modern Medical Thought, *Bull. Hist. Med.*, 1951, vol. 25, p. 248 [Essay, 33, p. 487].

[70]That is by diminishing the quantity of the humor through bleeding, phlegmagogues etc. or acting upon the quality involved according to the principle of *contraria contrariis curantur*.

[71]See Edelstein, *Peri aeron* etc. pp. 79–81; Deichgräber, *Die Epidemien* etc. p. 10 f. Von Brunn (*Gesnerus*, 1947), p. 14, doubts the exclusively prognostic character.

[72]Cf. Edelstein, *ibid.* Neuburger, *op. cit.*, p. 133, finds the essence of Hippocratic art "in the fact that it knew how, in individual cases, to decide which impressions collectively permitted of conclusions upon prognosis and indicated the occasion for therapeutic measures and the form they should take."

[73]One of the great difficulties presenting itself is the disregard of therapy. This has long been noticed and "Hippocrates" has been criticized for neglecting his patients. However, the patients received nourishment or they did not; in either case their "diet"—even if not prescribed by the physician—was right or wrong and somehow influenced the course of the disease. This consequence seems to follow from the premises of ancient dietetic medicine. Since the attitude to therapy is not quite the same in *Epidemics* I and III, I have limited myself to the former in spite of the generally accepted connection of the two books. The Hippocratic case histories have recently been discussed in detail by Pedro Laín Entralgo, *La Historia Clínica*, Madrid, Consejo Superior de Investigaciones Cientificas, 1950.

conceived as a process in time.[74] Thereby, disease becomes more than a symptom or a syndrome, designated by a popular or scientific name. The time-implied character of disease is also evident in that (first) part of *Epedemics I* which has led Deichgräber to coin the term "meteorological medicine."[75] Here the author described climatic events and the course of such diseases as showed seasonal variations of prevalence and character as they occurred during certain periods on the island of Thasos. Sporadic diseases are excluded and this part is less individualized. But even where the author deals with disease entities he does not view them as mere static combinations of symptoms but ascribes to them beginning and end, severity, complications, etc., in short imparts to the diseases a "history." So obvious is all this to us that we easily forget how essential the temporal concept of disease is for clinical medicine.[76] This concept could survive the particular prognostic motives from which it had originated as well as the physiological notions of the author,[77] and remain as a pattern of clinical study independent as it were from the philosophical "sciences." Small wonder then that the *Epidemics* became of interest to the empirical sect which denounced science. This interest, however, shows that the empirical sect does not represent a return to mere leechcraft. There is studied method in the empiricist's gathering of experience; it is merely a different form of research. Least of all does the methodist fall back upon the tradition of the leech, for he more than all others upsets the accustomed ways. The great methodist, Soranus, demands even of the future midwife that she should be literate "so that she may be able to grasp the art by theory too."[78]

Accustomed as we have become to scientific precision in modern medicine and its statistically proved therapeutic results, we have difficulties in conceiving of the clashes of the ancient sects as more than quibbles. But within the framework of ancient civilization the practitioner who wishes to overcome the narrowness of the craft in medical matters has no choice but to join a sect. This alone gives him the chance not only to enhance his prestige but to become a better, because broadly thinking, physician.[79] A final argument for this thesis seems to lie in the fact that even a dogmatist like Galen who loudly proclaimed "that the best physician must also be a philosopher" appears sincere in his medical demands and limitations upon

[74]Sigerist, *Antike Heilkunde*, p. 17, with regard to *Epidemics* writes: "Die ägyptische, die babylonische Literatur geben uns nur Augenblicksbilder. Schilderungen vom Verlauf einer Krankheit würden wir dort vergeblich suchen."

[75]Deichgräber, *op. cit.*, p. 12 f.

[76]See Otto Guttentag, On the Clinical Entity, *Annals of Internal Medicine*, 1949, vol. 31, p. 490, and Two Diagrams on the Clinical Entity, *The Journal of Pediatrics*, 1950, vol. 37, pp. 530–534.

[77]Thus the empiricists reinterpreted Hippocrates; see Karl Deichgräber, *Die griechische Empirikerschule*, Berlin, Weidmann, 1930, p. 319. The *Epidemics* are, of course, not the only Hippocratic work where disease is seen as a process; see e.g. the writing *On the Sacred Disease* which gives a complete pathogenesis culminating in the idea of the *kairos in treatment*. This shows how closely related etiological and prognostic writings could be (see p. 147).

[78]Soranus, *Gynaecia* I, 3, ed. I. Ilberg, 1927, p. 4, 19 (*Corpus Medicorum Graecorum*, IV).

[79]This holds good in principle; individually a good leech might have been a better practitioner than a theorizing physician.

philosophy. In the booklet bearing that title,[80] Galen claims that the majority of physicians, though would-be admirers of Hippocrates, do nothing to emulate him. They study neither astronomy nor its basic science, geometry, and even despise those who do so. They are ignorant of anatomy and think it useless to divide diseases into species and genera. They are so lacking in prognostic skill that "if anybody foretells a hemorrhage or a sweat, they call him a sorcerer and a narrator of marvels."[81] They are hardly able to ordain the sick man's regimen with a view to the future climax of the disease. Finally, they cannot even explain things properly.

It is not without interest that Galen thinks that the majority admire Hippocrates and, as he says, "declare him to be the first of all." *Hoi polloi* are not philosophical opponents to science but practical men who cannot be bothered. For this reason Galen does not simply admonish the physician to devote himself to scientific studies. The prerequisite for such study is a contempt for money. The true physician must have a balanced mind and follow truth. He must practice the logical method to know how many diseases there are as to species and genera and how to find the therapeutic indication for each. The same method will teach him the composition of the body of elements, tissues, and organic parts, and will be needed to prove things concerning the use and function of each part. "What then remains that the physician worthy of Hippocrates in his practice of the art be a philosopher? If, in order to discover the nature of the body, the difference of diseases, and the indications of treatment he must be trained in the theory of logic, if in order to practice these things diligently and steadfastly he must disdain money and must exercise self control, then indeed he has all the parts of philosophy: logic, natural science, and ethics."[82] At the end of the booklet, Galen says it would be foolish to argue over words. But as a matter of fact, his ideal physician is a limited philosopher, a man who is interested in ethics and science, and in logic because it is a tool for the latter.

Certain agnostic and eclectic trends in Galen's thought have long been obvious[83] and have received further confirmation from Galen's Synopsis of Plato's *Timaeus,* preserved in Arabic translation and quite recently published by Kraus and Walzer. Galen knows that Plato and Aristotle ascribe divinity to the stars, but he does not mention it. Likewise, he does not confirm, on his part, that the world has a soul.[84] This goes well together with his consistent refusal to pronounce on the essence of the human soul

---

[80]I used the edition by Ernst Wenkebach, Der hippokratische Arzt als das Ideal Galens, *Quellen u. Studien zur Geschichte d. Naturwissenschaften und der Medizin,* 1933, vol. 3, pp. 363–383. For a French translation see Ch. Daremberg, *Oeuvres anatomiques, physiologiques et médicales de Galien,* vol. 1, Paris, 1854, pp. 1–7.

[81]*Ibid.,* p. 379, 8 f.

[82]*Ibid.,* p. 382, 8–13.

[83]Eduard Zeller, *Die Philosophie der Griechen in ihrer geschichtlichen Entwicklung dargestellt,* 3. Theil, 1. Abtheilung. Dritte Auflage, Leipzig, 1880, p. 830 f.

[84]*Galeni Compendium Timaei Platonis* etc. edd. Paulus Kraus et Richardus Walzer, Londinii, 1951 (*Plato Arabus,* vol. 1), p. 13.

and the question of its immortality. "To know this," Galen states elsewhere, "is not necessary for the healing of diseases or the preservation of health; nor for ethical, practical and political philosophy. Indeed every one may call the latter as he wishes, separating it from theoretical philosophy."[85] Kraus and Walzer conclude that in cosmology and psychology, Galen tended towards the view of the sceptics.[86] I do not wish to argue the formal correctness of this statement. But I would think that Galen's indifference to contemplative philosophy is tinged by his being a physician. The physician must be a philosopher in so far as philosophy represents science and ethics; science will give him an understanding of nature and disease. Ethics will give him the attitude he needs to be a student of nature, and a guide for men whom he is to treat by diet, i.e. by regulating their way of life. And ethics, in Galen's mind, demands recognition of a divine providence.[87] Thus Galen can even admit that the immediate practical value of anatomy for the physician is limited, and can yet cultivate anatomy and physiology as studies which reveal nature and thus glorify God.[88]

We can now sum up by returning to our original problem. Having given a brief sketch of its history, we asked whether Greek medicine as a whole really followed the development mirrored in the books of its physician authors, or whether as a craft it might not have remained unchanged? Our answer was that Greek leechcraft, unaided by science or broad generalizing concepts may always have existed. But we suggested that, however great his skill, the mere leech was inferior to the physician whose philosophical in-debtedness expressed itself by his membership in one of the sects. We may imagine a broad stratum of practical men between the leaders whose ideas the literature reflects, and the practitioner bound by mere tradition. But even the latter will not have remained entirely unaffected by the thought trickling down to him; in this sense I believe that the literature from Hip-pocrates to Galen, incomplete as it is, contains the essential history of Greek medicine. And to this we may add an epilogue. In the Greek East, the date of Galen's death coincides with the end of the empiric and methodist sects. By the middle of the fourth century Galen has emerged as the great medi-cal authority next only to Hippocrates, and his true heir. From now on there is only one medical science, based on just those parts of philosophy which Galen accepted. And since, moreover, this science at an increasing rate is acquired from books, the break is prepared between the mere craftsman, the mechanic, and the learned doctor. In antiquity this break was never complete within the medical profession. Even the most learned

---

[85]Kühn edition, vol. 4, p. 764; the passage is quoted by Kraus and Walzer, *op. cit.*, p. 15, footnote 4. See also Zeller, *loc. cit.*

[86]*Op. cit.*, p. 15.

[87]*De placitis Hippocratis et Platonis,* IX, chs. 7 and 8 (ed. I. Mueller, Lipsiae, 1874, especially pp. 799 ff.).

[88]*On the Use of Parts,* XVII, 1. Galen claims that the search for the usefulness of parts constitutes the principle of a perfect theology which is of greater importance than all medicine. I think that this statement has to be understood in connection with Galen's pragma-tic evaluation of "theology" as indicated in *De placitis Hippocratis et Platonis, loc. cit.*

physician was still expected to have acquired the necessary skill and practical insight. But together with the systematization of Galen a tradition of medical science was formed that was to influence deeply the Latin West, even beyond the Middle Ages. The doctor is expected to have studied logic, he is to know astronomy, which often means astrology, and the study of human anatomy and physiology are integral parts of medicine, as are pathology, hygiene, and therapeutics. The transmittal of that tradition to the West transformed the physician of 400 B.C. into a physicus in the literal sense, while the craftsman found his own way of life in the guild.

9

On Galen's
Pneumatology*

As IS WELL KNOWN, Galen believed that the soul had three divisions to each of which a special anatomical seat could be allocated. He devoted his work *On the dogmas of Hippocrates and Plato* to the proof that the divine soul with which man thinks dwells in the brain, while passion (especially wrath) and desires have their principles in the heart and liver respectively. To this psychological division corresponds a physiological one. The brain houses the psychic spirit (πνεῦμα ψυχικόν) and forms the origin of the nerves which conduct sensations as well as voluntary impulses. From the heart the arteries containing blood and vital spirit (πνεῦμα ζωτικόν) depart, regulating the innate heat of the body and nourishing the psychic pneuma. The liver is the main organ of hematopoiesis and also the origin of the veins which carry nourishment to the rest of the body.

In its broad outlines, this sketch of the Galenic doctrine as far as the tripartite soul and its faculties are concerned, can be amply documented by references to some of Galen's fundamental works. It is equally true that the terms "pneuma" in general and "psychic spirit" and "vital spirit" in particular are frequently used by Galen. He may have accepted this terminology from Erasistratus who, as Galen writes, "says that the psychic spirit proceeds from the brain, the vital spirit from the heart."[1] As to the details of the sketch, they require many amplifications and qualifications. We shall discuss a few of them here, taking our starting point from the question: did Galen also assume the existence of a "natural spirit" (πνεῦμα φυσικόν) as a well defined third kind of pneuma?

In their outlines of the Galenic system, most of our textbooks give conventional sanction to the "natural spirit." It is supposed to have its seat in liver and veins in analogy to the psychic spirit of brain and nerves, and the vital spirit of the heart and arteries. It is true, of course, that Greek medicine, especially of the pneumatic school, knew of a natural spirit. Thus the pseudo-Galenic *Medical definitions* speak of a natural spirit in veins and arteries.[2] But this work reflects a system, according to which there are three forms of spirit: "Hexis," "Physis," and "Soul."[3] This system was influenced

---

Gesnerus (Aarau: H. R. Sauerländer & Co.), 1951, vol. 8, pp. 180–189.
[1] *De placitis Hippocratis et Platonis*, rec. I. Mueller, vol. 1, Lipsiae 1874, p. 245, 10–3. On the pneumatology of Erasistratus cf. G. Verbeke, *L'évolution de la doctrine du pneuma du stoïcisme à S. Augustin*, Paris–Louvain 1945, pp. 177–91.

[2] *Definitiones medicae*, nos. 73 and 74 (*Galeni Opera omnia*, ed. Kühn, vol. 19, p. 365). See also further below, note 33.

[3] Cf. *ibid.*, definitions 29, 95 and 96 (ed. Kühn, pp. 355, 371 and 372). See also Verbeke, *op. cit.*, p. 192f. On the chronology and provenience from the pneumatic school of the *Definitiones*

by Stoic philosophy, and Galen was neither a Stoic nor a follower of the so-called pneumatic school. As a matter of fact, some students of ancient pneumatology, e.g., Verbeke[4], do not mention the natural spirit at all in their discussion of Galen's views. Drabkin, on the other hand, has briefly stated that the natural spirit in liver and veins, though mentioned, had been "hardly incorporated into his system" by Galen and that only later ages had made the system symmetrical.[5] With this statement I find myself in substantial agreement.

In chapter 5 of book 12 of the *Method of treatment*, Galen writes: "Concerning the psychic spirit, we have clearly shown that the brain is its fount, so to speak, and that it is watered and nourished by inspiration and by the supply from the rete mirabile. Concerning the vital spirit, the demonstration has not been equally clear, yet it does not seem unlikely that it is contained in the heart and the arteries and that it too is chiefly nourished by the respiration and also the blood. And if there also is a natural spirit, this again should be contained in the liver and the veins."[6] I must admit that this is the only passage in Galen's work definitely speaking of the natural spirit and its seat in liver and veins with which I am so far acquainted.

Now it seems remarkable that Galen expresses himself so cautiously not only about the natural spirit, but the vital spirit as well. Yet there are ample references in his writings where Galen attaches no doubt to the existence of a vital spirit.[7] He seems to connect it with the "inborn pneuma"[8] which has to be sustained by external air. In the lungs the inhaled air is digested as food is in the liver. Through the pulmonary veins this product reaches the heart. Here as well as in the arteries it is further assimilated and transported to the various parts of the body. For special purposes, however, additional refinement is needed, above all for the nourishment of the psychic pneuma. The arteries of the rete mirabile serve this purpose which is realized in the ventricles of the brain.[9]

---

medicae see Max Wellmann, *Die pneumatische Schule*, Berlin 1895, p. 65 ff. The English reader will find a good discussion of the pneumatic views in Sir T. Clifford Allbutt's *Greek medicine in Rome*, London 1921, p. 224ff.

[4]See above, note 1.

[5]Morris R. Cohen and I. E. Drabkin, *A Source Book in Greek Science*, New York, McGraw–Hill Book Co., 1948, p. 486.

[6]Galen, *Methodus medendi*, XII, ch. 5; ed. Kühn, vol. 10, p. 839f.: τοῦ μὲν δὴ ψυχικοῦ πνεύματος ἐναργῶς ἐδείξαμεν οἷον πηγήν τινα οὖσαν τὸν ἐγκέφαλον,ἀρδομένου καὶ τρεφομένου διά τε τῆς εἰσπνοῆς καὶ τῆς ἐκ τοῦ δικτυοειδοῦς πλέγματος χορηγίας. τοῦ δὲ ζωτικοῦ πνεύματος οὐχ ὁμοίως μὲν ἐναργῶς ἡ ἀπόδειξις ἦν, οὐ μὴν ἀπίθανόν γε κατά τε τὴν καρδίαν αὐτὸ καὶ τὰς ἀρτηρίας δοκεῖν περιέχεσθαι, τρεφόμενον καὶ τοῦτο μάλιστα μὲν ἐκ τῆς ἀναπνοῆς, ἤδη δὲ καὶ τοῦ αἵματος. εἰ δέ ἐστί τι καὶ φυσικὸν πνεῦμα, περιέχοιτ᾽ ἂν καὶ τοῦτο κατά τε τὸ ἦπαρ καὶ τὰς φλέβας.

[7]E.g. *De placitis Hippocratis et Platonis*, book 7, p. 604: τὸ μὲν οὖν κατὰ τὰς ἀρτηρίας καὶ τὴν καρδίαν πνεῦμα ζωτικόν ἐστί τε καὶ προσαγορεύεται . . . p. 605: . . . τὸ ζωτικὸν πνεῦμα . . . τὴν ὕλην ἔχον τῆς γενέσεως ἔκ τε τῆς εἰσπνοῆς καὶ τῆς τῶν χυμῶν ἀναθυμιάσεως . . .

[8]*De usu partium*, rec. Georgius Helmreich, 2 vols., Lipsiae 1907–1909. See book 7, ch. 8; vol. 1, p. 392, 20f.: τῷ συμφύτῳ πνεύματι.

[9]*Ibid.*, p. 393f.; also book 9 ch. 4 (vol. 2, p. 12f.).

This picture of the seat and nourishment of the vital pneuma agrees with Galen's description of the heart as "the principle of the entire life,"[10] and the "home and fount of the innate heat by which the animal is supported."[11] Moreover, it agrees with the then customary designation of the left ventricle as the "pneumatic cavity."[12] Nor is it difficult to understand how the blood itself could also provide nourishment for the vital spirit. In his discussion with the followers of Erasistratus, Galen had made it abundantly clear that the arteries were not void of blood. And the arterial blood, as he did not tire of repeating, was fine and vaporous;[13] it could, therefore, easily nourish the vital spirit; Galen even suggested that the psychic spirit was an exhalation from useful blood.[14]

But the discussion with the followers of Erasistratus also brought him to the point where the above picture becomes obscured. This sect argued that, under normal circumstances, the arteries contained nothing but pneuma, the blood being restricted to the veins. Only under pathological conditions did blood enter the arteries through anastomoses with the veins. In his attempt to prove that in health too the arteries carried blood, Galen minimized the role of the pneuma in the arteries. Very little, if anything at all, of the inspired air reaches the heart, for we need a quality rather than a substance from the air.[15] Ligatures tied around the carotid arteries leave the animal breathing and moving, which proves that the brain is not in great need of the pneuma from the heart.[16] The psychic pneuma receives the bulk of its nourishment from respiration through the nose—an allusion to the theory of the ventilation of the anterior cerebral ventricles through an alleged communication with the nose.[17] Above all, in lesions of arteries no pneuma can be seen escaping. "As the blood in the arteries is relatively warm, so it is also relatively vaporous. However, no vapor, air, ether, or any pneuma at all appear to be contained in it as such."[18] In other words, there is no free pneuma in the arteries but only an admixture in the arterial blood.[19] It seems that in view of his own qualifications Galen was right in saying that the existence of a vital pneuma was not proved beyond doubt. Even if it was said that the pneumatic ingredient of the arterial blood constituted the vital pneuma, this ingredient was hardly a specific one, for the venous blood too contained pneuma.

[10]*Ibid.*, book 13, ch. 10; vol. 2, p. 269, 17: ἡ καρδία δ'ἀρχὴ τῆς συμπάσης ζωῆς.

[11]*Ibid.*, book 6, ch. 7; vol. 1, p. 318, 15–7.

[12]*Ibid.*, p. 318, 20–2. Of course Galen believed that the left ventricle contained blood too.

[13]See below.

[14]*Ibid.*, book 6, ch. 17; vol. 1, p. 361, 17–8. He seems here to have in mind arterial blood.

[15]*An in arteriis natura sanguis contineatur*, ch. 6; ed. Kühn, vol. 4, p. 725; *De usu respirationis*, ch. 3, *ibid.*, p. 484.

[16]*De usu respirationis*, ch. 5, *ibid.*, p. 503.

[17]*Ibid.*, p. 504 and *De usu partium*, book 8, ch. 10.

[18]*An in arteriis natura sanguis contineatur*, ch. 2; ed. Kühn, vol. 4, p. 707. And yet he claimed that the superficial arteries near the skin attracted external air and he differentiated between pneuma, vapor, and refined blood; see *On the natural faculties*, book 3, ch. 14, ed. A. J. Brock (Loeb Classical Library), p. 316. See also below, note 36.

[19]See J. Prendergast, *Galen's view of the vascular system in relation to that of Harvey*, Proc. Roy. Soc. Med., vol. 21, 1928, p. 1846.

On occasion Galen gives his reader the impression that the venous blood from the liver is not supposed to contain pneuma at all, in contrast to the arterial blood from the left ventricle of the heart.[20] But such extreme formulations can be counterbalanced by many references which, in the aggregate, weaken considerably the difference between composition and function of the venous blood, on the one hand, and the arterial, on the other.

The veins serve the main purpose of anadosis, i. e., transportation of proper nourishment to the organs. The chyle from the gastrointestinal tract reaches the veins of the portal system where it appears as crude blood. The main process of hematopoiesis is effected in the liver, the supposed origin of the veins,[21] which now offer to each part what it will attract, hold, assimilate, and eliminate by means of the natural faculties. In addition, the veins contain pneuma from three main sources. In the first place, the veins take the vaporous and useful part of the winds developed in the abdomen.[22] In the second place, the juices of chyle and blood can and do exhale some pneuma, so that even the psychic pneuma, to a small extent, may be engendered from the veins in the cerebral ventricles.[23] This is of importance in as far as the pneumatic content of the venous blood can substitute for the vital pneuma of the arteries. At any rate, the blood in the veins to some extent is vaporous; for its "thinnest and most vaporous" portion is attracted by the arteries through their anastomoses with the veins.[24] The arterial blood in turn, through these anastomoses forms a third source of pneuma for the veins. "The arteries and veins form synastomoses in the whole body (i.e., where the walls of the two kinds of blood vessels border upon each other[25]) and accept from each other blood and pneuma through some invisible and perfectly narrow paths."[26] The role which the pores in the intraventricular septum of the heart are supposed to play in this respect is too well known to need any comment. It is only necessary to add that in Galen's opinion the arteries which reach the intestines on their part also absorb a little food[27] in order to see the far-reaching parallel between arterial and venous blood. Neither of the two is without a pneumatic ingredient; the difference is one of degree. Whereas blood and pneuma are fine and thin in the arteries, they are crude and "smoky" in the veins. And whereas the arterial blood has a large pneumatic component, the latter is much smaller in the veins.[28] Just because the difference is only one of degree, both arteries and veins can supply the organs with food. Generally

[20]E.g., *De placitis Hippocratis et Platonis,* book 6, p. 566f.

[21]*De usu partium,* book 4, ch. 12.

[22]*Ibid.,* book 4, ch. 9; vol. 1, p. 214.

[23]*De placitis Hippocratis et Platonis,* book 3, p. 326, 4–6.

[24]*On the natural faculties,* book 3, ch. 14; ed. Brock, p. 316.

[25] *De usu partium,* book 6, ch. 17; vol. 1, p. 361, 2–5.

[26]*Ibid.,* book 6, ch. 10; vol. 1, p. 332, 14–7.

[27]*On the natural faculties,* book 3, chs. 13 (p. 308), 14 (p. 316f.), 15 (p. 318). *De usu partium,* book 4, ch. 17; vol. 1, p. 241, 25f.

[28]See e.g., *De usu partium,* book 6, ch. 16; vol. 1, p. 358, 5–9.

speaking, the organs take thinner food from the arteries, thicker food from the veins.[29] In particular, the nature of the organ will decide the kind of blood needed.[30] The spongy spleen shows a wide ramification of large arteries and the lungs receive blood from the right ventricle of the heart where it has assumed an almost arterial character.[31] The liver, on the other hand, has small arteries chiefly for cooling purposes. They do not absorb blood from the liver, nor do they have to feed its tissues with thin and vaporous food, "nor do they have to furnish the liver with much vital pneuma as they do some other organs."[32]

With these last words we are back at the vital spirit and the implied contention that it is carried in the arteries. After what has been said we need not reiterate the difficulties inherent in Galen's concept of the vital spirit; but we may well ask ourselves whether we have learned anything about a natural spirit. Is the latter identical with the pneumatic component of the venous blood? Perhaps. But in that case it would only be an inferior form of the pneuma contained in the arteries. Or as one might say, both veins and arteries carry blood mixed with natural spirit, but the veins have much blood and little vital spirit, whereas the arteries have little and purer blood, and more and thinner natural spirit. This indeed is stated in the pseudo-Galenic *Medical definitions.*[33] But in the Galenic system a natural spirit, as distinctly differentiated from the vital spirit, has little meaning. It has no specific function to fulfill, and, to the best of my knowledge, it is not mentioned in Galen's basic physiological works, viz., *On the dogmas of Hippocrates and Plato, On the natural faculties,* and *On the use of parts.* If this is true, we have to ask ourselves why Galen mentioned the natural spirit at all, in view of his obvious doubts. To answer this question we have to return to the passage in the *Method of treatment* and interpret it in the context of the chapter in which it occurs.

In this chapter Galen continues his discussion of syncope, which had been defined as an acute collapse of the faculties. The substance[34] of our faculties consists in the pneuma and the temperament of the solids. Galen makes some general remarks about this substance in the light of disease and therapy. The substance of the pneuma and the solid parts have to be

---

[29]*Ibid.*, book 4, ch. 15; vol. 1, p. 234, 3–8.

[30]*Ibid.*, book 6, ch. 10; vol. 1, p. 328, 11 ff.

[31]*Ibid.*, book 4, ch. 15. The arteries in the spleen also serve the additional function of altering the thick juice which the spleen receives from the liver through their pulsation and conveyance of heat from the heart.

[32]*Ibid.*, book 4, ch. 13; vol. 1, p. 225, 25f.

[33]Pseudo-Galen, *Definitiones medicae,* 73 and 74 (ed. Kühn, vol. 19, p. 365f.): (73) Φλέψ ἐστιν ἀγγεῖον αἵματος καὶ τοῦ συγκεκραμένου τῷ αἵματι φυσικοῦ πνεύματος . . . ἔχει δὲ πλεῖον τὸ αἷμα,ὀλιγώτερον δὲ τὸ ζωτικὸν πνεῦμα. (74) Ἀρτηρία ἐστὶν ἀγγεῖον αἵματος ἐλάττονος καὶ καθαρωτέρου καὶ τοῦ συγκεκραμένου φυσικοῦ πνεύματος πλείονος καὶ λεπτομερεστέρου . . . There remains the possibility that the end of definition 73 (ἔχει . . . πνεῦμα) may be a gloss, added as a parallel to another definition (no. 74, p. 366) according to which the artery carries vital spirit from the heart. This second definition seems Erasistratean in character. If this is true, then nos. 73 and 74 are a mixture of pneumatic and Erasistratean concepts.

[34]*Methodus medendi,* book 12, ch. 5; ed. Kühn, vol. 10, p. 837. ἡ οὐσία whereby Galen means the material substratum.

preserved so that they remain normal as far as possible in quality as well as quantity. However, the best one can do is to replace the loss of substance and to set aright a deviation from the well tempered condition. From such considerations Galen is led to make the statement quoted above about the psychic, vital and natural spirits.[35] "However," he adds, "we have discussed at very great length the substance of the faculties in the (work) on the dogmas of Hippocrates and Plato." He now turns to the substance and temperament of the solid parts of the body, and then comes back to the pneuma. This, he says, can be altered by vicious humors and the badness of the surrounding air, and besides by noxious potencies or the poison of venomous animals. The corruption of the substance of the pneuma can be due to psychic affection, severe pain, and too much movement (sleeplessness also belongs here), by exceeding thinness of the pneuma and porosity of the bodies containing it and, above all, by stoppage of breathing and want of food. All these demand careful correction. Psychic affections, in which the soul moves itself, are: sudden and vehement fear as well as very great joy (if they do not kill, they can at least render the pneuma exhausted and weak), grief, anguish, anger, worry, and much sleeplessness. There are also the active functions where the soul moves the body—in either event immoderate movements weaken the strength of the soul. Excessive pain (or work?) harms everybody. In all such cases the patients are weakened; some even die, be it that the pneuma is destroyed, be it that it is altered and sometimes partially dispersed—often both. The details of the manner by which damage is brought about, Galen says, need not be gone into here, but the very fact of the damage is important for the preservation of strength in disease. When the substance of the spirits which control us is rarified beyond the normal, it becomes weak, altered in its temperament, and easily dispersed. In the same manner, if the whole body has changed to immoderate porousness, the substance of the spirits is easily dispersed since it is now composed of thin particles and since the body does not support it. Therefore, one must neither unduly rarify the body of the patient if one intends to keep the pneuma within it, nor must one vigorously attenuate the content of the body by what is eaten and drunk. Morever, one must not only heed food and drink but also pay attention to the temperament and purity of the inhaled air. (The rest of the chapter deals with the solids and with details in the treatment of syncope.)

From this paraphrase we hardly learn anything new about the nature of the vital or natural spirit. The references to air and respiration, humors, food and drink do not carry us beyond what we already know. Nevertheless, two things do stand out. There is, first of all, the fact that Galen very often speaks of "the pneuma" in general and even where he uses the plural, "the spirits" are not specified. On the other hand, the detailed reference to psychic affections agrees very well with Galen's assured opinion of the psychic spirit and, to a lesser degree, vital spirit too.

---

[35]See text and above, footnote 6.

The existence of pneuma within the body as a requisite of animal life is a basic tenet of Galen's biological and medical doctrine. Equally basic is the assumption of one specific category of the pneuma, viz. the psychic spirit. It is the indispensable organ of the rational soul and the medium by which the function of the senses as well as nerves can be explained. Once the psychic spirit is acknowledged as a category, the remaining pneuma must also be accounted for. Life depends on respiration. Thus a special vital spirit is connected with the respiratory organs which in Galen's physiology include heart and arteries. But since the pneuma as such is really essential for life, the notion of a special vital spirit loses in clarity and Galen wavers between dogmatic affirmation and vagueness. Any further specification is really unessential.[36] It may be that there are passages in Galen's writings, preserved or lost, where he expresses himself more precisely about the natural spirit. At present I should like to make the following tentative suggestion. The term "natural spirit" was current at Galen's time. Tradition even had it that the ancients had assumed two spirits, the psychic and the natural.[37] He himself believed in the existence of pneuma in the venous blood. Thus he mentioned the natural spirit as a possibility at least. If it existed it had to be assigned a center. The liver, as a compact organ, was not altogether a suitable seat for any pneumatic substance. However, it was the seat of the concupiscent soul and of the natural faculty,[38] and the origin of the veins. If a natural spirit existed, it should have its seat in the liver. But the canonization of the three spirits came later. The Alexandrians and their heirs, the Syro-Arabic physicians, found it necessary to simplify and concentrate the older doctrines, especially Galen's profuse and often contradictory views. In the *Isagoge* of Joannitius[39] (Hunain ibn Ishaq) we read under the heading "De spiritibus": "Thus there are three spirits: first the natural which takes its origin from the liver; second the vital from the heart; and third the psychic from the brain. Of these the first is diffused from the liver over the whole body through the veins which have no pulse. The second is directed

[36]Galen can even contrast the psychic spirit with "all other spirits" (*De usu partium*, book 16, ch. 10; vol. 2, p. 420, 18/9). I do not believe that this refers necessarily to the vital and natural spirit since "pneuma" is a very general term. Even the stomach contains pneuma (*Natural faculties*, book 3, ch. 7, ed. Brock, p. 254). Although Galen at times distinguishes between pneuma and vapor in the arteries (see *ibid.*, book 3, ch. 15; p. 330), it is hard to tell where the distinguishing line should be drawn.

[37]Pseudo-Galen, *Introductio seu medicus*, ch. 9; ed. Kühn, vol. 14, p. 697: πνεύματα δὲ κατὰ τοὺς παλαιοὺς δύο ἐστί, τό τε ψυχικὸν καὶ τὸ φυσικόν. οἱ δὲ Στοικοὶ καὶ τρίτον εἰσάγουσι τὸ ἐκτικόν, ὃ καλοῦσιν ἕξιν. As to the psychic pneuma, Max Wellmann, *Die Fragmente der sikelischen Ärzte* etc., Berlin 1901, p. 137 (no. 44) and 142 (no. 59) gives two fragments in which Diocles of Carystus uses the term. Since the so-called Anonymus Parisinus is the doxographic source for these statements, Werner Jaeger, *Diokles von Karystos*, Berlin 1938, p. 215, has suggested that the term ψυχικὸν πνεῦμα may be due to later usage. With regard to Hippocratic works, such a reinterpretation can be proved. Thus in the discussion of epilepsy the Anonymus makes the author of *On the Sacred disease* speak of the psychic pneuma where the latter merely refers to inhaled air; cf. O. Temkin, *Epilepsy in an anonymous Greek work on acute and chronic diseases*, Bull. Hist. Med., vol. 4, 1936, p. 143.

[38]Galen, *Synopsis librorum suorum de pulsibus*, ch. 21; ed. Kühn, vol. 9, p. 492: ... τρίτην τὴν φυσικὴν (sc. δύναμιν) ὀνομαζομένην, ἧς ἀρχὴ τὸ ἧπάρ ἐστιν.

[39]I have used the text of the *Articella*, ed. Venice, 1491.

from the heart into the whole body by the arteries. And the third is directed from the brain into the whole body by the nerves. . . ." Here indeed we have the complete triadic formula as a theoretical axiom of medicine.

Our discussion of Galen's pneumatology, brief as it is, may yet allow us to end on a more general note. In the course of our analysis we have assembled passages which show Galen's opinions under different and divergent aspects. The mere fact that this can be done demonstrates the relative weakness of systematic concentration in Galen's writings. Galen has pronounced views to which he clings persistently. But it was in the philosophical and dialectic nature of ancient science that details were often worked out in argumentation against views of others. Galen's emphasis shifted according to the point he wished to make or the view he wished to combat. This does not mean that the niceties of his opinions cannot possibly be reconciled. But it does mean that such reconciliation, if attempted, needs elaborate interpretation. Thus the Galenic "system" of the late Alexandrian commentators and their heirs arises side by side with the Aristotelian systems of their philosophical colleagues.[40] The endurance of this scholastic interpretation speaks best for its quality, but it also has to be taken into account in our approach to Galen's thought.

[40]For the parallel activities of Aristotelian and Galenic commentators in late Alexandria see O. Temkin, *Geschichte des Hippokratismus im ausgehenden Altertum,* Kyklos, vol. 4, 1932, p. 43. I mention this parallel here again because the question arises whether divergent views in Galen's works can be explained by a development similar to the one shown for Aristotle by Werner Jaeger. In some important matter Galen did change his opinions, for instance with regard to the temporal relationship of liver and heart in embryological development (Galen, *De foetuum formatione libellus,* ch. 3; ed. Kühn, vol. 4, p. 662). Many more examples of this sort could undoubtedly be found in his works. On the other hand, his works are too well interconnected to make an explanation of all divergencies on this basis likely.

10

A Galenic Model
for Quantitative Physiological
Reasoning?*

INSTANCES of a quantitative approach to physiological problems are not very numerous in Greek physiology.[1] In the following example, Galen draws inferences from the urinary output to the activity of the kidneys. The example occurs in chapter seventeen of the first book of Galen's treatise *On the Natural Faculties*. It has received relatively little attention, though it is all the more interesting because its reasoning suggests a certain structural similarity with Harvey's calculation in support of the circulation of the blood.

Among the fundamental faculties *(dynameis)* of nature Galen counts the faculty of the bodily parts to attract, for nutritional purposes, what is appropriate for them.[2] For his belief in this attractive faculty he claims the authority of Hippocrates.[3] In particular, the formation of urine by the kidneys presupposes that the kidneys attract the thin, serous part of the venous blood.[4] According to Galen, any theory of urine formation which dispenses with the attractive faculty can be proved to be impossible,[5] a proof which he attempts in chapters 13–17 of Book I of *On the Natural Faculties*.

He first deals with Asclepiades, who altogether denied the kidneys a role in the production of urine. In a series of famous animal experiments Galen shows the errors of Asclepiades and his followers.[6] Having disposed of Asclepiades and other atomists, Galen offers as the only alternative to

*Bull. Hist. Med., 1961, vol. 35, pp. 470–475.
[1]Richard H. Shryock, "The history of quantification in medical science," *Isis*, 1961, 52: 215–37, and Owsei Temkin, "Nutrition from classical antiquity to the Baroque," *Human Nutrition, Historic and Scientific*, ed. Iago Galdston, New York: International Universities Press, Inc., 1960, pp. 78–97 (see p. 87).
[2]Galen, *On the Natural Faculties*, I, xii, 28, and 29 f.; pp. 44 f. and 48. Page references are to the edition of the Loeb Classical Library, where the Greek text is accompanied by the English translation of Arthur John Brock. In quoting from this work of Galen's I have utilized Brock's translation with changes where my understanding of the Greek text seemed to require them.
[3]*Ibid.*, I, xii, 29; p. 46 f. and I, xiii, 38; p. 60.
[4]*Ibid.*, I, xv, 58 f.; pp. 90 and 92. In bk. IV, ch. 5, of *De usu partium*, Galen explains the necessity for the presence of a thin and aqueous humor in the vena cava; bk. V., ch. 5, declares it the function of the kidneys to relieve the blood of all serous liquid, while the following chapter (6) relates that the kidneys must feed on this fluid. For the Greek text see Galen, *De usu partium libri XVII*, rec. G. Helmreich, 2 vols., Leipzig: Teubner, 1907–1909, vol I, pp. 199, 268, and 272.
[5]*On the Natural Faculties*, I, xv, 60; p. 92.
[6]*Ibid.*, I, xiii, 36–38; p. 58 f. See also Morris R. Cohen and I. E. Drabkin, *A Source Book in Greek Science*, New York, McGraw-Hill Book Co., 1948, p. 480 ff., and K. D. Keele, "Three

attractive action the propulsion of the blood to the kidneys, where the thin part would be filtered through as urine and the thick part retained.[7] This alternative too is declared impossible,[8] so that, in principle, the theory of attraction is the only remaining one. Nevertheless, Galen takes issue with Erasistratus and his followers: with the former for not having stated *how* the kidneys secreted urine,[9] with the latter for having suggested impossible explanations.[10]

The Erasistrateans, he claims, maintained a percolation of the watery part of the blood through the kidneys, this part (in contrast to the pure blood) allegedly being heavy enough to run downwards to the kidneys.[11] This view was given up by the Erasistrateans themselves, who then suggested that the serous part of the blood was diverted to the kidneys from the rest of the blood, because the two components separated like a mixture of oil and water. Galen parries with the obvious question why the serous fluid should flow into the renal veins, rather than into the other branches of the vena cava.[12]

With the disposal of the above two theories of the Erasistrateans there remains but one, "the worst doctrine of all, lately invented by Lycus of Macedonia," an anatomist and physician who probably lived in the early part of the second century[13] and had connections with the Erasistrateans.[14] "This Lycus," Galen writes, "declares, as though uttering an oracle from an inner sanctuary, that urine is *residual matter from the nutrition of the kidneys!*"[15] This assertion, repeated by Galen elsewhere,[16] is all we know of Lycus' theory of urine formation.

To understand Galen's subsequent reasoning we must proceed from the following assumptions: Both Lycus and Galen agreed that the urine was derived from the kidneys. Both were aware of the need of the parts of the body to nourish themselves and of the existence of what we would call metabolic processes in them, leading to the excretion of residual matter. But whereas Galen assumed that the kidneys attracted the watery and thin

---

early masters of experimental medicine—Erasistratus, Galen and Leonardo da Vinci," *Proc. Roy. Soc. Med.*, Section Hist. Med., July 1961, 54: 577–88.

[7]*On the Natural Faculties*, I, xv, 57; p. 88.

[8]*Ibid.;* p. 90 ff. Galen's argument is here vitiated by his ignorance of the systemic circulation, though he expressly allowed the renal arteries to carry blood to the kidneys, *De usu partium*, V, 5; ed. Helmreich, p. 268.

[9]*On the Natural Faculties*, I, xvi, 64; p. 98.

[10]*Ibid.*, I, xvii; p. 104 ff.

[11]*Ibid.*, I, xvii, 68; p. 106.

[12]*Ibid.*, I, xvii, 70; p. 108.

[13]On Lycus see the article by Kind in Pauly-Wissowa, *Real-Encyclopädie der classischen Altertumswissenschaft*, 13. Band, Stuttgart, 1927, cols. 2408–17.

[14]*Ibid.*, col. 2417.

[15]*On the Natural Faculties*, I, xvii, 70; p. 108.

[16]*De usu partium*, v, 5; ed. Helmreich, p. 268: "Yet if urine is residual matter of the nutrition of the kidneys—indeed Lycus the Macedonian reached such a point of ignorance as to approve even this—it is impossible to tell why the demiurge, who does nothing without purpose, implanted such large arteries and veins into the small bodies of the kidneys." The size of these vessels is apportioned to their carrying a large amount of fluid (the watery, thin part of the blood) to the kidneys. Argumentation from the size of blood vessels is not unusual in Galen.

part of the venous blood to find their nourishment and to let the rest pass as urine,[17] Lycus did not have recourse to selective attraction but assumed that the kidneys received the same food as other parts. Galen's argumentation against Lycus tries to show that to think of urine as residue without preceding selective attraction leads to absurdities.

Galen begins by pointing out that

the amount of urine passed every day shows clearly that it is the whole of the fluid drunk which becomes urine, except for that which comes away with the dejections or passes off as sweat or insensible transpiration.[18]

Proof for this assertion lies in the observation of persons carousing in winter and doing no work (so that there is a minimum of sweat) who drink "thin and diffusible" wine (which will be passed quickly). "These people rapidly pass almost the same quantity as they drink."[19]

Thus, under certain conditions, the intake of fluid and the output of urine shortly afterwards may be almost equal. This in itself seems so contradictory to Lycus' theory that Galen ridicules him as true to neither Erasistratus, Asclepiades, nor Hippocrates.[20] Nevertheless, Galen examines Lycus' argument on a broader basis.

Now it is agreed that all parts which are being nourished produce a certain amount of residual matter. But it is neither conceded, nor is it reasonable, that the kidneys alone, small bodies as they are, have four whole congii (about 14 quarts) and sometimes even more, of residual matter.[21] For the residual matter of each of the larger viscera must necessarily be greater: for instance that of the lung, if indeed it is proportionate to the size of the viscus, will doubtlessly be many times that in the kidneys, so that the whole thorax will become filled, and the animal will be suffocated forthwith. But, if somebody says that in each of the other parts the residual matter is produced in like manner,[22] through what kind of bladders is it excreted?[23]

Two points are thus made against the general assumption that urine is the residue of the metabolic process of the kidneys from the venous blood common to all parts: The larger viscera would have to show much more daily residual matter, and all organs would need bladders in analogy to the

---

[17]See the passages referred to in footnote 4, above, especially the end of ch. 6, bk. V, of *De usu partium.*

[18]*On the Natural Faculties,* I, xvii, 70; p. 108: *eis tēn adēlon diapnoēn.* On the meaning of *diapnoē* see Temkin, *op. cit.* (ftn. 1 above); p. 86, ftn.

[19]*Ibid.*, I, xvii, 71; pp. 108–111.

[20]*Ibid.;* p. 110 f.

[21]Fourteen quarts suggests a daily output of urine in diabetes, a disease which Galen assigned to the kidneys as an "atony" of their retentive faculty. In the two cases he encountered "the patients had an unquenchable thirst; they drank without measure and quickly passed as urine the liquid just as they had drunk it." (*De locis affectis,* VI, 3; ed. Kühn, vol. 8, p. 394).

[22]As the apparatus of the edition by Georg Helmreich (Claudii Galeni Pergameni *Scripta minora,* vol. III, Leipzig: Teubner, 1893, p. 153) shows, the manuscripts differ in the reading of this passage. Helmreich changed *isōs* to *ison* and was followed by Brock who translates (p. 111): "But if it be said that the residual matter is equal in amount in each of the other parts. . . ." Such a one-sidedly quantitative interpretation leads to difficulties, since in the following passage Galen assumes that the other viscera do not yield equal amounts.

[23]*On the Natural Faculties,* I, xvii, 71–72; p. 110 f.

kidneys. This is now applied to the earlier observation of the urinary output in a drinking bout, and this output is given a numerical value.

For if the kidneys in drinkers produce three or sometimes four congii of residual matter, there will be many more from each of the other viscera, and thus an enormous barrel will be needed to take the residual matters of all. Yet often a person urinates nearly all he has drunk, as if the entire drink were carried to the kidneys.[24]

Of course, the drink enters the blood and is not carried directly to the kidneys. But, the contrast between its rapid and almost total urinary elimination and the consequence of Lycus' theory which, by inference, postulates a barrelful of residual matter from the other viscera, makes that theory appear all the more absurd.

With the refutation of Lycus, all possible alternatives to Galen's doctrine of the attraction exercised by the kidneys have apparently been rejected, so that Galen's doctrine, the truly Hippocratic one, must be accepted.

I dwell purposely on this topic, knowing well that nobody else has anything to say about the function of the kidneys, but that either we must appear more foolish than the butchers if we do not agree that the urine passes through the kidneys; or if we acknowledge this, that then we cannot possibly give any other reason for the secretion than attraction.[25]

The method of proving one's own views by disproving all other possibilities has particular significance in the case of Lycus, because Galen's argument is based on the observation that the kidneys will quickly produce about 10–14 quarts (3–4 congii) of urine from about the same amount of wine ingested. This output cannot be mere residual matter. In an analogous manner, Harvey was to argue that, based on the estimated capacity of the left ventricle of the heart, the amount of blood propelled into the aorta in the course of half an hour, or even a day, led to values which could not be explained as derived from the ingesta or assumed as present in the veins at any one moment. The alternatives being excluded, the blood had to circulate.[26]

Obviously, the analogy is not altogether close. Galen's argument against Lycus lacks the conclusiveness and lucidity of Harvey's proof. It is far from clear as to details, and the above analysis can be no more than an attempt at an interpretation. Moreover, Harvey has the great advantage of being right from the modern point of view, whereas both Lycus and Galen are using a framework of biological thought which we no longer share. And, even though Galen may have proved his point against Lycus, the correctness of his own views presupposed in addition the refutation of Asclepiades and the Erasistrateans. Worst of all, the quantitative observation used against Lycus may also be turned against Galen himself. If the urine contains a

[24]*Ibid.*, I, xvii, 72; p. 110 ff.
[25]*Ibid.*, I, xvii, 72–73; p. 112 f.
[26]*De motu cordis*, ch. 9.

large portion of bilious and watery refuse discharged from the kidneys after they have retained the relatively small nourishing part of the blood serum, why then do the kidneys attract so much matter which they do not really need?[27]

Yet when all this has been said, a structural similarity between Galen's and Harvey's reasoning remains. This raises the question whether Harvey may have learned from Galen. There is little reason to doubt that Harvey was familiar with *On the Natural Faculties*, a basic medical text around 1600. The occurrence of our example in the book that describes some of Galen's best pieces of physiological experimentation is suggestive enough to allow the possibility of an "influence," perhaps a merely subconscious one. Beyond this, however, we cannot go at present.

[27]Galen is not altogether clear about the formation of urine from the serous blood attracted by the kidneys. *De usu partium*, bk. 4, ch. 6, makes the attracted and emitted fluids both equally thin and watery, whereas book 5, ch. 6 (end) and 7 (beginning), differentiate between blood retained and thin, bilious matter passed. At any rate, as indicated above (see ftns. 18 and 24), Galen must have thought that the kidneys retained an extremely small part for their nourishment.

11

History of Hippocratism
in Late Antiquity: The Third Century
and the Latin West*

T HE FIRST great medical author after Galen was Oribasius, who lived at
the time of the Emperor Julian, i.e., in the second half of the fourth
century.[1] This period between Galen and Oribasius, approximately a century and a half, is one of the most obscure epochs as far as the history of
medicine is concerned, and the reasons for this obscurity are several. It was
a time of unrest, full of internal and external struggles, so that the preconditions for a quiet, scholarly life were as remote as can be imagined. To this,
however, was added the much more serious matter of the period's changing interests. The pagan philosophy and religiosity of the preceding epoch,
eclectic in content, sophist in bearing, could rely on the favor of the broad,
educated public, which participated with interest in scientific discussion
and polemics. But in the third century, intellectual needs underwent a
transformation. The newly rising Neoplatonic philosophy gives evidence of
a repression of rational elements and of an ever increasing eclecticism,
aiming, however, more at satisfying the mystical aspects of life.[2] Yet in all
this, the upper stratum of society, with its still largely pagan culture, was
only reflecting in philosophy what was impelling the broader masses into a
profound religious movement, constantly adding new adherents to the
Mithras cult in the army, to Christianity among the people, especially in the
eastern provinces. These two currents, internally so closely related, also
soon intermingled. To the outward form of pagan philosophy was given
the deep content of Christian religiosity, and the latter adopted the
weapons of philosophy in the battle against other religions and against
heresy. It was historiography that was most severely affected by this
metamorphosis. The events of the third century presented so depressing a
picture that the effect on historians could only be crippling; indeed, there
are hardly any authors of importance, and besides most of the material has
been lost.[3] But when more peaceful times set in with Diocletian and Con-

*"Das 3. Jahrhundert und der lateinische Westen," chapter 2 of "Geschichte des Hippok-
ratismus im ausgehenden Altertum," *Kyklos, Jahrbuch für Geschichte und Philosophie der Medizin*
(Leipzig: Georg Thieme, 1932) 4: 18–28. Translation by C. Lilian Temkin.
[1]Cf. here and in the following pages the usual reference works. For brief accounts of most of
the names mentioned, F. Lübker, *Reallexikon des klassischen Altertums* (Leipzig–Berlin, 1914), is
also useful.
[2]Cf. M. Neuburger, *Geschichte der Medizin* (Stuttgart, 1911), 2:30ff.
[3]Cf. Gercke-Norden,*Einleitung in die Altertumswissenschaft*, 2nd.ed. (Leipzig–Berlin, 1912ff.),
and particularly the contributions of P. Wendland, E. Bethe, and E. Norden in vol. 1.

stantinus, history was of necessity seen in a different light. Since the world had gained a new content, it was this that attracted attention; the greatest historiographers of the following centuries are Christians; they are bishops, they write church history, incorporate political events, tell of philosophical and religious movements; yet medicine is seldom mentioned and then only incidentally.[4] And if one turns to medical literature itself, it is found to be scanty and to yield little information.

The history of medicine of late Antiquity, like the history of this change in culture in general, is usually seen as an aging, a stiffening, a withering away. If Antiquity is looked upon as an unbroken whole, as an isolated phenomenon, this conception is unavoidable. But if one looks at what follows, if the continuously flowing development is kept in mind, the negative judgments become positive ones. If one reminds oneself that the ancient world was outwardly tottering, that quite new thoughts and new feelings were becoming prevalent, if one considers also that men were not unaware of the upheaval around them, their efforts to salvage the tremendous treasures of a great past can be seen as the historical achievement of the first half of the millenium. Then the history of ancient medicine appears in this light: its fundamentals were laid down in the first period, in the sixth, fifth, and fourth centuries B.C.; these were developed further and on a broader basis in Hellenism and, finally, in late Antiquity, the material was worked in such a manner as to make it possible to bequeath it further. Admittedly, for this purpose the material had to be narrowed, to be concentrated and made more easily intelligible. Sacrifices had to be made to ensure the preservation of the essential.

Some of the emperors of the third century were quite well disposed toward culture—at least, some of their decrees compel one to conclude as much. Indeed, for medicine the external possibilities for activity were improved. Public educational institutions were established and even supplied with salaried professors.[5] While there had formerly been no licensure, the development of the institution of the *archiatros* led in this direction; exam-

---

[4]Some accounts are nevertheless interesting, e.g., those of the death of the emperor Maximinus (in Tarsus in 313) in Eusebius, *Ecclesiastical History*, IX, 10–14 (ed. Schwartz-Mommsen [Leipzig, 1903ff.] pp. 844ff.); and Lactantius, *De mort. persecutorum*, c. 49 (ed. Brandt-Laubmann, *Corpus scriptorum ecclesiasticorum latinorum*, vol. 27, fasc. 2 [1897], pp. 233ff.). Cf. E. Stein, *Geschichte des spätrömischen Reiches* (Vienna, 1928), 1:143. In contrast to these broad descriptions, Aurelius Victor is particularly struck by the fact that the emperor died a natural death, rather than by violence (*Hist. Aug. epitome*, p. 633a, in *Hist. Romanae script.* [Geneva, 1623]): "Maximinus apud Tarsum morte simplici periit." We find the same brevity in the statement concerning Galerius, *ibid.*:"Galerius Maximianus consumtis genitalibus defecit." Eusebius, *op. cit.*, VIII, 16, 2ff. (ed. Schwartz, pp. 788ff.) and Lactantius, *op. cit.*, chs. 33–35 (pp. 210ff.) enter into detail. Cf. Stein, *op. cit.*, p. 135.—It was a question of a carcinoma of the genital (penis?). Lanctantius, *loc. cit.* (p. 210, 8): "Nascitur ei ulcus malum in inferiori parte genitalium serpitque latius. medici secant curant," etc. I think Bloch's diagnosis of a phagedenic chancre (in Neuburger-Pagel, *Handbuch der Geschichte der Medizin*, vol. 1, [Jena, 1902], p. 497) very unlikely.

[5]Cf. R. Briau, *L'archiatrie romaine* (Paris, 1877), p. 113; Th. Puschmann, *Geschichte des medicinischen Unterrichts* (Leipzig, 1889), p. 83; although Lampridius, whom both cite as a source, must be used with the greatest caution.

inations and diplomas were given greater weight.[6] On the other hand, nothing of a more exact nature is known concerning the matter or manner of teaching. The silence of the sources invites conjecture. Stable institutions and stable faculties have a tendency to establish stable doctrines which can be handed on. They weaken the necessity for self-assertion through the most original, or original sounding, opinions in the contest of free competition; they focus on the material to be transmitted to the students in the form of certifiable knowledge. Even if the validity of this point of view were not completely admitted, since it cannot be documented, it nevertheless fits in well with the other factors.

The Galenic writings were still echoing with the quarrels of the sects and of individual physicians. Not even the second century, in which opinions had become so interwoven and which seems so eclectic, relinquished the fight. With Galen this note disappears—not permanently, but the difference becomes perceptible as soon as one crosses the threshold of the century. Little is known directly of the further existence of the schools. The Empiricists especially seem to have left the scene—no Empiricist fragments from this period have survived—so one of the most important schools is discounted, and from this negative circumstance we may conclude that eclecticism must have progressed further. Probably the Dogmatists had already gradually been outstripped by the Pneumatists, or, to express it more correctly, Dogmatism had gradually transformed itself more and more into the Pneumatic school. The general impression is that the differences in the schools slowly faded out behind the names. Galen, too, had drawn from many sources, but he had at least attempted to sort things out through his own contributions and systematic selection. But the more time passed, the more is absorbed of what seemed worth accepting from the heritage bequeathed under the great names, and these things were placed side by side. In the process, works attributed to great names and belonging to the more recent past inevitably stepped more into the foreground, especially when they also contained the knowledge of their predecessors. One name from the Greek past was, however, carried by all: that of Hippocrates. The only question was who, among later physicians, was to transmit him, in whose person he was to appear.

Since general historical sources proved unfruitful, the physicians themselves had to be approached. Here, however, similar difficulties are encountered, as in other literature of the period, and two circumstances must be emphasized as of fundamental importance and as valid also for the subsequent centuries. The first concerns the scanty transmission of writings, in part known only from excerpts in later works, particularly Oribasius and Aetius, which has resulted in complete uncertainty as to biographical dates. Apart from a few big names, like Oribasius, Aetius, Alexander of Tralles, Paulus of Aegina, the establishment of most rests on conjecture and conclusions of only limited certainty. In the course of medi-

[6]Cf. Th. Meyer, *Geschichte des römischen Ärztestandes* (Kiel, 1907), pp. 58ff.

cal historiography, few physicians of the period have not been ascribed to quite different centuries, with the result that it is difficult to decide who should be called in as a reliable witness. The second difficulty is still greater. When it is a question of the transmission of later physicians, a comparison of texts permits conclusions as to excerpting and borrowing. Yet the Hippocratic writings have passed through so many hands, have been exploited by almost all younger authors, that an investigation into the extent to which Hippocratic material was taken over directly appears for late Antiquity to be an almost impossible task. The more general and the more uncritical eclecticism becomes, the more difficult is it to sift out the older material. Thus, since analysis of content breaks down, there remains in most cases only the consideration of indirect relationships.

An illustrative example of the first point is to be found in the question of Aretaeus's period of activity. Looked at from the point of view of content, his book, apart from its language and dependence, presents a classic medical writing that can be put on an equal footing with the best works of the Hippocratic Corpus.[7] Compared to the majority of the Hippocratic books, its elaboration in a certain direction is admittedly unmistakable. The best descriptions of disease pictures go back to Aretaeus, descriptions which in some cases, e.g., in pneumonia and pleurisy, are exemplary.[8] He first gives the nosography of acute and chronic diseases, then the therapy. Aretaeus thus embodies most clearly the "Cnidian" tendency to set up firm disease pictures, and in this his concept of disease departs from that of the first and third books of the Hippocratic *Epidemics*.[9] Yet in its way, the nosography is truly classical, and chiefly because of this Aretaeus was formerly placed relatively early.[10] Doubts arose, however. His language is a strange, archaized Ionic which indicates a later period, and above all, the contents showed such extensive agreement with the Pneumatist Archigenes that dependence on him had to be presumed[11]—and on this basis Aretaeus belongs at the earliest to the end of the second century.[12] His book would then constitute an interesting proof of the survival of Pneumatist material—for which many other proofs can be found—and also an important contribution to Pneumatist doctrine. But he could not lay any claim to originality; seen in the context of Hippocratism, he would exemplify the repelling of the old classical literature.

In another Greek author, Philumenos, it is much the same. He appears to have drawn chiefly on Archigenes and Soranus; his dating, too, is not

[7]Neuburger, *op. cit.*, vol. 1, p. 338.

[8]I, ch. 10, and II, ch. 1 (ed. C. Hude, *Corpus medicorum Graecorum*, 2 [Leipzig–Berlin, 1923], pp. 12ff.). [English trans. by F. Adams, *The Extant Works of Aretaeus, the Cappadocian* (London, 1856)].

[9]Cf. my article: "Die Krankheitsauffassung von Hippokrates und Sydenham in ihren 'Epidemien'," *Arch. Gesch. Med.* 20 (1928): 327–52. [Addition: F. Kudlien argues for earlier date.]

[10]Cf. L. Choulant, *Handbuch der Bücherkunde für die ältere Medicin* (Leipzig, 1841), pp. 83ff.

[11]M. Wellmann, *Die pneumatische Schule bis auf Archigenes* (Berlin, 1895), p. 61.

[12]Wellmann, ibid., pp. 63–64; and in Pauly-Wissowa, *Real-Encyclopädie der classischen Altertumswissenschaft*, vol. 2 (1896), cols. 669–70.

quite certain.[13] But if we set these two authors aside, the well-known result is that we run into Latin authors, and with them a quite different kind of development is introduced.

The only author who can with certainty be put into the third century is Gargilius Martialis.[14] The improbability of his having been a physician is supported by the fact that his "Medicina ex oleribus et pomis" is but part of an agricultural work[15] and above all by his sometimes expressing himself in a manner not to be expected of a medical man.[16] Thus, on this account already, he fits into the company of the Latin writers Pliny and Celsus. His work presents a brief materia medica, a simple arrangement of medicinal herbs, giving their therapeutic value and indications for use. Of greater interest than the actual content are, however, the names of the authors cited[17] and, above all, the way in which they are cited; and in this Gargilius Martialis opens up the prospect of what is to come in Latin medical literature and also in the early Middle Ages. "The quotations in Gargilius Martialis himself show us already for the third century the principal authors of materia medica who have remained authoritative, and show them as such, side by side. Of the Greeks, Dioscorides and Galen, and with them *Plinius noster.*"[18] That materia medica stands in the foreground should not be considered a limitation, for it was of particularly great importance in the West in later times.

The three names of the Greeks, Dioscorides and Galen, and of the Roman, Pliny, are significant. Of the three, Galen was the youngest, and in this setting he is separated from the other, older, physicians and counts as one of the "younger" generation.[19] Gargilius Martialis must have had some, perhaps indirect, knowledge of Galenic pharmacology, for he is no stranger to the Galenic way of thinking and, above all, not to his qualitative theory of medicaments.[20] Yet there is here no question of Galenism, but

---

[13]Wellmann, *Die pneumat. Schule,* pp. 129–30. Idem, *Philumeni de venenatis animalibus eorumque remediis.* (*Corpus medicorum Graecorum,* X,1,1, [1908]), p. v; also *Hermes* 43 (1908): 373–404.

[14]Cf. Sudhoff-Pagel, *Kurzes Handbuch der Geschichte der Medizin,* 3rd and 4th ed. (Berlin, 1922), p. 125; Stadler, s.v. in Pauly-Wissowa, *op. cit.,* vol. 7, 1(1910), cols. 760–62.

[15]Cf. W. Puhlmann, "Die lateinische medizinische Literatur des frühen Mittelalters," *Kyklos* 3 (1930): 401. M. Wellmann, "Palladius und Gargilius Martialis," *Hermes* 43 (1908): 1–31.

[16]*Gargilii Martialis medicinae ex oleribus et pomis* I (*Plinii Secundi quae fertur una cum Gargilii Martialis Medicina,* ed. Valentin Rose (Leipzig, 1875), p. 133,1): "... omnium medicorum opinione compertum est, sed et nobis intellegere de usu licet"; LIII (p. 200,19): "vehemens hoc esse etiam domesticis in uxore servata experimentis probavi."

[17]Cf. the index in Rose's edition, p. 221.

[18]V. Rose, "Über die Medicina Plinii," *Hermes* 8 (1874): 65.

[19]Ch. 6 (ed. Rose, p. 140,6): "Veteres medici de cucurbita ita senserunt ut eam aquam dicerent coagulatam. Galenus umidae putat virtutis," etc.

[20]Ch. 4 (p. 138,1): "Non dubitatur coliandro refrigeratrix potestas datur, non tamen simplex, ut prudentissime Galeno videtur, sed sui quaedam portio austeritatis inmixta sit, inde quod quaedam ex eo vitia curantur quae numquam omnino sanaret, si sola virtute frigida niteretur." In Pliny, *Naturalis historia,* XX, 20 (ed. C. Mayhoff [Leipzig, 1892], p. 364,6): "Vis magna ad refrigerandos ardores viridi." The parallel passage in Galen, *De simplic. medicament, temperam. ac facult.,* VII, 43 (ed. Kühn, vol. 12, p. 36,8): σύγκειται γὰρ ἐξ ἐναντίων δυνάμεων πολὺ μὲν ἔχουσα πικρᾶς οὐσίας, ἥτις ἐδείκνυτο λεπτομερὴς ὑπάρχειν καὶ γεώδης, οὐκ ὀλίγον δὲ καὶ ὑδατώδους ὑγρότητος χλιαρᾶς κατὰ δύναμιν, ἔχει δέ τι καὶ στύψεως ὀλίγης.

only an indication that Galen has not been forgotten, that he has a reputation that lifts him above his more immediate contemporaries. Although he is repeatedly mentioned, he is at best coordinated with Dioscorides and is subordinate to Pliny, who is much closer to the Romans and whom Gargilius Martialis calls *Plinius noster.*[21] Pliny serves Gargilius in two respects. He is for him not only an authority but also a source assembling the older, Greek physicians, whom he hands down—and among them, Hippocrates.[22] Yet Gargilius Martialis has nothing to add to his name; it means little to him,[23] not much more than those of Diocles and Praxagoras, who follow shortly afterward.

Pliny's strong influence on Latin medical literature of late Antiquity was bound to be fatal for Hippocratism in the West; or, rather, the fact that he was able to exert such influence is an indication of the quite different paths upon which the West was entering. And this becomes still clearer with Quintus Serenus Sammonicus.

Quintus Serenus's "liber medicinalis" is a therapeutic anthology in hexameters, of strictly practical orientation.[24] It is in no way systematic;[25] indeed, no attempt at system is present. Instead, the author's intention is simply to state what the medicaments are to be used for, and this he does in a very popular manner. Humoral-pathological views have been taken over too and enter into the variegated list of indications.[26] This list is aimed partly at symptoms,[27] partly at disease species,[28] and sometimes just the organs are mentioned for whose maladies the medicaments are to be used.[29] Gargilius Martialis, too, had drawn from Pliny; but while Gargilius Martialis used Pliny himself, Quintus Serenus is already dependent on an adaptation and so knows him only indirectly.[30]

---

[21]Ch. 21 (p. 156,2): "sed recte Plinius noster adiecit," etc.

[22]Cf. Rose's index, p. 221.

[23]Cf. ch. 9 (p. 143,10), ch. 18 (p. 151,1), ch. 21 (p. 153,11).

[24]*Quinti Sereni liber medicinalis,* ed. F. Vollmer (*Corpus Medicorum Latinorum,* II,3), 1916. Cf. also Vollmer, "Nachträge zur Ausgabe von Q. Sereni liber medicinalis," *Philologus* 75, pp. 128–33, A. Baur, *Quaestiones Sammoniceae.* Diss. Giessen, 1886, and Gnüg, "Sprachliches zu Serenus Sammonicus," Beilage zum *Jahresbericht des Gymnasium Georgianum,* 1906, Hildburghausen, 1906.

[25]Cf. Rose, "Über die Medicina Plinii," pp. 32–33.

[26]Ch. 16 (ed. Vollmer, p. 16): "Tussi et choleribus medendis." Since the chapter headings seem to go back to Quintus Serenus himself (Vollmer, preface, p. xxiii), I use them as evidence.

[27]Ch. 13 (p. 13): "Oculorum dolores mitigando"; ch. 25 (p. 24): "Ventris dolori mitigando."

[28]Ch. 10 (p. 10): "Elephantiasi propellendae"; ch. 41 (p. 38): "Podagrae depellendae."

[29]Ch. 1 (p. 5): "Ad capitis curationem"; ch. 22 (p. 21): "Spleni curando."

[30]M. Cohn, "Historische Streifzüge (Quintus Serenus Sammonicus)," *Monatshefte für praktische Dermatologie* 28 (1899): 24–27, sees Quintus Serenus drawing on Galen (p. 25).—Cf. on the subject of Quintus Serenus's source, J. Keese, *Quomodo Serenus Sammonicus a medicina Pliniana ipsoque Plinio pendeat.* Diss. Rostock, 1916. Keese assumes the existence of an *editio maior* of the Medicina Plinii which was only later condensed into the version made known by Rose (cf. Keese's summary, pp. 66–67). Since Rose, "Über die Medicina Plinii," p. 35, places his version between 300 and 350, Quintus Serenus may well have lived in the third century. Cf. Vollmer's edition, preface, p. iii.

The medical content of Pliny's *Natural History* had become too extensive, and the need for a shorter, more concentrated version asserted itself. When such an edition was undertaken for the first time has not yet been determined with certainty, but in any case this was not the end of the matter: the task was undertaken several times in the course of the early Middle Ages.[31] One version hails in all probability from the fourth century but must be considered already in the present context, for it belongs in the direct line of development of late Roman medicine. The author of this *Medicina Plinii* has nothing original to offer; together with the material content he takes over Pliny's sharp attacks against the physicians, the difference being that the invective too takes on a coarser tone in the unknown compiler.[32] For the content of this *Breviarium* the same may be said as of the didactic poem of Quintus Serenus, namely, lack of system and poor conceptualization, which, in essence, go back to Pliny himself.[33]

It is very probable that this version was preceded by another somewhat more substantial one, about which, to be sure, nothing precise is known. Presumably, however, it was not very different in spirit and, as to dating, would have to be attributed to the third century. It was either from this older version or from the *Medicina Plinii* that Quintus Serenus now drew, and in so doing he ranges himself directly in the current leading away from the Greeks and Hippocrates.[34]

As the uncertain dating of the various versions indicates, the dates of Quintus Serenus's life, too, cannot be incontrovertibly established;[35] and this brings up a much more general aspect.

Tendencies peculiar to Latin medical literature develop clearly from the third century on, so that it is quite impossible to separate the single centuries from one another in anything but an artificial manner. Particularly in the realm of materia medica this period must be considered a unit, for what follows in literary production draws from the same sources and is enriched rather by the local coloring of its origin than by the absorption of thought along specific lines. Pliny, Dioscorides, Galen stand in the foreground, and what follows after Gargilius Martialis and Quintus Serenus differs in language and form but not in specific direction.

The known version of the *Medicina Plinii* was by no means the last; there were several subsequent ones.[36] But there exist also a number of writings

[31]Cf. the above footnote, also Rose's summary in "Über die Medicina Plinii," pp. 62–63 and Puhlmann, *op. cit.*, p. 413.
[32]*Plinii Secundi quae fertur una cum Gargilii Martialis medicina,* ed. Rose (Leipzig, 1875), p. 7,1: "Frequenter mihi in peregrinationibus accidit ut aut propter meam aut propter meorum infirmitatem varias fraudes medicorum experiscerer," etc. Ch. 6, p. 17,1:"scio certe quosdam medicos huius curationis sibi summam scientiam vindicasse et magnas mercedes poposcisse," etc. Cf. on Pseudo-Plinius also A. Köhler, "Handschriften römischer Mediciner," *Hermes* 18 (1883): 382–95.
[33]Cf. Rose, "Über die Medicina Plinii," pp. 32–33.
[34]Cf. Keese, *op. cit.*
[35]Cf. footnote 30 above.
[36]Cf. Rose, "Über die Medicina Plinii."

that show the same trend, though they put the other two authors more in the foreground. This is true first of all for Sextus Placitus Papyrensis[37] and for Marcellus Empiricus,[38] but also for the pharmacological part of the *Euporiston* of Theodorus Priscianus (i.e., Book I), which is based mainly on Galen.[39]

This entire pharmacological literature had nothing directly in common with Hippocrates, who in fact scarcely comes within its scope. Insofar, of course, as Hippocratic material is contained in Pliny, Dioscorides, and Galen, it is in part indirectly transmitted further. But this is hardly in any sense a matter of Hippocratism, for everything that distinguishes the Hippocratic writings is absent, and the name of Hippocrates is scarcely mentioned. Yet the picture would be distorted if one were unreservedly to generalize, imputing what is true for the pharmacological writings to the entire late Roman literature.

Theodorus Priscianus, just cited as a pharmacological author dependent on Galen, is dependent also in extensive parts of his work on the Methodists, chiefly on Soranus.[40] He should be stressed all the more in that he himself translated his work, originally written in Greek, into Latin.[41] Altogether, the tendency to change from Greek to Latin is noticeable in the fifth century in the western half of the empire,[42] for Greek seems to have been less and less understood. If Theodorus Priscianus bears witness to the penetration of the Methodists, he also constitutes evidence of yet another exchange between Greek and Roman medicine. Although he used Galen directly, it is after all possible that he had some personal knowledge of the Hippocratic writings, for he quotes Hippocrates in several places[43] and, indeed, in a curious formulation. Gargilius Martialis had spoken of *Plinius noster,* and this from the lips of a Roman was a thoroughly understandable expression of solidarity. In parallel fashion, Theodorus Priscianus designates Hippocrates as *Hippocrates noster,* and he does so repeatedly.[44] An explanation can perhaps be sought in the circumstance that for all these authors, insofar as they cite Hippocrates, he is the established founder of medicine, as Theodorus Priscianus himself expressed it: "Our Hippocrates, the originator of his profession,"[45] and as it becomes particularly clear in Cassius Felix. Yet again—and most clearly—at this time (447), Cassius Felix

[37]His *Liber medicinae ex animalibus,* ed. Howald-Sigerist *(Corpus Medicorum Latinorum IV)* 1927, together with *Antonii Musae de herba Vettonica liber, Pseudoapuleius,* et al., which also contains the evidence.

[38]See *De medicamentis liber,* ed. M. Niedermann *(Corpus Medicorum Latinorum V)* 1916, for evidence.

[39]*Theodori Prisciani Euporiston libri III,* etc., ed. V. Rose (Leipzig, 1894), preface, p. xix; Meyer-Steineg, *Theodorus Priscianus und die römische Medizin* (Jena, 1909), p. 31.

[40]Cf. Meyer-Steineg, *ibid.*

[41]Ed. Rose, p. 2,2: "in tuam gratiam nostro sermone digessi," etc. Cf. Sudhoff-Pagel, *op. cit.,* p. 127; Puhlmann, *op. cit.,* p. 402.

[42]The poet Claudianus is one example. Cf. Stein, *op. cit.,* p. 349.

[43]Cf. Rose's index, p. 552.

[44]Bk. I, ch. 17 (ed. Rose, p. 53,10): "quo Hippocratis nostri praecepta custodientes," etc., Bk. II, ch. 34, (p. 217,13): "hoc etenim etiam nostri Hippocratis nos instruxit auctoritas."

[45]II, ch. 7 (p. 121,14): "de his igitur Hippocrates noster, huius professionis auctor," etc.

represents the connection with the Dogmatic past of Greek medicine, as far as this designation of sects has anything more than historical significance in the fifth century. It is expressed in the title of his work: *A Book on Medicine, Translated from Greek Authors of the Logical Sect.*[46] One should not jump to the conclusion that he simply translated a Greek model into Latin; the only certain thing is that we are concerned with a Latinized compilation of physicians who belonged in a broad sense to the Dogmatic school.[47] They are almost exclusively Greeks, yet he mentions Vindicianus of the fourth century, the teacher of Theodorus Priscianus.[48] As was to be expected, his most important source is Galen; and Hippocrates, in complete agreement with Greek and particularly Dogmatic tradition, appears to him as the head of the school, as *dogmatum princeps,* as he says.[49] Although he often refers to him,[50] he mentions only two of his writings, quoting them usually in literal Latin translation. They are the *Aphorisms*[51] and the *Prognostics.*[52] Since both books were commented upon by Galen on the basis of the texts, it is not immediately possible to decide whether Cassius Felix had the original Hippocrates at his disposal, or a commentated edition. Indeed, the possibility exists that he used a much later edition, namely, a fourth century one. To this conclusion we are led by the circumstance that in two passages, after quoting the Hippocratic wording from the *Aphorisms,* he adds the explanation of the Iatrosophist Magnus,[53] who can be no other than the Magnus of whom Eunapius told, and who belonged to the circle of Alexandrian physicians of the fourth century.[54] Since Cassius Felix also knows Philagrius,[55] it seems certain that he is connected, even though loosely, with late Greek medicine of the fourth century.

It is in fact in Cassius Felix, and therefore in one of those Roman physicians who may most nearly be considered representatives of the Logicians, that we have an example of the relationship of Roman medicine to Hippocratism.

For Gargilius Martialis, Theodorus Priscianus, and Cassius Felix, Hippocrates is not much more than a concept grown shadowy, of which one knows that it is the name of a great physician, perhaps of the founder of medicine—but nothing more. Nowhere can one detect a truly living rela-

---

[46]*Cassii Felicis de medicina,* etc., ed. V. Rose, (Leipzig, 1879). Cf. also Wellman, s.v. Pauly-Wissowa, *op. cit.,* vol. 3 (1899), col. 1723.

[47]Ed. Rose, p. 1,3: "... placuit mihi ut ex graecis logicae sectae auctoribus omnium causarum dogmata in breviloquio latino sermone conscriberem."

[48]Rose, preface, p. iii, also his index, p. 259. Cf. Wellmann, Pauly-Wissowa, *loc. cit.*

[49]Ch. 1 (p. 3,2): "nam Hippocrates senior dogmatum princeps in aforismis sic ait." See also ch. 65 (p. 158,20).

[50]Cf. Rose's index, pp. 259–60.

[51]Ch. 1 (p. 3,3); ch. 32 (p. 64,15), and elsewhere.

[52]Ch. 35 (p. 75,14): "nam Hippocrates senior in suo prognostico sic ait"; ch. 18 (p. 27,5): "et sicut Hippocrates in prognostico dicit."

[53]Ch. 29 (p. 48,3): "sed omnia haec quinque secundum expositionem Magni iatrosophistae," etc.; ch. 76 (p. 182,9): "secundum expositionem Magni iatrosofistae."

[54]On this, cf. below. [The Iatrosophist Magnus is discussed in ch. 3, p. 41 of the German publication.]

[55]See Rose's index, p. 260.

tionship, even though only one of personal interpretation; Hippocrates is already a lifeless formula which, beyond the veneration due its age, cannot even claim to carry much more weight than other physicians, Galen, Soranus, Dioscorides, and above all Pliny. *Hippocrates noster* and *Plinius noster* illustrate, in the manner of slogans, the dulled sense of discrimination between the intellectually valuable and what was no more than practically usable. To be sure, Cassius Felix and Pliny's *Breviarium* still represent widely separated extremes, but even though this should not be overlooked, all currents flow little by little in the same direction. Roman medicine flows slowly into the Latin medicine of the Middle Ages, and any boundary between the two can only be erected by force.[56] If the Latin translations of ancient authors are added—and they, as well as Caelius Aurelianus, have not yet been considered, and very little is yet known of those belonging to this period—the transition from late Roman times to the early Middle Ages becomes still more blurred and unclear. Even though we bear in mind the fact that writings of Hippocrates, Galen, Soranus, Oribasius were translated directly into Latin,[57] this cannot essentially alter the relation of Roman medicine to Hippocratism, which has been investigated here in relatively independent writers.

It has been claimed that Roman medicine was distinguished by the predominance of the Methodists.[58] It is true that the Methodist school, which grew up in Rome and later came again to the fore in Soranus, through Caelius Aurelianus, left a heavier mark on the West than on the Greek-influenced world. Yet there is no question of an unqualified predominance. Galen was accepted at least as much as Soranus, and as pharmacologists Pliny and Dioscorides were scarcely typical representatives of the Methodists. It is altogether not permissible to tie Roman medicine to any one of the old schools; it is neither Dogmatic, nor Methodist, let alone Empiricist. It is, to be sure, oriented toward practical usefulness and the greatest possible avoidance of the theoretical and speculative, but this is expressed in a rather indiscriminate acceptance of anything that serves these ends, the provenience of the material playing a merely secondary role. This means, and it seems to be proved by the foregoing, that Roman medicine knew no Hippocratism in any vital sense. A great name—and not much more. And there is not even any Galenism, and this differentiates it from the medicine of the Greeks, which is still to be investigated.[59] Where the main attention was not directed to the scientific, where thought in scholarly form was not valued, where no importance was attributed to methodical execution, but where only bare facts, shortened and sum-

[56]Cf. Neuburger, *op. cit.*, p. 44; Sudhoff-Pagel, *op. cit.*, p. 155.

[57]Cf. V. Rose, *Anecdota graeca et graecolatina*, 2 vols., Berlin, 1864–70.

[58]Meyer-Steineg, *Theodorus Priscianus und die römische Medizin*, p. 26, and his "Thessalos v. Tralles," *Arch. Gesch. Med.* 4 (1911): 108, in which he replied to the criticism of Ilberg in *Neue Jahrbücher*, vol. 25.

[59]In this I agree with Meyer-Steineg (*Theodorus Priscianus*, p. 23): "Es ist wohl kaum zuviel gesagt, wenn man behauptet, dass Galen zwar für die mittelalterliche Medizin eine Epoche, für die römische dagegen nur eine Episode bedeutet.'

marized, were admitted, there Galen the systematist, the logician and sophist, could not possibly become a hero. Much was taken over from him, but he was not elevated to the status of a doctrine. Thus, in the West, too, Galen did not become the vehicle of Hippocrates; he, too, remained a great name, like Soranus, and side by side Hippocrates, Galen, and Soranus attain "mythical fame."[60] But there would be more to say about all this in connection with the medicine of the early Middle Ages on the basis of translations and compendia which were produced in the West.

Thus in Roman medicine a trend away from the Greek tradition is already perceptible in the third century, and gradually the estrangement of the two halves of the empire is noticeable also in the medical output. It is difficult to determine from contemporary sources what happened in Greek medicine itself in this period, and in particular the form of the relationship to Hippocrates. One has to rely more on conjecture, tempted by the silence of the time and by anticipatory projection into the future. After the rich productivity of the second century, a stagnation seems to have set in: medicine continued to be taught in the eclectic spirit of the immediate past, with Pneumatic doctrine exerting strong after-effects, but the circumstances of the time were not particularly favorable to widespread literary activity. There may well have been physicians who were efficient and who also let themselves be guided in their practical activity by the writings of Hippocrates, but they have scarcely attained prominence. The name of Galen must have been well remembered, for already in this century he comes more and more into the foreground. His whole stance was such that he must have had a group of disciples who carried his memory into the third century. It would seem that medical education was on a sufficiently high *niveau* to draw on the full work of Galen and of the chief Pneumatists, above all on Archigenes, but also on other schools; the simplification of doctrines did not really begin until the fourth century. It may be assumed that the preceding century offered enough material for an unproductive period to feed on, and at this time already Galen's all-comprehensive work must have borne fruit. To be sure, there is no evidence that he had already won his victory.[61] Although the open war between the sects had perhaps quieted down, tradition may nevertheless have been strong enough to allow other trends close to Dogmatism to assert themselves independently from Galen—and especially the late echoes of the Pneumatic school. But for the assessment of Hippocrates, this has little importance, for in reverence for his name all were united. It remained for the fourth century to bring victory to Galenic Hippocratism in particular.

[60]Cf. Rose, *Anecdota*, vol. 2, p. 115.
[61]Sudhoff-Pagel, *op. cit.*, p. 124.

12

Studies
on Late Alexandrian
Medicine

I. Alexandrian Commentaries on Galen's
*De Sectis ad Introducendos**

GALEN IS USUALLY considered the last great physician of antiquity. The medical work of the following four or five centuries is then either regarded as the decay of former greatness or related to the province of "Byzantine medicine" which lasted till the 15th century. Yet, both points of view fail to do justice to this period, especially to the activities of the medical school in Alexandria. For here, down to the 8th century,[1] Greek Medicine was not only taught but a new attitude was developed which we call "scholasticism" and which, later on, became so characteristic of the Mohammedan world as well as of mediaeval Europe.

To trace down the history of Alexandrian medicine from the 3rd to the 8th century A.D., to obtain a picture of its personalities and activities will be the object of a comprehensive work on which I am engaged. But first it is necessary to collect the texts, to establish a chronological basis and to identify, as far as possible, the various names which have been reported to us. Such preparatory work will be done in a series of articles which I intend publishing from time to time. I begin with the commentaries on Galen's *De sectis* since they give us some insight into the teaching activities of the Alexandrian school.

The Alexandrian commentaries on Galen's *De sectis* are divided into two parts, introduction and detailed commentation. In some manuscripts, however, the introduction alone is preserved. These introductions, since they discuss medicine as a whole, are of special interest and they will be the chief object of the present study.

TEXTS AND CHRONOLOGY

Since none of the following texts give direct information of the date of their composition, it is necessary to survey all of them briefly and by comparison and inferences to fix their chronology as far as possible. We shall begin with two Greek fragments which can be attributed to Alexandria and the 6th century A.D. Starting from them it will be possible to assign two comprehensive Latin texts to the same place and period. Finally, we shall

---

Bull. Hist. Med., 1935, vol. 3, pp. 405–30.
[1]Cf. Meyerhof (I), p. 409 and (III), p. 13.

have to discuss some Greek and oriental texts which, although certainly dependent on Alexandrian tradition, cannot be dated and placed with certainty.

1) Palladius, Εἰς Γαληνοῦ περὶ αἱρέσεων σχόλια, cod. Laurentianus plut. 74,11; saec. XIII, fol. 200r–211v.[2] Incipit: Τοῦ Γαληνοῦ τὸ περὶ αἱρέσεων σχόλιον ἀπὸ φωνῆς Παλλαδίου. Τῆς ἰατρικῆς τέχνης σκοπὸς μὲν ἡ ὑγίεια, τέλος δὲ ἡ κτῆσις αὐτῆς. Ὑπὸ τριῶν γενικωτάτων δυνάμεων διοικεῖται τὸ ἡμέτερον σῶμα etc.

This text, a part of which has been published by Rabe,[3] is a fragment. Its attribution to Palladius gives an indication of its chronology, for Palladius probably lived in Alexandria in the 6th century.[4] As far as I can see, it gives little more than an introduction (and even that in a fragmentary form) and stops abruptly soon after the beginning of the detailed commentation.

In this introduction the author intends to discuss medicine in relation to five questions: What does the name "ἰατρική" mean? Does medicine exist? What is medicine? How is it constituted? What is its goal?[5] But the answers to these questions are not clearly separated and a discussion of *De sectis* under the eight usual "capitula" mentioned in the two Latin texts[6] is missing. On fol. 209v. the introduction seems to be finished and the detailed commentation begins; this, however, is again interrupted on fol. 211r./v. by schematic tables and the whole ends with the words (fol. 211v.): ἐν μέρι γιγνόμενος σκιρός.[7]

The above mentioned general questions about medicine, a list of the main representatives of the three medical schools and a division of medicine into its various branches link this text with the group to be discussed next. But with its different wording it is of a separate type and holds a position of its own.

We shall now analyse three texts, all of which are closely related. They comprise one fragmentary Greek papyrus and two comprehensive Latin commentaries.

2) Papyrus 11739A of the "Staatliche Museen zu Berlin." This papyrus was edited and comprehensively analyzed by Ernst Nachmanson in 1925. It contains the fragment of an introduction to Galen's *De sectis*. Nachmanson arrived at the well substantiated conclusion that it hails from the pen of an Alexandrian Neo-Platonist and was written in the 6th century A.D. The title runs as follows: Προλεγόμενα τοῦ Περὶ ἐρέσεων Γαληνοῦ Ἀρχ... δου σοφιστοῦ ἐξήγησις.[8] From this Nachmanson reconstructed the name as Ἀρχ[ιμήδου] or Ἀρχ[ωνί]δου.[9]

3) The first volume of the Latin edition of Galen's works prepared by

---

[2]Cf. Diels, vol. II, p. 76.
[3]Rabe, pp. 561–62.
[4]Cf. Braeutigam, p. 35 ff. and Temkin, p. 74.
[5]Fol. 202r.-v.; cf. Rabe, p. 561.
[6]Cf. below.
[7]Then a different text starts under the title: Περὶ διαφορᾶς πυρετῶν; cf. Diels, II, p. 75.
[8]Cf. Nachmanson, p. 204.
[9]Cf. Nachmanson, p. 216.

Rusticus Placentinus and printed in Pavia in 1515 contains on fol. 6r.–12v. a Latin translation of Galen's *De sectis* together with an introduction and detailed commentation.[10] The introduction is attributed to one "Johannes Alexandrinus."[11]

A comparison of this introduction with the papyrus mentioned above shows that the whole content of the papyrus can be found almost verbally in the Latin introduction. As an example I quote the beginning of the papyrus opposite the corresponding passage in the Latin edition:

Papyrus 11739A[12]	Ed. Pap. fol. 6v.
Τοῖς τῆς ἰατρικῆς ἐρασταῖς καὶ ταύτης ἐφιεμένοις τυχεῖν καὶ διὰ τοῦτο πολλὴν σπουδὴν καὶ προθυμίαν ἐνδεικνυμένοις περὶ τὴν ταύτης κατόρθωσιν ἄξιον πρῶτον μαθεῖν τίς ἡ ταύτης φύσις.	Amantes igitur medicinam et desiderantes eam cognoscere: et propterea multam festinationem et desiderium habentes circa ipsius rei cognitionem: dignum est prius inquirere que sit eius natura.

This close connection with the papyrus suggests the probability that the introduction of the Latin edition was originally composed at about the same time as the papyrus, i.e., in the 6th century A.D. This inference is further confirmed by the end of the introduction where the author discusses Galen's book under the eight "capitula",[13] a scheme which, according to Praechter,[14] was not applied in such a form before the neoplatonic philosopher Ammonius and his school (*ca.* 500 A.D.). We can therefore say that the "terminus post quem" for the Latin introduction is the year 500 A.D.

4) The cod. Ambrosianus G 108 inf. contains on fol. 22r.–130r. Latin commentaries on the following Galenic writings: 1) *De sectis ad Introducendos* 2) *Ars medica* 3) *De pulsibus ad Introducendos* 4) *Methodus medendi ad Glauconem,* liber I.

Dr. Sigerist, to whom credit must be given for the rediscovery of these texts,[15] has pointed out that although the manuscript was written at the end of the 9th century, it is "in all probability but a copy of an older original," written in Ravenna, for which we have to go back as far as the 6th century A.D.[16] This contention is based on the work of Mørland who showed that the Latin translation of Oribasius was also written in or near Ravenna under the Ostrogoths.[17] This 6th century original was moreover a translation from the Greek, as the language clearly indicates. Furthermore it must go back to the work of an Alexandrian scholar, since the selection and

---

[10]The end of the translation and of the commentary seems not to be preserved. They go as far as *Scripta minora,* p. 29, 13. The end of the commentary on fol. 12v. apparently does not belong to it.

[11]Cf. Temkin, p. 68. I am only now able to classify this text, since Nachmanson's publication had previously escaped my attention.

[12]Nachmanson, pp. 204–05.

[13]Cf. Temkin, p. 68 and p. 186, below.

[14]Cf. Praechter, pp. 529–31; cf. also Rose (II), p. 206 and Braeutigam, p. 37.

[15]Daremberg, p. 257, apparently alludes to these texts.

[16]Cf. Sigerist, pp. 39–40.

[17]Cf. Mørland, p. 194.

arrangement of the Galenic books correspond to the conventions recorded of the Alexandrian school of medicine.[18]

The commentary on *De sectis* is contained on fol. 22r.–48v. It begins with an introduction (fol. 22r.–29v.) which is followed by detailed commentation (fol. 30r.–48v.) and which ends (fol. 48r./v.): Explicit scolia peri hereseon Galeni actio trigesima tertia feliciter. Ex voce Agnello Yatro Sophista ego Simplicius domino iuvante legi et scripsi in Ravenna feliciter.

If we compare this text with that of the Pavia edition we notice a very great similarity. The beginning of both introductions is the same:

Cod. Ambr. G 108 inf. fol. 22r.	Ed. Pap. fol. 6r.
Bonum aliquid divitiarum et oportunum vitae nostrae inventa est ars medicinae. Sanitatem enim operari et conservare promittit et exercere corpori per quam magna bonorum hominibus additur peritia et artes constant et omnis meditatio et disciplina procedit et ipsae animae operationes.	Bonum aliquid divitiarum et vite nostre oportunum adinventa est ars medicine. Sanitatem enim operari et conservare promittit et exercere: per quam magna bonorum utilitas hominibus additur: per quam etas et tempus et omnis medicatio[19] et disciplina procedit: et ipsius anime operationes.

This close congruency does not prevail through the whole of the two texts. The discrepancies become even so great that they indicate more than mere variants. On the other hand the similarity is strong enough to refer both texts to one type.[20]

From all these points we can conclude that the papyrus, the Pavia edition and the cod. Ambr. represent three versions of the same type of introduction and that this type goes back to Alexandria in the 6th century A.D. And the same must be true with regard to the detailed commentations represented by the Pavia edition and the cod. Ambrosianus.[21]

Whereas in the case of the cod. Ambr. we deal with an early mediaeval translation, the question arises at what time the text of the Pavia edition was translated and known in western mediaeval Europe, and whether it was a direct translation from the Greek or if it was first translated into Arabic and then from Arabic into Latin. This latter question can be answered by the fact that we find quite a few instances where obviously Greek words are used,[22] whereas any definite indications of Arabic terminology are lacking. Therefore the translation must have been made directly from the Greek.

---

[18]Cf. below.

[19]A marginal note indicates the variant: alius meditatio. Quite a number of variants in the Pavia edition can be found in the cod. Ambr. Perhaps the latter was known to the editor of the Pavia text.

[20]For the meaning of "type," cf. below.

[21]This contention is based on the fact that in the cod. Ambr. both introduction and detailed commentation hail from the same author. Since, however, the introduction and detailed commentations differ in some smaller points, it is quite possible that the latter were based on the work of previous Alexandrian scholars.

[22]Thus, for instance, speaking of rational faculties, the text says (fol. 6v.) : Rationales sunt tres : hpantasia (i.e., phantasia) : legismos (i.e., logismos) anime : et memoria.

But it is not the work of a Renaissance scholar, for the same text appears at a much earlier date: the cod. lat. Monacensis 5 of the 14th century[23] (fol. 12v.–20r.) gives the commentary together with the text of *De sectis*— although in a mutilated form, and here the introduction is ascribed to "Cascator."[24] Furthermore, the translation of the commentary was not only extant in the 14th century, it was also well known to the physicians of that period. For this we have two testimonies: Fol. 259v.–76r. of the cod. F. V 25 of the Biblioteca Nazionale in Turin contain a treatise on the plague written in the 14th century[25] which begins (fol. 259v.–60r.): "Bonorum honorabilium et vite nostre oportunum adinventa est scientia medicine, Johannes alexandrinus super commento libri secretarum magistri galiani.[26] Bonum est quod omnia appetunt, Aristotilis ethotorum primo.[27] Omnem autem malum tueri salutem laborat ac appetit mortem vero perniciemque deviat, Boecius de consolacione tercio.[28] Ideoque ut communiter actor libri secretarum galieni commento primo evidenter describit: Maximum est desiderium omni homini ad sanitatem facile ét custodire scienciam medicine festinare.[29] Et artis (?) medicinalis intencio sanitas et finis vera possessio eius ut galienus in principio libri praedicti."[30] From this we see that the author quotes Johannes Alexandrinus beside Aristotle, Boethius and Galen.[31] The second testimony is given by Mundinus' *Anathomia.* In the chapter "De anathomia ventris inferioris" he writes: "De membris autem officialibus sciendum quod in quampluribus ipsorum quantum ad anathomiam factam in mortuis sex sunt videnda ut dicit commentator alexandrinus in commento libri sectarum scilicet que ipsorum sit positio: que sit eorum substantia: et per consequens complexio: que sit eorum quantitas numerus figura: et continuitas eorum."[32]

Since the *Anathomia Mundini* was written in 1316,[33] the Latin translation of the commentary in question must have existed some time before,

---

[23]Cf. Diels, I, p. 60 and III, p. 30; cf. also Helmreich, pp. 247–48 and Temkin, p. 69.

[24]Cf. Helmreich, *loc. cit.,* who states that the same text is also contained in the cod. Monac. 490 and the cod. 1136 of the Universitaetsbibliothek, Leipzig, in mutilated form.

[25]Cf. Giacosa, p. 446.

[26]Cf. Ed. Pav. fol 6r.: Bonum aliquid divitiarum et vite nostre oportunum adinventa est ars medicine. "Secretarum" is written instead of "sectarum."

[27]Cf. Aristotle, *Ethica Nicomachea,* 1094 a.2: διὸ καλῶς ἀπεφήναντο τἀγαθόν, οὗ πάντ' ἐφίεται.

[28]Cf. Boethius, *Philosophiae consolatio,* III, 11: Omne namque animal tueri salutem laborat, mortem vero perniciemque devitat.

[29]Cf. ed. Pap. fol. 6v.: quoniam magnum est desiderium omni homini ad sanitatis factricem et custoditricem artem medicine festinare.

[30]Cf. Galen, *De sectis* (*Scripta minora,* III, p. 1): Τῆς ἰατρικῆς τέχνης σκοπὸς μὲν ἡ ὑγίεια, τέλος δ' ἡ κτῆσις αὐτῆς.

[31]Otherwise there is no connection between this text and that of the Pavia edition; cf. Temkin, p. 68.

[32]Anathomia Mundini emendata per Doctorem Melerstat, fol. A III. The passage refers to ed. Pav. fol. 9v.: In mortuis etiam fit anothomia propter VI occasiones scilicet numerum: et substantiam membrorum: et positiones locorum: et magnitudinem : et scema : et alterutrum communicationes.

[33]Cf. Choulant, p. 91.

roughly speaking at the beginning of the 14th century. Of translators from the Greek up to this time we know above all Alphanus (11th century), Burgundio of Pisa (1110–1194),[34] Bartholomaeus of Messina, William of Moerbeke (13th century) and Nicolaus of Reggio (first part of the 14th century).[35] I am unable to say whether we owe the translation to any of these men, but it is nevertheless worth mentioning that Burgundio of Pisa is said to have translated Galen's *De sectis* into Latin.[36]

To sum up so far, we can say that the Greek and Latin texts reveal the existence of two types of Commentaries on Galen's *De sectis*. One type is represented by the text in the cod. Laur. plut. 74,11, ascribed to Palladius. The other type is represented by the Papyrus 11739A, the commentary in the Pavia edition ascribed to Johannes Alexandrinus and the commentary in the cod. Ambr. G. 108 inf. ascribed to Agnellus. Both types go back to the same place and period, namely Alexandria in the 6th century A.D.

In addition I give an account of a Greek and two Arabic texts which cannot be fixed chronologically.

5) Cod. Vindobonensis med. 35 (fol. 329r.–59v.)[37] shows schematic tables analysing the contents of various Galenic writings. The title of the whole runs as follows (fol. 329r.): ᾽Αρχὴ σὺν θεῷ τῶν διαιρέσεων πασῶν τῶν ⟨Γαλ⟩ ηνείων πραγματειῶν ἀρχόμενος ἀπὸ τοῦ περὶ αἱρέσεων τελευτῶν δὲ εἰς τὴν θεραπευτικήν, whereupon the following pages (till fol. 332) are devoted to *De sectis*. The schemes at the beginning, especially the division of medicine into two or five parts and the list of representatives of the sects, correspond so much to the foregoing texts that dependence on Alexandrian material must be inferred. It is, however, not possible to decide whether the text is simply a copy of an Alexandrian original or if it is a systematic extract by some mediaeval scholar.

The same is the case as regards the two Arabic texts whose first pages I have investigated.

6) Cod. add. 23407 of the British Museum. According to the catalogue[38] this manuscript contains summaries of the following Galenic writings: *De sectis, Ars medica, De pulsibus ad Theutram, Ad Glauconem de Methodo medendi,*[39] *De Elementis secundum Hippocratem, De Temperamentis, De Facultatibus naturalibus, De Anatomia ad Tyrones* (i.e., *De Ossium Dissectione, De Musculorum dissectione, De Nervorum dissec., De Venarum dissec.*). The catalogue states also

---

[34]Cf. Buonamici, p. 3.

[35]Cf. Schoene (II), p. 6; Ackermann, p. lxvii, states that the translation of "De sectis" in the Pavia edition was done by Nicolaus of Reggio. But fol. 6r. of this edition names Nicolaus as the translator or the "Subfiguratio empirica" only.

[36]Cf. Buonamici, p. 31. Helmreich, pp. 247–48, however, does not think Burgundio the translator.

[37]Cf. Costomiris, p. 381. Costomiris refers to Lambecius' catalogue (VI, 151) which I was unable to obtain.

[38]Cf. Cat. suppl., pp. 629–30.

[39]The Cat. suppl. (p. 629) gives the title as "Summarium Alexandrinorum in librum priorem Galeni ad Glauconem de naturae nomine . . . الطبيعة اسم فى ." I have not seen this part of the manuscript.

that some of these texts are extracts by Hunain ibn Ishaq, others are Alexandrian summaries translated by him, while others again are simply given as Alexandrian summaries without indication of a translator's name.[40] To this latter group belongs the "Summarium Alexandrinorum ad Librum Galeni de medicorum sectis . . . via expositionis et elucidationis"[41] which is contained on fol. 2v.–2ov. The introduction (fol. 2v.–3v.) deals with the divisions and subdivisions of medicine, names the three sects of Dogmatists, Empiricists and Methodists and gives a list of the main representatives of these three schools. The commentation on the first chapter (fol. 3v.–4v.)[42] begins with two definitions of medicine and goes on with a more detailed characterisation of the three sects. The commentation on the second chapter deals with the different kinds of experience,[43] etc.

Comparison between this and the previous texts shows that the contents are closely related and that the Arabic text was dependent on some Alexandrian material. But in its composition it is different and in its introduction much shorter than any of the genuine commentaries mentioned above and, therefore, we must conclude either that the Alexandrians themselves wrote such summaries which, however, are not known from Greek or Latin manuscripts, or that the Syrians or Arabs compiled such summaries from more extensive Alexandrian sources.[44]

7) Cod. Arund. Or. 17 of the British Museum. This manuscript represents a "Liber Compendium Sedecim Galeni; Expositio Yaḥya al-Nahawi."[45] Fol. 2v.–3r. give a brief account of the 16 Galenic books[46] and fol. 3r.–5v. contain the "compendium" of *De sectis.*[47] The indication of the pages alone shows that this "compendium" is much shorter than the above "summary." This is also the case with regard to the introduction which starts immediately with the three sects and their representatives. It is, therefore, an even more concise extract than the "summary," although the list of the names again proves its historical connection with the Alexandrian school.

Due to the uncertainties connected with them the three last mentioned texts will be used only as additional material.

---

[40]Ritter-Walzer list quite a number of manuscripts containing these "Summaries" which they have recently found in Constantinople.

[41]Cat. suppl., p. 629.

[42]Fol. 3.: شرح الباب الاول من كتاب جالينوس

[43]Fol. 4 v.: شرح الباب الثانى اجزاء التجربة خمسة

[44]According to the Arabian historians such summaries were written by the late Alexandrian scholars, cf. Meyerhof (I), p. 394 ff. and Temkin, p. 75 ff., where I suggested that the canon of 16 Galenic books was either established in Alexandria not before the second half of the 6th century, or that it was a later invention of the Syrians and Arabs themselves. Since the question of the authorship of the summaries and compendia is closely connected with that of the canon, its definitive answer does not fall within the limits of this study.

[45]*Catalogue*, p. 217 and Meyerhof (II), p. 16.

[46]Cf. footnote 44.

[47]Fol. 3r.: كتاب الفرق وعدد الفرق واسما اهلها

ANALYSIS OF CONTENT

Having established a chronological basis for our material we shall now survey its contents, analysing its composition, and discussing some points in more detail.

As to the detailed commentations, it may suffice to say that the two Latin texts and that of the cod. Laur. correspond on the whole to the other already known Alexandrian commentaries as edited by Dietz. The Pavia edition gives the text of *De sectis* itself, whereas the others contain lemmata from the writing. They therefore presuppose that the Galenic book was read at the same time. As to the two Arabic texts, they are more rounded in their literary form and it is difficult to say whether they were not read independently.

For the introduction the text of the cod. Ambrosianus may serve as the basis of our analysis, since it gives the clearest arrangement. The introduction of this text is divided into eight "actiones" which again are subdivided into smaller paragraphs usually called "theoriae." [48] The *actiones* 1–6 represent a general introduction into medicine whereas the *actiones* 7–8 introduce *De sectis*.

The opening remarks of a protreptic character are calculated to stimulate beginners[49] and then it is pointed out that one has to start with an inquiry into the nature of the subject and with the question of its objective existence[50] (first *actio*).[51] Now medicine really exists as an art for it possesses both substance and purpose.[52] But its nature can be found out by definition only[53] and this definition must be derived from the substance and the purpose. There results the statement that medicine is an art dealing with

---

[48]The end of the first *actio* runs (fol. 22r) : Finit scidion (σχίδιον?) et actio prima. Then the next *actio* starts: Dicentes scidion cum domino incipimus et de ipso agon est exponere medicinam.

[49]Fol. 22r.: Bene et nos utilitatis finem artis praeponentes suscitamus audientium animos etc. The protreptic character of this *actio* stands in parallel to similar openings in other non-medical commentaries. Thus the very beginning of our text: "Bonum aliquid divitiarum et oportunum vitae nostrae inventa est ars medicinae" looks like a slight variant of a passage quoted by grammarians, e.g., *Scholia in Dion. Thr.*, p. 106, 22–25: Τούτων μάρτυς τῶν λεχθέντων Ἵππαρχος ὁ κωμικός, διά τινος τῶν αὐτοῦ κωμῳδιῶν λέγων πολλῷ γάρ ἐστι κτῆμα τιμιώτατον Ἅπασιν ἀνθρώποισιν εἰς τὸ ζῆν τέχνη.

[50]Fol. 22r.: Unde necessarium nobis est naturam ipsius cognoscere quia et omnis res quae constat propriam aliquam naturam habet a qua separtita est et veluti ab aliquo sequestrata et in quibus Platon philosophus veluti filios ita et discipulos admonet dicens Quia oportet nos scire si hoc ipsum quod dicitur aliquid est ut et hoc ipsum quod inchoat aliquis discere proprietatem ipsius et scire debet.

[51]Fol. 22r.

[52]Fol. 22v: Nos enim dicimus quia medicina ars est et aliquid est; habet subiectum habet et finem quomodo et aliae artes.

[53]Here the text discusses definitions in general and gives the following example (fol. 23v.) : Substantialis orismos est quando dicimus accipientes hominem et dicimus quia homo est animal rationale mortale sensu capax et disciplinae. This definition is also used in non-medical writings, cf. *Scholia in Dion. Thr.*, p. 107, 31–32: οἷον τί ἐστιν ἄνθρωπος; ζῷον λογικὸν θνητὸν νοῦ καὶ ἐπιστήμης δεκτικόν and Walz, p. 18 and Elias, p. 4, 17.

human bodies and effecting health[54] (second *actio*).[55] Philosophers base their inquiries into a subject on four questions: does the subject exist? what is it? how is it constituted? what is it for? These questions must also be applied to medicine.[56] The first and last questions are dealt with very briefly since they have been answered already. The answer to the second question repeats the definition given in the preceding *actio* and explains, furthermore, the nature of an art in general.[57] Concerning the third question, how medicine is constituted, the text points out that medicine is "speculative" as well as "active," "perfective" and "possessive"[58] (third *actio*).[59] The fourth *actio*[60] gives a list of different definitions of medicine and names the three sects and their chief representatives. The fifth *actio*[61] subdivides the theoretical part of medicine, whereas its practical part is subdivided in the sixth *actio*.[62] The seventh and eighth *actiones*[63] discuss the writing *De sectis* under the eight "capitula" of: 1) *intentio auctoris* 2) *si codex est eius proprius* 3) *utilitas* 4) *ad quam partem medicinae iste liber pertinet* 5) *qualis praetitulatio libri sit* 6) *quis ordo legendi* 7) *in quot dividitur particulas* 8) *modus doctrinae.*[64]

On the basis of this short review we can recognize the method and aim of this introduction into medicine. The method is logical and dialectic throughout, for the text proceeds from definition to definition in continuous argument with opposing opinions. As to its aim, the pupil is taught 1) the position of medicine compared to that of philosophy and other arts, 2)

---

[54]Fol. 24v.–25r.: . . . dicamus quia medicina ars est circa corpora humana occupata, operans sanitatem. Cf. Elias, p. 6, 2–3: τέχνη περὶ τὰ ἀνθρώπεια σώματα καταγινομένη ὑγείας περιποιητική. Cf. Nachmanson, p. 210–211.

[55]Fol. 22r.–25r.

[56]Fol. 25r: Dicamus nunc de quattuor titulis quibus utuntur philosophi in arte medicina. Primo si est, secundo quid est, tertio qualis est, quarto propter quid est.

[57]Fol. 25r: Sed quia artem memoravimus dicamus quid est ars. Ars est congregatio universalis in relinquendo et exercitando ad unumquemque finem utilis in vita. The cod. Laur. writes (fol. 202r) : ἡ τέχνη ἐστὶ σύστημα ἐκ καταλήψεως ἐγγεγυμνασμένον ἤτοι συγγεγυμνασμένον πρός τι τέλος εὔχρηστον τῶν ἐν τῷ βίῳ which corresponds to Pseudo-Galen's *Introductio*, Kuehn, XIV, 685 and *Definitiones medicae*, Kuehn, XIX, 350. According to the *Scholia in Dion. Thr.*, p. 108, 31–32, it is stoic: Οἱ δὲ Στωικοὶ λέγουσι: "τέχνη ἐστὶ σύστημα ἐκ καταλήψεων ἐμπειρίᾳ ἐγγεγυμνασμένων πρός τι τέλος εὔχρηστον τῶν ἐν τῷ βίῳ."

[58]I quote here from the Pavia edition which is clearer in this passage than the cod. Ambr. Ed. Pap. fol. 6v : Speculativa quidem ut quando in semetipso requirit medicus et contemplator corpus humanum si simplex est aut compositum . . . (fol. 7r). Est et activa medicina qua incidit medicus et operatur. . . . Est et perfectiva que relinquit in corpore nostro perfectum aliquid. Dico namque sanitatem : potest etiam vocari possessiva : quia et revocat ad extra naturam et iam factam sanitatem custodit : ne iterum incidat in egritudinem. As regards the conception of medicine as a τέχνη μικτή, cf. Englert, p. 87.

[59]Fol. 25r-v. The four questions mentioned in this *actio* go back to Aristotle 89, b 23, as Rabe, p. 543, has shown. The Pavia edition does not mention them at all although it practically gives the answers to them. The cod. Laur. asks 5 instead of 4 questions; cf. above.

[60]Fol. 25v–26r.

[61]Fol. 26r–27r.

[62]Fol. 27r–v.

[63]Fol. 27v–29r.

[64]This corresponds to the arrangement of the Pavia edition, cf. Temkin, p. 68. The arrangement in the cod. Ambr. is slightly different but the eight points are substantially the same.

present and past definitions of medicine together with a historical outline of the three schools, 3) the branches of medicine.

Leaving the first point for the next section, we shall now analyse points two and three viz. the definitions of medicine, the historical account of the three sects and the divisions of medicine, as given by our texts.

a) Definitions of medicine

The definition of medicine as the art which deals with human bodies and effects health is supplemented in the texts by reports of older definitions, formulated by earlier physicians and philosophers.[65] Hippocrates is said[66] to have defined medicine as addition and subtraction, whereas for Plato it was the balance between repletion and evacuation. Both definitions can easily be identified.[67] The definitions attributed to Alexander Philalethes differ in the cod. Ambr. and the Pavia edition. The "regimen of the healthy and therapy of the sick" of the cod. Ambr. and the "regimen, the guardian of health and the cure of sickness" of the Pavia edition are corroborated as definitions in other Greek texts, without, however, any confirmation of the authorship of Alexander Philalethes.[68]

Aristotle, moreover, is credited with definitions which not only lack uniformity but obviously contradict one another. In the cod. Ambr. he is quoted as having said: "Medicina est philosophia corporis philosophia est medicina (animae?)," and this is acclaimed in the statement: "Iuste sic dixit quia medicina et philosophia duae sorores sunt" etc. In the Pavia edition on the other hand, the definition, "Medicina est philosophia corporis" is attributed to an anonymous group of people *(medicinam sic diffiniunt)*, whereas Aristotle himself is quoted as having said "philosophia et medicina due sorores sunt" and "philosophia est medicina anime." The following considerations may help to clear these difficulties: 1) None of these alleged definitions can be found in Aristotle's extant works. 2) The neoplatonic philosopher Elias states that it is the physicians who define medicine as the philosophy of the bodies and philosophy as the medicine of the souls.[69] 3) The sentence "philosophia et medicina due sorores sunt" corresponds to the grammarians' usage of calling grammar a sister of medicine and seems, therefore, to be based on a formula for comparing two arts.[70] From this we

---

[65]For the history of the ancient definitions of medicine, cf. Englert, pp. 4–31.

[66]See Appendix for passages concerned quoted from both the cod. Ambr. and the Pavia edition.

[67]Cf. Hippocrates, *De Flatibus* (CMG. I, 1, p. 92,8–10); Plato, *Symposium*, 186, b–d; cf. Englert, pp. 6 and 16.

[68]Kuehn, XIV, p. 687,9–11 : οἱ δὲ νεώτεροι οὕτως ὡρίσαντο. ἰατρική ἐστιν ἐπιστήμη, ὑγιείας μὲν τηρητικὴ, νόσων δὲ ἀπαλλακτικὴ etc. Kuehn, XIX, p. 351,5–7 :οἱ δὲ πλείους οὕτως ὡρίσαντο. ἰατρική ἐστι τέχνη διαιτητικὴ ὑγιαινόντων καὶ θεραπευτικὴ νοσούντων. Dietz, I, p. 239, 7–9: ἔλεγε τοίνυν ὁ Μνησίθεος, ὅτι ὁ ἰατρὸς ἢ τοῖς ὑγιαίνουσι φυλάττει τὴν ὑγείαν, ἢ τοῖς νοσήσασι θεραπεύει τὰς νόσους etc.

[69]Elias, p. 9,6–9 :οἱ γὰρ ἰατροί... τὴν ἰατρικὴν ὡρίσαντο φιλοσοφίαν σωμάτων, τὴν δὲ φιλοσοφίαν ἰατρικὴν ψυχῶν.

[70]*Scholia in Dion. Thr.*, p. 2,5–9: ἰατρική... Ἧς ἀδελφή ἐστιν ἡ γραμματική. Further, in the detailed commentations this definition is attributed to Plato (ed. Pap. fol. 7v.) : ut Plato

may conclude that probably none of these definitions really hail from the pen of Aristotle. They represent later interpretations of his ideas (as expressed for instance in Ethica Nicom. VII, 15)[71] which were then attributed in a rather contradictory manner to Aristotle himself.

The last definition: "Medicina est disciplina sanorum egrotantium atque neutrorum" is referred to Herophilus by the Pavia edition. The cod. Ambr. attributes it in the introduction to Heracleides of Erithraea, but the detailed commentation corrects this statement in favour of Herophilus.[72]

b) The sects and their representatives

All texts (except the fragmentary papyrus) give lists of the chief representatives of the three schools, although the names vary. Among the Greek and Latin texts the shortest list is given by the cod. Vind. which names:[73]

For the Empiricists: Acron of Agrigentum, Philinus of Cos, Serapion of Alexandria, Sextus, Apollonius.[74]

For the Dogmatists: Hippocrates, Diocles, Praxagoras, Philotimus, Erasistratus, Asclepiades.

For the Methodists: Themison, Thessalus, Menemachus, Soranus.

The lists in the cod. Ambr. and the cod. Laur. are identical with the above, except that the first adds Galen to the Dogmatists whereas the latter adds Mnaseas to the Methodists.[75] Only the Pavia edition gives a much longer and more complicated list.[76] As to the two Arabic texts, the names are rather corrupt but with the help of the Latin and Greek parallels they can be reconstructed.[77] Such lists probably became sources of information for the later Arabic historians who however, confused the chronology.[78]

---

philosophus dixit : philosophia et medicina sunt duo sorores : quia philosophia curat quae sunt anime vitia : humores corporis curat medicina.

[71]Cf. also Rose (I), pp. 107–115. For these references I am indebted to Dr. Edelstein, personal communication.

[72]

cod. Ambr. fol. 30v.	Ed. Pap. fol. 7v.
Ista Herofili definitio est ubi dicit medicina est disciplina sanorum egrotantium atque neutrorum.	Sed Erophili diffinitio dicit : medicina est disciplina sanorum et egrotantium atque neutrorum.

It is not quite certain whether this definition which was used by Galen (*Ars medica*, Kuehn, I, p. 307) and referred by him to Herophilus (cf. Schoene (I), pp. 24–26) was actually formulated by the latter (cf. Englert, pp. 24–25). The discrepancy between the cod. Ambr. and the Pavia edition in the introductions and their congruity in the detailed commentations may suggest that the detailed commentations in both texts were dependent on older patterns. The Arabic "summary" refers the Platonic definition of medicine as "the knowledge of health and disease" (cf. Plato, *Charmides*, 171a and Englert, pp. 16 and 18) to Soranus!

[73]Fol. 329r.; cf. Kroehnert, p. 60.

[74]Cf. Deichgraeber, p. 40.

[75]Where the name of Menemachus would be expected, the cod. Laur. writes: Μενενδος. I do not know whether this is a wrong spelling of Menemachus or of Menodotus.

[76]Cf. the appendix.

[77]Cf. the appendix.

[78]Acron of Agrigent who is named in both Arabic texts may serve as an example. *An-Nadim*, p. 286, places him at the time between Parmenides and Plato which roughly corresponds to the truth. According to Ibn Qifti he lived after Johannes Grammaticus! (Cf. *Ibn Qifti*, p. 56. I

c) Divisions of medicine

The Arabic Summary and the cod. Vindob.[79] relate that some people divide medicine into two parts, whereas others divide it into five parts. The first division distinguishes between theory and practice, subdividing theory into physiology, aetiology and semeiology and practice into hygiene and therapy. The division into five parts starts immediately with physiology, aetiology, semeiology, hygiene and therapy and differs, therefore, from the first only in so far as it ignores the distinction between theory and practice. As to the further subdivisions, both schemes are practically identical.

Both schemes hail from Greek sources. But whereas the division into five parts goes back further than the 6th century,[80] the distinction of theoretical and practical branches of medicine seems to have become important at that period, as witnessed by many Greek and Latin texts.[81] This distinction, as we shall see, has more than superficial significance.

HISTORICAL INTERPRETATION

It is now our task to enquire into the literary character of our texts and to place them in the general scientific activities of their time.

Immediately the question of their authorship arises, although the possible inferences are not very fruitful. Palladius, the author of the cod. Laur., under whose name some other medical commentaries and treatises are known,[82] probably lived in the 6th century.[83] Johannes Alexandrinus to whom the introduction of the Pavia edition is ascribed, is usually identified with the commentator of Hippocrates' *De natura pueri,* and of the 6th book of the Hippocratic Epidemics, printed in the *Articella.*[84] But here again we do not know when he lived nor do we possess any information about his

---

see no reason why the name of Acron should here be corrected into Ahron as suggested by Meyerhof (II), p. 15.)

[79]Cod. add. 23407 of the British Museum, fol. 2v.; cf. Cat. Suppl. p. 629. Cod. Vind. fol. 329:

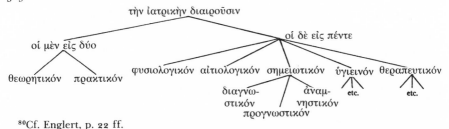

[80]Cf. Englert, p. 22 ff.

[81]In our texts this division appertains to the cod. Laur., and the two Latin texts. Cf. also Dietz, II, pp. 246–49 and Englert, pp. 23–24 and 31. I do not include here a complete exposition of the subdivisions of medicine obtaining in my material, since they correspond substantially to those in De Renzi, I, pp. 87–88.

[82]Cf. Diels, II, pp. 75–76.

[83]Cf. p. 179, above.

[84]Cf. Temkin, p. 67 ff.

personality,[85] except that he was evidently a Christian. The same inference can be drawn concerning Agnellus, the Iatrosophist of the codex Ambrosianus, who so far is an entirely new name.[86] New too is Ἀρχιμήδης or Ἀρχωνίδης as Nachmanson reconstructed the name of the sophist who wrote the papyrus. Yahya an-Nahwi who is mentioned in the Arabic "Compendium" is, in the Arabian tradition, identical with Johannes Grammaticus, as Meyerhof has pointed out. But according to Meyerhof, this is a mistake on the part of the Arabians who wrongly attributed medical writings to him.[87]

These names, therefore, do not lead us far and furthermore they probably do not even in all cases indicate original authors. Praechter has shown that in the commentaries on Aristotle which hail from the 5th and 6th centuries, we have to deal with lecture notes which were often published under the name of the pupil, or where a teacher made use of the notes of his predecessor.[88] The same is also true with regard to late commentaries on grammatical writings, where again the multitude of names can be explained in the same way.[89] This also elucidates the similarity between some of the texts, on the basis that they are either notes of the same lecture taken down by different pupils, or notes from the pen of the same teacher, with additions, variations and corrections.[90]

Similar arguments are also valid for our material, as has been suggested by Nachmanson in the case of the papyrus,[91] but the cod. Ambrosianus is again the best example. The explicit on fol. 48r.-v.: "Ex voce Agnello yatro Sophista ego Simplicius domino iuvante legi et scripsi in Ravenna feliciter" reveals Agnellus as the teacher and Simplicius as the pupil. "Ex voce" is the Latin rendering of the Greek ἀπὸ φωνῆς. Besides, the division of the text into "theoriae" and "actiones" corresponds to the Greek terms θεωρίαι and πράξεις, and these again, according to Praechter,[92] represent the arrangement of the material during the lectures. A third argument is given by the repeated mentioning of different opinions and their refutation, obviously a dialectic procedure, e.g. (fol. 22v): "Stant enim rursum altercantes et inquirunt nos dicentes quia quot modis subiciuntur quae subiecta sunt? Et dicimus quia tribus modis" etc.

[85]Cf. Meyerhof (II) and Temkin, *loc. cit.*

[86]For Johannes Alexandrinus this seems indicated in a passage of the detailed commentation where the author says (ed. Pap. fol. 12r.) : Oravi namque pro vobis. Oratio est triplex : aut necessaria; aut impossibilis: aut possibilis. Necessaria quemadmodum deum debemus orare pro peccatis nostris etc. Cf. Temkin, p. 68 where, however, I wrongly interpreted the neoplatonic conception (cf. Nachmanson, p. 207 and p. 215) of the perfection of philosophy in the assimilation to God as Christian. As to Agnellus, the cod. Ambr. says on fol. 41v.: Simili modo faciunt et sacerdotes quando volunt baptizare prius exorcismus utuntur et sic baptizant ut accipientes signum crucis mundi ad baptismum veniant. It is possible that Agnellus is identical with Anqilaus of the Arabian historians, although the cod. Ambr. (fol. 57v.) quotes one "angeleo sophista" who could also be identified with Anqilaus.

[87]Cf. Meyerhof (II), p. 16. [But cf. Essay 14 in this volume, on Alexandria.]

[88]Cf. Praechter, pp. 523–26.

[89]Cf. *Scholia in Dion. Thr.*, p. xii.

[90]Cf. Praechter, *ibid.*

[91]Cf. Nachmanson, p. 216.

[92]Cf. Praechter, pp. 532–33.

Although not as obviously as in the cod. Ambrosianus, the other texts, nevertheless, also reveal their character as lecture notes. The text of the Pavia edition says on fol. 9v.: "Nunc iterum in presenti actione dogmatici empericos accusant" etc. And on fol. 7v.: "Et quidam opponunt Galenum dicentes: quare dixit ex quibus" etc. The cod. Laurentianus indicates the teacher in the title: ἀπὸ φωνῆς Παλλαδίου. Even the Arabic "summary" is reminiscent of the controversies current in the school, when it says that some people divide medicine into two parts, others into five.

The fact that all these texts are lecture notes not only explains the variety of names, but also gives the reason why we could only classify them according to types. For all we can say is that the group comprising the papyrus, the Pavia edition and the cod. Ambrosianus represents one type of lectures, whereas the cod. Laurentianus represents a different type, and that the Arabic texts give abstracts which reflect similar activities.

The literary character of our texts indicates at the same time their place in the teaching of medicine of their period, for they are lecture notes on Galen's *De sectis,* which was the first book to be read in the medical curriculum of Alexandria. Galen himself had already recommended *De sectis* as a suitable introduction to his works[93] and a later Arabian author informs us that Alexandrian teachers had put together four Galenic books, headed by *De sectis,* and had addressed the collection to beginners.[94] Logically, therefore, the reading of the introductory medical textbook had to be preceded by an introduction into medicine as a whole and further, the cod. Laurentianus goes to great length to prove the necessity of implanting right dogmas into the minds of beginners.[95]

The procedure reflected in our introductions is, moreover, exactly analogous to contemporary procedures in the teaching of philosophy[96] and scientific disciplines in general.

The study of philosophy started with the reading of Aristotle's logical books, preceded by Porphyrius' *Eisagoge.* Thus the preface to the commentaries on this latter writing developed into a general introduction into philosophy.[97] The parallelism between the philosophical and the medical curricula goes even further. Although the late Alexandrian philosophers were Neo-Platonists, they read Aristotle first, and Plato later.[98] In medicine, instead of Aristotle and Plato, we find the names of Galen and Hippocrates and the introduction to the Pavia edition, in discussing the superiority of Galen or Hippocrates, says that since Hippocrates laid the foundation of

---

[93]Galen, De Ordine librorum suorum ad Eug. (*Scripta minora,* II, pp. 83, 23–84,4).

[94]Cf. *Hunain ibn Ishaq,* pp. 4–5. The four books are those commented on in the cod. Ambr.; except that the latter contains a commentary on the first book only of Galen's Methodus medendi ad Glauconem.

[95]Cod. Laur., fol. 201r.: οὕτω δεῖ καὶ ἡμᾶς ποιεῖν καὶ πρῶτον τὰς τῶν νέων ψυχὰς προεκκαθαίρειν ἐκ τῶν μοχθηρῶν δογμάτων καὶ οὕτω λαβεῖν χρηστὰ δόγματα etc.

[96]This has been suggested by Nachmanson (pp. 208–09 and 214–16) on the basis of the papyrus edited by him.

[97]Cf. Praechter, pp. 526–27 and Nachmanson, pp. 214–16.

[98]Praechter, p. 526 : "Denn mit Aristoteles begann das Studium, um zu Platon fortzuschreiten."

medicine, he ought to be introduced first; but since he is too difficult for beginners to follow, Galen is taken up first.[99]

But not only are the introductory medical writings related to corresponding philosophical works. Rabe has analysed late Greek introductions into rhetoric connected with the commentaries on Hermogenes' *Status*, and has demonstrated the influence of the neoplatonic arrangement upon them. Similar conditions obtained with regard to the study of grammar. Here the *Ars grammatica* by Dionysius Thrax formed the basic textbook[100] and the Scholia to it also contain introductions which in many ways are similar to the philosophical, rhetorical and medical introductions. Here too definitions of "art" are given,[101] the different kinds of arts are discussed,[102] the differences between ἐπιστήμη, τέχνη, ἐμπειρία and πεῖρα are explained[103] and seven or eight "capitula" are applied to the writing which is to be commentated.[104]

Thus the commentaries on *De sectis* only represent the medical example of a type of introduction into the study of arts, prevalent too in philosophy, grammar and rhetoric. All these introductions evince neoplatonic influence and they are all intimately connected. For Nachmanson has already shown that not only do the medical introductions reflect philosophical ideas and terminology, but that also the neoplatonic writers very often use medical exemplifications.[105] This wide use of medical exemplifications is found too among the rhetoricians,[106] while Rabe went so far as to consider passages of the cod. Laurentianus excerpts from rhetorical writings.[107] Finally, the same is also true with regard to grammar: The physician compares his procedures with those of the grammarian[108] and, vice versa, the grammarian exemplifies his art by medical comparisons.[109]

The teachers of these various disciplines all wrote from a philosophical point of view. That does not mean that they were necessarily philosophers by profession, but it makes it very difficult to decide to what vocation they originally belonged.[110] As to medicine we usually call them "Iatrosophists,"

[99]Ed. Pap. fol. 7r.: Videndum est deinde quis in medicina gloriosior extitit. Hippocras namque antiquior fuit tempore, Galenus posterior. Sed Hippocrates veluti semina nobis tradidit, Galenus autem semina illa excoluit et propagavit et perfectionem imposuit. Ergo Hippocrates introducendus esset : non tamen secundum dignitatem : sed tanquam gloriosus. Sed quia ad introductionem opus est persuasione: non enim tantam profunditatem aures introducendorum possent percipere, Galenum assumamus : et librum eius de introductione in medio constituamus : ut et opulentia et eius dulcedine adiuti : quod querimus inveniamus.

[100]Cf. Christ, pp. 427–28.

[101]Cf. *Scholia in Dion. Thr.*, p. 106 ff.

[102]Cf. *ibid.*, p. 110.

[103]Cf. *ibid.*, pp. 112–13.

[104]*Ibid.*, p. 123,25 and p. 159,6.

[105]Cf. Nachmanson, p. 210 ff. This seems to have been the case as regards mathematical commentaries too; cf. Deichgraeber, p. 328.

[106]Cf. Walz, IV, p. 8.

[107]Cf. Rabe, p. 562.

[108]Cf. Nachmanson, pp. 207–08 and 216 for the papyrus; ed. Pap. fol. 6v.: Ostendimus autem et grammaticam artem que habet subiacentiam et perfectionem etc.

[109]Cf., e.g., *Scholia in Dion. Thr.*, pp. 2 and 158; cf. also Deichgraeber, pp. 125 and 328.

[110]A comprehensive term for them seems to have been "technographoi." Cf. Sextus Em-

leaving open the question whether they were philosophers who were also interested in the exegesis of medical texts, or whether they were physicians who treated their subject philosophically and with some knowledge of the other arts. For in late Alexandria the theory of medicine was considered a philosophical subject in which even Christian theologists were interested and, on the other hand, it was impossible to teach medicine scientifically without some knowledge of philosophy.[111]

The iatrosophists were first of all teachers of medical theory and it is indeed doubtful whether all of them were engaged in medical practice. For of Magnus of Nisibis, an Alexandrian iatrosophist of the second half of the 4th century A.D., it is said that, basing his arguments on Aristotle, he was stronger in dialectic discussions than in therapeutics;[112] and of Gesius, another Alexandrian iatrosophist, his biographer deems it necessary expressly to state that he was efficient in the practice as well as in the teaching of medicine.[113]

Thus it would seem that the division of medicine into theory and practice as seen in our texts, was more than a logical arrangement. It appears indeed to reflect the medical life of the time, when the theory of medicine was taught by the iatrosophists, while medical practice was largely in the hands of such physicians as Alexander of Tralles, Aëtius and Paulus of Aegina whose writings are handbooks of practical medicine.[114]

APPENDIX

1. *Definitions of medicine.*   Comparative excerpts from the cod. Ambrosianus and the Pavia edition.

Cod. Ambr. fol. 25v.–26r.	Ed. Pap. fol. 7r.
Primus Ypocrates dixit, quia medicina est abiectio et detractio. Abiectio est addere cibos digestibiles et nutrire corpus; detractio est quod superfluum fuerit per flebothomum aut catarticum subtrahere. Secundus est Alexander amicus veritatis qui dixit, quia medicina est dieta sanorum terapeutica aegrotorum. Dieta hoc est gimnizare lavacra et alia quaeque talia quae circa aegrotum fiunt. Tertius Platon	Hippocrates sic diffinivit. Medicina est adiectio et detractio. Adiectio ad hoc quod minus. Detractio ut superfluum est. Ut enim agricola a superfluis et spinosis que fructus suffocant terram emendare festinat: et sic seminat: sic et medicus agricola est humani corporis: et festinat que sunt superflua deducere: et quibus indiget introducere: per flebothomiam etenim deducuntur superflua: et per curationes catartici:

---

piricus, *Adv. math.*, XI, 8; *Scholia in Dion. Thr.*, p. 165,2 : Τῶν τεχνογράφων οἱ μὲν; cf. *Ibid.*, pp. 556,18 and 564,34. As to its use in rhetoric, cf. Spengel, I, p. 427,12 : Ἔνιοι μὲν τῶν τεχνογράφων etc.

[111]Cf. Schemmel, p. 440 ff. and Temkin, p. 45.

[112]Eunapius, *Vitae Sophist*, p. 498 (Boissonade) : Μάγνος ... τῇ περὶ τῶν σωμάτων τῶν προαιρετικῶν φύσει τὸν Ἀριστοτέλην ἐς τὸ δύνασθαι λέγειν συνεφελκυσάμενος σιωπᾶν μὲν ἐν τῷ λέγειν τοὺς ἰατροὺς ἠνάγκαζε, θεραπεύειν δὲ οὐκ ἐδόκει δυνατὸς εἶναι καθάπερ λέγειν.

[113]Suidas, s.v. Gesius :καὶ μέγα κλέος εἶχεν οὐ μόνον ἰατρικῆς ἕνεκα παρασκευῆς, τῆς τε διδασκαλικῆς καὶ τῆς ἐργάτιδος, ἀλλὰ καὶ etc.; cf. Schemmel, p. 441.

[114] Cf. Puschmann, p. 140.

philosophus dixit, medicina est superinundans aut diminuens. Iste dicebat duo esse cupidines in hominibus unum bonum et alterum malum. Malum qui trahit mentes nostras ad inferioras partes furtum facere adulterare et his similia. Bonum qui levat mentes nostras ad caelestia et superiora, id est facere elemosina et his similia. Quartus Aristotelis philosophus dixit, quia medicina est philosophia corporis philosophia est medicina † † Iuste sic dixit, quia medicina et philosophia duae sorores sunt, quia et ambae artes hominibus prosunt. Medicina curat quae sunt corporis vitia, philosophia curat quae sunt animae vitia. Quintus Eraclides erithresus dixus (?) bene dixi eritreus, quia est et alius eraclides tarentinus. Ipse dixit, quia medicina est disciplina sanorum aegrotantium atque neutrorum. Sanum est corpus quod ex nativitate proponit operationem; infirmum est corpus quod non utiliter proponit operationem; neutrum est corpus quando ex aegritudine relevantur et neque infirmi sunt neque bene sani.

nec non per sudorem et clistere: sed et hec per accidentia. per abstinentiam autem dum introducit bonos cibos: que superflua sunt purgat. Alexander amator veritatis medicinam diffinivit ita. Medicina est dieta custodiens sanitatem: et curans egritudinem. Quoniam medicine non solum sufficit ut curet egritudinem: sed etiam ut sanitatem custodiat in sanis hominibus. Aristoteles autem volens ostendere quod medicina satis coniungitur philosophie dixit. Philosophia est medicina anime. Festinat namque philosophus anime passiones curare: que multe et diverse sunt: ut cupiditas et libido: ingens furor extra rationem: et multa huiusmodi: que omnia in egrota anima philosophus festinat mitigare et refrenare. Medicinam sic diffiniunt. Medicina est philosophia corporis, quia medicus philosophicat circa corpus hominis: primum inquirens elementa et secundum temperationes: humores membra et operationes. Diffinivit etiam Aristoteles ita philosophia et medicina due sorores sunt. Divinus autem Plato due sunt inquit cupidines idest mores in corpore nostro: una sanitatis et altera egritudinis. Et diffinivit medicinam sic dicendo. Medicina est temperantia corporis adversus plenitudinem et inanitionem. Quia qui cognoscit bonam et malam cupidinem optimus est medicus. Et bene dixit bonam et malam cupidinem: quia in sanis hominibus pulchritudo et equalitas membrorum delectat visus aspicientium: languentium autem corpus fedum et insuave videtur. Erophilus autem sic diffinivit medicinam. Medicina est disciplina sanorum languentium et neutrorum. Cui videtur Galenus consentire. Et hic diffinitio sibi dicitur placere.

2. *Representatives of the three schools.*

Ed. Pap. fol. 7r.: Sed nunc videamus qui medicinam constituerunt: et eos auctores secundum sectas suas nominemus. Empericam namque sectam Serapion et Apollonius senior: et Apollonius iunior et Eraclitus Nichomacus Gautica Menedoctus. Sextus affer. Logicam sectam: Hippocras: Paragoras; Diocles: Erasistratus: Crisippus: Herophilus: Leufastus: Asclepiades: Galenus: illi empericam: isti logicam constituerunt. Methodicam sectam: Thesion: Thesilus: Dionysius: Manaseus: Phylon: Olimpicus: Seranus: Menemacus: Avidianus invenerunt.[115]

Cod. add. 23407 of the British Museum, fol. 3 v.:[116]

والذين قاموا بتثبيت فرقة اصحاب التجارب اقرون الاقراغنطينى
وفيلقوس العوامى وسرافيون الاسكندرانى وسنطس وابولونيوس
والذين قاموا بتثبيت فرقة اصحاب القياس ابقراط وديوقيلس
وفركساغورس وقولوطيمس وارسطراطس واسيقليباذس والذين
قاموا بتثبيت فرقة اصحاب الحيل ناميس الاديغى وثاسلس
وميانانداس(؟)[117] وميناساوس(؟) وسورانس.

BIBLIOGRAPHICAL ABBREVIATIONS

Ackermann	J. Chr. G. Ackermann, Historia literaria Claudii Galeni. In: *Claudii Galeni opera omnia,* ed. C. G. Kuehn, Vol. I, Lipsiae, 1821.
An-Nadim	*Kitāb al-Fihrist,* hrsg. von G. Flügel, I, Leipzig, 1871.
Braeutigam	W. Braeutigam, *De Hippocratis epidemiarum libri sexti commentatoribus,* Diss. Koenigsberg, 1908.
Buonamici	F. Buonamici, Burgundio Pisano. In: *Annali delle Università Toscane,* Vol. 28, Pisa, 1908.
Catalogue	*Catalogus codicum manuscriptorum orientalium qui in Museo Britannico asservantur.* Pars secunda, Londini, 1852.
Cat. suppl.	*Catalogus codicum orientalium Musei Britannici,* Partis II Supplementum, Londini, 1871.
Choulant	L. Choulant, *History and Bibliography of Anatomic Illustration,* translated and edited by Mortimer Frank, Chicago, 1920.
Christ	W. v. Christ, *Geschichte der Griechischen Litteratur,* II, 1; 6th ed., Muenchen, 1920.
CMG	*Corpus medicorum Graecorum,* I, 1; Lips. et Berol., 1927.
Cod. Ambr.	Cod. Ambrosianus G 108 inf.
Cod. Laur.	Cod. Laurentianus plut. 74,11.
Cod. Vind.	Cod. Vindobonensis med. 35.
Costomiris	A. G. Costomiris, Etudes sur les écrits des médecins Grecs. In: *Revue d. études Grecques,* II, Paris, 1889.
Daremberg	Ch. Daremberg, *Histoire d. Sciences méd.* I, Paris, 1870.

[115]For this list cf. also Wellmann, pp. 368–71.

[116]The photostatic copy which I have used is not always clearly legible. I have transcribed the passage to the best of my ability. The names mentioned could be reconstructed as follows: For the Empiricists, Acron of Agrigent, Philinus of Cos, Serapion of Alexandria, Sextus, Apollonius. For the Dogmatists: Hippocrates, Diocles, Praxagoras, Philotimus, Erasistratus, Asclepiades. For the Methodists: Themison of Laodicaea, Thessalus, Menemachus (? or Menodotus?) Mnaseas (?), Soranus. The list in the cod. Arund. Or. 17 is substantially the same.

[117]In this as well as in the following word the reading is very uncertain since the diacritical points seem to be missing.

Diels
H. Diels, *Die Handschriften der antiken Aerzte*, 3 volumes, Berlin 1905–1908.

Dietz
F. R. Dietz, *Apollonii Citiensis, etc. Scholia in Hippocratem et Galenum*, 2 volumes, Regimontii Prussorum, 1834.

Deichgraeber
K. Deichgraeber, *Die Griechische Empirikerschule*, Berlin, 1930.

De Renzi
S. De Renzi, *Collectio Salernitana*, I, Napoli, 1852.

Ed. Pap.
Latin edition of Galen's works prepared by Rusticus Placentinus, Vol. I, Pavia, 1515

Elias
Eliae in Porphyrii Isagogen et Aristotelis Categorias Commentaria, ed. A. Busse, Berolini, 1900 (*Commentaria in Aristotelem Graeca*, XVIII, 1).

Englert
L. Englert, *Untersuchungen zu Galens Schrift Thrasybulos*, Leipzig, 1929.

Giacosa
P. Giacosa, *Magistri Salernitani nondum editi*, Torino, 1901.

Helmreich
G. Helmreich, Galeni libellum Περὶ αἱρέσεων τοῖς εἰσαγομένοις In: *Acta seminarii philologici Erlangensis*, Vol. II, Erlangen, 1881.

Hunain ibn Ishaq
Ḥunain ibn Isḥāq, Ueber die Syrischen und Arabischen Galen-Uebersetzungen. Zum ersten Male herausgegeben und uebersetzt von G. Bergstraesser, Leipzig, 1925.

Ibn Qifti
Ibn al-Qifṭī's *Ta'rīḫ al-Ḥukamā'*, ed. J. Lippert, Leipzig, 1903.

Kroehnert
O. Kroehnert, *Canonesne Poetarum scriptorum artificium per antiquitatem fuerunt?* Diss. Königsberg, 1897.

Kühn
C. G. Kühn, *Claudii Galeni opera omnia*, Lipsiae, 1821 ff.

Meyerhof (I)
M. Meyerhof, Von Alexandrien nach Bagdad. In: *Sitzungsberichte d. Preuss. Akademie d. Wissensch. Phil.-Hist. Klasse*, 1930, XXIII, 389–429.

Meyerhof (II)
M. Meyerhof, Joannes Grammatikos (Philoponos) von Alexandrien und die arabische Medizin. In: *Mitteilungen d. Deutschen Instituts für Aegyptische Altertumskunde in Kairo*, Bd. II., 1931, 1–21.

Meyerhof (III)
M. Meyerhof, La fin de l'École d'Alexandrie d'après quelques Auteurs Arabes. In: *Archeion*, XV, 1, 1933, 1–15.

Mørland
H. Mørland, *D. lateinischen Oribasiusübersetzungen.* Osloae, 1932 (Symbolae Osloenses Fasc. Supplet. V.).

Nachmanson
E. Nachmanson, Ein neuplatonischer Galenkommentar auf Papyrus. In: *Minnesskrift utgiven av Filologiska Samfundet i Goeteborg*, Goeteborg, 1925, 201–17.

Papyrus
Cf. Nachmanson.

Praechter
K. Praechter. In: *Byzantinische Zeitschrift*, XVIII, 1909, 516–538.

Puschmann
Th. Puschmann, *A History of Medical Education.* Transl. and ed. by E. H. Hare, London, 1891.

Rabe
H. Rabe, Aus Rhetoren-Handschriften. In: *Rheinisches Museum für Philologie*, N. F. 64, 1909, 539–90.

Ritter-Walzer
H. Ritter and R. Walzer, Arabische Übersetzungen Griechischer Aerzte in Stambuler Bibliotheken. In: *Sitzungsberichte d. Preuss. Akad. d. Wissensch. Phil.-Hist. Klasse*, 1934, XXVI, 801–46.

Rose (I)   V. Rose, *Aristoteles Pseudepigraphus*, Lipsiae, 1863.
Rose (II)   V. Rose, Ion's Reisebilder und Ioannes Alexandrinus. In:
                    Hermes, V, 1871, 205–15.
Schemmel   F. Schemmel, D. Hochschule v. Alexandria im IV. u. V.
                    Jahrhundert P. Ch. N. In: *Neue Jahrbücher f. d. klass. Al-
                    tert.*, 1909, 438–57.
Schoene (I)   H. Schoene, De Aristoxeni Περὶ τῆς ʽΗροφίλου αἱρέσεως
                    etc. Diss. Bonn, 1893.
Schoene (II)   H. Schoene, *Galenus de partibus artis medicativae*, Greifswald,
                    1911.
Scholia in Dion. Thr. *Scholia in Dionysii Thracis Artem Grammaticam*, rec. A. Hilgard
                    (*Grammatici Graeci*, I, 3), Lipsiae, 1901.
Scripta minora   *Claudii Galeni Pergameni Scripta minora*, 3 volumes, Lipsiae,
                    1884–1893.
Sigerist   H. E. Sigerist, The medical literature of the early Middle
                    Ages. In: *Bulletin of the Institute of the History of Medicine,
                    The Johns Hopkins University*, II, 1934, 26–50.
Spengel   L. Spengel, *Rhetores Graeci*, I, Lipsiae, 1853.
Temkin   O. Temkin, Geschichte des Hippokratismus im ausgehen-
                    den Altertum. In: *Kyklos*, IV, Leipzig, 1932, 1–80.
Walz   Chr. Walz, *Rhetores Graeci*, IV, Stuttgartiae et Tubingae,
                    1833.
Wellmann   M. Wellmann, Z. Gesch. d. Med. i. Altert. In: *Hermes*, 35
                    1900, 349–84.

13

The Byzantine Origin
of the Names for the Basilic
and Cephalic Veins*[1]

THE NAMES "vena basilica" and "vena cephalica" are so reminiscent of the Greek words βασιλικὸς and κεφαλικὸς that it was natural to assume the existence of a φλὲψ βασιλικὴ and a ψλὲψ κεφαλικὴ in ancient Greek authors. But in 1879 Joseph Hyrtl, a leading anatomist and an authority for anatomical nomenclature, denied the existence of either Greek designation. According to Hyrtl, they are Latin renderings of the Arabic al-bāsilīq and al-qīfāl.[2]

Hyrtl's contention has been accepted widely,[3] though not unanimously;[4] for twenty years after Hyrtl, Macalister argued convincingly against Hyrtl's hypothesis of the Arabic origin of the terms.[5] Hyrtl had not tried to explain the meaning of al-bāsilīq and al-qīfāl, and Macalister stressed the point that these words and related forms have no meaning in Arabic and the related semitic languages, Hebrew and Syriac, except as borrowings from the Greek. Macalister quoted from the Latin translation of the pseudo Galenic *Anatomia vivorum*, which he believed to stem from a Syriac source, composed after 840 A.D. He concluded his discussion of the two terms with the words: "Farther back I have not yet traced these words, but some Greek text must have existed from which the words have come."[6]

Actually, the Arabic terms appear in the translation by Ḥunain ibn Isḥāq and his nephew Ḥubaish of book 10 of Galen's "Anatomical Administrations". In an excursion on phlebotomy at the elbow, we hear of three kinds of possible injuries:

"Together with the vein al-ʿakhal (lit. the black), which is in the very middle of the veins in the bend of the elbow, a small nerve is cut which is situated there. Or, together with the large vein, al-bāsilīq on the inner side,

*From *XVIIe Congrès International d'Histoire de la Médecine*, vol. 1: *Communications*, Athens, 1961, pp. 336–39.
[1]With the support of a grant from the American Philosophical Society.
[2]Joseph Hyrtl, *Das Arabische und Hebräische in der Anatomie*, Vienna, 1879, pp. 76 and 97; and *Onomatologia Anatomica*, Vienna, 1880, pp. 69 and 103.
[3]For instance, Charles Singer and C. Rabin, *A Prelude to Modern Science*, Cambridge University Press, 1946, p. 7, note 42.
[4]For instance, Hermann Triepel, *Die anatomischen Namen, ihre Ableitung und Aussprache.* 25. Auflage von Robert Herrlinger. Munich, 1957, pp. 18 and 21.
[5]A. Macalister,"Archaeologia anatomica III. The veins of the forearm," *Journal of Anatomy and Physiology*, 1899, *33* (n.s. *13*) : 343–49.
[6]*Ibid.*, p. 348.

the artery situated underneath is cut. Or, together with the vein *al-qīfāl* of the shoulder, the origin of the sinewy muscle is cut."[7]

The editor, Max Simon, considered the Arabic words additions by the translators, rather than part of the Galenic text, and was herein followed by Singer and Rabin.[8]

At any rate, in their Arabic forms, basilic and cephalic can be traced as far back as the late 9th century. And the same, roughly speaking, holds true of the Latin vena cephalica.

Vena cephalica is found in the Codex Bruxellensis 3701–15 in two short phlebotomy texts attributed to Hippocrates.[9] I quote the following examples: "In brachio incidimus venas tres, cephalicon, meson et epaticon....[10] Caephalica vena est quae a capite habet principatum....[11] Caephalica vena incidimus propter causas capitis et oculorum suffusionis et pro impetus vel tumoris grandis oculorum".[12]

The occurrence in these texts of the 10th century which predate Constantinus of Africa and Arabic influence by a hundred years, proves that there existed a term φλὲψ κεφαλική which entered both Arabic and Latin literature. But can this expression and the corresponding φλὲψ βασιλική actually be traced to Greek sources?

During my research in the summer of 1956 I chanced upon a number of Greek texts which mention the cephalic and basilic veins.[13] Thus the Parisinus graecus 2224, on fol. 68v states: "In each arm we cut three veins, in the right arm the cephalic, the catholic, and the hepatic."[14] The occurrence of 'catholic' vein where we would have expected 'median' vein, is particularly interesting. Now the same Paris codex contains another text studied more than 100 years ago by Daremberg, who quoted the following passage: "... bleed him from another vein, the so called median (μέση); some

---

[7]Max Simon, *Sieben Bücher Anatomie des Galen*, 2 vols., Leipzig, 1906; see vol. 1, p. 58, and vol. 2, p. 42; also Singer and Rabin, *loc. cit.*

[8]Simon, *op. cit.* vol. 2, p. 269 f., and Singer and Rabin, *loc. cit.*

[9]The first of these texts, ("Incipit perid fleotomia Yppocratis") was published by Arthur Morgenstern, *Das Aderlassgedicht des Johannes von Aquila* etc., Thesis, Leipzig, 1917. It was Morgenstern's publication which alerted me to the existence of the name vena cephalica in pre-Arabic western literature; cf. my review of Singer and Rabin in *Bull. Hist. Med.*, 1953, 27: 393–96. The title of the second text is: "Epistula de incisione fleotomi quem conposuit Yppocrates de incisione venarum." On the Codex Bruxellensis 3701–15 and both texts see Augusto Beccaria, *I codici di medicina del periodo presalernitano*, Rome, 1956, pp. 112–17.

[10]Cod. ms. fol. 10v, Morgenstern *op cit.*, p. 66.

[11]Cod. ms. fol. 10v, Morgenstern *op. cit.*, p. 67. The "Epistula de incisione fleotomi" begins similarly (fol. 11r): "Hoc est vena caephalica, a capite habet principatum."

[12]Cod. ms. fol. 11r, Morgenstern *op cit*, p. 71; cf. Temkin, *op. cit.* p. 396. How variable the terminology was, evinces from another text (or chapter?) of the same Brussels ms. (fol. 11v: "Qualis venas sunt incidendas") where we read: "In brachio enim tres sunt venae quae fleotomantur necessariae. Capitalisque superior et media quae dicitur matricalis et tercia inferior cubito proxima et dicitur iusana."

[13]Owsei Temkin in *Year Book of The American Philosophical Society.* 1957, pp. 448–50.

[14]Cod. Parisinus graecus 2224 fol. 68v: ... εἰς ἕκαστον βραχίονα τέμνομεν τρεῖς, εἰς μὲν τὴν δεξιὰν χεῖρα κεφαλικήν, καθολικήν, καὶ ἡπατικήν.

people call this vein καθολική, and some call it βασιλική."[15] Here then we meet with the basilic vein in Greek. Daremberg was interested in the name καθολική rather than βασιλική.[16] Writing before Hyrtl, he had not thought of doubting the Greek origin of 'basilic'. If Daremberg's excerpts had not been overlooked by Hyrtl and apparently by others after him, the whole hypothesis of the Arabic provenience of the names for these veins might never have been born.

For completeness' sake, I mention that the codex Parisinus graecus 36, on folios 96 r–99 r contains a text entitled: "Selections on phlebotomy by Paul of Aegina from the works of Hippocrates and Galen," in which both κεφαλική and βασιλική occur.[17] Moreover, I have found the cephalic vein, sometimes referred to as κρανιακή, mentioned in a number of other Greek texts.[18]

We can therefore say that the terms for the cephalic and basilic veins can be traced in Greek, and must have existed by 850. In the material analysed by me, the term "cephalic vein" occurs more frequently than the term "basilic vein." Moreover, the latter designation is by no means fixed, as is best shown by the alternative "catholic vein".

We have so far treated the question of the origin of our terms as a matter of anatomical nomenclature. To show their Greek origin, reference to the existing Greek manuscripts alone would have sufficed. I have chosen the longer route via Arabic and Latin translations for two reasons. First, because they give us a terminus ad quem which the relatively late Greek manuscripts (15th to 17th centuries) do not provide. Can we establish a terminus a quo? Our material does not suffice to give a clear answer. If we exclude the occurrence in the Arabic translation of Galen's "Anatomical Administrations," we can say that the words have not been found in any classical anatomical and surgical text. But an argumentum ex silentio is, of course, a weak one. A hint, however, is provided by the kind of material which we studied. The Arabic, Latin, and Greek texts—and this is my second reason for taking them all into consideration—discuss the veins within the context of phlebotomy. From this point of view our investigation takes on added significance. We are not primarily dealing with the ter-

---

[15]Ch. Daremberg, *Notices et extraits des manuscrits médicaux grecs, latins et français*. Paris, 1853, p. 29: Ὅταν φλεγμαίνουσιν αἱ λεγόμεναι σιαγόνες ... φλεβοτόμησον τοῦτον κρανιακήν ... φλεβοτόμησον αὐτὸν ἄλλην φλέβα τὴν λεγομένην μέσην, τινὲς δὲ λέγουσι ταύτην καθολικὴν καί τινες λέγουσιν αὐτὴν βασιλικήν.

[16]*Ibid.* footnote 1.

[17]Cod. Parisinus gr. 36 fol. 96v: Ἐκ τοῦ βραχίονος Γ, κεφαλικήν, μέσην, ἡπατικήν, ἥ α ἐστὶν ἡ κεφαλικὴ ἀπὸ κεφαλῆς ἔχουσα τὴν ἀρχὴν καὶ συμβάλλουσα ὑπὲρ τὸν ὦμον καὶ τοῦ βραχίονος. Fol. 98v: ἡ μὲν καθόλου φλεβοτομία ὅλον τὸ σῶμα ὠφελεῖ, ἡ δὲ ἐπάνω τῆς βασιληκῆς (sic) φλέβα ὠφελεῖ (?) ἐς ὅλον τὸ πρόσωπον καὶ εἰς τοὺς ὀδόντας. There is considerable similarity between this and related Greek texts and the Latin phlebotomy texts of the Cod. Bruxellensis 3701 mentioned above. I intend to investigate the question of their relationship further.

[18]Cod. Parisinus graecus 2303 fol. 79r–82r: Ἑρμηνεία τῆς φλεβοτομίας. Cod. Parisinus graecus 2320 fol. 13v–14v: Περὶ ἐκ ποίων τόπων φλευοτομεῖν, Ἱπποκράτους. This text suggests Latin influence as does Parisinus graecus Coislin 335, fol. 47r–49v (?): φλεφοτομία λέγεται etc.—British Museum, Cod. Addit. 17,900, fol. 272r–272v (?) Περὶ φλεβοτομίας etc.

minology of the learned anatomist, but with that of the practical man. We are dealing with a type of literature which includes uroscopy, pulse lore, brief dietetic rules, medical astrology, prescriptions, etc. Ideler's *Physici et Medici Graeci minores* gives us good and well known examples. It is a type of practical literature which we find in Greek as well as Latin manuscripts. The texts are often very short, not clearly separated as to beginning and end, and their style far from elegant. This type of literature reflects everyday medical practice. I do not doubt that this literature existed in classical antiquity, but it is only from the early Byzantine centuries on that abundant material has been preserved. Here, I believe, our terminology either originated or came to the fore, and such fanciful names as catholic vein, and basilic vein were coined. Incidentally, the name basilic, i.e., royal vein, is no more fanciful than Morbus regius, the royal disease, for jaundice. We are dealing with the period of the *Capsula eburnea* and perhaps also with that of the Five Picture Series. If our hypothesis is correct, then our terminological study not only solves a problem of anatomical terminology, but gives us a more exact approach to the practice of medicine in the centuries of Oribasius and Paul of Aegina.

14

Byzantine Medicine: Tradition
and Empiricism*

I

ACCORDING to the textbooks, Byzantine medicine extends from A.D. 330 to A.D. 1453. But this long period is not uniform in itself. It must be divided into two phases: one which extends to 642, the year of the Arab entry into Alexandria, the other including the subsequent period when Constantinople formed the center of medical practice.[1]

The Alexandrian period, seen in the perspective of antiquity, was a period of considerable formative power. It did not merely continue what had been done and known before. Out of the works of Galen it created a medical system that was to endure for a thousand years. It was still heathen, even though some of its teachers became Christians.[2] Medicine of the period of Constantinople was Christian. It accepted rather than shaped a tradition.

However, as Meyerhof has shown in detail, the school of Alexandria survived the Arabic conquest till about A.D. 700.[3] Syrians and Arabs were more direct heirs of the last phase of Alexandrian medicine than was Constantinople.[4] Early Arab medicine lies like a wedge between our knowledge of medicine in Alexandria and Constantinople. It gives us much valuable information but it does not always reveal when and where the events it relates took place.

Byzantine medicine thus represents the formation as well as the continuation of a tradition, broken and unbroken. It also represents the cultivation of practices of which some have a clear origin while that of others is obscure.

We shall first discuss the formation of the Galenic system in Alexandria.

---

*From *Dumbarton Oaks Papers* (The Dumbarton Oaks Center for Byzantine Studies), 1962, vo. 16, pp. 97–115.

[1]Max Neuburger, *Geschichte der Medizin,* II (Stuttgart, 1911), 97. The articles by Iwan Bloch on "Griechische Aerzte des dritten und vierten (nachchristlichen) Jahrhunderts," and "Byzantinische Medizin" in Neuburger-Pagel, *Handbuch der Medizin,* I (Jena, 1902), 481–91 and 492–568 still form an important basis for any survey of Byzantine medicine. For a recent discussion of many aspects of Byzantine medicine. see *XIIe Congrès international d'histoire de la médecine, Athènes-Cos, 4–14 Septembre 1960,* 2 vols. (Athens, 1960).

[2]Owsei Temkin, "Geschichte des Hippokratismus im ausgehenden Altertum," *Kyklos* (Leipzig), 4 (1932), 1–80.

[3]Max Meyerhof, *Von Alexandrien nach Bagdad* (Berlin, 1930) Sitzungsberichte der Preussischen Akademie der Wissenschaften, Phil.-Hist. Klasse, 23 (1930).

[4]It must, moreover, not be overlooked that from 616 to about 628 Alexandria was under Sassanian rule.

We shall then turn to the obscure interlude before later Constantinopolitan medicine emerges more clearly. Finally, we shall select a few aspects of tradition and empiricism apparent during this later period.[5]

II

When Galen died in Rome around A.D. 200, he left a reputation as physician and philosopher, and a body of writings which would have filled considerably more than the twenty-two volumes of the Kühn edition that have come down to us in Greek. These works were partly logical and philosophical, and it is here that the greatest losses have been suffered. Others belonged to anatomy and physiology, if we may stretch modern terms; still others dealt with a great variety of medical topics, including materia medica. Finally, there was a series of commentaries on several works attributed to Hippocrates, by then considered the greatest of all physicians. In these commentaries, and also in others of his books, Galen tried to prove that Hippocrates was to medicine what Plato was to philosophy, and that he, Galen, was the true interpreter and follower of Hippocrates.[6]

Galen thus bridged more than five hundred years of development. A victory for Galen meant, in the first place, a defeat for those medical sects which were not Rationalist, i.e., which did not base medicine on anatomical dissection, physiological experiment, and speculation about causes both hidden and evident. Galen debated with the sects of the Empiricists and Methodists, and a book "On Sects" which he himself intended for beginners became one of the elementary texts in Alexandria. "For it is useful to learn what is good and to reject what is bad. We reject the empirical and methodical art, and we take to ourselves the rational art which is pure and useful,"[7] writes a commentator of the early sixth century with regard to this work.[8]

As a sect, the Methodists never were strong in the Greek East. Of Empiricists we hear little after A.D. 200; their successors, the Empirics of the Middle Ages, were a different breed: The Empiricists had been learned men, philosophical defenders of observation as the only source of knowledge.[9] Empirics were practitioners who had little but experience on which to draw.

---

[5]The following is no more than an attempt to put together some selected topics, on which I am still working, in a picture that undoubtedly will need many corrections and elaborations.

[6]For this and the following, see Temkin, "Geschichte des Hippokratismus."

[7]Cod. Ambrosianus, G 108 inf., fol. 28ʳ: *Utile est enim discere quae bona sunt et quae mala sunt rennuere. Rennuimus impiricam et methodicam, suscepimus logicam mundam et utilem artem.*

[8]On the dating and provenience of the text, see Owsei Temkin, "Studies on Late Alexandrian Medicine: I. Alexandrian Commentaries on Galen's *De sectis ad introducendos*," *Bulletin of the History of Medicine*, 3 (1935), 408, [Essay 12, p. 180].

[9]Karl Deichgräber, *Die griechische Empirikerschule* (Berlin, 1930), and Ludwig Edelstein, "Empirie und Skepsis in der griechischen Empirikerschule," *Quellen und Studien zur Geschichte der Naturwissenschaften und der Medizin*, III, 4 (1933), 45–53.

Galen's victory meant the unification of medicine, a unification which was to last till the days of Paracelsus in the sixteenth century. Since it recognized anatomy, physiology, and pathology as sciences basic to medicine, it drew the outlines of medicine as we still know them today.

This was achieved by the second half of the fourth century and is reflected in the works of Oribasius, the friend of the Emperor Julian the Apostate. Oribasius had compiled a compendium "from the writings of Galen only."[10] Then followed Oribasius' *Collections,* a large encyclopedia of medical knowledge that aimed at presenting each subject in the words of the author who had best treated it. It was a reference work, as were the encyclopedias of Alexander of Tralles and Aetius of Amida in the sixth century, and it served the added purpose of protection against the repetitious treatment of the same matters,[11] already felt to be a nuisance in the fourth century. Among the authors cited by Oribasius, Galen holds the first rank and is excerpted more frequently than anyone else.

There are a number of facts that explain the preference given to Galen. He was the last of the original medical scientists; he linked medicine and philosophy; he admired Plato, yet in method he followed Aristotle. Like Ptolemy[12] he had thrown his net very far; apart from technical works on the surgical disciplines, he offered information on all medical subjects from anatomy to uroscopy and drug lore. Above all, he presented a medical theory that penetrated all his works and united them, and was at the same time able to incorporate a wealth of anatomical, clinical, and pharmacological detail.

Galen was very much aware of his eminence. Lacking any discernible trace of humor, he took himself *au grand sérieux,* did not shun controversy, or hesitate to make his superiority very clear. Oribasius who, incidentally, was a countryman of Galen's, admired him because, as he says, in following the principles and opinions of Hippocrates, Galen made use of the most exact methods and definitions.[13] In his animal anatomy, Galen's exactness as a dissector has rarely been surpassed. In his pharmacology, he tried to introduce an exact grading of the potency of drugs which would fit a similar exactness in gauging the nature of diseases, so that a cold disease could be counteracted exactly by a hot remedy. This, in particular, would appear as Hippocratic since the principle of *contraria contrariis curantur* was considered a truly Hippocratic maxim.[14]

In the nineteenth century, when Galen was generally held to have been the main obstacle to medical progress during the Middle Ages, his greatness was denied, and what had once been seen as virtue was now viewed as tiresome self-glorification and senseless verbiage. This gave rise to

---

[10]Oribasius, *Collectionum medicarum reliquiae* 1, 1, ed. Ioannes Raeder (Leipzig-Berlin, 1928) (Corpus Medicorum Graecorum VI, 1, 1,), 4, 3–6.

[11]*Ibid.,* 4, 12: περιττὸν δὲ νομίσας εἶναι καὶ παντελῶς εὔηθες τὸ ἐγγράφειν τὰ αὐτὰ πολλάκις.

[12]Festugière, *La révélation d'Hermès Trismégiste,* I (Paris, 1950), 2 ff.

[13]Oribasius, *op. cit.,* 4,17.

[14]For references, see Temkin, "Geschichte des Hippokratismus," 38.

Wilamowitz von Moellendorff's notorious phrase "Seichbeutel Galen."[15] Yet, unjust as is this description of Galen as a windbag, it nevertheless points to weaknesses in Galen's writings; weaknesses, that is, if viewed by a professor who had to teach Galenic medicine. Galen's writings were too numerous to be read in their entirety, his style was prolix, and his underlying medical theory, though consistent in its essential features, was expressed unevenly. Since many of his writings served particular purposes, they accentuated different things at different times.[16] The late Alexandrian iatrosophists, i.e., the teachers of medicine, thus took it upon themselves to make a selection of Galenic works to be read in the schools, to comment upon them, and to summarize them. They fulfilled a similar task for the works of Hippocrates.[17] The theoretical study of medicine leaned heavily on these two authorities, just as the study of philosophy leaned on Aristotle and Plato. The late Neoplatonic teachers began with Porphyry and Aristotle; the iatrosophists, similarly, began with Galen.

Before turning to the late school of Alexandria, we must, however, take a somewhat broader view of medical activities from the middle of the fourth century to the beginning of the seventh, or, to express it in authors, from Oribasius to Paul of Aegina.

As the works of the great encyclopedists, especially Oribasius and Aetius of Amida, show, the ascendancy of Galen did not imply a disregard of all other authors before him, nor the suppression of all originality after him. Even heretics were utilized if they had been prominent in some field, as Soranus had been in gynecology. Side by side with Galen, Dioscorides was studied and excerpted as the great pharmacologist. A beautifully illustrated edition of his materia medica was prepared for the princess Juliana Anicia in Constantinople around A.D. 500. Jacob Psychrestus practiced in Constantinople in the fifth century. Himself a pagan, he was credited by pagan sources[18] with almost divine attributes. So extraordinary are his diagnostic and therapeutic abilities said to have been, that he was generally named · "Savior," like the healing god Asclepius.[19] His nickname Psychrestus was taken to indicate a therapeutic bias in favor of a liquifying diet, "because he saw that most people were very busy and covetous of money and always lived a life full of grief and worry."[20]

Jacob Psychrestus received a salary from the city, which probably means that he served as a public physician.[21] General as this institution had been

---

[15]U. v. Wilamowitz-Moellendorff, *Isyllos von Epidauros* (Berlin, 1886) 122, note 12: "... der unerträgliche seichbeutel Galen."

[16]Owsei Temkin, "Galen's Pneumatology," *Gesnerus* (Aarau) 8 (1951), 180–89, esp. 189 [Essay 9, p. 161].

[17]For details, see Meyerhof, *Von Alexandrien nach Bagdad* and Temkin, "Geschichte des Hippokratismus," esp. 51–80.

[18]The main source for Jacob Psychrestus is Damascius' Life of the Philosopher Isidoros which Rudolf Asmus, *Das Leben des Philosophen Isidoros von Damaskios aus Damaskos* (Leipzig 1911), reconstructed in German translation, chiefly from the Suda and Photius.

[19]*Ibid.*, 73,14–16.

[20]*Alexander von Tralles*, ed. Th. Puschmann, II (Vienna, 1879), 163.

[21]Asmus, *Das Leben des Philosophen Isidoros*, 74.

since the fifth century B.C., the duties connected with it are still imperfectly known. Jacob's biographer relates that he did not exact money from his patients; rather, he tried to persuade the rich among them to aid the poor.[22] This tends to corroborate the view that public physicians were not forbidden to collect fees from the poor, and that the institution was not a form of socialized medicine.[23]

Medical practice of the period followed the older tradition of treating diseases by regimen and drugs. A number of prescriptions associated with the real or pretended names of their authors appear in this late literature, the admixture of superstitious remedies increasing steadily. Even Alexander of Tralles admits amulets on the ground that a good physician must do everything the art orders him to do.[24] Alexander is credited with having introduced colchicum into the treatment of gout,[25] a disease that was prevalent in Byzantium. It figures among the diseases for which the Code of Justinian contains a special ruling: "The disease of podagra does not represent an excuse from [the performance of] personal duties. If, however, you say you are so much afflicted by the disease of the feet as not to be able to serve your own interests, go to the governor of the province; if he establishes the truthfulness of your excuses he shall not suffer you to be called for physical duties."[26] As late as the thirteenth century at least, two monographs were devoted to this disease, one by Demetrius Pepagomenus, the personal physician of Michael Palaeologus.[27] There were excellent descriptions of other diseases too, e.g., diphtheria.

If we are to believe Fulgentius, surgery must have been practiced with particular devotion in Alexandria around A.D. 500. He has Calliope complain that she would have found peace in that city had it not been for "Galen's family, which is more cruel than wars and which is so ingrafted into almost all of Alexandria's narrow streets that one can count more little surgical butcher stalls than dwelling places."[28] Ample experience was to be gained in Alexandria. Paul of Aegina mentions a prescription which he picked up there.[29] Sergius of Rēshʿainā, the translator of medical and philosophical works into Syriac, visited Alexandria in the early sixth century. Constantinople had its visitors too. The Frankish physician Roevalis

---

[22]*Ibid.*

[23]Owsei Temkin, "Changing Concepts of the Relation of Medicine to Society in Early History," in *Social Medicine, Its Derivations and Objectives,* ed. Iago Galdston (New York, 1949), 3–12, esp. 11, note 11.

[24]Alexander von Tralles, ed. Theodor Puschmann, I (Vienna, 1878), 571–73.

[25]Fielding H. Garrison, *An Introduction to the History of Medicine,* 4th ed. (Philadelphia, 1929), 124. Alexander, however, mentions prescriptions against gout containing colchicum (hermodactylum), which he credits to "some persons" (vol. 2, 561). In particular, he refers to Jacob Psychrestus' receipts against gout containing the *hermodactylon* medicine (vol. 2, 565, 571).

[26]*Codex Iustinianus* X, 51, 3, ed. P. Krueger (Berlin, 1895), 422.

[27]Bloch, "Byzantinische Medizin," 565. The other author was Ioannes Chumnus.

[28]Quoted (in Latin) by F. Schemmel, "Die Hochschule von Alexandria im IV. and V. Jahrhundert P. Chr. N.," *Neue Jahrbücher für das klassische Altertum* (1909), 448–57, see esp. 441.

[29]Paulus Aegineta IV, 49, 2; ed. I. L. Heiberg, I (Leipzig-Berlin, 1921) 371, 26. (*Corpus Medicorum Graecorum,* IX, 1).

cured a boy by operating "as he had once seen the physicians act in the city of Constantinople."[30]

No doubt good practical training in medicine could be obtained.

But theory was taught in the schools from books. The late Alexandrians were Galenists; they followed the man, yet did not try to imitate him. They interpreted his anatomical works, perhaps they even dissected, as we shall hear later. But they did not try to use dissection and physiological experiment as tools for research.

According to Eunapius, around A.D. 350 Zenon of Cyprus established a famous school.[31] He was trained in both medical rhetoric and medical practice, while his famous pupils followed him in one or the other direction or in both. Among his pupils was Oribasius, as well as Magnus of Nisibis who excelled more in rhetoric than in practice. By medical rhetoric, Eunapius means dialectic skill. Thus Magnus proved that patients who had been cured by other doctors were still sick.[32] "At Alexandria a public school was especially assigned for him to teach in, and everyone sailed thither and attended his lectures, either merely in order to see and admire him or to enjoy the advantages of his teaching."[33]

Eunapius' portrait of Zenon and his pupils supplies us with some important facts. There was no separation between medicine and surgery, but there was a potential separation between dialectic and practical ability. A man could be a philosopher, orator, and physician, all at the same time, as we know of Asclepiodotus that he studied philosophy with Proclus, and medicine with Jacob Psychrestus.[34] There also was a *diadoche,* a succession in teaching.[35] The public school given to Magnus possibly means that he was provided with a lecture room, a sort of provision the state would make for doctors.[36]

All this becomes pertinent when we approach the men who taught during or after the late fifth century. Their names appear as authors of commentaries in Greek, Latin, or Arabic; two lists, one of four, the other of seven names, are given by the Arabic historians of medicine.[37] Some of the names, such as Gesius, Damascius, and John the Grammarian, are well known in philosophical literature. The titles ascribed to these men vary: philosopher, iatrosophist, physician, or a combination of these.[38]

---

[30]Gregory of Tours, *Historia Francorum,* X, 15, ed. W. Arndt and Br. Krusch (Hannover, 1885), 426 (Mon. Germ. Hist., *Script. rer. Meroving.,* I): . . . *sicut quondam aput urbem Constantinopolitanam medicos agere conspexeram. . . ."*

[31]Eunapius, *Lives of the Sophists,* with an English translation by W. C. Wright (Loeb Classical Library, 1922), 528 ff.

[32]*Ibid.,* 530.

[33]*Ibid.,* 533.

[34]Asmus, *Das Leben des Philosophen Isidoros,* 86 and 76.

[35]Eunapius, *Lives of the Sophists,* 530: οἱ διάδοχοι Ζήνωνος.

[36]*The Scriptores historiae Augustae* (Severus Alexander XLIV, 4), translated by F. Magie, II (Loeb Classical Library, 1924), 267.

[37]For details see Meyerhof, *Von Alexandrien nach Bagdad,* 9ff. and Temkin, "Geschichte des Hippokratismus," 51 ff.

[38]See the titles of the commentaries published by F. R. Dietz, *Apollonii Citiensis, Stephani,*

I shall resist the temptation to speculate on the date and identity of the iatrosophists, particularly the four mentioned in an Arabic "History of Physicians," which Professor Franz Rosenthal edited in 1954.[39] Instead, let us see what the late Alexandrians are supposed to have done and how far this is borne out by works at our disposal. "Those four Alexandrians were the ones who commented on the books of Galen, made synopses of them, abridged them, and gave brief résumés of some books and discussed others at length."[40] Elsewhere we read that one of the four[41] acted as editor and was the head of what seems to have been a group.

A Latin manuscript at Milan contains commentaries on four Galenic works: On the Sects for Beginners, the Medical Art, On the Pulse for Beginners, and the Therapeutics for Glaucon.[42] Their titles and the order of their arrangement agree well with what Ḥanain ibn Isḥāq, the famous Nestorian translator of the ninth century, tells about them in his essay on the Syriac and Arabic translations of Galen. "The teachers, who in antiquity used to teach medicine in Alexandria, made a book in five parts out of four Galenic treatises [the four books of the Milan manuscript] and named it 'for beginners.'"[43] The first of these books, On the Sects for Beginners, usually contained a lengthy introduction to medicine comparable to Porphyry's philosophical *Eisagoge*. That philosophy really served as the pattern is attested by the following passage from the Milan manuscript: "Indeed, we must read in an orderly fashion, as the divine Plotinus, the philosopher, also states."[44] Most commentaries on Galenic as well as Hippocratic books discuss the place which each particular book should hold in the study of Galenic or Hippocratic works.

Synopses (or summaries) of Galenic works exist in Arabic in a number of manuscripts.[45] I have been studying the summaries contained in a manuscript of the British Museum.[46] Again the four books for beginners come first, then follow others whose titles I shall not enumerate here. The synopses, as far as I have studied them, are so colorless and devoid of

Palladii, Theophili, Meletii, Damascii, Ioannis, Aliorum Scholia in Hippocratem et Galenum, 2 vols. (Königsberg, 1834).

[39]These four are Anqīlāūs and the three mentioned *supra*. Franz Rosenthal "Isḥāq B. Ḥunayn's Ta'rīḫ Al-Aṭibbā'," *Oriens*, 7 (1954), 69.

[40]*Ibid.*, 79.

[41]I.e., Anqīlāūs, see Meyerhof, *Von Alexandrien nach Bagdad*, 10–12, who cites both Ibn al-Qifti and Ibn Abī Uṣaibi'ah.

[42]On the manuscript, Cod. Ambros. G 108 inf., see *supra*, note 8, and Augusto Beccaria, *I codici di medicina del periodo presalernitano* (Rome, 1956), 288–293, also *idem*. "Sulle tracce di un antico canone latino di Ippocrate e di Galeno. I," *Italia medioevale e umanistica*, 2 (1959), 1–56.

[43]G. Bergsträsser, Ḥunain ibn Isḥāq, *Ueber die syrischen und arabischen Galen-Uebersetzungen* (Leipzig, 1925), p. 5 of the Arabic text. The Milan MS contains only the first book of Galen's *Methodus medendi ad Glauconem*.

[44]Cod. Ambros. G 108 inf., fol. 28ʳ; *Debemus enim secundum ordinem legere, quemadmodum et divinus Plotinus philosophus dicit.*

[45]H. Ritter and R. Walzer, "Arabische Übersetzungen griechischer Ärzte in Stambuler Bibliotheken," *Sitzungsberichte d. Preuss. Akad. d. Wissensch.*, Phil.-Hist. Klasse, 26 (1934), 801–46, also R. Walzer, "Codex Princetonianus arabicus 1075," *Bull. Hist. Med.*, 28 (1954), 550–52.

[46]Brit. Mus. Cod. add. 23407.

personality, and are so governed by the principle of schematic divisions and subdivisions that their Greek origin seemed unproved to me, in spite of the appearance of Ḥunain's name as the translator. I was, therefore, glad to come across a passage corroborating to some minor degree the Greek provenience of the original. Referring to structural abnormalities of parts of the body, the text states: "This, for instance, happened to," then follows a word which looks like Būsīṭ⟨e⟩s, a meaningless form.[47] A marginal note offers the explanation: "Būsīṭ⟨e⟩s, this is a man. Homer the poet mentions that he was in the army; his chest and his back were misshapen," etc.[48] This is an obvious reference to Thersites. Illustration by means of a Homeric pseudo-hero could be expected from a Greek author, while the Arabic reader needed an explanation.

The monotony and colorless schematism which make the reading of these summaries so tiresome a task also tinge the commentaries. Only occasionally do we obtain a glimpse of the school room. An aged commentator of the Hippocratic Aphorisms, in interpreting the changes which the stature of the body underwent with age, supposedly told his pupils: "If you wish to understand exactly what Hippocrates said, take me as an example for your argument: 'for this one was large in his youth and good-looking, but in his old age he became bent for the reason stated.'"[49]

Such light touches are rare. What prevails is a dry didactic tone such as is found also in the late commentaries on Aristotle. In the manuscripts, commentaries as well as compendia often go under different names, though the differences in content may be a matter of variants only.[50] The impression gained is that of an established opinion which the choice of lecturer does not materially affect. It is very difficult to find out whether the lecturer is a Christian or a pagan. A science had been created that was neutral to religion and could, therefore, be passed on to Christians, Mohammedans, and Jews alike.

III

In the main we have so far relied on Byzantine material, supplemented by oriental sources. Now, however, we must turn to more questionable matters where it is hard to tell whether tradition continues or a different path branches off.

We shall begin with a detail. We repeatedly find brief but very exact outlines of the constitutive parts of medicine. On a few pages, they present

[47]Fol. 27ʳ.
[48]*Ibid.*, Būsīṭs huwa rajulun ḏakara 'ūmīrus al-shā'iru 'annahu kāna fī-l-'askari wakāna 'aḥdaba fī ṣadrihi waẓahrihi etc.
[49]Dietz, *op. cit.*, vol. 2,343, note 4 (from Stephanus' commentary on Hippocrates, Aphorism II, 54): ἐνταῦθα γενόμενος ὁ τρισευδαίμων σοφιστὴς Γέσιος, καὶ τὸν ἀφορισμὸν τοῦτον ἐξηγούμενος, ἀστείως φερόμενος, τοῖς ἀκροαταῖς ἔλεγεν · εἰ βούλεσθε ἀκριβῶσαι τὸ ὑφ' Ἱπποκράτους λεγόμενον, ἐμὲ αὐτὸν ὑπόθεσιν τοῦ λόγου ποιήσασθε. οὗτος γὰρ ἐν νεότητι μακρὸς ἦν καὶ εὐπρεπὴς τοῖς ὁρῶσιν, ἐν δὲ γήρᾳ κεκυφὼς ἐγένετο κατὰ τὴν εἰρημένην αἰτίαν.
[50]In this connection, see Marcel Richard, Ἀπὸ φωνῆς, *Byzantion*, 20 (1950), 191–222.

the whole Galenic system of medicine in a remarkably concentrated form. I quote a few lines from the Milan manuscript: "We shall now say into how many parts medicine is divided. Into two: theory and practice. Theory is divided into three: physiology, etiology, semeiotics. Physiology is divided into six: elements, temperaments, humors, very solid parts of the body, faculties, operations."[51]

If we compare this with the corresponding lines of an Alexandrian summary, extant in Arabic translation,[52] and again with a commentary by Palladius of the sixth century and one by Theophilus,[53] probably of the seventh century, we shall find almost literal agreement. If, however, we turn to a distinctly Arabic product, the so-called *Questions (masā'il)* of Ḥunain ibn Isḥāq, we note both agreement and disagreement. "Into how many parts is medicine divided? Into two parts.—Which are they? Theory and Practice.—And into how many parts is theory divided? Into three parts.—And which are they? The theory concerning the natural things from which results the science of disease by the deterioration (*bizawāli*) of these natural things from their conditions, and the theory concerning the causes, and the theory concerning the signs.—How many are the natural things? Seven things.—And what are they? The elements, the temperaments, the humors, the parts of the body, the faculties, the actions, *and the spirits.*"[54]

The subdivision of Physiology has increased from six to seven, the spirits having been added. Surely this is a small matter? Galen and his Alexandrian followers also frequently mentioned the spirits, the *pneumata*. But there is disagreement. "How many are the spirits? Three.—And which are they? The natural spirit, the vital spirit, and the psychic spirit. And the natural spirit is sent from the liver and runs in the veins into the whole body and serves the natural force. And the vital spirit is sent from the heart" etc.[55]

Ḥunain ibn Isḥāq definitely enumerates three *pneumata*, among them the natural *pneuma* in the liver and veins. But Galen had practically disregarded the natural *pneuma*.[56] Such late Constantinopolitan authors as John

---

[51]Cod. Ambros. G 108 inf. fol. 26ʳ: *Dicamus nunc in quot partes dividitur medicina? In duas, Theoreticon et practicon. Theoreticon dividitur in tres, Fisiologicon, ethiologicon, simioticon. Fisiologicon dividitur in sex: In elementis, in temperantia naturae, in umoribus, in firmissimis corporis locis, in virtutibus, in operationibus.*

[52]Brit. Mus. Cod. add. 23407, fol. 2ᵛ.

[53]Dietz, *op. cit.*; vol. 2,246. For Palladius, see Giovanni Baffioni, "Scolii inediti di Palladio al *De sectis* di Galeno," *Bolletino del comitato per la preparazione della edizione nazionale dei classici Greci e Latini,* N.S. fasc. VI (Rome, Accademia Nazionale dei Lincei, 1958), 69 and 75. Palladius calls medicine a τέχνη μικτή because it comprises theory and practice.

[54]Oxford, Bodleian Library, Cod. Marsh 16, fol. 56ᵛ. The italics are, of course, mine. While reading proof, I find that the commentary on Galen's *De sectis* printed in the Latin edition of Galen's works by Rusticus Placentinus, vol. 1 (Pavia, 1515), fols. 6ʳ–12ᵛ, and ascribed to Joannes Alexandrinus, also divides physiology into these seven parts. See Baffioni, *op. cit.,* 75. I am at present unable to ascertain whether the "spirits" are subdivided as by Ḥunain ibn Isḥāq. On the commentary, see Temkin, "Studies on Late Alexandrian Medicine," and on its author *idem,* "Geschichte des Hippokratismus," 67 ff.

[55]*Ibid.,* fol. 60ᵛ.

[56]Temkin, "Galen's Pneumatology."

Actuarius who lived in the fourteenth century speak of it as a matter of course, and it occurs in Greek texts which are perhaps considerably earlier. But just how late we may go, I do not know.[57] To this example we may add another of the canon of sixteen Galenic books that Arabic authors connect with John the Grammarian, i.e. John Philoponus, and a corresponding canon of twelve Hippocratic works.[58] I pass over the details of this complicated question; suffice it to say that so far, to the best of my knowledge, no Byzantine source, Alexandrian or Constantinopolitan, is known to refer to this canon of exactly sixteen books, although their summaries are extant in what seem to be Arabic translations from the Greek.

These examples may serve to illustrate a number of possibilities regarding the transmission of tradition from Alexandria to Constantinople. We must take into account the possibility that the Arabic tradition incorporated developments which took place in Alexandria but did not reach Constantinople, or, if they reached that city, did not receive the attention which the Arabs gave them. Because Byzantine medicine always had been Greek medicine, its dependence on Alexandria in later times was less than was that of the Orient, where Greek medicine had been introduced through Alexandria.[59] Consequently, it is very difficult to determine exactly where Syrians and Arabs began to add their own. Where in Ḥunain's *Questions* do the Alexandrians end and Ḥunain begin?

Were the *Questions* or, if you like, their Latin paraphrase,[60] ever translated into Greek? I do not yet know. The whole problem of the translation of medical books from Latin, Syriac, and Arabic into Greek[61] needs a much more thorough treatment than it has received so far. Our ignorance on this

[57]G. Helmreich, *Handschriftliche Studien zu Meletius* (Berlin, 1918) (Abhandlungen der königl. Preussischen Akademie der Wissenschaften, Jahrgang 1918, Philosophisch-historische Klasse, Nr. 6), publishes from a Munich manuscript Anecdota which he thinks suggestive of Meletius' authorship (p. 41). Here we read (p. 44): Φλέψ ἐστι σῶμα νευρῶδες, ἀγγεῖον αἵματος καὶ τοῦ συγκεκραμένου τῷ αἵματι φυσικοῦ πνεύματος etc. See also *supra,* note 54.

[58]This has been discussed in detail by Meyerhof, *Von Alexandrien nach Bagdad; idem,* "Joannes Grammatikos (Philoponos) von Alexandrien und die arabische Medizin," *Mitteilungen des Deutschen Instituts für Ägyptische Altertumskunde in Kairo,* 2 (1931), 1–21, and Temkin, "Geschichte des Hippokratismus," 51 ff.

As Meyerhof, partly following Furlani, has shown, the Arabs caused great confusion regarding John Philoponus, whom they connected chronologically with the Arab conquest of Alexandria. Meyerhof believes that the entire medical literary activity ascribed by them to John Philoponus must be considered apocryphal. Franz Rosenthal, on the other hand, thinks that Isḥāq b. Ḥunayn's *Ta'rīḫ al-aṭibbā',* which he edited and translated in *Oriens,* 7 (1954), 55–80, actually is based on John Philoponus' *Ta'rīḫ,* as claimed by Isḥāq. I am at present inclined to believe that, all exaggeration and falsification notwithstanding, the tradition making John Philoponus a commentator of medical writings has a foundation in fact, though it remains to be seen just how far his activities in this direction went. As footnote 65 *(infra)* shows, John Philoponus certainly was acquainted with Galenic works.

[59]What Richard Walzer "Filosofia islamica," *Le Civiltà dell' Oriente,* 3 (1958), 416, writes of ancient philosophy is equally true of medicine.

[60]The *Isagoge* of Joannicius printed in the various editions of the *Articella,* a medieval collection of basic medical texts.

[61]See Aristote Kousis, "Quelques considérations sur les traductions des oeuvres médicales orientales et principalement sur les deux manuscrits de la traduction d'un traité persan par Constantin Melitiniotis." Πρακτικὰ τῆς 'Ακαδημίας 'Αθηνῶν, 14 (1939), 205–20.

point is a serious hindrance to understanding Byzantine medicine in its later phase.

Commentaries play such a great role in the tradition of Byzantine medicine that they have had to be discussed, dull as they are and confusing as are the details, which I have simplified as far as I could. But our discussion should have enabled us now to approach a problem of wider significance that will close our consideration of Alexandria and at the same time introduce us to Constantinople.

In speaking of the Galenic system, we had in mind the physician Galen. Undoubtedly the school paid particular attention to his medical works. But what about the philosopher Galen? The question is all the more fascinating since Walzer pointed out the great role which Galen's philosophy played in Christian theology.[62] Galen was accepted by orthodox Christianity and even highly admired by a heretical sect of Adaptionist tendencies which originated in Galen's lifetime and tried to rationalize Christianity in philosophical terms. "Thus some of them make a laborious study of Euclid, they admire Aristotle and Theophrastus, and some of them almost worship Galen."[63] Walzer is probably right in saying that this makes sense only in reference to the philosopher Galen. His philosophical works were still studied in the sixth century and exerted a great influence. Of the philosopher Marinus we hear that, being constitutionally unable to follow the sublime explanations of Plato's Parmenides by his teacher Proclus, he dragged the discussion down to the level of the "forms," "for the ideas of Firmus and of Galen attracted him more" etc.[64] Somewhat later, John Philoponus not only quotes Galen's work *On Demonstration,* but calls him "an excellent scientist" who "understands philosophical problems not less thoroughly than his special science."[65] Simplicius likewise speaks of him as "the most learned Galen" and the "admirable Galen" in passages which also refer to Galen's work *On Demonstration.*[66]

Yet, when Ḥunain ibn Isḥāq wanted to translate this work, he and his friends were unable to find a single complete Greek manuscript of it, in spite of a search that took them to Mesopotamia, Syria, Palestine, and

---

[62]Richard Walzer, *Galen on Jews and Christians* (Oxford University Press, 1949), *passim.*

[63]Walzer, *Galen on Jews and Christians,* 77. The passage occurs in Eusebius, *Hist. Eccl.* V, 28. To this should be added Galen's influence on ethics, traced in the Arabic tradition by R. Walzer and recently discussed by Roger Paret, "Notes bibliographiques sur quelques travaux récents consacrés aux premières traductions arabes d'oeuvres grecques," *Byzantion,* 29–30 (1959–1960), 387–446, see 416 ff. and 434 ff. (See now R. Walzer, *Greek Into Arabic* [Cambridge, Mass., 1961]).

[64]Asmus, *Das Leben des Philosophen Isidorus,* 89. Photius, *Bibliotheca,* ed. I. Bekker (Berlin, 1824), 351a, 33: ταῖς Φίρμου καὶ Γαληνοῦ τὸ πλέον ἐννοίαις ἐπισπώμενος.

[65]Joannes Philoponus, *De aeternitate mundi contra Proclum,* xvii, 5; ed. Hugo Rabe (Leipzig, 1899), 599f.: Γαληνὸς ... ἀνὴρ φυσικώτατός τε καὶ οὐδὲν ἧττον τῆς ἰδίας ἐπιστήμης τὰ κατὰ φιλοσοφίαν ἠκριβωκὼς θεωρήματα ... οὗτος οὖν ἐν τῷ δ' λόγῳ ἧς αὐτός συνέγραψεν ἀποδεικτικῆς πραγματείας φησὶν....

[66]Simplicius, *Comment. in Arist. Phys.* 218 b 21; ed. Diels (Berlin, 1882), 708: ὁ θαυμάσιος Γαληνός; in 219a 14–bg; p. 718: ὁ πολυμαθέστατος ... Γαληνός. Iwan von Müller, *Ueber Galens Werk vom wissenschaftlichen Beweis* (Munich, 1895) (Abhandlungen der K. bayer. Akademie der Wiss. I. Cl. xx Bd., 2. Abth.), 60, 66, 68, cites the above remarks of John Philoponus and Simplicius in their full context.

Egypt.[67] Most of Galen's logical works have shared the same fate. This is all the more surprising as the understanding of Galen's system and of his scientific approach to medicine postulated a training in logic and methodology.

To understand the fate of the philosopher Galen, one must keep in mind that he was made up, so to speak, of two persons: the natural theologian, the author of *On the Use of Parts*, and, the methodologist and logician. It is not always obvious which of the two is meant when Galen is praised. *On the Use of Parts* was meant by Galen himself to be a philosophical, rather than a strictly medical, treatise. It demonstrates the absolute perfection with which the Creator, i.e. Nature, has shaped the human body and all its parts out of the available material. It was necessary only to identify the Demiurge with the one God to possess a work which on every page sang His praise. *On the Use of Parts* became a major source of information for all who dealt with the structure and function of the human body. In this work Galen often exhorts the reader to study the structure of a part by autopsy, words being insufficient to describe it.[68] Theophilus also repeatedly refers his readers to the anatomists who practice dissection.[69] Theophilus' words do not sound as if they were empty echoes of Galen's. It may not be impossible that in late Alexandria, as well as in Constantinople in the seventh century, animals were dissected as a demonstration of anatomical data, rather than to find anything new. Be that as it may, the existence of this book and its theological significance certainly helped to promote Galenism among Neoplatonists and Christians alike.

The situation is different regarding the methodologist and logician Galen. Whatever a few men thought of them, Galen's books on these topics were of doubtful value and dispensable. *On Demonstration* especially, as Müller's analysis shows, emphasized the value of reason and experience in medicine. But, in the late Byzantine world, experience, apart from training and the superstitious reliance on remedies proved by experience only, no · longer meant much. And Galen the logician was dispensable because the students could be expected to study Aristotle's *Organon*. Galen's very close-

---

[67]Bergsträsser, Hunain ibn Isḥāq, p. 38f. See also I. von Müller, *op. cit.*, 3 ff.

[68]William L. Straus, Jr. and Owsei Temkin, "Vesalius and the Problem of Variability," *Bull. Hist. Med.*, 14 (1943), 609–13. For Galen as a philosopher, see also Owsei Temkin, "Greek Medicine as Science and Craft," *Isis*, 44 (1953), 224 f. [Essay 8, p. 151] and Walzer, *op. cit.*, 142 ff.

[69]Theophilus Protospatharius, *De corporis humani fabrica, libri V*, ed. G. A. Greenhill (Oxford, 1842), 123, 126f., 191, 202.

In this connection, Mr. Cyril Mango has kindly reminded me of Theophanes, *Chronographia*, ed. C. de Boor, I (Leipzig, 1883), 436, where he relates the torture of a certain Christianos. After his hands and feet had been cut off "the physicians convened and they cut him up, while alive, from pubes to thorax, in order to apprehend the structure of man." Afterwards he was burnt. A. Blanchet, "Contribution à l'histoire de l'anatomie," *Comptes rendus du deuxième congrès international d'histoire de la médecine, Paris, 1921* (Évreux, 1922), 235f., cites and translates the story and points out its importance. Remarks like that cited *infra* (note 84) from Theophilus, viz., that physicians examined the afflicted parts in insanity and amnesia, may possibly refer to similar incidences or to post mortem autopsies. Nowhere, however, is there an indication of the desire to learn new anatomical facts.

ness to peripatetic philosophy favored his assimilation and set limits to it. Seen, one-sidedly perhaps, from the point of view of medicine, the university of Alexandria has little to do with Neoplatonism. The vague use of this term for philosophy after Plotinus is misleading. In Alexandria, a man could receive his formal philosophical training from the Aristotelian commentators and could then continue his medical education with the iatrosophists, some of whom conceivably had been his teachers before. Justinian closed the University of Athens in 529, but left Alexandria unmolested. Its medical curriculum had begun to resemble that of the later medieval universities; medicine was becoming scholastic.

The inference that we have drawn concerning the philosopher Galen explains the fate of his writings and the position assigned to him during the formative period of scholastic medicine. Throughout the Middle Ages there remained a latent tension between Aristotle and Galen. Moreover, though Galenism was the all-embracing medical system, minor or major revolts within this system did take place. One of them is documented by the "Controversy (*Antirrhētikos*) with Galen" of Simeon Seth, the contemporary of Psellus and physician of Michael Ducas. This short chapter, edited and translated by Daremberg,[70] has quite recently been analyzed by Dr. Magnus Schmid, who rightly characterizes it as an attack upon the logical inconsistency of Galen's treatise *On the Natural Faculties,* possibly motivated by Aristotelian tendencies, rather than a revolt against his biological thought.[71] Simeon Seth, who accuses Galen of prolixity, feels obliged to refute passages of his works by demonstrative methods (μεθόδοις ἀποδεικτικαῖς). He obviously does not think highly of the followers of Galen to whom he addresses himself. "Perhaps," he says in conclusion, "by contradicting your words, I shall convert some of your followers, not to a different opinion but so as to prove that no man is infallible. For God alone always effects the good in the same fashion."[72]

One cannot help asking who the "followers" of Galen were at a time when all physicians were Galenists. Simeon Seth obviously has a particular group in mind "by whom you would not be more pleased than I am," he tells Galen.[73] They are the people who consider Galen "as something divine."[74] This has a very similar ring to the reproaches heaped upon the Adoptionists of the third century,[75] the forerunners of the Byzantine Paulicians. But before rushing to the conclusion that we are dealing with a chapter in religious history, we must at least envisage another possibility. Simeon Seth was the great Orientalist of Byzantine medicine. A dietetic text

[70]Ch. Daremberg, *Notices et extraits des manuscrits médicaux grecs, latins et français, des principales bibliothèques de l'Europe* (Paris, 1853), 44–47 and 229–33.

[71]Magnus Schmid, "Eine Galen-Kontroverse des Simeon Seth," *XVIIᵉ Congrès international d'histoire de la médecine,* I, 491–95 (Discussion, II, 123).

[72]Daremberg, *op. cit.,* 47.

[73]Daremberg, *op. cit.,* 45: ἐδέησέ μοι τοῖς σοῖς προ[σ]διαλεχθῆναι ὀπαδοῖς, οἷς εἴπερ ἑώρακας, οὐκ ἂν ἐπ' αὐτοῖς εὐηρέστησας, ὥσπερ οὐδ' ἐγώ.

[74]Daremberg, *op. cit.,* 44: Πρὶν μὲν ὁμιλῆσαι Γαληνὲ τοῖς θεῖον τί σε χρῆμα λογιζομένοις.

[75]See *supra,* p. 212.

which selected the best, not only from the Greek materia medica but also from Persian, Arabic, and Indian sources is ascribed to him.[76] To this eclectic, an enthusiastic limitation to Galen may have looked like one-sidedness, which he detested: Galen was not the only one who could effect the good.

IV

Though Christianity was not a conspicuous feature of Alexandrian medicine, in the Constantinopolitan era it became a constitutive element. The Christian tradition in medicine went back to the Greek Fathers of the Church, as is amply borne out by Frings's recent publication.[77] Medicine entered into such theological disputes as the argumentation against the Manichaeans: the evil that exists in animals and plants can be utilized by man, who has reason and medicine to help him.[78]

The ancient medical tradition did not always fit smoothly into the Christian civilization. In the tenth century Theophanes Nonnus, upon the command of Constantinus Porphyrogenitus, composed a synopsis in the form of an epitome of the medical art, from which I cite the beginning of the chapter on epilepsy:

Epilepsy is a convulsion of the whole body together with a damaging of the governing functions. Sometimes the cause is situated in the brain itself, sometimes in all its ventricles, blocking the passages of the psychic pneuma, so that people fall and froth. This laymen (οἱ ἰδιῶται) call "a demon." The ventricles are blocked by phlegm or melancholic humor. Sometimes the disease also originates because of sympathy with the mouth of the stomach. Sometimes auras ascend from another part, such as the hand or foot, to the brain, and people fall down.[79]

There is a considerable amount of superstitious belief in this chapter, but those superstitions relate to remarkable curative powers of various substances, etc., not to anything supernatural. The demoniac notion of epilepsy is simply attributed to laymen. This is just the kind of situation to which Psellus refers in his *Dialogue on the Operation of Demons,* when he had the monk Marcus tell about possession by subterranean demons:

"But Marcus," said I, "physicians persuade us to be of another way of thinking, for they assert that such affections are not produced by demons, but are occasioned by an excess or deficiency of humors, or by a disordered

---

[76]*Syntagma de alimentorum facultatibus, prooemium,* ed. B. Langkavel (Leipzig, 1868), 1. I am not concerned here with the interdependence of Simeon Seth and Psellus (see Bloch, "Byzantinische Medizin," 562 and 563), which can hardly be decided before both authors are better known in their medical relationship. Simeon Seth's orientalistic knowledge is assured apart from the *Syntagma.*

[77]Hermann Josef Frings, *Medizin und Arzt bei den griechischen Kirchenvätern bis Chrysostomos* (Diss. Bonn, 1959).

[78]*Ibid.,* 8.

[79]Theophanes Nonnus, *Epitome de curatione morborum,* chap. 36; rec. I. S. Bernard, I (Gotha-Amsterdam 1794), 144f.

state of the animal spirits, and accordingly they endeavor to cure them by medicine or dietetical regimen, not by incantations or purifications." Marcus replied: "It is not at all surprising if physicians make such an assertion, for they understand nothing but what is perceived by the senses, their whole attention being devoted to the body."[80]

Conflicts could arise also where the Scriptures and the teaching of medical science disagreed. For this I would like to cite Theophilus Protospatharius who is usually placed in the seventh century. There is no absolute certainty about this date, nor about the identities of all the medical authors of the time who bore the name Theophilus, though I see no cogent reason to differentiate between the writer of books on the pulse, urine, and faeces, the commentator on the Hippocratic Aphorisms, and the author of a work on the Fabric of the Human Body. Theophilus also stands fully in the tradition of antiquity: his book on urine builds on his Alexandrian predecessor[81] and his commentary on the Aphorisms[82] does not diverge substantially from that of others. Yet references to the deity which occur here and there leave no doubt that he was a Christian.[83] His book on the human body is an anatomical text frequently quoting Hippocrates, largely dependent on Galen, but also intent on glorifying God. The difficulty arises when Theophilus bears witness to the Galenic, i.e. medical, belief that the brain is the seat of the principal part of the soul:

> I cannot tell the why or how of Homer's saying that the principal part of the soul is in the heart. He is followed by most of the Hellenes, nay even by Divine Scripture, for it says: "Wherefore do arguments arise in your hearts?" Indeed, the physicians examining the loss of reason and of memory, and the afflicted part from which it arises, have found nothing but the brain. Therefore, they apply things fitting for therapy: salves, vapor baths, and other remedies, to the head, not to the heart.[84]

The step from Theophilus to Meletius, the next author of a work On the Fabric of Man, takes us to a different intellectual climate. Unfortunately, the dating of Meletius is even more uncertain than that of Theophilus. Meletius is often cited in medical literature; so a knowledge of his biography would provide an anchoring point for further chronological orientation. Meletius' book is put together from Galenic and pseudo-Galenic works, from the Bishop Nemesius of the fourth century, from Gregory of Nyssa, Gregory Nazianzen, and Basil the Great.[85] Meletius states that many of the ancient sages and physicians have dealt with man's body and soul. "Regarding the body, their endeavors are known and admitted by all men who are willing to learn and who show industry, and they have been ob-

---

[80]*Psellus' Dialogue on the Operation of Daemons,* Eng. transl. by Marcus Collisson (Sydney, 1843), 35.

[81]Theophilus, "De urinis" in I. L. Ideler, *Physici et medici graeci minores,* I (Berlin, 1841), 261.

[82]Dietz, *Scholia,* II, 236–544, has published the commentary of Theophilus together with that of Stephanus and extracts from others.

[83]For instance, the end of "De urinis," *op. cit.,* 283.

[84]Theophilus, *De corporis humani fabrica,* IV, 31; 184,15.

[85]The sources have been analyzed by Helmreich, *Handschriftliche Studien zu Meletius,* 56–62.

served to be facts. However, what the Greeks philosophized about the soul has been proved vain. For they were not able to ascertain anything true about its essence or to show what it is by nature."[86] These are just the sentiments we would expect from a monk whose book has such a strongly teleological and even theological flavor that it has, undeservedly, received relatively little attention from medical historians. While Theophilus was a high dignitary at court, Meletius was a monk in the monastery of the holy Trinity in Asia Minor.[87] His name also occurs in manuscripts as a commentator on Hippocrates;[88] this would not be surprising in a monk who could be credited with book learning. But, apart from telling us where he comes from, Meletius gives us also considerable information about himself and the state of the profession. In an appended treatise On the Soul, Meletius speaks about individuality. This is defined as composed of peculiarities the sum of which is not to be found in anybody else. "And well is it said 'in nobody else.' For the peculiarities of Meletius, since he is an individual, cannot be perceived in anybody else: such as being a Byzantine, a physician, short, blue-eyed, snub-nosed, suffering from gout, having such and such a scar on the forehead, being the son of Gregory. For all these things assembled have constituted my friend Meletius; they cannot be perceived in anybody else."[89]

Then follows a definition of a person, and again Meletius illustrates: "for instance, my friend Meletius when, standing, he reads or bleeds or cauterizes somebody, proves himself separated from the rest of the brethren."[90]

Monk, physician, and surgeon: this combination must be seen against the background of Christianity, medical learning and empiricism.

In the early Middle Ages of the Latin West, the monasteries and cathedral schools became the places where medicine as a science and art found a modest refuge. There followed the lay school of Salerno and then the medical faculty of the medieval university. In the realm of Constantinople, too, monasteries and ecclesiastical schools seem to have been the main teaching centers of medicine,[91] but on a scale and with a spirit of learning that surpassed the West before the thirteenth century. This, perhaps, is not surprising, since available here was the ancient literature which the West had to acquire by a slow process of translation. But in another direction also Byzantium was surpassing the West: the development of the hospital and its role in the medical care of the sick.

---

[86]Meletius, Περὶ τῆς τοῦ ἀνθρώπου κατασκευῆς, ed. J. A. Cramer, *Anecdota Graeca,* III (Oxford, 1836), 5.

[87]*Ibid.,* 1: παρὰ Μελετίου μοναχοῦ θέματος τοῦ ᾿Οψικίου, βάνδου ᾿Ακροκοῦ, χωρίου Τιβεριουπόλεως, μονῆς λεγομένης Τρεῖς, ἤτοι τῆς ἁγίας Τριάδος.

[88]See H. Diels *Die Handschriften der antiken Aerzte,* II (Berlin, Akademie der Wissenschaften, 1906), 63.

[89]Meletius, ed. Cramer, 154, 32–155,5.

[90]*Ibid.* 155,10–12.

[91]Friedrich Fuchs, *Die höheren Schulen von Konstantinopel im Mittelalter* (Leipzig-Berlin, 1926) (Byzantinisches Archiv, Heft 8), must be consulted throughout.

Hospitals all through the Middle Ages fulfilled a broad function of housing persons needing shelter and care. The foundation of the first Christian hospital is ascribed to Basil the Great.[92] The Basilias in Caesarea, established in the seventies of the fourth century, became renowned; there nurses and medical attendants were available, as well as animals to carry burdens, and escorts.[93]

Constantinople also had its hospitals, and Justinian engaged in building them.[94] Anna Comnena describes the so-called orphanage, the wonderful foundation of her father Alexius.[95] But from a medical point of view all these hospitals were overshadowed by the hospital founded by Eirene, the wife of John Comnenus in 1136. Attached to the monastery of the Pantocrator, it had 50 beds for the sick: 10 for surgical cases, 8 for acute and severe diseases, 20 for common diseases, and 12 for women. Each of the divisions had two physicians—which makes sense only if we assume limited hours of duty and multiple occupancy of each bed. There was an outpatient department, and lower medical personnel. The physicians of the hospital also took care of the sick brethren in the monastery of the Pantocrator.[96]

The mention of escorts by Basil the Great has led to an identification of these persons with the so-called *parabalani* or *parabolani* or *parabalanin* found in the law codes, and this, in turn, has led to some unsupported views about them. Supposedly, they were the reckless persons who did not mind exposing themselves to plague or leprosy when searching in the city for the sick, to bring them to the hospital.[97] The one-sided connection of the *parabalani* with hospitals appears to me a doubtful interpretation. The indubitable fact of their holding an office connected with the care of the

[92]For the following, see: Karl Sudhoff, "Aus der Geschichte des Krankenhauswesens im früheren Mittelalter in Morgenland und Abendland," reprinted in *Sudhoff's Arch. Gesch. Med.*, 21 (1929), 164–203; E. Jeanselme et L. Oeconomos, "Les oeuvres d'assistance et les hôpitaux Byzantins au siècle des Comnènes," *Ier Congrès de l'histoire de l'art de guérir, Anvers, 1920* (Antwerp, 1921), 239–56. The whole development of Byzantine hospitals has now been reviewed thoroughly by A. Philipsborn, "Der Fortschritt in der Entwicklung des byzantinischen Krankenhauswesens," *BZ*, 54 (1961), 338–65. This article became available to me only after my MS had gone to press.

[93]Sudhoff, *op. cit.,* 167: τοὺς νοσοκομοῦντας, τοὺς ἰατρεύοντας, τὰ νωτοφόρα, τοὺς παραπέμποντας.

[94]Procopius, *Buildings* (Loeb Classical Library, 1940), *passim*.

[95]Anna Comnena, *Alexias*, XV, 7.

[96]Sudhoff, *op. cit.,* 174f. E. Jeanselme et L. Oeconomos, "Les oeuvres d'assistance et les hôpitaux Byzantins au siècle des Comnènes," 247. Pan S. Codellas, "The Pantocrator, the Imperial Byzantine Medical Center of XIIth Century A.D. in Constantinople," *Bull. Hist. Med.,* 12 (1942), 392–410. See also Philipsborn, "Der Fortschritt ... " 354–55 who (355, note 21) refers to G. Schreiber, "Byzantinisches und abendländisches Hospital" in *Gemeinschaften des Mittelalters* (Münster, 1948) (not available to me), as giving "die beste Darstellung mit Kommentar."

[97]C. F. Heusinger, "Die Parabalanen oder Parapemponten der alten Xenodochien," *Janus*, 2 (1847), 500–25 is basic for the view connecting hospitals and Parabalani and is still referred to by Sudhoff, "Aus der Geschichte des Krankenhauswesens," 177, and by Alexandre Philipsborn, "La compagnie d'ambulanciers 'Parabalani' d'Alexandrie," *Byzantion*, 20 (1950), 185–90.

sick *(qui ad curanda debilium aegra corpora deputantur),*[98] and the experience in healing required of them,[99] seem to indicate their function: they formed a lower class of medical personnel in contrast to the physicians.[100] The law insisted that they be selected from among guildsmen and put them under the control of the Church. Regardless of whether they also formed a religious group, or were otherwise employed by the patriarch, I share the view that they functioned similarly to the *dipotatoi* or *despotatoi* in the Byzantine army,[101] an ambulance corps whose duty it was to collect the wounded or incapacitated and give them aid.

An incident that took place during the wars of Alexius may here be cited: George Palaeologus had been wounded in the head by an arrow. He summoned "one of the empirics" who were in the army.[102] This man, however, was not able to extract the arrow; so the shaft was cut off and the head bandaged, and fighting continued. The story does not resound to the credit of these "empirics" in the army, but it would agree with the character of *parabalani* and *dipotatoi.*

A matter of anatomical terminology leads us further into the empirical aspect of Byzantine medicine. We still use the terms cephalic vein and basilic vein for two veins situated in the bend of the elbow. In Arabic and Latin writings we can trace the term cephalic vein as far back as the ninth century, and the synonym "cranial vein" occurs in Meletius.[103] The terms have not been found in classical Greek authors, and where they occur later, in Greek, Latin, and Arabic works, they are, at first at least, always mentioned in connection with phlebotomy. I believe them to be of Greek provenience, and to stem from the language of everyday practice.[104]

This practice, in contrast to the works of the ancients and the commentaries on them, and to the more literary products of Byzantine medical authors, has left many traces. Greek medical manuscripts are replete with shorter or longer texts, badly composed, badly marked as to beginning or end, and often transmitted anonymously or under pseudonyms. These writings range from phlebotomy, diagnosis from blood, urine, faeces, medical astrology, brief dietetic rules, to recipes and their collection in so-called

---

[98]*Cod. Justinianus* 1, 3, 18, and *Cod. Theod.* 16, 2, 43.

[99] *Cod. Just.* 1, 3, 18: *qui pro consuetudine curandi gerunt experientiam.*

[100]I seem to be in agreement with the views expressed by H. Grégoire in *Byzantion,* 13 (1938), 283. Philipsborn's remark, *Byzantion,* 185, that *curare* may have a broader meaning than "to treat" does not prove that the broad meaning was intended here.

[101]The parallel between the two bodies was noticed but not heeded by Heusinger *op. cit.,* 507. See also Philipsborn, *Byzantion,* 189.

[102]Anna Comnena, *Alexias* IV, 4: ed. A. Reifferscheid, I (Leipzig, 1884), 138,26: μετακαλεσάμενός τινα τῶν ἐμπείρων. I cannot agree with Georgina Buckler, *Anna Comnena* (Oxford University Press, 1929), 148, who refers to this passage as signifying "doctors in the specialized sense which corresponds with our word 'empiric,'" apparently giving the latter term a meaning of commendation.

[103]Meletius, *op. cit.,* 119f: ἡ ὠμιαία, ἣν καὶ κρανιακὴν λέγομεν ἡ μέση τε, καὶ ἡ ἔσω· τὴν μὲν οὖν μέσην καθόλου καλοῦμεν, ὥσπερ τὴν ἔσω σπληνικήν.

[104]Owsei Temkin, "The Byzantine Origin of the Names for the Basilic and Cephalic Veins," *XVIIᵉ Congrès international d'histoire de la médecine,* I, 336–40 [Essay 13].

iatrosophia. The *istrosophion* is a handbook listing diseases and the remedies appropriate to them. The most outstanding is ascribed to John Archiatrus[105] about whom we know nothing.[106] We encounter this work in many manuscripts,[107] usually in such disarray that one cannot help feeling deep sympathy with its future critical editor. This and other *iatrosophia* may have been in special demand at the hospitals,[108] and additions or interpolations were made as experience dictated.

In speaking of this literature of everyday practice, I do not mean to convey the idea that its authors were necessarily uneducated men. Such a division does not seem feasible to me. Works on urine, for instance, were composed by Theophilus as well as John Actuarius. The latter's composition comprised no fewer than seven books. It is the emphasis on quick orientation and application, rather than on theory, that defines this literature. The impossibility of excluding recognized authorities from authorship reflects the impossibility of drawing a sharp line between the medically interested philosopher and the professional medical man.

Agapius, one of the philosophers in Alexandria who resisted the Emperor Zeno, as well as an "iatrosophist," went to Constantinople where he founded a school and amassed a fortune.[109] Psellus, the most outstanding Byzantine scholar, also wrote medical treatises on diet. Nicephorus Blemmydes' education had reached the study of philosophy when he turned his back upon it and for seven years cultivated medicine "logically and practically,"[110] having been bred to this art which was his father's profession.

This is by no means an exhaustive list.[111] The question as to how persons became physicians who did not learn medicine as a craft from their father or, presumably, a master, needs further elucidation.[112] There may not be a general formula for the answer to the problem, which is not restricted to Byzantium. Hospitals may have played a role here, as the mārastān did in Arabic medicine. John Actuarius studied philosophy with Planudes when he was urged to remain in Constantinople, where he could also further his education at the hospital.[113]

Seen from a modern point of view, the practical medical literature of the

[105]Daremberg, *Notices et extraits,* 22 ff.

[106]Aristoteles Kouses, in Ἐπετηρὶς Ἑταιρείας Βυζαντινῶν Σπουδῶν, 6 (1929), 379ff, tries to identify him with another unknown author named Ioannes.

[107]Diels, *Die Handschriften der antiken Aerzte,* II, 52.

[108]Daremberg, *Notices et extraits,* 22ff.

[109]Asmus, *Das Leben des Philosophen Isidorus,* 115.

[110]Nicephorus Blemmydes, *Curriculum vitae et Carmina,* ed. Aug. Heisenberg (Leipzig, 1896), 3 (see also pp. lxxxiv and lxxxviiif.): ἅμα καὶ ἰατρικῆς ἐπιμελόμενος λογικῶς τε καὶ πρακτικῶς · πατρικὴ γὰρ ἄσκησις ἡ τέχνη κἀμοὶ σύντροφος ἄχρις ἐτῶν ἑπτὰ περατώσεως.

[111]Fuchs, *Die höheren Schulen von Konstantinopel im Mittelalter,* mentions a considerable number of names, esp. pp. 5, 6, 62, 72, and *passim.*

[112]This question should be examined in connection with the history of the organization of the Byzantine medical profession. As far as I can see, for such a history we possess at present scattered references only.

[113]Fuchs, *op. cit.,* 61. According to Philipsborn, "Der Fortschritt...," 355, the Pantocrator contained the first place for the instruction of physicians outside of the universities (as part of philosophy) and the school of the Patriarch.

Constantinopolitan phase, much like that of the western Middle Ages, seems the least interesting, with the exception of its pharmacological part. Anatomy, physiology, and pathology we may critize but will understand. Yet it is difficult to understand how people could rely on a lore which to us lacks a basis in reality. Even if we admit that urinoscopy and similar predecessors of "laboratory medicine"[114] contained here and there a valuable observation and that bleeding may have helped in some cases, the bulk of such observations and practices, let alone the downright superstitions, is hard to appreciate. We must conclude that life creates a need for managing human affairs regardless of whether or not they can truly be managed by the means at hand.

Byzantine medicine reached its climax with John Actuarius, about a hundred years before the fall of Constantinople. With him, the practice of writing synopses and abridgements is reversed: full-length books appear from his pen. John Actuarius knows that he has something to say. Yet I hesitate to include him in my discussion. He lived at a time when the West had produced its great figures of scholastic medicine and when the influence of the West would have to be taken into account. As far as I know, even the necessary philological preparation for such a task has not yet been made.

Instead, we shall use as a summary of Byzantine medicine its reflection in the *Timarion,* the anonymous satire of the twelfth century.[115] Timarion is severely ill, his liver is affected, he has lost much bile. Two demons appear and drag his soul to Hades. "This is the man," they say, "who has lost the fourth of his component elements, and he cannot be allowed to continue to live on the strength of the remaining three; because a sentence of Asclepius and Hippocrates has been written out and posted up in Hades, to the effect that no man may live when one of his four elements is wanting, even though his body may be in good condition."[116]

Poor Timarion, in Hades, has to face the tribunal which benefits from the expertness of great doctors. But his counsel for the defense is optimistic: Asclepius, since his deification, rarely attends the meetings, Hippocrates mumbles dubious aphorisms, Erasistratus is an ignoramus anyhow, and "the god-like Galen" whom the counsel "respects more than the others"[117] has been granted leave of absence. He is pondering some omissions in his work on fevers and believes that the additions may become longer than the whole work.

Timarion presupposes a remarkable knowledge of medical literature on the part of its readers. Acquaintance with the Hippocratic aphorisms is

---

[114]I adopt this designation of modern medicine from Erwin H. Ackerknecht, *A Short History of Medicine* (New York, 1955), 157.

[115]Adolph Ellissen, *Timarion's und Mazari's Fahrten in den Hades* (Leipzig, 1860) (Analekten der mittel- und neugriechischen Literatur, 4).

[116]*Timarion,* 13; p. 56. The translation of the above passage is from H. F. Tozer, "Byzantine Satire," *Journal of Hellenic Studies,* II (1881), 247.

[117]*Timarion,* 29; 72: Ὁ γε μὴν δαιμόνιος Γαληνὸς ὃν ἐγὼ μᾶλλον τῶν ἄλλων δεδίττομαι.

needed for an appreciation of Hippocrates' peculiar behavior. The reader who has not heard of Erasistratus' famous diagnosis of a case of love sickness[118] will not understand the reference to his bragging to everybody about it. The joke about Galen's contemplating the publication of revisions which would be even bigger than his original book implies a familiarity with Galen's verbose style. *Timarion* is a satire for intellectuals, which Molière's comedies about physicians were not, and there is another point where such a comparison falls short: the author of *Timarion* calls Galen "god-like" and does not deny his respect for the great medical authority of the time.[119] Finally, Timarion is saved; the experts find that he has lost the secreted bile which is not identical with the constitutive element—a fine enough point which, however, enables the doctors to reconcile their theory with reality. *Timarion* does not step out of the Byzantine world; the satire mocks, but accepts, the traditions and practices of Byzantine medicine.[120]

[118]Galen, *Opera,* ed. Kühn, XIV (Leipzig, 1827), 630ff., and Plutarch's life of *Demetrius,* chap. 38. R. Walzer, *"Fragmenta graeca in litteris arabicis 1* Palladios and Aristotle," *The Journal of the Royal Asiatic Society* (1939), 412, note 6, emphasizes the role of this story in the Greek and Oriental tradition.

[119]See *supra,* note 117.

[120]Some of the material utilized in this article was gathered with the support of a grant from the American Philosophical Society.

IV

Medicine:
Renaissance to Twentieth
Century

15

The Elusiveness
of Paracelsus*

Two of the greatest historical figures of the medical past are also among its most elusive ones. The literature on Hippocrates and Paracelsus is abundant just because it is provoked by so many unanswered questions. In the case of Hippocrates, this is easy to understand. Of his life we know barely more than that he was a contemporary of Socrates, born on the island of Cos, a teacher of medicine, well known in his days. Of the more than 60 books that go under his name, none can be attributed to him with certainty. And from the scanty remarks of Plato, the basic tenets of his theory do not emerge with unequivocal clarity or any degree of completeness. Thus the elusiveness of Hippocrates is grounded in a paucity of facts.

The same cannot be said of Paracelsus. Although there are very important gaps in our knowledge of his life, the data at our disposal are by no means negligible. He was born ca. 1493 in Einsiedeln, Switzerland, of a father, Wilhelm Bombast of Hohenheim, who was a practicing physician, and of a mother who was subject to the monastery of Einsiedeln. Around 1502 father and son moved to Villach, a town near the important mining centers of Carinthia.[1] Then, it is true, we have a large gap until we meet Paracelsus in Salzburg where, in 1525, he was suspected of involvement in the peasants' war.[2] In 1526 he planned to settle in Strasbourg where he acquired citizenship. The register refers to him as "Theophrastus von Hohenheim der Artzney Doctor. . . ."[3] But the next year he moved to Basel where the city government had called him as town physician and professor. In Basel he stayed from March 1527 till February 1528 when he had to flee in order to escape arrest by the authorities whom he had attacked after previous quarrels with the other doctors and a patient.[4] His itinerary during the succeeding thirteen years is fairly well known. There are his wanderings in southern Germany, St. Gall, and elsewhere in Switzerland, his

*Bull. Hist. Med., 1952, vol. 26, pp. 201–17.
Read at the New England Conference on Renaissance Studies, Harvard University, May 9, 1952.
[1]See Karl Bittel, Die Kindheit Theophrasts in Einsiedeln, Nova Acta Paracelsica, 1944, vol. 1, pp. 37–44.
[2]See Karl Sudhoff, Paracelsus, Leipzig, Bibliographisches Institut, 1936, p. 17.
[3]Ibid., p. 22, and Ernest Wickersheimer, Paracelse à Strasbourg, Centaurus, 1951, vol. 1, pp. 356–65. This article is very interesting since it re-publishes the entire record of Paracelsus' testimony given at Basel concerning a law suit taking place in Strasbourg (see below), and publishes, for the first time, the diary entries of Nicolas Gerbel of Strasbourg concerning his consultation of Paracelsus.
[4]Albrecht Burckhardt, Wie lange und in welcher amtlichen Stellung war Paracelsus in Basel? Correspondenz-Blatt für Schweizer Aerzte, 1914, vol. 44, pp. 356–68.

visits to Vienna and Carinthia, and finally his death in Salzburg in 1541. Even the texts of his will, and of the inscription on his tomb, where the name Philip appears instead of the heathenish Theophrastus, have been transmitted.

There are many more details of his life which we know for certain, even the appearance of the man is preserved in at least two authentic portraits by August Hirschvogel from 1538 and 1540. At any rate, this very short outline shows that Paracelsus' biography is not a mere fragment to us. And concerning his writings—the medical, scientific, and philosophical works, genuinely Paracelsian, fill 14 volumes in the edition by Sudhoff. The theological writings are not as easily accessible; their edition has not proceeded beyond one volume in the parallel series.[5]

In short, compared not only with Hippocrates but with many others, Paracelsus leaves us in a fortunate position. And yet he has remained elusive as a man, and as a medical thinker. Why?

The fight about the personality of Paracelsus began in his own lifetime. He had followers and admirers as well as enemies and detractors. By the end of the 18th century, the enlightened Dr. J. G. Zimmermann could write of him that "he lived like a pig, looked like a coachman and took most pleasure in the company of the loosest and lowest mob . . ." and that "all his writings seem to have been written during intoxication."[6] Romanticism of the early 19th century found new sympathies for Paracelsus, and the racism and nationalism of recent years made him a heroic figure of phantastic proportions. But those who wish to avoid condemnation and adulation of Paracelsus and who wish to study him objectively, find themselves confronted with a great difficulty. Paracelsus himself is the main source for his evaluation, and almost at the outset we seem forced to take this source on trust or to reject it. One example may suffice to illustrate the situation. As early as 1527 in his Basel program, Paracelsus called himself "Doctor of both medicines,"[7] which meant doctor of medicine and surgery. Did he really possess the degree of a medical doctor? No diploma has been found, no entry in the matricles of any university. But why doubt his assertion? Because his colleagues at Basel had already spread rumors of its nonexistence[8] and because Paracelsus later also called himself Doctor of Holy

[5]Theophrast von Hohenheim, gen. Paracelsus, *Sämtliche Werke* 1. Abteilung: Medizinische, naturwissenschaftliche und philosophische Schriften, herausgegeben von Karl Sudhoff. 14 vols., Munich, 1922–1933. 2. Abteilung: Theologische und religionsphilosophische Schriften, herausgegeben von Wilhelm Matthiessen. 1 vol., Munich, 1923.

[6]Walter Artelt, Paracelsus im Urteil der Medizinhistorik, *Fortschritte der Medizin*, 1932, vol. 50, no. 22. Zimmermann's judgment obviously goes back to Oporinus' letter to Weyer.

[7]"utriusque medicinae Doctor ac Professor"; ed. Sudhoff, IV, p. 3.

[8]In a draft of his report to the city council of Basel, summer 1527, Paracelsus complained that some doctors "reden mir auch schmelich zu, man wiss nit, woher oder ob ich doctor sei oder nit,—mit beger inen im collegio auf ir fragen zu antworten etc." (ed. Sudhoff, IV, p. 153). This passage apparently has been understood as implying that Paracelsus could not present a diploma, an inference which, as Burckhardt, *l.c.* p. 364, has pointed out, is not compelling. Paracelsus complains about the rumor as if it were a libel. The incident at Sterzingen where Paracelsus was denied recognition as a doctor is explained by him as due to the mayor's never having seen doctors "in zerissen lumpen an der sonnen braten." (Ed. Sudhoff, IX, p. 562). The mayor did not believe Paracelsus—with or without diploma.

Writ,[9] although certainly he was no doctor of divinity. Then why accept his medical degree? Because when called as a witness in a lawsuit, according to the record he testified upon the oath which he had sworn at the University of Ferrara upon his doctorate. The actual record of this testimony was rediscovered by Burckhardt[10] and it thus seems established that Paracelsus received an M.D. degree at Ferrara—provided of course that we are willing to accept his word. The question is not without interest. A Paracelsus who went through the medical curriculum of his days and the Latin disputations required would be a rebel like Luther to whom he was likened during his life-time. A Paracelsus who decked himself with clothes which he never possessed and then attacked all rightful bearers of these same clothes would be a suspicious fellow indeed.

We may go further and even ask whether Paracelsus really was as successful in his cures as is generally assumed. What do we really know about them and how are we to judge?[11] To hear Paracelsus speak, the doctors of his time were inefficient compared with himself,[12] and the very inefficiency of contemporary medicine was one of the main points of his attack. This may well be, but does not prove his own prowess. Of his therapeutic maxims as they appear in his books, some are excellent, others are mere superstitions as judged by any modern standard. Therapeutic maxims prove neither cures nor malpractice. Oporinus who, for some time, was Paracelsus' amanuensis praises his master's great skill in the treatment of various diseases.[13] In 1526, Paracelsus cured the publisher Froben, a feat which redounded greatly to his fame; but a year later Froben was dead, killed by poisonous remedies, Paracelsus' enemies whispered.[14] Some of Paracelsus' consilia for patients are not very enlightening; his letter to Erasmus in which he diagnosed the humanist's state of health is hard for us

---

[9]See Henry M. Pachter, *Paracelsus*, New York: Henry Schuman, 1951, p. 58, and K. Goldammer, Neues zur Lebensgeschichte und Persönlichkeit des Theophrastus Paracelsus, *Theologische Zeitschrift*, 1947, vol. 3, pp. 191–221. Goldammer has collected all passages where Paracelsus refers to himself as a teacher of theology and explains them as consequences of Paracelsus' doctrine of religious office. "*Sein 'Doctor der Heiligen Geschrift' ist eine religiöse Amts- und Gemeindeaufgabe*, die er sich gestellt wusste, *kein Universitätstitel*" (ibid., p. 206).

[10]Albrecht Burckhardt, Nochmals der Doktortitel von Paracelsus. *Correspondenz-Blatt für Schweizer Aerzte*, vol. 44, 1914, pp. 884–87. The whole record is now conveniently found in Wickersheimer, *op. cit.*

[11]Th. Oettli, Paracelsus und St. Moritz, *Schweizerische medizinische Wochenschrift*, 71, 1941, pp. 1121–25, has put the question very well (p. 1124): "Dieser Mann, der so treffliches über die Grundlagen des Arzttums geschrieben hat—war er selber ein grosser Arzt? Sicher ist, dass ihm manche Heilung da glückte, wo vor ihm andere Aerzte sich umsonst bemüht hatten. Aber es muss schon zu seinen Lebzeiten schwer gewesen sein, ein Urteil über sein Können zu gewinnen. Er zog von Stadt zu Stadt, von Land zu Land, nirgends Fuss fassend. Für einen Arzt bedeutet dies, dass er selten oder nie in die Lage kommt, den Grad und die Dauer seiner Heilungen zu kontrollieren."

[12]Preface to Paragranum, ed. Sudhoff, VIII, p. 34: " . . . und die grossen cur, so ich durch vil königreich, sprach und lendern treffentlichen bewiesen hab uber ander arzt, uber ir patronen und all bücher, und curas volbracht, die inen in allen iren büchern nicht müglich waren."

[13]The entire letter of Oporinus is to be found in German translation in Sudhoff, *Paracelsus*, p. 46–49.

[14]R. Julius Hartmann, *Theophrast von Hohenheim*, Stuttgart and Berlin, Cotta, 1904, p. 60.

to understand and was not entirely understandable to Erasmus either.[15] A few neutral references to the treatment of patients, neutral because not designed to enhance or to belittle Paracelsus, do not allow one to draw any inferences, perhaps because of their brevity and paucity. He seems to have set great store by urinoscopy as evinces from the records of his examinations of Claus and Gerbel in Strasbourg.[16] In the legend, Paracelsus survives as a great healer, but legend also celebrates him as a great sorcerer.[17]

It is admittedly difficult to judge the results of any medical practice of the past, and to raise the question as to Paracelsus' success does not necessarily mean to deny it. Yet these and other questions have to be asked in order to make us realize how elusive his personality has remained. It must be added that our uncertainty is not helped by a historical method that has constructed an imaginary route of his travels from the mere mentioning of place names in his works regardless of the context, and that makes him a "feldscher" in the army of the low countries because of some vague reference to his deeds during the Netherlandish and other wars.[18] The same doubtful method has traced the development of his youth from some autobiographical remarks which are given without any clear references as to the periods of his life.[19] Unfortunately, the literature on Paracelsus abounds in uncritical constructions, assumptions, and interpretations. Here, critical objectivity could at least help to remove some of the fog.[20] But critical objectivity will still have to reckon with the ambiguity which seems rooted in Paracelsus' character. The name Paracelsus appears in 1529 in connection with an astrological prognosis on the fate of Europe.[21] Among the speculations about the meaning of the word Paracelsus, that which explains it as a latinization of the family name von Hohenheim is the most

[15]For the consilia see ed. Sudhoff, IX, p. 661 ff.; X, p. 1 f. and 574 ff.; XI, p. 279 ff. For the letter to Erasmus see *ibid.*, III, p. 379, and for Erasmus' reply, Sudhoff, *Paracelsus*, p. 24 f., and Pachter, *op. cit.*, p. 146 (English translation).

[16]*See* Wickersheimer, *op. cit.*, pp. 357 and 359.

[17]Article "Paracelsus" in *Handwörterbuch des deutschen Aberglaubens*, vol. IX, Berlin, 1941, col. 59 ff. See also Donald Brinkmann, Mythos und Logos im Weltbild des Paracelsus, *Nova Acta Paracelsica*, I, 1944, pp. 109–34.

[18]As far as I can see, the claims for Paracelsus as an army surgeon rest mainly on the passage in the Spital-Buch, ed. Sudhoff, VII, p. 374: "dieweil ich auch im Niderland, in der Romanei, in Neapolis, in Venedischen, Denemerkischen und Niderlendischen kriegen so treffentliche summa der febrischen aufbracht und ob den vierzigerlei leibkrankheiten, so in denselben funden worden, in gesundheit aufgericht." (See R. Julius Hartmann, *op. cit.*, pp. 25 and 181, notes 56 ff. In note 57, Hartmann mentions an article in vol. 4 of the "Abhandlungen der königlichen Societät der Wissenschaften zu Kopenhagen" which is supposed to prove that Paracelsus served as physician in the army of King Christian II of Denmark. The article is mentioned in Ersch-Gruber, *Allgemeine Encyklopädie der Wissenschaften und Künste*, 3. Sect. 11. Theil, 1838, p. 286, but was accessible neither to Hartmann nor to me.)

[19]I refer here to the preface to the first Tractat of book 1 of the Grosse Wundarznei (ed. Sudhoff, X, p. 19 ff.), a book that dates from 1536.

[20]See Bittel, *loc. cit.*, p. 37 f. See also George Rosen, Some recent European publications dealing with Paracelsus, *Journal of the History of Medicine*, 1947, vol. 2, pp. 537–48.

[21]See Paracelsus-Museum Stuttgart, Paracelsus-Dokumentation, Referat-Blätter. A 44: *Para und Paracelsus*, 1943 (Dr. Bittel).

likely as far as rational meaning is concerned.[22] But does the rational intent suffice? If the name had been coined merely to fascinate the hearer, it could not have been done better. Through the centuries the name has exerted a peculiar magic. Paracelsus was a magician[23] and there is at the core of the magician's personality an elusiveness which, though not identifiable with willful deceit, yet instinctively avoids precision and lucidity.

From the man we pass to his works, only to meet with great external obstacles to their understanding. The idiom he used adds to the difficulties of an as yet grammatically undeveloped German language which lacked the adequate vocabulary and stylistic suppleness for the scientific content he wished to express. But these external obstacles, which Gundolf[24] has analyzed, are not decisive. When Paracelsus heaps scorn upon the doctors and apothecaries, he expresses himself only too clearly. Where he speaks of the physician's duty, of the dignity of medicine, and of the distress of the sick, he finds words of a poignancy that makes him one of the most moving German authors of the Reformation period. Where the underlying thought is quite clear to us, it reveals itself through the cover of the style. But where the thought is strange we meet with difficulties more serious than the unfamiliar style.

An example may serve us as illustration and guide. It is taken from the first of Paracelsus' "Eleven treatises of the origin, causes, signs, and cures of individual diseases," medical sketches supposedly written about 1520, and it concerns the pathology and treatment of dropsy.[25] We have chosen this short essay because of its relative simplicity, and the absence of the Paracelsian neologisms which were already the despair of his contemporaries.

According to Paracelsus, the nature of dropsy is expressed in its German name, Wassersucht; for essentially it is water, or rather a resolutus liquor, that is a fluid generated from the solution of tissues.[26] Paracelsus describes the disease as a gradual swelling of the body from the feet upwards "until the spirit of life is drowned in it, like a man in a flood that overtakes him." The patient has a feeling of pressure in the epigastric region and oppression around the heart, he coughs and is short of breath. "All these things are the disease called 'Wassersucht.' And in the end it reddens the urine,

---

[22]For this as well as other interpretations see Bittel, *ibid.* For the purpose of the present discussion it matters little whether the name Paracelsus was coined by himself or invented by others and subsequently accepted.

[23]I use the word magician to characterize the author of the Astronomia Magna and the prophecies on Europe. Paracelsus' personality has facets which do not impress me as harmoniously united. Franz Strunz, *Theophrastus Paracelsus*, Salzburg-Leipzig, Pustet, 1937, p. 49: "... dieses aufreizend Widerspruchsvolle, das im seelischen Knotenpunkt seines Charakters liegt und seiner so schwer deutbaren Persönlichkeit die Farbe gibt...."

[24]Friedrich Gundolf, *Paracelsus*, Berlin, Georg Bondi, 1927.

[25]"Elf Traktat von Ursprung, Ursachen, Zeichen und Kur einzelner Krankheiten," I. Von der Wassersucht; ed. Sudhoff, I, p. 3 ff. I have chiefly used the first version (pp. 3–9) for the following analysis. I wish to emphasize that in selecting this essay I have chosen an example of *one* type of Paracelsian pathology. I am aware that Paracelsus also knows of other types of pathological interpretation, e.g., the alchemistic, which, however, is hardly less elusive.

[26]This interpretation is suggested by the first paragraph of the second version (p. 10) where Paracelsus lays great stress on the difference between real water and dropsical fluid.

splits open the skin, seeps through and there may be thirst. In some it increases quickly, in other slowly, according to the impression from the heavens; and in the same course they die."[27] The clinical description is brief but masterly; its latter part refers to his explanation of the disease which rests upon three concepts: the power of the heavens, the nature of the earth, and the microcosm.

Paracelsus believes in a correspondence between the macrocosm, the outer world, and the microcosm, i.e., man. The macrocosm consists of the visible heavens with their higher elements of air and fire, and of earth and water, the lower elements. The elements are not the physicochemical principles of the Aristotelian-Galenic tradition; they are the sources from which and in which things are generated and grow: plants from earth, minerals from water. The elements are the mothers that bring forth the manifold species of things. And the heavens and lower elements exist in man too, but invisibly. Nevertheless, the same processes that can be observed in the macrocosm also go on in the microcosm and account for many diseases. Since man's inner nature is invisible, the physician has to rely on the observation of the external world and then find the correspondence in the inner. This finding of the correspondence Paracelsus called anatomy, in contrast to the ordinary anatomy of which he did not think very highly.

Of the microcosm you have here to know that it is constituted of the four elements and that it is these elements, but invisibly so. For formed as it is in the image of Him who created things, it has yet remained a creature. Therefore it is in part earth and must have the heavens, must have the air, must have fire etc. just like our Earth, to be understood internally just as the Earth is understood externally. This constitution entails destruction from which diseases grow, if measure and temperance do not prevail.[28]

Now the life of the visible earth depends on the heavens and their impressions, rain and dew. Without the latter, everything on earth will die. But if the earth receives them beyond measure, death will follow too. "As the rain corrupts the earth, makes it too moist, drowns it, interrupts its functions, if the heavens in their impressions cause a downpour beyond temperance and measure, so it also covers man in his earth and pours down on him; this is the dropsy with which this chapter deals."[29]

This interpretation of the disease leads to its prognosis and treatment. The prognosis again contains flashes of lucid clinical description:

If the patients cough continuously and lose their color and the moon rules their lack of breath, for it is from her that the rain and impression of this disease go forth, and if thereupon there is a breaking open, spontaneous seepage, and the mouth and eyes turn yellowish, the nose becomes sharp, the fingers become thin and form wrinkles, the urine decreases and thickens, nature has quite abandoned this patient

[27]Ed. Sudhoff, I, p. 3.
[28]*Ibid.*, p. 5.
[29]*Ibid.*, p. 4.

and there is little hope of bringing her back; but without these signs there is good hope.[30]

The treatment, just as the pathology, has to rest upon the philosophy of the earth, the astronomy of the heavens, and on "physica which teaches you to know the microcosm, what it is and what you have under your hands."[31] The treatment is alchemistic, that is it prefers chemically prepared remedies whose essential nature is to counteract the invisible microcosmic forces. A large accumulation of water has first to be removed by "mercurial essences" (probably mercurial oxide);[32] then sulphur and a metallic "crocus," i.e., oxide, have to be administered.[33] The sulphur is supposed to act like a sun dispelling the rain in the microcosm, while the metallic crocus will dry the body of the patient.

In analyzing this example we have to distinguish between the scientific philosophy and the scientific method. Interconnected as the two are, they are yet not identical. Various attempts have been made to outline the scientific philosophy of Paracelsus; the task has proved very difficult and there is no general agreement. We are here not concerned with the difficulties of Paracelsian thought, and it may suffice to give a few examples of the manner in which reconstructions of his philosophy have been attempted. We know that the macrocosm-microcosm parallelism had been popular since antiquity.[34] We also know that Paracelsus, a firm believer in the Bible, was deeply influenced by the accounts that God "formed man of the dust of the ground, and breathed into his nostrils the breath of life" (Genesis 2,7) and yet "created man in His own image, in the image of God . . ." (*ibid.*, 1,27). Because of these common origins there is thus for Paracelsus a correspondence between the outer world and man on the one hand, and between man and God on the other.[35] We also know that the heavens, to Paracelsus, represent not only the conditions of climate and weather, but also the conditions of time and change, so that the varying combinations of stars and planets mark the moments for cosmic and human events.[36] Thus the world can be conceived as becoming older and exhibiting new diseases just as man's diseases change with the periods of his life. Again, a study of the works of Paracelsus teaches us that he believed all bodies to be composed of

[30]*Ibid.*, p. 7.
[31]*Ibid.*, p. 6.
[32]See the second version, p. 17. This seems one of the earliest diuretic uses of mercurial compounds.
[33]For the interpretation of some of Paracelsus' chemical terms see the "Verzeichnis alchemistischer Ausdrücke" in Ernst Darmstaedter, *Die Alchemie des Geber*, Berlin, Springer, 1922, p. 185 ff.
[34]Adolf Meyer, *Wesen und Geschichte der Theorie von Mikro- und Makrokosmos*, Bern, 1900; George Perrigo Conger, *Theories of macrocosms and microcosms in the history of philosophy*, New York, 1922.
[35]Bodo Sartorius Freiherr von Waltershausen, *Paracelsus am Eingang der deutschen Bildungsgeschichte*, Leipzig, Meiner, 1936, p. 187.
[36]J. D. Achelis, Zur Grundstruktur der paracelsischen Naturwissenschaft, *Kyklos*, 1, 1928, p. 47.

the three chemical principles of sulphur, salt, and mercury.[37] And since sulphur constituted the combustible principle, it begins to appear logical that it should be prescribed to act as a microcosmic sun that would dispel the invisible rain causing dropsy.

In this manner it seems at least possible to piece together the groundwork of Paracelsus' scientific philosophy.[38] And if Paracelsus were but a philosopher, this task, difficult as it is, would suffice to make his works understandable, just as the works of other Renaissance philosophers. However, Paracelsus was a physician and a scientist, i.e. an investigator, and the method of his investigation is not revealed by a mere description of his metaphysical schemes. Returning to our example, we may, for instance, ask why Paracelsus had to think of dropsy as the result of an invisible rain? It seems to me that there is no answer to this question. With equal right we might imagine an analogy of flooding rivers swelled by the snow which a premature sun had caused to melt. Or, to give another example, what justification has Paracelsus in interpreting an epileptic attack as a thunderstorm, which strikes suddenly but passes soon, leaving the country to recover?[39] The picture may have something compelling, but it remains a picture. There is no necessity for its choice. In other words, we may be able to describe and apprehend the fixed results of Paracelsus' thought; but its movements seem to lack necessity; it is here that Paracelsus eludes us. And unfortunately it is also here that we are relatively little helped by modern scholarship. A glimpse at the bibliography published by Sudhoff[40] in the *Acta Paracelsica* and continued by Betschart[41] in the *Nova Acta Paracelsica* shows that among the books and articles which have appeared since 1900 those dealing with the life of Paracelsus, his philosophical, scientific, and general medical significance far outweigh the studies devoted to his investigation of definite diseases.

It now remains to characterize this elusiveness more sharply and to ask whether and how Paracelsus can justify it. In his macrocosmic analogies, Paracelsus presents us with pictures which he expects us to see just as he sees them. Paralleling art and science, Benesch has spoken of "Paracelsus'

[37]This chemical theory is one of the best known aspects of Paracelsus' doctrines and is mentioned in all histories of chemistry. On the other hand, the extreme difficulty of exactly interpreting Pracelsus' chemical procedures is indicated by Ernst Darmstaedter, *Arznei und Alchemie: Paracelsus-Studien*, Leipzig, Barth, 1931 (Studien zur Geschichte der Medizin, 20).

[38]Our conviction of man's essential unity seems to stimulate us to the attempt at systematizing the thoughts and acts of historical personalities. In the case of Paracelsus, such a procedure seems unusually doubtful, especially if it relies on gathering passages from various of his writings. One could quite easily compose a list of conflicting statements. Here as so often, certain basic ideas recur, whereas others change or even contradict one another. In Paracelsus, the ratio of the latter to the former impresses me as being great. H. Kayser, Das Formendenken des Paracelsus, *Nova Acta Paracelsica*, 1, 1944, pp. 103–08, has stressed the difficulties of systematizing Paracelsus' doctrines, and has pointed to the latter's "Formendenken," and especially the "Bildbegriffe" (image concepts) as one of the main roots of these difficulties.

[39]O. Temkin, *The falling sickness*, Baltimore, Johns Hopkins Press, 1945, p. 162 f.

[40]Karl Sudhoff, Nachweise zur Paracelsus-Literatur. Beilage zu *Acta Paracelsica*, 1–5, 1930–32.

[41]P. Ildefons Betschart, Paracelsus-Bibliographie, *Nova Acta Paracelsica*, 1, 1944, pp. 182–92.

intuitive, artistic approach toward nature" and, together with others, has referred to his "interpretation of nature."[42] I too think that Paracelsus' scientific method can rightly be called intuitive and interpretative. Negatively this is evidenced by his dislike of discursive proof, scholastic or otherwise. Paracelsus condemns a science based on human reasoning as sheer phantasy. This is more than an attack on the scholastic belief in authority; it is an attack on the rationality of the world. On the positive side, his intuitive method is evidenced by his predilection for example. It has long been remarked that Paracelsus has a liking for analogies. This in itself would be of little importance since analogy had been a scientific tool from the days of antiquity. With Paracelsus, however, the analogy almost takes the place of the parable in the New Testament. To make his reader see the truth of his interpretation, Paracelsus has no other means but to lead him as near as possible through examples. Hence the style of Paracelsus is marked by a series·of statements connected by analogies or by open or hidden biblical references. It fits none of the great scientific methods, be they scholastic, mathematical, classificatory, purely descriptive, or even experimental in the modern sense. And these pictures, these visions are offered as interpretations of what is otherwise hidden and obscure in its causes.[43]

This procedure finds its justification in the *Labyrinthus medicorum errantium,* one of the Carinthian writings of 1538, the other two being his *Seven Defensiones* and the *Book on the Tartaric Diseases.* The physicians who rely on the written books err and find themselves in a labyrinth. "Nevertheless," Paracelsus says, "a disciple cannot exist without a master; the disciple must learn from the master. And I wondered again and again where the master might be who would teach, since the scribblers cannot be deemed masters. This made me think if there were no book on earth, no physician at all, how would one then have to learn? And I realized that medicine can very well be learned without a human master. How, and in what manner, I have here put together, the very books that are the truly basic ones for the invention of all arts and theory."[44] These truly basic books are heavens, the elements, the anatomy of the macrocosm and microcosm, alchemy, etc., many of which we have already met as fundaments of the Paracelsian philosophy of science. They are the books whose study Paracelsus recommends "in the light of nature."

Much has been written about the meaning Paracelsus gives to the "lumen naturale."[45] It will suffice to point out that he believes in its illuminating function. The natural light helps us to see things as they really are in

[42]Otto Benesch, *The art of the Renaissance in northern Europe,* Harvard University Press, 1947, pp. 50 and 51.
[43]See Kayser, *op. cit.* and Hans Fischer, Die kosmologische Anthropologie des Paracelsus als Grundlage seiner Medizin, *Verhandlungen der naturforschenden Gesellschaft in Basel,* 52, 1940–41, pp. 267–317; see especially p. 285.
[44]Labyrinthus medicorum errantium, ed. Sudhoff, XI, p. 103.
[45]On this concept see among others Fritz Medicus, Paracelsus in der philosophischen Bewegung seiner und unserer Zeit, *Nova Acta Paracelsica,* I, 1944, pp. 45–68; Hans Fischer, *op. cit.;* and especially von Waltershausen, *op. cit.*

nature, it reveals what otherwise is invisible.[46] We can now understand why Paracelsus speaks in pictures and how his intuitive method justified itself. At the same time we know that we cannot follow him, at least not everywhere. Only when he describes phenomena which we can see with our own eyes or test by our own experience do we share his intuition. Thus we admire the passages in which he reveals himself as a master of clinical observation. The Paracelsus who travels from land to land, who turns the leaves of the codex naturae with his feet[47] in order to observe new diseases, is the Paracelsus we understand. But when he turns to the study of the other books, his visions become strange and he eludes us. When he describes the course of dropsy as it may develop in severe cardiac insufficiency, or recommends mercurial drugs, he and we see in the same light. But when he declares dropsy a rain, the light of nature shines for him while we remain in darkness.

Modern science distrusts intuition. Paracelsus was not a modern scientist,[48] but he too set conditions for its use. The investigation of nature will yield certainty if undertaken in confidence in God. He is the author of the book of Nature, He is the first of the books that Paracelsus recommends to the student. "Thus every perfect gift comes from God who bids us ask, seek, and knock and who says that what we ask in His name shall be given unto us. Hence there follows that we are not given stones or serpents for bread, but something better. Now every student of nature should know that he has to get to know nature in this manner."[49]

To the written books of authority with their trust in reason, Paracelsus has thus opposed a method that relies on God and the experience of nature. The scholastic books stand condemned because their truth cannot be proved; the scholastic dispute leads in a circle from the book back to the book.[50] Proof has to be found outside of this circle, viz, in works, the healing of the sick, and by its inefficiency, the medicine of the Galenists reveals itself as false.[51] Obviously, however, the same demand for practical proof can be made of Paracelsus. His intuitions would be worthless if his method did not lead to better results. Hence he must claim to be the better

[46]Von Waltershausen, *op. cit.*, p. 106.

[47]Paracelsus, Seven Defensiones, translated by C. Lilian Temkin (Four Treatises of Theophrastus von Hohenheim called Paracelsus, ed. Henry E. Sigerist, Baltimore, Johns Hopkins Press, 1941, p. 29): "Scripture is explored through its letters; but nature from land to land. Every land is a leaf. Such is the *Codex Naturae;* thus must her leaves be turned."

[48]H. Fischer, *op. cit.*, p. 285, rightly contrasts Paracelsus' intuitive knowledge gained in the light of nature with modern physical science. See also Kayser, *op. cit.*

[49]Labyrinthus medicorum errantium, ed. Sudhoff, XI, p. 173.

[50]*Ibid.*, p. 177: "es ist etwas mer dan spöttig, das die erzt so gar nit wöllen in die rechten bücher der erznei, sondern verzeren ir zeit unnüzlich in den erdichten büchern, dero buchstaben tot ist und im sentenz kein leben, *als sie dan auch durch ir werk bezeugen* und betrachten nicht, so einer spreche, das buch der erznei ist falsch, das sie es nicht könten probiren das gerecht were als alein mit demselbigen buchstaben. so ein buch probirt sol werden, so muss probirt werden aus dem aus dem es ist. das euangelium aus Christo, aus im ist es, das natürlich buch aus der natur, aus der natur ist es." (italics mine).

[51]See the italicized passage above. *Ibid.*, p. 175: "... und on die bücher des rechten grunts seints alles tote buchstaben, das ist, sie bringen die kranken mer zum tot dan zum leben.

physician and to have cured where his adversaries failed. The question as to whether Paracelsus really was a successful practitioner thus shows itself as a very important one. We may not be able to answer it, but we can understand why Paracelsus must boast and why he cannot permit any doubt of his ability to cure. For this alone yields the objective justification of his interpretation of nature. The elusive character of the man and the elusive nature of his thought, therefore, are but two aspects of the same thing.

At this point we may begin to wonder just how seriously Paracelsus should be taken when he refers to the heavens, the elements, etc. as books. Our first reaction is to take this manner of speech as a mere simile, used to contrast nature to the "paper books" as Paracelsus calls them.[52] If this is the case, Paracelsus appears peculiarly persistent in his use of the simile. He refers to the world as a library,[53] countries are leaves of the book of nature,[54] stars are compared to words and their combinations to meaningful sentences.[55] Somewhere Paracelsus even maintains that every profession is based on its own book: theology on the Bible, jurisprudence on the corpus juris. It is, therefore, at least worth while trying to take his simile seriously,[56] especially after the lesson Professor Singleton[57] has taught us regarding Dante's *Vita nuova*.

We were able to confirm the opinion that Paracelsus interpreted nature; and we know that Paracelsus refers to nature as a book written by God. "And nobody may make a book or a text: it is nature who makes the text, the physician makes but the gloss."[58] From this point of view, Paracelsus' own works are but glosses to the book of nature. Now the task of the glossator is to facilitate the understanding of the text; and if we are right, then the purpose of Paracelsus as an author is to facilitate the understanding of nature, notably for those who are not able to read the text by themselves. Such a view seems to give the answer to a difficulty frequently encountered in Paracelsus' works. Repeatedly he breaks off a discussion with the suggestion that the reader find the rest by himself. In one place, for instance, where he refers the reader to his own clinical experience, he says: "Thus it is necessary that a physician have great experience, not only

[52]*Ibid.*, p. 174: "die bücher des papirs."

[53]Das Buch von den tartarischen Krankheiten, ed. Sudhoff, XI, p. 92.

[54]See above, note 46; also ed. Sudhoff, XI, p. 92.

[55]Labyrinthus, ed. Sudhoff, XI, p. 175 f. Since the "book"—similes abound in the Carinthian writings which are all of the same period, I have used them as main references.

[56]A. Koyré, Paracelse, *Revue d'Histoire et de Philosophie religieuses*, 1933, pp. 46–75, and 145–63; see p. 58.

[57]Charles S. Singleton, *An essay on the Vita Nuova.* Harvard University Press, 1949. This work contains instructive material on "the book of nature" and similar expressions; see especially pp. 34 ff. and 131 ff.

[58]Labyrinthus, ed. Sudhoff, XI, p. 182. Paracelsus here alludes to the "glosses" added to medieval texts; the modern reader may take the term in the approximate sense of a commentary. Cf. Singleton, *op. cit.* and Beryl Smalley, *The study of the Bible in the middle ages*, Oxford, Clarendon Press, 1941, p. 35. For medical glosses see Max Neuburger, *Geschichte der Medizin*, vol. 2, Stuttgart, Enke, 1911, p. 375.

of what is in the book; rather, the sick should be his book; they will not fail him; in them he will not be deceived. But the physician who is satisfied with the letter—the letter is dead and he too is dead; these two kill the patient also."[59]

Strictly speaking, he who searches in the light of nature does not need any books, but will gather his own experience. It has rightly been observed that Paracelsus' idea of experience is an individualistic one,[60] just as is Luther's idea of faith based on the interpretation of God's word. Nevertheless, Paracelsus cannot refrain from writing paper books and putting before the reader what he believes to be the right interpretation of nature,[61] just as Luther soon led his followers to a new form of orthodoxy. But at any moment Paracelsus will remember his role as a mere commentator and refer the reader back to his own search. It is just at such moments that we are most acutely aware of our inability to interpret nature. For our physical and biological science has followed a different direction.[62] And it is not by chance that Paracelsus appears most modern to us where we too have recourse to an interpretative method, viz., in analytical psychology and psychiatry.[63]

A comparison with Galilei's reference to the book of nature is instructive. There are obvious parallels: Galilei speaks of the true book of philosophy as Paracelsus speaks of the true book of medicine. To the books written by the phantasy of men, both oppose the book of nature. But here a decisive difference becomes visible. Galilei claims that the book of nature is not written in the ordinary alphabet, but in "triangles, squares, circles, spheres, cones, pyramids, and other mathematical figures." Therefore "this book can only be read by means of mathematics."[64] But since mathematics can be learned, this means that man can acquire a method that will make the book of nature readable. Such a method is lacking in Paracelsus. There are indications that chemistry could have supplied it. In his work on the tartaric diseases, Paracelsus hints that an examination of the urine of the patients as well as of their food might reveal the substances whose ingestion causes these metabolic diseases.[65] But chemically such an analysis was not possible at the time. It is one of the many glimpses Paracelsus had of a science approaching ours,[66] of a way out of the interpretation of nature. As it was,

[59]Tartarische Krankheiten, ed. Sudhoff, XI, p. 85.

[60]Wilhelm Matthiessen, *Die Form des religiösen Verhaltens bei Theophrast von Hohenheim, gen. Paracelsus.* Diss. Bonn. Düsseldorf, 1917, p. 5 ff.

[61]Paracelsus does not altogether exclude the possibility of learning from a book, provided that it be understood in the light of nature, just as the Gospel is a spur to seek the eternal life in its author (Labyrinthus, ed. Sudhoff, p. 200 f.) See also below, note 66.

[62]Since a "meaning" only can be interpreted, an interpretation of nature becomes impossible as soon as nature is no longer believed to be meaningful.

[63]It is, therefore, understandable that Paracelsus has received the attention of psychiatrists. See C. G. Jung, *Paracelsica*, Zürich, Rascher Verlag, 1942; I. Galdston, The psychiatry of Paracelsus, *Bull. Hist. Med.*, 24, 1950, pp. 205–18.

[64]Cf. Wilhelm Dilthey, *Gesammelte Schriften*, vol. 2, Leipzig–Berlin, Teubner, 1921, p. 259.

[65]Ed. Sudhoff, XI, p. 94.

[66]In the same work, p. 17, Paracelsus suggests that a written book of real value could be composed if all physicians described the species of tartaric diseases prevalent in their coun-

Paracelsus attempted to read a book written in an unknown language, and he had to rely on the technique of the philologist who tries to decipher a strange inscription. The assumed meaning of some letters and words must support the reading of the rest. Thus in our example of dropsy we questioned the necessity of interpreting the disease as an invisible rain. However, this interpretation is partly supported by the immediately following interpretation of consumption as a lack of rain, as a drought.[67] Since the same vision explains two diseases, Paracelsus could consider it as confirmed by nature.

The main consequence of the lack of a rational or otherwise objective method was a preoccupation with language and terminology. Paracelsus did not care for the humanist's learned interests. "As to the names which dropsy has, be it in Latin, Greek, Arabic or Chaldaic, never mind their etymology, for here the languages play with one another and make sport like cats with mice; such study is useless."[68] But the glossator of the book of nature must be sure that his words denote things as they really are. Since the text of the book cannot be changed, all efforts have to concentrate upon the terminology of the gloss. Here the glossator and the magician Paracelsus meet and so are born the yliaster and cagaster and other monsters of a terminology which, as Achelis has shown, is rooted in the very structure of Paracelsian science.[69] That the preoccupation is not merely due to a lack of preexisting convenient terms, but to a concern with proper medical and scientific language, can be exemplified by the name "tartaric diseases" which Paracelsus coined. The old names, stone and gravel, are inadequate because the concretions found in the bladder, kidneys, and elsewhere are not real stones. The old names are metaphors. "And this I declare, because it is a lack of skill to use metaphora in medicine and nothing but an error to give names metaphorically."[70] He chooses the name tartaric because of the identity of the matter formed in these diseases with the concretions found in wine casks.[71] Again we have an example of the possibility of establishing an objective science by proving the real identity of the two. As it is, the identity largely rests on analogy and does not even give the only reason for the new name. "Moreover, mark my words, the name I give to this disease is tartara, that is aegritudo tartari or tartareus morbus, taken from tartaro which is called tartarum by its inborn name; tartarum because it yields an oil, a water, a tincture, a salt which inflames and burns the sick like a hellish fire, for tartarum is the hell."[72] Since Paracelsus offers this etymology

---

tries. He compares such a book to a map from which everybody can learn even if he has not travelled himself. This passage strikes me as approaching the modern concept of inductive science. At the same time it is an example of a positive evaluation of books (see above, note 61).

[67]Ed. Sudhoff, I, pp. 9 and 24.

[68]*Ibid.*, p. 3.

[69]J. D. Achelis, Zur Terminologie des Labyrinthus Medicorum, *Acta Paracelsica*, 1930, pp. 33–39. On the magic element of Paracelsus' terminology, see Jung, *op. cit.*, p. 60 f.

[70]Tartarische Krankheiten, ed. Sudhoff, XI, p. 20.

[71]*Ibid.*, pp. 19–23.

[72]*Ibid.*, p. 21.

instead of the alleged metaphors, we may assume that to him the connection between the substance that causes hellish pain and the name of the disease that means hell is a real one. In short, the magic glossator is not satisfied with referring to a thing, but wishes to express the thing itself.

But our main concern is not with the magician Paracelsus; we tried to explain the elusive character of the physician, as far as a separation is possible. The aim of this paper is to facilitate the reading of Paracelsus' medical works. Paracelsus cannot be approached like a modern doctor who is sure of his training and his usefulness. Nor can his works be read like modern medical publications. There are passages that appeal to us directly; we mentioned a few, we might have mentioned many more. But there are provinces where Paracelsus remains elusive; not because of a complicated philosophy, but because of an approach that may yield personal conviction, yet does not allow objective certainty. Paracelsus' enmity towards medieval scholasticism should not mislead us into seeing in him a modern scientist. If we know what not to expect, we may be in a better position to understand. The famous Lichtenberg once asked: "If a head and a book clash and the sound is hollow, is that sound always in the book?"[73] In one form or another, this question has again and again been raised by the readers of Paracelsus. Who should decide whether the man was a genius, though hard to understand, or a charlatan, and not worth while reading? In our opinion the question is wrongly put. A man can be intrinsically elusive and yet worth while reading.

[73]I am indebted to Professor Ludwig Edelstein for this aphorism; see G. Chr. Lichtenberg, *Aphorismen* (E 103) *Deutsche Literaturdenkmale des 18. und 19. Jahrhunderts*, No. 136, Berlin, 1906, p. 23.

16

Zimmermann's Philosophy
of the Physician*

THE SEVENTEENTH and eighteenth centuries were destined to give birth to scientific ideas of fundamental importance for the shaping and development of European culture. We call Galileo the founder of modern physics, we attribute the invention of calculus to Newton and Leibniz, with Descartes the modern philosophical spirit becomes conscious of its individuality, Linné creates for botany a system and a methodological foundation. And it is not different in medicine. When Harvey had opened a new physiological way of thinking with his discovery of the circulation of the blood, solutions to the problems of life and sickness were sought through physics and chemistry, anatomy became the scientific basis of medicine, Sydenham, Boerhaave, Hoffmann, Stahl initiated a new way of clinical teaching, and with Morgagni came the dawn of the era of pathological anatomy. This science knows only one judge, namely human reason; nature is its legal code, and its verdict depends on proof. In the seventeenth century, in the strength of its newness, it immediately attempts monumental perfection: in all fields systems arise—in medicine we find them in iatrophysics and iatrochemistry—and where detailed knowledge is lacking it is impatiently replaced by new dogmas. Only gradually do ambitions become more modest, quieter, and the intensive creative urge gives way to extensive investigative industry, and the system yields to encyclopedic collections. This new science is at first limited to a small circle of men; it is international, but it takes hold of the scholars, not of the nations; its Latin tongue is uniform but dead, the exchange of thoughts brisk and intensive but confined to a small circle, through correspondence. To become alive and penetrate the consciousness of people in general, this science had to rid itself of its cumbersomeness and emerge from the oligarchic exclusivity of the scholarly world, an eventuality which was not yet possible in the aristocratic-feudalistic society of the seventeenth century. For this a social regrouping was required, the creation of a new public embracing wide circles, and this possibility arose only in the eighteenth century with the gradual emancipation of the bourgeoisie. Thus the eighteenth century is given the task of affording the new science, which was constantly broadening factually, a new avenue of development—and the process which now takes place we are accustomed to call the Enlightenment. Starting in England, the Enlightenment arrived in Germany via France around the mid-

*"Zimmermann's Philosophie des Arztes," *Schweizerische medizinische Wochenschrift* (Basel: Benno Schwabe & Co., 1928), 58: 1215–18. Translation by C. Lilian Temkin.

dle of the eighteenth century. There Leibniz had been the representative of the new science, and in Boerhaave's pupil Albrecht von Haller, Germany possessed the greatest physiologist of the century. It was now the task of the Enlightenment to adopt the language of the people, i.e., to write in German, to help the new, modern ideas to triumph over superstition and intellectual torpor. It no longer addressed only the scholars but all who were prepared to let reason prevail and to absorb the new body of ideas. Enlightened man has become its public, education its ideal. Such is the spirit we encounter in the philosophical physician J. G. Zimmermann, and it is on this basis that his work *On Experience in the Medical Art* [*Von der Erfahrung in der Arzneykunst,* 1763–64] is to be understood.

His affiliation with the Enlightenment stands out in Zimmermann's conception of experience. He does not consider it his task to set up a fundamental theory of experience and in doing so to get lost in long-winded philosophical discourse; he makes no attempt to set up an original, independent philosophy; instead, he takes over the ordinary English and French opinions, in order to demonstrate the fundamental principles on which medical experience is based. "This entire work is to contain a chain of principles the knowledge and application of which constitute experience" (I, p. 5). These principles, and thus experience also, are not intended to yield pure knowledge, but they have a definite meaning and are bound up with practical duties: "Experience in medicine is that skill in the art of protecting man from diseases, of knowing those which do occur, and of relieving and curing them, which is acquired through well-made and well-considered observations and experiments" (I, p. 46). Experience, therefore, is less a matter of possessing knowledge than a skill to act correctly, and as the bearer of this experience may be seen the "experienced physician," whose principles and abilities Zimmermann investigates. What differentiates true from false experience, how one should act if one is to be correct and reasonable, which superstitious beliefs should be fought, all these questions are meant to separate the educated physician from the raw empiric, the enlightened individual from the mob.

The philosophic principles to which Zimmermann clings are not derived from the ponderous system of the Leibniz–Wolff school. He holds much more to a sensualism such as Locke initiated and which the Enlightenment gladly adopted without giving it metaphysical depth. More and more this sensualism took hold of the minds of Europe, and we know that not even Kant could resist it but, on the contrary, was profoundly stimulated by it. We need not read far to find proof of Zimmermann's sensualistic stance. At the very beginning he says: "We attain knowledge through our senses and understanding" (I, p. 2). This basis appears assured to him, and he does not speculate about it but proceeds immediately to investigate the correct use of the senses and of the understanding in his own field, that of medicine.

From these brief indications it can already be seen that Zimmermann is bent on pursuing a philosophical bias, that he is less concerned with discovering new facts and opening new paths than with pointing out which principles a true and reasonable medicine must always follow. But even this formulation would be too broad, for he is not concerned with investigating the concepts that make up the great, broad, scientifically based edifice of medicine, he has no desire to set up a profound, ponderous, logical system of medicine; he wants to discover the principles a physician must follow and to consider the human prerequisites involved.

Zimmermann was certainly a thoroughly trained physician; he had done scientific work under Haller, but he wanted to remain a physician, to practice rather than become a scientist. Thus his work too concerns the physician and not medical science, and he writes a philosophy of the physician, not really a philosophy of medicine. The time of the great medical systems was past, but there had arisen the task of bridging the gap between the learned physician and the rank and file of the public. The physician had to leave the isolation of his study, he had to broaden his horizon along cosmopolitan lines, remaining objective and not becoming superficial in the process; and, on the other hand, the people must be enlightened, they must be shown the advantages of the well-instructed physician over the unskilled and the quack, and they must be warned of the latter. This twofold task is fulfilled by the book *On Experience,* which, written in clear German, can be understood by every really educated person and is indeed meant for far wider circles than the physicians. It is a pedagogical accomplishment, an educational philosophy of the physician in the spirit of the Enlightenment. Zimmermann presents his line of thought convincingly and with straightforward consistency. At first he speaks of experience in general and finds the three elements that make up true experience, namely, learning, the spirit of observation, and genius. He says, in fact: "Learning gives us historical knowledge, the spirit of observation teaches us to see, genius to draw the conclusions" (I, p. 47). Having reached this standpoint, he proceeds to investigate the role to be played by each component. Accordingly, there now follow three sections comprising the whole work, the first dealing with learning, the second with the spirit of observation, and the third, forming the entire second book, with genius. The work was not continued beyond this point but remained a torso.

The truly experienced physician will not despise learning but will rather base his knowledge upon it. Learning is to be understood as the knowledge to be derived from the study of what physicians had thought and observed in earlier times. Zimmermann calls this knowledge which is transmitted through learning "historical," and what the Enlightenment understood by history, and why it prized it, he expresses as follows: "History itself is nothing but a collection of observations whose purpose is knowledge of man and the world" (I, p. 159). This concept of history differs essentially from our own. For us today, understanding historical events means learning to grasp them in the spirit of their time; we are aware of the differences in character of historical epochs, and we know that truths can only be measured in their temporal context. This feeling for history was not yet in the possession of the Enlightenment, which lacked the necessary relativity for such a yardstick. Truths for them are valid and equal at all times, and a period which did not yet possess the rational truths was simply a "dark" age, not yet "enlightened." Progress was absolutely uniform, consisting in a quantitative enrichment of knowledge, not in a qualitative permutation of the Zeitgeist. The paucity of Zimmermann's appreciation of history becomes quite clear if we read his description of Paracelsus, who for him is a drunkard, a vagrant, a mystagogue. This corresponds also to his idea of the value of studying other physicians, particularly the ancients. The physician is obliged to widen his horizon, for his personal life does not suffice to allow him to gather enough experience. The widening occurs in the first place spatially, geographically, in that he must know what is happening amongst other peoples in other parts of the world, but also in time, historically. Diseases have been roughly the same at all times, they needed the same therapy, and if we read with diligence what Hippocrates, Galen, Sydenham, Boerhaave, and others observed, we raise ourselves above the limitations of our personal lives and the few cases we ourselves see. In this way, from many cases described in the course of time, we become acquainted with the physiognomy, the history of the diseases, and understand them.[1] For Zimmermann the old physicians are teachers, without intermediary: he is unaware of living in different times, in changed circumstances, with new opinions and truths—for him the history of medicine runs a uniform, unwavering course.

Though armed with this historical knowledge, the physician is still not capable of fulfilling the demands of his profession, for it confronts him with the isolated case and requires him to be able to recognize it and classify it. For this book-knowledge does not suffice: he must be able to see, and here the spirit of observation comes into its own.

In the seventeenth century the great English physician, Sydenham, had pointed to the necessity for exact knowledge of the individual disease pictures, for the ability to distinguish them from one another and to describe them carefully. He called for an orderly "historia morborum," and the eighteenth century followed his shining example. To this period we owe a considerable number of good disease pictures, e.g., the description of morbus maculosus by Werlhof, that of rubella by Hoffmann, etc. Thus it must have been the duty of a good doctor in the eighteenth century, as it is today, to observe a case of sickness exactly in order to recognize the disease type involved, i.e., to make a correct diagnosis. This necessitated first of all a knowledge of diseases in general, and then the correct interpretation of the symptoms in the case at hand. It is this observation of the symptoms and their interpretation that is incumbent upon the spirit of observation. But parallel to this task of classification there runs another, namely, the prognostic evaluation of all the changes in the patient, and it is on this

---

[1]"Der Mensch ist unter gleichen Umständen allenthalben gleich, denn seine meisten Krankheiten sind in Ansehung ihres Anfanges, Fortganges und Ausganges so beständig als die Pflanzen, die in beständiger Ordnung aus gleichen Samen, in dem gleichen Erdreich, immer gleich blühen, wachsen und vergehen" (I, p. 231).

account that good observation is absolutely indispensable for the physician, for without it he stands blind and helpless before his patient. Zimmermann indicates the "phenomena and signs of diseases" as the object of observation. It is not altogether easy to define exactly the difference for him between phenomena, accidents, and signs in diseases. Roughly, he visualizes the phenomena and accidents as the symptoms exhibited by the patient—cough, fever, sleeplessness, etc.—and the observing physician's task is to differentiate between what is essential and nonessential, to recognize and stress what is characteristic for the disease picture. The signs are more concerned with prognosis, with what is to be viewed as favorable or unfavorable, with what promises cure or indicates death. He writes in detail about the signs derived from the pulse, respiration, urine, state of mind, i.e., the psychic changes. Broadly speaking, it may be said that the phenomena constitute symptomatology, the signs semiotics, although it must be noted that in Zimmermann the difference is often blurred. The Hippocratic stance of the eighteenth-century physician is marked by the fact that for him psychic changes are just as important as purely somatic ones. For him man is body and mind, still an indissoluble unit, completely at one with himself; the psyche changes in sickness just as the body does, and the physician must be as much psychologist as scientist.

Granted that historical information and observation yield grouping and evaluation of diseases, that they are for the physician the indispensable basis of all knowledge of the patient and of all treatment, they still do not constitute ultimate knowledge, for there remains the overriding question why, the question of etiology. Here, however, mere observation is inadequate; here the search for causes begins, and this demands more than the simple ability to see. It requires speculation; the physician must not only observe, he must draw conclusions. The healing art draws conclusions in two ways: by analogy and by induction. Here Zimmermann associates himself closely with Bacon, professing a logical procedure in medicine fully in agreement with procedure in the natural sciences. (Even a hundred years later Oesterlen was to write a logic of medicine built entirely on the principle of induction.) Analogy and induction construct a bridge to the material that observation has furnished. This material is thoroughly mastered and understood only when one can infer what the causes of the case in hand are, how the case can be explained, and to the working of what factors it can be attributed. Zimmermann gives a list of these factors and interprets their mode of operation: he perceives them in the air, in food and drink, in movement and rest, sleeping and waking, etc. Thus the patient's every circumstance, all his functions must be considered if, via correct conclusions, one is to reach a judgment of the nature of the disease and what brought it about. But in order to pursue these conclusions to the end, to reach this judgment, more is needed than erudition and observation: for this genius is required.

The conceptual framework out of which experience is built up consists, as we saw, of historical knowledge, observation of facts, and insight by analogy and inductive reasoning. This furnishes the logical structure and sketches the model of the factual content of experience. But Zimmermann is not satisfied with these intellectual conditions; he subordinates these elements to a principle stemming from a completely different, not strictly logical, point of view. Historical knowledge he ranges with erudition, inquiry into the facts with observation, the process of conclusion with genius. Here he introduces concepts that lie outside logic, that do not represent unadulterated cognitive elements, but come from psychology. The question is not merely how is medical experience theoretically possible, but under what human psychological conditions does it come to be. He is not investigating a simple faculty of reason: he is delineating the constitution of the true physician. Experience needs a historical foundation—and so the physician must possess [learning and] the spirit of observation; experience is crowned in the logical conclusion as to the causes—and so the physician must be a man of genius.[2] Zimmermann's work is distinguished by the leavening of a logical investigation with psychological analysis by the actual physician, and it is this that makes of it a philosophy of the physician, who thereby stands in the center of attention.

Zimmermann's doctrine of genius is perhaps (as Bouvier has already emphasized) the most original part of his work, often involving formulations reminiscent of quite modern ideas. "Thus the genius of the healing art is reduced to its first principles as the art of surveying and combining in a flash a great number of scattered data, of proceeding from these combinations to clear conclusions, from the known to the unknown" (II, pp. 17–18). Today we should probably no longer speak of genius: for us the meaning of this concept has changed. But we speak of intuition, and in so doing we come close to what Zimmermann meant. This man, then, already realized that intuition is an indispensable asset for the physician. However important erudition may be, without the spirit of observation and without genius, it remains dead book-learning, and the scholar is still not a physician.

For us today, to similar problems a further one has been added: what is the relationship of the practitioner to his science, i.e., what is the physician's place in medicine? Close as Zimmermann is to us by reason of the emphasis he placed on the physician's personality, he could not confront this question, for it did not yet lie within the spirit of the age.

However great the progress of medical science since the dawn of modern times, however much its theoretical knowledge had been broadened, it was nevertheless still unitary, with no essential separation of scientist and physician. They were, when all is said and done, still united in a single person; there was really no medical man who was not at the same time a physician. The initiation of this separation was reserved to the nineteenth century,

[2]"Der ist ein schlechter Arzt, der durch seine Handlungen zeigt, dass er keine Gelehrsamkeit, keinen Beobachtungsgeist und kein Genie hat" (II, p. 114). "Learning and" had obviously dropped out of the German text and has therefore been added in brackets.—O.T.

particularly from Virchow on. Where the objective presuppositions were lacking, it was not possible to pose a question which makes sense only on the basis of such presuppositions. In the eighteenth century, emphasis on the physician had necessarily had a different meaning, and we touched on this in the introduction. Zimmermann's task is to show his profession and the educated world how the physician must be constituted, if he is to represent something in life, if he is to be called upon to play a part, and win respect. He arrives at a solution to the problem by two routes: He polemicizes sharply against the raw empirics, the "practici," as he calls them, who do not know what they are really doing nor why they do it, who run after the rabble and pander to it, who become assimilated into the mob, who are the enemies of all knowledge and lucid enlightenment. On the other hand, he tries to prove that the true physician must blend erudition with receptive senses, intellect with wit; in short, that he must at the same time be scholar, man of the world, and philosopher. Philosophy is the grand ideal of the eighteenth century, philosophy not in the weightiest sense, and at this time little burdened with metaphysics, but signifying rather an intellectual attitude expressed in contrast to the character of the mob. He who despises superstition and prejudice, he who is able to "demonstrate all his claims with indisputable evidence" (I, p. 111), or at least strives to do so, he raises himself thereby above the "common crowd," becoming a philosopher and a man of culture and enlightenment. Zimmermann writes a philosophy of the physician in which the physician, in his true character, appears as a philosopher, and he thereby legitimizes him in the eyes of his era. But at the same time, he influences the physicians, showing them that the healing art demands a philosophical, enlightened attitude, and that they distinguish themselves from the mob only through a philosophical spirit. For "it is the lack of philosophical spirit that has so long made rabble of most physicians, for they could not be cleverer than their century" (I, p. 114).

We must therefore define Zimmermann's historic achievement in his book on experience as not only the demonstration of the role experience plays in medicine, but the delineation of the type of physician required by his age and needed by medicine itself for its further development.

Two hundred years after Zimmermann's birth, we shall not conclude these remarks about the philosophy of the physician from a bygone epoch without thinking briefly of our own situation. Our problems are largely of a different kind; in the nineteenth century, we have experienced medical developments such as Zimmermann could not even suspect. We demand of philosophy something deeper and more serious; we are moved by many questions that at that time had not yet arisen. Physician and medical science, medicine and natural science, the future of our profession, these are just a few arbitrarily selected examples. But one thing we have in common with that time, the yearning for a physician's philosophy capable of satisfying the demands of our time, and we remember the old Hippocratic saying that the physician who is also a philosopher becomes god-like.

17

Wunderlich,
Schelling and the History
of Medicine*

WUNDERLICH is remembered as one of the founders of clinical thermometry, as an early fighter for scientific medicine in Germany, and as a spirited historian of medicine. It is, therefore, not surprising to find one of his early scientific publications, "Fever," given the subtitle: "Historical-physiological investigations."[1] The historical part of the long essay appeared in the same volume (though not the same issue) of the *Archiv für physiologische Heilkunde* which was prefaced by the famous attack of the editors on contemporary German medicine,[2] and which also contained Wunderlich's article on medical journalism.[3] The latter article initiated a controversy with Haeser over the aims of medical historiography. Wunderlich insisted on a history of medicine that would be useful, in that it would trace those ideas which were of concern to the current theory and practice of medicine.[4] From this point of view, Wunderlich's methods, as well as his remarks on medical historiography in his essay on fever, deserve some attention.

Wunderlich pursues his historical discussion of fever from Hippocrates to Johannes Müller (whose physiological interpretation of fever as an affection of the spinal cord impressed him as "the height of the physiological point of view"),[5] Stilling, Henle, and Stannius.[6] Summing up the historical part of his investigation, Wunderlich asks whether it represents a mere list of errors, or whether the history of the doctrine of fever is a developmental history ("Entwicklungsgeschichte"). He affirms the latter alternative, though he denies a regular and steady change. "To attempt always in every detail and peculiarity to demonstrate the idea which is unconsciously asserting itself is an unnatural manner of dealing with history, totally at variance with an objective view of events. It is not in such fortuitous matters that the historian must find the development of the idea; he must rather demon-

---

Gesnerus (Aarau: Sauerländer), 1966, vol. 23, pp. 188–95.

[1]Carl August Wunderlich, Das Fieber. Historisch-physiologische Untersuchungen, *Arch. physiol. Heilk. 1* (1842) 266–94 and 351–400, 2 (1843) 6–62.

[2]Roser and Wunderlich, Über die Mängel der heutigen deutschen Medicin und über die Nothwendigkeit einer entschieden wissenschaftlichen Richtung in derselben, *ibid.,* pp. i–xxx.

[3]Wunderlich, Die medicinische Journalistik, *ibid.,* pp. 1–42.

[4]Owsei Temkin and C. Lilian Temkin, Wunderlich *versus* Haeser: a controversy over medical history, *Bull. Hist. Med. 32* (1958) 97–104. Here (p. 103) literature on contemporary historiography is cited.

[5]Wunderlich, Das Fieber, p. 398.

[6]*Ib.,* pp. 399 and (1843) p. 10, footnote.

strate that it proceeds on its way in spite of accidents and episodic incidents." [7]

To speak of "Entwicklungsgeschichte" and to trace the development of a concept or an idea, was not uncommon in 1842. But in the opening pages of his essay Wunderlich supplied a basis for his historical thinking which shows some personal characteristics.

The essay opens with the following quotation from the philosopher Schelling: "In accordance with a general rule, Science, like every kind of culture, seems after the age of unconsciousness to arrive at conscious clarity and fulfillment only by way of opposition and splitting off." [8] Wunderlich says that he "put this sentence of the celebrated philosopher of our time at the head and would like to use it as a motto and as a shield for the following essay." The sentence is to serve as a motto because "it announces the historical and psychological fact" whose validity for some part of medical science Wunderlich is going to show. Besides, the sentence is to shield him against the increasing custom of considering morally suspect all medico-historical research that does not appear in the garb of enthusiasm, tactfully cloaking the past. [9]

For Wunderlich, scientific progress is not an arithmetical progression. It is an organic process; it consists in a continuous sequence of annihilation and formation. What comes later spares as much of what went before as it needs for its own existence. Of the ideas of our predecessors few only remain, and even they are modified. On the other hand, the steps in the development can be traced not only through various periods; these steps also find their representation in our own time. Historical investigation, therefore, embraces present problems. In the present era, examples "for all and sundry steps (Sprossen) of the intellectual ladder will [easily] be discovered: from the lowest, most limited aspect to the clear recognition and penetration of the subject," i.e., fever. [10] This, we may add, is a parallel in the realm of ideas to the law of recapitulation in biology.

Wunderlich refers to the investigation of the origin and development of scientific ideas, concepts, and knowledge as "the scientific treatment of history." Such scientific treatment enjoys much greater license than "antiquarian historiography." For the scientific treatment, questions of priority

---

[7] *Ib.*, p. 399f. (translation by C. Lilian Temkin). For the convenience of the English reader, quotations are given in translation; lack of space unfortunately forbids the addition of the German original.

[8] Wunderlich, *op. cit.*, p. 266, with reference in the footnotes. The quotation is from Schelling's Vorläufige Bezeichnung des Standpunktes der Medicin nach Grundsätzen der Naturphilosophie, *Jahrbücher der Medicin als Wissenschaft*, ed. by A. F. Marcus and F. W. J. Schelling, Tübingen, Cotta, 1806, *1:* 165–206, where it reads (p. 166): "Nach einem allgemeinen Gesetz scheint die Wissenschaft, wie jede andre Art der Bildung, nach dem Zeitalter der Bewußtlosigkeit erst durch Gegensatz und Trennung hindurch zur selbstbewußten Klarheit und Vollendung gelangen zu müssen." Wunderlich does not quote accurately; in particular he omits the word 'andre' before 'Art der Bildung,' and he ends the quotation with 'können,' instead of 'müssen.'

[9] Wunderlich, *loc. cit.*

[10] *Ib.*, p. 268.

will be subordinate. Representative men who were able to handle the idea in its purest, most comprehensive, and most influential form are of greater interest than are men who showed the first traces of an idea.[11]

As Wunderlich understands it, history will not try to belittle the talent and the relative merits of our predecessors. But it will not claim for them unsurpassable excellence or suggest a return to their so-called classicality. History is the judge of things, for it is history which has judged the errors of the past. The mere fact that we exist, that we know the past and yet think differently, suffices to condemn the past. "Retrogression is only possible in science if we forget and ignore our predecessors.... The man who becomes enthusiastic about them and takes them as his model remains stuck at their level. He who recognizes their errors steps over them. What we need, what raises us above the past and makes us worthy of the present, is the recognition of where and why man has failed."[12]

2

The history of science as a critical debate with earlier opinions goes back at least as far as Aristotle. But in the form given by Wunderlich, it rests on assumptions that belong to the period around 1800. Wunderlich's image of the history of ideas as a continuous destruction and creation, where each step leaves its mark so that all the steps still exist in the present, has its counterpart in the ideas of Herder, Kielmeyer, Schelling and Hegel, where history and ontogeny blended into a picture of "development."[13] This picture, to which historical, philosophical, and biological work had contributed, could be expected to be in Wunderlich's mind, and he could rightly cite Schelling as a source of his philosophy of history.

In 1841, Schelling had followed a call to the University of Berlin, where he was welcomed with great expectations. Thus Wunderlich's reference to "the celebrated philosopher of our time" is understandable. But there was more involved than an opportune gesture. When Wunderlich turns to the history of the doctrine of fevers in Germany, he says that many an ingenious attempt at a better comprehension of what is called fever is found among German physicians in the beginning of the nineteenth century. Unfortunately, their wish to investigate a priori the final principles of things led to a neglect of detailed knowledge, without which all speculation in medicine is useless and fatal. Such a criticism of speculative medicine is not surprising, but the subsequent admission is significant: "To be sure, sometimes along these paths [i.e., a priori speculations] an ingenious idea was also gained regarding the conditions of fever; for it cannot be denied that in the beginning of this century, thoughtful, philosophical men had turned to the problems of medicine."[14]

---

[11]*Ib.*

[12]*Ib.*, p. 267 (translation by C. Lilian Temkin).

[13]Owsei Temkin, German concepts of ontogeny and history around 1800, *Bull. Hist. Med.*, 24 (1950) 227–46 [Essay 27].

[14]Wunderlich, *op. cit.*, p. 380. In contrast to Germany, Wunderlich characterized English modern medicine as "poor in ideologies" (p. 376: "arm an Ideologieen").

Wunderlich then continues with his criticism of this phase of German medicine. Yet he is relatively restrained; his full wrath is reserved for the following generation: "This fanciful era was followed by a period which offers even fewer results to the historian looking for progress; it did not even produce speculations, leave alone positive enrichment. This was the intellectually barren time of medical eclecticism. To look back upon this sad desert is painful. Whereas our neighbors pursued theoretical discussions and exact research with enthusiastic zeal, the German medical writings of this period (third decade and beginning of the fourth) with few exceptions are the expression of a hopeless intellectual poverty, of a repellent absence of taste, and a complete lack of talent for observation, even of the urge to observe."[15]

Wunderlich's relative respect for the early romantic era (in contrast to the period from about 1820 to 1834, when the first volume of Müller's *Handbook of Physiology* appeared) is corroborated by his remarks on the Brunonian system, on Röschlaub, and on some adherents of the school of Naturphilosophie. "The Brunonian doctrine contains the basic formula of physiological medicine;" it could have led to a transformation of medical science, had it not been for the ineptness of its followers. Röschlaub was different; he tried to elaborate his theory of excitement ("Erregungstheorie") in a physiological sense. "He can be regarded as the German who, earlier than anybody else, clearly conceived the relevancy of a physiological medicine."[16] The Erregungstheorie imperceptibly passes into the doctrines of the so-called school of Naturphilosophie, and "the writings of these theoreticians contain many a good remark, many a good idea."[17] In this context Wunderlich quotes books by Troxler (of 1803) and Kieser (of 1817). To be sure, Wunderlich is thinking above all of the theory of fever, and his praise is followed by criticism of the distance from concrete problems and of the lack of objective observation. Nevertheless, with all its reservations this acknowledgment is worth noting.

Wunderlich does not stand alone among his reforming contemporaries in seeing a good side in the German medicine of the early nineteenth century. Jacob Henle, in the opening article of the competing *Zeitschrift für rationelle Heilkunde*,[18] which he began to edit together with C. Pfeuffer in 1844, also made rational medicine depend on physiology. Fundamentally the two are even identical. The study of the abnormal influences teaches something about the forces of the healthy organism. For a short time, this was forgotten when Naturphilosophie introduced the genetic point of view into medicine and thereby opened an entirely new field for research. On the basis of the development of organs and by the comparison of parts which correspond to one another all through the scale of organisms, one inquired into the significance of the organs and the reason of their exis-

---

[15]*Ib.*, p. 380f.
[16]*Ib.*, p. 387. For the appreciation of Brown's system see also p. 357.
[17]*Ib.*, p. 388.
[18]J. Henle, Medizinische Wissenschaft und Empirie, *Zeitschrift für rationelle Medicin* (Schultheß, Zürich) *1* (1844) 35.

tence, rather than into their purpose and use. This led to physiological explanations, to an insight into the plan of organization and what is essential in every compound organ. "One must have experienced what joy results from seeing the same idea embodied in a thousand forms and the most complicated structure developing from the simplest beginnings, in order to understand, and to pardon, the zeal with which the coryphaei of physiology followed the direction of comparative anatomy exclusively."[19]

This reference to the work of Goethe, Doellinger, Meckel, and Johannes Müller is not surprising from Müller's pupil and friend. Henle was more closely connected with the past than were Wunderlich and such pupils of Müller's as Virchow, Helmholtz, Du Bois-Reymond, and Brücke. Henle too adds that medicine profited next to nothing from that movement, except for a theory of congenital anomalies. A healthy reaction against the reveries of some philosophical physiologists, important discoveries in the realm of physics, organic chemistry, and even of physiology had cured physiology of its one-sidedness and restored to honor the experimental method, which had been forgotten or even rejected.[20]

Henle's remarks merely go to show that Wunderlich did not stand alone among medical reformers in allowing a good side to the past, and undoubtedly many others could be cited. Henle does not define chronological boundaries, and perhaps this was not essential for him, since he was speaking of physiology, and particularly of that part of physiology which Rudolphi, as far back as 1821, had claimed for German scientists.[21] Wunderlich, on the other hand, was speaking of medicine, with special reference to one subject, the doctrine of fever. The fact that, in 1842, a man of Wunderlich's stature could appeal to Schelling's authority, is interesting. That he perceived many different strands within the history of German medicine during the three and a half decades before 1834, strands which he evaluated differently, should induce us to pay attention to these various strands also, especially when we trace romantic influences in Germany or abroad.[22]

Would it be justifiable then to say that Wunderlich was indebted to Schelling and his Naturphilosophie? As stated before, Wunderlich, like so many historians of this time, was under the influence of the philosophy of history which Schelling had helped to shape. But I do not believe that we have to establish close bonds between Wunderlich and Naturphilosophie in the field of medical science. Wunderlich's qualified respect for the latter, apart from the acknowledgment of individual sagacity, is largely due to his appreciation of a philosophical view of medicine. This appreciation is expressed in his *Wien und Paris* of 1841, where Wunderlich compared French and German science. German science, he states, is marked by an inclination

[19]*Ib.*, p. 29.
[20]On the rejection of physiological experiment see Owsei Temkin, Basic science, medicine, and the romantic era, *Bull. Hist. Med.* 37 (1963) 97–129 (especially p. 120 ff.) [Essay 26, 365ff.].
[21]K. A. Rudolphi, *Grundriss der Physiologie*, vol. 1, Dümmler, Berlin 1821, p. 2. Rudolphi is thinking of general physiology.
[22]In Wunderlich's *Geschichte der Medicin*, Ebner und Seubert, Stuttgart 1859, the distinctions, though still present, appear weakened because of the greater historical distance.

to philosophical penetration. To be sure, the strong influence of the recent philosophical systems was largely misleading, yet "if only the poetical-philosophical ideas of the but recently passed period were to be changed for the sober tendency and the keen, unbiased logic of the present, incalculable profit could be foretold for medicine."[23] German physiology, as Wunderlich thought, had partly solved this task already: indeed, a mere comparison of the physiology of a Johannes Müller with that of Magendie enabled one "to enjoy the salutary sentiment of patriotic pride."[24]

In other words, Wunderlich demands a philosophical penetration of medical science, in preference to the unsystematic approach of positivistic fact-finding. But philosophy need not, and should not, be identified with "Naturphilosophie" in the historically restricted meaning of the word.

These ideas of Wunderlich's have some bearing on the historiography of medicine in Germany. It seems important to have an open mind for the positive effects of the philosophical movements of the early nineteenth century. Their influences should not be denied where they can be demonstrated. Nevertheless, Wunderlich's attitude raises doubts whether we are not sometimes going too far in this direction. The tendency towards systematization, often with pronounced metaphysical undertones, has long been observed in German science, especially of the nineteenth century. However we may explain this tendency, to see in it a constant after-effect of Naturphilosophie seems one-sided. Rather it would seem that Naturphilosophie itself was an early manifestation of the same tendency, of which the materialism of the mid-century, and many systematized theories were other manifestations. In as far as historical phenomena usually are interconnected, such a view does not exclude connecting threads; on the other hand, it safeguards us from overrating their strength. Wunderlich favored a philosophical approach; he even complained that "the newest philosophy of our era has as yet had little effect upon us," i.e., on medical men.[25] Thus he could perceive the kindred spirit in the work of Schelling and his contemporaries, and of the philosophically minded Johannes Müller, without himself being a romantic in medicine.[26]

[23]Carl August Wunderlich, *Wien und Paris*. Ein Beitrag zur Geschichte und Beurtheilung der gegenwärtigen Heilkunde in Deutschland und Frankreich, Ebner und Seubert, Stuttgart 1841, p. 21.

[24]*Ib.*, p. 22.

[25]*Ib.*, p. 21: "So hat namentlich die neueste Philosophie unseres Zeitalters bis jetzt auf uns noch wenig gewirkt." I do not know what philosophers, if any, Wunderlich has in mind.

[26]In some respects Wunderlich's attitude as sketched in this article makes him appear as a forerunner of Virchow; see Erwin H. Ackerknecht, *Rudolf Virchow*, University of Wisconsin Press, Madison 1953, p. 48, and especially p. 146ff.

18

The European
Background of the Young
Dr. Welch*

IT WAS IN Europe, in Bad Homburg, in the fall of 1927, that I first remember meeting Dr. Welch at a gathering of German medical historians. This acquaintance was renewed in the Leipzig Institute of the History of Medicine. I offer these personal remarks because they may explain
why I wished to speak on the *European* background of the young Dr. Welch.
His biography by Simon and James Flexner,[1] based as it is on an extensive
study of all personal documents, leaves little space for the discovery of new
biographical data. But it occurred to me that some of the facts set forth by
the Flexners might gain in perspective if supplemented by German
sources. These latter might offer an additional commentary on the two
years, from 1876 to 1878, that Dr. Welch spent in Germany and with which
alone my remarks will be concerned.

Dr. Welch sailed for Europe on April 19, 1876.[2] Personal inclinations,
the influence of various associates, and general currents of the time had
determined his goal and aims. Pathological anatomy had been cultivated by
his teachers at the College of Physicians and Surgeons: Alonzo Clark,
Henry Berton Sands, Charles McBurney and, above all, Francis Delafield
with whom he worked in pathology after his graduation.[3] He wished to
become a professor of pathological anatomy, if possible at the Johns Hopkins University, and his name had already been recommended to President
Gilman.[4] But it was clear to him that, as yet, he was unprepared for such a
position. He possessed a microscope, yet did not know how to use it.[5] He
had to study histology and the place to do this was Germany. His own
teachers, it is true, had been reared in the French tradition.[6] But the pilgrimage of American doctors to Germany for postgraduate work had al-

---

Bull. Hist. Med., 1950, vol. 24, pp. 308–18. [Read at the 23rd annual meeting of the
American Association for the History of Medicine, Welch centenary celebration, May 21,
1950.]
[1]Simon Flexner and James Thomas Flexner, *William Henry Welch and the heroic age of American medicine*, New York, The Viking Press, 1941.
[2]*Ibid.*, p. 76.
[3]*Ibid.*, p. 63 ff.
[4]*Ibid.*, p. 71 ff.
[5]*Ibid.*, p. 64.
[6]According to Walter B. James' article in Kelly and Burrage, *Dictionary of American medical
biography*, New York–London, Appleton, 1928, p. 315 f., Francis Delafield "had acquired in
Germany a conviction of the overwhelming importance of practical studies in pathological
anatomy." I have been unable to obtain details about Delafield's studies in Germany.

ready begun. Abraham Jacobi directed his "attention especially to the great position of German medical science in the world."[7] Wood, among others, told him to study microscopy in Germany.[8] Of course, there was no certainty of his receiving the Hopkins position, and things being what they were, medical practice might turn out to be a necessary alternative. But even in this case, "absorbing a little German lore" would put him in a more favorable position.[9] Thus Dr. Welch set out with the hope to become a competent pathologist or at least to perfect himself in some clinical knowledge, preferably neurology in which his teacher Seguin, himself a pupil of Charcot,[10] had interested him.

On Dr. Welch's own testimony it was Seguin who directed him to Strasbourg,[11] which had passed from French into German hands but five years before. The Germans were determined to wean the Alsatians from their attachment to France and, to further this purpose, they had decided to create a model university in Strasbourg, appointing some of the best men as professors. Although they failed in their major aim, they had succeeded in establishing an excellent new university. Especially in pathology and histology, the fields of Dr. Welch's immediate studies, conditions were almost ideal. Von Recklinghausen, the pathologist, was one of Virchow's most outstanding pupils. Waldeyer was not only a briiliant anatomist, but before accepting the chair of normal anatomy in Strasbourg, had taught pathology in Breslau.[12] Moreover, these two men were on such good terms that they wished their institutes to be housed in the same building.[13] Thus the transition from von Recklinghausen's institute, where Dr. Welch was studying gross pathology, to Waldeyer's course in normal histology must have been easy enough. Nor was Waldeyer unaccustomed to American students. In his autobiography he gives the names of three Americans who had worked with him during his Strasbourg period. They were: George Livingston Peabody, Landon Rives Longworth, and A. J. Lanterman.[14] Dr. Welch's name, as you see, is not among them. This, however, is understandable, since he merely participated in a regular course, whereas Longworth and Lanterman, at least, had done actual research work. Longworth's article, "Ueber die Endkolben der Conjunctiva," appeared in the *Archiv für mikroskopische Anatomie* in 1875, although the work had apparently been done in 1874.[15] It deals with the existence of terminal bodies of sensitive nerves in

[7]Flexner and Flexner, *op. cit.*, p. 70.

[8]*Ibid.*, p. 74.

[9]*Ibid.*, p. 76.

[10]Walter L. Burrage in Kelly and Burrage, *op. cit.*, p. 1088.

[11]Flexner and Flexner, *op. cit.*, p. 78.

[12]Wilhelm von Waldeyer-Hartz, *Lebenserinnerungen*, Bonn, Friedrich Cohen, 1921, p. 128.

[13]*Ibid.*, p. 150.

[14]*Ibid.*, p. 159: "Aus den Vereinigten Staaten Nordamerikas arbeiteten bei mir Peabody, Longworth und Lanterman, der die nach ihm benannten kerbförmigen Bildungen der markhaltigen Nervenfasern im Strassburger anatomischen Laboratorium entdeckte, die gleichzeitig und völlig unabhängig von Schmidt in New-Orleans aufgefunden wurden."

[15]L. R. Longworth (Cincinnati, Ohio), Ueber die Endkolben der Conjunctiva, *Archiv für mikroskopische Anatomie*, 11. Bd., 1875, pp. 653–60. Some editorial remarks made by Waldeyer

the conjunctiva. Incidentally, the same volume contains another anatomical work by an American, W. T. Alexander from Boston, also from the Strasbourg anatomical institute, entitled "Bemerkungen über die Nerven der Dura mater" (Remarks on the nerves of the dura mater).[16] Whether Waldeyer failed to mention Alexander because this paper had not been prepared under his guidance, or whether he had forgotten Alexander, I am unable to decide. Lanterman's preliminary notice on the minute structure of mylienated nerve fibres is dated Strasbourg, August, 1874.[17] He must, therefore, have been at work at approximately the same time as Longworth. Lanterman, contemporaneously with, but independently from H. D. Schmidt in New Orleans, described the clefts which are still known under the name of Schmidt-Lanterman clefts or incisures.

Now all three of these American pupils of Waldeyer had one thing in common: they had graduated from the College of Physicians and Surgeons a few years before Dr. Welch.[18] Under these circumstances I wonder whether his going to Strasbourg was quite the "leap in the dark" he represented it to be to his sister.[19]

In Strasbourg, Welch had devoted himself chiefly to attending laboratory courses: a demonstration course in gross pathology with von Recklinghausen, normal histology with Waldeyer, and physiological chemistry with Hoppe-Seyler.[20] The next stage, Leipzig, marked his acquaintance with the German methods of actual research. He now took up pathological histology with Wagner who assigned to him a case of lympho-sarcoma for investigation, and, more important perhaps, he stumbled into Ludwig's physiological institute. I use the word "stumbled," because Welch would later have it that he had really gone to Leipzig in order to attend Heubner's course on nervous diseases and that Heubner's shift from psychiatry to pediatrics had left him with free time which led him to Ludwig.[21] The Flexners have

---

suggest that the work had been done about a year before (see p. 657) and that the manuscript had been completed a considerable time before its publication (see p. 659). Besides, according to his biography in Kelly-Burrage, *op. cit.*, p. 757, Longworth returned home in the fall of 1874.

[16]W. T. Alexander aus Boston, Bemerkungen über die Nerven der Dura mater, *ibid.*, pp. 231–34.

[17]A. J. Lanterman (Cleveland), Bemerkungen über den feineren Bau der markhaltigen Nervenfasern. Vorläufige Mittheilung. *Centralblatt für die medicinischen Wissenschaften*, vol. 12, 1874, pp. 706–09. The more detailed publication with illustrations appeared in the *Archiv für mikroskopische Anatomie*, vol. 13, 1877, pp. 1–8.

[18]For Longworth and Peabody see Kelley-Burrage, *op. cit.*, pp. 757 and 951. Polk's *Medical and surgical directory of the United States*, 1886, p. 182, lists A. J. Lanterman in Buena Vista, Colorado, as having been graduated by the College of Physicians and Surgeons in 1868.

[19]Flexner and Flexner, *op. cit.*, p. 78. William T. Councilman, in turn, during his postgraduate studies in Europe, 1880–1883, went to von Recklinghausen in Strasbourg and to Cohnheim who then held a chair in Leipzig. He was to become Dr. Welch's first associate in 1884 in Baltimore. See Alan M. Chesney, *The Johns Hopkins Hospital and the Johns Hopkins University School of Medicine*, vol. 1, Baltimore, The Johns Hopkins Press, 1943, p. 90 f. It would also be interesting to know who the other Americans were to whom Welch alludes as fellow students in Strasbourg (see Flexner and Flexner, *op. cit.*, p. 80 f.).

[20]For this and the following see Flexner and Flexner, *op. cit.*, pp. 78–84.

[21]*Ibid.*, p. 84.

pointed out that in his letters home Welch did not mention Heubner at all and that this is all the more remarkable since he would hardly have failed to acquaint his father, who was somewhat impatient of his son's theoretical bent, with the practical nature of his intended study. Apparently Heubner, in 1876, was still giving his course on psychiatry and Welch attended it. But even though the lectures were delivered, they failed to arouse enthusiasm.[22] For Heubner himself writes in his autobiography that he had no liking for the matter, that he was repelled by the hopelessness of psychiatric therapy, and that he refused to consider an associate professorship in psychiatry on which he was sounded out by the Leipzig medical faculty in 1877.[23] Thus, whether from an excess of free time or disappointment over Heubner's course, Dr. Welch found himself in Ludwig's laboratory. In Carl Ludwig, Dr. Welch discovered a man who lived for research and who taught his advanced students the spirit in which it had to be pursued. Ludwig put Dr. Welch on some microscopic investigation of "the nervous apparatus of the heart."[24] Although his results were not published, the work had the much greater importance of admitting Welch into the community of active scientific investigators. The impression Ludwig made on Welch is, perhaps, best exemplified by a statement of February 1877 when he referred to Ludwig and Claude Bernard as "undoubtedly the two greatest living physiologists."[25] As far as Ludwig is concerned, this statement is not without interest and you will permit me a personal comment in this connection. As a medical student at the University of Leipzig, I attended courses in the physiological institute which had once been directed by Ludwig. Some of Ludwig's original apparatuses were still standing around and there was even an "Institutsgehilfe" who could look back to the days of Ludwig. The memory of the master was very much with us; we were very conscious of the fact that one of the most outstanding German physiologists had taught in this same place. Nevertheless, I wonder whether we should unhesitatingly have named Ludwig as *the* greatest German physiologist of the later 19th century. In our minds, his name would have competed with those of Du Bois Reymond and Helmholtz. But there is no doubt that Ludwig was the most outstanding teacher, having an especially high number of foreign pupils,[26] and I think that this has given Ludwig an even greater reputation abroad than he possessed at home.

The year 1877 was to become one of the most decisive years in Dr. Welch's life. The work with Wagner, Ludwig, and the zoologist Leuckart, left its stamp not only on his appreciation of scientific research but also on his whole philosophical outlook. Besides, he met John Shaw Billings and

[22]*Ibid.*, p. 474, and Simon Flexner, William Henry Welch, a biographical sketch, *Science*, n.s., vol. 52, 1920, pp. 417–33, see p. 420.
[23]Wolfgang Heubner (ed.), *Otto Heubners Lebenschronik*, Berlin, Julius Springer, 1927, p. 103 f.
[24]Flexner and Flexner, *op. cit.*, p. 86.
[25]*Ibid.*, p. 85.
[26]See also George Rosen, Carl Ludwig and his American students, *Bull. Hist. Med.*, vol. 4, 1936, 609–50.

spent an evening with him in Auerbach's Keller. This meeting made Welch decide upon another year in Germany and also led to a strengthening of the ties with the Johns Hopkins University. Finally, Ludwig and his assistant, Kronecker, inveighed upon him to turn to Breslau and continue his pathological studies with Julius Cohnheim.[27]

In the sound motion picture which is to conclude this session you will hear Dr. Welch refer to the beautiful summer of 1877 in Breslau. He will mention to you Salomonsen's article in the *Berliner klinische Wochenschrift* of March 16, 1914, which gives reminiscences of that time.[28]

This article of Salomonsen's is indeed so vivid in its description and so important for the association of Cohn, Cohnheim, Weigert, Ehrlich, Heidenhain, Koch, Lassar, and others that Dr. Welch, himself, in later years, consulted it to refresh his memory.[29] In 1931, when he once more visited Europe, Dr. Welch was asked to speak on his reminiscences of Robert Koch before the medical society of Berlin. In his diary he mentions his attempts at getting hold of Salomonsen's "book"—Sudhoff finally succeeded in tracing the article for him. Welch read it and entered an extract in his diary, probably for further reference. At the same time he added some reminiscences of his own. Thus he writes that Cohnheim, at that period, was "little interested in mere pathological histology, rather scornful of pretty stainings.—'Was malen Sie heute, Herr Welch'[30] he would say in looking at my haematoxylin stained sections. Weigert scolded me for bringing haematoxylin into the microscopical course and impressing Cohnheim with its value—said I had made trouble for the Assistants as C(ohnheim) wanted them to use haematoxylin in these student courses."

To understand this remark it is necessary to realize, as Salomonsen informs us, that Cohnheim was chiefly interested in experimental work so that his assistant, Carl Weigert, was the real anatomist in the institute.[31] Weigert and even more so the "master dyer,"[32] Ehrlich, still a medical student, were of course pioneers in the use of new staining methods in histology and bacteriology. But whatever benefit Dr. Welch may have derived from his association with Weigert—it was Cohnheim with whom he had come to study, and it was in line with Cohnheim's investigations in pathological physiology that he undertook and finished his important research on pulmonary edema.

[27]For this paragraph see Flexner and Flexner, *op. cit.*, pp. 86–94.

[28]Carl Jul. Salomonsen, Lebenserinnerungen aus dem Breslauer Sommer-Semester 1877, *Berl. Klin. Wchschr.*, vol. 51, 1914, pp. 485–90. This article, was also used by Flexner and Flexner, *op. cit.*, and Heymann (see footnote 37). The English translation by Mrs. C. L. Temkin appears below [*Bull. Hist. Med.*, vol. 24 (1950)], pp. 333–51.

[29]The information in this paragraph is derived from a diary (box 209, diary no. 37) of Dr. Welch's which Dr. Sanford V. Larkey kindly made available to me. It is part of the Welch material deposited in the Welch Medical Library of the Johns Hopkins University.

[30]"What are you painting today, Mr. Welch." It is not customary in Germany to use the title of "doctor" in addressing one's medical colleagues.

[31]See the English translation of Salomonsen's article by C. Lilian Temkin, below [*Bull. Hist. Med.*, vol. 24 (1950)], p. 336.

[32]Hauptfärber," see *ibid.*

We may here raise the question whether Dr. Welch can be considered a pupil of Cohnheim in his general approach towards pathology. Cohnheim is remembered as the representative of pathological physiology. This is not to be understood as if Virchow and his school lacked interest in the experimental approach or in any way underrated the significance of the physiological interpretation of pathological phenomena. Nor does it mean that Cohnheim, himself a pupil of Virchow's, underrated the importance of morphological studies, both macroscopic and microscopic. The difference, such as it existed, was rather one of emphasis upon what constituted general pathology. Virchow's concepts of general pathology had emerged in close association with his fundamental work on cellular pathology.[33] To some extent, at least, cellular pathology was to replace the older medical systems. Whether or not it is justifiable to consider cellular pathology a system too, one cannot quite escape the impression in reading Cohnheim's "Introduction" to his *Lectures on General Pathology* and his inaugural address of 1878 "On the tasks of pathological anatomy," that he, just as Ludwig many years before,[34] tried to avoid any overemphasis of the cellular theory. "Far be it from me to deny our indebtedness to these manifold [pathological] systems for many a great and important advance in pathology; but they have as such, whatever be the names they bear, a purely historical interest. General pathology knows no other direction and no other classification than that which obtains in physiology, and following this science, we shall in succession treat of the pathology of the circulation, digestion, respiration, nutrition, etc."[35] Now I think that Welch succeeded in avoiding a onesided attachment to pathological anatomy or physiology. Though decidedly influenced by both Ludwig and Cohnheim, he returned, after the summer in Breslau and some weeks in Vienna, to Strasbourg and to von Recklinghausen,[36] Virchow's staunch pupil. Nor would onesidedness have suited the American scene where Welch was to perform his work. Thorough post-mortem dissection, microscopic technique, and pathological experiment had all to be naturalized: there was no room for cultivation of one at the expense of the others.

I cannot take leave of that summer in Breslau without commenting on Dr. Welch's relationship to bacteriology, in whose history a new chapter was just being written. As you know, Robert Koch, then residing in Wollstein, had demonstrated his epoch-making experiments on the anthrax bacillus to the botanist Cohn in Breslau in the spring of 1876, almost one year before Welch's arrival in the city. Cohnheim was called in and Weigert too

---

[33]This is especially evident in *Die Vorlesungen Rudolf Virchows über allgemeine pathologische Anatomie*, Jena, Gustav Fischer, 1930.
[34]Ludwig's lack of enthusiasm for cellular pathology has been noted by Flexner, *Science*, n.s., vol. 52, 1920, p. 422. I have tried to sketch Ludwig's attitude in "Metaphors of human biology," *Science and civilization*, ed. Robert C. Stauffer, Madison, University of Wisconsin Press, 1949, p. 173 [Essay 20, p. 273].
[35]Julius Cohnheim, *Lectures on general pathology*, vol. 1, London, The New Sydenham Society, 1889, p. 11.
[36]Flexner and Flexner, *op. cit.*, p. 107 f.

witnessed the demonstration.[37] From then on there was close contact between Koch and the Breslau workers. Of interest to us is Koch's short visit to Breslau on June 6, 1877.[38] This I believe to be the event to which Dr. Welch refers in his diary:[39] "It was on the occasion of one of these visits that he [i.e., Koch] came one day to Cohnheim's laboratory and spent an hour or more with Cohnheim—Afterward Cohnheim introduced me to Koch in the laboratory, and was full of enthusiasm about his discovery. At this time Koch's special interest was in the reproduction of bacteria—fresh and stained—by microphotography." I mention this entry because there is some uncertainty about the date as well as the nature of this early encounter with Koch.[40] And here we are confronted by a somewhat puzzling problem. In 1877, Welch met the leaders in German bacteriology: Cohn, Koch, Klebs (whom he visited in Prague), Weigert; his intimate friend, Salomonsen, was a pioneer in the new science; his teacher Cohnheim had expressed enthusiasm over Koch's work. Yet all this made little impression upon Welch. On his return stay in Strasbourg, von Recklinghausen pointed out the significance of bacteria to him, but when Welch passed through Paris on his way home, he apparently had no thought of visiting Pasteur.[41] To be sure, Welch was busy with his experiments, but he had time to attend other lectures, and at any rate it is his lack of interest and appreciation that strikes us. Perhaps we come a little nearer to the solution if we consider the peculiar position of bacteriology in 1877. There were still a number of men who denied to bacteria any decisive etiological rôle. For instance Fischer, the Breslau surgeon, had not yet espoused Lister's antiseptic treatment.[42] However, the group of radical sceptics was fast shrinking. The idea that microorganisms could and did cause diseases was being widely recognized. But the question as to what diseases exactly were of bacterial origin was far from solved and the uncertainty proved a disturbing element. In a paper of 1877, Carl Weigert defined his own position as follows:[43]

---

[37]Bruno Heymann, *Robert Koch,* vol. 1, Leipzig, Akademische Verlagsgesellschaft, 1932, p. 150.

[38]This date is established by the note in Cohn's diary: "Dr. Koch besuchte am 30.6. das Institut" (Heymann, *op. cit.,* p. 195).

[39]See above, note 29.

[40]Flexner and Flexner, *op. cit.,* p. 100 f., believe the meeting between Koch and Welch to have taken place some time between October 15 and 18, when Koch demonstrated his work on anthrax to the London physiologist, Burdon Sanderson (Heymann, *op. cit.,* pp. 210–12). By that time, however, Salomonsen had already left Breslau, so that his own reminiscences (see this *Bulletin,* p. 334) must refer to June 6. Besides, he mentions that Koch paid a short visit to Cohnheim's institute which well agrees with Dr. Welch's remark. Since Welch in his own letters home apparently did not mention Koch at all and, in later years, does not seem to have been certain of the details of this encounter, the question of the date remains somewhat doubtful.

[41]Flexner and Flexner, *op. cit.,* pp. 101 and 109.

[42]Salomonsen, this *Bulletin* [vol. 24 (1950)], p. 345. Fischer's conversion to antisepsis must have taken place soon afterwards; see *Festschrift zur Feier des hundertjährigen Bestehens der Universität Breslau,* ed. G. Kaufmann, 2. Teil, Breslau, 1911, p. 302.

[43]Carl Weigert, *Gesammelte Abhandlungen,* vol. 2, Berlin, 1906, p. 426.

I believe that in some cases (recurrent fever and anthrax) the action of bacteria has been proved with such certainty as is attainable for scientific investigations, that in a series of other cases this action can be assumed as probable but that in a great many cases it cannot yet be assumed with any certainty.

And Cohnheim in the above mentioned address in 1878 expressed himself in a somewhat similar vein:[44]

For the whole very important group of infectious diseases, the *Contagium animatum* of earlier authors is at present no longer a hypothesis and science today quite rightly demands of the pathologist that in each infectious disease he find the parasitic organisms to which it owes its origin. The only point where unity has not yet been reached is the question as to how far the territory of infectious disease should be staked: there are authors who attribute an infectious character even to the malignant tumors, and there are others who do not hesitate to refer every so-called cold, every catarrh, to an infection.

Taking these two statements by adherents of the bacteriological school together, we see that only for relapsing fever and anthrax was a bacterial etiology accepted as strictly proved, that the infectious nature of even a common cold was still open to doubt and that the demonstration of pathogenic microorganisms for individual diseases was a research problem. In other words, in 1877, bacteriology was not yet a field with well established methods which could be learned and taught. It was not yet a domain of those pathological sciences which Dr. Welch had come to make his own. Even the German pathologists who, in principle, recognized the rôle bacteria played, held somewhat aloof from the development of bacteriology.[45] Relatively few of them took an active interest in the matter. With Koch's appointment to Berlin, bacteriology became combined with hygiene and even men like von Recklinghausen, originally enthusiastic over the new insight, distanced themselves from a science which they began to consider as a competitor.[46] All this has to be remembered if we ask for the reasons why Dr. Welch showed such slight response to bacteriology during his first European journey. It was only during his subsequent years in New York that bacteriology developed to an extent which made its study imperative.[47] Dr. Welch's second trip, in 1884–85, culminating in a course with Koch in Berlin, was undertaken for this purpose.[48] That Welch's previous failure to be impressed by bacteriology can be explained by the requirements of

[44]Julius Cohnheim, *Gesammelte Abhandlungen*, Berlin, 1885, p. 615.
[45]Address by Dr. William H. Welch on the history of pathology. *Bull. Hist. Med.*, vol. 3, 1935, p. 13. Even the surgeon Theodor Billroth in a letter of August 9, 1877, wrote despairingly about the difficulties of obtaining positive proof of bacterial etiology; see Heymann, *op. cit.*, p. 200.
[46]B. Naunyn, *Erinnerungen Gedanken und Meinungen*, München, Bergmann, 1925, pp. 370 and 431. Otto Lubarsch, *Ein bewegtes Gelehrtenleben*, Berlin, Julius Springer, 1931, p. 25.
[47]Flexner, *Science*, n.s., vol. 52, 1920, p. 429.
[48]Flexner and Flexner, *op. cit.*, p. 137 f.

American medical science as it then existed is further documented by the similar experiences of Welch's main competitor, T. Mitchell Prudden. For Prudden, too, studied pathology in Germany and he too had to go back in order to attend school again with Robert Koch.[49]

The few remarks offered may have shown that Dr. Welch's assimilation of German science was partly determined by the conditions of that science in 1876–78. Partly it was determined by his own sense of what would be needed in the United States, especially with regard to the study and teaching of medicine. I have stressed the early, though loose, ties that bound Dr. Welch to the future of Johns Hopkins. I should supplement this by pointing out that Dr. Welch's interest was not limited to medical science but extended to medical education as well. In January 1877, two months after the meeting with Billings, he remarked: "I think that the mainspring of German thoroughness lies in their preliminary education. No man can study medicine or any profession who has not gone through a course of study at least equal to a college course at Yale and Harvard."[50] Impressions like these fitted very well into the ideas concerning premedical education voiced by Billings and President Gilman.[51] But having said all this, I have to add that Dr. Welch did not accept everything he found in Germany. From the picture Salomonsen and the Flexners have given us, we have reason to assume that Dr. Welch met his German colleagues with an open mind, ready to learn and to accept what impressed him as good. He seems to have entered with ease into friendly relations with his professors and fellow students. But he was not attracted by the more clamorous and overbearing aspects of German student life. In the beginning of this paper, I said that I met Dr. Welch in Germany in 1927. At that time, he impressed me by the patience with which he listened even to the youngest speaker and by his dignified yet friendly and utterly unassuming manner. I think he listened rather than talked. And I like to believe that when he was in Germany some fifty years earlier, his attitude had been fundamentally the same. It was one of the remarkable things about Dr. Welch that he was wise in his youth, yet remained young in his older years. This may, perhaps, allow us to draw a parallel in spite of the lapse of years. Although Europe, and especially Germany, exerted a great influence upon the young Dr. Welch, they only formed a background for his development. He was always conscious that his roots and his future lay across the sea, in America.

[49]*Biographical sketches and letters of T. Mitchell Prudden, M.D.*, Yale University Press, 1927, p. 52.

[50]Flexner and Flexner, *op. cit.*, p. 91.

[51]Chesney, *op. cit.*, p. 45 ff.

19

The Era
of Paul Ehrlich*

THE ERA OF Paul Ehrlich is the period in which Germany exerted a preponderant influence in the affairs of the world. Ehrlich was about
seventeen years old when France was defeated by Prussia and the German
states which Bismarck welded into a new Empire. When Ehrlich died, the
first World War had just entered into its second year. Thus his manhood
extends over the era of Bismarck and Wilhelm II, when Germany played
the role of a world power, proud of her army and her "Kultur." In the
wake of the Franco-Prussian War, the German university of Strasbourg was
founded, largely with the aim of counter-balancing the French influence in
Alsace. University professors were esteemed as perhaps never before, and
the Geheimrat was almost a minor deity. It was a time of great achievements in all the sciences. All over the world, German had to be studied by
scientists no less than by students of the humanities who wanted to keep
abreast of new methods and results. If the professor was well aware of what
others owed to his rank, he also remembered what he owed to his position:
never ceasing hard work, thoroughness and self-criticism in his investigations, objectivity in viewing the results of others. It was the devotion to his
calling that had raised the German professor to a pinnacle, not the mere
worship of a title, widespread as such worship might be.

Yet achievement is not always identical with inner strength and greatness. The time of classical German philosophy and literature was a matter
of the past. With some exceptions, the greatest names in the history of
German sciences of the nineteenth century had made their debut prior to
1870. Among historians, Ranke was a very old man, and of Mommsen's
Roman History the first three volumes had appeared in the late fifties.
Liebig, the great chemist, died in 1873. Henle the anatomist, Virchow the
pathologist, Helmholtz and Carl Ludwig the physiologists, the clinicians
Frerichs, Traube and Wunderlich had long occupied chairs of their own.
Altogether, the debates over fundamental philosophical and scientific issues had lost vigor because of lack of opposing factions. To be sure, Dar-
winism was a lively topic, but its radical defense by Haeckel dated back to
1868. In 1872, Du Bois-Reymond read a paper "On the Boundaries of the
Knowledge of Nature" which he concluded with the words: "Yet, when the
Scientist finds himself confronted by the riddle of matter and force, and
their ability to think, he is obliged once and for all to pronounce the most

*Bulletin of the New York Academy of Medicine (New York Academy of Medicine), 1954, vol. 30,
pp. 958–67.

difficult of judgments: 'Ignorabimus' " [we shall never know].[1] Now what is left for the scientist in the face of such philosophical resignation? Research that will lead to positive results, especially those useful in human life.

Science and learning in the Germany of that period were not private affairs. Unless the individual found a position in a public institution, he remained an outsider. And public institutions were integrated into the state. Plans to establish a university in Frankfurt, the seat of Ehrlich's Institute, dependent solely upon the plans of its private founders, came to naught when the Mayor opened a meeting with a copy of the Statutes of the Prussian State in his hand and read: "The universities are creations of the State."[2] This state made itself felt in many respects as a protector as well as a supervisor. Virchow might defy Bismarck; among his younger colleagues a certain aloofness from politics, leaving this field to the ordained rulers, became widespread. The political events found a relatively weak echo at the universities. Professors and students alike mostly came from well-to-do homes. Students did not work their way through college and aspirants to an academic career needed private means while waiting for an appointment. Arbitrariness at the helm of the state bred arbitrariness lower down. In the Prussian cabinet for cultural affairs, Friedrich Althoff came to rule as a veritable autocrat. As Ehrlich's example shows, he could be of the greatest help in furthering talented men. But his treatment of professors dependent upon his approval did not help to strengthen their moral backbone. Moreover, the official policy of the state, Prussia as well as Germany, became anti-Semitic under the influence of Adolf Stoecker, the court chaplain in Berlin. It was an anti-Semitism that did not allow a Jew to become a full professor unless he was baptized. In medicine, particularly, the influence of the state went further than in many other European countries, let alone the United States. Public health found a central body in the Reichsgesundheitsamt, established in 1876. In 1880 Robert Koch was appointed to this organization which combined the functions of an institute for bacteriological and epidemiological research with a public health agency. That the state should have a hand in controlling drugs, especially vaccines that needed standardization and careful preparation, was almost a matter of course, as was the inspection of meat, isolation and disinfection in cases of infectious disease, compulsory smallpox vaccination of babies and school children, and the many other major and minor regulations where the paternalism of the state met with the national respect for administrative wisdom. When a scientific meeting was held at Königsberg, Virchow and a colleague of his took a walk along the coast, stomping with difficulty through the sand at the bottom of the dunes. They were hailed by some ladies suggesting that on this special occasion they take the easier though prohibited path on top of the dunes. Virchow not only refused but got angry and excited and continued stomping through the sand, holding forth about the lack of understanding among ladies for laws that served the common good and that had to be obeyed by everybody on all occasions.[3] From 1881, this paternalism of the state took a new departure when Bismarck initiated a program of social insurance that was to include compulsory sickness insurance as well.

It hardly needs saying that the government enforced its requirements for obtaining a license to practice medicine as a physician. This presupposed a secondary education with a strong classical note and a prescribed minimum of years of medical studies at a university. Certain courses, as well as a few official examinations, were required before the license was issued which was valid in all German states. The degree of M.D. was subject to the writing of a thesis and an additional oral examination. But it is the leeway that the German system of medical education allowed to the student which needs to be stressed in connection with Paul Ehrlich's development. Apart from the minimum requirements, the medical student was free to choose his courses, to change his universities, and to devote almost as much time to his studies as he desired. Anatomy, physiology, pathology, etc. were presented to him as sciences, each in its own right. If he felt attracted by any of them he was not only free to concentrate his energies upon it, but almost from the beginning it was made possible for him to engage in investigative work of his own. To the mediocre student, the absence of a rigid curriculum was a danger, often a temptation to waste years in idleness and an excessive consumption of beer. To the good student it was an opportunity to find his own way, free from spoon feeding. Above all, it was an ideal training ground for future scientists. The system was based upon the identity of teaching and research and fostered a veneration for research which hardly found its equal anywhere else.

We characterized the time of Paul Ehrlich as the period of preponderant German influence, on a scene, we now have to add, where medicine became increasingly international. The formation of international societies and congresses falls largely within these years. The problems to be attacked and the methods to be used for their solution tended to become the same in all countries. This increasing uniformity was necessitated by the intrusion of exact scientific research into all fields of the healing art, including its practice.

Around 1860 there were as yet few skills which a good doctor could not have acquired from a practical course in gross anatomy, the example of a good preceptor, and books. The ophthalmoscope introduced by Helmholtz in 1851, and the laryngoscope invented by Manuel Garcia in 1855 were just coming into their own and might require additional training. As to the progress in pathology and experimental physiology—what was there that could not be followed by reading the literature? Changing concepts of disease were interesting but not of vital importance as long as they had little practical bearing. The first sweeping change, I think, came in the wake of Virchow's cellular pathology of 1858, with its transition from gross anatomical description to microscopic study. To anybody, untrained in the use of the microscope and not acquainted with normal histology, the new doctrines must largely remain ununderstandable. More important, perhaps, were the practical applications of microscopy which extended all the way from a reliable postmortem diagnosis to the examination of urine sediment. Here then was a need to learn a whole new branch of science, not only an isolated technique as, for instance, cystoscopy. The experience of William Welch who went to Strasbourg to study pathology and had first to take a course in normal histology with Waldeyer illustrates our point.[4]

Microscopy owed a good deal of its progress to improvements in staining of specimens. In the fifties, von Gerlach had popularized the use of carmine as a stain. Julius Cohnheim under whom Carl Weigert spent many years in Breslau and in Leipzig, and who for some time was Ehrlich's teacher, was one of the masters in the development of staining methods. Cohnheim used gold chloride and aniline blue in his famous studies on inflammation of 1867.[5] Leukocytes ingested aniline blue that had been injected into the blood stream; they were thus tagged and their appearance in inflamed tissue proved that they had found their way through the walls of the blood vessels and were identical with the pus corpuscles. This epoch-making paper of Cohnheim's is worth mentioning not only as an example of the interest in staining methods but also because it played a part in the controversy between the two leading pathological schools in Germany. Cohnheim's investigation centered around keratitis and demonstrated that here too the changes in the blood vessels—at the periphery of the cornea—are the first phase of inflammation. Thereby he contradicted Virchow on a point of great theoretical importance.[6] Without personal animosity, the differences between the two were yet to develop into an opposition between the morphological and experimental schools. To Virchow and his pupils pathology, that is the study of disease, was becoming more and more pathological anatomy;[7] to the adherents of Cohnheim it meant, above all, physiology and experimentation. The difference was really one of emphasis rather than excluding principles. However, it seems that Cohnheim and his circle stood closer to the rise of bacteriology. And the emergence of this new science, even more than pathology, forced the practitioner to abandon the old ways and to keep step with scientific progress.

The debt which bacteriology owes to Pasteur is so well known that we need not dwell upon his early work. Around 1876 the question was not so much whether microorganisms could cause disease; rather it was which diseases are caused by microorganisms and how can claims in this direction be proved.[8] The answer to the latter question was given by Robert Koch's famous postulates. It took a longer time to survey the domain of infectious diseases; it is not quite surveyed even now. Nevertheless, in 1882 when Koch announced his discovery of the tubercle bacillus, the immediate value of bacteriological techniques could no longer seriously be doubted, where the diagnosis of relapsing fever, anthrax, actinomycosis, gonorrhea, leprosy, typhoid, malarial fever, and tuberculosis was concerned. It goes without saying that the correct diagnosis often had its immediate consequences for prognosis and prophylaxis. This meant that a physician could not be satisfied with reading in books about the progress of bacteriology; he had to be able to handle the new methods required or at least to be able to avail himself of expert services. The speed with which one new discovery followed another must have contributed to the growing sense of a changing time. Two years later, in 1884, diphtheria, cholera, tetanus had been added to the list and, at the same time, antiseptic surgery was constantly gaining new triumphs.

Antiseptic surgery did not presuppose much bacteriological refinement. It rested on the simple assumption that surgical infection was carried to the wound by hostile microorganisms that could be destroyed by a chemical agent, carbolic acid. This assumption almost strikes us as too simple. But the anecdotes about the surgeons who, after careful antiseptic preparation, continued to operate with a scalpel that had fallen to the floor, and similar stories indicate that to the generation of the seventies and eighties a great effort was needed to grasp the underlying principle. That we think of Lister's teaching as simple merely goes to prove how different the outlook of younger men who, like Ehrlich, grew up with the changed views must have been from that of the generation before him.

Antiseptic surgery, which in the nineties was to be succeeded by aseptic surgery, made the healing art more efficient in its cure of disease. For a number of years surgery seemed superior to internal medicine. *Circumstare et verba facere,* to stand around and talk, was all the internist seemed to be able to do while the surgeon snatched people away from imminent death by boldly removing an inflamed appendix or a cancer of the stomach. Therapeutic successes of internal medicine were relatively slow to come because they needed an elaboration of so many factors: immunology, experimental physiology, and pharmacology. Though many of the results were achieved later, the foundation nevertheless was established during the years under discussion.

As with the rise of bacteriology, so with immunology the name of Pasteur is intimately connected. In 1879 he discovered the possibility of immunization against infectious disease by attenuating the culture of the responsible virus. This discovery led to great practical results; but the physiology of immunity remained dark. Two theories arose in short succession seemingly excluding each other. Metchnikoff made "phagocytosis" the main line of defense; harmful particles were removed by cells that acted the role of policemen. However, this theory was not adequate to explain protection against dissolved toxic substances; here a humoral theory looked more promising and the promise found an early fulfillment in von Behring's invention of antitoxic sera for tetanus and diphtheria. But this brings us so close to the borderline of Ehrlich's own contributions that we had better turn to another aspect of developments in internal medicine.

In a paper of 1878, Julius Cohnheim made an attack directed, as I believe, against men like Brown-Séquard and Claude Bernard,* although

*Cohnheim's attack only mentions "the chairs and institutes for experimental pathology which, in a neighboring state, exist at several universities." As far as I can see this would fit France, where Brown-Séquard held the chair of "Comparative and Experimental Pathology" in Paris from 1869 to 1872 to be succeeded by Vulpian, 1872–1887; cf. Prévost, A. *La faculté de médecine de Paris.* Paris, A. Maloine, 1900, p. 46f.

he did not mention the great experimental physiologists by name.[9] Cohnheim claimed that experimental pathology should be in the hands of clinicians who encountered disease at the bedside or pathological anatomists who studied its appearance on the postmortem table. The physiologist, because lacking the necessary contact with morbid phenomena, would tend to raise and answer physiological questions. I do not know whether Cohnheim actually had in mind Claude Bernard's *Introduction to Experimental Medicine* that had appeared in 1865. But his attack is understandable from the point of view of German conditions. Much of what this book was fighting for had become reality in Germany. Not only pathologists like Cohnheim, but clinicians too combined the clinical, anatomical, and experimental approach. As examples we may choose Frerichs and Traube who represented internal medicine at Berlin—in disharmony we must say, for they were bitter personal enemies. Now Traube is usually remembered as one of the founders of German experimental pathology. As far back as 1846 he had declared that "it is the experiment, added to passive observation, which can make pathology too what it wishes to become, an exact science."[10] But it is not always remembered that Frerichs also was an experimentalist. As a young professor he had become famous through his article on "Digestion"—a purely physiological subject—and shortly afterwards his work on kidney disease that utilized animal experiments. More than Traube, Frerichs was also versed in chemistry.[11] One of his greatest pupils, Naunyn, tells us about Frerichs' attitude towards his assistants of whom Ehrlich later was to be one. "He accepted each one from the very first day as a man who unquestionably could and would do everything the position required of him. So confident was he, unfortunately, of this that he never gave us any instructions as to how we should do anything; indeed, he scarcely said what he wanted done, and he actually managed to have everything done to his satisfaction without any such explanations." A little later on Naunyn adds: "It was just as much a matter of course that we should make scientific investigations and produce able pieces of work, as that we should perform our clinical duties to his satisfaction. What this work should be and how we did it was again entirely up to us, for he let us come and go and do whatever we wished, however we wished."[12] It is only necessary to point out that Naunyn in turn had as his pupil Minkowski whose work on the pancreas and diabetes was one of the preconditions for the discovery of insulin, in order to perceive the clinical tradition of the Frerichs' school in which chemistry and animal experiment combined with pathology to render medicine scientific.

We might expect that the search for exactness in medicine would lead such a school to therapeutic nihilism which had plagued medicine around the middle of the century. But this was hardly the case. Frerichs, a consultant with a very large clientele, was saved by his faith in "proved" remedies from falling into the pitfall.[13] The younger generation was saved by association with experimental pharmacology. Historically speaking the new pharmacology stemmed from the same root as experimental medicine; it really was a part of the latter. In 1873 there appeared the first issue of the

"Archives for experimental pathology and pharmacology"[14] edited by the clinician Naunyn, the pathologist Klebs, and Schmiedeberg, professor of pharmacology. The first three articles are characteristic: an investigation of blood coagulation in the living animal; a discussion of the effect of quinine on blood; and a contribution to the knowledge of micrococci; even the budding discipline of bacteriology was represented.

The nature of the new pharmacology needs a word of explanation. Schmiedeberg, in his textbook, defined it as "the science of the changes brought about in the living organism by chemically active substances, except foodstuffs, without regard as to whether such substances are used for curative purposes or not."[15] In other words, the pharmacologist merely investigates "the living processes under the influence of drugs."[16] He is a biologist. It is up to the physician then to choose those drugs he wishes to use in therapy. Pharmacology and materia medica stand in the relationship of a pure science and its application. The science exists regardless of its application, while application should not be made without the backing of science.

We characterized the time of Ehrlich as one of achievement. We set out to trace its general features and then tried to sketch the situation in medicine during Ehrlich's formative years. It was a peaceful time that allowed a man to concentrate on the work at hand, sometimes without looking up and seeing wider horizons. To unravel the mechanism of things may have occupied the mind more than to know their interconnection. As has been pointed out, public health was submerged by bacteriological studies[17] and medicine treated man as an organism with little soul inside.* Yet the end of our survey showed a belief in the superiority of science over its applications, and in conclusion we may ask what this belief embodied. We shall try to solicit the answer from the Englishman, Thomas Huxley, who became something of a philosophical spokesman for many biologists of the late nineteenth century. In an address of 1866, Huxley[18] looked back upon the great pestilence that had ravaged London about 200 years before. "Surely," he exclaimed, "it is true that our countrymen are less subject to fire, famine, pestilence, and all the evils which result from a want of command over and due anticipation of the course of Nature, than were the countrymen of Milton; and health, wealth, and well-being are more abundant with us than with them?" Remembering the repeated epidemics of Asiatic cholera and typhoid, the high incidence of tuberculosis and venereal disease which then prevailed we might not grant a positive answer with the assurance Huxley expected. However that may be, the speech goes on to say that in the eyes of many contemporaries, natural knowledge is nothing "but a sort of fairy godmother, ready to furnish her pets with shoes of swiftness, swords of sharpness, and omnipotent Aladdin's lamps, so that they may have telegraphs to Saturn, and see the other side of the moon, and thank God they are better than their benighted ancestors." To which

---

*Although the beginnings of psychoanalysis fall within the 1890's, it was of relatively little influence before the first World War.

Huxley contemptuously replied: "I think I would just as soon be quietly chipping my own flint axe after the manner of my forefathers a few thousand years back, as to be troubled with the endless malady of thought which now infests us all, for such reward."[19] The "practical benefits" as he calls them are but incidental. "I say that natural knowledge, seeking to satisfy natural wants, has found the ideas which can alone still spiritual cravings. I say that natural knowledge, in desiring to ascertain the laws of comfort, has been driven to discover those of conduct, and to lay the foundations of a new morality."[20]

We may no longer share such a robust faith in the spiritual value of natural science. Nevertheless, we have to recognize it as an expression of the striving of many scientists in the time of Paul Ehrlich. It was the existence of such faith that made them value their work beyond the immediate results they achieved.

REFERENCES

1. Du Bois-Reymond, E. H. *Reden von Du Bois-Reymond,* ed. by Estelle Du Bois-Reymond. Leipzig, Veit & Co., 1912, v. 1, p. 464.
2. Wachsmuth, R. Die Gründung der Universität Frankfurt. Frankfurt a. M., 1929, p. 2.
3. Waldeyer, H. W. G. *Lebenserinnerungen.* 2.ed. Bonn, F. Cohen, 1921, p. 246f.
4. Flexner, S., and Flexner, J. T. *William Henry Welch and the heroic age of American medicine.* New York, Viking Press, 1941, p. 78f.
5. Cohnheim, J. Ueber Entzündung und Eiterung, in his *Gesammelte Abhandlungen,* Berlin, A. Hirschwald, 1885, pp. 173–245.
6. Ackerknecht, E. H. *Rudolf Virchow, doctor, statesman, and anthropologist.* Madison, Univ. of Wisconsin Press, 1953, p. 118.
7. Ackerknecht, E. H. Reference 6, p. 55.
8. Temkin, O. European background of the young Dr. Welch, *Bull. Hist. Med.* 24:227–46, 1950 [Essay 18].
9. Cohnheim, J. Ueber die Aufgaben der pathologischen Anatomie, in his *Gesammelte Abhandlungen,* Berlin, A. Hirschwald, 1885, pp. 605–22.
10. Traube, L., *Gesammelte Beiträge zur Pathologie und Physiologie.* Berlin, A. Hirschwald, 1871, v. 1, p. ivf.
11. Naunyn, B. *Erinnerungen, Gedanken und Meinungen.* Munich, F. Bergmann, 1925, p. 126.
12. Naunyn, B. Reference 11, pp. 132 and 134.
13. Naunyn, B. Reference 11, p. 132.
14. *Archiv für experimentelle Pathologie und Pharmakologie,* vol. 1, 1873. The three articles cited were by Naunyn, Binz, and Klebs.
15. Schmiedeberg, O. *Grundriss der Arzneimitellehre.* 2.ed. Leipzig, F. C. W. Vogel, 1888, p. 1.
16. Schmiedeberg, O. Reference 15, p. 3.
17. Galdston, I. Humanism and public health, *Bull. Hist. Med.* 8:1032–39, 1940.
18. Huxley, T. H. On the advisableness of improving natural knowledge, in his *Methods and results,* New York, Appleton, 1902, p. 28.
19. Huxley, T. H. Reference 18, pp. 30 and 31.
20. Huxley, T. H. Reference 18, p. 31f.

V

Basic Medical Sciences
and Biology

20

Metaphors of Human
Biology*

ANALOGIES are not in good usage among modern scientists. And of all
analogies the metaphor is almost the worst, for it smacks of rhetoric
rather than of sober and factual description of things.[1] We are all prone to
compare human life to a candle that slowly burns down, or our bodies to
prisons for our souls. But although we may think that such fanciful images
are good enough for casual or poetical expressions, we expect the biologists
to keep aloof from metaphorical concepts. Thereby, however, we under-
rate the power of the metaphor. I believe that metaphors have exercised
considerable influence over the biologists' thought. For this thesis I propose to give some examples and then to inquire into the reason for this
peculiar habit of mind.

Instead of searching for the oldest metaphor for the human organism,
let us discard chronology and turn our attention to the term "organism"
itself. We are immediately aware that we are here dealing with a concept
which suggests a social counterpart. When we speak of an organism we
think of a natural object where all parts function so as to maintain the
existence of the whole. Now this biological order also seems applicable to
human society, as is expressed in the old parable by which Menenius Ag-
rippa is said to have brought back the revolting plebeians from the Mons
Sacer, where they had seceded in 494 B.C.[2] Jealous of the stomach that
received all the good things for which they had to work, some other organs
of the body decided to go on strike. But as a result, they too starved until
they finally recognized that the stomach was as important to them as they to
the stomach, and that in order to exist the body needed the proper service
of each part. The moral of this story was obvious. The stomach is the
patrician caste, the other parts are the plebeians, the body as a whole is the
Roman state. Disregarding this parable, it is indeed hard to say which side

---

*"Metaphors of Human Biology," in Robert C. Stauffer, editor, *Science and Civilization*
(Madison: The University of Wisconsin Press; © 1949 by the Regents of the University of
Wisconsin), pp. 169–94.
[1]According to Aristotle (*Poetics*, ch. 21, 1457 b.) analogy is but one among several pos-
sibilities of forming metaphors. However, it is the metaphor based on analogy which we have
in mind here and which according to Alfred Biese, *Die Philosophie des Metaphorischen*
(Hamburg–Leipzig, Voss, 1893) has played a fundamental role in nearly all branches of
human life. The use of analogy in science goes, of course, beyond the metaphorical. See Agnes
Arber, "Analogy in the History of Science," *Studies and Essays in the History of Science and
Learning, Offered in Homage to George Sarton on the Occasion of His Sixtieth Birthday*, ed. M. F.
Ashley-Montagu (New York, 1947), 219–33.
[2]Livy, II, 32,9.

271

of the comparison between organism and the state was the primary one. Yet, once in existence, the comparison served not only the statesman and political thinker but the biologist as well. Moreover, the differences in social organization were reflected in the different pictures of biological organization. Thus Alcmaeon, one of the old pre-Socratic philosophers, defined health as a balance between the various qualities constituting the body. Significantly enough, the Greek word which he used for balance, "isonomia," also connoted equality of political rights. In further accord with the political theory of the Greeks, he described disease as a "monarchy" of any one of the qualities.[3] Some six hundred years later the Greek city-state had lost its freedom. The Roman Empire ruled the world not only by its armies but also by its laws expressed in the maxim: To each his own.[4] This did not imply everyone's having equal claims; rather, it meant that everybody ought to share according to his rank. In the second century Galen, the last of the ancient anatomists and experimental physiologists, used this concept of justice again and again to make the anatomy of the human body understandable.[5] The various parts of the body differ in size: this is only just, because Nature has apportioned their size to the usefulness of their functions.[6] Some parts have few nerves: this too is just, for they do not need much sensitiveness.[7] As we shall see later, the comparison with a social organism was not Galen's main biological metaphor. Nevertheless he found the concept of social justice valuable just as he used the simile of the food supply of a city for explaining the function and name of the veins of the portal system, which carried chyle to the liver just as many routes carried food to the city's bakeries.[8]

In more recent times the metaphor of the state was utilized in a much stricter sense by Virchow in establishing his cellular pathology. As Hirschfeld has shown,[9] there existed a remarkable parallel between Virchow's biological views and his liberal political opinions. The cell, Virchow maintained, was the fundamental unit of life. All plants and animals were sums of these vital units. It was the relationship between the cells that determined the structure and function of the multicellular organism. "Hence it becomes evident that the composition of a larger body, the so-called individual, always amounts to some kind of social institution."[10] This cell state, moreover, was patterned after a republic. There was no special organ, no single cell representing the individual. Individuality as some-

---

[3]See John Burnet, *Early Greek Philosophy* (4th ed., London, 1930), 196, who also gives the Greek text of the passage.

[4]*Corpus iuris civilis* (3 vols., Berlin, Weidmann, 1889), "Institutiones," recognovit P. Krueger, I:1: "Iustitia est constans et perpetua voluntas ius suum cuique tribuens."

[5]For a general statement see Galen, *De usu partium*, V, 9 (ed. G. Helmreich, Leipzig, 1907), 1:277 f, see also *ibid.*, I,17 (1:36), I,22 (1:59), II, 16 (1:116).

[6]*Ibid.*, III, 10 (1:171).

[7]*Ibid.*, V, 9.

[8]*Ibid.*, IV, 2 (1:196).

[9]Ernst Hirschfeld, "Virchow," *Kyklos* (1929), 2:106–16.

[10]Rudolf Virchow, *Die Cellularpathologie* (2nd ed., Berlin, 1859), 12.

thing simple and integral was altogether a subjective phenomenon of our minds without corresponding biological parallel.[11]

We shall find the biological significance of Virchow's metaphor best if we dwell briefly upon the biological controversy which in the fifties raged between the physicists, systematists, and the followers of the cellular theory. In 1852 Carl Ludwig, one of the leaders of the German materialistic school, published the first volume of his textbook of physiology,[12] which quite seriously attempted to erect a physiological system upon the actions of chemical atoms and physical molecules. Characteristically enough, the book began with a chapter on "the physiology of atoms."[13] Since atoms were the elements of all matter, the first task of the physiologist was to find the significance of various atoms and atom groups for the process of life. What this "process of life" was, and how this concept entered into a system that was supposed to recognize nothing but physical forces, Ludwig did not say. But Ludwig remained consistent in not recognizing cells as vital units. The relative unimportance which the cells played in Ludwig's thought was demonstrated by the fact that their discussion was relegated to the second volume in connection with the physiology of nutrition.[14] Both Virchow and the systematists were united in their attack upon this radical form of materialism. Virchow was rather impatient with the "scientific prudishness" which saw in vital processes nothing but a mechanical result of the inherent molecular forces.[15] Even if it were granted that in a remote past life had originated from these forces, today at least it was a demonstrable truth that life did not exist outside of cells, that there was no spontaneous generation of cells, and that vital phenomena rested in the cells. But from here on the paths of Virchow and the systematists parted. In the same year, 1855, in which Virchow published his article on "Cellular Pathology," where his famous formula "omnis cellula a cellula" appeared,[16] Reichert criticized this article in a comprehensive and instructive review.[17] He blamed Virchow for having adopted an atomic view of the organism. Virchow, he claimed, rightly admitted the principle of organization for the cell, only to give it up in the explanation of the animal as a whole, and to construct the latter from cells as if they were atoms composing an inorganic body. In this criticism of the cellular theory Reichert coincided with certain views which Thomas Huxley had expressed in 1853.[18] This article of Huxley's has not

[11]*Ibid.,* 260. See also Virchow, "Atome und Individuen" in *Vier Reden über Leben und Kranksein* (Berlin, 1862), 73 f.

[12]I have had at my disposal the second edition: Carl Ludwig, *Lehrbuch der Physiologie des Menschen* (2 vols., Leipzig-Heidelberg, 1858–61).

[13]*Ibid.,* 1:16.

[14]*Ibid.,* 2:229.

[15]Rudolf Virchow, "Zellular-Pathologie," *Virchows Archiv* (1855), 8:23.

[16]*Ibid.*

[17]"Bericht über die Fortschritte in der mikroskopischen Anatomie im Jahre 1854," *Archiv für Anatomie, Physiologie und wissenschaftliche Medicin,* ed. J. Müller, 1855, Appendix. See also E. S. Russell, *Form and Function* (London, 1916), 192.

[18]Thomas Henry Huxley, "The Cell-Theory," reprinted in *The Scientific Memoirs of Thomas*

received the attention it deserves. We here deal with the young Huxley, the follower of von Baer, who still defended the constancy of species. For Huxley as for the embryologists, Wolff in the eighteenth century and von Baer in the early nineteenth, animal individuality did not so much consist in organization as in the course of development that leads from conception to death. This development "is a continually increasing differentiation of that which was at first homogeneous." The cells "are not instruments, but indications" of this development.[19] In other words, the law of the organic individual determines the differentiation into cells.

But for Virchow, as we have seen, the adult organism was not an individual. How then was he to save its existence as an organized whole? His answer was to take refuge in the concept of the cell state. "There is then no danger that we may lose the unity of the living organism by our multiplicity of vital foci. . . . It is a free state of individuals with equal rights though not with equal endowments, which keeps together because the individuals are dependent upon one another and because there are certain centers of organization without whose integrity the single parts cannot receive their necessary supply of healthful nourishing material."[20] In other words, the metaphor of the cell state for Virchow was not a mere manner of speech, but an integral part of his biological theory. It was a means of preserving the unity of the organism which he, as a physician who had to treat human beings, could not possibly give up. At the same time, the metaphor helped him to avoid admitting an objective form for this unity. A society, or even a state, has no objective form; it has no morphology. The metaphor of the organism as a society is, therefore, just as inadequate as the reverse analogy of society as an organism so popular among sociologists of the nineteenth century.[21]

At this point we have to clarify our use of the term "metaphor." Virchow, apparently, was quite serious in comparing organism and society. At any rate he seems not to have been unduly bothered by the problem of borrowing, for biological purposes, a concept belonging to another field. It is only under our critical analysis that the metaphorical nature becomes clearly visible. All of the comparisons which we are discussing derive their strength from the belief that they are true and valid biological notions. To refer to them as metaphors in itself already throws doubt upon their validity.[22] This

---

Henry Huxley, ed. M. Foster and Ray Lankester (London, 1898), 1:242–78. In a certain sense this article is a continuation of a paper, "Upon Animal Individuality," which Huxley had delivered on April 30, 1852, and which is abstracted, *ibid.*, 1:146–51.

[19]*Ibid.*, 277.

[20]Virchow, *op. cit.* (see note 15), 25.

[21]For a detailed discussion and criticism see Adolf Meyer, *Wesen und Geschichte der Theorie vom Mikro- und Makroskosmos* (Bern, 1900) and George Perrigo Conger, *Theories of Macrocosms and Microcosms in the History of Philosophy* (New York, 1922).

[22]The interplay between the positive phase of establishing philosophical metaphors and the negative phase of revealing them as mere metaphors has been well described by Biese, *Die Philosophie des Metaphorischen*, 106, 226. Biese on page 159 also alludes to the role which the metaphor of the cell state played among biologists of the nineteenth century.

discrepancy between original belief and present criticism is especially marked in the comparisons of the organism with a work of art and with a machine, which we shall discuss next.

The term "organism" is of relatively modern origin. It is only the term "organ," meaning instrument, that has a venerable past. Plato spoke of the eye as an instrument of the senses.[23] Aristotle and Galen used the term "organ" very frequently. It was compatible with the picture of an instrument that an organ or part of the body could be visualized as operating mechanically.[24] But the Greek biologists of the Aristotelian tradition did not forget that an instrument has an artist who designs it and a master who uses it. The artist to them was divine nature and the master, the soul. Whether in part or as a whole, the human body was conceived as an instrument of the soul, formed so as to suit the requirements of the soul.[25] "For the body," says Galen, "is the instrument of [the soul] and because of this the parts of the animals differ greatly from one another since the souls also do. For some animals are brave, others cowardly, some are wild, others tame, some are social so to speak and industrious, while others are solitary. But in all of them the body is adapted to the fashion and faculties of the soul. Thus the body of the horse is endowed with strong hoofs and a mane for it is a quick and proud animal and not without spirit."[26] It is Galen's ambition to prove for all parts of the human body the perfect adaptation of structure to function, even to social demands and passing fashion. This endeavor at times leads to rather ridiculous statements, as, for instance, when Galen proposes the following explanation for man's beard:

Indeed, the hair on the lower part of the face not only covers the jaw but also serves as an ornament. For a man, particularly in advanced years, looks more stately if his face is nicely surrounded by hair. And for this reason nature left the prominences of the cheeks and the nose bare and free from hair, since otherwise the whole visage would have become fierce and brutal and not at all suitable for a civilized and social being.[27]

Behind this is Galen's conviction that the divine craftsman, the demiurge, has created man as a sublime work of art.[28] This metaphor of the work of art must be taken literally, against the background of Greek civilization. Just as the workman did not count in the highest ranks of ancient society, so the demiurge did not necessarily hold the highest place among the gods.[29] And indeed, his abilities were rather limited. He did not create the world out of nothing; he had to use matter with all its imperfections.[30] Therefore

[23]Plato, *Republic*, 508 b.
[24]See Galen, *De usu partium*, VII, 14.
[25]See Aristotle, *De partibus animalium*, I, 1 (642 a) and I, 5 (645 b, 15 ff.).
[26]Galen, *De usu partium*, I, 2 (ed. Helmreich), 1:1, line 14–p. 2, line 4.
[27]*Ibid.*, XI, 14 (2:154, lines 4–12).
[28]*Ibid.*, IV, 1 (1:195), and V, 4 (1:260).
[29]Thus the demiurge in Plato's *Timaeus* is not the highest god.
[30]This becomes especially clear from Galen's polemic against the biblical concept of God, *De usu partium*, XI, 14. An interesting remark on the ancient concept of the creating deity occurs

275

he could not prevent disease from befalling the human body; all he could do was to shape his material so as to foresee all possible dangers and safeguard against them in the best possible way. One might almost say that Galen, the physician, conceived his demiurge in the likeness of a divine physician given the task of framing man's body in a manner best calculated to secure his life and that of his race and to equip him for life's duties and pleasures.[31]

The metaphor of the divine work of art does not disappear when the organism begins to be likened to a machine. In the *Discours de la méthode,* Descartes alludes to a structure conceivable for the human body that would make it respond to external impressions without the influence of the will. This, he adds, would not be surprising if we think of "the divers automata, or moving machines," which the industry of man can construct from relatively few pieces, compared with the manifold parts composing the animal body. We shall then consider the body "as a machine which having been made by the hands of God is disposed incomparably better and has in itself more attainable movements than any of those that can be invented by men."[32] Here, too, the body is perceived as a divine work of art; yet by changing the accent a new concept has emerged. For Galen, the demonstration of divine art is the main aim; everything in the body, animal and human alike, is understandable only from the point of view of its instrumentality to the soul. For Descartes, the body functions according to mechanical laws. It does not need a soul; indeed animals are not supposed to have a soul at all. The idea of divine workmanship in analogy to human automata merely serves to explain the possibility of such a marvelous construction. From a biological point of view, Descartes' identification of the body with a machine is a metaphor by which he tries to give a concept of an organized natural object regulated merely by matter and motion. The metaphor has its obvious weakness. A machine is built for a purpose. Thus the clocks, mills,[33] and automata which Descartes mentions all serve human purposes. But what is the purpose of a soulless animal? This question is unanswerable to Descartes, since he rejects the quest for final causes from his philosophy. However, the metaphor assumes significance immediately if applied to the concept of man who has a rational soul totally distinct from his body. For the purpose of man's conscious and purposeful life, the body can indeed be considered as a machine that will run according to the manipulations of the machinist. And it will run all the better if it has no purpose of its own, if it is stripped of teleological assumptions and of the vegetative and animal soul with which the ancients had endowed it. There

---

in the latest novel by Thomas Mann, *Doctor Faustus,* translated by H. T. Lowe-Porter (New York, 1948), 15 f.

[31]Nature's purpose in building the body is directed toward the preservation of the individual's life and of that of his species and towards making life pleasant. See Galen, *De usu partium,* VI, 7 (ed. Helmreich), 1:318.

[32]"Discours de la méthode," part 5, *Oeuvres de Descartes,* edited by Charles Adam and Paul Tannery (Paris, 1902), 6:55 f.

[33]"Traité de l'homme," *ibid.* (Paris, 1909), 11:120.

must be no other forces at work than those which can be measured and calculated and there must be no other will than that imposed by man's rational will.

In two essays written some seventy years ago Thomas Huxley praised Descartes as having grasped the spirit of the most advanced physiology.[34] Indeed, Descartes' metaphor of the body machine proved most fruitful in many respects. In the first place, it made room for a more active attitude toward the body. Galen had imagined the human organism to be so perfectly constructed that an improvement was not even thinkable. Besides, nature was constantly at work to protect and cure. If, for instance, a wound had been inflicted, it was her first intention to glue the severed edges together.[35] Incidentally, we still bear witness to this ancient principle when, in surgery, we speak of healing by the first intention. But a machine has only a certain number of regulations, which in many cases may prove insufficient to restore the damage. One of the consequences of the Cartesian concept, as Neuburger has shown,[36] was a difference in the evaluation of the healing power of nature and of medical interference. The Galenists upheld the healing power of nature whereas many Cartesians tended to stress its limitations. Boyle, for instance, who followed Descartes in the metaphor of the human machine, argued elaborately that many natural reactions in disease were not beneficial but harmful and that the physician, therefore, had to combat rather than encourage them—this, in spite of Boyle's belief that the human body had been fashioned by God with infinite wisdom.[37] Once this belief weakened it could be asked whether the body was a good or a bad machine. Thus Helmholtz, in considering the eye as an optical instrument, found it so full of defects that he for one would have felt justified in returning it to the optician who had dared to sell it to him.[38] And perhaps it is not by chance that the period of the nineteenth century which made the most fruitful applications of the metaphor of the body machine also became interested in "dysteleology." By this theory Haeckel designated organs which were useless, and dysteleology found its practical culmination in the removal of the healthy appendix as an altogether useless and dangerous part.[39] In the days of Galen this would have been rank heresy.[40]

The most fruitful application of the metaphor of the machine came with

---

[34]"On Descartes' 'Discourse Touching the Method of Using One's Reason Rightly and of Seeking Scientific Truth'" and "On the Hypothesis that Animals Are Automata, and Its History" in: Thomas H. Huxley, *Method and Results* (New York, 1898). See especially page 184.

[35]Galen, "Ars medica," ch. 29, *Opera omnia* (ed. Kühn, Leipzig, 1820), 1:385.

[36]Max Neuburger, *Die Lehre von der Heilkraft der Natur im Wandel der Zeiten* (Stuttgart, 1926), 49 ff.

[37]See *ibid.*, 51 ff.

[38]H. Helmholtz, *Popular Lectures on Scientific Subjects,* translated by E. Atkinson (New York, 1883), 219. It has, however, to be added that this criticism by Helmholtz is directed only against the optical aspect of the eye, not against its total physiological efficiency.

[39]Ernst Haeckel, *Die Welträtsel* (Leipzig, n.d.), 162 f.

[40]Asclepiades was the kind of heretic who did not subscribe to the maxim that nature does nothing in vain.

the development of thermodynamics and the discovery of the law of the conservation of energy. So fruitful indeed has this mataphor proved that it is still widely used. The first as well as the second law of thermodynamics can be expressed in terms of an engine. The first law formulates the impossibility of building a *perpetuum mobile*.[41] The second law rests upon the experience that "it is impossible to construct a periodically functioning engine which effects nothing but the lifting of a weight and the cooling of a reservoir of water."[42] Considered as an engine, the body must be subject to both these laws. Conversely, it would seem that the validity of these laws would prove the body to be an engine. But an engine is not merely defined by thermodynamic laws and, therefore, the applicability of these laws does not yet make the body an engine. The "living" machine, be it a cell[43] or the organism as a whole, exhibits features which make it unique if compared with lifeless machines. It is one thing to speak of mechanisms by which certain functions are made possible, and quite another to speak of the entire living unit as a machine. In a booklet which Carl Oppenheimer published in 1921, he denied that man was *one* machine; rather, he believed that he represented a large system of many small engines. And this system he compared to an entire factory.[44] True, Oppenheimer made this comparison only in passing, but it is nevertheless interesting to dwell upon it for a moment. Here we deal with another metaphor, for a factory is an economic unit of which the actual machinery is but a part; organization and productivity enter as equally important factors and productivity implies a definite purpose. The metaphor of a factory is related to the term "animal economy" which formerly, more than now, was used for physiology and on which Dr. Ackerknecht has made some pertinent remarks.[45]

The economic metaphors suffer from the same inadequacy as Virchow's sociological metaphor of the cell state; they do not account for the biological phenomenon of form. On the other hand they avoid the great weakness of the machine metaphor which presumes somebody outside the machine for whom it exists and who will make use of it. On the presupposition of Descartes, as we have seen, this somebody outside was the rational soul. It is indeed surprising to see how deep-rooted and widespread this Cartesian dualism still is. But it is also noteworthy that it has become an insufficient basis for modern psychiatry. All psychoanalytical and psychosomatic theories which assume bodily reactions to unconscious psychic processes endow the body with qualities which do not belong to the idea of a machine. As I have pointed out elsewhere, in some respects they show closer affinity

[41]See Max Planck, *Vorlesungen über Thermodynamik* (7th ed., Berlin-Leipzig, 1922), 38.
[42]*Ibid.*, 87.
[43]See D. R. Goddard in: Rudolf Höber, *Physical Chemistry of Cells and Tissues* (Philadelphia, 1945), 373.
[44]Carl Oppenheimer, *Der Mensch als Kraftmaschine* (Leipzig, 1921), 53, 59.
[45]Erwin H. Ackerknecht, "Metabolism and Respiration from Erasistratus to Lavoisier," *Ciba Symposia* (1944), 6:1815.

to the old Platonic and Galenic idea of the tripartite soul than to the organistic psychiatry of the later nineteenth century.[46]

But I think the time has now come when we should take stock of what we have found so far. We have discussed a few metaphors by which the human organism has been compared to society, a work of art, a machine or engine, and an economic unit. All these comparisons were taken from realms outside human biology and I have, therefore, felt justified in calling them metaphors. Short as the analysis has had to be, it has brought out features common to all these metaphors. They were not always mere figures of speech, but integrating concepts used by biologists in guiding their thought. However, we have had to take notice of the fact that they were all open to criticism; being metaphors they were not adequate to their subject. Why then did biologists resort to such metaphors? Why the need to use an image outside one's professed domain?

In the first place it is relatively easy to show that each of the metaphors discussed corresponded at one period or another to a certain general view of events transcending the realm of biology. Neither for Galen nor for the mechanists of the seventeenth century did the animal body stand alone as a divine work of art. A contemptible part like the foot moved Galen to a comparison with the sun and to an enraptured hymn upon the divinity of nature.[47] And to Boyle, the machine of the body was but a part of the great machine of the universe.[48] Helmholtz measured the heat produced by muscular movements as a step toward proving the conservation of energy as a general law of physics. And Virchow viewed the body in the light of his concept of a just human society. Perhaps it is not saying too much of the metaphors of human biology which we have discussed to call them only variations of that greatest of all biological metaphors whereby the organism is called a microcosm, a little world, as compared with the macrocosm, the large world.

The theme, microcosm-macrocosm, is indeed very old and its variations are more manifold than can be mentioned here.[49] In the classical and explicit form which it reached in the late Middle Ages and Renaissance it consisted of a point by point concordance between the world and animal life. If we take Paracelsus as our guide we see that it led him, in the first place, to attribute birth, age, and death to the world: "Now the sky too was a child, it too had its beginning and is predestined to its end, like man, and death is in it and around it."[50] Secondly, the sky had its organs which corresponded to those of man. And finally: "Big man also sickens just as

---

[46]Owsei Temkin in *Bull. Hist. Med.* (1944), 16:519.

[47]Galen, *De usu partium*, III, 10 (ed. Helmreich), 176.

[48]" . . . that great machine the world . . . that smaller engine the human body." Quoted from Neuburger, *Die Lehre von der Heilkraft*, 52.

[49]See the books by Meyer and Conger quoted in note 21.

[50]*Four Treatises of Theophrastus von Hohenheim Called Paracelsus*, ed. Henry E. Sigerist (Baltimore, 1941), 20.

the little one."[51] Thus the picture is completed on its macrocosmic side. On the microcosmic side, this correspondence leads to a medical theory of the proper understanding of diseases, and especially of their courses. The physician cannot study directly the genesis and development of diseases inside the body. Paracelsus did not believe in the study of anatomy based on the dissection of dead bodies. Instead he believed in a cosmic anatomy which would teach the physician the correlation between astronomical bodies and human organs and make him recognize human diseases from telluric events: "He that knoweth the origin of thunder, winds and storms, knoweth where colic and torsions come from . . . he that knoweth what the planets' rust is and what their fire, salt and mercury, also knoweth how ulcers grow and where they come from as well as scabies, leprosy and serei."[52]

This correspondence between macrocosm and microcosm is based on a belief that macrocosm and microcosm are related like father and son. After God had created heaven and earth and all creatures he formed a mass which contained an extract from everything created. This mass was what the Bible called the "limus terrae," "the dust of the earth" of which God formed man in His likeness. "Out of this 'limus' the creator of the world made the little world, the microcosm, that is man. Thus man is the little world, that is man has all properties of the world within himself. . . . Thus the big world is a father of the little world. For this reason there exists in the little world the kind of the dragons, the kind of snakes, the generation of vipers and adders, also the nature of wolves, sheep, etc., also of all elements, likewise health and disease. For each child takes after the kind of his father."[53] This concept even allows a literal explanation of the beast in man. If some people are vipers or wolves it is because the essence of these animals entered into the composition of Adam.

There is still another variant of the macrocosm-microcosm idea which connects it more closely with the metaphor of the organism as a state from which our discussion started. Not only the animal but the state has been for ages likened to the universe.[54] In particular it was the sun whose commanding position among the stars was identified with that of the king.[55]

> And therefore is the glorious planet Sol
> In noble eminence enthron'd and spher'd
> Amidst the other; whose med'cinable eye
> Corrects the ill aspects of planets evil,
> And posts, like the commandment of a king,
> Sans check, to good and bad . . .

---

[51]Theophrast von Hohenheim, *Medizinische, naturwissenschaftliche und philosophische Schriften* (ed. Karl Sudhoff, Munich, 1924), 8:168.

[52]*Ibid.*, 176. According to M. Höfler, *Deutsches Krankheitsnamen Buch* (Munich, 1899), 652, "serei" in Paracelsus means a skin affliction.

[53]Theophrast von Hohenheim, *Schriften* (ed. Sudhoff, Munich-Berlin, 1929), 12:37. See also Meyer, *Wesen und Geschichte*, 57 ff.

[54]See Conger, *Macrocosms and Microcosms*, passim.

[55]See E. M. W. Tillyard, *The Elizabethan World Picture* (New York, 1944), 83.

These lines, from Shakespeare's *Troilus and Cressida* (Act I, scene 3), may stand for many which could be adduced from ancient to modern times. But just as the sun could be connected with the king so it could also be connected with the heart.[56] And all three pieces were most intricately and significantly combined in one of the greatest works of human physiology, Harvey's *De motu cordis*, which in 1628 announced the discovery of the circulation of the blood. The dedication of this book to Charles the First begins:

> Most Gratious King, The Heart of creatures is the foundation of life, the Prince of all, the Sun of their Microcosm, on which all vegetation does depend, from whence all vigor and strength does flow. Likewise the King is the foundation of his Kingdoms, and the Sun of his Microcosm, the Heart of his Commonwealth, from whence all power and mercy proceeds.[57]

One might be inclined to dismiss these and the following words as the euphuistic style of the body physician Harvey, were it not for the fact that the heart appears again as the sun of the microcosm in the decisive eighth chapter of the book which introduces the idea of the systemic circulation. "So the heart is the beginning of life, the Sun of the Microcosm, as proportionably the Sun deserves to be call'd the heart of the world, by whose vertue and pulsation, the blood is mov'd, perfected, made vegetable, and is defended from corruption and mattering." And again, in chapter seventeen we read: "The heart is as it were a Prince in the Commonwealth, in whose person is the first and highest government every where; from which as from the original and foundation, all power in the animal is deriv'd, and doth depend."[58]

In both of these passages, the comparisons have a definite biological meaning. In the latter Harvey compares the heart with the ruler of the state, because the heart originates first, because it does not depend on other organs, notably brain and liver, but has the organs of its movements in itself—"as if it were some internal animal"—so that all the rest of the body depends upon it. Harvey here uses the Aristotelian metaphor of the heart as the "acropolis" and "the supreme power."[59]

But the comparison of the heart with the sun is of even more startling character, for it elucidates Harvey's very concept of circulation. The sun makes vapors rise from the earth; these vapors in turn become condensed and change into rain which moistens the earth. Hence things are generated and storms and meteors arise "from the circular motion of the sun, by coming and going." Likewise in man, the blood reaches all parts of the body while warm and nutrient, but is itself cooled and worn out so that it returns

[56]See *ibid.*

[57]*The Anatomical Exercises of Dr. William Harvey De Motu Cordis 1628: De Circulatione Sanguinis 1653*, the first English text of 1653 now newly edited by Geoffrey Keynes (London, 1928), vii.

[58]*Ibid.*, 59 f., 115.

[59]Aristotle, *De partibus animalium*, 670 a, 23–26, and *Parva naturalia*, 469 a, 5. See also John G. Curtis, *Harvey's Views on the Use of the Circulation of the Blood* (New York, 1915), 44 f.

to the heart, "the fountain so to speak or the domestic deity of the body," in order to be perfected. From here it is distributed again "and all this depends upon the motion and pulse of the heart. Therefore the heart is the principle and sun of the microcosm."[60] Mark the double analogy in this comparison. The circulation of the blood is likened to the circulation of moisture. The latter depends upon the circuit of the sun just as the former depends upon systole and diastole of the heart.

The implications of this analogy for Harvey's fundamental beliefs as well as for some of his mystically inclined followers have been pointed out by Curtis[61] and, above all, by Pagel.[62] Here too we see the Aristotelian Harvey who still clings to a geocentric cosmology with its old ideas about the nature of the heavenly bodies. What a contrast this concept is to the mere mechanical description of the circulation of the blood for which alone we are inclined to praise Harvey! And, on the other hand, this metaphor of the sun of the microcosm allows Harvey, in a few paragraphs, to indicate his notions of the physiological significance of the blood for the life of the whole organism.[63] In a book full of metaphors, these particular ones of sun, king, and heart serve the purpose of sketching a whole system of physiology which, it may be added, is not modern at all. But this does not give us the right to dismiss them as an antiquated byplay in an otherwise admirably modern piece of research.

Our contention that all of the metaphors mentioned are only variants of the theme of macrocosm-microcosm needs qualification. The macrocosm is not necessarily the universe of heaven and earth as it was for Paracelsus, Harvey, and Boyle; it may simply be some wider realm which seems to give order and meaning. Virchow's interest, for instance, lay in the concept of a just society. With this qualification it may be said that the metaphors we have discussed, in the beginning at least, helped to place the organism in some scheme and thereby give meaning to its existence. They served to co-ordinate the interests of our human life and the science of life. When the picture of the world and the spheres of interest changed, the metaphors of human biology tended to change, too.

We should, of course, not forget that most of the metaphors mentioned could be used the other way around. That is to say, the organism could be used as a primary concept and the world, society, or economic units could then be explained by conceiving them as organisms. This indeed has been done and is still being done with the same result of co-ordinating life and a wider order of things.[64] Moreover, it is possible that upon closer scrutiny,

---

[60]William Harvey: *Exercitatio anatomica de motu cordis et sanguinis in animalibus* (Frankfurt, 1628), ch. 8, p. 42.

[61]Curtis, *op. cit.*, p. 154 ff.

[62]Walter Pagel, "William Harvey: Some Neglected Aspects of Medical History," *Journal of the Warburg and Courtauld Institutes* (1944), 7:146; "The Vindication of 'Rubbish,'" *Middlesex Hospital Journal* (Autumn, 1945); "A Background Study to Harvey," *Medical Bookman and Historian* (1948), 2:407–09.

[63]See especially the last-named paper by Pagel.

[64]See the works of Biese, Meyer, and Conger.

human biology would not appear as the only science in which metaphors have been used in order to give unity to our concept of the world. The metaphors in science may appear to be a kind of indicator for our prevailing convictions.[65] But aside from this possibility it seems to me that in human biology special reasons prevail. The phenomenon of the living organism is hard to define; our modern textbooks usually shy away from the task. Moreover, in dealing with human biology the difficulty is substantially increased. We speak of human biology as if it were a well-defined province of science. But are we really agreed upon the nature and scope of human biology? From biology we inherit all the problems of the living organism. To this is superadded the question how far the field of biology reaches in human affairs. There are some who would like to give a biological explanation even to history and ethics. Others there are who would exclude from the field of biology anything not purely somatic. Either extreme has to justify its position. This justification is not the mere scientific inference from facts but is usually a decision made a priori and for reasons not inherent in biology itself. The realm and nature of human biology, it seems to me, is defined by convictions entering from outside. Therefore, the language too comes from outside; it is metaphorical. The use of metaphors in human biology is not an aberration from which even great men have failed to escape. On the contrary, by using metaphors which they believed to represent adequate and true concepts, Aristotle, Galen, Paracelsus, Harvey, Descartes, Virchow, and Helmholtz shaped concepts of human biology which conformed with their own thoughts and feelings and with the thoughts and feelings of their times.

[65]Biese, in *Die Philosophie des Metaphorischen,* has stressed the integrating function of the metaphor in general and in philosophy in particular. Meyer, in *Wesen und Geschichte,* 109 ff., speaking of the theory of microcosm-macrocosm, admits the usefulness of metaphorical analogies but criticizes the theory for having assumed real similarities at the expense of scientific exactness. Meyer's criticism is certainly valid and in the past similar criticism has served to unveil metaphors. For instance, van Helmont said of Paracelsus: "To wit, he translated the Metaphor of a Microcosme into the truth itself." *Oriatrike* (London, 1662), 237. I am indebted to Dr. Lloyd G. Stevenson for this reference. However, a metaphor consciously and consistently used as a mere figure of speech is not likely to exert great influence in science because of the probable lack of confidence in its validity. It is the transcendence of legitimate metaphorical speech into real identification which has proved stimulating as well as dangerous.

2 1

Was Servetus Influenced by Ibn an-Nafīs?*

UNTIL A FEW years ago the Spanish heretic, Michael Servetus, was generally considered the first to have described pulmonary circulation.[1] Now, however, we know that in this discovery Servetus had been anticipated about three hundred years before by an Arabic physician, Ibn an-Nafīs. This fact was laid down in 1924 in the thesis of Muhyī ad-Dīn aṭ-Ṭaṭāwī.[2] Since this thesis was never printed, it is through two important publications of M. Meyerhof that we have become more fully acquainted with the details of Ibn an-Nafīs' life, work, and discovery.[3]

In many respects the statements of Ibn an-Nafīs and Servetus show definite similarity, and the question arose whether Servetus might possibly have been acquainted with Ibn an-Nafīs' work. It was, however, not possible to establish any such connection. Ibn an-Nafīs' "Commentary on the Anatomy in the Canon of Ibn Sīnā" has not been translated into Latin[4] and no intermediary source is known. It had, therefore, to be assumed that Servetus developed his theory independently from Ibn an-Nafīs.[5]

It seems to me that this result can be furthermore supported by some internal evidence. Meyerhof has already pointed out that Servetus expresses two ideas not to be found in Ibn an-Nafīs: "Was Servede mehr hat, ist ausser der 'gelben' Farbe des oxydierten Blutes, die er möglicherweise an Schlachttieren beobachtet haben kann, sein Argument, das ich oben nicht wiedergab, dass die Lungenarterie zu dick sei, um allein der Er-

*Bull. Hist. Med., 1940, vol. 8, pp. 731–34.

This article was prepared about two years ago as a contribution to the intended "Festschrift" for the 70th birthday of Professor Max Neuburger. In publishing it now in the Bulletin I wish to express my esteem for the great Viennese historian of medicine.

[1] The expression "pulmonary circulation" has to be used with the necessary qualifications pointed out by M. Neuburger, "Zur Entdeckungsgeschichte des Lungenkreislaufes," *Arch. Gesch. Med.*, 23, 1930, pp. 7–9.

[2] Cf. Meyerhof in *Isis*, p. 102.

[3] "Ibn an-Nafīs und seine Theorie des Lungenkreislaufs" in *Quellen und Studien zur Geschichte der Naturwissenschaften und der Medizin*, Band 4, Berlin, 1935, pp. 37–88, and "Ibn An-Nafīs (XIIIth cent.) and his theory of the lesser circulation," *Isis*, No. 65 (Vol. XXIII, I), 1935, pp. 100–20.—Cf. also S. Haddad and A. Khairallah, "A Forgotten Chapter in the History of the Circulation of the Blood," *Annals of Surgery*, 104, 1936, pp. 1–8.

[4] Sarton, *Introduction to the History of Science*, Vol. II², Baltimore, 1931, p. 1100 cites "Ebenefis philosophi ac medici expositio super quintum canonem Avicennae ab Andrea Alpago bellunensi ex arabico in latinum versa. This is a part of the Latin Ibn Sīnā edition of Venice 1547." I have not seen this work, but since the 5th book of the Canon deals with pharmacology, it has scarcely any bearing upon the present subject.

[5] Cf. Meyerhof, *Isis*, pp. 119–20. Cf. also Goyanes, J., *Miguel Serveto, teologo, geografo y medico, etc.*, Madrid, 1933, pp. 219–23.

nährung der Lunge zu dienen." [6] But whereas these could be interpreted as merely additional arguments of Servetus, there are, besides, two anatomical points where his conception is *different* from that of the Arab:

1. Ibn an-Nafīs is very definite about the impossibility of any blood passing directly from the right to the left cavity of the heart. To quote Meyerhof's translation, he says: *"But there is no passage between these two cavities;* for the substance of the heart is solid in this region and has neither a visible passage, as was thought by some persons, nor an invisible one which could have permitted the transmission of blood, as was alleged by Galen. The pores of the heart there are closed and its substance is thick." [7] And again: "Therefore the contention of some persons who say that this place"—i.e., the septum—"is porous, is erroneous." [8] Servetus, on the other hand, does not mention the pores at all. Speaking of the transmutation of venous into arterial blood, he says: "Demum, paries ille medius, cum sit vasorum et facultatum expers, non est aptus ad communicationem et elaborationem illam, *licet aliquid resudare possit."* [9] The admission that a little blood may sweat through into the left cavity makes it even likely that Servetus would not have absolutely denied the existence of pores. For, as is proved by the first edition of Vesalius' *Fabrica,* it was just through such invisible pores that blood was believed to *sweat through.* [10]

2. The other point refers to the way in which Ibn an-Nafīs and Servetus visualized the passage of blood from the pulmonary artery to the pulmonary vein. Ibn an-Nafīs believed that "there exist perceptible passages... between the two [blood-vessels]." [11] After some blood had "filtered through" the wall of the pulmonary artery it would find "the great quantity of air distributed in the cells of the lung and is mixed with it in order to acquire the aptitude to generate the vital spirit." [12] Then, we may complete the picture; it would filter into the pulmonary vein which, according to Ibn an-Nafīs, "has thin substance in order to facilitate the reception of the transsuded [blood] from the vein in question." [13] Servetus' remarks on this subject suggest quite a different theory, although he is not very explicit about it. After the above quoted passage concerning the septum of the heart he adds: "Eodem artificio, quo in hepate fit transfusio a vena porta ad venam cavam propter sanguinem, fit etiam in pulmone transfusio a vena

[6]Meyerhof, *Quellen und Studien,* p. 87. For the interpretation of Servetus' designation of the color of arterial blood as "flavus" cf. Izquierdo, J. J., "A New and More Correct Version of the Views of Servetus on the Circulation of the Blood," *Bulletin of the Institute of the History of Medicine,* Vol. V, Baltimore, 1937, p. 920.

[7]Meyerhof, *Isis,* p. 116.

[8]*Ibid.,* p. 117.

[9]*Christianismi Restitutio,* reprint edition of 1791, p. 171. (Italics mine.)

[10]Vesalius, *De Humani Corporis Fabrica,* Basileae, 1543, p. 589: "Ex his foveis nullae (quod sensu saltem comprehendi licet) ex dextro ventriculo in sinistrum penetrant, adeo sane ut rerum Opificis industriam mirari cogamur, qua per meatus visum fugientes ex dextro ventriculo in sinistrum sanguis resudat."

[11]Meyerhof, *Isis,* p. 116.

[12]*Ibid.,* p. 117.

[13]*Ibid.,* p. 116. The "vein in question" is the pulmonary *artery.*

arteriosa ad arteriam venosam propter spiritum."[14] But he does not describe exactly how he imagined the transition of the blood from the portal vein to the vena cava. He supports his contention of a communication between the two ventricles via the lungs by the equally unclear argument: "docet coniunctio varia, et communicatio venae arteriosae cum arteria venosa in pulmonibus."[15] But then, in a different connection, he develops a surprising hypothesis. Since Servetus believed the blood to be the seat of the soul he had to reconcile this view with the obvious physiological rôle of the nerves. This he did by assuming that in the brain the arteries, by means of the meninges, continued into the nerves. This connecting part he considered a new kind of vessel, and he thought that a similar type of vessel was also to be found in the lungs, connecting the pulmonary artery with the pulmonary vein: "Hi plexus intima omnia cerebri penetrant, et ipsos cerebri ventriculos interne succingunt, vasa illa secum complicata, et contexta servantes, usque ad nervorum origines, ut in eos sentiendi et movendi facultas inducatur. Vasa illa miraculo magno tenuissime contexta, tametsi arteriae dicantur, sunt tamen fines arteriarum, tendentes ad originem nervorum, ministerio meningum. Est novum quoddam genus vasorum. *Nam sicut in transfusione a venis in arterias, est in pulmone novum genus vasorum, ex vena et arteria:* ita in transfusione ab arteriis in nervos est novum quoddam genus vasorum ex arteriae tunica in meninge: cum praesertim meninges ipsae suas in nervis tunicas servent."[16] This suggests that Servetus visualized the blood as passing from the pulmonary artery via some kind of linking vessel, made up by vein and artery, directly into the pulmonary vein.

SUMMARY

The contrasting views of Ibn an-Nafīs and Servetus may be stated as follows:

1. Ibn an-Nafīs denies the existence of pores in the septum of the heart. Servetus is silent on this point and does not exclude the possibility of blood sweating through.

2. Ibn an-Nafīs thinks that the blood filters through the wall of the pulmonary artery, mixes with the air in the lungs, and then filters into the pulmonary vein. Servetus believes that the blood passes from the pulmonary artery into the pulmonary vein by way of intermediate vessels.

If these interpretations are correct it would mean that in two rather important anatomical details Servetus differed from Ibn an-Nafīs. This difference in its turn would give support to the belief that he had no knowledge of his Arabic predecessor.

[14]*Loc. cit.*, p. 171.
[15]*Ibid.*, p. 170.
[16]*Ibid.*, pp. 171–72. (Italics mine.)

22

Vesalius
on an Immanent Biological
Motor Force*

GALENIC DOCTRINE explained the nutrition of the parts of the body by the four natural faculties which attracted, retained, and assimilated food, and discharged the surplus.[1] These faculties served every part, as well as the body as a whole. In attracting food, the stomach, for instance, fulfilled its own desire and, at the same time, served the digestive process of the organism.

The doctrine was not altogether clear regarding the mechanisms whereby attraction, retention, and discharge were effected. Galen likened attraction to the magnet; he also spoke of an "innate tension," present in all parts of the body, though in variable strength, whereby surplus material could be passed on from the stronger to the weaker part. These then were possible explanations for the passage of nutritive material or waste products between neighboring parts. On the other hand, Galen attributed attraction, retention, and discharge to the contraction of three sets of fibres. He referred to the contractions of these fibres above all where gross movements of whole organs or of sizable parts of organs were concerned. However, Galen himself did not explicitly state the distinction between the two modes of motion. It is here that Vesalius intervened by differentiating between motions serving the nutrition of an individual part and motions serving the nutrition of other parts (or of the body as a whole). The latter motions were effected by fibres, whereas none were involved in the former.

The relevant passage from Vesalius' *Fabrica* is here offered in English translation.[2] Vesalius' view does not represent any revolutionary departure, nor shall we here inquire into possible forerunners for his view. Nevertheless, the text to be quoted contains the interesting statement that "the motions that are particular to all parts and do not aid other parts are effected completely without the help by fibres, by a force simply implanted in the parts." By this statement Vesalius recognized a principle of motion as a general property of living tissue. In doing so, he may have prepared the way for later authors who considered all parts of the body irritable.[3]

---

*Bull. Hist. Med., 1965, vol. 39, pp. 277–80.
[1]For the subsequent remarks on Galenic notions see Owsei Temkin, "The classical roots of Glisson's doctrine of irritation," *Bull. Hist. Med.*, 1964, *38*: 297–328 [Essay 23].

[2]The translation follows the first edition of the *Fabrica* of 1543. I have compared the text with that of the second edition of 1555, p. 436 f., and found a number of minor changes. The readings of 1555 have been noted where they clarify or change the meaning.

[3]Walter Pagel, "Vesalius and the pulmonary transit of veinous blood," *J. Hist. Med. and Allied*

The above statement is of interest also in relation to Vesalius' known recognition of "contractility as an immanent property of muscular tissue."[4] Vesalius believed the muscular flesh, which contained and strengthened the ligamentous fibres, to be the proper substance of the muscle, as well as the main instrument of motion.[5] In the light of our passage, one would have to assume that Vesalius thought of muscular flesh as an instrument of voluntary motion, since he allowed other motions to fibres without flesh.[6] Whether such an inference is warranted, or whether Vesalius offers statements not always reconcilable, has to be left to a systematic investigation of the *Fabrica* not attempted here. Nevertheless, as they stand, the passages further accentuate the transitional role of Vesalius' physiology between the Galenic system and its later critics.[7]

TRANSLATION[8]

The membranous tendons of the muscles, though for the most part woven from a single kind of fibre, are in the present context classed as instrumental parts, rather than as similar parts;[9] the same applies to the tunic of the vein, built of three kinds of fibres.[10] Fibres of this sort are named *ines* by the Greeks, and in substance, form, and color they correspond to the fibres of the muscles, yet in action they differ very much from them. For the latter, covered[11] by the fleshy substance of the muscles, are in charge of voluntary motion, whereas the former, not enveloped by any flesh,[12] are in charge of natural motion. Indeed, as we achieve the motions that depend on our will by the help of the fibres in the muscles, so the

---

Sc., 1964, *19*: 327–41, has elucidated the possible role of Vesalius in breaking ground for later work on the circulation of the blood.

[4]M. Roth, *Andreas Vesalius Bruxellensis*, Berlin: Reimer, 1892, p. 152. See also C. D. O'Malley, *Andreas Vesalius of Brussels: 1514–1564*, Berkeley and Los Angeles: Univ. of California Press, 1964, p. 162.

[5]*Fabrica* (1543) p. 222.

[6]According to Alexander Berg, "Die Lehre von der Faser," *Virchows Arch. f. path. Anat.*, 1942, *309*, p. 351, it was Falloppio who distinguished between fleshy fibres as instruments of voluntary motion and fleshless fibres as the means of involuntary (natural) motions. However, our passage establishes such a distinction already for Vesalius. Interestingly enough, Falloppio in his *Observationes Anatomicae*, Venice: Marcus Antonius Ulmus, 1561, fols. 114–17, stated that in the veins, the fibres existed potentially rather than actually and were incapable of active spatial movements. Among the arguments against the contraction of the fibres, Falloppio (fols. 115 v and 116 r) mentioned their lack of flesh.

[7]See above, ftn. 3, as well as Walter Pagel and Pyarali Rattansi, "Vesalius and Paracelsus," *M. Hist.*, 1964, *8*: 309–28.

[8]Andreas Vesalius, *De humani corporis fabrica libri septem*. Basel: Oporinus, 1543; book 3, ch. 1, pp. 257 *(bis)*—258 *(bis)*.

[9]"Instrumental parts" are those which serve as organs. "Similar parts" are those which are divisible into similarly constructed parts. Roughly speaking, they correspond to what we call "tissues."

[10]O'Malley, *op. cit.*, pp. 95, 166, and 294 f., discusses the controversy in which Vesalius became involved with Corti over the fibres of the veins, Falloppio's criticism of Vesalius, and the latter's final admission of his error. On Falloppio see above, ftn. 6.

[11]*Fabrica* (1555) adds: *maxima ex parte*, "to a very large extent."

[12]*Fabrica* (1555) adds: *eiusmodi*, "of this kind."

natural motions, which serve the entire body, are executed by certain fibres interwoven in organs which are servants of the whole body.[13] To be sure, not all natural motions are performed by fibres of this kind, but only attraction, retention, and expulsion of material of some sort. But at present I do not call that force attractive, retaining, and expelling which, by Nature, is implanted in every single part for its nutrition. Rather I so designate the force whereby some parts of the body fulfil a common service for the whole body. For the attraction of the food through the gullet into the stomach, of the blood from the vena cava into the right ventricle of the heart, of air from the veinous artery[14] into the left ventricle of the heart, of semen into the uterus, of blood into the veins, of spirit into the arteries is deemed[15] utterly different from the attraction by whose aid those parts entice to themselves the nourishment which is familiar to them and by which they are individually fed. Again, the excretory faculty by which the stomach propels into the intestines the food which it has prepared; by which the upper intestines in turn thrust it forth into the lower intestines; by which the heart sends blood into the lungs; and into the big artery [sends] vital spirit with the blood that runs with an impetus through the body;[16] by which one part of the vein continuously distributes blood into the next; by which the uterus discharges the fetus; and the bladder urine—[this excretory faculty] is quite different from the one by which the aforesaid parts cast off the refuse of their own nourishment. Moreover, the retention of food and drink in the stomach; of the fetus in the uterus; of urine in the bladder; of blood in the veins; and of spirit[17] in the heart is considered utterly different from the retention by whose help the heart, the stomach, the bladder, and the uterus preserve for themselves, and retain, their familiar nutriment.

Accordingly, the motions that are particular to all parts[18] and do not aid other parts are effected completely without the help of fibres, by a force simply implanted in the parts. But the parts which must take upon themselves attraction, retention, or expulsion, of help to, and useful for, other parts, or even for the whole body, claim for themselves certain fibres for this function by whose help they accomplish it. And as there are three kinds of motion, so three kinds of fibres have been constructed[19] by Nature: viz. straight, oblique, and transverse.

[13]See my comments above concerning Vesalius' view on muscular contraction.
[14]I.e., the pulmonary vein.
[15]*Fabrica* (1543): *censetur; Fabrica* (1555): *mihi censetur,* which stresses the subjective element.
[16]This refers to the pulsation of the arteries.
[17]*Fabrica* (1555) adds: *ac sanguinis pariter,* "and blood as well."
[18]*Fabrica* (1555) adds: *similiter,* "in like manner."
[19]*Fabrica* (1543): *constructum est; Fabrica* (1555): *constructum esse credimus,* "we believe to have been constructed." Here again (see ftn. 15 above), Vesalius introduces a subjective element.

23

The Classical Roots
of Glisson's Doctrine
of Irritation*

THE HISTORY of physiological irritability is usually traced back to Francis Glisson (1597–1677). On the authority of Albrecht von Haller, we even consider him responsible for the term *irritabilitas* (irritability),[1] which he introduced as a biological concept. "Francis Glisson, who discovered the active force of the elements of our bodies, was the first who invented the word *Irritability*, which he attributes to a *natural perception*, that is not accompanied with any sensation, and depends upon Archaeus who is the framer of his own body."[2] In this statement Haller clearly refers to Glisson's *Tractatus de ventriculo et intestinis* of 1677.[3] Here indeed, Glisson used the word irritability to denote a biological property not dependent on consciousness or on the nervous system. Glisson's ideas on irritability as expressed in the *Tractatus* have been analyzed and interpreted so often, that we need not present them here.[4]

In crediting Glisson with the invention of the word *irritabilitas*, Haller made a mistake which, as far as I can see, has been shared by medical historians.[5] Actually, the word was used by Apuleius in the second century A.D. to denote the emotion of anger which Plato had placed in the heart.[6] Moreover, connecting irritability with the late *Tractatus de ventriculo* of 1677, Haller neglected to pay attention to the occurrence of the same word in Glisson's *Anatomia hepatis*, which appeared in 1654.[7] This is all the more

---

Bull. Hist. Med., 1964, vol. 38, pp. 297–328.

[1] I repeated this erroneous notion in my introduction to the re-edition of the English translation of Haller's *A Dissertation on the Sensible and Irritable Parts of Animals,* Baltimore: The Johns Hopkins Press, 1936 (see p. 2).

[2] Haller, *ibid.,* p. 42 f.

[3] This is made even more obvious in Haller's ensuing analysis of Glisson's notion. In his *Bibliotheca anatomica,* t. 1, Tiguri: Orell, Gessner, Fuessli, 1774, p. 452, Haller likewise associates Glisson's contribution to irritability with the *Tractatus* of 1677 and explicitly states: "ipsum demum nomen excogitavit."

[4] Apart from the usual text books, I mention here: G. H. Meyer, "Glisson's Irritabilitäts- und Sensibilitätslehre," *Arch. f. d. ges. Med.,* 1843, 5: 1–17.—Ch. Daremberg, *Histoire des sciences médicales,* t. 2, Paris: J.-B. Baillière, 1870, pp. 650–72.—Alexander Berg, "Die Lehre von der Faser als Form- und Funktionselement des Organismus," *Virchows Arch. f. path. Anat.,* 1942, *309:* 333–460 (see pp. 386–90).—E. Bastholm, *The History of Muscle Physiology,* Copenhagen: Munksgaard, 1950. The dissertation of C. Müller, *Francisci Glissonii theoremata de perceptione, appetitu et motu,* Berlin, 1846, which Daremberg, *op. cit.,* p. 652 ftn., cites, unfortunately, was not available to me.

[5] Even Daremberg, *op. cit.,* pp. 650–51, is not clear as to where the noun first appears.

[6] Apuleius, *De dogmate Platonis* I, 18 (*Opera omnia,* ed. G. F. Hildebrand, pars II, Leipzig, 1842, p. 210).

[7] I have had at my disposal the edition published in Amsterdam by Johannes a Ravensteyn in

---

remarkable, since Haller did not claim a total neglect of the *phenomena* of irritability before Glisson.[8] Modern historians are well aware of the fact that Glisson, in 1654, expressed opinions on irritability which he modified subsequently,[9] till they reached the form given to them in the *Tractatus de ventriculo* of 1677.[10] In particular Glisson's views on the anatomy and physiology of the biliary vessels have received careful attention.[11]

Beginning with Glisson's views on biliary discharge, I shall attempt, first, to analyze his ideas about irritability as expressed in the *Anatomia hepatis*. I shall then try to relate these ideas to traditional, notably Galenic, physiology. "The classical roots of Glisson's doctrine of irritation" has been chosen as a title because irritation, rather than irritability in the strict sense, is the guiding concept in this phase of the general history of irritability.[12,13]

I. "IRRITABILITY" IN THE *Anatomia hepatis*

1

Glisson's notions of irritability in the *Anatomia hepatis* are mainly related to the discharge of bile. He divides what he calls vessels of the liver into gall bladder (*vesicula fellea*), cystic duct (*meatus cysticus*), hepatic duct (*porus*

1659. All references to the *Anatomia hepatis* are to this edition. An interesting analysis of the work has just been published by Stanley E. Bradley, "The splanchnic circulation," in Alfred P. Fishman and Dickinson W. Richards, *Circulation of the Blood: Men and Ideas*, New York: Oxford Univ. Press, 1964, pp. 659–65.

[8]Haller, *Bibliotheca anatomica, loc. cit.:* "De irritabilitate nemo ante Glissonium rectius cogitavit . . . ." which allows some earlier thought.

[9]This modification leads via Glisson's *Tractatus de natura substantiae energetica, seu de vita naturae*, London: Flesher, 1672. The role of this book in the development of Glisson's thought will not be discussed here. It is not directly concerned with irritability, much as it may have helped Glisson to work out a philosophical fundament for the ideas of the *Tractatus de ventriculo et intestinis* before he published the latter. For analysis of the work, see Henri Marion, "Francis Glisson," *Revue philosophique*, 1882, *14*: 121–55. This is supposed to be a French rendering of the author's *Franciscus Glissonius quid de natura substantiae sive vita naturae senserit*, Thesis, Paris 1880 (not available to me); see E. Gley, *Essais de philosophie et d'histoire de la biologie*, Paris: Masson, 1900, p. 3, note 1. Heinrich Heinrichs, *Die Ueberwindung der Autoritaet Galens durch Denker der Renaissancezeit*, Bonn: Haustein, 1914 (Renaissance und Philosophie, 12. Heft), contains an important examination of Glisson's two *Tractatus* of 1672 and 1677 respectively. (I am indebted to Dr. Robert Multhauf for having drawn my attention to this book). Walter Pagel, "The reaction to Aristotle in seventeenth century biological thought," in E. Ashworth Underwood (ed.), *Science, Medicine, and History*, Essays in the Evolution of Scientific Thought and Medical Practice Written in Honour of Charles Singer, vol. 1, London and New York: Oxford Univ. Press, 1953, pp. 489–509, has examined Glisson's work from the point of view of Aristotelian vitalism.

[10]Among others see Daremberg, *op. cit.* and E. F. Adolph, "Early concepts of physiological regulations," *Physiol. Rev.*, 1961, *41*: 737–70 (see p. 752).

[11]Edward A. Boyden, "The pars intestinalis of the common bile duct, as viewed by the older anatomists (Vesalius, Glisson, Bianchi, Vater, Haller, Santorini, etc.)," *Anat. Rec.*, 1936, *66*: 217–32.—[Editorial] "Glisson on gall bladder pain," *J. Hist. Med. & Allied Sc.*, 1955, *10*: 112–13 (contains a translation by B. L. Ullman of ch. 30 of the *Anatomia hepatis*).—Adolph, *op. cit.*,—Erik Nordenskiöld, *The History of Biology*, New York: Tudor Publishing Co., 1942, p. 148.

[12]This includes the spectrum of notions related to irritability without necessary occurrence of the noun.

[13]The present article is intended as an installment toward such a general history of irritability, on which I am engaged; see Owsei Temkin, "Scientific medicine and historical research," *Perspectives Biol. & Med.*, 1959, *3*: 70–85 (p. 82 f.).

bilarius or *ductus hepaticus*),[14] and common duct (*ductus communis*).[15] These vessels have a proper coat, the description of which reads in part:

The tunica propria of these vessels also has fibres of every kind; viz. straight, transverse, and oblique. Unless I am mistaken, the oblique ones are more copious in the gall bladder, the transverse ones, however, in the other vessels. With the help of these fibres, all these vessels are ready to contract more or less, as well as to dilate, a matter which will be discussed at greater length later.

Finally, this tunic (after the fashion of other fibrous parts) is endowed with veins, arteries, and nerves. . . .[16] And, from its having nerves, we conclude that these same parts are sensible and subject to pain and irritation [*irritationi*].[17]

In particular, the gall bladder is endowed with "a small nerve, from the sixth pair,[18] by whose help this part must be considered sensible [*sensibilis*]."[19]

The gall bladder obtains bile through the *truncus* which has its roots in the liver;[20] the hepatic duct obtains bile from its small ramifications in the liver.[21] At the juncture of gall bladder and cystic duct, an *anulus fibrosus* is to be found, which can be assigned to either the bladder or to the duct. The *anulus* narrows the duct and thereby prevents incidental emptying of the bladder.[22] Further, the oblique insertion of the common duct into the duodenum acts like a valve, impeding regurgitation of bile and the entrance of any fluid from the intestinal canal into the biliary vessels.[23]

On the basis of the above anatomical and physiological data, Glisson envisages the following mechanism regulating the flow of bile from the gall bladder.[24] The presence of the *anulus fibrosus* makes it impossible for any humor to flow out of the gall bladder, unless it be expelled by some contraction or compression of the bladder.[25] This raises the question as to what causes contraction of the gall bladder. Glisson assumes a continuous flow of bile from the liver to the bladder, which under normal conditions is moderately full.[26] However, beyond this point a process comes into play which

[14]*Anatomia hepatis,* p. 169: "Dicitur canalis, sive porus *bilarius;* item meatus, vel ductus *hepaticus. . . .*"

[15]*Ibid.,* p. 159.

[16]A few remarks about the blood vessels have been omitted.

[17]*Ibid.,* p. 160 f.

[18]The vagus nerve of modern terminology.

[19]*Ibid.,* p. 165. The nerve supply to the liver and pain related to the liver are discussed in chapter 30, which has been translated by Professor Ullman (see above note 11).

[20]*Anatomia hepatis,* pp. 162 ff., 165, and 193. The *truncus* enters the gall bladder near the *anulus fibrosus,* about which see below.

[21]*Ibid.,* pp. 165, 171.

[22]*Ibid.,* p. 167. Boyden, *op. cit.,* p. 224, note 10, identifies the *anulus fibrosus* with "the so-called 'Tobiens Sphincter' (1853) or the 'collum-cysticus sphincter' recently predicated by Luetkens ('26)."

[23]*Anatomia hepatis,* ch. 16; pp. 174 and 175. Boyden, *op. cit.,* has translated and analyzed Glisson's description of the insertion of the common duct into the duodenum and, p. 221, has particularly stressed Glisson's assignment of "ring-like fibres" to this part, now called the sphincter of Oddi, which Glisson saw "contract by spontaneous motion."

[24]Cf. Adolph, *op. cit.*

[25]*Anatomia hepatis,* ch. 20; p. 213.

[26]*Ibid.,* ch. 20, *Propositio prima;* p. 212: "Vesicula fellea, suapte natura, et quandiu integra sanitate fruimur, semper moderate plena est."

Glisson describes under the proposition: "The gall bladder, when more than usually filled, and irritated [*irritata*], is relieved through the cystic duct."[27]

... if the gall bladder is uncommonly distended and is stuffed with more humor (than is its use and wont, or than it can easily bear), it is by necessity compelled to contract strongly, and to break down the restraint of its *anulus* and to emit the surcharge of the humor until it has regained its moderate fulness. For when this new burden[28] (the cause of the aforementioned irritation)[29] has been removed, the bladder spontaneously rests and permits the *anulus fibrosus* to draw together again and to prevent the exit of the remaining humor.

Immediately afterwards, Glisson supplies a general explanation of the above action, which, because of the importance of the terminology used, will also be cited.

The general reason of this is that all sensitive [*sensitivae*] parts (among which the bladder is numbered, since it receives a little nerve from the sixth pair) are irritable [*irritabiles*]. Therefore, as soon as they are distended beyond their wont, or more than they can bear conveniently, or are otherwise burdened or provoked [*lacessuntur*], they enter into immediate opposition. If the parts thus irritated [*irritatae*] are hollow, membranous, and fibrous, their resistance must needs occur through a contraction of all fibres, until their cavity is reduced to a smaller compass and some part at least of the humor contained therein is removed to the outside, all of which holds true of the gall bladder.[30]

At the insertion of the common duct into the intestine, similar events take place. As long as the insertion is closed, the bile flows back into the gall bladder.

This return goes on until the quantity or quality of the humor powerfully irritates [*irritaverit*] the vessels so as to effect excretion. When this happens, the oblique insertion is forced to cede to the greater force, and it permits the vessels to deposit what is burdensome [*molestum*] into the intestines, whereupon it soon closes again.[31]

The resistance of the insertion is not easily overcome. Hence a relatively large amount of bile must accumulate, and the discharge into the intestines does not take place by a constant trickle; rather the bile enters at intervals and then in a large quantity.[32] Moreover, a number of pathological conditions may change the picture. In the first place, fibres and tunics of the intestines may evince a certain tenseness,[33] as is experienced after an astringent potion. On the other hand, the fibres (especially of the sphincter

---

[27]*Ibid.*, ch. 20, *Propositio quinta;* p. 220: "Vesicula fellea plus solito impleta, atque irritata, per meatum cysticum exoneratur."

[28]*Ibid.*, p. 221: "Sublato enim novo hoc onere," i.e., the surplus bile.

[29]*Irritationis.*

[30]*Ibid.*, p. 221.

[31]*Ibid.*, ch. 20, *Propositio nona;* p. 230.

[32]*Ibid.*, ch. 20, Propositions nine and ten.

[33]*Ibid.*, ch. 20, *Propositio octava*, p. 228: "Fibrarum, tunicarumque intestini *tensitas* (nam sic loqui libet) constrictionem hanc facile roboraverit" (italics in the text). Glisson used the word *tensitas* repeatedly in his *De rachitide sive morbo puerili tractatus*, the first edition of which appeared in 1650 (I have used the third edition, Leyden, 1671).

Oddi, as we would say) may be in a state of weakness and relaxation. Then the discharge takes place drop by drop, as in persons affected by a paralysis of the urinary bladder, when the urine escapes slowly and imperceptibly all the time. Or the biliary vessels may be excessively irritated, in which case a condition analogous to stranguria or tenesmus prevails.[34]

The *Anatomia hepatis* was not the first book in which Glisson used the concept of irritation to explain organic self-regulation. In the treatise *De rachitide* of 1650 Glisson had discussed the factors that accounted for the distribution of the blood in the peripheral parts of the body. Among these factors he counted the irritation of the heart as well as of the arteries. The blood was thrust by the arteries into the peripheral parts with a certain pressure which gave rise to counter pressure in the receiving parts. This resistance provoked (*proritari*) the arteries to increase the pressure and make the pulse stronger. Where the resistance was weak, a strong pulse was not likely to be found. If the resistance was greater, without however subduing the arterial pressure, the pulse became more vigorous, other things being equal. Glisson exemplified this theory by reference to what happened when parts of the body became cold or hot owing to climatic conditions, or when the body moved, or when its parts were inflamed or contused. But strong resistance of the parts might yet fail to irritate the arteries effectively. In that case, resistance dulled the impetus of the blood instead of intensifying it.[35] Irritation, then, was a principle of which Glisson made operational use as early as the *De rachitide.* Its theoretical analysis was left to the *Anatomia hepatis,* to which we have to return.

The very last chapter of the *Anatomia hepatis* deals with "the action and use of the lymph ducts or aqueous channels."[36] This chapter includes Glisson's speculations on the nutritive fluid carried by the nerves. The doctrine of nervous fluid, widespread though it was in the seventeenth century, concerns us only in so far as Glisson makes irritation the propelling force of this fluid. Irritation, he argues, takes place from plenitude, from acrimony, and from *vigoratio* of the nerves,[37] a term which Daremberg renders by *mise en activité,*[38] and which we may translate by "activation."

Plenitude, being always molesting, necessarily stimulates (*exstimulet*) the part it burdens, an idea which we have already met in the discussion of the discharge of bile from the gall bladder.

Acrimony of humors easily produces irritation. Normally, nutritive juice is not mordant. However, in sickness it can happen that this juice becomes

---

[34]*Anatomia hepatis,* Propositio decima; p. 232: "Fallit iterum, si vasa fellea ad excretionem moliendam summopere irritata fuerint. Idem enim tunc temporis ductui huic versus intestina contingit, quod in *stranguria* vesicae urinariae collo evenire solet, aut sphincteri ani in *tenesmo,* sive continuo desidendi conatu."

[35]*De rachitide,* ch. 10; pp. 94–103.

[36]*Anatomia hepatis,* ch. 45; p. 482: "De actione et usu lymphaeductuum, sive canalium aquosorum."

[37]*Ibid.,* p. 547 ff.

[38]Daremberg, *op. cit.,* p. 664.

acrid and, by plucking (*vellicando*) the nerves, induces fluxes. Finally, "activation [*vigoratio*] of the nerves (for we cannot express it otherwise) necessarily expels any humor that may have been in them."[39] This activation can have three causes: perception (or sensation), desire (*appetitus*), and muscular movement.[40] A sense of pain, as well as a sensation of pleasure, activates the nerves. Desire too, if violent, "imparts strength to the nerves and provokes them [*irritat*] to motion, just as fear produces trepidation and, at the same time, causes a cold sweat. Perhaps the other psychic dispositions too stir up [*incitantur*] the nerves through all kinds of provocations [*irritamentis*]."[41] Movement and exercise heat our bodies and thus add tension (*tensio*) and strength.

2

We have now become acquainted with the manner in which Glisson operates with such words as "stimulate," "irritable," "irritation," "to irritate," "irritated." A large part of the terminology which is still used today in connection with the doctrine of irritability is represented, except the word itself. However, the absence of this abstract noun is no impediment to Glisson's explanations, which take it for granted that fibres and organs are "irritable."

Glisson obviously assumes that his readers will understand his diction. Where terms that are new or unusual occur, he excuses himself, as for instance in the case of *tensitas* and *vigoratio*.[42]

Though Glisson's terminology concerns physiological events, it is frankly psychological and even anthropomorphic.[43] The various parts behave like irritated people: they react because they have been "burdened" or "provoked."[44]

But with all this, Glisson cannot suppress a doubt regarding the relationship of irritable part and irritation. He tries to resolve this doubt in chapter forty-four, presenting the following argument.[45]

Subsequent to the intake of cathartics or emetics, a large amount of bile is evacuated, an amount much larger than that evacuated at other times. Nobody doubts that this difference presupposes irritation of the biliary vessels. However, this irritation could not take place if the biliary vessels were deprived of all sense. "Indeed, all irritation indicates the existence of perception: for whatever is provoked is immediately aroused into freeing itself from the injury that has been inflicted." But perception requires the

---

[39]*Anatomia hepatis*, p. 548: "Nervorum *vigoratio* (nam sic loqui cogimur). . . ."

[40]*Ibid.*, p. 549: "Tres autem sunt hujust vigorationis causae: nimirum *perceptio*, sive *sensatio; appetitus;* et motus *musculorum*."

[41]*Ibid.*,

[42]See above, notes 33 and 39.

[43]Marion, *op. cit.*, p. 127: "C'est sous les traits du plus naïf anthropomorphisme que sa théorie apparaît pour la première fois dans l'*Anatomie du foie*."

[44]See above, note 13.

[45]Because of the importance of this chapter a translation will be published in a subsequent issue of this *Bulletin* [This has not been done.].

presence of nerves. Without nerves, perception would not be possible, nor the subsequent motion which is implied in irritation. The argument can also be built on the anatomical fact that gall bladder and hepatic duct are endowed with nerves. Parts so endowed are sensitive and motive, hence irritable. "Indeed, whatever perceives an injury inflicted from some other source and engages in ridding itself of it will properly be said to be irritated." Therefore, the biliary vessels are "capable of irritation" (*irritationis capaces*).

This is a crucial point in Glisson's position, reached by 1654 as far as his doctrine of irritation[46] is concerned. From what we heard about the "activation" of nerves and the three causes involved, we obtain an approximate picture of how Glisson visualized the activation of the biliary vessels. Apparently he had no difficulty in assigning perception and motion to the same nerve, since he considered them two stages of one phenomenon: irritation. However, he ran into a difficulty in postulating nervous action for a bodily process that takes place involuntarily and unconsciously. Motion mediated by nerves was usually considered psychic motion, i.e., exercised through the will. Glisson expressly says that the motion of the biliary vessels is not to be interpreted as psychic motion. What he has in mind is the kind of motion "we find in the stomach and intestines whereby a harmful thing is expelled."

In thus referring to the expulsion of harmful agents by the stomach and intestines, Glisson again must have counted on some understanding on the part of his readers. At the same time he was referring to the activity of organs with which his *Tractatus de ventriculo* of 1677 was to deal. In this treatise the fibres were to be assigned "irritability" as their natural property. There is here an obvious connection between the two books. The difference in Glisson's position is characterized by the role assigned to the term irritability when it finally appears in the *Anatomia hepatis*.

Irritation, Glisson reasons, can be original or by consensus with other parts showing original irritation. In view of his previous discussion of original irritation of the biliary vessels, he now concentrates on irritation by consensus. It involves the stomach and the intestines. If the latter organs are excessively irritated so that vomiting or diarrhea ensues, bile is also discharged in the vomited material or the stool. The explanation lies in the common nerve supply of these organs. In particular, the consensus affects that part of the hepatic nerve which enters into the common capsule of the porta. The biliary vessels are stimulated and compressed, and the vena portae is goaded into effecting a quicker transport of the abundant amount of blood.

The advantages of this irritation by consensus are threefold. First, the participation of the biliary vessels effects a beneficial general evacuation, and the abstersive power of bile facilitates ridding the body of all kinds of impurities. Second, in cases where the biliary vessels have become insensi-

---

[46]Marion, *op. cit.*, p. 128 rightly states that the concept of "irritation rather than of irritability" predominates in the *Anatomia hepatis*.

ble, their irritation can still be brought about by their consensus with the stomach and intestines. "This kind of irritability by consensus (if I may say so) has not been granted to them in vain."[47] Finally, the consensus operates in both directions. The healthy irritation of the biliary vessels can impart itself to stomach and intestines, which now are better disposed to eliminate the plentiful supply of bile.

Here then, for the first and only time, as far as I am aware, the term *irritabilitas* occurs in the *Anatomia hepatis.* As elsewhere,[48] Glisson apologizes for the strange word, though the Latin text does not allow a clear decision whether the parenthesis refers to "irritability" only, or to "irritability by consensus." However, this question is of minor importance, because the introduction of the noun merely refers to one particular abnormal condition and is mainly a matter of convenience. Nevertheless, the appearance of the noun is characteristic for Glisson's scholastic turn of mind. Having presumed that certain parts were "capable of irritation," he proceeded to establish a "capability of being irritated," when the context made the use of such a term convenient.

II. THE GALENIC DOCTRINE OF IRRITATION

As Glisson sees it, irritation is the experience by some part of the body of a molesting sensation with ensuing attempts to remove the offending agent. In the *Anatomia hepatis,* Glisson believes this sensation (or perception) to be mediated by nerves which also mediate the movements towards removal of the agent. In the *Tractatus de ventriculo,* a "natural perception," independent of nerves, is assumed. Consequently, the parts of the organism, especially fibres, by themselves are assigned the capacity of being irritated, and this capacity is called "irritability." Glisson thereby generalizes a term introduced, but casually, in the *Anatomia hepatis.* Whatever philosophical reorientation was needed to bring about this change in outlook, "irritation" remains a central phenomenon for Glisson.[49]

The position which Glisson held in 1654 is of importance, because "irritation" and allied terms were presented in a manner close to the general understanding of the time. Glisson was justified in counting on his readers' familiarity with such words as irritation, irritable, to irritate, to stimulate, because these notions were imbedded in the Galenic physiology in which he and most of his medical contemporaries had been reared.

1

In Galenic parlance, the bile of the present context is yellow bile (in contrast to black bile).[50] This bile is notoriously sharp and biting and exerts

---

[47]*Anatomia hepatis,* p. 481: "Ideoque istiusmodi per consensum irritabilitas (ut sic dicam) haud frustra illis concessa est."

[48]See above, notes 33, 39, and 42.

[49]R. S. Peters (ed.), Brett's *History of Psychology,* New York: Macmillan, 1962, p. 613: "Glisson obscured his teaching by speaking of this irritability as a perception of irritation...."

[50]For Galen's teachings on liver and gall bladder, see Nikolaus Mani, *Die historischen Grund-*

a cleansing action on all organs.[51] Galen reasons that if much bile were introduced into the stomach, the latter, stung by the sharpness of the bile, would undergo a violent peristaltic movement, and the undigested food would be expelled through the cardia (i.e., by vomiting) or through the pylorus.[52] In reality, the bile enters the duodenum[53] and purges the intestines of the harmful phlegmatic humor produced by them and by the stomach.[54] But when *pure* bile passes the intestines, they become ulcerated, corroded, and rotten.[55]

The mechanism whereby the gall bladder is filled and emptied, as well as the underlying theory of this mechanism, is discussed in Galen's *On the Natural Faculties*.[56] The gall bladder functions according to the same principles as do the stomach, intestines, the urinary bladder, the uterus, and other parts.

Thus when the stomach is sufficiently filled with the food and has absorbed and stored away the most useful part of it in its own coats, it then rejects the rest like an alien burden. The same happens to the bladders,[57] when the matter attracted into them begins to give trouble either because it distends them through its quantity or stings[58] them by its quality.[59]

In the uterus, miscarriage as well as normal delivery is explained on a similar basis, so that Galen can sum up by claiming that

In all organs, then, both their natural effects and their disorders and maladies plainly take place on analogous lines, some so clearly and manifestly as to need no demonstration, and others less plainly, although not entirely unrecognizable to those who are willing to pay attention.[60]

In the stomach, the uterus, and the urinary bladder, the mordant action of the contents is obvious because manifested to our conscious feeling.

---

lagen der Leberforschung, 1. Teil, Basel-Stuttgart: Schwabe, 1959 (Basler Veröffentlichungen zur Geschichte der Medizin und Biologie, Fasc. IX), especially pp. 65 f. and 73–77.

[51]Galen, *On the Use of Parts*, V, 4; ed. G. Helmreich, vol. 1, Leipzig: Teubner, 1907, p. 261; French translation in Ch. Daremberg, *Oeuvres anatomiques, physiologiques et médicales de Galien*, (hereinafter cited as Daremberg), 2 vols., Paris: Baillière, 1854–1856, vol. 1, p. 346. For the whole subject of Galen's theory of digestion and nutrition, see Theod. Meyer-Steineg, "Studien zur Physiologie des Galenos," *Sudhoffs Arch. f. Gesch. d. Med.*, 1913, 6: 417–48.

[52]Galen, *ibid.;* ed. Helmreich, pp. 261 f.; Daremberg, *ibid.*

[53]*Ibid.;* ed. Helmreich, p. 259. Daremberg, p. 344, ftn. 1, points out Galen's inconsistencies in locating the ending of the common bile duct. In *On the Natural Faculties*, III, 5; Loeb ed. p. 244, Galen states that the gall bladder eliminates the bile daily into the stomach.

[54]Galen, *On the Use of Parts*, V, 4; ed. Helmreich, p. 259; Daremberg, p. 344 f.

[55]*Ibid.*, V, 10; ed. Helmreich, p. 279; Daremberg, p. 363. (Italics mine.)

[56]The passages are selected *ad hoc* and do not follow the systematic order of the book; nor do they exhaust Galen's theory of irritation and its application to physiology, pathology, and therapy; cf. above, ftn. 13.

[57]The gall bladder and the urinary bladder.

[58]*Daknon*, i.e., biting or stinging. This is one of many plastic expressions for irritating Galen and other ancients used. We too, of course, speak of mustard as "biting" and of alcohol as "stinging" when applied to a wound. The Greek equivalent for the Latin *irritare* is *erethizein*, a term also used by Galen in the present context, e.g., when he says that a dead fetus dissolved into bad ichors "irritates [erethizēi] and bites [daknēi] the coat of the uterus." (*On the Natural Faculties*, III, 12. English translation by Arthur John Brock, Loeb Classical Library, p. 286–87.)

[59]Galen, *On the Natural Faculties*, III, 12; Loeb ed., p. 285 (Brock's translation).

[60]*Ibid.*, p. 287.

This does not apply, however, in the case of the bladder alongside the liver, whence it is clear that it possesses fewer nerves than do the other organs.[61] Here too, however, at least the physiologist must discover an analogy. For since it was shown that the gall-bladder attracts its own special juice, so as to be often found full, and that it discharges it soon after, this desire to discharge must be either due to the fact that it is burdened by the quantity or that the bile has changed in quality to pungent and acrid.[62]

Galen claims that bile, in contrast to food and even to urine, changes rapidly, a contention which conflicts with claims made elsewhere.[63] At any rate, he concludes:

Now, if there be clear evidence in relation to the uterus, stomach, and intestines, as well as to the urinary bladder, that there is either some distention, irritation [*dēxis*], or burden inciting each of these organs to elimination, there is no difficulty in imagining this in the case of the gall-bladder also, as well as in the other organs,—to which obviously the arteries and veins also belong.[64]

Anatomically, the gall bladder is equipped with the means for contraction. Though, according to *On the Use of Parts*, it possesses only one tunic, this tunic is provided with longitudinal, transverse, and oblique fibres. The transverse fibres, in particular, serve expulsion; when all three kinds of fibres contract simultaneously, the whole organ becomes contracted.[65]

2

The above passages from Galen's *On the Use of Parts* and *On the Natural Faculties* show far-reaching parallels with Glisson's views on the nature of the bile and its evacuation into the intestinal canal. Galen's presentation easily fitted into the language of the Renaissance. Vesalius, discussing the place where bile enters the intestinal canal, argues that the stomach would not have been the right place of entry.

For if the bile flowed into the stomach, the latter (as Galen rightly affirms) would be perpetually provoked to discharge by the mordacity of the bile.[66]

As it is, the bile "irritating and biting at the intestines, . . . urges and stimulates them to discharge the faeces."[67] Similarly, Fernelius, speaking of the common duct, considers it the organ

[61] In *On the Use of Parts*, V, 8; ed. Helmreich, p. 274; Daremberg, p. 359, Galen states that the gall bladder receives a branch from the nerve supplying the liver, but that this branch is thin and hard to see.

[62] *On the Natural Faculties*, III, 12; Loeb ed., pp. 287–89 (Brock's translation).

[63] *On the Use of Parts*, V, 10; ed. Helmreich, p. 280; Daremberg, p. 364, Galen says that even after the death of an animal the gall bladder can be removed and inspected for a long time without showing any change and that nature rightly endowed the liver and gall bladder with little feeling (and very small nerves) because the residues they harbored did not incommodate them.

[64] *On the Natural Faculties*, III, 12; Loeb ed., p. 289 (Brock's translation).

[65] *On the Use of Parts*, V, 11; ed. Helmreich, p. 282 f.; see Daremberg's footnote, p. 366.

[66] Vesalius, *Fabrica*, Basel: Oporinus, 1543, lib. V, c. viii; p. 510: "Nam si ventriculo bilis influeret, tum ille (uti Galenus recte affirmat) huius mordacitate perpetuo ad excernendum iritaretur. . . ."

[67] *Ibid.* "Deinde intestina iritans et mordens, ad faeces excernendas invitat, et stimulat. . . ." For this passage I have used the translation of Boyden, *op. cit.*, p. 220, ftn. 9.

whereby the excess of bile is thrust out and expelled. For by it the intestines are wont to be aroused and provoked to the ejection of the faeces, as if a sharp goad had been employed, while the faeces themselves are tinged with a yellowish color.[68]

Guided by the example of the gall bladder, we can now inquire into the premises on which Galen based his explanation of the discharging mechanism of various organs. We must remember that, in contrast to Glisson's *Anatomia hepatis*, Galen, in the writings cited, faced the task of elaborating principles that would hold good for many organs, of which the gall bladder was but one. In particular, he devoted much attention to the stomach and intestines, which were to become the subject of Glisson's later work.

Galen believed the organism and its parts to be endowed with a discharging faculty to which he gave various names, such as "propellent," "excretory,"[69] "secretive."[70] It is the fourth of the natural faculties that serve the nutrition of the organs. Each part attracts the food it needs, retains it, alters (assimilates) it, and propels the surplus.[71] In so far as the discharging faculty expels those things which are foreign to the organs,[72] it has equal significance for physiology, pathology, and therapeutics. Physiologically, it serves the elimination of waste material as well as the delivery of the fetus. Since waste material by itself is foreign to the body and harmful unless removed, there is an obvious connection between physiological and pathological conditions. In disease, the discharging faculty has to rid the body of noxious substances, thereby leading to the crisis.[73] Miscarriage, abortion, normal delivery, as well as the expulsion of a disintegrating fetus, are all explained by the activation of the discharging faculty.[74] "In all organs, then, both their natural effects and their disorders and maladies plainly take place on analogous lines."[75]

Just as there is a connection between physiological and pathological conditions, so also there exists a connection between pathology and therapy in the discharge of material. To illustrate the forcefulness of the discharging faculty, Galen points to cases of ileus where intestinal content, to be vomited, has to traverse the small bowel, the pylorus, stomach, and esophagus.[76] In this disease "the inflamed intestine is unable to support

[68]Fernelius, *Physiologia*, I, c. 7; in *Universa medicina*, Geneva: Samuel de Tournes, 1679, p. 13 f.: "... quo bilis exuperantia exigitur atque expellitur. Haec enim solent intestina ad faecum dejectionem quasi adhibito stimulo acui et irritari, ipsae autem faeces subflavo colore infici."

[69]For instance, *On the Natural Faculties*, III, 3, Loeb ed., p. 230, line 6 (*proōstikē*), line 16 (*apokritikē*), line 25 (*apokritikē te kai proōstikē*).

[70]*Ibid.*, III, 5; Loeb ed., p. 244: *ekkritikē*.

[71]For a summary, see *On the Natural Faculties*, III, 8; Loeb ed., p. 274; see also Meyer-Steineg, *op. cit.*, above, ftn. 51. The four faculties as a basis of Galenic physiology and pathology have recently been discussed by Lester King, *The Growth of Medical Thought*, Chicago: Univ. of Chicago Press, 1963, p. 43 ff.

[72]Galen, *On the Natural Faculties*, III, 5 beginning; Loeb ed., p. 244.

[73]*Ibid.*, I, 13; Loeb ed., p. 60, see also Brock's comment, p. 61, ftn. 3.

[74]*Ibid.*, III, 12; Loeb ed., p. 286; see also above, ftn. 58.

[75]*Ibid.*, Loeb ed., p. 287 (Brock's translation).

[76]*Ibid.*, III, 13; Loeb ed., p. 298.

either the weight or the acridity of the waste substances and so does its best to excrete them, in fact to drive them as far away as possible." [77] What is here done by nature can also be done therapeutically, for instance by purgative drugs: in both cases, internal irritants (*dierethizonta*) account for the movements. [78] Another example may be taken from Galen's *Hygiene*. When food begins to become spoiled in the stomach, passage of the spoiled substance is most salutary. "But in persons in whom it does not pass, one must provoke [*erethisteon*] passage by means of painless cathartics." [79]

We may then say that for Galen provocation of the discharging faculty explains physiological, pathological, and therapeutic phenomena of the same order as those with which Glisson is dealing. It is, therefore, hardly surprising to find Glisson also thinking of this faculty. He says of bile that it "may simply pluck the excretory faculty of the bile vessels because of its acrimony or its amount," [80] and that it possesses qualities whereby "it goads the excretory faculty of the intestines." [81]

To this must now be added that the psychological and anthropological way of thinking notable in Glisson prevails in Galen too. Galen claims that the phenomena

testify that there must exist in almost all parts of the animal a certain inclination towards, or, so to speak, an appetite for their own special quality, and an aversion to, or, as it were, a hatred of the foreign quality. And it is natural that when they feel an inclination they should attract, and that when they feel aversion they should expel. [82]

In short, for both Galen and Glisson irritation as a biological phenomenon is akin to the psychological reaction of man in a state of provocation and anger.

3

Up to a point, Galenic physiology allowed Glisson to count on his reader's understanding of his explanation of the physiology of the gall bladder. Galen's doctrine of the discharging faculty offered the common ground. [83]

[77]*Ibid.*, Loeb ed., p. 303 (Brock's translation).

[78]*Ibid.*, Loeb ed., p. 300.

[79]Galen, *De sanitate tuenda*, VI, 7; ed. K. Koch, p. 182 (Corpus Medicorum Graecorum V, 4, 2, Leipzig and Berlin: Teubner, 1923).

[80]Glisson, *Anatomia hepatis*, p. 160: "Sin vero bilis cum impetu descenderit; aut vasorum felleorum excretricem facultatem, ob acrimoniam sui, aut copiam, plurimum vellicaverit. . . ." Similarly, p. 201. P. 230: "Alioquin enim, nisi vis excretoria in istis vasis [i.e., biliary vessels], obliquae insertionis in contrarium molimini praepolleret, natura utique suis rebus male consuluisset."

[81]*Ibid.*, p. 414: " . . . excretricem intestinorum facultatem extimulat."

[82]Galen, *On the Natural Faculties*, III, 6; Loeb ed., pp. 247–49 (Brock's translation). Brock, p. 248, ftn. 1, points out the "use of psychological terms in biology."

[83]Daremberg, *op. cit.*, (ftn. 4), p. 659, speaks of "le souvenir des facultés naturelles de Galien qu'on retrouve dans la théorie de Glisson." In the *Anatomia hepatis* the parallel is stronger than in the *Tractatus de ventriculo*, where Daremberg's dictum of "un mélange souvent inextricable, des facultés naturelles de Galien et de l'archéisme de Van Helmont" (p. 256) holds true. Augustus Gottlob Weber, *Commentatio de initiis ac progressibus irritabilitatis*, Diss. Halle 1782, also

However, Glisson believed sensation and nerves to be indispensable for the process of irritation. In exploring Galen's position in this matter, we are led to a paradoxical conclusion. Especially in his *On the Use of Parts*, Galen easily appears in agreement with Glisson. But the Galen of *On the Natural Faculties* and particularly Galen the interpreter of Plato's *Timaeus* can also be seen as admitting sensation without nerves. There is thus an ambiguity in Galen's teaching which, in retrospect, would allow us to connect him with the *Anatomia hepatis* as well as with the *Tractatus de ventriculo*.

Galen listed the discharging faculty among the natural faculties, which by definition were independent of the rational soul, i.e., of feeling and voluntary motion.[84] Though in many cases, such as in the normal passage of food through the alimentary canal, our consciousness is not involved, still, we become painfully aware of any molestation. In child labor this is obvious even under normal conditions, but the urinary bladder offers perhaps the most striking example. Galen said that it "continues to collect urine up to the time that it becomes uncomfortable through the increasing quantity of urine or the irritation [*dēchtheisan*] caused by its acidity. . . ."[85] Anatomically, sensation presupposed nerves according to Galenic doctrine. In line with this reasoning, Galen assigned to the nerves a threefold purpose: sensibility in the organs of perception, movement in the organs of locomotion, and "to all others [i.e., organs] the recognition of distressing things."[86] Hunger, for instance, is a sensation which Galen located in the cardia, and he classified the latter among the organs of perception, like the inside of the hand.[87] Generally, however, he said of the organs of nutrition that none of them was a sense organ or an organ of movement. Hence

the nerves given to all of them had needs be small and for the third use only, so that they might be able to distinguish what would cause distress. For if this too were lacking and they were insensible of the sufferings within them, nothing would prevent animals from being destroyed in a very short time. For as it is now, when we feel a sting [*dēxeōs*] in the intestines, we forthwith hasten to get rid of the distressing thing. If, however, [the intestines] were completely insensible, they would, I think, easily become ulcerated and would all be corroded and made to putrify by the waste material that collects and flows into them daily. . . .[88]

The sensibility of an organ, moreover, depends on the number and volume of the nerves with which it is supplied.[89] Thus the gall bladder

---

points out the parallel between Galen's natural faculties and the doctrine of irritability. Generally speaking, Weber goes too far in finding traces of "irritability" in a large variety of ancient authors; at the same time he is satisfied with a very superficial analysis of the congruences.

[84]Galen, *On the Natural Faculties*, I, 1; Loeb ed., p. 2.

[85]*Ibid.*, III, 5; Loeb ed., p. 245 (Brock's translation).

[86]Galen, *On the Use of Parts*, V, 9; ed. Helmreich, p. 277; Daremberg, p. 361. See K. D. Keele, *Anatomies of Pain*, Springfield, Ill.: Thomas, 1957, p. 49.

[87]Galen, *On the Use of Parts*, V, 9. On the complicated theory of hunger with its interplay of "natural" and "psychic" faculties see Meyer-Steineg, *op. cit.*, p. 442f.

[88]*Ibid.*, V, 10; ed. Helmreich, p. 278; Daremberg, p. 363.

[89]See above, ftns. 61 and 62; *On the Use of Parts*, XVI, 1 and 2; also, Keele, *op. cit.*, pp. 49 f. and 52.

possesses fewer nerves than the stomach, uterus, and urinary bladder. But is noci-perception always associated with awareness of pain or discomfort? Galen does not seem to offer a clear answer to this question. He believed that the brain, the seat of sensation and volition, extended to the very organs via the nerves, which conducted the psychic pneuma or a light-like principle.[90] Hence pain was "felt" in the organs when the nerves were involved, hence organs became anesthetic or paralyzed when the nerves were cut, ligated, or otherwise affected so that the communication between organ and brain was impeded.[91] According to this explanation, however, pain and discomfort always ought to be perceived consciously, and yet Galen admitted that no consciousness of discomfort accompanied the irritating action of bile on the gall bladder.[92] His attempt to solve the difficulty by allowing fewer nerves to the gall bladder seems to imply that sensitivity could be quantitatively diminished, till there was just enough of it left for the organ but not enough for conscious perception. Interesting as such a hypothesis is, there is no certainty of its having been maintained by Galen.[93]

Regarding the manner in which organs effected a discharge, Galen offered two possibilities. In the first place, every part had its *tonos symphytos*,[94] an innate tension. The different parts of the body were not in a constant dynamic equilibrium. Not only were some parts stronger than others in absolute terms (e.g., the heart had a greater attracting power than the liver),[95] their relative strength also varied under different circumstances. If the tension of a part, temporarily at least, became weaker than that of its stronger neighbor, the latter would be able to pass on its surplus material to it. A passage from stronger to weaker parts and a deposit in the weakest would thus explain the condition of a morbid flux.[96]

The other mechanism, already explained in relation to the gall bladder, was more often cited by Galen. The discharge of waste material, just as the attraction of food[97] and its retention, depended on the fibres in the tunics

---

[90]The idea of the *pneuma psychikon* is too well known to need elaboration. For the light-like principle see below, ftn. 100.

[91]The main passage is in Galen, *De Hippocratis et Platonis placitis*, VIII, 7; ed. Kühn, vol. 5, pp. 641 and 644. For a good summary see Hermann Siebeck, *Geschichte der Psychologie*, erster Theil, zweite Abtheilung, Gotha: Perthes, 1884, p. 191 f., also Theodor Meyer-Steineg, "Studien zur Physiologie des Galenos," *Sudhoffs Arch. f. Gesch. d. Med.*, 1912, 5: 172–224 (pp. 222–24). I think that Meyer-Steineg's argument is vitiated by his crediting Galen with a notion of "stimulation" *(Reiz)* foreign to him.

[92]See above, ftn. 61.

[93]It is, however, true that such quantitative notions made Galen believe that deep or light sleep depended on the relative quantity of the influent faculty from the brain to the rest of the body; see *De symptomatum causis*, I, 8; Kühn ed. vol. 7, p. 144.

[94]*On the Natural Faculties*, III, 13; Loeb ed., p. 296. The occurrence of this Stoic notion in Galen is important in view of the role the tonus was to play in the physiology of Stahl and his followers; see below, p. 314.

[95]*Ibid.*, p. 293.

[96]*Ibid.*, p. 296.

[97]At least attraction of food at a distance; see Meyer-Steineg, *op. cit.*, *Sudhoffs Arch. f. Gesch. d. Med.*, 1913, 6: 431 f. In attracting its food from the immediate surroundings, the attracting faculty acted similarly to a magnet. (See *On the Natural Faculties*, III, 15.)

of the organ. Straight (longitudinal) fibres served attraction, and oblique fibres retention. The discharging faculty acted through the transverse fibres; it was the motions of these fibres which performed the excretory functions.[98] The presence of nerves was not postulated for this function, since these fibres did not constitute muscles.[99]

4

Galen tried to distinguish between natural organs (primarily those of the abdomen) and the psychic organs, (subject to sense perception and will). All organs, natural and psychic alike, needed veins and arteries, because they underwent metabolic change and had their share in the bodily heat. In so far, then, even the psychic organs were also "natural," otherwise they would not be alive. However, the functions of the natural organs were inborn; and these functions, therefore, could be damaged only if the organs themselves were damaged. The psychic organs, on the other hand, needed nerves to supply them with the principles of sensation and movement, "as the sun furnishes light to all things on which it shines."[100] They could lose their function without being hurt themselves, when their communication with the brain was intercepted.[101]

This seemingly clear distinction was complicated by the occurrence of discomfort and pain in the natural organs and by their being supplied with nerves which made noci-perception possible. Whether or not this perception was bound to be conscious was a question to which we were not able to find a clear answer in Galen. To this ambiguity is now added another major difficulty. Could the natural faculties be denied sensation and motion altogether, or was some sort of sensation and motion necessarily associated with them, though not of the kind carried by the nerves?

All the facts confirm, Galen said,

that the stomach, uterus, and bladders possess certain inborn faculties which are retentive of their own proper qualities and eliminative of those that are foreign.[102]

But how did these organs recognize "their own proper qualities" to be attracted and retained, and "those that are foreign" to be eliminated? This question concerned the natural organs not only of the animal body; it also concerned plants, which lived by the natural faculties.

The organic nature of plants and their ability to nourish themselves were

---

[98]*On the Use of Parts*, IV, 17; ed. Helmreich, p. 242; Daremberg, p. 328. *Ibid.*, V, 11; ed. Helmreich, p. 282 f.; Daremberg, p. 366; and *On the Natural Faculties*, III, 11; Loeb ed., p. 280 and *ibid.*, III, 13; p. 300. See also above, ftn. 65.

[99]See below, ftn. 142. Nevertheless, *On the Use of Parts*, XVI, 5; ed. Helmreich, vol. 2, p. 395; Daremberg, vol. 2, p. 172; assigned spinal nerve fibres to the intraperitoneal organs, endowing them with force and vigor. See Keele, *op. cit.*, p. 48 f.

[100]Galen, ed. Kühn, vol. 8, p. 67.

[101]Essentially, the above paragraph represents a summary of Galen, *De locis affectis*, I, 7; ed. Kühn, vol. 8, pp. 66–68; see Daremberg, vol. 2, pp. 504–505.

[102]Galen, *On the Natural Faculties*, III, 5; Loeb ed., p. 245 (Brock's translation).

issues on which Plato and Aristotle too had speculated. According to Aristotle, plants had neither locomotion nor sensation,[103] but they possessed a kind of soul which they shared with animals. This soul was the capacity to grow, to be nourished, to continue to live "as long as they are able to absorb food,"[104] and to decay.[105] "This capacity to absorb food," Aristotle added, "may exist apart from all other powers, but the others cannot exist apart from this in mortal beings."[106] Hence Aristotle assumed that the sensitive faculty of animals included the nutritive,[107] whereas plants "have the nutritive faculty only."[108] Aristotle's "nutritive soul"[109] reappeared in Galen's "vegetative soul," which he admitted as a synonym for "nature" in animals and man.[110]

Galen's own answer to the problem is given in his interpretation of a short passage of Plato's *Timaeus*.[111] As Galen stated it, the problem was: "In what way do we say that they [i.e., the natural faculties] attract what is familiar, but reject what is foreign?"[112] This seemed to presuppose a discriminatory perception of what was familiar and foreign. And this, in turn, seemed to presuppose a sensory function on the part of the natural faculties. The solution, according to Galen, was to be found in Plato's attribution to plants of a genus of sensation different from sight, hearing, smell, taste, and touch. Plants can merely discover what is nourishing, and what is not.

Hence Plato seems to me to speak rightly when he says that plants have sensation, namely of what is familiar and what is foreign, and thus may suitably be called living beings, since, at the same time, they are not without autonomous movement. But because such inquiry is not necessary for medical philosophy, I am content—having gone as far as the limit of the plausible, and that merely in order to be consistent—to praise Plato, who calls plants living beings and says that they partake only of a discriminating perception of things familiar and foreign. If considered accurately,

---

[103]Aristotle, *On the Soul*, 410 b 23 and 435 b 1. Since the Aristotelian and Platonic views on the subject are not discussed here *per se*, I refrain from citing literature on the subject.

[104]*Ibid.*, 413 a 30; English translation by W. S. Hett (Loeb Classical Library), p. 75.

[105]*Ibid.*, 411 a 30, 411 b 28, 413 a 25. Aristotle (*ibid.*, 412 a 14) defines life as autonomous nutrition, growth, and decay, a definition which obviously includes plants. In 412 a 28 he refers to a living body (including plants) as organic (*organikon*), i.e., possessing organs. This, as far as I see, embodies the notion, though not the word, of "organism."

[106]*Ibid.*, 413 a 31; Hett's translation, p. 75.

[107]*Ibid.*, 414 b 31.

[108]*Ibid.*, 414 a 33; Hett's translation p. 81; see also 415 a 2.

[109]*Ibid.*, 415 a 23.

[110]Galen, *On the Natural Faculties*, I, 1; Loeb ed., p. 2.

[111]Plato, *Timaeus*, 77 B: "For everything, in fact, which partakes of life may justly and with perfect truth be termed a living being. Certainly that being which we are now describing [i.e., plants] partakes of the third kind of soul, which is seated, as we affirm, between the midriff and the navel, and which shares not at all in opinion and reasoning and mind but in sensation, pleasant and painful, together with desires." Translation (adapted) by R. G. Bury (Loeb Classical Library), pp. 203–205.

[112]Galen, *De substantia facultatum naturalium;* ed. Kühn, vol. 4, p. 764. As Karl Kalbfleisch, "Zu Galenos," *Philologus*, 1896, 55: 689–694, has shown, this fragment is really part of Galen's *Peri tōn heautōi dokountōn*, of which G. Helmreich published another fragment in *Philologus*, 1894, 52: 431–434.

this seems to be of the category of what is pleasant and unpleasant. For on no other account can one say that they attract the familiar or assimilate it to themselves, except for the sake of enjoyment and the pleasure engendered in them. But, as I said, for medicine it suffices to know this alone, that they attract the familiar, whereby they are also nourished, but reject the foreign. For ethical philosophy the exact inquiry into such things is even more useless, wherefore Plato did not have it in mind either.[113]

Elsewhere Galen again confirmed his interpretation of Plato:

For in the commentaries on the natural faculties[114] we have shown that they [i.e., plants] possess a cognitive faculty for familiar substances, which nourish them, and for foreign substances, which harm them. Hence they attract the familiar substances but turn away and reject the foreign. Therefore Plato said that the plants participate in a special genus of sensation, for it makes known what is familiar and what is foreign.[115]

Finally, Galen dared his detractors, who derided him for distinguishing three faculties and for locating

in the brain the principle of the nerves and purposeful movements, and also of the five senses; in the liver the principle of blood and veins and of nourishment of the body, as well as of making known what is familiar substance and what foreign in this respect; in the heart, the principle of arteries, inborn heat, and pulsation.[116]

Like the plants, the vegetative (i.e., natural) organs of the body possessed a special kind of sense informing them of what was to be retained and what to be rejected. This principle was situated in the liver; in Platonic terms it was the concupiscent soul.[117]

This means that all organic beings possessed such a sense rooted in their nature, as well as some kind of motion, since rejection or discharge could not be accomplished otherwise. These, sensation and motion, had to be independent of the psychic soul and of the nervous system, since their principle was in the liver.

To sum up: The Galenic doctrine of irritation could be understood in two different ways. Irritation meant an attempt by an organ (or a part of it) to eliminate material which the organ experienced as disturbing. To the extent that such experience and action were directly credited to the dis-

---

[113]Galen, *De substantia;* ed. Kühn, vol. 4, p. 765 f.

[114]Schröder (see the following footnote), p. 42, discusses the question whether this refers to *On the Natural Faculties.*

[115]Galen, *In Platonis Timaeum commentarii fragmenta,* ed. H. O. Schröder, Leipzig-Berlin: Teubner, 1934 (Corpus Medicorum Graecorum Supplementum I), p. 11.

[116]*Ibid.,* p. 12.

[117]Paul Kraus and Richard Walzer (editors and translators), *Galeni compendium Timaei Platonis,* London: Institute Warburg, 1951 (Plato Arabus, vol. 1), p. 81: "Deinde dixit: Et creavit Deus—qui honore et maiestate eminet—plantas propter hominis nutrimentum, et in eis unam animae speciem, id est concupiscentem, posuit." See also p. 15, and p. 26 of the Arabic text.

charging faculty possessed by every living part, irritation was dependent on perception *sui generis;* it was not dependent on the awareness of pain or on the existence of nerves. To the extent that the perception of an injuring agent was believed a function of the nerves, the latter appeared essential. Through them a feeling of discomfort or pain was experienced in the organ. Whether or not this feeling was always accompanied by awareness remains a moot question.

Galen himself probably thought that he had offered a consistent explanation of the interplay of "natural" and "psychic" faculties and of the role of nerves in the phenomenon of irritation. He did not overlook the need for integrating vegetative organs into the animal organism. The heart, lungs, and abdominal organs all have a share in the nerves, "so that they partake of some sensation and may not be plants altogether."[118] But this statement gives a formal consistency rather than a real synthesis of divergent modes of accounting for the phenomena of irritation. Even within the framework of the classical tradition the doctrine of irritation could present itself in different ways.[119] The differences became marked when parts of the Galenic physiology were abandoned. We have already seen this in Glisson, and it is to be seen also in Caesalpinus and Harvey, both of whom preceded Glisson.

III. CAESALPINUS AND HARVEY

1. *Caesalpinus*

The *Quaestiones medicinales* of Caesalpinus contain a chapter entitled: "Animals completely deprived of the sense of touch cannot be nourished."[120] This title supports an Aristotelian thesis, as is to be expected of Caesalpinus, the peripatetic philosopher. But the argument leans heavily on Galen; indeed, Caesalpinus uses the ambiguities in Galen's doctrine to convict him out of his own statements.

Caesalpinus states that nutrition is accomplished by attraction, retention, concoction, and expulsion of the excrements. Attraction presupposes a feeling of familiarity with the substances needed. On the other hand, nature does not expel what is foreign "unless she is irritated."[121] Neither of

---

[118]Galen, *On the Use of Parts,* VI, 18; ed. Helmreich, vol. 1, p. 365; Daremberg, p. 447. See Mani, *op. cit.,* p. 65 ff.

[119]On Galen's theory of consciousness in general, see Hermann Siebeck, *Geschichte der Psychologie,* p. 336 f. Siebeck (p. 180) rightly says of Galen: "Dass er gelegentlich der stoischen Unterscheidung von Seele und Physis zustimmt, scheint ihn nicht abgehalten zu haben, bei eingehender Erwägung die wirkliche Beseelung bis auf die Pflanzen auszudehnen." In evidence of this Siebeck (note 53, p. 497) refers to the passage in Galen's commentary on the *Timaeus* cited above. In fairness to Galen it has to be added that he discussed the phenomena of irritation rather than conceptualizing irritation, as Glisson did.

[120]Andreas Caesalpinus, *Quaestionum peripateticarum lib. V, Daemonum investigatio peripatetica, Quaestionum medicarum libri II, De medicament. facultatibus lib. II.* Venice: apud Iuntas, 1593, fol. 226 r.: "Privata omnino sensu tactus animalia nutriri non posse. Quaest. xiii."

[121]*Ibid.,* fol. 226 v.: "nisi ab aliis irritetur."

these two phenomena could happen without the sense of touch, the food sense according to Aristotle, who concluded that animals must die if deprived of this sense.[122]

But Galen, as Caesalpinus argues, leans on Plato, taking it that the natural soul[123] possesses the sense to distinguish between the familiar and foreign, though this sense is different from the five senses. Thus Galen asserts that natural organs "have an inner power by which they bring about their actions, while the psychic ones have a power which flows into them from a principle, as the light from the sun."[124] In consequence of this thought, natural actions can be damaged only if the organs themselves are affected, whereas psychic actions can suffer if the organs are intact yet their power prevented from flowing into them from the principle.

Yet according to Aristotle, Caesalpinus avers, plants have no sensation.[125] Hence the nutrition takes place "without any recognition of the food."[126] Animals, on the other hand, need the sense of touch, which is their food sense. Their nerves, as Galen pointed out, extend to the viscera "so that they may feel what brings pain." According to Galen, the purpose of their endowment is "that the irritated parts[127] may expel what molests them and retain the beneficial." This proves that sensation is necessary for natural actions. Galen carefully explains this by drawing attention to the dire consequences that would befall animals if noxious excrements were allowed to accumulate in the organs of nutrition because of a lack of sensation. Moreover, as Galen has it, a blow on the spine can lead to a loss of feeling in the internal parts and to a suppression of urine and excrements.[128] However, contrary to Galen's belief, this can happen before these parts are inflamed, which shows that their function suffers by consensus[129] when the psychic faculty does not reach them via the nerves. Furthermore, if, as Galen has it, all movement starting from a natural faculty is brought about by fibres, "and if the fibres are nervous bodies and endowed with sense,"[130] they must originate from the same organ as the nerves and sensation. In fact, the movements are called natural because they are involuntary, as are movements in epileptic convulsions, rigor, or hiccup. "For, although these movements may take place in the muscles or in the nervous parts,[131] or in the brain itself, they are nevertheless natural, be-

---

[122]Caesalpinus here refers to Aristotle, *De anima*, 414 b 7 and 435 b 4.

[123]Caesalpinus, *op. cit.*, fol. 226 v.: "In hoc igitur laudat [i.e., Galen in *De substantia facultatum naturalium*] Platonem: quod animae naturali sensum quendam tribuerit domesticorum et alienorum discretivum."

[124]Caesalpinus here refers to Galen's *De locis affectis*, I, 7; ed. Kühn, vol. 8, p. 66.

[125]The reference is to Aristotle, *De anima*, 435 b 1.

[126]Caesalpinus, *op. cit.*, fol. 226 v.

[127]*Ibid.*, fol. 226 v.: "particulae irritatae."

[128]The reference is to Galen's commentary 3, ch. 51, on Hippocrates' *De articulis*, ed. Kühn, vol. 18 A, p. 562 f.

[129]Caesalpinus, *op. cit.*, fol. 227 r.

[130]*Ibid.*, fol. 227 r.: "fibrae autem nervosa corpora sunt et sensu praedita." For the meaning of *nervosa*, see below, ftn. 134.

[131]*Ibid.*: "in partibus nervosis," see below, ftn. 134.

cause they are brought about involuntarily by the excreting faculty, provided that the faculty has been irritated by the sense of a noxious thing." [132]

Caesalpinus draws a distinction between nutrition of plants and of animals, a distinction made explicit in the rest of the chapter, which deals with
various pros and cons of his thesis. Because they are fixed, plants do not
select food as animals do. "The spirit suffices for the attraction of nourishment from the soil into the roots and for the distribution from the roots
into the twigs, without any distinguishing sense, unless we call the intelligence by which nature is guided, sense." [133] In animals, however, attraction
and elimination of food are dependent on a sense of touch, though we may
not be aware of the sensation, and on the natural movements which result
from irritation of the discharging faculty, different from the "psychic"
movements only in being involuntary. This latter opinion is bolstered by
the declaration of fibres as "nervous bodies." To remove the possible objection that allegedly non-sentient parts (bone, cartilage, the medulla of the
brain) can be nourished, Caesalpinus, at the end of the chapter, emphasizes
"that there is no particle in the animal that does not receive some measure
of power of feeling."

For the bones participate more or less in sense through the membranes which are
called periostea, the teeth through the nerves distributed to their roots, the flesh of
the intestines, the brain, and the spinal cord, through their membranes. The sense
is more exquisite in the membranes, because their substance is nervous. [134]

Caesalpinus' argument fundamentally circles around the denial of sensation different from, and independent of, the senses, particularly that of
touch, a sensation that would be in the parts of animals and plants. In
consequence of this thesis, he asserts that all parts of the body are supplied
with nervous elements to give them sensation, and the fibres are declared
to be nervous bodies, though the exact meaning of these assertions remains
unclear. Together with his Aristotelian bias, Caesalpinus accepts the
Galenic doctrine of the discharging faculty and the role of irritation.

2. *Harvey*

As is well known, Harvey refuted Galen's explanation of the diastole of
the heart. During the diastole, which Galen had attributed to contraction of
the heart's longitudinal fibres, [135] the heart, in Harvey's view, was passive,
the initial force coming from the blood that rose like a fermenting sub-

[132]*Ibid.:* "irritata tamen virtute per sensum rei noxiae."

[133]*Ibid.*, fol. 227 r-v.

[134]*Ibid.*, fol. 227 v. Caesalpinus' views of "nervous" parts in general, and membranes in
particular, is not altogether clear. This unclarity was inherited from Galen. Though Galen
distinguished between nerves, ligaments, and tendons, he bequeathed an unclear notion of
"nervous bodies." In his Commentaries on Hippocrates' Aphorisms (ed. Kühn, vol. 17 B, p.
783) he says: "They [i.e. *neurōdea sōmata*] are cords [*tonoi*], ligaments, muscles, and tendons."
By *tonoi* he may mean nerves. On the Use of Parts, XVI, 2; ed. Helmreich, vol. 2, p. 379;
Daremberg, vol. 2, p. 160, however, expressly denies nerves to ligaments.

[135]Galen, *On the Use of Parts*, VI, 8; ed. Helmreich, p. 320; Daremberg, vol. 1, p. 402.

stance.[136] The active role of the heart consisted in its contraction due to the forced dilation and leading to a propulsion of the blood. Harvey considered this explanation equally valid for the embryonic heart and for that of the adult.

For, as there are two parts in a pulsation, viz.: distension or relaxation, and contraction, or diastole and systole, and, as distension is the prior of these two motions, it is manifest that this motion proceeds from the blood; the contraction, again, from the vesicula pulsans of the embryo in ovo, from the heart in the pullet, in virtue of its own fibres, as an instrument destined for this particular end. Certain it is, that the vesicle in question, as also the auricle of the heart at a later period, whence the pulsation begins, is provoked [*irritari*] to the motion of contraction by the distending blood.[137]

By the contraction of the auricles, the blood is propelled into the ventricles, "and the ventricles, thus replete and distended, are stimulated [*sollicitant*] to contraction, and this motion always precedes the systole, which follows immediately afterwards."[138]

Harvey, as does Glisson shortly afterwards, made the fibres contract when they were forcibly distended. From all that has been said before, this must have seemed understandable on the basis of contemporary Galenic principles. However, Harvey differed from Galen in declaring the heart a muscle,[139] and he differed from Aristotle in assigning supremacy to the blood over the heart.[140] Both points have an important bearing on Harvey's view of irritation.

Galen emphatically denied that the heart was a muscle.[141] Though heart and muscle both showed fibres surrounded by flesh, the fibres are of different kinds. Those of the muscle are "parts of nerves and ligaments," whereas "the heart has a particular kind of fibres as have the tunics of artery and vein, the intestines and stomach, uterus, and both bladders. For in all these organs, too, the particular flesh will be seen enveloping the

---

[136]Harvey, "Second Disquisition to John Riolan"; Robert Willis (translator), *The Works of William Harvey, M. D.*, London: Sydenham Society, 1847, p. 132; Guilielmi Harveii *Opera omnia*, a Collegio Medicorum Londinensi edita, London, 1763, p. 132. For this whole section see also John G. Curtis, *Harvey's Views on the Use of the Circulation of the Blood*, New York: Columbia Univ. Press, 1915, especially ch. VII.

[137]Harvey, *Anatomical Exercises on the Generation of Animals*, exercise 51, Willis' translation, p. 375 (adapted); *Opera*, p. 391.

[138]Harvey, Letter to R. Morison, Willis' translation, p. 604; *Opera*, p. 621. Curtis, *op. cit.*, p. 89: "The circulation of the blood then, according to the final view of its discoverer, is maintained by a self-regulating mechanism worked by causes operating within the blood itself, the 'principal part' of the body. The systolic muscular contractions of the walls of the ventricles are caused by direct mechanical stimulation (in modern language) due to diastolic distension by blood of the relaxed muscular walls of these chambers. The blood which distends the ventricles is driven forcibly into them by the auricular systole, the muscular walls of the auricles having been stimulated to contract by diastolic distention due likewise to blood."

[139]Harvey, *An Anatomical Disquisition on the Motion of the Heart and Blood in Animals*, ch. 17; Willis, pp. 82 and 387.

[140]Harvey, *On Generation*, exercise 51; Willis' translation, p. 373.

[141]Galen, *Administrationes anatomicae*, VII, 8; ed. Kühn, vol. 2, p. 609 ff. Charles Singer (translator), *Galen on Anatomical Procedures*, London and New York: Oxford Univ. Press, 1956, p. 181 ff.

fibres particular to them." [142] Whereas muscles through their nerves are subject to will, "the power of pulsation has its origin in the heart itself . . . by the high virtue of some special element in its nature." [143]

Harvey, however, called the heart a muscle because it acted and functioned like a muscle, "namely to contract and move something else, in this case, the charge of blood." [144] On the other hand, "neither the heart *nor anything else* can dilate or distend itself so as to draw aught into its cavity during the diastole, unless, like a sponge, it has been first compressed, and as it is returning to its primary condition." [145] This denied Galen's "attraction" through contraction of the longitudinal fibres and tended to confuse the theory of the natural faculties altogether. Indeed, Harvey substituted a modification which rested on his un-Aristotelian assumption of the supremacy of the blood.

Harvey's embryological investigations indicated to him that the blood was the "primogenate" particle embodying the primary vital principle. [146] All the parts of the body received life from the blood; [147] the cardiovascular apparatus was constructed for impelling and distributing the blood. [148] Aristotle's thesis of the primacy of the heart was tenable only if by heart was understood "that which first appears in the embryo of the chick in ovo, the blood to wit, with its containing parts—the pulsating vesicles and veins, as one and the same organ." [149] The blood possessed both sense and motion, [150] and Harvey went so far as to say that "the blood perceives things that tend to injure by irritating, or to benefit by cherishing it." [151] Since blood appeared in the body prior to the brain, all sensation and motion could not proceed from the brain. When the latter is as yet nothing but "a limpid fluid," the mucilaginous body of the embryo, "if lightly pricked, will move obscurely, will contract and twist itself like a worm or caterpillar, so that it is very evidently possessed of sensation." [152] What the physicians called natural movements and actions, i.e. those not subject to our will, were independent of the brain but indicated the presence of sensation,

---

[142]Galen, *De temperamentis*, II, 3; ed. Kühn, vol. 1, p. 602; ed. G. Helmreich, Leipzig: Teubner, 1904, p. 58 f. See also Berg, *Die Lehre von der Faser*, p. 347.

[143]Galen, *Administrationes anatomicae*, VII, 9; Singer's (*op. cit.*) translation, p. 184.

[144]Harvey, *Motion of the Heart and Blood*, ch. 17; Willis' translation, p. 82.

[145]Harvey, *Motion of the Heart and Blood*, ch. 17; Willis' translation, p. 80 f. (italics mine); see also *ibid.*, ch. 2, p. 23.

[146]Harvey, *On Generation*, exercise 51, Willis' translation, p. 373. Since the statement of the primacy of the blood also occurs in Harvey's *Lectures on the Whole of Anatomy*, fol. 73 r and 75 r (pp. 175 and 180 of the annotated translation by C. D. O'Malley, F. N. L. Poynter and K. F. Russell, Berkeley and Los Angeles: Univ. of California Press, 1961), these observations seem to precede the *Motion of the Heart and Blood*.

[147]Willis' translation, p. 377.

[148]*Ibid.*, p. 374.

[149]*Ibid.*, exercise 52, p. 387.

[150]*Ibid.*, p. 381: "Now that both sense and motion are in the blood is obvious from many indications, although Aristotle denies the fact."

[151]*Ibid.*, p. 380; *Opera*, p. 396; "eum et irritantis injuriam et foventis commodum persentiscere manifestum est."

[152]*Ibid.*, exercise 57, Willis' translation, p. 430.

"inasmuch as they are aroused, provoked, and changed thereby."[153] Harvey illustrated this first of all by various morbid conditions of the heart, attributed to causes afflicting its sensation. "For whatever by its divers movements strives against irritations [*irritamenta*] and troubles must necessarily be endowed with sensation."[154] There followed examples: the stomach must have a sense whereby it could distinguish between what is noxious and useful. Even the flesh distinguished poison from non-poison. Various affections, inconveniences, and irritations [*irritamenta*] of the uterus did not depend on the brain or the *sensus communis;* still, they could not be deemed to occur without any sense.

For that which is wholly without sense is not seen to be irritated [*irritari*] by any means, neither can it be excited [*excitari*] to motion or action of any kind. Nor have we any other means of distinguishing between an animate and sentient thing and one that is dead and senseless than the motion excited by some other irritating [*irritante*] cause or thing, which as it incessantly follows, so does it also argue sensation.[155]

This declaration, in which motion excited by irritation indicated sensation and separated living from lifeless things, is very reminiscent of Glisson.[156] Yet there is this difference: Glisson of the *Anatomia hepatis* postulated the intermediacy of nervous function; Harvey established a clear-cut separation between what was consciously perceived by the *sensorium commune,* i.e. the brain, and "a certain sense or form of touch which is not referred to the common sensorium, nor in any way communicated to the brain, so that we do not perceive by this sense that we feel."[157] In particular, there existed a psychic sense of touch as distinct from a natural sense of touch, the latter not communicated to the *sensorium commune* and representing a different species. Likewise, purposeful muscular motions were distinct from mere muscular contraction and movement. Convulsive motions from an irritating (*irritante*) cause were like the uncoordinated movements of a decapitated cock or hen.

All this is summed up in Harvey's following statement:

We therefore conceive the fact to be that all the natural motions proceed from the power of the heart, and depend on it; the spontaneous motions, however, and those that complete any motion which physicians entitle a psychic motion, cannot be performed without the controlling influence of the brain and common sensation.[158]

Galen, denying the muscular nature of the heart, had classified it with the other viscera that attract, retain, and discharge.[159] Harvey, declaring

---

[153]*Ibid.,* p. 431 (Willis' translation, adapted); *Opera,* p. 449: "utpote a quo excitentur, irritentur et permutentur."

[154]*Ibid.,* (Willis' translation); *Opera,* p. 450.

[155]*Ibid.,* p. 432 (Willis' translation, adapted); *Opera,* p. 450 f.

[156]See above, p. 295.

[157]Harvey, *On Generation,* exercise 57, Willis' translation, p. 432.

[158]*Ibid.,* p. 433 (Willis' translation); *Opera,* p. 452. By "power of the heart" Harvey, in consequence of what he said before, must refer to the blood propelled by the heart.

[159]Galen, *On the Use of Parts,* VI, 8; ed. Helmreich, p. 320; Daremberg, vol. 1, p. 402.

the heart a muscle and refusing it any sucking power, had put himself into clear opposition to Galen. By his peculiar vitalization of the blood, which even allowed it to react to irritation, he had also come to group the motion of the heart with the other natural motions. Fibres contracted, but so did all living tissue, which, when irritated, revealed its power of sensation through its motion. There existed a sense of touch different from the conscious sense and independent of the brain. Here Harvey differed not only from Caesalpinus, but also from the Glisson of the *Anatomia hepatis.* He came closer to the "natural perception" of the Glisson of the *Tractatus de ventriculo.*[160]

IV. CONCLUSION

Glisson's doctrine of irritation has been shown to be deeply rooted in the classical tradition, which means the teaching of the schools prevailing during the first half of the seventeenth century. With the possible exception of anatomy, this teaching, in the schools of medicine, was largely based on Aristotelian science and Galenic medicine, and Glisson's ideas of 1654 were planted in Galenic physiology. Though Galen did not conceptualize "irritation" as Glisson did, both dealt with the same kind of phenomena in a very similar way. Galen's explanation of the phenomena of irritation was not unequivocal. Caesalpinus, adhering to Aristotle, rejected the idea of a cognitive element in the natural faculties, an idea much more consonant with Harvey's views in spite of the latter's well-known divergences from Galen.

While paying attention to the Galenic roots of Glisson's doctrine, we have omitted from our consideration other influences, possibly that of Campanella, and particularly that of van Helmont.[161] As far as I can see, van Helmont's influence is not yet noticeable in the *Anatomia hepatis,* though it is obvious in the *Tractatus de ventriculo.* Why and when Glisson turned to van Helmont is a question made all the more interesting, because Galen's "Platonizing" passages and the example of Harvey permitted a natural perception without the intermediacy of nerves. Yet in the *Tractatus de ventriculo,* natural perception was identified with the *Archeus.*[162] Whatever van

---

[160]Walter Charleton, *Enquiries Into Human Nature,* London, 1680, p. 109, may have been the first to point to the relationship between Harvey (and Campanella) on the one hand and Glisson on the other. Campanella and Harvey, Charleton states, called natural touch (as distinct from the animal sense of touch) what "Dr. Glisson, coming after to consider the thing more Metaphysically, and founding the very life or substantial Energie of Nature wholly upon the same, denominated . . . *Perceptio Naturalis,* thereby to distinguish it from all the Senses, as well internal, as external. . . ." See Richard A. Hunter and Ida Macalpine, "William Harvey: his neurological and psychiatric observations," *J. Hist. Med. and Allied Sc.,* 1957, *12*: 126–139 (p. 129). [I overlooked that Harvey's concept of irritability was mentioned by Joseph Needham, *A History of Embryology,* 2nd ed., New York: Abelard-Schuman, 1959, p. 143.]

[161]For van Helmont's contribution to the history of irritability, see Francis B. Anstie, *Stimulants and Narcotics, Their Mutual Relations,* London: Macmillan, 1864, p. 31 ff.; Rudolf Virchow, "Reizung und Reizbarkeit," *Virchows Arch. f. path. Anat.,* 1858, *14*: 1–63 (p. 8 f.); Walter Pagel, *Jo. Bapt. van Helmont,* Berlin: Julius Springer, 1930, p. 75 ff.; *idem,* "Helmont. Leibnitz. Stahl," *Sudhoffs Arch. f. Gesch. d. Med.,* 1931, *24*: 19–59.

[162]Glisson, *Tractatus de ventriculo,* p. 161: "Natural perception (or the Archeus) knows well-

Helmont's own indebtedness to the classical tradition may have been,[163] he could hardly be considered a traditionalist. The association of the *Archeus* with natural perception, as Haller's testimony shows,[164] helped to obscure Glisson's relationship to Galenic medicine. In some respects, this is symptomatic of events in the history of medicine in the seventeenth and early eighteenth centuries. Galen's notion of an inborn tonus (*tonos symphytos*)[165] which goes beyond that of the postural muscular tonus, the history of which Sherrington[166] also traced back to Galen, is another example for the viability of classical biology.

Possible "roots" and "influences" apart, how significant was the doctrine of irritation? Glisson's ideas of 1654 were overshadowed by his later elaboration of the concept of irritability. As Virchow once remarked, irritation presupposes irritability.[167] Much of what we discussed in this essay concerned the attributes which organs must possess in order to exhibit irritation. For Glisson, life was marked by the unity of perception (*perceptio*), striving (*appetitus*), and motion (*motus*). This unity was implied in his explanation of irritation of 1654,[168] it was made explicit in the *Tractatus de natura substantiae energetica,* and it was reiterated in the *Tractatus de ventriculo*.[169] Glisson's extension of the principle of life to all matter, important though it is for his philosophical position,[170] is of little concern in our present context, which is limited to biological phenomena. Within the biological context this unity can also be read into Galen's views of the natural faculties, especially the discharging faculty, and Harvey's criteria of life, even if the three factors were not equally accentuated.

But it must not be overlooked that "irritation" is fundamentally oriented towards pathology, where it still has its assured place. Galen and Glisson used it to elucidate physiological processes of a kind where an obstacle had to be overcome, or where foreign, molesting, or potentially harmful matter was to be eliminated. This limited its physiological usefulness. Galen could

---

nigh innumerable things which are hidden to sense, and it knows the whole workshop [*fabrica*] of the body, having fashioned the workshop, and the use of the parts, and the manner in which everything is to be done."

[163]See Pagel, *op. cit.* (above ftn. 9) and, *idem, The Religious and Philosophical Aspects of van Helmont's Science and Medicine,* Baltimore: Johns Hopkins Press, 1944, p. 26.

[164]See above, p. 290.

[165]See above, p. 303.

[166]C. S. Sherrington, "Note on the history of the word 'tonus' as a physiological term," *Contributions to Medical and Biological Research,* Dedicated to Sir William Osler in Honour of His Seventieth Birthday, vol. 1, New York: Hoeber, 1919, pp. 261–268.

[167]Rudolf Virchow, *op. cit.,* ftn. 161 above, pp. 1 and 63. On p. 7 f. of this article Virchow offers a definition of "irritation" substantially identical with that of Glisson, though adapted to the cell; see Erwin H. Ackerknecht, *Rudolf Virchow,* Madison: Univ. of Wisconsin Press, 1953, p. 152. On Virchow as a vitalist *ibid.,* p. 50. For contemporary criticism of Virchow's theory of stimulus and irritation as vitalistic and dependent on Broussais, see Anstie, *op. cit.,* pp. 49 and 52–54.

[168]See above, p. 295.

[169]Heinrich Heinrichs, *op. cit.* (above ftn. 9); pp. 61, 62 (for the *Tractatus de natura substantiae energetica*), and pp. 64–65 (for the *Tractatus de ventriculo*).

[170]Heinrichs, *op. cit.,* has assembled a number of parallels with Aristotle and Suarez; see also Pagel, *op. cit.* (above, ftn. 9), p. 503 ff.

connect it with the discharging faculty; but he had to find different interpretations for physiological events which we attribute to irritability as a reaction to change in the environment. By crystallizing the notion of irritability out of the concept of irritation, so to speak, Glisson in 1677 clarified the physiological presupposition implied in "irritation." Thereby he helped to initiate the period in the history of "irritability" when this concept was no longer onesidedly oriented towards pathology.[171]

Today, we tend to replace physiological irritability by "excitability." However, one of the functions of the historiography of ideas is to make us aware of hidden ingredients in our conceptual tools. For this purpose we must beware of destroying or changing the images associated with the words we use. We have stressed the dependence of irritation on the picture of an angry man. As long as we speak of irritability we also preserve the association with this particular mental state. When we speak of excitability we change the association.

How far psychological associations are still present in the minds of modern physiologists is a question on which I am not going to enter here.[172] As far as scientists of the nineteenth century are concerned, the dependence of the explanation of somatic processes on psychological analogies can easily be demonstrated.[173] Just as Galen and Glisson (and, we may add, Bichat and many others) before him, so Claude Bernard too had to deal with the problem of unconscious perception. By referring to reflex action, he was able to circumvent some of the difficulties that had beset Galen,[174] Harvey, and Glisson. Thus Claude Bernard could write:

One might think that there is no sensibility in the internal organs. Indeed, we are not conscious of any manifestations of their sensibility. However, though the nerves which they receive are ordinarily unable to transmit the impressions of conscious sensibility, they [i.e., the organs] nevertheless have a particular sensibility, without consciousness, to which the name *reflex sensibility* has been given.[175]

But, reflex or not, the meaning of sensibility had to be explained. How Bernard thought about it evinces from his subsequent discussion. Upon the arrival of food in the stomach, movement and secretions take place (as Beaumont had observed).

---

[171]In van Helmont's *Archeus* Glisson may have found a broader biological basis than Galen's discharging faculty offered him; see Pagel, "Helmont. Leibnitz. Stahl," p. 23.

[172]It seems at least permissible to raise the question whether words like "stimulus" and "response" are quite free from psychological associations.

[173]The very plea made by Ewald Hering for liberation from psychological terminology and the difficulties which he admitted are characteristic. Ewald Hering, "In wie fern ist es möglich, die Physiologie von der Psychologie sprachlich zu trennen?", *Deutsche Arbeit*, 1901–1902, *I*: 946–951. (I am indebted to Professor Maurice Mandelbaum for a copy of this article.)

[174]Galen had to ascribe to degrees of consciousness such acts as breathing and moving in one's sleep; see Siebeck, *Geschichte der Psychologie*, p. 273 f. (Professor Ludwig Edelstein has drawn my attention to this discussion); and Georges Canguilhem, *La formation du concept de réflexe aux XVIIᵉ et XVIIIᵉ siècles*, Paris: Presses universitaires de France, 1955, p. 15 f.

[175]Claude Bernard, *Leçons sur la physiologie et la pathologie du système nerveux*, vol. 1, Paris: Baillière, 1858, p. 321.

There obviously exists a perceived sensation (*une sensation perçue*); one can become certain of this by cutting the nerves which are distributed to the organ: from that moment on the reaction is impeded, and the arrival of food in the stomach causes there neither movements nor secretions.[176]

To speak of sensation perceived by the stomach can have meaning only if conscious perception serves as the model. Similarly Glisson had argued for the gall bladder that discharge of bile depended on perception and that this perception, as well as the ensuing motion, depended on the presence of nerves. Let us say then that he, as well as Galen, had used a psychological model.

The naive and ubiquitous use of such models by the old physiologists has led to the accusation of animism and anthropomorphism. The history of irritability shows that the facts leading to the accusation cannot be denied. The designation of such modes of thinking as anthropomorphic is quite correct. But before turning this designation into an accusation, it will be worth while to consider why men like Galen and Glisson, who were no fools, so easily accepted anthropomorphic explanations. Galen was shocked by the atomism of Asclepiades and the mechanistic thinking of Erasistratus, both of which he deemed inadequate and attacked in *On the Natural Faculties*. Whatever we may think about the possibility today of reducing physiology to the level of physics, we know that such a possibility did not exist in previous centuries. If we disregard metaphysical or religious reasons for preferring the one or the other, we have to admit that psychological models were not necessarily more fantastic than mechanical ones for such processes as assimilation of food, growth, and reaction to stimuli.

The very success in elucidating the mechanical component of a complex biological process could bring into relief the need for a different explanation of the remaining part of the process. Harvey, who showed that the circulation of the blood could be attributed to the pumping action of the heart, at the same time had recourse to fermentation and irritation to account for the heart's diastole and systole. His appeal to irritation, which Descartes suspected as an appeal to an occult faculty,[177] was biologically more fruitful than Descartes' own reference to the action of heat. Haller's great contribution was the freeing of the phenomena of irritability from both anthropomorphic and mechanistic models and the subjecting of them to experimental biological criteria.

---

[176]*Ibid.*, p. 322.

[177]This point has been brought out by J. A. Passmore, "William Harvey and the philosophy of science," *The Australasian J. Philosophy*, 1958, *36*: 85–94. (Professor Maurice Mandelbaum kindly brought this article to my attention.)

24

The Philosophical
Background of Magendie's
Physiology*

D
R. OLMSTED has published a biography of François Magendie presenting a lucid and instructive account of life and work of this
"pioneer in experimental physiology and scientific medicine in XIX century France."[1] He follows him from his birth in 1783 through his scientific
and medical career in Paris until the year 1855 when he died much honored, though not equally well liked. In the course of this narrative Magendie's work, above all his physiological experiments, is discussed in detail
and with an instructiveness which only a fellow physiologist could supply.
Magendie's achievements as well as his failures become understandable.
The famous controversy regarding priority in what is commonly known as
the law of Bell and Magendie is decided in Magendie's favor on the basis of
a painstaking investigation. Moreover, Magendie the experimental pharmacologist, hygienist and medical practitioner is not neglected. Altogether,
it can be said that the picture of the man and of his work is drawn in a
manner which makes this book a standard biography.

Just because of its biographical thoroughness, Dr. Olmsted's present volume invites a question of a more general nature. In how far was Magendie,
whose personal character and scientific aim are so clearly delineated, dependent upon a philosophical current of his time, and in how far did he
himself give a new direction to this current? It is to this question that a
tentative answer will be proposed in the following pages.[2]

1

At first glance an investigation into Magendie's philosophical background does not seem promising. The man who compared himself to a

*Bull. Hist. Med., 1946, vol. 20, pp. 10–35.

[1] J. M. D. Olmsted, François Magendie, pioneer in experimental physiology and scientific medicine in
XIX century France. With a preface by John F. Fulton. New York: Schuman's, 1944. xvi + 290
pp., illustrated.

[2] The complexity of the subject and the present impossibility of gaining access to much
important source material make it impossible for me to attempt more than a preliminary
answer. Nevertheless I think the indications which suggested themselves to me worth publishing if only as the tentative beginning of a more comprehensive scheme. In course of time I
intend to analyze the relation between physiology and philosophy in the 19th century and
such future work may offer the opportunity of correcting or amplifying what is said here.

I wish to take this opportunity to thank Dr. Erwin H. Ackerknecht for several bibliographical suggestions, particularly the book by Cailliet and the article of v. Hayek (see below notes 79

scavenger in the realm of science[3] and who led a lifelong fight against hypotheses and systems might be expected to lack all interest in philosophical questions. Indeed, if philosophy is limited to some traditional metaphysical problems like the existence of God and the immortality of the soul, Magendie's occasional remarks are vague and disconnected from his main work. In his "Précis élémentaire de physiologie" which appeared in 1816–1817,[4] Magendie wrote:

> The human intellect consists of phenomena so different from all others in nature, that they are referred to a particular being, regarded as an emanation from the Divinity.
>
> The belief in this being is too consolatory for the physiologist to doubt its existence; but the strictness of language and logic at present observed in physiology requires the human intellect to be treated as the result of the action of an organ.[5]

A few pages later he said:

> Whatever may be the number and diversity of the phenomena which belong to the human intellect, however different they may appear from all the other phenomena of life, and however evidently they may be dependent upon the soul, it is necessary to consider them as the result of the action of the brain, and not in any measure to distinguish them from other phenomena which depend upon organic action.[6]

From these quotations it is clear that as a physiologist Magendie treated the human intellect as a function of the brain. This in itself is very important, but does it mean that, beyond physiology, he recognized the soul as a divine emanation? Or were these remarks meant ironically? Or were they an outgrowth of mere religious and philosophical indifference which did not think it worth while to offend publicly prevailing sentiments?

Such questions are more easily raised than answered. Besides, the impression cannot be avoided that they do not touch the core of Magendie's interests which seem to have been absorbed by his scientific work. During his last fatal illness, he remarked to a colleague: "You see me here completing my experiments; never has the science to which I have devoted all my energies appeared to me surrounded by more grandeur. The forces of life, so marvellously integrated, awaken to make each of us a passing instrument which upon extinction is regenerated. At least I have been able, during my limited course, to place a few landmarks on the road which leads to Truth, the only power to which I have subordinated my reason."[7] This solemn

---

and 113). These suggestions were made while Dr. Ackerknecht was still on the staff of the Johns Hopkins Institute of the History of Medicine, when I frequently had stimulating talks with him concerning various phases of my above mentioned project.

[3]Cf. Claude Bernard, *Leçons sur les effets des substances toxiques et médicamenteuses.* Paris, 1857, p. 12 f. Cf. also J. M. D. Olmsted, *Claude Bernard, physiologist.* New York and London: Harper and Brothers, 1938, p. 25.

[4]In the following abbreviated as "Précis." For the English quotations from this work I used the translation by J. S. Forsyth which appeared under the title of *"An elementary summary of physiology. By F. Magendie,"* London, 1825. This will be abbreviated by "Summary."

[5]*Summary* I, p. 104 f. (cf. *Précis* I, p. 154).

[6]*Summary* I, p. 115 (cf. *Précis* I, p. 170).

[7]P. Flourens, *Éloge historique de François Magendie.* Paris, 1858, p. 57.

remark reveals Magendie's impersonal concept of science, but it also suggests that he felt no need to step beyond the boundaries of medicine and physiology.

It is, therefore, all the more interesting to see that Magendie, at one time in his life at least, took an interest in philosophical literature. The title-page of his doctoral thesis[8] carries the following motto:

> Il faut ménager le temps de ses lecteurs.
> jamais on ne saurait en être trop avare.[9]
> DESTULT [*sic*] TRACI, *Elémens d'idéologie.*

This sentence is taken from the second part of the "Éléments d'idéologie" by Destutt de Tracy (1754–1836),[10] the French philosopher, who used the term "idéologie" as designating the science of ideas which was to replace the older metaphysical systems. Destutt de Tracy was one of the leaders of the "idéologues" who had aroused Napoleon's suspicious contempt.[11] The other head of this school was the physician Cabanis (1757–1808), whose fame chiefly rests on his "Rapports du physique et du moral de l'homme," part of which was published in 1798–99, while the first complete edition appeared in 1802. These two men stood in the philosophical center of a large but loosely connected group of intellectuals who, with more or less accuracy, have been called idéologues. It is significant that Magendie's first publication already indicated some connection with their work.

But before this lead is followed further, another circumstance has to be mentioned which points to a connection between Magendie's physiological work and some broad principles guiding it. In 1809, the year following his graduation, Magendie brought out "Quelques idées générales sur les phénomènes particuliers aux corps vivans."[12] In a chapter headed "Revolt from Bichat 1809," Dr. Olmsted[13] has analyzed the salient points of this essay against the background of a résumé of Bichat's doctrines. He has found that it already announces "the general principles to which he [i.e. Magendie] was to adhere for the whole of his career." And Dr. Olmsted adds that "the paper is unique" among Magendie's publications since it does not describe any experimental or other observations.[14] In other

---

[8]*Essai sur les usages du voile du palais, avec quelques propositions sur la fracture du cartilage des côtes.* Paris, 1808.

[9]For translation cf. Olmsted, *Magendie*, p. 18.

[10]*Élémens d'idéologie. Seconde partie. Grammaire.* Par le Cen. Destutt-Tracy. Paris, an XI = 1803, p. x. A second edition of the first part with the sub-title *"Idéologie proprement dite"* appeared in 1804, while the third part, *"Logique,"* was published in 1805. The fourth and fifth parts, called *"Traité de la volonté et de ses effets,"* I was able to use in the second edition of 1818.

Since Magendie's thesis dwelt on phonetical questions, this may have conceivably led him to consult the second part of Destutt de Tracy's work which included a discussion of the origin of words. However, once attracted, his interest certainly increased as will become clear further on.

[11]Cf. Picavet, *Les idéologues*, Paris, 1891, p. 21 ff.

[12]Cf. Olmsted, *Magendie*, pp. 20 and 271. Unfortunately, I have not been able to obtain a copy of this essay.

[13]*Ibid.*, p. 19 ff.

[14]*Ibid.*, p. 34.

words, Magendie, outstanding throughout his life for his "distrust of theory and firm faith in experiment,"[15] conceived his program largely on theoretical grounds.

It, therefore, seems worth while asking whether such theoretical opinions as underlined his physiological work were related to some current philosophical thought of his time, more specifically to the "idéologie" with which he had already been acquainted as a medical student.

2

Physiology is confronted with philosophical issues on two sides. At one end, so to speak, it touches upon the relationship between matter and life, while at the opposite end it meets the problem of body and mind. On both points Magendie expressed himself in no uncertain terms, so that his historical position can be fixed with some degree of certainty.

Descartes had made the human body a mere machine assigning the mind to the realm of pure spiritual existence. The idéologues, on the other hand, made the mind a mere function of the body. It was Destutt de Tracy who said: "One has but an incomplete knowledge of an animal if one does not know its intellectual faculties. Ideology is a part of zoology, and it is particularly in man that this part is important and deserves to be examined thoroughly."[16] Small wonder then that in the early decades of the 19th century Destutt de Tracy was considered the head of French materialism, and Heinrich Heine, comparing French and German philosophers, called him "the Fichte of materialism."[17]

In a passage which has remained famous, Cabanis had said: "In order to form a correct idea of the operations from which thought results, one must consider the brain as a particular organ, especially destined to produce it; just as the stomach and intestines are destined to effect digestion, the liver to filter the bile, and the parotid, maxillary and sublingual glands to prepare the salivary juices." And once again comparing the functions of stomach and brain, he had added that "the brain, in some way, digests impressions and that organically (organiquement) it effects the secretion of thought."[18] This passage became the mainstay of the popularizers of materialism in the middle of the 19th century.[19]

As has already been remarked, Magendie too had insisted that the physiologist had to treat intellectual phenomena as the result of the action

[15]*Ibid.*, p. 33.
[16]Destutt de Tracy, *Élémens d'idéologie*, I, p. xiii.
[17]H. Heine, Französische Zustände (letter of June 2, 1842), *Sämtliche Werke*, Leipzig, Reclam, 4. Bd., p. 285.
[18]P.-J.-G. Cabanis, *Rapports du physique et du moral de l'homme*. Huitième édition augmentée de notes etc. par L. Peisse. Paris, 1844, p. 137–138.
[19]Cf. *ibid.* p. 138, editor's note. Cf. also F. A. Lange, *Geschichte des Materialismus*, zweite Aufl., 2. Buch, 1. Hälfte, Leipzig u. Iserlohn, 1874, pp. 134, 152 and 288;—J. T. Merz, *A history of European thought in the nineteenth century*, vol. II, third unaltered edition, Edinburgh and London, 1928, p. 469 f.;—G. H. Lewes, *The history of philosophy from Thales to Comte*, 3rd ed., vol. II, London, 1867, p. 375.

of the brain just as any other phenomenon depending on organic action. Such a study, if strictly adhering to observation and avoiding any hypothetical ideas, would become purely physiological and would not belong to metaphysics exclusively.[20] And then he continued with a paragraph important enough to be cited in full:

> However this may be, the study of the intellect does not at present form an essential part of physiology; a science is specially devoted to it, I mean *ideology*. Those who wish to acquire enlarged views of this interesting subject, must consult the works of Bacon, Locke, Condillac, Cabanis, and especially the excellent work of M. Destutt Tracy, entitled *Elemens d'Ideologie*. We shall at present confine ourselves to some of the fundamental principles of this science.
>
> The innumerable phenomena which constitute the human intellect, are only modifications of the faculty of feeling. If they are attentively examined, this truth will be easily acknowledged, which is fully set forth by modern metaphysicians.[21]

Together with Destutt de Tracy, Magendie distinguishes the following "four principal modifications of the faculties of feeling"; *sensibility, memory, judgment* and "the *desires* or *will*."[22] To each of them he devotes a short section, the last one being of special interest since it contains a few remarks on the science of morals and on understanding. Happiness results from the satisfaction of our desires whereas lack of such satisfaction leads to unhappiness. "*Morals* are a science whose object is to give the best possible direction to our desires."[23] In particular, we ought to avoid hurtful things and should not desire things which we cannot attain. *Understanding* is achieved by combinations and inter-reactions of the simple faculties. It is characterized by the faculty of generalizing, viz. the creation of signs which represent ideas, thinking by means of these signs and the formation of abstract ideas. But only in a state of society is man able to develop this faculty of generalizing. Moreover, cultivation of the mind depends on ease in procuring a living and on satisfaction of all the wants of man's organization. This is the case in civilized countries, whereas in "hunting nations, in hordes of savages, the rustic slave, etc."[24] man's understanding will remain imperfect, since it must constantly be directed towards the one end of satisfying his needs.

The latter ideas are expounded at greater length in the following sections "Of Instinct and Passions" and "Of the Passions." Nature has given instinct to all animals with the twofold aim of the preservation of the individual and of the species. In man, whose instincts are "enlightened" because they are accompanied by a knowledge of the ends, two kinds can be found. The *animal instinct*, relates to his various needs from hunger, thirst, etc., down to the tendency to live in a society, whereby the path for the development of the various stages of civilization is opened. The *social in-*

---

[20]Magendie, *Summary* I, p. 115 f. (*Précis* I, p. 171).
[21]*Ibid.*, p. 116 (*Précis* I, p. 171).
[22]*Ibid.*, p. 116 (*Précis* I, p. 172).
[23]*Ibid.*, p. 120 (*Précis* I, p. 177).
[24]*Ibid.*, p. 121 (*Précis* I, p. 179).

stinct is the response to new needs which arise with man's living in civilized society under conditions of freedom from want and of leisure. The sentiments that now stand in the foreground are a desire for a lively feeling of existence and the love of idleness. The former leads to an ever increasing craving for excitement, since sensations become blunted by experience, "hence the ennui which incessantly torments man when civilized and unoccupied."[25] On the other hand, "the want of lively existence is balanced by the love of repose or idleness, which acts so powerfully upon the opulent class of society. These two contradictory feelings modify each other, and from their reciprocal action arises the love of power, of consideration, fortune, etc. which afford us all the means of satisfying both."[26] The social instinct, as a "vital phenomenon" also depends on organization.[27] It is, therefore, not opposed to the animal instinct.

The natural wants influence the social, and these in their turn modify the former; when we also recollect that age, sex, temperament, etc. forcibly alter every kind of want, we shall be able to conceive the difficulty of studying human instinct: and in fact this point of physiology is at present scarcely even roughly sketched.[28]

Passions are but extreme and exclusive forms of instinctive feelings and can, therefore, also be divided into animal and social, the latter being "merely the social wants carried to a high degree."[29] If gratification of passions leads to their appeasement, happiness may result, but if it only leads to more irritation, misfortune is bound to arise. Social wants further understanding which goes to explain the relatively high intellectual capacity of members of "the higher class of society."[30] But it is on the passions that the greatness of human actions depends, be they good or bad. "Great poets, heroes, great criminals and conquerors are empassioned men."[31]

Having reached this peak of his psychological doctrine, Magendie still does not deny its sensualistic origin. The passions are internal sensations: therefore they have no definite *seat* and Bichat was wrong when he made them reside in organic life. They result from the action of the nervous system in general and of the brain in particular: therefore they can be as little explained as any other vital actions. "One should observe, direct, calm, or extinguish them, but not explain them."[32]

---

[25]*Ibid.*, p. 123 (*Précis* I, p. 182).

[26]*Ibid.*

[27]*Précis* I, p. 180: "L'autre genre d'instinct naît de l'état social; sans doute il dépend de l'organisation: quel phénomène vital n'en dépend point?"

[28]*Summary* I, p. 123 (*Précis* I, p. 183).

[29]*Ibid.*, p. 125 (*Précis* I, p. 184).

[30]*Ibid.*, p. 124 (*Précis* I, p. 183: "la classe aisée de la société").

[31]*Ibid.*, p. 125 (*Précis* I, p. 185).

[32]*Précis* I, p. 185. In a footnote (*Summary* I, p. 125), Magendie adds that "this would be the place to treat of the use of the different parts of the brain, in the understanding and instinctive faculties," if the subject were not "too conjectural or too little known to be considered in an elementary work." This might be taken as an allusion to Gall's doctrine, and it is not impossible that Magendie was interested in Gall's theory of innate instincts and passions as depending on the organization of the brain, without following him into his phrenological system.

Even in the discussion of sensibility, memory, judgment and will where Magendie claimed but to outline the science of ideology and indeed followed the arrangement of Destutt de Tracy, he frequently went his own way. In his views of instinct and passions he seems to be even more independent of any direct model. "Without being entirely new, the ideas which he sets forth concerning the instinct and the passions are for the greater part not to be found in our elementary works on physiology, and from this point of view they give a real advantage to the one under discussion."[33] This praise by a contemporary reviewer extends particularly to those parts of the "Précis" where Magendie applies these ideas to the relationship between sensations, motions, the will and instinct and passions.[34] The discussion is preceded by a distinction between the "cry or native voice" and the "acquired voice, or voice properly so called."[35] The cry is independent from man's intellectual achievements, it is a mere consequence of his organization and serves to "express our most simple instinctive wants, our natural passions."[36] It is the kind of language that evokes joy, pity, dread, etc. in others and which man possesses in common with most animals. Voice properly so called must be learned, i.e. acquired. It presupposes not only hearing and intelligence, but also a state of social existence. It is the "social voice" and speech and singing are its modifications.[37]

Man alone is gifted with *speech*, which is the most powerful means of expression possessed by the mind; he alone also attaches a meaning to the words which he pronounces, and to the arrangement which he gives them; without his intellect he could not speak. In fact, most idiots cannot speak; they articulate sounds vaguely, which have, and can have, no signification.[38]

Singing, like voice and speech, is the effect of society. It supposes an ear and understanding. It is generally employed to signify [peindre] instinctive wants, passions, different states of mind: joy, sorrow, successful or unsuccessful love, excite different kinds of songs.

Singing may be articulate. Then instead of expressing feelings only, it becomes the means of expressing most acts of the understanding, but particularly those which are connected with the *social* passions.[39]

As a subject which he had already approached in his doctoral thesis, the physiology of the voice was sufficiently near to Magendie to receive more than casual attention. But in principle the remarks made here could serve as paradigms for more general considerations. All those movements which are called "gestures" (gestes) are intended to express our intellectual and

---

[33]Review by Chamberet of the first volume of the *Précis* in: *Journal de médecine, chirurgie, pharmacie, etc.*, 1816, t. 36, p. 291.

[34]*Ibid.*, p. 291. Cf. *Summary* I, pp. 204–211 (*Précis* I, pp. 300–310).

[35]*Summary* I, p. 151 ff. (*Précis* I, p. 224 ff.).

[36]*Ibid.*, p. 152 (*Précis, p.* 225).

[37]*Ibid.*, p. 153 (*Précis*, p. 227: "la parole et le chant ne sont que des modifications de la voix sociale").

[38]*Ibid.*, p. 155 f. (*Précis*, p. 230). The statement concerning idiots is accompanied by a reference to "Pinel, *Traité de la Manie*, pag. 167."

[39]*Summary* I, p. 157 (*Précis* I, p. 232 f.).

instinctive acts and can be divided into those intimately connected with organization which "are to the motions, what cry is to the voice"[40] and those that "may be termed *acquired or social gestures,* from their analogy to acquired voice."[41] Just as a person, born deaf, will not develop a social voice, so a person blind from birth will not acquire social gestures.[42]

Magendie now raises the question in how far our attitudes and motions are dependent upon our will. Willful actions presuppose an idea of the motion to be produced. Whereas the will can determine what motion should result, it cannot direct the contractions of the individual muscles which make the motion possible; this part is purely instinctive. Magendie cites Legallois as having supplied the experimental basis for this contention.

His [i.e., Legallois] experiments have demonstrated that the will is more particularly seated in the cerebrum and cerebellum. The direct cause of motion appears, on the contrary, seated in the spinal marrow. If the spinal marrow is separated from the rest of the brain by a section behind the occipital bone, the will is prevented from determining and directing the motions; but the latter are not the less produced; it is true that as soon as the separation is made they become very irregular in extent, rapidity, duration, direction, etc.[43]

This demonstration of the essential rôle which instinct plays even in voluntary motions and attitudes now closes the circle. Not only do voice and gestures express instinctive feelings and passions but motions are also dependent upon "natural passions and all the instinctive phenomena which are developed in the social state."[44] Passions can excite and strengthen motions, and they can also make them impossible: "hence the art of pantomime is employed with success in painting violent passions."[45]

It might not be impossible to annotate this outline with various references showing to what authors Magendie could have been indebted. More important than such details, however, is the general observation that at his time it was almost customary among medical scientists to deal with psychological and sociological questions. And here again, the heirs of the philosophers of the 18th century had set the tone. Cabanis' "Rapports" had tried to prove that man's body and mind should be seen from a common angle.[46] Destutt de Tracy had declared that the study of man's mind was a province of zoology.[47] Even Bichat, though somewhat reluctant to accept the radicalism to which the idéologues had pushed Condillac's doctrine,[48] paid much attention to the interdependence between the functions of

[40]*Ibid.,* p. 205 (*Précis,* p. 302).
[41]*Ibid.,* p. 206 (*Précis,* p. 302).
[42]*Ibid.,* p. 206 (*Précis,* p. 302).
[43]*Ibid.,* p. 209 (*Précis,* p. 306).
[44]*Ibid.,* p. 210 (*Précis,* p. 308).
[45]*Ibid.*
[46]Cf. Lewes, *op. cit.,* p. 368 ff.
[47]Cf. above, p. 320 and G. Boas, *French philosophies of the romantic period.* Baltimore, 1925, chaps. 1 and 2.
[48]Cf. below, p. 332.

man's organism and the society in which he lived. Bichat, just as Cabanis' friend Alibert (1768–1837) and others who had lived through the turmoil of the French revolution, studied the effects of political passions on human health,[49] and in the early decades of the 19th century the physiological aspects of passions became a favorite theme among French medical authors,[50] culminating in Alibert's treatise of 1825.[51] Obviously, therefore, Magendie did nothing unusual in projecting physiology into the realm of sociology. If anything, Magendie was even relatively restrained in this respect, for he wished to exclude from his work what he did not consider pertinent to physiology and medicine, as for instance the origin of language and the invention of the alphabet. "This knowledge," he said, "would undoubtedly be curious and useful, but it is not indispensable, and besides does not belong to physiology."[52]

3

As far as the relationship between body and mind is concerned, Magendie not only accepted the basic doctrines of the idéologues but openly acknowledged his indebtedness to them. Such an acknowledgement will not be found regarding the way Magendie visualized the relationship of matter and life. Nevertheless, a parallel can be perceived which goes far to explain Magendie's vitalistic attitude.

Descartes' vision of the animal organism as a machine acting according to mechanical laws had deeply influenced philosophers as well as physicians of the 17th century. A reaction had set in during the 18th century under the influence of Stahl in Germany and Bordeu and Barthez in France, and towards the turn of the century, vitalism, in one form of another, was accepted by most medical men. Under these circumstances, the ideas of Cabanis are significant since he was the physiologist of the "idéologie."

Cabanis is not a very concise thinker. At first glance it might seem as if life to him were nothing but a complicated interplay of general physical laws. He denied the distinction between inanimate and living matter as "chimerical" and maintained that, under certain conditions, inanimate matter was capable of becoming organized, alive and sensitive.[53] At the bottom of all natural phenomena there was a tendency of bodies to come together. If this tendency expresses itself in different laws and, consequently, different properties, this depends upon "the condition in which the isolated elements find themselves, and the circumstances under which they

---

[49]Cf. Bichat, Recherches physiologiques sur la vie et la mort, in: *Anatomie générale précédée des recherches physiologiques* etc., nouvelle édition, t. 1, Paris, 1818, p. 41. As early as 1795, Alibert had published an article "De l'influence des causes politiques sur les maladies et la constitution physique de l'homme"; cf. L. Brodier, *J.-L. Alibert*, Paris, 1923, p. 383 and *passim*.

[50]Cf. Brodier, *op. cit.*, p. 266 ff.

[51]Cf. *ibid.*, p. 265 ff. and 384. The title was: "Physiologie des passions, ou nouvelle doctrine des sentiments moraux."

[52]Magendie, *Summary* I, p. 153 f. (*Précis* I, p. 227).

[53]Cabanis, *Rapports*, p. 471 f.

meet."[54] All this sounds mechanistic enough, almost like an attempt at generalizing the concept of gravitation for all branches of science. But it is contradicted and partly even reversed by a second line of thought.[55] In Cabanis' view we may succeed in discovering the *conditions* under which life emerges from lower forms, but in all probability we shall never be able to penetrate to the *causes* which determine the organization of matter.[56] Cabanis extends this agnostic attitude towards sensibility which for him is "the unique and common principle of the vital faculties."[57] We may study its phenomena but are unable to fathom its cause which cannot be a proper object for research. The operations of the nervous system with which sensibility is closely connected are not to be explained by mere physical or chemical hypotheses; their explanation must be looked for in the living body itself.[58] Thus in spite of his denial of a distinction between inanimate and living matter, Cabanis, to all practical purposes, reintroduced vitalistic ideas. And on top of this he raised the question as to whether the tendency of all matter towards some center of attraction (gravitational, chemical, etc.) was not itself a kind of "universal instinct," still vague in mere gravitation, but attaining its highest form in human intelligence. "Are the other attractions to be explained by sensibility, or are sensibility and the intermediate tendencies between these two terms to be explained by gravitation?"[59] Cabanis leaves little doubt that he favors an anthropological interpretation of nature based on introspective experiences.[60] Now, the idéologues were heirs to the sensualistic philosophy of Condillac (1715–1780), and the idea of sensibility as the metaphysical center of man and the universe may be called a logical consequence of radical sensualism. But from this concept according to which gravitation is a primordial form of the human will, there is but a short step to Schopenhauer who indeed cited Cabanis in support of his thesis that will was at the core of the phenomena of nature.[61]

Whether Magendie followed Cabanis in his metaphysical speculations remains uncertain, but there is a remarkable analogy between the ways in which the two men considered the interdependence of physical and vital phenomena in physiology. Expounded at great length in the "Rapports," the doctrine is stated more succinctly in Cabanis' "Coup d'oeil sur les révo-

---

[54]*Ibid.*, p. 491.

[55]Cf. *ibid.*, p. 492, editor's note.

[56]*Ibid.*, p. 469.

[57]*Ibid.*, p. 111.

[58]*Ibid.*, p. 505. This reference is particularly remarkable in view of the fact that for Magendie too the vital actions of the nervous system above all were excepted from physico-chemical analysis; cf. C. A. Wunderlich, *Geschichte der Medicin*, Stuttgart, 1859, p. 319. Wunderlich is one of the very few historians to connect the names of Cabanis and Magendie directly: "Die Gewebsanatomie Bichat's und Cabanis' Auffassung des Organismus haben die zahlreichen und meisterhaften Untersuchungen Magendie's vorbereitet" (p. 319).

[59]*Ibid.*, p. 491 f.

[60]*Ibid.*, p. 492.

[61]Cf. Paul Janet, Schopenhauer et la physiologie française. Cabanis et Bichat. *Revue des deux mondes*, troisième periode, 1880, t. 39, pp. 35–59. E. Schiff, *Pierre Jean Georges Cabanis, der Arzt und Philosoph*, Diss. Berlin, 1886, p. 54.

lutions et sur la réforme de la médecine," [62] a book that was written in the year III of the revolution, [63] but not published until 1804. In a footnote of this work, Cabanis refers to his "friend Boyer," [64] the great surgeon who was also the friend of Magendie's father and Magendie's first medical teacher. [65] Cabanis here distinguishes several degrees of existence among natural objects. There are first of all those which do not show any organization and are subject to the general law of physical masses only. Next come the bodies such as crystals and salts which show distinct characteristics due to particular laws of formation. The vegetable kingdom represents the third degree, and the fourth and final degree is reached with the animals, all of which are endowed with feeling. In this chain of beings, "the characteristic laws of each class are found again, in certain respects, in the preceding or following class." [66] Two consequences follow from this position. On the one hand, it is impossible to reduce completely the laws of animal life to mere physics and chemistry as the iatrophysicists and iatrochemists had tried to do. Cabanis attacked them with no less vigor than did Bichat and other vitalists. On the other hand, since the laws of a lower class still operate in the higher ones, physics and chemistry need not be entirely banned from animal physiology. "Some phenomena of the animal economy, from certain points of view at least, belong to simple mechanics. Others are a direct consequence of the structure of the organs and of their mutual relationships. There are phenomena that result from the laws to which the course of fluids in a system of pipes is subjected. There are also such as are purely chemical whereas others, finally, are exclusively due to the action of sensibility." [67]

If in this quotation "vital force" were substituted for "sensibility," Magendie might have identified himself with the views expressed. For Magendie admits that brute and living bodies differ as to form, composition and the laws governing them. Brute bodies are "subjected entirely to attraction and chemical affinity," whereas living bodies are "partly subjected to attraction and chemical affinity, partly subjected to an unknown power." [68] This analysis into a *partly* physical and chemical and a *partly* vital element remained one of the most remarkable features in Magendie's physiology. [69] Even in his "Phénomènes physiques de la vie," published in 1842, he was just as emphatic in proving that physics has a place in physiology as he was serious in his warning not to explain everything "by the laws

[62]P. J. G. Cabanis, *Coup d'oeil sur les révolutions et sur la réforme de la médecine.* Paris, an XII—1804.

[63]*Ibid.*, p. v: "L'ouvrage suivant a été écrit dans l'hiver de l'an III."

[64]*Ibid.*, p. 324, note: "Quand j'écrivois ceci, l'Anatomie de mon ami Boyer n'existoit pas encore."

[65]Cf. Olmsted, *Magendie*, p. 9.

[66]Cabanis, *Coup d'oeil*, p. 257.

[67]*Ibid.*, p. 258.

[68]Magendie, *Summary* I, p. 3 (*Précis* I, p. 4).

[69]Cf. Olmsted, *Magendie*, pp. 33, 83 and 202.

which hold sway over inorganic matter."[70] It would be misleading to over-look the fact that Magendie went incomparably further than did Cabanis in realizing the importance of physics and chemistry. But it has also to be stressed that his vitalism was more deeply rooted than merely in the prevailing influence of Bichat.

It is possible to pursue the analogy between the vitalism of Magendie and that of the "idéologues" in some more detail. The "vital force," according to Magendie, is an unknown power and this and similar terms merely conceal "the absolute ignorance in which we always have been, and perhaps always shall be, respecting the cause of life."[71] Vital phenomena can be reduced to "nutrition" and "vital action" which are closely interrelated. "Nutrition," fundamentally, is an intimate movement of particles, fresh ones replacing old ones in the organs. "This movement allows no explanation. At the present state of physiology it can by no means be related to the molecular movements which are governed by chemical affinity."[72] By "vital action," Magendie designates such phenomena as the formation of bile by the liver and muscular contraction. And just as in nutrition so in vital action too the mechanism consists in an inexplicable molecular movement. "There occurs in the organ which acts an insensible molecular movement, as inexplicable as the nutritive movement. No vital action, however simple, is an exception in this respect."[73]

Magendie's emphatic insistence that vital force was just a term to hide our ignorance, must not obscure the fact that he took this admission of ignorance very seriously. Observation and experiment might lead to an exact knowledge of vital actions; but here investigation had to rest, further analysis being hopeless. Perhaps this is one of the reasons why Magendie, as an experimenting physiologist, concentrated on vivisection where the vital phenomena could be studied as such.

The problem of vital force had also been taken up by Destutt de Tracy. Feeling and movement (internal as well as external) constitute life; though movement may be considered the prior faculty since even purely intellectual perceptions presume some movement taking place in our organs.[74] The "vital force" (force vitale) is the cause of the movements though we do not know how the latter are brought about. But since we have to acknowledge the reality of life as contrasted with death, we also have to acknowledge a vital force.

Thus life is something: also life it is which effects that as long as a body is endowed with it, that body has the power of assimilating to its substance the bodies with which it is in suitable contact, whereas, as soon as it is dead, all the elements

---

[70]Quoted by Olmsted, *ibid.*, p. 203, note.

[71]Magendie, *Summary* I, p. viii f. (*Précis* I, p. iv).

[72]Magendie, *Précis* I, p. 20.

[73]Magendie, *Summary* I, p. 16 (*Précis* I, p. 22). The ideas on nutrition and vital action were already propounded in his essay of 1809; cf. Olmsted, p. 28.

[74]Destutt de Tracy, *Élémens d'idéologie*, I, p. 246 f. However, in vol. 4, p. 494, he admits that sensibility may be "une propriété universellement répandue dans toute la nature." His attitude in this respect is fundamentally the same as that of Cabanis.

which compose it, disintegrate, separate and enter into new combinations with the surrounding beings, following new laws of affinity. We do not know of what this vital force consists; we can only picture it to ourselves as the result of attractions and chemical combinations which for a time give birth to a particular order of facts and soon, by virtue of unknown circumstances, return to the realm of more general laws, which are those of unorganized matter.[75] As long as it endures, *we are alive: that is, we move and feel.*[76]

To sum up: Both Magendie and Destutt de Tracy believe in the autonomy of animal life, an autonomy expressed by the concept of vital force. But the vital force is not on a par with physical and chemical forces.[77] It represents the integration of molecular movements on a new and higher level. Since we are unable to fathom the principle of this integration, we cannot consider the human organism a mere machine as Descartes had done before. With Destutt de Tracy and Cabanis, Magendie was rooted in the sensualistic tradition which went back to Condillac and Locke and which did not identify itself with the mechanical rationalism of Descartes.[78]

4

It is hardly necessary to point out that Magendie was not a "disciple" of Cabanis and Destutt de Tracy, if by this word is meant the faithful adherent of a detailed body of doctrines. The "idéologie," after all, was nothing but a philosophical background for him, a background which he shared with many of his contemporaries. In fact, the circle of men with varying shades of opinion who have been named "idéologues"[79] is so wide that the term is not free from vagueness. This circumstance makes it desirable to comment briefly on at least two physiologists, viz. Richerand and Bichat, because Magendie had to compete with the textbook of the former and the ideas of the latter.

[75]A similar idea occurs in Bichat's *Anatomie générale* (cf. above, note 49), p. 18. On Bichat's relationship to the idéologues, cf. below, p. 331 f.

[76]Destutt de Tracy, *op. cit.,* I, p. 248 f. A striking parallel to the last sentence occurs in the opening of Legallois' Expériences sur le principe de la vie (*Oeuvres*, t. 1, Paris, 1830, p. 33): "Parmi les facultés propres aux animaux, celles qui les caractérisent éminemment sont la faculté de sentir et celle de se mouvoir, et l'on peut dire que le véritable but de l'organisation d'un animal est de produire et d'entretenir ces deux facultés. Quels que soient les moyens intérieurs ou extérieurs, les ressorts secrets ou apparens que la nature emploie pour cela, et quel que soit l'état actuel de ces moyens et de ces ressorts, dès qu'un être sent et se meut spontanément, c'est un animal vivant et qui a le sentiment de son existence."

[77]Destutt de Tracy (*op. cit.,* p. 247) is careful to point out that our power of spontaneous movement does not constitute a new physical force.

[78]Destutt de Tracy, *Élémens d'idéologie*, IV, p. 491 ff., argues against Descartes' concept. On the fate of mechanistic ideas in 18th century France cf. L. C. Rosenfield, *From beast-machine to man-machine,* New York, 1941, particularly ch. 2 and pp. 195 ff. On the connection between sensualism and French physiology and psychology cf. Sudhoff-Pagel, *Kurzes Handbuch der Geschichte der Medizin,* 3. u. 4. Aufl., Berlin, 1922, pp. 333 f., 351 and 359 ff., where Cabanis' influence is also mentioned.

[79]Cf. particularly the standard work by Picavet (see above, note 11) and E. Cailliet, *La tradition littéraire des idéologues,* Philadelphia, 1943 [Memoirs of The American Philosophical Society, vol. 19, 1943].

A superficial glimpse at Richerand's "Nouveaux éléments de physiologie" suffices to show how wide-spread was the influence of Cabanis and Destutt de Tracy during Magendie's formative years. Balthasar-Anthelme Richerand (1779–1840), famous as a surgeon and the rival of Dupuytren, had been a favorite disciple and friend of Cabanis. His textbook of physiology, which was first published in 1801, immediately became very popular inside as well as outside France, going through one edition after another till by 1832 it had expanded into three volumes.[80] It is said that the appearance of this text decided Cabanis to refrain from publishing the manuscript of a treatise on physiology which he himself had prepared.[81] The inclusion of Richerand among the idéologues, therefore, seems justified.

Richerand's "Elements" are modeled after Haller's "First Lines of Physiology"—such at least is the contention of the author.[82] The name of Condillac appears already in the preface, to be mentioned again and again in the work, particularly in those sections which deal with sensations.[83] But Richerand also takes issue with Condillac. Thus he blames him for having left "much doubt and uncertainty" regarding the individual faculties of the soul until Destutt de Tracy brought final clarity into the matter.

> The merit of dispersing the mist which covered this part of metaphysics, remained for M. Tracy. His Elements of Ideology, leave nothing to be wished for on this subject. I shall extract some of its main results, referring the reader for the rest to the work.[84]

Another point where Richerand deviated from Condillac concerns the external senses as the sole portal for sensations. Condillac had claimed that our ideas were derived from the impressions we receive through our external sense organs. Cabanis had considered this explanation insufficient and had added those impressions which resulted from the functions of internal organs.[85] These internal impressions, in the opinion of Cabanis, accounted for instinctive actions, and he noted "that the order which nature had established in this regard is extremely favorable for the preservation and the well-being of animals."[86] Destutt de Tracy laid much stress on

---

[80]Cf. A. Bonnet, article "Richerand" in: *Nouvelle biographie générale*, t. 42, Paris, 1863, cols. 253–255; Olmsted, *Magendie*, p. 66. In the following I make use of the American edition: *Elements of Physiology*, by A. Richerand. Translated from the French by G. J. M. De Lys, with notes by N. Chapman. Philadelphia, 1813.

[81]Cf. Peisse in: Cabanis, *Rapports*, p. xxxiii, note 3.

[82]Cf. Richerand, *op. cit.*, p. v.

[83]*Ibid.*, ch. VII: "Of Sensations."

[84]*Ibid.*, p. 400. This reference to Destutt de Tracy is similar to that made by Magendie in the latter's "Summary." Cf. above, p. 321. Another striking similarity occurs on p. 408 f. of Richerand's *Elements*: " . . . in a word, the knowledge of moral and intellectual man, belongs to the science known by the name of metaphysics or psychology, of analysis of the understanding, but better described by that applied to it by the writers of our days, ideology. On this science, you may consult, with advantage, the philosophical works of Plato and Aristotle among the ancients; of Bacon, Hobbes, Locke, Condillac, Bonnet, Smith, Cabanis, and Tracy among the moderns."

[85]Cabanis, *Rapports*, p. 118.

[86]*Ibid.*, p. 120.

these internal sensations which he believed present in all "sentiments" and "passions."[87] Richerand likewise accepted this step beyond Condillac. "But we are compelled to acknowledge with Cabanis, two sources of ideas quite distinct from each other: the external senses, and the internal organs. . . . Instinct, as the author just quoted has very justly observed, springs from impressions received by the interior organs, whilst reasoning is the produce of external sensations . . ."[88]

The differentiation between the realms of external and internal sensations finds, of course, a striking parallel in Bichat's distinction between the two lives of man, the animal and the organic. Indeed, Broussais (1772–1838) suggested that Bichat had adopted this idea from Cabanis.[89] The question of Bichat's relationship to the idéologues is a very complicated one,[90] confused by personal recriminations. Thus Cabanis made it rather clear that in his opinion Bichat had appropriated some of his views without giving proper credit; but he did not say to which views he was referring.[91] Richerand quite generally accused him of plagiarism. Praising Bichat's "Anatomie générale," Richerand added: "That glory would be complete, if in that book, and yet more, in his other works, he had done his predecessors, as well as his contemporaries, the justice they had a right to expect from him."[92] Bichat's relative and collaborator, Buisson, on the other hand, said that others had appropriated for themselves the distinction which Bichat, in his "Recherches physiologiques sur la vie et la mort," had established between the central and ganglionic nervous systems.[93] Richerand seems to have defended himself against such suspicions when he stated that his own researches on the sympathetic nerves went back as far as the year VII, "before anything that has appeared on the same subject."[94]

These accusations and counter-accusations reveal two things. In the first place, they serve to make clear that, through mutual influence or otherwise, Bichat and the idéologues show far-reaching agreement. This is particularly true with regard to Richerand and from this point of view, Magendie's revolt against Bichat is also a revolt against Richerand, and his reproach of systematizing may have been directed against the former as

---

[87]Destutt de Tracy, *Élémens d'idéologie*, I, pp. 37–39 and 422.

[88]Richerand, *op. cit.*, p. 392.

[89]F.-J.-V. Broussais, *Examen des doctrines médicales et des systèmes de nosologie*, t. 2, Paris, 1821, p. 389. Richerand, *op. cit.*, p. 72, claimed that the idea belonged to Grimaud. On this whole question cf. Arène, *op. cit.* (note 90), p. 779, and M. Genty, Bichat et son temps, chaps. 4 and 5, *La médecine internationale*, July 1934–Sept. 1935.

[90]Cf. on this subject A. Arène, Essai sur la philosophie de Xavier Bichat, *Arch. d'anthropol. crim.*, Oct.–Nov., 1911, pp. 753–825.

[91]Cabanis, *Rapports*, p. 48.

[92]Richerand, *op. cit.*, p. 19.

[93]M. F. R. Buisson, Précis historique sur Marie-François-Xavier Bichat, in Bichat's *Traité d'anatomie descriptive*, t. troisième, terminé et publié par M. F. R. Buisson. Paris, an XI (1802), p. xix, footnote. Cf. also Picavet, *op. cit.*, p. 435 f.

[94]Richerand, *op. cit.*, p. 57, footnote. I do not know whether this note already occurred in the first edition. On Richerand's hostile attitude towards Bichat cf. Genty, *loc. cit.* (note 89), and G. Genty, *Bichat, médecin du Grand Hospice d'Humanité*. Clermont (Oise), 1943, p. 24 f.

well as the latter.[95] But the strained relationship also suggests that Bichat was not in harmony with all the ideas of the idéologues. These differences apparently related to metaphysical questions. Condillac, sensualist that he was, still believed that it was the soul that felt, the organs of the body being its agents.[96] Cabanis and Destutt de Tracy, however, had little use for the soul; to them feeling became a biological phenomenon or even a general attribute of matter.[97] Now there is no doubt that Bichat was strongly influenced by Condillac[98] and it is not certain that he was willing to abandon the soul altogether. It is Condillac rather than Cabanis who made him say: " . . . for the brain is to the soul what the senses are to the brain; it transmits to the soul the impressions conveyed to it by the senses, as the senses convey to the brain the impressions made upon them by external objects."[99] Likewise, he remarked that the pleasure, pain and indifference which accompany our sensations are "by no means seated in the organs, which receive or transmit the sensation, but in the soul."[100] And a little later he warned against insisting upon the principles of physiology where they endangered those of morality. "The one, and the other are equally solid, though sometimes at variance."[101]

Statements like the above suggest that from the point of view of systematic philosophy, a line has to be drawn between Bichat and the idéologues.[102] But in the framework of the present article which is centered upon Magendie these metaphysical differences do not yield any clear lead. Magendie and even Richerand also mention the soul, yet this fact is hardly sufficient to class them with Bichat against Cabanis. Moreover, the outcry against materialism in the early 19th century, rightly or wrongly, included Bichat,[103] for the differences paled before the similarities. Nevertheless, regarding some basic problems more closely related to physiology, Magendie seems to have stood closer to Cabanis than to Bichat. He did not agree with Bichat's distinction between animal and organic life, yet he accepted Cabanis' distinction between external and internal sensations in the following words:

All sensations coming from within, arising independently of external agents, have been collectively designated by the denomination of *internal sensations,* or *sentiments.*

Their consideration was neglected by the metaphysicians of the last age; but this has now become the object of the study of many distinguished authors, particularly

[95]Cf. Olmsted, *Magendie,* p. 66.
[96]Cf. M. Frischeisen-Köhler and W. Moog, *Die Philosophie der Neuzeit bis zum Ende des XVIII. Jahrhunderts.* 12. Auflage, Berlin, 1924, p. 433 f. [Ueberwegs Grundriss der Geschichte der Philosophie III]. Cf. Condillac, Traité des sensations, in: *Oeuvres complètes de Condillac,* t. 3, Paris an VI. 1798, p. 51, note.
[97]Cf. above, pp. 325 f. and 328.
[98]Cf. Arène, *op. cit.,* p. 754 ff and 803.
[99]Xavier Bichat, *Physiological researches on life and death* (translated by F. Gold), with notes by F. Magendie (translated by G. Hayward). Boston, 1827, p. 30 f.
[100]*Ibid.,* p. 49.
[101]*Ibid.,* p. 50.
[102]Cf. Arène, *op. cit.* p. 822, note 1, who rightly points to Bichat's disdain of "philosophy."
[103]Cf. Arène, *op. cit.,* pp. 784 and 824 f.

of Cabanis, and M. Destutt-Tracy, and their history is one of the most curious parts of ideology.[104]

Moreover, in asserting that physics and chemistry had their legitimate place in physiological research, Magendie took an attitude which could more easily be reconciled with Cabanis' than Bichat's contentions. According to Bichat the vital properties of the tissues rather than their physical qualities decided all the phenomena of life. Since the former were opposed to physical and chemical laws, any attempts at mathematical exactness were eo ipso futile. Cabanis' argument was not so much a biological as a historical one. The dogmatic systems of iatrochemists and iatrophysicists had failed, attempts at measuring the muscular force necessary for digestion or of the heart had brought nothing but misleading and contradictory results:[105] therefore it was wrong to expect a solution of *all* medical problems from the exact sciences, for no more than a small province could be allowed to them.[106] Magendie quite agreed that physics and chemistry must not dominate physiology *exclusively*.[107] But the historical data of Cabanis could be countered by arguments taken from more recent history:

... even in the time of Bichat it could not be denied that it was to the progress of these same sciences, that was owing the explanation of many very important phenomena; that by it was ascertained what takes place in respiration, and by what means a living body always supports itself between certain limits of temperature, etc.[108]

This quotation, of course, refers to the famous experiments by Lavoisier and Laplace on respiration and animal heat. Flourens[109] as well as Claude Bernard[110] have stressed the influence of Laplace on Magendie's early development and the testimony of these two men has to be accepted. It is likewise certain that Laplace and the chemist Berthollet (1748–1822) took an active interest in Magendie's work,[111] just as (together with Corvisart)

[104]Magendie, *Summary* I, p. 94 (*Précis* I, p. 138).

[105]Cabanis, *Coup d'oeil*, p. 246 f.

[106]*Ibid.*, p. 246, note: "Sans doute les phénomènes de la vie peuvent, sous quelques points de vue, se prêter au calcul: mais ces points de vue sont en général peu importans" etc. In a final note to his *Du degré de certitude de la médecine* (nouvelle éd., Paris, an XI—1803, p. 161 f.) Cabanis even says: "Il faut convenir, de plus, que certaines parties de la physique animale, telles que l'appréciation des forces musculaires, la théorie de la vision, peut-être même celle de l'audition, ne paroissent guère pouvoir être traitées complètement, sans le secours des mathématiques." Magendie himself did by no means subscribe to an unwarranted extension of mathematical methods (cf. below, note 131), on the contrary, he has been blamed for neglecting measurement; cf. Wunderlich, *op. cit.*, p. 319 f. This somewhat narrows the gap between him and Cabanis (and even Bichat) whose main attack was directed against pretended mathematical exactness.

[107]Cf. above, p. 327 f.

[108]Bichat, *Physiological researches* etc., p. 80, note.

[109]Flourens, *op. cit.*, p. 20 f.

[110]Claude Bernard, *Rapport sur les progrès et la marche de la physiologie générale en France*, Paris, 1867, p. 6, and *Leçons sur les effets des substances toxiques et médicamenteuses*, Paris, 1857, p. 7.

[111]Cf. P. Mentrier, Documents inédits concernant Magendie, *Bulletin de la Société Française d'Histoire de la Médecine*, 1926, t. 20, p. 254, and Olmsted, *Magendie*, p. 152.

they had sponsored that other physiological experimentalist, Legallois.[112] The two famous men, both connected with the Ecole polytechnique,[113] encouraged the process of experimental physiology, and Magendie, in turn, was inspired by the example set by the exact scientists and particularly by Laplace.

The rôle which Magendie played in making physiology an experimental science will have to be discussed further in the following section. But just because Laplace has been brought into such close relationship to this rôle,[114] it has to be pointed out that Laplace himself has been numbered among the idéologues.[115] Cabanis had praised Laplace's lectures on probability,[116] and in his "Essai philosophique sur les probabilités," Laplace spoke of psychology as a mere extension of physiology. The sensorium in the brain, being continuously modified by impressions from the nerves, was the seat of sensation and thought.[117]

The argument of the present section offers a possible answer to the question why so little attention has been given to Magendie's affiliation with the ideas of the idéologues. These ideas were so current among contemporary physiologists that they seemed hardly worth while mentioning. What singled Magendie out was not his conformity with, but his departure from tradition. This departure will have to be discussed in the following final section.

5

It is not very surprising to find Magendie leaning towards the philosophy of the idéologues. The group had its social center in the salon of Madame Helvétius at Auteuil where Cabanis had met Condillac, Holbach, Jefferson, Franklin, Turgot and Destutt de Tracy, and where, among others, the physicians Richerand, Alibert, Pinel, Pariset and Moreau de la Sarthe were wont to assemble.[118]

Many of these men had become actively associated with the revolutionary movement. When the "Institut" was founded in 1795, its class of "sciences morales et politiques" had a "section de l'analyse des sensations et des idées,"[119] and this section was the academic center of the school. But in 1802 Chateaubriand published "Le génie du christianisme" in which he

[112]Notice biographique sur M. Legallois, *Bulletin de la Faculté de Médecine de Paris*, 1814, no. 5, p. 105 f.

[113]Cf. F. A. v. Hayek, The counter-revolution of science, *Economica*, new series, 1941, vol. 8 [pp. 9–36, 119–150 and 281–320], p. 17. I mention this relationship because I believe that v. Hayek has somewhat over-emphasized the contrasts between engineers and physicians.

[114]Cf. Olmsted, *Magendie*, p. 19 f. and *passim*.

[115]Cf. Picavet, *op. cit.*, p. 169 ff. and Cailliet, *op. cit. passim*.

[116]Cabanis, *Rapports*, p. 43, footnote.

[117]Laplace, *Essai philosophique sur les probabilités*, cinquième éd., Paris, 1825, p. 219 ff.

[118]Cf. Peisse in: Cabanis, *Rapport*, pp. xiii and xxiii and P. Delaunay, La médecine et les idéologues: L. J. Moreau de la Sarthe, *Bull. Soc. Franç. d'Hist. de la Méd.*, 1920, 14, pp. 24–60; cf. pp. 37 ff.

[119]Peisse, *loc. cit.*, p. 61.

attacked the "sophists"; in 1803 Napoleon reorganized the Institut and suppressed the section and in the following years the fight against "materialism" and for cultural and political restoration became more pronounced and successful.[120] But even after the return of Louis XVIII in 1815, the idéologues were by no means silenced.[121] In 1818, Pinel and Bricheteau wrote an article on "Idéologie" in which they stated: "It is doubtless not necessary for the physician to make a profound study of ideology, although he must on no account be ignorant of its fundamental principles...."[122] In 1832, following the revolution of 1830, the section de l'analyse etc. was resuscitated under Guizot as the section of philosophy, and Broussais was chosen to represent the medical point of view.[123] Gradually, however, the names of Cabanis and Destutt de Tracy became a historical memory. Claude Bernard does not seem to have been influenced by the works of these men in a directly formative way, though sensualism of course remained very much alive among physicians and biologists. Magendie thus appears as a connecting link between the idéologues proper and the physiologists succeeding him. The son of an ardent revolutionary and himself "an extreme liberal,"[124] Magendie was naturally attracted towards a philosophy which in his youth was a living issue.

The revolutionary background of the idéologues is very noticeable in their claim to metaphysical agnosticism, their rejection of systems and their emphasis on positive facts. "Analysis" was the catchword of the movement, an analysis that was to reveal simple constituent phenomena and their relations, but not first or final causes. Analysis was, therefore, opposed to the systems erected upon theological or metaphysical presuppositions, or derived from one-sided generalizations. Systems of this kind were denounced as loudly during the 1790's as was the political tyranny of the kings. In philosophy, physiology and medicine, the old systems had to be done away with if an edifice of reliable knowledge, founded on well established facts, was to be erected.

"Rational analytic philosophy," Cabanis said, "must begin to march according to the facts after the example of all those parts of human science that have acquired veritable certitude."[125] And with an eye upon medicine, he wrote: "The real treasures of the sciences lie in the constant and recognized truths and not in the display of systems. They are measured by exactness and not by number or the apparent grandeur of the ideas. Even when the methods of investigation are perfectly sure, one cannot repeat the application to the same objects too many times."[126] Similar views could be

[120]Cf. Boas, *op. cit.*, p. 26.

[121]Ferraz, *Etude sur la philosophie en France au XIXe siècle. Le socialisme, le naturalisme et le positivisme.* Paris, 1877, p. 239.

[122]*Dictionaire des sciences médicales par une société de médecins et de chirurgiens*, vol. 23, Paris, 1818, p. 473.

[123]Cf. Peisse, *loc. cit.*, p. 62.

[124]Cf. Olmsted, *Magendie*, p. 91 f.

[125]Cabanis, *Rapports*, p. 129.

[126]Cabanis, *Coup d'oeil* (see above, footnote 62), p. 269 f.

quoted from Alibert's "Quelques réflexions sur la valeur des systèmes dans l'étude des sciences" which appeared in 1797,[127] and Bichat, speaking of first causes, said:

Of what importance besides to us are these causes? Is it necessary to know the nature of light, of oxygen and caloric to study their phenomena? Without the knowledge of the principle of life, cannot we analyze its properties? In the study of animals let us proceed as modern metaphysicians have done in that of the understanding. Let us suppose causes, and attach ourselves to their general results.[128]

The latter reference to the "modern metaphysicians" must be interpreted as including the idéologues.[129] Indeed, whatever differences may have existed between the latter and Bichat, there was agreement upon the necessity of a positivistic approach to physiology. Here was the connecting link with the tradition of Albrecht von Haller[130] as well as with the exact sciences.[131]

The beginning of Magendie's preface to his "Précis" sounds almost like a summary of these views. He states that "every natural science may exist under two different forms, 1. systematic; 2. theoretical." The systematic form is based on "gratuitous suppositions," on "principles established *a priori*," and facts are sought for only to uphold a hypothesis. The theoretical form, on the other hand, rests on facts; "the learned endeavour to verify them, and to multiply them as much as possible, and afterwards study the relations of the different phenomena, and the laws to which they are subject." The method of the systematic form is "synthetic," that of the theoretical form is "analytic."[132]

These words might as well have been written 20 years before. But then the preface takes a turn which puts it in a provocative contrast to Magendie's predecessors. Before the time of Galileo and Bacon, he continues, almost all natural sciences were systematic, whereas since then they have become theoretic and analytic and more perfect from day to day. Yet physiology has not shared in this process, it has remained systematic.

If we attentively examine the manner in which it is treated in the best works, we shall find it founded upon mere suppositions, to which every one attaches at pleasure, the numerous phenomena of life, thinking that he is explaining them satisfac-

[127]Cf. Broider, *op. cit.*, pp. 242 ff. and 383.

[128]Bichat, *Physiological researches* etc., p. 77.

[129]Bichat was, of course acquainted with that part of Cabanis' *Rapports* which had been published in the *Mémoires* of the Institut since he refers to it in his *Recherches physiologiques, loc. cit.*, p. 89.

[130]Cf. Albrecht von Haller, *A dissertation on the sensible and irritable parts of animals*, Baltimore, 1936, pp. 7–8.

[131]On the formulation of French positivism by D'Alembert and other scientists before Comte cf. H. Gouhier, *La jeunesse d'Auguste Comte et la formation du positivisme* II, Paris, 1936 [Travaux et mémoires de l'Université de Lille, Nouv. sér.—Droit—lettres, 18], pp. 5–62, and v. Hayek, *op. cit.*, p. 11 ff. Magendie cites D'Alembert with approval in his *Summary* II, 2, p. 7, note (*Précis* II, p. 251), for his contention that experiments are the only promising path where a mathematical treatment of phenomena is impossible.

[132]Magendie, *Summary* I, vii f. (*Précis* I, p. i ff.)

torily. What in fact are the *vital* or *animal* spirits of the ancients, the *faculties* of Galen, the *moving* and *generating principle* of Aristotle, *the archeus, the vital principle, power* and *properties*, &c. which have been successively adopted to explain the animal functions, but arbitrary suppositions, which served through many ages to conceal the absolute ignorance in which we always have been, and perhaps always shall be, respecting the cause of life?[133]

This passage has a certain similarity with one written by Bichat who had condemned as futile "the archeus of van Helmont, the soul of Stahl, the vital principle of Barthez, the vital power of others."[134] By including the vital properties in his list, Magendie obviously aimed at Bichat himself, and there is indeed little doubt that Bichat, Richerand[135] and many of his contemporaries appeared as systematizers to Magendie. But his statement that physiology, fourteen years after Bichat's death, was still in its systematic form and consequently "still in its infancy" shows more than an attack upon Bichat's theories. It reveals the point where Magendie had developed beyond the tradition of the idéologues.

When Cabanis insisted upon a reform of medicine which would discard hypotheses and, instead, reorganize the mass of factual observations and experiments he was moved by a spirit of optimism. "Twenty-five or thirty years would suffice today to verify all observations (except perhaps those which refer to the epidemic constitutions). The same amount of time would also suffice for repeating all experiments and ascertaining their results."[136] If it is remembered that this was written in the year III of the revolution, "twenty-five or thirty years" would come near the publication of Magendie's "Précis." But then Cabanis conceived of this medical reform somewhat in the manner of those revolutionaries who thought that with the king and feudalism abolished, all the good qualities of man would soon assert themselves. After all, the idéologues believed in the perfectibility of man, and the temper of the time made men expect perfection soon. Just as the revolution ended in the splendor of Napoleon's empire, so the battle against hypotheses and one-sided theories often ended in new systems incorporating old and new facts. For this, the experimentalist and speculative physiologist Bichat was an outstanding example. And even the name of Laplace who wished "that every science be nothing but a unity of rigorously connected facts"[137] is bound up with an astronomical hypothesis. The desire to give a synthesis was strong among most idéologues though not always admitted. "In fact, I have not made a system," Destutt de Tracy answered a criticism that his system was inexact. He claimed only a collection of facts. If the latter fitted so well together as to deserve the name of a system, it would simply be that of nature herself and could not be called inexact. If, on the other hand, it contained badly observed facts (as very

[133]*Ibid.*, p. viii f.
[134]Bichat, *Physiological researches*, p. 76 f.
[135]Cf. Olmsted, *Magendie*, p. 66.
[136]Cabanis, *Coup d'oeil* etc., p. 275.
[137]Flourens, *op. cit.*, p. 21.

probably it did) they disrupted the connection of the others and there was no longer any general system. Instead of speaking of an inexact system, the critic ought to have unmasked the wrong facts.[138]

Magendie could hardly have taken exception to the logic of this argument. His criticism of contemporary physiology was not based on a philosophy opposed to that of the idéologues, but on applying the same philosophical arguments under different circumstances. Endowed with an uncompromising temperament, he perceived that the physiologists of the revolution had not kept faith with their own premises. Recognizing the value of physical and chemical contributions, he turned against the dogmatic rejection of these sciences from physiological research. Declaring physiology to be backward compared with other sciences, he refuted the claim of Bichat and Richerand to have employed physiological principles as solid as Newton's concept of gravity.[139] By contending that physiology, in 1816, was still in its infancy, he denied that it was ready for a systematic synthesis. In the preface of the "Précis" he proclaimed his aim of helping to put physiology upon equal terms with the most advanced sciences.

It must take the analytic course and theoretic form.... There will therefore above all be found in this work facts which I have directly verified as much as was in my power, either by observation upon the healthy or diseased subject, or by experiments upon living animals. Among these facts will be found many which are new.[140]

The idéologues had insisted upon facts and Magendie was, therefore, praised by men like Pinel.[141] But the idéologues and those close to them had hardly been prepared to acknowledge that in physiology the sum total of available facts was lamentably small. They welcomed new discoveries, but their writings show their belief that the facts were already largely assembled and would stand out clearly as soon as they were sifted and properly arranged. Such at least was Cabanis' avowed conviction[142] and Bichat, great anatomist and experimentalist that he was, deplored above all that the physiologist had not yet learned to go back from the phenomena to the underlying vital properties in the manner in which the chemist and physicist referred everything to affinity, gravity, elasticity etc.[143] Even Magendie at first seems to have been satisfied with a criticism of methods and concepts.[144] Yet his whole life work, as so clearly depicted by Dr. Olmsted, evinces not only his insistence on facts but, above all, his striving for new facts, so that his work more and more took on the character of a mere conglomeration of experimental results. The older Magendie became and

[138]Destutt de Tracy, *Élémens d'idéologie,* III, p. 280 f., note.
[139]Cf. Olmsted, *Magendie,* p. 64.
[140]Magendie, *Summary,* I, p. ix (*Précis* I, p. iv f.).
[141]Cf. Olmsted, *Magendie,* p. 43 f.
[142]Cf. above.
[143]Cf. the "Considérations générales" at the beginning of Bichat's *Anatomie générale.*
[144]Cf. Olmsted, *Magendie,* p. 27 f.

the further the influences of his youth receded, the stronger this tendency seems to have grown. This is Magendie, as Claude Bernard knew him.[145]

Facts can be valued for various reasons. In the first place, they represent truth, and herein Magendie and the idéologues agreed. If assembled in large numbers, facts may lead to an integrating theory affording a wide perspective. With the qualifications that Destutt de Tracy and Laplace had given to the term, the idéologues believed that such a "system" could be built in their time, a belief which Magendie did not share. Yet he too believed in the perfectibility of medicine; the time would come when, with the help of physics and chemistry, the body of exact knowledge would have assumed such proportions as to make medicine equal to its task.[146]

In the meantime, the fight for truth and limited knowledge as opposed to vague opinion had to go on relentlessly, though it implied therapeutic nihilism. This was "the scepticism which germinated into scientific medicine."[147] Entering upon this path, Magendie stepped out of his ideological background and became a protagonist of the medical positivism of the 19th century.

[145]Cf. *ibid.*, p. 238 f.

[146]Magendie, *Phénomènes physiques de la vie*, 4 vols., Paris 1842; vol. 1, p. 17: "Quant à nous, nous voulons vous diriger dans le sens du perfectionnement de la médecine; or, la médecine ne peut se perfectionner sans des connaissances positives sur les grands phénomènes de la nature." *Ibid.*, vol. 4, p. 2 f.: ". . . les effets des maladies sont étudiés depuis long-temps, ils sont en grande partie connus; remontons à leurs causes; tâchons de les découvrir, étudions-les patiemment une à une, et alors nous pourrons peut-être modifier leurs effets nuisibles avec avantage. C'est là, n'en doutez pas, qu'il faut nous rallier; c'est vers ce but qu'il faut diriger tous nos efforts. L'entreprise n'est pas aisée, car rien n'est tenace et persistant comme une idée absurde passée dans le domaine public, et il y en a beaucoup de ce genre aujourd'hui dans la théorie et la pratique de la médecine; mais vous le savez, Messieurs, plus l'oeuvre est difficile, plus il est glorieux de l'entreprendre, et lors même que nous n'aurions réussi qu'à mettre nos successeurs sur la voie de l'achever un jour, nous croirions avoir assez dignement rempli notre tâche."

[147]Olmsted, *Magendie*, p. 155.

25

Materialism in French and German Physiology of the Early Nineteenth Century*

AROUND 1800 French physiologists elaborated a doctrine which stood in contrast to the beliefs of their great countryman, the philosopher Descartes. Descartes had clearly separated man's body and soul, the body was a mere mechanical machine, bare of sensation, thought and will which belonged to the soul as a spiritual entity. Yet for Cabanis, Bichat, Richerand, and many others including the young Magendie, the body could not be understood as a mere machine. Whether vital properties were believed to counteract the physical and chemical processes or whether a vital force was assumed to cover our ignorance regarding nutrition and so-called vital actions, the result was the same in so far as the laws of inanimate nature were declared insufficient to explain all the manifestations of life. But if the body was thus given autonomy, the soul on the other hand was deprived of the position Descartes had assigned to it. Passions, instincts, thought and will could be studied as phenomena dependent upon our external and internal sensations and, therefore, upon our biological organization.

In an article dealing with the philosophical background of Magendie's physiology,[1] I have tried to show in more detail how this attitude was rooted in the sensualistic philosophy which had been developed by Locke and Condillac and had been brought to a radical formulation by the so-called idéologues during the French revolution. "Feeling" and "sensibility" most clearly manifested in animals became the central phenomenon for an explanation of nature as well as the mind. Cabanis, the physiologist among the idéologues, even went as far as to suggest that gravitation and chemical affinity might be primordial forms of sensibility.[2] Obviously such an attitude was a favorable ground for a vitalistic biology. On the other hand, the mental activities of man too were reduced to sensibility, whereby man was put on a par with animals. It was this elimination of an independent spiritual principle that was decried as materialism. It mattered little whether physiologists as, for instance, Bichat retained a belief in the soul, if only the soul could be neglected in physiological research and as long as psychology was a mere province of physiology.

*Bull. Hist. Med., 1946, vol. 20, pp. 322–327.
[1]O. Temkin, The philosophical background of Magendie's physiology, Bull. Hist. Med., vol. 20, pp. 10–35, 1946 [Essay 24].
[2]Cf. ibid., p. 20 [p. 326].

I think that we find an echo of this "vitalistic materialism" in Balzac who has been credited with the intention of presenting the physiology of contemporary French society in his cycle of novels.[3] In "La peau de chagrin" he describes a wild orgy where the participants, drunk with wine, exhibit their lowest passions. "The resemblances to animals inscribed upon the human features and so curiously demonstrated by the physiologist reappeared vaguely in the gestures and the attitudes of the body. Here was a book ready written for some Bichat, if he had been present, cool and sober."

Balzac sees the animal in man and to him passions rather than abstract material forces are the elements which decide man's actions. Passions and instincts were considered deeply rooted in man's biological organization by many physiologists of the time: "Great poets, heroes, great criminals and conquerors are empassioned men," Magendie wrote in 1816 in his textbook of physiology.[4]

Some peculiarities of this vitalistic materialism stand out in better relief if we now compare it with the materialism of the German physiologists.[5] During the early decades of the last century when the idealistic systems of Fichte, Schelling and Hegel dominated, the few German physiologists who, like Ernst Heinrich Weber, kept aloof from the romantic "Naturphilosophie"[6] were little given to any philosophizing at all. Paradoxically enough, the German physiologists began to exert a philosophical influence upon popular thought most strongly after they had broken away from the philosophy of nature. This event can be placed in the late thirties, about ten years before the revolution of 1848. It cannot be doubted that, as Dr. Ackerknecht has shown,[7] this materialistic bias of the medical men was related to the revolutionary movement of '48. And it was just because of its political significance that the materialistic tendency was most noticeable where it was directed against the belief in man's spiritual character. In France as well as in Germany a denial of the soul could be used as a denial of theological claims and of the rule by divine right of kings. In 1846 Carl

[3]W. Dilthey, Die drei Epochen der modernen Ästhetik und ihre heutige Aufgabe, in: *Gesammelte Schriften*, 6. Band, Leipzig-Berlin, Teubner, 1924, p. 244: "Balzac wollte methodisch in einem zusammenhängenden Zyklus von Romanen die Physiologie der damaligen französischen Gesellschaft geben: der Zusammenhang der menschlichen Leidenschaften mit dem sozialen Boden, auf dem sie wachsen, und die pathologische Bedingtheit der Personen, in denen diese Leidenschaften entstehen, beschäftigen ihn vornehmlich." I am indebted to Dr. L. Edelstein for this reference. Cf. also P. Lamy, *L'introduction à l'étude de la médecine expérimentale, Claude Bernard, le naturalisme et le positivisme*, Paris, 1928, p. 8 f and E. Cailliet, *La tradition littéraire des idéologues*, Philadelphia, The American Philosophical Society, 1943, p. 152 f.

[4]F. Magendie, *An elementary summary of physiology*. Translated from the French by J. S. Forsyth, London, 1825, I, p. 125. Cf. also Temkin, *op. cit.*, p. 16 [p. 322].

[5]For this and the following cf. J. T. Merz, *A history of European thought in the nineteenth century*, vol. 2, third ed., Edinburgh and London, 1928; F. A. Lange, *Geschichte des Materialismus*, 2. Aufl., II, Iserlohn, 1875; E. Rádl, *Geschichte der biologischen Theorien seit dem Ende des siebzehnten Jahrhunderts*, 2 vols., Leipzig, 1905–1909, especially II, pp. 80–84.

[6]Cf. C. Ludwig, *Rede zum Gedächtniss an Ernst Heinrich Weber*, Leipzig, 1878, p. 6 f.

[7]E. H. Ackerknecht, Beiträge zur Geschichte der Medizinalreform von 1848, *Sudhoffs Arch. Gesch. Med.*, vol. 25, 1932, pp. 61–109 and 113–83; cf. p. 86 f.

Vogt wrote: "I think that every scientist if thinking at all consistently will reach the opinion that all the faculties which we comprise under the name of psychic actions are nothing but functions of the cerebral substance, or, to express myself somewhat crudely, that thoughts have about the same relation to the brain as bile has to the liver or urine to the kidney."[8] These words which scandalized the world were not much more than a repetition of a similar thought expressed by Cabanis almost half a century before.[9]

And yet, German materialism as it developed among physiologists from 1838 on showed a different pattern from its French predecessor. To be sure, not all French physiologists had been vitalists. One has but to mention Dutrochet who coined the terms of endosmosis and exosmosis in order to realize that mechanistic doctrines were by no means lacking in French physiology.[10] But it seems fair to say that in Germany such attempts were overshadowed by a veritable campaign against the assumption of a vital force, a campaign where the first shot was fired by Theodor Schwann in 1839 in the same work that contained his interpretation of the cellular origin of the animal organism.[11] Neither Schwann nor Schleiden whose names are so intimately connected were materialists.[12] Schwann was a very religious person and Schleiden in 1863 published one of the most violent attacks against the materialism in modern German science.[13] But they attacked vitalism, and Schwann in particular presented the problem as an alternative between the following views: either the organism is endowed with a force which forms it as a whole according to some idea, or the organism is subject to forces which act according to blind necessity, forces which are inherent in matter itself. Schwann decided for the latter alternative. But how to account for the purposefulness of organic structure? Schwann did not deny purposefulness, but he transferred it from biology to the world as a whole, and from a vital force to the Creator. God had created matter and its forces, so that by following their blind laws they nevertheless produced a purposeful whole. Only in degree were organisms more purposeful than, for instance, the planetary system.[14]

[8]Carl Vogt, *Physiologische Briefe für Gebildete aller Stände.* Stuttgart and Tübingen, 1845–1847, p. 206.

[9]Cf. Temkin, *op. cit.,* p. 14 [p. 320].

[10]Cf. A. R. Rich, The place of R.-J.-H. Dutrochet in the development of the cell theory, *Bull. Johns Hopkins Hospital,* vol. 39, 1926, pp. 330–365. Cf. also below p. 343.

[11]Th. Schwann, *Mikroskopische Untersuchungen über die Übereinstimmung in der Struktur und dem Wachstume der Tiere und Pflanzen.* Hrsg. von F. Hünseler, Leipzig, 1910 [Ostwald's Klassiker der exakten Wissenschaften, Nr. 176].

[12]Cf. Rádl, *op. cit.,* II, pp. 65–73.

[13]M. J. Schleiden, *Ueber den Materialismus der neueren deutschen Naturwissenschaft,* Leipzig, 1863.

[14]Schwann, *op. cit.,* p. 183 ff. However, Schwann admitted that in man as a free being, a principle substantially different from matter had to be recognized; cf. *ibid.,* and E. Du Bois-Reymond, *Reden,* 2. Aflg., hrsg. von Estelle Du Bois-Reymond, 2 vols., Leipzig, 1912, vol. 1, p. 289. The admission of Schwann's put him in basic agreement with Descartes (cf. Du Bois-Reymond, *op. cit.,* II, p. 497), so that antivitalism once again started where it had set out in the 17th century. It may be mentioned that of contemporary physiologists Flourens too has been considered a Cartesian, although in his youth he had been a friend of the idéologue Destutt de Tracy. Cf. *Nouvelle biographie générale,* Paris, Didot, t. 18, 1857, cols. 11–14; A. Schopenhauer,

Schwann's whole argument against purpose in biology is not without interest. Many physiologists before Schwann had denounced final causes only to use a downright teleological language in large sections of their works.[15] Where vitalism prevails, teleology is easily excused. But for the antivitalist the problem is a very difficult one, and was especially difficult in the days before Darwin. Schwann's solution of shifting the problem from biology to the world as a whole served as a model for many materialists during the following decade. Lotze's famous article on life and vital force which appeared in 1842 [16] attacked the assumption of a specific living matter as distinguished from inorganic matter and the unclear use of the concept of force by the vitalists. But in discussing the purposefulness of the organism Lotze used an argument very similar to that of Schwann. Vogt too, materialist that he was, nevertheless spoke rather naively about the plans of nature and of the Creator.[17] Even Du Bois-Reymond tried to argue away inconvenient biological teleology by referring to the apparent purposefulness of many other cosmic phenomena.[18] However, there was this difference, that Du Bois-Reymond merely played with an idea which for Schwann had been a serious conviction. Since the mechanistic doctrine had to prevail and organization could not be explained, it was simply ridiculed out of the discussion.

With Du Bois-Reymond we reach one of those German physiologists who did most to prepare the ground for mechanistic materialism. In 1841 he is yet torn between opposing sentiments, yet he quotes with approval Dutrochet's opinion: "The more one advances in the knowledge of physiology, the more reasons one will have for stopping to believe that the phenomena of life are essentially different from the physical phenomena."[19] By 1842 he and Brücke have sworn to fight for the truth that all forces active in the organism must be reducible to attractive and repulsive components.[20] Towards the end of 1845 he announces his acquaintance with Helmholtz and writes: "In addition to Brücke and my own humble self this is ... the third organic physicist of the alliance."[21] A fourth ally in the fight for a mechanistic physiology was found in Carl Ludwig. The program of the new school was formulated in the preface of Du Bois-Reymond's "Investigations Concerning Animal Electricity" of 1848 where the author predicted the

Die Welt als Wille und Vorstellung, 2. Band, Leipzig, 1919, p. 328 ff. [Sämtliche Werke, hrsg. Otto Weiss]; F. Picavet, *Les idéologues*, Paris, 1891, p. 434.

[15]Cf. E. Nordenskiöld, *The history of biology*, New York, 1942, p. 327 for Lamarck. Similar contradictions occur in Cabanis and many other physiologists down to our own days; cf. C. Singer, *A short history of biology*, Oxford, 1931, p. 213 f.

[16]H. Lotze, Leben, Lebenskraft; in Wagner's *Handwörterbuch der Physiologie*, I. Braunschweig, 1842, pp. ix–lviii.

[17]Vogt, *op. cit.*, pp. 3 f., 50, 62 *et passim*.

[18]Du Bois-Reymond, *op. cit.*, I, p. 20 f. This passage originally occurred in the preface to Du Bois-Reymond's *Untersuchungen über thierische Elektricität*, 1. Band, Berlin, 1848, pp. v–lvi, a large part of which was republished in the *Reden* under the title "Über die Lebenskraft."

[19]*Jugendbriefe von Emil Du Bois-Reymond an Eduard Hallmann*, hrsg. von Estelle Du Bois-Reymond, Berlin, 1918, p. 98.

[20]*Ibid.*, p. 108.

[21]*Ibid.*, p. 122 f.

day when physiology would dissolve completely into biophysics and biochemistry.[22] Analytical mechanics was the ideal science in whose terms all natural events should be described if possible. This aim at physical exactness and mathematical interpretation on the part of leading German physiologists contrasted with the methods and views of the most outstanding French physiologists. Bichat, Legallois, Magendie and even Flourens and Claude Bernard did their most important experiments on living animals where vital phenomena could be studied as such. For the older of these men, at least, this was a consequence of their vitalistic background.[23] Although Magendie insisted that physics and chemistry be given a suitable province in physiology, he did not insist on mathematical treatment.[24] Helmholtz and Du Bois-Reymond, on the other hand, were physicists in the realm of organic nature. It was characteristic for the former that his work on the preservation of energy was closely connected with the attempt at disproving any special vital force.[25] It was characteristic for the latter that as late as 1857, i.e., 9 years after the first volume of his "Investigations Concerning Animal Electricity" had been published, he had to ask Ludwig's help in mastering the art of vivisection.[26]

But in the preface of this work Du Bois-Reymond went further than pleading for a mechanistic concept of man's body. He believed that if the analytical mechanics of vital processes could only be pushed far enough, then, in principle at least, it would even reach the problem of personal freedom.[27] This statement he later on revoked and admitted that consciousness could not be explained mechanically.[28] Nevertheless, the statement shows that by 1848 some German physiologists had advanced to a position that recognized only matter and force. Its essence was characterized in the formula in which the philosopher Feuerbach summarized Moleschott's popular text on food: "Der Mensch ist, was er isst"[29]—man is what he eats. To the vitalistic materialists in France man was but an animal. To the mechanistic materialists in Germany he became but a passing constellation of lifeless particles of matter.

[22]Du Bois-Reymond, *Reden*, I, p. 21 (cf. above footnote 18).

[23]In spite of his insistence on determinism in biology, Claude Bernard did not believe in a purely mechanistic explanation of life. In his *Leçons sur les phénomènes de la vie*, t. 1, Paris, 1878, he wrote (p. 50 f.): "Les phénomènes vitaux ont bien leurs conditions physico-chimiques rigoureusement déterminées; mais en même temps ils se subordonnent et se succèdent dans un enchaînement et suivant une loi fixés d'avance: ils se répètent éternellement, avec ordre, régularité, constance, et s'harmonisent, en vue d'un résultat qui est l'organisation et l'accroissement de l'individu, animal ou végétal." For the latter phenomenon he admits the term of "force vitale" and says metaphorically (p. 51): "la force vitale dirige des phénomènes qu'elle ne produit pas; les agents physiques produisent des phénomènes qu'ils ne dirigent pas." But the vital force is never directly accessible to the physiologist.

[24]Cf. Temkin, *op. cit.,* note 106.

[25]Cf. L. Koenigsberger, *Hermann von Helmholtz*, 1. Bd. Braunschweig, 1902, pp. 58 ff. 81 ff. and 92.

[26]Estelle Du Bois-Reymond [ed.], *Zwei grosse Naturforscher des 19. Jahrhunderts. Ein Briefwechsel zwischen Emil Du Bois-Reymond und Karl Ludwig.* Leipzig, 1927, p. 146 f.

[27]Du Bois-Reymond, *Reden*, I, p. 9.

[28]*Ibid.,* p. 23.

[29]J. Moleschott, *Für meine Freunde*, Giessen, 1894, p. 208.

26

Basic Science, Medicine, and the Romantic Era*

The Fielding H. Garrison Lecture†

THE NAME of Garrison is usually associated with a text-book and a bibliographical work, both cited the world over.[1] To me, Fielding H. Garrison is the name of a friend, the first to welcome me upon my arrival in the United States, and whose office, once filled with cigar smoke, lined with books, and with an old-fashioned roll-top desk standing in the center, I occupied for many years after his death in 1935. I remember him as a kind but sensitive man, a lover of literature and of music. When asked to deliver the Garrison lecture, I therefore thought it opportune to speak on a subject that might fall within the realm of his interests.[2]

I propose to begin with the controversy that started among medical men in England in 1814, follow it for a decade, and discuss some of its wider implications. Since the controversy arose over physiology, involved medicine, and fell into a period of predominantly romantic orientation in western cultural life, I have chosen for this lecture the somewhat cumbersome title: Basic Science, Medicine, and the Romantic Era.[3]

*Bull. Hist. Med., 1963, vol. 37, pp. 97–129.
†This article represents a revised and extended form of the lecture delivered at the thirty-fifth annual meeting of the American Association for the History of Medicine, Los Angeles, California, May 4, 1962.
[1]Fielding H. Garrison, *An Introduction to the History of Medicine.* 4th ed., Philadelphia and London: Saunders, 1929.—Leslie T. Morton, *Garrison and Morton's Medical Bibliography.* 2nd ed., New York: Argosy Bookstore, 1954.
[2]See Garrison's editorial, "The romantic episode in the history of German medicine," *Bull. New York Acad. Med.,* 1931, 7: 841–64.
[3]The present article does not deal with the subject of "romantic medicine" per se. From the large literature on that subject I mention here the following: Paul Diepgen, *Deutsche Medizin vor hundert Jahren; ein Beitrag zur Geschichte der Romantik.* Freiburg: Speyer und Kaunrer, 1923.—Ernst Hirschfeld, "Romantische Medizin," *Kyklos,* 1930, 3:1–89.—Werner Leibbrand, *Die speculative Medizin der Romantik.* Hamburg: Claasen, 1956.—Walter Pagel, *Virchow und die Grundlagen der Medizin des XIX. Jahrhunderts.* Jena: G. Fischer, 1931. (Jenaer medizinhistorische Beiträge, Heft 14).—Karl E. Rothschuh, "Ansteckende Ideen in der Wissenschaftsgeschichte, gezeigt an der Entstehung und Ausbreitung der romantischen Physiologie," *Deutsche med. Wchnschr.,* 1961, 86: 396–402.—George Rosen, "Romantic medicine: a problem in historical periodization," *Bull. Hist. Med.,* 1961, 25: 149–58, has pointed out the inadequacy of regarding "Romantic medicine solely in relation to German Romanticism" (p. 157).

I. THE CONTROVERSY [4]

a) *The Abernethy–Lawrence phase*

In 1814, John Abernethy, the famous London surgeon, delivered before the Royal College of Surgeons a series of anatomical lectures, the first two of which were published in the same year.[5] Expounding what he believed to be doctrines of John Hunter and referring to the work of the chemist, Humphry Davy, Abernethy tried to distinguish between body, life, and mind as separate entities.

Life, so he claimed, had its own principle; it was not the same as the organization of the body; it depended on a subtle substance, similar to, though not necessarily identical with, electricity. Just as life should be thought superadded to structure, so the mind, in turn, should be conceived of as superadded to life.[6]

The lectures were not distinguished by clarity. The *Edinburgh Review*[7] decried Abernethy's "bombast about genius, and electricity, and Sir Isaac Newton,"[8] and denied that he had correctly interpreted John Hunter's theories, which were obscure and untenable anyhow. We need not enter here upon Hunter's views or their interpretation, especially since this has been recently touched upon by Goodfield.[9] The importance of the review lies in its championship of a chemical explanation of life. Abernethy had dealt with muscular and nerve fibres; he had based his argument on the phenomenon of irritability. The reviewer took for his example the assimilation of food and drew consequences entirely at variance with Hunter and Abernethy alike.

Abernethy's lectures of the following year, at least in the printed version,[10] took no notice of the review. But in 1816 he was criticized in a form

---

[4]Apart from the titles to be cited further below, see the following items on this controversy: George Macilwain, *Memoirs of John Abernethy, F.R.S.* 2 vols., London: Hurst and Blackett, 1853 (see vol. 2, p. 1 ff.).—John M. Robertson, *A Short History of Freethought Ancient and Modern.* 2 vols., 3rd ed., London, 1915.—Alice D. Snyder, *Coleridge on Logic and Learning,* With Selections from the Unpublished Manuscripts. New Haven: Yale Univ. Press, 1929.—John L. Thornton, *John Abernethy.* London: distributed by Simpkin Marshall Ltd., 1953.—C. D. Darlington, *Darwin's Place in History.* New York: Macmillan, 1961. See especially pp. 16–24 and 100–01. This book, which came to my attention only after the delivery of the Garrison Lecture in its original form, places the Lawrence controversy in an anthropological rather than a physiological context. I am indebted to the publication for some of the bibliographical information given on p. 100 f.

[5]*An Enquiry into the Probability and Rationality of Mr. Hunter's Theory of Life;* reprinted in: John Abernethy, *Introductory Lectures,* Exhibiting some of Mr. Hunter's Opinions Respecting Life and Diseases, Delivered before the Royal College of Surgeons, London, in 1814 and 1815. New ed., London: Longman et al., 1823.

[6]*Ibid.,* pp. 40 and 79.

[7]*Edinburgh Rev.,* 1814, 23: 384–98.

[8]*Ibid.,* p. 386.

[9]G. J. Goodfield, *The Growth of Scientific Physiology.* Physiological Method and the Mechanist-Vitalist Controversy, Illustrated by the Problems of Respiration and Animal Heat. London: Hutchinson, 1960, p. 108. Macilwain, *op. cit.* (above, n. 4), vol. 2, p. 8 ff., argues at length the correctness of Abernethy's interpretation of Hunter's doctrines.

[10]*Part of the Introductory Lecture for the Year 1815, Exhibiting Some of Mr. Hunter's Opinions Respecting Diseases.* Reissued in Abernethy, *Introductory Lectures* (above, n. 5).

he could not possibly overlook. In the preceding year the College had appointed William Lawrence, (1783–1867) as a junior lecturer. Lawrence already enjoyed a reputation in London and, in later years, was to become one of the most outstanding English eye surgeons.[11] He was one of the founders of physical anthropology[12]—but also something of a *bête noire*. While still a pupil of Abernethy, he had objected to the latter's interpretation of Hunter's views,[13] and now, in 1816, he attacked his erstwhile teacher publicly, though indirectly. His lectures[14] began with expressions of esteem and praise for Abernethy, yet in substance they contradicted all the latter held dear. They admittedly depended on the views of Cuvier, the great French zoologist, still alive at the time, and of Bichat, the founder of modern histology, who had died so young in 1802. Lawrence firmly believed in the dependence of function on structure. Structure or organization "means the peculiar composition, which distinguishes living bodies," and "functions are the purposes, which any organ or system of organs executes in the animal frame."[15] To this teleological definition of function, Lawrence added Bichat's doctrine of vital properties, of which sensibility and irritability were deemed the most remarkable. "To such properties we refer, in our ultimate analysis of the functions, as the mechanician does to elasticity, when he is explaining the motions of a watch, or the astronomer to gravitation, in accounting for the course of the heavenly bodies."[16] Lawrence admitted that the many endeavors to establish a connection between the texture of organic parts and their vital powers had been unsuccessful and that here, as in all other branches of human knowledge, "an observation of the succession of events" is all we can rely on.[17] But he was quite sure that there was no separate principle of life. The reference to Abernethy was made very explicit by the rejection of any analogy between electricity and life. The fiction of a subtle, invisible, animating matter

[11]Norman Moore, article on Lawrence in *Dictionary of National Biography (D.N.B.)*, vol. 11, New York: Macmillan, 1909, p. 727 f.—Obituary on Lawrence in *Brit. M. J.*, 1867, 2: 36–37.—[W. S. Savory], "Sir William Lawrence, Bart.," *St. Barth. Hosp. Rep.*, 1868, 4: 1–18. My identification of the anonymous writer with Savory rests on Moore's authority.—W. R. LeFanu, "Past presidents: Sir William Lawrence, Bart.," *Ann. Roy. Coll. Surg. England*, 1959, 25: 201–02.

[12]In concentrating on the physiological opinions of Lawrence rather than on his anthropological views, I effect a somewhat artificial separation. Nevertheless, this seems justifiable, because the controversy was mainly over basic physiological questions.

[13]John Abernethy, *The Hunterian Oration for the Year 1819*. London: Longman et al., 1819, Postscript, p. 59. See also Macilwain, *op. cit.* (above, n. 4), p. 33. According to Thornton, *op. cit.* (above, n. 4), p. 132, Lawrence's indenture is dated April 4, 1799.

[14]*Introduction to Comparative Anatomy and Physiology; Being the Two Introductory Lectures Delivered at the Royal College of Surgeons, on the 21st and 25th March, 1816.* This will be referred to as *Introduction.* I have used the edition included in William Lawrence, *Lectures on Comparative Anatomy, Physiology, Zoology, and the Natural History of Man; Delivered at the Royal College of Surgeons in the Years 1816, 1817, and 1818.* London: Carlile, 1823. This book comprises under separate title pages the above named *Introduction* as well as the *Lectures on Physiology, Zoology, and the Natural History of Man, Delivered at the Royal College of Surgeons*, cited below, n. 27.

[15]Lawrence, *Introduction*, p. 52.

[16]*Ibid.*, p. 62.

[17]*Ibid.*, for further discussion, see below.

Lawrence compared with the personifications in ancient and medieval myths.

> Thus we find at last that the philosopher with his archeus, his anima, or his subtle and mobile vital fluid is about on a level, in respect to the mental process, by which he has arrived at it with the
>
> > "Poor Indian, whose untutor'd mind,
> > Sees God in clouds, and hears him in the wind."[18]

This was clear enough and forced Abernethy to reply. The reply came with Abernethy's *Physiological Lectures* of 1817, again before the Royal College of Surgeons.[19] Now Abernethy attacked, pleading advocacy of "the cause of Hunter versus Cuvier and others."[20] At the same time he tried to forestall the accusation of nationalistic bias. While eulogizing John Hunter, who had anticipated much of Cuvier's work, Abernethy nevertheless paid high tribute to the latter. His treatment of Lawrence was different. Without mentioning the name, Abernethy included him in what he called the party of modern skeptics.[21] Abernethy tried to force his antagonists into this alternative: either acknowledge a vital principle, or acknowledge yourselves materialists. The vital forces "must either be the attributes of the atoms which compose an organized body, or of some subtle and invisible substance superadded to, and inherent in it."[22] The skeptics, he alleged, were afraid of a substance superadded to structure, because belief in such a substance might lead to belief in a soul, thereby endangering "the privileges of scepticism," viz. the assurance that "gratifying their senses, and acting as their reason dictates, for their own advantage, independently of all other considerations" was true philosophy.[23]

Abernethy thus by insinuation imputed materialism, both metaphysical and ethical, to his adversary. He was not surprised that French anatomists and physiologists should write in a vein esteemed "in a nation where the writings both of its philosophers and wits have greatly contributed to demoralize the people." But that in England, after Hunter's work, "the mere opinions of some French anatomists, with respect to the nature of life, should be extracted from their general writings, translated, and extolled, cannot, I think, but excite the surprise and indignation of any one fully apprized of their pernicious tendency."[24] The anatomist was bound to perceive that intelligence had operated in ordaining the laws of nature.[25]

---

[18]*Ibid.*, p. 77.

[19]Abernethy, *Physiological Lectures, Exhibiting a General View of Mr. Hunter's Physiology, and of His Researches in Comparative Anatomy.* Delivered before the Royal College of Surgeons in the Year 1817. 2nd ed., London: Longman, 1822.

[20]*Ibid.*, p. 16.

[21]*Ibid.*, p. 36 f.: "In becoming the advocate of Mr. Hunter's Theory of Life, I knew I should irritate what many might consider as a very formidable Party ... I shall include all the individuals who compose this party, under a general denomination, which I think appropriate to them, and call them the Modern Sceptics."

[22]*Ibid.*, p. 44.

[23]*Ibid.*, pp. 46 and 47.

[24]*Ibid.*, p. 52.

[25]*Ibid.*, p. 331.

> Tongues in the trees, books in the running brooks,
> Sermons in stones, and good in every thing.[26]

If Lawrence had ignored Abernethy's accusations, the matter might perhaps have ended here. But by replying immediately, i.e., in his course of the same year,[27] and by protesting loudly, he added substance to them. Lawrence protested against the allegation that there was a party of modern skeptics.[28] He reaffirmed his belief that the animal functions were inseparable from the animal organs. He now was emphatic "that life then, or the assemblage of all the functions, is immediately dependent on organization."[29] He did not shy away from connecting the human mind with the functioning of the brain and the external senses. "Physiologically speaking," that is, "because the theological doctrine of the soul and its separate existence" rested "on a species of proof altogether different."[30] He protested "against the attempt to stifle impartial inquiry by an outcry of pernicious tendency."[31] Science should unite men rather than "encourage controversy, and inflame national rivalry." But almost immediately afterwards, commenting on the French scientists of his own days, he himself did not refrain from political remarks. "It is perhaps yet too soon to determine how these and similar pursuits may be influenced by the recent political changes in France. Hitherto, however, science has not partaken in the triumph of legitimacy." Many French scientists had gone to the new world. He invited his listeners to rejoice that there is a

vast region of the earth, lavishly endowed with nature's fairest gifts, and exhibiting at the same time the grand and animating spectacle of a country sacred to civil liberty; where man may walk erect in the conscious dignity of independence, that

> "Lord of the lion heart and eagle eye,"

and enjoy full freedom of word and action, without the permission of those combinations or conspiracies of the mighty, which threaten to convert Europe into one great state prison.

He ended with a prophesy. The American people, he said, "may reach in our lives as gigantic a superiority over the worn-out despotisms of the old world, as the physical features of America, her colossal mountains, her mighty rivers, her forests and her lakes, exhibit in comparison with those of Europe."[32]

[26]*Ibid.*, p. 340.
[27]The reply is part of "Lecture I. Introductory to the Course delivered in 1817," of Lawrence's *Lectures on Physiology, Zoology, and the Natural History of Man*, Delivered at the Royal College of Surgeons. London: J. Callow, 1819 (henceforth to be quoted as Lawrence, *Lectures*). According to Darlington, *op. cit.* (above, n. 4), p. 100, this is the original, first edition of the work. For other editions see Darlington, *ibid.*, and above, n. 14.
[28]Lawrence, *Lectures*, p. 5.
[29]*Ibid.*, p. 7.
[30]*Ibid.*, p. 8. The passage continues: "These sublime dogmas could never have been brought to light by the labours of the anatomist and physiologist. An immaterial and spiritual being could not have been discovered amid the blood and filth of the dissecting-room...."
[31]*Ibid.*, p. 15.
[32]*Ibid.*, pp. 36 and 37.

b) The controversy becomes generalized.

Lawrence's *Lectures on Physiology, Zoology and the Natural History of Man* appeared in 1819. Of these *Lectures* we have analyzed the first, directed against Abernethy. Here, the main issue was over the principle of life and the relationship of mind to brain. In the remaining lectures, this physiological issue was bolstered by arguments which all but denied the existence of an immaterial soul and made it hard to remember that Lawrence was speaking "physiologically" only.[33] Moreover, in these lectures Lawrence argued against those "who regard the Hebrew Scriptures as writing composed with the assistance of divine inspiration, and therefore commanding our implicit assent; who receive, as a narrative of actual events, authenticated by the highest sanction, the account contained in Genesis of the formation of the world, the creation of man and animals, and their dispersion over the face of the globe."[34] Apart from his skepticism regarding the descent of all men from Adam and Eve, and the gathering of representations of all animals before Adam and then again in the ark, Lawrence doubted the inspired character of the Old Testament altogether.[35]

Lawrence thus became involved in anthropological and geological debates into which we need not follow him. It was above all his alleged denial of an immaterial soul, combined with his doubts about the revelation of the Old Testament and his general skepticism, which assigned him his place in 1819, by which time others had raised their voices too. The whole matter has to be understood against the broader background of the conditions of the post-Napoleonic era.

By 1793 the initial enthusiasm which the French Revolution had aroused abroad have given way to widespread horror and opposition. In England, the war which began in that year and almost uninterruptedly lasted till the downfall of Napoleon, impeded travel to France,[36] while strong governmental measures were taken against any manifestations of Jacobine sentiments or reform tendencies. In 1814, the continent again became open to England, and from late 1815 Europe was dominated by the Quadruple Alliance of Austria, England, Prussia, and Russia. In France, the monarchy was restored under Louis XVIII. The Holy Alliance between the rulers of Austria, Prussia, and Russia was the bond for a policy of suppression of national and democratic threats to the established order and the monarchic principle. England was not a partner to the Holy Alliance. But the removal of the military threat of France did not lift the dread of Jacobinism. In the spring of 1817, bills were passed by Parliament suspending habeas corpus and directed, above all, against seditious meetings.[37] The

---

[33]See below, n. 149.

[34]Lawrence, *Lectures,* p. 247 f.

[35]*Ibid.,* p. 248 ff.

[36]This does not imply that England and France were cut off from all mutual exchange of scientific information; see Henry Guerlac, "Some Daltonian doubts," *Isis,* 1961, 52: 544–54 (p. 549). There is, however, a difference between a restricted scientific intercourse and a free flow of ideas.

[37]Horace Twiss, *The Public and Private Life of Lord Chancellor Eldon,* With Selections from His Correspondence. 2 vols., Philadelphia: Carey and Hart, 1844, vol. 2, p. 17.

memory of Pitt and the precedents of 1794 were evoked; the dread of French influence was kept alive by the fears concomitant with the unrest of the Industrial Revolution.[38]

Among the British travelers who for the benefit of their countrymen described post-Napoleonic France was Lady Sidney Morgan, accompanied by her husband, Sir Thomas Charles Morgan.

Lady Morgan was an Irish novelist who previously had aroused the anger of the *Quarterly Review*.[39] Her husband, a Cambridge M.D., was a practicing physician in 1817, when his wife's book on France[40] appeared.[41] He provided "Appendices" to the work, and one of these dealt with the state of medicine in France. The book and its authoress were greeted by the *Quarterly Review* in no uncertain terms:

Our charges (to omit minor faults) fall readily under the head of—Bad taste— Bombast and Nonsense—Blunders—Ignorance of the French Language and Manners—General Ignorance—Jacobinism—Falsehood—Licentiousness, and Impiety.[42]

Dr. Morgan was dismissed briefly with the advice to confine his writings to the only matters he understood, viz., those of the apothecary shop.[43] The general direction of Dr. Morgan's thoughts on physiology, which he was to elaborate two years later in his *Sketches of the Philosophy of Life*,[44] was clearly indicated in the appendix, where he declared that "in profound and comprehensive views the French must be considered as superior to ourselves . . ." and that the spirit of French philosophy had given French medical works "a decided excellence in those parts of the science, which are purely ideal."[45] No doubt, if there was a party of modern skeptics, as Abernethy had said, Morgan had to be counted among its members.

In many respects, Morgan's physiological opinions agreed with those of "his friend, Mr. Lawrence, (whom to name is to praise) one of the most enterprising physiologists and enlightened surgeons of the present generation."[46] Both Lawrence and Morgan represented the tradition of the French physiological school. But Morgan aggressively combined French physiological theories with the moral and political ideas of the French

---

[38]Harriet Martineau, *The History of England during the Thirty Years' Peace: 1816–1846*. 2 vols., London: Knight, 1849–1850; vol. 1, books I and II.—*Cambridge Modern History*, vol. 10, 1907, p. 578. During the revolutionary period, anti-Jacobine sentiments had led to attacks upon Erasmus Darwin, see Norton Garfinkle, "Science and religion in England, 1790–1800," *J. Hist. Ideas*, 1955, *16*: 376–88.

[39]George Sampson, *The Concise Cambridge History of English Literature*. New York: Macmillan, 1941, p. 891.—J. A. Hamilton, article on Lady Sydney Morgan in *Dictionary of National Biography*, vol. 13, 1909, pp. 924–26.

[40]Lady Morgan, *France*. 3rd American ed., 2nd with the Addition of an English Translation of the French Words and Phrases. Philadelphia: M. Thomas, 1817.

[41]J. M. Rigg, article on Sir Thomas Charles Morgan in *D.N.B.*, vol. 13, 1909, p. 933.

[42]*Quart. Rev.*, 1817, *17*: 260–86 (April and July).

[43]*Ibid.*, p. 285 f.

[44]T. C. Morgan, *Sketches of the Philosophy of Life*, London: Colburn, 1819.

[45]Lady Morgan, *France*, appendix no. III, p. xlix.

[46]Morgan, *Sketches of the Philosophy of Life*, p. 424, ftn.

idéologues.[47] The following citation from Cabanis, the medical philosopher of revolutionary France, appeared in French on the title page: "There is no doubt that the physical needs depend directly upon the organization; but do the moral needs not equally depend on it, though in a less direct or less perceptible manner?" There are also statements which are reminiscent of utilitarian principles.[48] Altogether while not denying God and an immortal soul, Morgan left little room for their meaningful existence.

Now the storm broke against Lawrence, Morgan, and some kindred spirits. In the postscript to his *Hunterian Oration* of 1819, Abernethy, it is true, added some explanations to his previous statements about the party of modern skeptics in general and its French sponsors in particular in a language more conciliatory than before. Probably the most interesting remark was made "with respect to the subject of nationality." He wished to bring to Lawrence's consideration the following sentence which he remembered having heard in Mr. Coleridge's lectures: "There can be no sincere cosmopolitan, who is not also a patriot."[49]

As the remark shows, Abernethy had been attending the Philosophical Lectures delivered by Samuel Taylor Coleridge in the winter and spring of 1818–1819.[50] Coleridge, on his side, is said to have been in the audience that listened to Abernethy's Hunterian Oration[51] and, on March 15, 1819, Coleridge made science the subject of his lecture. Coleridge scholars have long been aware that he was actively engaged in "the vitalist—mechanist controversy which after John Hunter's death divided his students . . . into two schools" and that he "naturally defended the vitalist position."[52] They have, moreover, been able to trace probable references to statements made by the leaders of the quarrel.[53] We can, therefore, be brief on this point.

[47]Morgan quotes Magendie as well as Bichat (see *ibid.*, p. 212). On Morgan as a follower of Cabanis see Robertson, *op. cit.* (above, n. 4).

[48]For instance, p. 293 f. For the physiological connections of the French *idéologues* and the English utilitarians, see Elie Halévy, *The Growth of Philosophic Radicalism*. Transl. Mary Morris. [Reprinted] Boston: The Beacon Press, 1955, p. 434 ff.

[49]Abernethy, *Hunterian Oration*, p. 66. Kathleen Coburn (ed.), *The Philosophical Lectures of Samuel Taylor Coleridge.* London: Pilot Press, 1949, p. 236 ftn., and p. 422.—Alice D. Snyder, *Coleridge on Logic and Learning*, p. 25.

[50]Coburn, *op. cit.*, p. 28, and Snyder, *op. cit.*, p. 25.

[51]Coburn, *op. cit.*, p. 24.

[52]Coburn, *ibid.*, p. 60. Not only did Coleridge place Abernethy in the same rank as Cuvier (Coburn, *ibid.*, p. 175), he also followed Abernethy in affirming (elsewhere) "that whatever is grandest in the views of Cuvier is either a reflection" of the light spread by Hunter, "or a continuation of its rays"; see Alice D. Snyder, *S. T. Coleridge's Treatise on Method* as Published in the Encyclopaedia Metropolitana. London: Constable, 1939, p. 21. Of the considerable literature on Coleridge's biological views I mention here James Benziger, "Organic unity: Leibniz to Coleridge," *Publications of the Modern Language Association of America*, 1951, 66: 24–48, and M. H. Abrams, *The Mirror and the Lamp*, Romantic Theory and the Critical Tradition. [Reprinted] New York: The Norton Library, 1958, especially chs. vii and viii. As far as I know, the mutual dependence of Abernethy and Coleridge has not yet received the attention it may deserve; it may well go back before 1819.

[53]In particular, the following passage is believed to refer to Lawrence (Coburn, *op. cit.*, p. 353 and notes on p. 457): "For we have been assured, not in old times, but even in our own, that mind is a function of the brain, that all our moral and intellectual being are the effects of organization . . ."

Bichat's definition: "Life is the sum of all the functions by which death is resisted," appeared to Coleridge as "the vilest form . . . of modern materialism."[54] "To explain organization itself we must assume a principle of Life independent of organization," for organization, to Coleridge, "is nothing but the consequence of life, nothing but the means by which and through which it displays itself."[55]

Coleridge brought Abernethy's position before a popular audience, and attacked a philosophy with which he disagreed. The anonymous author[56] of the *Cursory Observations*, who designated himself "one of the people called Christians,"[57] and the Reverend Thomas Rennell[58] attacked the *spokesmen* of this philosophy, above all Lawrence and Morgan. The anonymous author, addressing himself to Lawrence, stated: "Instead of contemplating physiology, in its reference to surgery and medicine, you have exhibited it as the road to materialism in metaphysics, to faction in politics, and to infidelity in religion."[59] Thereby he neatly summarized the main points on which the attack by him and others was to rest. To follow the attack and counter-attack in all its details would transcend the limits of this lecture.[60] The following discussion is meant as an illustration of the character of the controversy in its broadened form.

Rennell's was probably one of the most important early voices. As far back as 1813 he had attended the lectures of the surgeon and anatomist Charles Bell and had found the latter "engaged in maintaining the principles of the English school of Physiology, and in exposing the futility of the opinions of those French philosophers and physiologists, who represented life as the mere physical result of certain combinations and actions of parts, by them termed Organization."[61] Rennell was Christian Advocate in the

---

[54]*Ibid.*, p. 356. Possibly Coleridge said "purest" instead of "vilest" (see *ibid.*, ftn.).

[55]*Ibid.*, pp. 356 and 358. On the other hand, life must not be confounded with soul. "For I think too highly of my responsible nature, to confound it with a something by which I am not distinguished from the merest animal." (*Ibid.*, p. 359).

[56]Darlington, *op. cit.* (above, n. 4), p. 101: "probably William Grinfield, M. A. Oxon."

[57]*Cursory Observations Upon the "Lectures on Physiology, Zoology, and the Natural History of Man, Delivered at the Royal College of Surgeons, by W. Lawrence, F.R.S. . . ."* in a Series of Letters Addressed to That Gentleman; with a Concluding Letter to His Pupils. By one of the People Called Christians. London: T. Cadell and W. Davies, 1819.

[58]*Remarks on Scepticism*, Especially as It is Connected with the Subjects of Organization and Life. Being an answer to the views of M. Bichat, Sir T. C. Morgan, and Mr. Lawrence, upon those points. By the Rev. Thomas Rennell, A. M. Vicar of Kensington, and Christian Advocate in the University of Cambridge. 2nd ed., London: F. C. and J. Rivington, 1819. P. 136: "As many of the observations which I have here made upon the Lectures of Mr. Lawrence, resemble those which appeared in the British Critic of July, 1817, it may be perhaps necessary to say that the author of both is the same person." This review not having been accessible to me, I can only surmise that it attacked Lawrence's *Introduction*.

[59]*Op. cit.* (above, n. 57), p. 8.

[60]To treat the whole controversy in detail would require a systematic search of the literature far beyond what I have been able to do. Apart from the fact that a few titles, known to deal with the controversy, were not accessible to me, I cannot tell how many more may have escaped my attention altogether. To judge by my more or less accidental encounters, I believe that there is a considerable literature of works implicated in the controversy though not forming a declared party to it.

[61]This is Bell's statement. Charles Bell, *The Hand*, Its Mechanism and Vital Endowments as

University of Cambridge. As such he was motivated to write by the observation that the treatises criticized "strike deep at the root of all Religion, both natural and revealed." Rennell, like Abernethy before him, feared that once a separate principle of life was denied, denial of an immortal soul would soon follow. Moreover, he wanted to save science as the domain for natural theology. From Newton down, scientists and natural philosophers had been among the firmest believers. "To this representation, the French school of natural philosophy constitutes a lamentable exception." Incidentally, not only French science was accused of irreligious tendencies. The *Quarterly Review* believed to have traced Lawrence's dependence on "the free-thinking physiologists of Germany."[62]

An even more uncompromising attack than Rennell's was made by "an Oxonian Resident in London" in *A Letter to John Bull*. The title of this pamphlet[63] indicated the direction of the attack. The publisher Carlile through spreading the work of Thomas Paine, Lord Byron through his irreverence, and Lawrence through his materialism were undermining belief in the Bible and the immortality of the soul, were destroying hope or dread of future reward or punishment, and thus depriving the people of due respect for authority, civil as well as divine. In the section particularly devoted to Lawrence we read:

Life they say is a mere quality of organized substance, and mind is inseparable from a sound brain, for both depend upon material organs! Life therefore is the principle of organization and intellect of brain! What then forsooth are operations of intellect? Why, merely organic impulses. And what is thought? Why, merely affections of the brain! Our desires and motives therefore are merely modifications of the brain,—and our crimes and virtues are attributable merely to the *structure* of the brain![64]

The author of the pamphlet took hope in the success of the Bible Society;[65] deploring the acquittal of the English satirist Hone, he thanked Heaven for the conviction of the publisher Carlile.[66]

Evincing Design. 3rd ed., London: William Pickering, 1834, p. ix f. These remarks may, of course, be tinged by the events of the intervening years.

[62]*Quart. Rev.*, 1820,22, no. 43: 1–34 carried a review article on Abernethy's *Inquiry* of 1814 and his *Physiological Lectures* of 1817 (see above, ns. 5 and 19), Lawrence's *Introduction* of 1816 and his *Lectures* of 1819 (see above, ns. 14 and 27), Morgan's *Sketches* of 1819 (see above, n. 46), Rennell's *Remarks* (see above, n. 58), the *Cursory Observations* (see above, n. 57), and "A Letter to the Rev. Thomas Rennell, From a Graduate in Medicine 1819." The last named item was not available to me. On p. 4, the reviewer writes: "And we have traced him [i.e. Lawrence], in like manner, still more frequently transcribing into his own pages materials of the same description from the free-thinking physiologists of Germany." Lawrence had dedicated his *Lectures* to Professor I. G. Blumenbach and revealed a very impressive knowledge of German scientific literature.

[63]*The Radical Triumvirate*, or, Infidel Paine, Lord Byron, and Surgeon Lawrence, Colleaguing with the Patriotic Radicals to Emancipate Mankind from All Laws Human and Divine. A Letter to John Bull, from an Oxonian Resident in London. London: Francis Westley, 1820.

[64]*Ibid.*, p. 22.

[65]*Ibid.*, p. 8.

[66]*Ibid.*, p. 3: "A jury of your own Englishmen—a jury,—the bulwark of English liberty—who doubtless were enlightened with a few rays of *reforming* wisdom, have boldly acquitted one

The attacks came to a climax in March 1822 with the ruling of Lord Eldon in the law suit of Lawrence versus Smith. Lawrence had invoked the protection of copyright against the publisher Smith, who had pirated his *Lectures on Physiology.*[67] An injunction had been obtained, restraining the defendant from selling the pirated edition. The defendant now moved to dissolve the injunction. His lawyers argued that the work should not enjoy a copyright, because of passages which "were hostile to natural and revealed religion, and impugned the doctrines of the immateriality and immortality of the soul."[68] The other side denied this and tried to disprove the interpretations of the defendant. The Lord Chancellor, Lord Eldon, was confronted with an interesting legal situation. If Lawrence's lectures were irreproachable, the pirated edition would be suppressed and the sale of the book be limited. If, however, the lectures were potentially criminal, they could not enjoy the protection of the law. Consequently the book could then be sold in unlimited editions. Lord Eldon was quite aware of the paradox but said:

Looking at the general tenour of the work, and at many particular parts of it, recollecting that the immortality of the soul is one of the doctrines of the Scriptures, considering that the law does not give protection to those who contradict the Scriptures, and entertaining a doubt, I think a rational doubt, whether this book does not violate that law, I cannot continue the injunction.[69]

Now the publisher Carlile issued an edition which contained not only the *Lectures* which Lord Eldon had failed to protect, but also the *Introduction* of 1816, which had originated the scandal.[70] To this edition was prefixed the following ironic dedication:

This edition of these important lectures is dedicated to John, Earl of Eldon, Lord

culprit, who tried to laugh us out of our old religion; and I was apprehensive they would have acquitted another. But thank Heaven! a few stubborn friends to old times and old doctrines and usages remain, and a virtuous jury have bestowed upon him the reward which he merited." On William Hone see the article by H. R. Tedder in *D.N.B.*, vol. 9, pp. 1137–41, and on Richard Carlile that by G. J. Holyoake, *ibid.*, vol. 3, pp. 1009–12. Hone's trials for sedition and blasphemy are described in detail by Martineau, *op. cit.* (above, n. 38), vol. I, p. 144 ff.
It is interesting to compare Lawrence's enthusiastic references to America, cited above, with the following utterances of the pamphleteer (p. 44 f.): "The state of religion in America is most awful. Extensive societies exist throughout the United States, formed professedly with the intention of eradicating the Christian religion.—Very few acknowledge God to be the governor of nations; and they express it to be unconstitutional to refer to the providence of God in their public acts and memorials. Hence social subordination has ceased. Parents have no authority over their children, masters have no control over their servants, tutors and physicians have no command over their pupils."
[67]Darlington, *op. cit.* (above, n. 4), p. 100, mentions an edition by J. and C. Smith, though giving 1823 as the year.
[68]Edward Jacob, *Reports of Cases Argued and Determined in the High Court of Chancery During the Time of Lord Chancellor Eldon. 1821, 1822, 2&3 Geo IV.* London: Joseph Butterworth and Son, 1828, pp. 471–74; see p. 471.
[69]*Ibid.*, p. 473 f. According to J. M. Rigg's article on Lord Eldon in the *D.N.B.*, vol. 17, pp. 987–94, the latter had acted similarly in other areas. See also Twiss, *op. cit.* (above, n. 37), vol. 2, p. 394, and Martineau, *op. cit.* (above, n. 38), vol. 1, 409.
[70]See above, n. 14.

High Chancellor of England, as the result of his injustice in refusing to establish the author's right of property in them. By the Publisher.

Carlile was not alone in taking Lawrence's part.[71] Thomas Forster, a physician, scientist, and phrenologist who, under the pseudonym "Philostratus," published a pamphlet with the formidable title: *Somatopsychonoologia,* felt included in the party to which Abernethy had referred. He thought that Lawrence had been accused wrongly of having "written against revelation and the historical and miraculous proofs of the eternity of the soul."[72] From a physiological point of view he considered Lawrence right and Abernethy wrong. The assumption of vitality and intelligence as inherent properties of atoms involved less difficulty than did the distinction of three essences. Physiology should be allowed free and unshackled inquiry which need not be feared, since religion did not need the support of science. Yet in contrast to Lawrence and his followers, Forster not only maintained the irrelevancy of science for the true faith, but injected a religious note of his own. Religion rested on faith and miracles. The Catholic religion represented "the original and general faith of Europe," while "the method adopted by certain protestant christians of mixing their own peculiar modes of profane reasoning with religious mysteries . . . combined with the mutual contradictions of disunited schismatics"[73] had slowly undermined religious faith since the reformation. Forster evinced an enthusiasm for the middle ages which was in the best romantic tradition of the day.

In spite of these and possibly several other dissenting voices, there was little doubt as to whose sentiments carried the day. Philostratus was duly answered by Anti-Philostratus, who thought that "to suppose that any person would believe that material atoms could of *themselves* originate animal and vegetable organisms, possessing life and perception, is an opinion too absurd, we should think even for a physiological materialist. It would be to give to those atoms design and intelligence. But what absurdity is there that such philosophers will not maintain?"[74]

The reaction to Morgan's *Sketches of the Philosophy of Life* was so unfavorable, we are told, that it induced him to retire from medical practice.[75]

---

[71]Holyoake, *op. cit.* (above, n. 66), p. 1012, lists the following title among Carlile's own publications: "'An Adress to Men of Science, calling upon Them to stand forward and Vindicate the Truth . . .' 1821." It would be interesting to see whether this bears on the Lawrence controversy.

[72]Philostratus, *Somatopsychonoologia:* Showing that the Proofs of Body, Life and Mind, Considered as Distinct Essences, Cannot be Deduced from Physiology, but Depend on a Distinct Sort of Evidence; Being an Examination of the Controversy Concerning Life carried on by MM. Laurence, Abernethy, Rennell, and Others. London: Hunter, 1823, ftn. 5. My attention was drawn to this pamphlet as well as to the reply by Anti-Philostratus (below, n. 74) by Edward L. Margetts, "The early history of the word 'Psychosomatic.'" *Canad. M.A.J.,* 1950, *63*: 402–04 (revised reprint). On Forster see also note 132 below.

[73]Philostratus, *op. cit.,* p. IV f.

[74]Anti-Philostratus, "On somatopsychonoologia," *London M. Repository,* 1823, *19*: 368–71, see p. 370.

[75]Rigg, *op. cit.* (above, n. 41).

Nevertheless, in 1822, Morgan brought out his *Sketches of the Philosophy of Morals* which he dedicated to Destutt de Tracy, the leader of the French *idéologues*.[76] The book is a continuation of his former work into the sphere of social science. Its "Preface containing some observations on 'the remarks on scepticism' of the Rev. T. Rennell" reveals something of the bitterness that Morgan felt in consequence of the concerted attacks. He was aware that the present moment (1822) was not favorable "to the obtaining of a fair hearing."[77]

Lawrence was faced with the choice between recanting or resigning his appointment as Surgeon to the Royal Hospitals of Bridewell and Bethlem. He withdrew his *Lectures* from circulation and promised not to reprint them and to refrain from future publications "on similar subjects."[78] Although he admitted "that the publication of certain passages in these lectures was *highly improper*,"[79] this, apparently, did not constitute a change of heart. At some time, he sent a copy of his lectures to William Hone, with a letter of transmittal in which he characterized his withdrawal of the book as an act of expediency and assured Hone of his high respect "for the possession of much greater courage in these matters than had fallen to his own lot."[80] Lawrence also visited Carlile during the latter's fatal illness in 1843.[81]

To sum up: as far as public reaction was concerned, the debate that had begun as a controversy between Abernethy and Lawrence ended with a defeat of the skeptical party.

II. THE HISTORICAL PLACE OF THE DEBATE

We now have to inquire into the meaning of the controversy for the history of physiology and medicine. This meaning has to be distinguished from the significance of the controversy for the general history of philosophy and for the history of freedom of thought and of the press. We are not concerned with the *Weltanschauung* of the participants as long as it does not throw light on the situation of physiology and medicine of the period. For this very reason we must first of all judge the pertinence of some of the general arguments.

The opponents of Lawrence claimed that he had misused his professional office to express heretical opinions, while Lawrence's faction defended the freedom of scientific inquiry. Accusation and defense rested on whether certain problems did or did not belong into the realm of the medical sciences. Lawrence and Morgan explicitly claimed that there was no place for an immaterial principle in physiology, and that the belief in an immortal

---

[76]T. C. Morgan, *Sketches of the Philosophy of Morals*. London: Colburn, 1822.
[77]*Ibid.*, p. xxviii.
[78]*Brit. M. J.*, (*op. cit.* above, n. 11), p. 36 f.
[79]*Ibid.*, p. 37.
[80]Darlington, *op. cit.* (above, n. 4); see also above, n. 66.
[81]Holyoake, *op. cit.* (above, n. 66), pp. 1010 and 1011.

soul had to be supported on different grounds.[82] Their denial of a physiological role of the soul was taken as a denial of its existence. It may be said that if Lawrence had not brought up the subject of an immaterial principle, the accusation would not have been made. But the fact that science does not today operate with an immaterial soul does not prove that such could as easily be the case around 1820. The debates over phrenology and "psychiatry"[83] do not point in any such direction. In 1829 Prichard, famous as an anthropologist and psychiatrist, denied that "judgment" was connected with any operation of the brain.[84] While the theological faction, rightly or wrongly, complained about an invasion of its territory by physiologists, Rennell in turn was censured for not having understood the dispute among the physiologists. Even the polite "Philostratus" said that Rennell was "running wild in the unknown regions of anatomical science."[85] According to Morgan, "the whole subject in dispute among physiologists concerns the existence of a *material* principle of life; nor would any philosopher in these days investigate the action of an immaterial agent, whose operations, *ex vi termini,* are placed beyond the reach of our comprehension."[86]

Why then did the opposition insist on a separate principle of life, different from organization? Obviously, such a principle would be an added safeguard against the identification of mind with function of the brain. But since the day of Descartes, at least, body and soul had been separated without necessarily endangering the belief in immortality. As Prichard was to show, an immaterial conscious principle could well be combined with a "chemical and mechanical doctrine of physical life."[87] Not unlike Schwann later, Prichard declared the cause governing organization and vital existence to be "nothing more or less than the energy of the Deity, operating continually through the universe, in preserving and renewing the various tribes of beings, in a manner scarcely less wonderful than at the period when they were first called into existence."[88] The principle of organization, which Lawrence and Morgan accepted, could thus be used in the interest of natural theology, which Rennell and his friends wished to preserve. Lawrence himself had borne witness to this in unmistakable terms:

The philosophic naturalist, guided by comparative anatomy, discovers at every step striking peculiarities in the economy of animals, founded on corresponding arrangements of organization. We must take refuge either in verbal quibbles, or in an

[82]Actually Morgan, *Sketches of the Philosophy of Morals,* p. xi, contended that the "longing after immortality" had prompted the adoption of the notion of an immaterial soul.

[83]Owsei Temkin, "Gall and the phrenological movement," *Bull. Hist. Med.,* 1947, *21:* 275–321—Editorials in *Am. J. Psychiat.,* 1951, *107:* 628 and 868–69.

[84]J. C. Prichard, *A Review of the Doctrine of a Vital Principle, as Maintained by Some Writers on Physiology.* With Observations on the Causes of Physical and Animal Life. London: Sherwood, Gilbert, and Piper, 1829, p. 188 f.

[85]Philostratus, *op. cit.* (above, n. 72), p. 52.

[86]Morgan, *Sketches of the Philosophy of Morals,* p. xiii.

[87]Prichard, *op. cit.* (above, n. 84), p. 81.

[88]*Ibid.,* p. 123. For Schwann see Russell, *op. cit.* (below, n. 121), p. 180 f.

exaggerated and unreasonable scepticism, if we refuse to recognize in this relation between peculiarity of structure and function those designs and adaptations of exalted power and wisdom, in testimony of which all nature cries aloud through all her works.[89]

The sincerity of these lines is not denied by the preceding illustrations of the foolishness of "the physico-theologists," who considered it "their duty to point out the end and purpose contemplated by the Creator in every natural arrangement."[90] Morgan's attitude differed somewhat. Though speaking of "organization" and "harmony" in the arrangement of animal organs, he showed no enthusiasm for final causes or design. As a follower of Cabanis, he shared the latter's vacillation between radical materialism and agnostic empiricism.[91]

From the point of view of the opposition, Lawrence was not to be trusted. He denied man's immortal soul, he doubted the Bible, he was as Abernethy had rightly felt, one of the "skeptical party." Even the author of the *Letter to John Bull*, who was not a subtle philosopher, had thrown into the debate the name of Hume, who "endeavored to introduce scepticism by perplexing cause and effect."[92] Indirectly at least, and through his emphatic agreement with Thomas Brown,[93] Lawrence was an heir to Hume's skepticism, as was pointed out in detail by Lady Mary Shepherd in a book that appeared anonymously in 1824.[94]

The controversy thus appears as part of a prelude to the Bridgewater Treatises, financed by a bequest of Francis Henry Egerton, eighth Earl of Bridgewater, who on his death in 1829 lef the sum of £8000 for the publication of a work *On the Power, Wisdom, and Goodness of God, as manifested in the Creation; illustrating such work by all reasonable argument, as for instance the variety and formation of God's creatures in the animal, vegetable, and mineral kingdoms; the effect of digestion, and thereby of conversion; the construction of the hand of man, and an infinite variety of other arguments; as also by discoveries ancient and modern, in arts, sciences, and the whole extent of literature.* The Bridgewater Treatises are too well known to need discussion here. What may deserve emphasis is the fact that the testator had signed his will under the date of

---

[89]Lawrence, *Lectures*, p. 52.

[90]*Ibid.*, p. 51.

[91]For Morgan, see his *Sketches of the Philosophy of Life*, especially pp. 29 f., 32 f., 61, 85, 187, 208, and 216 f. For Cabanis, see Owsei Temkin, "The philosophical background of Magendie's physiology," *Bull. Hist. Med.*, 1946, 20: 10–35; especially p. 20 [Essay 24, p. 325 f.].

[92]*The Radical Triumvirate*, p. 46.

[93]Lawrence, *Lectures*, p. 78, n. According to Halévy, *op. cit.* (above, n. 48), p. 435, "Brown had felt the influence of the French ideologists quite as much if not more than that of Hume." Morgan, *Sketches of the Philosophy of Morals*, p. 2, ftn., expressed himself disparagingly of "the Scotch school," accusing it of retrograding rather than advancing science. I do not know whether this was meant to include Thomas Brown.

[94]*An Essay upon the Relation of Cause and Effect*, Controverting the Doctrine of Mr. Hume, Concerning the Nature of That Relation; with Observations upon the Opinions of Dr. Brown and Mr. Lawrence, Connected with the Same Subject. London: T. Hookham, 1824. My identification of Lady Shepherd as the author of the book rests on the authority of the Library of the University of Illinois, from which I obtained a copy of this work by interlibrary loan.

25th of February, 1825,[95] when the controversy was still alive, and that biological examples apparently were foremost in his mind. The work on the hand was entrusted to Charles Bell, an early defender of the English school of physiology and enemy of the French believers in mere organization. In 1819 Bell sided with Abernethy, and his later book on *The Hand* with its romantic illustrations proved a very successful venture.

The defeat of the skeptical party in the name of patriotism and religion gave English physiology and biology a setting different from that of continental Europe. This difference extended into the following decades and still showed itself in the specifically British reaction to Darwin's theory of descent.

III. VITAL PROPERTIES, ORGANIZATION, AND EXPERIMENT

Non-medical men were drawn into the controversy because of its philosophical, political, and religious implications, but the concepts used by these participants throw some light upon physiological and medical thought of the time.

The debate has been referred to as a "vitalist-mechanist controversy"— which it was not. Abernethy and those siding with him had several reasons for looking for a principle of life apart from organization. They did not find the transition from life to death necessarily accompanied by any obvious structural changes. Second, in "the great chain of living beings" life was found connected with "a vast variety of organization yet exercising the same functions in each."[96] Moreover, a long tradition, upheld by John Hunter, had it that life was inherent in blood, i.e. an amorphous mass.[97]

Obviously, these men were vitalists, but so were Bichat and Lawrence with their belief in vital properties and the significance of organization. As far as the latter were concerned, their vitalism expressed itself in placing sensibility and contractility on a par with gravity, elasticity, and other basic forces of inanimate matter. Goodfield has introduced the felicitous distinction between "explanatory vitalists" and "descriptive vitalists."[98] Abernethy would have to be classed with the former and so would his partisan Charles Bell, who, in 1819, published *An Essay on the Forces which Circulate the Blood.*[99] The booklet was dedicated to Abernethy, to whom he expressed

---

[95]From the "Notice" in Charles Bell, *The Hand*, p. V. On Bell's connection with the Bridgewater Treatises, see Benjamin Spector, "Sir Charles Bell and the Bridgewater Treatises," *Bull. Hist. Med.*, 1942, *12*: 314–22. On the Treatises in general, see Charles C. Gillispie, *Genesis and Geology.* Cambridge: Harvard Univ. Press, 1951, pp. 209–16, 246 f., 298, and *passim*.

[96]Abernethy, *An Enquiry* (above, n. 5), p. 16.

[97]*Ibid.*, p. 48; and Abernethy, *Hunterian Oration* (above, n. 13).

[98]Goodfield, *op. cit.* (above, n. 9), p. 75.

[99]Charles Bell, *An Essay on the Forces Which Circulate the Blood;* Being an Examination of the Difference of the Motions of Fluids in Living and Dead Vessels. London: Longman and Co., 1819.—See Gordon Gordon-Taylor and E. W. Walls, *Sir Charles Bell, His Life and Times.* Edinburgh and London: Livingstone, 1958, p. 165 ff. My attention was drawn to Bell's *Essay* by Dr. Lloyd G. Stevenson.

gratitude for the stand taken against the pernicious French influences.[100] In the first part of the essay, Bell claimed that the heart could not possibly overcome the force of cohesive attraction of the blood. He suggested that "the living coats" of the blood vessels might exert an influence on the blood, whereby "the common attraction of cohesion is dismissed."[101] Not satisfied with endowing life with its own forces, Bell credited it with the ability to suspend physical laws of matter, an opinion shared by others.[102]

To "descriptive vitalists" such explanations would hardly be acceptable. "That animals obey those general laws which regulate matter and motion in all other cases," was "too obvious to be a subject of question" for Lawrence.[103] But the *operation* of the natural laws to which all bodies were subject was, in the case of living bodies, constantly modified by the vital powers.[104] This introduced an element of uncertainty and complexity into vital processes, so that they became unfit for exact quantitative determination. The original moving forces of animal functions, it was generally thought, could not be explained by mechanics and chemistry.[105] The mechanical speculations of men like Boerhaave and of the adherents of the medico-chemical and animistic systems were due to partial views and distorting notions to be guarded against.[106] Morgan formulated the contrasting attitude of the French physiologists as "having traced the functional powers to certain elementary formations which they term 'tissues,' and being wholly unable to carry their investigations further, they consider these tissues as the elements of their science; exactly as the chemists consider certain substances elementary, subject to the correction of ulterior discoveries."[107]

The claim that irritability could not be reduced beyond muscular fibres, nor sensibility beyond nervous fibres, quite literally meant that nobody had been able to do so. It may be observed that Virchow, some thirty years later, replacing the tissues by the cells, evinced impatience with those who wished to reduce vital processes to molecular forces.[108] In Virchow's days

[100]*Essay*, pp. i–viii. On p. iv appears an attack on Lawrence, who is referred to as "your [i.e., Abernethy's] younger colleague in the chair of the College of Surgeons."
[101]*Ibid.*, pp. 19 and 20.
[102]See Gordon-Taylor and Walls, *op. cit.* (above, n. 99), p. 167. William Whewell, in his *History of Scientific Ideas*, 3rd ed., vol. 2, London: John W. Parker and Son, 1858, eliminated a general "vital principle" (p. 189), and carefully excluded the "soul" from the conception of life (p. 194). But, having done so, he still claimed (p. 203 f.): "As the vital functions became better and better understood, it was seen more and more clearly at what precise points of the process it was necessary to assume a peculiar vital energy, and what sort of properties this energy must be conceived to possess. It was perceived where, in what manner, in what degree, mechanical and chemical agencies were *modified, over-ruled, or counteracted*, by agencies which must be hyper-mechanical and hyperchemical." (Italics mine.)
[103]Lawrence, *Lectures*, p. 69 f.
[104]*Ibid.*, p. 71.
[105]Goodfield, *op. cit.* (above, n. 9), p. 61: " ... to believe that physics and chemistry would eventually give the physiologist all the explanatory factors he needed was a complete act of faith."
[106]Lawrence, *Lectures*, pp. 70–76.
[107]Morgan, *Sketches of the Philosophy of Morals*, p. xiv.
[108]Owsei Temkin, "Metaphors of human biology." In Robert C. Stauffer (ed.), *Science and*

there was a strong insistence, among German physiologists at least, that physical laws were the final laws of all natural phenomena, and even Virchow did not deny this postulate *qua* such. In the days of Abernethy and Lawrence, reducibility was postulated by very few. Men like "Philostratus" (Thomas Forster) were exceptions in Britain as well as elsewhere. Morgan, as a follower of Cabanis, was attracted by the idea, yet "in the present state of our knowledge" assigned it "rather to the province of poetry than of physiology."[109] Lawrence did not quail before the accusation of having endowed mere atoms with the potential production of intelligence. Yet his reluctance to reduce vital properties to general physical causes was supported by philosophical reasons that went beyond the failure of all trials in that direction. With Thomas Brown,[110] he denied that the relationship of cause and effect had any other meaning than that of an invariable temporal sequence. Concerning the attempts to find some necessary connection between a substance and its properties, he had this to say:

... however strong the feeling may be which leads us to believe in some more close bond, we can only trace, in this notion of necessary connexion, the fact of certainty or universality of concurrence. Nothing more than this can be meant, when a necessary connexion is asserted between the properties of sensibility and irritability, and the structures of living muscular and nervous fibres.[111]

Lawrence's adversaries were right in characterizing this attitude, a joint product of French *idéologie* and British empiricism,[112] as skeptical. Perhaps, "empirical" would have been a better word, for Lawrence continued:

This language does not explain, how the thing takes place; it is merely a mode of stating the fact. To say that irritability is a property of living muscular fibres, is merely equivalent to the assertion, that such fibres have in all cases possessed the power of contraction. What then is the cause of irritability? I do not know, and cannot conjecture.[113]

Lawrence apparently failed to see that the insistence on mere factual concomitance could be a release from further research. In the long run, this kind of empiricism satisfied nobody, neither those looking for a vital principle, nor those looking to physics and chemistry for the explanation of vital properties. Claude Bernard also doubted the use of calculation in the study of living beings.[114] However, a comparison of his resolute deter-

---

Civilization. Madison: Univ. of Wisconsin Press, 1949, p. 173 [Essay 20, p. 273]. Erwin H. Ackerknecht, *Rudolf Virchow*, Doctor, Statesman, Anthropologist. Madison: Univ. of Wisconsin Press, 1953, p. 49 f.

[109]Morgan, *Sketches of a Philosophy of Life*, p. 217. See also above, n. 91.

[110]Lawrence, *Lectures*, p. 78 ftn.

[111]*Ibid.*, p. 81.

[112]In this connection see Erwin H. Ackerknecht, "Elisha Bartlett and the philosophy of the Paris clinical school," *Bull. Hist. Med.*, 1950, 24: 43–60, and Halévy, *The Growth of Philosophic Radicalism*, p. 434 f.

[113]Lawrence, *Lectures*, p. 81 f.

[114]Claude Bernard, *Introduction à l'étude de la médecine expérimentale*. Paris: Baillière, 1865, p. 226 ff.

minism[115] with the empiricism of the group represented by Lawrence will suffice to show the gulf between their respective theories of physiological research. Regarding the practice of research, a comparison is altogether difficult, since Morgan was a physician and philosopher (though of little originality) rather than a scientific investigator, while Lawrence was an anatomist, a follower of Cuvier, rather than an experimentalist.

The skeptical party confessed ignorance of the connection of vital properties and their material substratum. But the latter was designated as texture; it was organized. In the period under discussion "organization" was a favored though frequently misused term. Dr. John Barclay, the Edinburgh anatomist, rightly criticized the confusion between "organization" and "organism."[116] The term "organism" had been used by Stahl and his followers to designate the opposite of mechanism. But the expression "organized body" was preferred for living beings. The *Encyclopédie* of Diderot and d'Alembert defined *organization* as an "arrangement of the parts which constitute the living bodies,"[117] while *organisme* was not listed. With the French Revolution, when "organizing" became a prominent activity, the social meaning of organization also became popular. Carnot had "organized victory,"[118] and Napoleon was *un génie organisateur.*[119]

In 1790, Kant, in his *Critique of Judgment,* defined an organized being as a product of Nature, in which a part existed by means of the others and for others as well as for the whole. In contrast to a machine, the parts also produced one another. To this he added in a footnote: "Thus in a recently undertaken complete transformation of a great people into a state, frequent and very skillful use has been made of the word 'organization' for the system of magistracies etc., even for the entire body politic."[120] Cuvier expressly referred to Kant when he differentiated between the part of a living body which had the ground of its existence in the whole, in contrast to the dead body where each part possessed it in itself.[121]

---

[115]*Ibid.,* p. 240 ff.

[116]John Barclay, *An Inquiry into the Opinions, Ancient and Modern, Concerning Life and Organization.* Edinburgh: Bell and Bradfute, 1822, p. 340. This was part of Barclay's criticism of Lawrence, whose empiricist attitude he considered an imitation of Blumenbach (p. 333). Barclay was opposed to Abernethy's subtile substance as the cause of life (p. 490) as well as to Morgan, whom he classified among the submissive followers of Cabanis. He ascribed to Morgan "the hypothesis, that all the phenomena of organization as well as the other phenomena of life may be explained upon physical principles" (p. 385).

[117]*Encylopédie, ou Dictionnaire raisonné des sciences, des arts et des métiers.* Nouvelle éd., vol. 24. Geneva: Pellet, 1778, p. 2.

[118]Article by G. Héquet in *Nouvelle biographie générale,* vol. 8, Paris: Didot, 1854, cols. 788–800; see col. 792.

[119]*Nouveau petit Larousse illustré.* Paris: Librairie Larousse, 1947, p. 725.

[120]Immanuel Kant, *Kritik der Urteilskraft,* par. 65, in *Sämtliche Werke,* vol. 6. Leipzig: Inselverlag, 1924, p. 264, ftn.

[121]G. Cuvier, *Leçons d'anatomie comparée,* vol. 1, Paris, an VIII, p. 6: ". . . selon l'expression de Kant, la raison de la manière d'être de chaque partie d'un corps vivant réside dans l'ensemble, tandis que, dans les corps bruts, chaque partie l'a en elle-même." See E. S. Russell, *Form and Function.* London: John Murray, 1916, p. 35. Morgan, *Sketches of a Philosophy of Life,* p. 33, ftn., quotes this passage in English, referring to "the usual mysterious language of Kant." Kant

"Organization," with its biological and social meaning was (and is) a concept allowing manifold applications. Professor Ackerknecht has recently pointed out how Cuvier's work in comparative anatomy served as a pattern for the comparative approach in many fields.[122] In biology, the plans according to which animals were built allowed an insight into the various adaptations of structure, function, and environment. Presence or absence of organs, differences in their number, shape, texture, etc., threw light on the functions they served. On the other hand, experiment destroyed organic unity. Although Lawrence did not reject animal experimentation, he nevertheless echoed Cuvier's views of its limitations.[123] "We cannot analyze an animal of the higher orders, and observe the simple result of each organ by itself; for, if we destroy one part, the motion of the whole machine is stopped." In this predicament, "comparative observations afford some assistance. The animals of inferior classes are so many subjects of experiment ready prepared for us; where any organ may be observed under every variety of simplicity and complication in its own structure: of existence alone, or in confirmation with others."[124]

The encouragement of comparative anatomy as a tool for answering physiological questions at the same time implied discouraging the emulation of the physical sciences. Moreover, as mentioned before, organization meant a teleological relationship between the organism and its part. Cuvier made extensive use of final causes "a most happy and successful use," Prichard said.[125] Lawrence believed that the doctrine of final causes had "suffered more from the ill-judged efforts of its friends, than from the attacks of its enemies," and that one could not "seriously doubt that our stomachs were expressly constructed for digestion, our eyes for seeing, and the rest of our organs for the purpose which they so admirably fulfil."[126] In the days before Darwin, the purposefulness of the structure of the organism either had to be explained away, or ascribed to divine design, or accepted without any explanation of its validity.[127] In any case, it was dif-

---

apparently was known to Lawrence, since he mentions him in other contexts. L. Pearce Williams, "The physical sciences in the first half of the nineteenth century: problems and sources," *Hist. Sc.*, 1962, *1*: 1–15, draws attention to the influence Kant exerted upon such British scientists as Humphry Davy and Faraday through the medium of Coleridge.

[122]Erwin H. Ackerknecht, "On the comparative method in anthropology," in Robert R. Spencer (ed.), *Method and Perspective in Anthropology*, Papers in Honor of Wilson D. Wallis. Minneapolis: Univ. of Minnesota Press, 1954, see p. 119 ff. Even the historical literature on the biological principle of organization is so large that I must refrain from any attempt at listing it.

[123]Cuvier, *op. cit.* (above, n. 121), p. V f. On Cuvier's criticism of animal experimentaion see Owsei Temkin, "The dependence of medicine upon basic scientific thought," in Chandler McC. Brooks and Paul F. Cranefield (eds.), *The Historical Development of Phsyiological Thought.* New York: Hafner, 1959, p. 12.

[124]Lawrence, *Lectures,* p. 91.

[125]Prichard, *op. cit.* (above, n. 84), p. 69.

[126]Lawrence, *Lectures,* pp. 50 and 51.

[127]George G. Simpson, "Biology and the nature of science," *Science,* 1963, *139*: 81–88; see p. 86.—Goethe's lack of interest in teleology, echoed by Johannes Müller (see below), rested on his pantheistic concept of nature, where all existence carried its own dignity. See Russell, *op. cit.* (above, n. 121).

ficult for the biologist to evade a declaration of his faith. Conversely, it is understandable that comparative studies based on the principle of organization found great favor during the romantic period which hoped for an insight into and understanding of the plans of God or Nature in the created world.

Under these circumstances, the positivistic physiologist might prefer the experimental approach for which Haller in the eighteenth century had set the great example. Indeed, animal experimentation was cultivated extensively. But it did not stand in the forefront of research and was not favored.[128] If we take Charles Bell as representing the prevailing mood and Magendie as a prophet of things to come, a comparison of their attitudes is instructive. We shall not enter upon questions of priority regarding the law named after both. Following the late Professor Olmsted,[129] we shall merely underline the different roles which experiment played in Bell's *Idea of a New Anatomy of the Brain* of 1811, and in Magendie's paper of 1822. Bell's description of his experiments occurs in about the middle of the pamphlet and takes three short paragraphs.[130] The experiments encouraged Bell in the view he had taken, i.e., they supported a complicated thesis on functional differences of the brain and nerves. By contrast, Magendie's article opens with the words: "For a long time I have wanted to try an experiment in which I should cut in an animal the posterior roots of the nerves which take their rise from the spinal cord."[131] Here the experiment was the main object, regardless of what Magendie may or may not have wanted it to prove.

Bell performed his experiments reluctantly. He, as well as his friend Abernethy, was opposed to vivisection, as were other medical scientists, above all in England where, as Dr. Stevenson has shown, antivivisection was related to religious sentiment.[132]

However, these sentiments would hardly have gathered such strength if the physiologist could have pointed to obvious practical results, as we can

[128]Richard H. Shryock, "The history of quantification in medical science," *Isis*, 1961, 52: 215–37; p. 229: "For their part, physicians and biologists tended, during the early 1800's, to view physiologic experiments as random procedures. They held that functions were best revealed by morphologic studies." The role of experimentation has just been discussed by Walther Riese, "The impact of romanticism on the experimental method." *Studies in Romanticism*, 1962, 2: 12–22.

[129]J. M. D. Olmsted, *François Magendie*, Pioneer in Experimental Physiology and Scientific Medicine in XIX Century France. New York: Schuman's, 1944, p. 93 ff.

[130]Charles Bell, *Idea of a New Anatomy of the Brain;* Submitted for the Observation of His Friends. N.p.n.d., pp. 21–22.

[131]Quoted from Olmsted, *François Magendie*, p. 100.

[132]For Bell and Abernethy see Macilwain, *Memoirs of John Abernethy*, vol. 1, pp. 194–207. K. A. Rudolphi, *Grundriss der Physiologie*, vol. 1, Berlin: Dümmler, 1821, p. 7, thinks that animal experiment, as a rule, does not need vivisections, "least of all such cruel ones as we find described to our disgust in some recent physiological writings." This may be an allusion to Legallois and Magendie.—Lloyd G. Stevenson, "Religious elements in the background of the British anti-vivisection movement," *Yale J. Biol. & Med.*, 1956, 29: 125–57. Thomas Forster (Philostratus) was also a co-founder of the Animals' Friend Society (*ibid.*, p. 132). The debate over the existence of a soul in animals connects our controversy with the antivivisection movement.

now, and if his faith in experimental physiology had been supported by the philosophy of the time. Such was not the case. The *Gazette médicale de Paris* of June 12, 1830, in a *feuilleton* article on Magendie, asked: "what point of physiological doctrine, treated by him and his experiments, has acquired the authority of demonstrated truth? . . . M. Magendie, by experiment, proves that one vomits without a stomach, M. Maingault, by another experiment, proves that one vomits without muscles."[133] However much antagonism to Magendie may have dictated that article, it had its deeper reason in prevailing opinions of leading biologists.

For this, the criticism of contemporary experimentation by the young Johannes Müller in an inaugural lecture of 1824, "On the Need of Physiology for a Philosophical View of Nature"[134] offers an instructive illustration. The author was soon to become the outstanding comparative anatomist, embryologist, and physiologist of Germany, the teacher of Henle, Virchow, Helmholtz, to mention but a few of the most famous names of German medical science. In 1824 he was twenty-three years old, had already won a prize for a piece of experimental research, and had written a dissertation couched in the language of *Naturphilosophie,* the philosophy of Nature connected with the names of Schelling and Oken.[135] Although the lecture undoubtedly was philosophical to a degree which makes its understanding difficult for us, it was not in the line of *Naturphilosophie* which, indeed, it attacked. It followed Goethe in deprecating the use of teleological reasoning since "in Nature everything exists for its own sake."[136] The essay also followed Goethe in its constructive part. It praised the insight which the biologist gained by a patient and faithful observation of nature, and of her ways of shaping and changing plants and animals. To this Müller contrasted experiment. "Observation: simple, unwearied, industrious, honest, without prejudice;—experiment: artificial, impatient, busy, shifting, passionate, unreliable."[137] This picture of the experimental physiologist is the very opposite of the one Claude Bernard was to draw some forty years later! Müller said that a physiologist who experimented much, met with an unfavorable response. One of the reasons for frivolous experimentation was the promise it held of obtaining at least some kind of result.

[133]"Fragmens d'histoire et de biographie médicales contemporaines. (M. Magendie)," *Gaz. méd. de Paris,* 12 Juin 1830, *1:* 223–26. The article is mentioned by Olmsted, *François Magendie,* p. 174.
[134]Johannes Müller, "Von dem Bedürfnis der Physiologie nach einer philosophischen Naturbetrachtung." Reprinted in Adolf Meyer-Abich, *Biologie der Goethezeit.* Stuttgart: Hippokrates Verlag, 1949, pp. 256–81. This essay has also been discussed by Riese, *op. cit.* (above, n. 128), p. 19.
[135]Wilhelm Haberling, *Johannes Müller, das Leben des Rheinischen Naturforschers.* Leipzig: Akademische Verlagsgesellschaft, 1924, pp. 36 f., 38 f., 56 ff.
[136]Müller, *op. cit.* (above, n. 134), p. 267: "In der Natur hat nichts, was einer physiologischen Untersuchung unterworfen ist, einen Zweck. Alles ist in der Natur um seiner selbst willen da." See above, n. 127.
[137]Müller, *ibid.,* p. 269: "Die Beobachtung schlicht, unverdrossen, fleissig, aufrichtig, ohne vorgefasste Meinung;—der Versuch künstlich, ungeduldig, emsig, abspringend, leidenschaftlich, unzuverlässig."

Physiological experiments were largely fallacious because, in contrast to chemical experiments, the reaction of the animal intervened between the experimental conditions we create and the result we obtain. Only if the same experiment were repeated with "innumerable modifications,"[138] if the conditions for the functioning of an organ were isolated and then removed, could we count on a reliable result. Müller welcomed recent experiments on the nervous system where the nerves were cut—possibly a reference to the law of Bell-Magendie. Müller did not reject experiment, but he certainly did not expect salvation from experimentation.

All this suggests that there was no easy way to be a *mere* scientist.

IV. BASIC SCIENCE AND MEDICINE

Since the days of Aristotle there have been in existence a science of physiology, cultivated in the spirit of philosophical inquiry, and medical physiology cultivated because—and in as far as—it is a basis for medical theory and practice. The relationship between the two approaches has varied with the times, and so has the relationship of medicine to its basic science. During the last hundred years, medicine has come to place an almost unprecedented reliance on physiology. This juncture was reached when experimental physiology became the foundation of experimental medicine. Reliance is placed on the *method* that has been elaborated: However far removed from immediately practical concerns a project may be, it will produce results that will eventually prove of practical medical value, provided that the project is scientifically sound. For this reason the drawing of a border line between physiology as such and medical physiology has become an increasingly doubtful task.

To say that physiology, in the time of our controversy, had not *yet* attained the status which it has today would be stating the obvious. It would also be stating it in the language of hindsight. We know the path along which physiology developed; but none of the contemporaries of Abernethy and Lawrence knew it. Experimentalists like Magendie (whom we mention as a representative of many) had a faith which itself was a factor in shaping the future. The prevalent trend in medicine, as is well known, was to rely on real or alleged experience. This empirical character is attested by voices of the time, some of which would have agreed with us that medicine was "merely" empirical,[139] while others approved of the empirical orientation.

Morgan may be cited in evidence for the latter point of view. We met him as the most aggressive protagonist of French physiology, praising French

---

[138]*Ibid.*, p. 272.

[139]According to Lawrence, *Lectures*, p. 57 f., general anatomy and physiology must be cultivated. "From this quarter we must expect the future improvement of our profession; not from the addition of new medicines to a catalogue already too long; not from fresh accessions to that mass of clinical observations, which lie unread on the shelves of our medical libraries." See below, n. 157. Müller, *op. cit.* (above, n. 134), p. 280: "In England und Frankreich ist aus Einsicht des Ungrundes der Hypothese die Medicin auf die verständige Empirie beschränkt."

medical works for their "decided excellence in those parts of the science, which are purely ideal." [140] But he added immediately: "In all that is more particular and practical, the works of the English physicians are by very many degrees superior and more valuable." Waxing enthusiastic, he declared, in words which he might have borrowed from us: "It is no longer sufficient to know disease; the physician must cure it. He must wield with courage and dexterity the weighty weapons, which modern discoveries have placed in his hands..." [141] The weighty weapons which, in his estimate, placed the doctor of 1816 far above Hippocrates were: the bark, mercury, antimony, and opium,[142] in other words the puking, purging, and salivating which in the United States contributed to a revolt from orthodox medicine.

Morgan explained the discrepancy between advanced theory and lagging practice by the empirical character of the latter. "It is, however, in physic, as in the other natural sciences; theory, however ornamental, however calculated to impose, by the air which it gives of connected and perfect knowledge, has done, *and will do,* little towards the enlargement of its domain." [143] Morgan's defense of empirical practice in medicine harmonized quite well with the defense of an empiricist attitude in basic science.

In his comments on French medicine of 1816, Morgan also stated that "wherever indeed the French surgeons have crossed the path of physic, they have largely contributed to its advancement; and the most considerable steps that have been made in the art, were taken since the branches have been taught in common." [144] This attested for France the leading role of surgery, a role which was equally shared by the British surgeons. Abernethy, Bell, Astley Cooper, Brodie, Lawrence were the foremost names of the British medical profession around 1820. The leaders of our controversy were surgeons, addressing an audience of surgeons.

Abernethy, in line with his conservative and anti-French attitude, believed that by opposing the traditional division of medicine into medicine and surgery, "we would subvert the institutions of society." [145] Such apprehensions do not seem to have beset Lawrence. However, much as the two differed in their principles and views, circumstances and inclinations combined to make the critics of both Abernethy and Lawrence question the appropriateness of their discourses for the instruction of a surgical audience. Both believed in the necessity of presenting their subjects from a broad point of view and of inculcating right principles in the minds of their listeners. Both, in the names of Hunter or Cuvier, followed an anatomical line of thought. Abernethy, for instance, cited Cuvier's description of vessels arising from the digestive cavities of "medusae and similar animals"

[140]Above, n. 45.
[141]Lady Morgan, *France,* p. lxiii.
[142]*Ibid.*
[143]*Ibid.,* p. L (italics mine).
[144]*Ibid.,* p. xlix.
[145]Abernethy, *Hunterian Oration,* p. 31.

and exhausting their contents "in deposition, effusion, and transpiration." Mr. Hunter, he added, "injected the vessels of medusae from the digestive cavity, in some of the specimens preserved in the Museum in the year 1779." Having thus defended Hunter's priority, Abernethy pointed out the physiological consequence: "In animals thus nourished, in which there is no circulation, there can be no distinct respiratory organs; neither do they want them, for their blood or nutritive fluid, is every where exposed to circumambient air."[146] This method did not explain physiological mechanisms, a fact of which Abernethy was aware.[147] He acknowledged that an investigation of function needed animal vivisection, a method which he abhorred.[148] But the method, though it did not explain, helped towards an "understanding" of an organism. The method was in line with the idealistic morphology of the romantic age, and so was Lawrence's interest in the natural history of man. On the other hand, his comparisons of man and animals corroborated his denial of the existence of an immaterial principle.[149] These comparisons allowed him to judge favorably the phrenological work of Gall and Spurzheim, who had offered a rescue "from the trammels of doctrines and authorities" and had directed attention to nature, whose instructions could not deceive us.[150]

The materialistic science of the mind, which Lawrence defended in the controversy, had far-reaching medical implications. Those who considered "mental operations as acts of an immaterial being," Lawrence said, quite consistently represented insanity as a disease of the mind, rather than of the brain, and recommended "moral treatment." Lawrence turned resolutely against this notion of insanity as well as against the moral treatment. "Mental derangements" were "symptoms of diseased brain,"[151] and "these symptoms have the same relation to the brain, as vomiting, indigestion, heartburn, to the stomach; cough, asthma, to the lungs; or any other deranged functions to their corresponding organs."[152]

He, Lawrence, had hardly seen a single brain of an insane person, examined by him after death, which did not show obvious marks of disease. His view, that the material cause of mental disease was in the brain, was no more subject to doubt than "that impaired biliary secretion has its source in the liver, or faulty digestion in the stomach."[153] It is easy to trace in such

[146]*Idem, Physiological Lectures* (above, n. 19), pp. 204–05.

[147]*Ibid.*, p. 265: "We find indeed, in many instances, organization adapted to function, and yet it is highly improbable that we shall ever be able to explain function by means of our knowledge of organization."

[148]Abernethy, *Hunterian Oration*, p. 25, speaking of Haller: "He saw no mode by which function could be scientifically investigated, except by experiments made on living animals; yet in detailing these, we find frequent evidences of his being disturbed by those 'compunctious visitings of nature' which every good mind must necessarily feel at inflicting sufferings on unresisting or subdued sensitive creatures, over which nature has given us dominion."

[149]Lawrence, *Lectures*, pp. 104 and 237.

[150]*Ibid.*, p. 247. On phrenology as a science of the mind, see Temkin, "Gall and the phrenological movement."

[151]Lawrence, *Lectures*, p. 111.

[152]*Ibid.*, p. 112.

[153]*Ibid.*, p. 113.

utterances the ideas of Cabanis;[154] in the following, one may also suspect an attack upon men like Pinel, Tuke, or Heinroth.

Indeed they, who talk of and believe in diseases of the mind, are too wise to put their trust in mental remedies. Arguments, syllogisms, discourses, sermons, have never yet restored any patient; the moral pharmacopoeia is quite inefficient, and no real benefit can be conferred without vigorous medical treatment, which is as efficacious in these affections, as in the diseases of any other organs.[155]

It is not surprising that theologians, philosophers, and politicians alike turned against Lawrence's views on the soul as the core of his heresy. An anonymous late-comer to the debate, whom Lawrence's *Lectures* had escaped at the time of their publication, printed a tract, entitled *Thought not a Function of the Brain*.[156] Its main thesis was that spirit, being proved by our consciousness and the consensus of men, its reality could not be denied, and that "the co-existence" of spirit and matter in one being involved no contradiction and was, therefore, possible. The booklet also pointed out that thought was not on a par with material secretions, and that insanity was not part of a diseased brain in the sense in which suppuration was a particular state of a wound.

The prominence of theological and philosophical arguments in our controversy must not hide the fact that to Abernethy and Lawrence it was of one piece: philosophical, physiological, and medical at the same time. General anatomy and physiology, as Lawrence had it, must furnish the principles of researches and studies, if the science of medicine was to be

permanently raised above its early state of an empirical and blind belief in the virtue of herbs, drugs, and plasters, or above its more modern but equally deplorable condition of servile submission to the dogmas of schools and sects, or subjection to doctrines, parties, or authorities.[157]

Lawrence was, first of all, a surgeon. In 1823, when the controversy was at its height, the *Lancet* was founded. Lawrence became a member of the reform party which gathered around its editor, Thomas Wakley, to uphold the interests of the medical profession at large. In 1826, Lawrence presided over a mass meeting of members of the Royal College of Surgeons against its Council and officers.[158] But in 1827 he accepted membership in the Council of the Royal College of Surgeons, and the reform party had lost one of its most impressive leaders. Here his personal reaction seems to have followed the same pattern as in the controversy we have traced.[159]

---

[154]Temkin, "The philosophical background of Magendie's physiology," p. 14. [p. 320].
[155]Lawrence, *Lectures,* p. 112.
[156]*Thought not a Function of the Brain:* A Reply to the Arguments for Materialism Advanced by Mr. W. Lawrence in His Lectures on Physiology. London: C. and J. Rivington et al., 1827. The preface of the book is signed C. It is interesting that the author, though he does not seem to be a physician, devotes only seven out of a total of eighty pages to a discussion of "the reasons alleged by Mr. Lawrence . . . against the inspiration of the writings of Moses" (p. 74).
[157]Lawrence, *Lectures,* p. 57 f.
[158]S. Squire Sprigge, *The Life and Times of Thomas Wakley.* London: Longmans, Green and Co., 1897, p. 185.
[159]*Ibid.,* p. 209. It has been suggested (see Thornton, *John Abernethy,* p. 81) that Lawrence

V. CONCLUSION

Viewed within the history of biology and medicine as a whole, the British debate contained little that was new, and it is doubtful that it exerted any serious influence on the European continent.[160] In 1867, Savory could write, with a backward glance:

> The doctrine (if it can be so called) which then prevailed concerning the nature of Life, and the weakness of which Lawrence exposed with an unsparing hand, has long since become a dogma of the past; and in the discussion of this great question it is only fair to state that he was far in advance of his time. And, again, his view of the other chief subject, the relation of mind to brain, which was then denounced so fiercely, is (whether right or wrong) identical with that of many of the most enlightened physiologists of the present day.[161]

How the change in sentiment came about is known, in outline at least.[162] The reform movement played its role, and so did a multitude of factors including developments in the physical sciences. To single out one: Criticism on chemical grounds, which had attacked Abernethy's lecture of 1814, began to threaten vitalism, after Wöhler prepared urea in the laboratory in 1828. As early as 1829, Ducrotay de Blainville wrote that "it has been possible for some organic compounds, though their number is still small, to be formed entirely in our laboratories (such is the urea which M. Voehler has just demonstrated to be nothing but a cyanate of hydrated ammoniac)."[163] How in the face of this and related facts, he asked, was it possible to deny that truly chemical processes went on in the organism? A few years later, Johannes Müller, in the introductory chapter of his Textbook of Human Physiology, referred to Wöhler's discoveries as being the ones (and the only ones) where organic compounds had been produced artificially. As a convinced vitalist, he consoled himself with the thought that urea was at the very border of organic substances, and that it was an excretion rather than a component of the animal body.[164] In 1852,

---

may have been the person who surreptitiously passed Abernethy's lecture notes to Wakley, who began publishing them in the *Lancet* in 1824. Abernethy sued Wakley, and the matter eventually reached the Lord Chancellor, i.e., Lord Eldon (see Thornton, *ibid.*, pp. 79–85 and 167, and Sprigge, *op. cit.* (above, n. 158), p. 89 ff.).

[160]However, this and the possible repercussions in America remain to be examined. H. Haeser, *Lehrbuch der Geschichte der Medicin und der epidemischen Krankheiten*, vol. 2, 3rd ed., Jena: Gustav Fischer, 1881, p. 955, mentions "the storm" caused by Lawrence's *Lectures* in England.

[161]*St. Barth. Hosp. Rep.* (above, n. 11), p. 3.

[162]In this connection see A. W. Benn, *The History of English Rationalism in the Nineteenth Century*. 2 vols., London-New York: Longmans, Green and Co., 1906.

[163]H. M. Ducrotay de Blainville, *Cours de physiologie générale et comparée.* 2 vols., Paris, 1829, vol. 1, p. 31: "... quelques composés organiques, quoiqu'en petit nombre encore, ont pu être formés de toutes pièces dans nos laboratoires (telle est l'urée que M. Voehler vient de démontrer n'être qu'un cyanite d'ammoniaque hydraté)..." I mention this and the following data because Professor McKie in rightly pointing out that Wöhler's was not a true synthesis has limited the significance of his discovery more than is due, I believe. D. McKie, "Wöhler's 'synthetic' urea and the rejection of vitalism: a chemical legend." *Nature*, 1944, 153: 608–10, and Goodfield, *op. cit.* (above, n. 9), p. 126.

[164]Johannes Müller, *Handbuch der Physiologie des Menschen*, vol. 1. 3rd rev. ed., Coblenz: Hölscher, 1838, p. 3.

Moleschott, a leader of the German materialists, commenting on Liebig's hope that someday the compounds of which proteins and muscular fibres consisted would be synthesized, said, "And the deed is greater than faith and hope. The deed is the preparation of urea from cyanic acid and ammoniac."[165]

In 1832, Goethe and Cuvier died, and the temper of the time was changing. In France, men like Magendie and Louis began to set the tone. In 1832, the aging Broussais, who had made his career through battles with systems and principles,[166] felt misgivings over something new, over the "scientific anarchists," as he called them, who denounced induction, deduction, and argument as theory and system. The mine of observation was almost exhausted, he thought, and the time had come to return to reasoning and controversy, "now . . . when religious, scientific, and governmental inquisitions can no longer stop the élan of thought nor falsify the judgment of the observer."[167] Wrong as it would be to draw generally valid consequences from such a remark, it seems nevertheless permissible to read into it a yearning for a time when men battled for understanding of the world as much as for an increase in positive knowledge.

For better or worse, science and philosophy were not desegregated to the degree they are now. The controversy we have followed was an episode illustrating that state of affairs. Its episodal character may explain why the great British historian of science, William Whewell, did not relate it in his major works. But it does not explain why in his discussion of biology, vitalism, and final causes, he seems to avoid reference to works that were implicated. Perhaps the matter was still too painful; particularly since some of the protagonists were still alive. At any rate, his silence helped to dim the memory of an event that derives some interest from its intricate interdependence of such ideas as vitalism and empiricism, such sciences as zoology and physiology, the political, economic, and religious situation of post-Napoleon England, the personal character of Abernethy and Lawrence, the status of medicine, and the romantic temper of the time.

---

[165]Jacob Moleschott, *Der Kreislauf des Lebens.* Mainz: Victor v. Zabern, 1852, p. 351: "Und mehr als Glaube und Hoffnung ist die That. Die That aber ist die von Liebig und Wöhler geleistete Darstellung des Harnstoffs aus Cyansäure und Ammoniak." See also p. 345 f. It has to be added that Moleschott knew that before Bunsen, Playfair, and Rieken it was believed impossible to synthesize cyanide (*ibid.*, p. 345).

[166]Erwin H. Ackerknecht, "Broussais, or a forgotten medical revolution," *Bull. Hist. Med.,* 1953, 27: 320–43.

[167]F.-J.-V. Broussais, *Mémoire sur la philosophie de la médecine.* Lu à l'Académie des Sciences le lundi 8 octobre 1832.

27

German Concepts
of Ontogeny and History
around 1800*

1

IF WE LOOK at Haller's *Elementa Physiologiae* we find the first part of the last volume devoted to conception, embryology, and birth. The second part then takes up the subject of "Human life and death."[1] It starts with *growth* which gradually slackens until man has reached his *status*. "Then," Haller says, "man is most perfect and happy as far as his condition allows. The nerves feel acutely, the muscles enjoy full strength, and he is conscious of desire as well as apt for fertile love."[2] The *status* is succeeded by the *decrementum* which ends with *death* when "the cadaver rots" and "the immortal soul remains."[3] Waning life "is a sad topic yet abundant in material. Indeed, while the body was still on the increase, while the extending forces still held the upper hand over the resisting forces, the animal body nevertheless hardened on all sides."[4] Now, however, these negative forces are no longer balanced and man's body marches towards its end. The religious opinions met with in the *Elementa* cannot disguise the fact that Haller's analysis is largely mechanistic.[5] He conceives of the process of life as of two systems of forces acting in different directions. This point of view was also compatible with a vitalistic physiology as expressed, for instance, in Bichat's famous formula of life as the totality of the functions resisting death. Whether explained mechanistically or on the basis of vital properties, the process of life remained a sequence of events determined by conflicting forces rather than by a law of its own.

Most physiologists of the 19th century came to deal chiefly with the physiology of some adult but otherwise ageless organism.[6] Embryology and, above all, the physiology of man's ages did not receive much attention;

---

*Bull. Hist. Med., 1950, vol. 24, pp. 227–46.
This is a revised version of a paper read before the History of Science Society, Boston, Mass., December 29, 1949.
[1]Albertus Haller, *Elementa physiologiae*, tomus octavus, Bernae, 1766. The title of the whole volume is: "Fetus hominisque vita." The first part (liber 29) is entitled "Fetus," the second (liber 30) "Vita humana et mors."
[2]*Ibid.*, pars 2, p. 48.
[3]*Ibid.*, p. 348 (table of contents).
[4]*Ibid.*, p. 68.
[5]For a discussion of the religious issues involved see below p. 388.
[6]Joh. Heinr. Ferd. Autenrieth gave his *Handbuch der empirischen menschlichen Physiologie* (2 vols., Tübingen, 1801–2) the subtitle, "Lehre von der Natur des erwachsenen Menschen im gesunden Zustande," excluding embryology, which as he said (vol. I, p. xv) "Usually filled but one chapter of most physiologies."

their discussion was usually relegated to the beginning or end of the text. Richerand[7] gave an interesting reason for this practice when he said:

I have placed after generation, an abridged account of life and death, in which will be found whatever did not belong to any of the preceding divisions. The necessity of this appendix, containing the history of the different periods of life, that of the temperaments and varieties of the human species, that of death and putrefaction, arises from the impossibility of introducing into the particular history of the functions, these general phenomena in which they all participate.

Today we have eliminated the discussion of "the phases of man's life" and of death almost entirely from our texts. Death, as Dr. Guttentag[8] states, is hardly even listed in the indices of modern textbooks of physiology. Partly this is due to the elaboration of embryology, pediatrics, endocrinology, and other special disciplines which deal with the problems of aging or with certain age groups. But I think that to some extent this is due to a tendency to consider death a pathological rather than a physiological phenomenon. Primitive unicellular organisms, it is argued, can die, but they need not die. They can survive through division in an endless series of generations. Even in man our tendency goes towards doubting a predetermined boundary of life. Some 150 years ago, Blumenbach,[9] the famous anthropologist and physiologist, wrote: "Thus we are conducted to the ultimate line of physiology—to death without disease, to the senile ευθανασια which it is the first and last object of medicine to procure...." This positive accent on senility and death seems somewhat surprising today. If we think of medicine in the perspective of a future we seem more likely to hope that senility may become a preventable disease and that death may be pushed further and further into a vague distance. And indeed, if the process of life is nothing but the interplay of physical forces that can be understood and then controlled, it would not be illogical to hope for a progressive advance in the prolongation of this process. If, however, the process of life, because of some inner law, leads necessarily through the different ages and to death, then such hopes are nothing but wishful thinking. It was such a concept of life in which each stage has its definite place that gained momentum among some German physiologists around 1800. The rise of this movement is closely related to embryology on the one hand and to history on the other.

2

The rise of German embryology begins in 1759 with the publication of Caspar Friedrich Wolff's *Theoria generationis*. This publication marks the

[7]A. Richerand, *Elements of Physiology,* translated by G. J. M. De Lys (American ed. by N. Chapman and J. D. Godman), Philadelphia, 1823, p. 84.

[8]Otto E. Guttentag, On the clinical entity, *Annals of Internal Medicine,* 1949, vol. 31, p. 489. This paper provides an interesting discussion of the "irreversibly finite course of life."

[9]J. F. Blumenbach, *The Institutes of Physiology,* transl. from the Latin of the third and last edition by John Elliotson, 2nd ed., Philadelphia, 1817, p. 369. The Greek word in the quotation means "euthanasia."

beginning of a successful fight against the prevailing theory of preformation, according to which the female ovum or the male spermatozoon possesses the main characteristics of the individual so that ontogeny is basically an unfolding of what already exists. Like some others before him,[10] Wolff opposed preformation by a theory of epigenesis and the authority of neither Haller nor Bonnet was great enough to obliterate his name in Germany. It is a mistake, though often repeated, that Wolff's *Theoria generationis* was forgotten or failed to make a serious impression and that it took the German translation of Wolff's other work, *On the Formation of the Intestines,* to remind the world of him. It is true that the latter essay remained practically unknown until Meckel's translation in 1812.[11] It is equally true that the emphasis in these two works is placed differently. But I am afraid that Goethe is partly responsible for the misapprehension that in 1790, when he published his *Metamorphosis of Plants,* preformation still prevailed and Wolff was unknown. Goethe learned of the *Theoria generationis* only around 1792,[12] but this was due to his own oversight, not to that of his contemporaries.[13] Moreover, by that time epigenesis, in Germany, had found an even more aggressive and popular protagonist in Blumenbach, whom we mentioned before. At any rate, before the century had passed, epigenesis, though not without qualifications,[14] was accepted by leading German biologists and philosophers,[15] to mention only Herder, Kant, and Schelling among the latter.[16]

[10]See Wilhelm His, Die Theorien der geschlechtlichen Zeugung, *Archiv für Anthropologie,* 1870, vol. 4, pp. 197–220, 317–32; 1872, vol. 5, pp. 69–111. F. J. Cole, *Early Theories of Sexual Generation,* Oxford, 1930. Tadeusz Bilikiewicz, *Die Embryologie im Zeitalter des Barock und des Rokoko,* Leipzig, 1932, p. 103 ff. Joseph Needham, *A History of Embryology,* Cambridge University Press, 1934, p. 190 ff. Arthur William Meyer, *The Rise of Embryology,* Stanford University Press, 1939, p. 54 ff. Bentley Glass, Maupertuis and the beginning of genetics, *Quarterly Review of Biology,* 1947, vol. 22, pp. 196–210.

[11]Caspar Friedrich Wolff, *Über die Bildung des Darmkanals im bebrüteten Hühnchen.* Übersetzt und mit einer einleitenden Abhandlung und Anmerkungen versehen von Johann Friedrich Meckel, Halle, 1812. The Latin original that appeared in the *Novi Comment.* of the St. Petersburg Academy in 1768–69 was not available to me.

[12]In his "Entdeckung eines trefflichen Vorarbeiters," dated 1817, Goethe said: "... und ich freue mich bekennen zu dürfen, dass ich seit mehr als fünfundzwanzig Jahren von ihm und an ihm (i.e., Wolff) gelernt habe." This indicates his first acquaintance with Wolff between 1790 and 1792. In the "Annalen oder Tag- und Jahreshefte," an entry under the date of 1807 reads: "besonders suchte man von Caspar Friedrich Wolfs Theoria generationis sich *immer mehr* (italics mine) zu durchdringen." This sounds like a renewed and intensified reading of the *Theoria generationis.*

[13]J. H. F. Kohlbrugge, Historisch-kritische Studien über Goethe als Naturforscher, *Zoologische Annalen,* 1913, Bd. 5, pp. 83–228; see p. 201 and especially p. 218, note 14, where Kohlbrugge names a number of authors, including Herder, who mentioned Wolff before 1790, and rightly says: "Wir haben in bezug auf Wolff scharf auseinander zu halten, dass seine ersten Schriften weite Verbreitung fanden ... während nur eine ... unbeachtet blieb. Die ersteren hätte Goethe schon vor 1790 kennen sollen."

[14]For instance, I. H. F. Autenrieth, *Observationum ad historiam embryonis facientium, pars,prima,* Tubingae 1797, p. 2, writes: "Nos igitur evolvi organa, ubi germina eorum conspicimus, formari, ubi nullum eorum rudimentum antea apparuit, dicemus." See also footnote, 16, below.

[15]Cf. His, *loc. cit.,* vol. 5, p. 106.

[16]Kant, *Kritik der Urteilskraft,* § 81. Kant's arguments for epigenesis which he accepted together with Blumenbach's concept of the nisus formativus are interesting. He rejects the idea of the formation of organisms out of dead matter by mere mechanical laws. Likewise, he

Wolff's *Theoria generationis*[17] presents a somewhat puzzling sequence of ideas. Its main part deals with the development of plants which is conceived as a chapter in the physiology of nutrition and growth. Under the influence of an "essential force" and a specific nutrient substance, annual plants develop their various parts step by step and the continuation of the same process leads subsequently to a withering away until the cycle is begun anew in the following year. Throughout this part, the "essential force" often seems identical with what we should call osmosis so that the impression of a mere mechanical interpretation becomes very strong.[18] It is only in the subsequent parts that the teleological nature of the process is stressed and Wolff's strong antimechanistic bias clearly exhibited. In principle, Wolff considered his theory of plant development as elucidating the ontogeny of animals too.[19] However, the part dealing with animal embryology is not only shorter, but the complication of the subject leads to a great emphasis on descriptive observation. This latter aspect predominates in the essay *On the Formation of the Intestines,* where the specific approach to be followed in animal embryology is stressed. Plants reveal the general elementary processes of ontogeny. In animals, on the other hand, the actual changes must be followed in the various organic systems and must be described individually since they differ from one another.[20]

Whatever one may think of Wolff's general theories, the fact remains that epigenesis teaches the emergence of something new so that the initial germ and the end product have no similarity, although they are still one and the same thing. If the observer puts aside all theory, then he sees under

---

rejects preformation as supernaturalistic. Epigenesis has the advantage of being better founded in facts and of granting nature a maximum of creative power. Consequently he considers epigenesis as a system of "generic preformation," because "the productive ability of the procreators regarding the inner appropriate predispositions (zweckmässige Anlagen) with which their stock was endowed, that is the specific form, was virtually preformed." Goethe, in his remarks on "Bildungstrieb," arrived at similar conclusions: "... und wenn wir keine Präformation denken mögen, so kommen wir auf eine Prädelineation, Prädetermination, auf ein Prästabiliren, und wie das alles heissen mag, was vorausgehen müsste bis wir etwas gewahr werden könnten." In other words, the theory of epigenesis, as accepted in Germany around 1800, contained a strong teleological element and was, therefore, a compromise between preformation (rejected in the form of emboîtement) and mere mechanistic explanation. For Herder and Schelling see below. C. O. Whitman in a series of lectures (*Biological Lectures* delivered at ... Wood's Hole, 1894, Boston, 1896, pp. 205–272) has shown the complexities of Bonnet's preformistic theories.

[17]The German translation by Paul Samassa, *Caspar Friedrich Wolff's Theoria generationis (1759),* 2 vols., Leipzig, 1896 (Ostwald's Klassiker der exakten Wissenschaften, nos. 84 and 85) is more easily accessible than the two Latin editions (Halle, 1759 and 1774). The German *Theorie von der Generation,* Berlin, 1764, unfortunately was not available to me.

[18]This may, in part, account for the attempt to make Wolff a monist in the sense of the 1860's; cf. Alfred Kirchhoff, *Die Idee der Pflanzen-Metamorphose bei Wolff und bei Goethe,* Berlin, 1867, p. 14, and, by the same author: Caspar Friedrich Wolff, *Jenaische Zeitschrift für Medicin und Entwickelung,* 1868, vol. 4, pp. 193–220 (especially p. 216 f.).

[19]Wolff, *Theoria generationis, Expositio* § 32, and *passim.*

[20]Wolff, *Über die Bildung des Darmkanals,* p. 67: "Bei den Thieren erkennt man dagegen (i.e., in contrast to plants) mehrere Entstehungsweisen, mehrere dadurch veranlasste Thätigkeiten, mehrere dadurch erzeugte Producte, welche die Theile des Thiers darstellen; zwischen denen daher keine Beziehung, so wie in dem einen nicht der Grund des anderen erkannt wird." Cf. also *ibid.,* p. 69 f.

the microscope—and let us stress the fact that Wolff and many other German embryologists made considerable use of the microscope[21]—changes taking place from day to day which he could not foretell. His observations form a chronicle of events which makes it possible to understand the peculiarities of the grown animal. It is the history of this development which relates how a potentiality became an actuality,[22] and the temptation will be great to ascribe ontogeny to an entelechy or a formative instinct (the nisus formativus of Blumenbach) or a genetic force which unconsciously[23] realizes an end.

This analysis may prepare us for what really happened in the minds of Döllinger and his pupils, Pander and Carl Ernst von Baer, who most successfully continued Wolff's work and at the same time thought of ontogeny and man's ages in historical terms. But since so little is commonly known about Döllinger, the head of the school, a few biographical remarks may not be amiss.[24]

3

Born in 1770 in Bamberg, Döllinger, after medical studies at home and abroad, returned to his native city where, in 1794, he was appointed professor of "the institutes of medicine and botany." Bamberg was approaching the zenith of its medical fame. Moreover, when Schelling visited the city, "Naturphilosophie" began to reign supreme. In 1802 Döllinger was transferred to Würzburg. At first Schelling and Döllinger were on the friendliest terms, but in 1806 an estrangement took place.[25] The years in Würzburg until 1823, when he moved to Munich, were the most fruitful ones of Döllinger's life as a creative scientist. He died in 1841.

We may now begin our discussion of Döllinger's work with a paper of 1814, *On the Value and Significance of Comparative Anatomy*, the main object of which he defines as the quest for the laws of formation whereby new life instinctively realizes a certain type.[26] Teleological reflections about the use-

[21]For Döllinger, in particular, we have von Walther's (p. 63; see below, footnote 24) testimony that he was interested in the use as well as manufacture of the microscope. George Oberhäuser, who later went to Paris from where he supplied German physicians with microscopes, had served his apprenticeship as a mechanic in Würzburg where Döllinger was professor. See Justus Thiersch, Zur Geschichte des Mikroskopes (George Oberhäuser), *München. med. Wchnschr.*, 1933, vol. 80, p. 1671, and Richard H. Shryock, *The Development of Modern Medicine*, New York, 1947, p. 170, n. 2.

[22]Johannes Müller, *Handbuch der Physiologie des Menschen*, Coblenz, 1837–1840 (vol. 1 in third edition) Bd. 1, 1, p. 24: "Der Keim ist das Ganze, *Potentia*, bei der Entwickelung des Keimes entstehen die integrirenden Theile des Ganzen *actu*" (italics in the text). See also above, footnote 16.

[23]The role which the concept of the "unconscious" played in German romantic science has been brought out by Alexander Gode-von Aesch, *Natural Science in German Romanticism*, Columbia University Press, 1941.

[24]The following biographical data are chiefly based on J. Friedrich, *Ignaz von Döllinger*, I, München, 1899, and Ph. Fr. v. Walther, *Rede zum Andenken an Ignaz Döllinger*, München, 1841.

[25]Friedrich, *loc. cit.*, pp. 47–50.

[26]Ignaz Doellinger, *Ueber den Werth und die Bedeutung der vergleichenden Anatomie*, Würzburg, 1814, p. 21: "Der erste Trieb, womit sich die Lebendigkeit äussert, ist das Bilden, dieses geht

fulness of parts, Döllinger thinks, do not belong to comparative anatomy. Some parts have no use at all and the fact that in the organism all organs must be compatible is a condition for its existence rather than a principle by which to comprehend it.[27] It is not difficult to recognize Goethe's concept of morphology as well as Goethe's aversion to teleology in this document of 1814. Döllinger was an ardent admirer of Goethe although I can only speculate about the way he had become acquainted with Goethe's views at such an early date.[28] Probably Schelling had a share in it,[29] or the botanist, Nees von Esenbeck, who at that time was residing at Sickershausen near Würzburg.[30] In the following year, 1815, Carl Ernst von Baer came to Würzburg as Döllinger's pupil and in turn persuaded Pander to join them in early 1816. One day when all three were on their way to visit Nees von Esenbeck, Döllinger expressed the wish that a young scientist should investigate anew the development of the chick under his direction. Pander acceded to the task; Döllinger generously turned over to him his own material and the result was Pander's famous thesis on *The History of the Metamorphosis Which the Incubated Egg Undergoes during the First Five Days.*[31] The thesis appeared in 1817 and was followed by the *Entwickelungsgeschichte des Hühnchens im Eye,*[32] d'Alton, another of Goethe's protégés, having also cooperated.[33] The two works continue Wolff's observations and form the basis of the theory of germ layers.

I have given the German title of Pander's second publication because of the word *Entwickelungsgeschichte,* "history of development." Carl Ernst von Baer's even more important book of 1828 also carried the word *Entwickelungsgeschichte* in its title.[34] What did Döllinger and his school mean by "history" of development?

In his *Entwickelungsgeschichte der Thiere* of 1828 von Baer sums up his results as follows: "The history of the development of the individual is the

---

nach einem, in der Lebendigkeit selbst gegründeten Typus vor sich; dieser Typus muss erfüllt, und durch die Gebilde dargestellt werden...."

[27]*Ibid.,* pp. 20–22 and 24 f.

[28]With the exception of the *Metamorphosis of Plants,* Goethe's morphological writings began to appear in print in 1817 only.

[29]Goethe's relationship with Schelling, who was connected with the University of Jena from 1798 to 1803, as well as with other scientists in Jena has been noted by Kohlbrugge, *op. cit.,* pp. 85, 105 n. 9, 146 ff.

[30]Christian Gottfried Daniel Nees von Esenbeck (1776–1858) had studied medicine in Jena where he was influenced by Schelling and became Goethe's friend. In 1802 he retired to Sickershausen where he remained until 1817 when he became professor of botany in Erlangen. *Allgemeine Deutsche Biographie,* vol. 23, 1886, p. 368 ff., and Erik Nordenskiöld, *The History of Biology,* New York, 1942, p. 289.

[31]Ch. Pander, *Dissertatio inauguralis sistens historiam metamorphoseos, quam ovum incubatum prioribus quinque diebus subit,* Wirceburgi, 1817.

[32]Pander, *Beiträge zur Entwickelungsgeschichte des Hühnchens im Eye,* Würzburg, 1817.

[33]The episode which led to Pander's investigations as well as the relative share of Döllinger, Pander, and d'Alton are discussed by von Baer in his autobiography: *Nachrichten über Leben und Schriften des Herrn Geheimraths Dr. Karl Ernst von Baer, mitgetheilt von ihm selbst,* zweite Ausgabe, Braunschweig, 1886, p. 192 ff., and in von Baer's *Entwickelungsgeschichte* (see footnote 34) p. V f.

[34]Karl Ernst v. Baer, *Über Entwickelungsgeschichte der Thiere,* erster Theil, Königsberg, 1828.

history of the growing individuality in every aspect."[35] The context leaves little doubt that history is here taken in a more than descriptive sense. But if we wish to understand its full meaning we must turn to Döllinger's fragmentary *Elements of Physiology*[36] which began to appear in 1836, five years before his death.

This peculiar work is an attempt to expand a treatise on embryology into a physiology of man's entire life. Having remarked that life is a process from imperceptible beginnings to death, and that there is a constant change of building and destruction going on within the body, Döllinger writes in the introduction: "In this course of life and passing of existence the single phenomenon itself cannot have any significance for itself; for everything that at a certain time appears as part of the process has its peculiarity only by what preceded it and thus prepared it and gave rise to it. And its value consists merely in its contribution to the establishment of a coming stage of development. Thus, the knowledge of individual human existence cannot truly be other than historical. . . ." And the introduction ends in the following general definition: "Physiology should be a history of what happens and how it happens in the course of man's individual process of life, according to his generic character." The process of life, for Döllinger, is no longer a mere result of conflicting forces but a process in which each phenomenon has its "historical place" and a definite significance for what precedes and follows.[37] It would be easy to translate this introduction into Hegelian terms and to say that for Döllinger life is a process in which each phenomenon is but a moment within the totality.

In this emphasis on the course of life, Döllinger and his school stood not alone among their romantic contemporaries. Burdach in his six volumes of *Physiology as a Science of Experience,*[38] which he wrote in cooperation with von Baer, Rathke, Valentin, Johannes Müller, and others, attempted something similar. The first three volumes are devoted to "The history of life" and deal respectively with generation, embryology, and the ages of man including death. Here too, the traditional order is reversed. What used to be relegated as an appendix to the end of a text, now emphatically was placed in the foreground. But whereas Burdach, in the remaining volumes, re-

---

[35]*Ibid.*, p. 263: "Die Entwickelungsgeschichte des Individuums ist die Geschichte der wachsenden Individualität in jeglicher Beziehung."

[36]I. Döllinger, *Grundzüge der Phsyiologie*, Regensburg und Landshut, 1836. The book stops abruptly on p. 368 in the middle of a sentence. See also below, footnote 40.

[37]*Ibid.*, p. 4: "Somit kann auch die Erkenntniss des individuellen menschlichen Daseins in ihrer Wahrheit lediglich nur eine *historische* seyn, wobei es zwar ursprünglich auf die richtige Auffassung einer jeden dem Lebensprozess angehörenden Erscheinung ankömmt, deren wissenschaftliche Tendenz aber nur darin gefunden werden mag, dass überall eine *historische* Ansicht hervorleuchte, und deren Forschungen durch das Bemühen für jede einzelne Erscheinung im Gange des Lebens die *historische* Stelle, und ihre Beziehung auf das, was vor ihr war und nach ihr seyn wird, damit also auch ihre Bedeutung im Gesammtlebensprozesse, auszumitteln, geleitet werden" (italics mine).

[38]Karl Friedrich Burdach, *Die Physiologie als Erfahrungswissenschaft*, Leipzig, vols. 1–3 (second edition), 1836–38; vol. 4, 1832; vol. 5, 1835; vol. 6, 1840. The individualistic and "historical" element of romantic medicine is also discernible in its case histories; see Owsei Temkin, Studien zum "Sinn"-Begriff in der Medizin, *Kyklos*, 1929, vol. 2, p. 56.

verted to functional physiology,[39] Döllinger pushed the "historical" approach to the extreme and endeavored to integrate not only embryology and histogenesis, but all functions of the grown organism into one. To achieve this aim he had to take up the embryological account again and again and yet try to preserve the continuity of the process as a whole. Moreover, he had to introduce metaphysical principles in order to include death as a determining point in the development of the individual. This is brought out very clearly in his discussion of the physiology of circulation. The universe, he says, uses adult progenitors as instruments in order to maintain existing species by the production of new individuals. Thus the newly conceived individual, as far as its body is concerned, exists as a part of the earth and, in the beginning, as a part of the maternal organism. Its task now is to separate itself from the mother. In birth it achieves independent life which, from this moment on, it has to maintain against the surrounding cosmic forces. The second task then is to achieve freedom from these forces and to establish its egoistic principle even more validly. This leads to "a second birth, natural death, resulting in the autonomous transfer to a third sphere of life." Consequently, for Döllinger, the real life of a human individual has two main periods: "The first period is the embryonic life before birth, the second (period) begins with birth and continues until natural death. Thereby two main periods are also given in the genesis of the circulatory system (Blutbahnbildung)."[40] It is strange to find such reasoning in a chapter on the cardiovascular system; no wonder that the work was never completed.[41]

So far we have shown the existence of a concept of "historical" physiology among German biologists and its close association with the rise of epigenetic principles in embryology. Embryology indeed was the science in which Germany stood foremost at a time when it was behind other countries in most branches of positivistic research. The importance of the embryological studies reveals itself not only in the contemporary achievements of Meckel, Oken, Pander, von Baer, and others, but likewise in their bearing upon the future of general anatomy. The romantic anatomists and physiologists, being so greatly interested in embryology, were wont to use the microscope and to inquire into the genesis of tissues as well as of organic form. Thus, in 1824 Döllinger could write:

A perfect and in every respect satisfactory anatomy to which, as we say, the fundament has already been laid,[42] must give the time and manner of origin of all

---

[39]Vols. 4–6 are devoted to: "Die Lehre vom bestehenden Leben" and deal with what we may call "vegetative" physiology. Three more volumes, dealing with "animal" physiology had been intended, as well as a tenth "Band . . . der die Geschichte des Lebens auf Erden überhaupt und des Menschengeschlechts insbesondere zum Gegenstand hätte" (vol. 6, p. 610).

[40]Döllinger, *Grundzüge der Physiologie*, p. 279; see also *ibid.*, p. 323 f.

[41]H. Eichhorn, in his obituary of Döllinger, *Medicinisches Correspondenz-Blatt bayerischer Aerzte*, 1841, zweiter Jahrgang, pp. 173–76 and 186–89, ascribes (p. 188) the abrupt ending of the book to publications by J. Müller and R. Wagner which made the published part obsolete.

[42]Döllinger here refers to the work of J. Fr. Meckel which has been well reviewed by Rudolf Beneke, *Johann Friedrich Meckel der Jüngere*, Halle, 1934.

formations of the human body. It must determine with precision their particular *tissues* and how, afterwards, one differentiates from the other. It must separate the connection of the organs, it must narrate how the parts grow and, while growing, change as to form and *tissue*, how they change their position, how what is separated becomes connected and what is simple gradually dissolves into something many-fold. It must exactly describe the structure at the point of completed growth, the perfect fulfillment of the concept of individual life. It must, in the subsequent periods, show the causes of natural death in the changes of formations and *tissues*. And, finally, it is also its task to establish the laws which result from an attentive consideration of the natural differences of the human race.[43]

On the other hand, in his practical microscopic work, the embryologist encountered "vesicles,"[44] "globules,"[45] "granules,"[46] or similar bodies in the primordial embryo. Whether or not these bodies sometimes were identical with what we call cells,[47] the fact remains that to the embryologist their existence seemed a reality. Anatomists like Cuvier and Bichat might neglect the microscope; anatomists interested in the "history" of the human organism could hardly do without it.[48] Thus the ground was being prepared for the subsequent emergence of the cellular theory.[49] It has one of its roots in the predilection for genetic anatomy and physiology, that is embryology, which Johannes Müller had praised as the science in which "nature herself reveals the plan of her thoughtful operations."[50]

Now it is well known that the idea of "development" exerted a common influence upon all branches of romantic thought. Contemporaneously with

---

[43]Ignaz Döllinger, *Von den Fortschritten, welche die Physiologie seit Haller gemacht hat,* München, 1824, p. 13 (italics are mine).

[44]Wolff, *Theoria generationis,* § 6 ff.

[45]*Ibid.,* § 168. Carl Ernst von Baer, *Entwickelungsgeschichte, passim,* devotes much energy to tracing the fate of the "Kügelchen" in the development of the chick.

[46]Pander, Beiträge, § 1, p. 4 and *passim.*

[47]J. Walter Wilson, Dutrochet and the cell theory, *Isis,* 1947, nos. 107 and 108, pp. 14–21, has pointed out the fallacies in identifying the "globules" and "cellules" of older anatomists with cells in the modern sense. In emphasizing the work of German romantic biologists, I do not wish to overlook the contributions of French scientists like Dutrochet, Milne Edwards, Raspail, and others. For the whole history of the cellular theory see Marc Klein, *Histoire des origines de la théorie cellulaire,* Paris, 1936 (Actualités scientifiques et industrielles, 328).—John R. Baker, The cell-theory: a restatement, history, and critique, *Quarterly Journal of Microscopical Science,* 1948, vol. 89, pp. 103–125, and 1949, vol. 90, pp. 87–108, subsumes the early attempts under the heading "The globule-theory" (I am indebted to Dr. Erwin H. Ackerknecht for this reference).

[48]This should not be interpreted as if the historical school had been the only one interested in embryology or microscopy. On the other hand, it may help to answer the question, raised by Richard H. Shryock (*The Development of Modern Medicine,* New York, 1947, p. 170), as to why the microscope was exploited by German rather than French physicians and biologists. The younger Meckel, though an outstanding embryologist, made little use of the microscope; but it is perhaps significant that he was strongly influenced by Cuvier and stood in opposition to speculative Naturphilosophie (See Beneke, *op. cit.,* pp. 21, 29 ff., 98, 110).

[49]The title of Schleiden's contribution, "Beiträge zur Phytogenesis," is in itself suggestive. E. Küster, in *Hundert Jahre Zellforschung* by L. Aschoff, E. Küster, W. J. Schmidt, Berlin, 1938 (Protoplasma-Monographien, Bd. 17), pp. 6–7, has stressed Schleiden's ontogenetic approach.

[50]J. Müller, Jahresbericht über die Fortschritte der anatomisch-physiologischen Wissenschaften im Jahre 1833, *Archiv für Anatomie, Physiologie und wissenschaftliche Medicin,* 1834, p. 2.

"historical" physiology, historical work in the strict sense flourished in Germany where Niebuhr in 1811, with the publication of the first volume of his Roman history, initiated a new historiography. Was there an inner relationship between these two movements? I shall try to show that it was the idea of ontogenetic development in particular that linked the philosophy of nature and of history.[51] For this purpose we must once more return to the 18th century and the struggle between the followers of preformation and epigenesis.

4

Among the early adherents of epigenesis in Germany we find Herder, the erstwhile pupil of Kant and mentor of the youthful Goethe. In the *Ideen zur Philosophie der Geschichte,* which began to appear in 1784, Herder is quite outspoken in his rejection of preformation and uses the term "genesis" to express the true nature of embryonic development.[52] Genesis to Herder is the equivalent of the German word "Bildung," a term so dear to Goethe.[53] Speaking, further on, of the "genetic force,"[54] he not only quotes Wolff's *Theoria generationis* but shows himself well acquainted with its contents.[55] However, here his agreement with Wolff ends. The invisible force which is at work manifests itself in the formation of the embryo, but it must have the type of this manifestation in itself. "The new creature is nothing but a materialized idea of creative nature which never thinks otherwise than by acting."[56] This platonic element of the organism as representing an idea is

---

[51]Morris Cohen, *The Meaning of Human History,* La Salle, The Open Court Publishing Company, 1947, p. 13, has pointed out the influence of embryology upon "the notion of continuous development through a definite series of stages."

[52]Johann Gottfried Herder, *Ideen zur Philosophie der Geschichte der Menschheit,* book 5, II: "Präformierte Keime, die seit der Schöpfung bereit lagen, hat kein Auge gesehen; was wir vom ersten Augenblick des Werdens eines Geschöpfs bemerken, sind wirkende organische Kräfte."

[53]*Ibid.* In this section, Herder opposes "Bildung" (genesis) to both preformation and epigenesis. "Sieht man diese Wandlungen ... so, dünkt mich, spricht man uneigentlich, wenn man von Keimen, die nur entwickelt würden, oder von einer Epigenesis redet, nach der die Glieder von aussen zuwüchsen. Bildung (genesis) ist's, eine Wirkung innerer Kräfte, denen die Natur eine Masse vorbereitet hatte, die sie sich zubilden, in der sie sich sichtbar machen sollten." At that time, Herder was not yet acquainted with Wolff's *Theoria generationis* which, according to Rouché, he read only while working on the second part of the *Ideen;* see Max Rouché, *La philosophie de l'histoire de Herder,* Paris, 1940, p. 198. This was partly in line with the qualifications with which German philosophers and biologists accepted epigenesis (see above, footnotes 14 and 16).

The accent placed on "Bildung" raises the question as to Goethe's influence who, on his own testimony, conversed daily with Herder when the latter worked on the first part of his *Ideen.* While Goethe's influence cannot be excluded, the fact that Goethe, at this time, was not conversant with Wolff's work speaks for the independent progress of Herder's studies.

[54]Herder, *Ideen,* book 7, IV: "Die genetische Kraft ist die Mutter aller Bildungen auf der Erde, der das Klima feindlich oder freundlich nur zuwirkt."

[55]*Ibid.* "Aus Kügelchen, zwischen welche Säfte schiessen, wird ein lebender Punkt ... das Herz erzeuge sich nicht anders als durch eine Zusammenströmung der Kanäle, die schon vor ihm waren." These thoughts seem to be derived from Wolff, rather than Harvey whom Herder also cites.

[56]*Ibid.;* see also Rouché, *op. cit.,* p. 200.

382

fundamental for romantic biologists—we still find it dogmatically confirmed in Johannes Müller's *Physiology* as late as 1840.[57] Ontogeny, then, is the materialization of this idea, and though it may involve mechanisms, it will not be the mere result of an interplay of forces. Now if this is true, the ages of man and his death must also be planned by nature. Herder immediately proceeds to confirm this necessary consequence. The genetic force does not leave the creature it formed, but goes on to sustain it until it weakens in old age. But here we seem to be confronted with a difficulty. For just how long does the genetic force remain active within us and why does it weaken? These questions also must have their answer if the ages of man are to be explained as immanent necessities of life. Herder hints at the answer and Schelling states it quite clearly. Nature is not interested in the individual but only in the species to which it belongs. Though the individual represents an idea, this idea is that of its species. Nature therefore will sustain individuals until they are grown up and able to reproduce. When men and women love each other, they feel desires and have illusions. "Sweetly deceived creatures," Herder exclaims, "enjoy your time! Yet know that it is not your little dreams but the greatest view of nature which you, pleasantly compelled, are thereby advancing."[58] And Schelling adds that after the time for reproduction has passed nature turns against the individual and destroys it.[59]

So much is necessary to explain how physiologists who accepted such ideas could think of human life as a "historical" process. There remains the question as to whether they were justified in using the term "historical." The answer to this question depends largely on what is meant by "history." Schelling, the father of "Naturphilosophie," had stated that nature herself might be considered historically, not so, however, natural objects.[60] We may agree with him and concede that the "history" of development (Entwicklungsgeschichte) is no real history. Let us therefore consider the role ontogeny played in the development of truly historical thought. We shall then perhaps find a synthesis on a higher level.

With so many of his contemporaries, Herder believed in a "scala

---

[57]J. Müller, *Handbuch*, Bd. 2, Abtheilung 3, p. 505. The relationship of German biologists and physicians, including Döllinger, von Baer, Burdach, and Johannes Müller to romantic philosophy has been brought out by Werner, *Schellings Verhältnis zur Medizin und Biologie*, Diss. Leipzig, Paderborn, 1909. For Johannes Müller see, in particular, Martin Müller, *Über die philosophischen Anschauungen des Naturforschers Johannes Müller.* Leipzig, 1927.

[58]Herder, *Ideen*, book 2, II; see also Arthur O. Lovejoy, Some eighteenth century evolutionists, *Popular Science Monthly*, 1904, vol. 65, p. 331.

[59]Erster Entwurf eines Systems der Naturphilosophie, in *Schellings Werke*, herausgegeben von Manfred Schröter, 2. Hauptband, München, 1927, p. 51: "Von diesem Augenblick an, da das Gemeinschaftliche gesichert ist, wird die Natur das Individuelle verlassen, wird aufhören in ihm thätig zu seyn, oder vielmehr, . . . sie wird anfangen darauf entgegengesetzte Wirkungen auszuüben; von nun an wird das Individuelle eine Schranke ihrer Thätigkeit seyn, welche sie zu zerstören arbeitet." This writing dates of 1799.

[60]System des transzendentalen Idealismus (1800), *loc. cit.*, p. 588. The general difference between the "historical" and the "scientific" method and its bearing upon morphology have been well formulated by Thienemann, *loc. cit.* (see footnote 61), p. 273 f.

naturae," a chain of beings from the lowest to the highest, man.[61] This chain was linked not only by perfection of forms, but also by an ascent of functions. In plants, nutrition and reproduction are the only organic forces. They still predominate in the lowest animals, which also possess something analogous to sense and voluntary movement. With higher forms irritability and then sensibility step to the foreground, while the power of reproduction is weakened.[62] Herder believed that the chain of being had come into existence successively. Species had perished in the revolutions of the earth and higher forms had been built from the lower material.[63] Herder did not believe in descent.[64] The creation of higher forms was the work of the genetic force which also manifested itself in the development of the individual. The genetic force was, therefore, the common link between ontogeny and creation of new species.

This being the case, it was not far fetched to assume, on the basis of an identical genetic force, the existence of a parallelism between ontogenetic development and the scale of beings. Kielmeyer, the friend of Cuvier, in his famous speech of 1793,[65] drew this consequence by suggesting the so-called law of recapitulation couched in physiological language.[66] Sensibility, irritability, and the force of reproduction appear in the embryo in a sequence similar to their relative distribution in the scale of nature. A morphological formula was added by Autenrieth in 1797.[67]

Herder's influence on Kielmeyer is so obvious that it has escaped the notice of neither modern historians nor Herder's own contemporaries.[68]

[61]August Thienemann, Die Stufenfolge der Dinge, der Versuch eines natürlichen Systems der Naturkörper aus dem achtzehnten Jahrhundert, *Zoologische Annalen*, 1909, vol. 3, pp. 185–274. Arthur O. Lovejoy, *The Great Chain of Being*. Harvard University Press, 1936.
[62]Herder, *Ideen*, book 3, II.
[63]*Ibid.*, book 10, II and V.
[64]This has been elaborately proved by Max Rouché, *Herder précurseur de Darwin?* Paris, 1940.
[65]Carl Friedrich Kielmeyer, Ueber die Verhältnisse der organischen Kräfte untereinander in der Reihe der verschiedenen Organisationen, die Geseze und Folgen dieser Verhältnisse. Reprinted, with notes by Heinrich Balss, in *Sudhoffs Archiv*, 1930, vol. 23, pp. 247–67.
[66]Em. Rádl, *Geschichte der biologischen Theorien*, 1. Theil, Leipzig, 1905, p. 262. J. H. F. Kohlbrugge, Das biogenetische Grundgesetz. Eine historische Studie, *Zoologischer Anzeiger*, 1911, vol. 38, pp. 447–53. E. S. Russell, *Form and Function*, London, 1915, p. 89 f.
[67]Autenrieth, *Observationum* etc., p. 24 f.: "Plura ad comparandos diversos embryonis se evolventis status cum constantibus inferiorum animalium formis in interna structura partim evidentissima, et quaedam, quae in adulto Afro minus, quam adulto Europaeo ex reliquiis embryonis mutata videntur, progressus opusculi exhibebit. Verum semper ad id attendendum erit, in serie organisationum sensim sensimque partes plane novas communi omnium trunco se addere, aliis interdum in totum evanescentibus, ... et homini suas proprias in formatione idiosyncrasias esse et dari series extra animalia quasi cohaerentes, nequaquam in uno eodemque individuo unquam obvias. ..." Neither Kielmeyer nor Autenrieth was the discoverer of the law of recapitulation. To mention the 18th century only: Haller (according to Autenrieth, *ibid.*, p. 20), Bonnet (see Lovejoy, *The Great Chain of Being*, p. 285), and John Hunter (see Needham, *loc. cit.*, p. 203), had already anticipated it in varying degrees of clearness. I here use the term "law of recapitulation" merely in the sense "that animals in the course of their embryonic development pass through stages corresponding to the mature forms lower in the scale" (S. J. Holmes, K. E. von Baer's perplexities over evolution, *Isis*, 1947, nos. 107 and 108, p. 9). There is some reason to believe that Kielmeyer really thought of descent; see Heinrich Balss, Kielmeyer als Biologe, *Sudhoffs Archiv*, 1930, vol. 23, p. 276 ff.
[68]Johann Eduard Erdmann, *A History of Philosophy*, English translation edited by W. S. Hough, vol. 2, London, 1890, p. 572. Balss, Kielmeyer als Biologe, *loc. cit.*, p. 287 (Carl

Schelling, in 1799, even quoted the pages of Herder's *Ideen* to which Kiel-meyer was indebted.[69] And at the same time Schelling incorporated Her-der's and Kielmeyer's ideas into his own system.[70] The chain of being is nature's endless attempt at achieving an ideal product.[71] In this she con-stantly fails, because each species develops sexual differentiation, and any differentiation of functions is incompatible with the ideal. Thus nature tries again and a higher species results. On the other hand, the embryo of each species up to the point where it develops sexual characteristics, runs through all stages of organization. Hence Schelling arrives at a formula for the law of recapitulation which is surprisingly modern since it implies that the series of species is determined by an ontogenetic series.[72] But to Schel-ling too, the species themselves are immutable.[73] If viewed singly, they are but the manifest failures of nature to create the absolute product. But if all species were viewed as embryological stages in the development of one ideal organism, then this ideal organism could be considered as converging towards the final product.[74] In other words, the chain of being would be but one process of ontogeny. Moreover, if we knew how organic functions had combined in course of time to form the different species with their different organs, we should have a real history of nature instead of mere natural history.[75]

It is easy to perceive in this system the basis for Oken's claim that man was the complete animal, all other species being but persistent forms of his ontogeny.[76] And Döllinger must still have been under the influence of similar thoughts when, in 1824, he wrote that all products of nature could

Siegel's *Geschichte der deutschen Naturphilosophie*, Leipzig, 1913, to which Balss here refers, was unfortunately not accessible to me). According to E. Jacobshagen (cited by Beneke, *Johann Friedrich Meckel der Jüngere*, pp. 112 and 152), Herder's *Ideen* were the starting point for the whole biological movement around 1800 including not only Kielmeyer but also Goethe, Cuvier, and Pfaff. [Jacobshagen was the lecturer referred to above, p. 30. His *Allgemeine ver-gleichende Formenlehre der Tiere*, 1925 (cited by Beneke), has not been available to me.]

[69] Schelling, *Erster Entwurf eines Systems der Naturphilosophie*, *loc. cit.*, p. 195, footnote. It must, however, not be overlooked that certain similar ideas of Vicq d'Azyr, which Thienemann, *loc. cit.*, p. 252 ff., has outlined, may also have influenced Kielmeyer.

[70] Kuno Fischer, *Geschichte der neuern Philosophie*, sechster Band: Friedrich Wilhelm Joseph Schelling, Heidelberg, 1872–1877. Balss, Kielmeyer als Biologe, *loc. cit.* Oskar Walzel, *German Romanticism*, translated by A. L. Lussky, New York-London, 1932, pp. 18–20. Hegel, Vor-lesungen über die Geschichte der Philosophie, in *Georg Wilhelm Friedrich Hegel, Sämtliche Werke*, Jubiläumsausgabe in zwanzig Bänden, herausgegeben von Hermann Glockner, Stuttgart, vol. 19, p. 648, writes: "Erst später (i.e., after 1798), in Bezug auf Herder'sche und Kielmeyer'sche Schriften,—wo von Sensibilität, Irritabilität und Reproduktion, ihren Gesetzen, z.B. dass je grösser die Sensibilität, desto geringer die Irritabilität u.s.f. gesprochen wird . . . fasste er (i.e. Schelling) dann . . . die Natur in Gedanken-Kategorien auf, und machte allgemeine be-stimmtere Versuche wissenschaftlicher Ausführung."

[71] For this and the following see Schelling, Erster Entwurf, *loc. cit.*, p. 43 ff.

[72] *Ibid.*, p. 53: " . . . die Verschiedenheit der Organisationen reducirt sich zuletzt allein auf die Verschiedenheit der Stufen auf welchen sie in entgegengesetzte Geschlechter sich tren-nen." Rádl, *op. cit.*, p. 259, is partly right in saying that Schelling stressed "den Stufengang jener (i.e., physiological) Prinzipien, nicht den der Formen." However, Schelling, *loc. cit.*, p. 74, showed himself aware of the need for correlating these principles with definite organs.

[73] *Ibid.*, p. 32 ff.

[74] *Ibid.*, p. 64.

[75] *Ibid.*, p. 68.

[76] Lorenz Oken, *Elements of Physiophilosophy*, from the German by Alfred Tulk, London,

be considered as experiments which had to precede man, the acme of creation.[77] This was an echo from Herder and Robinet.[78]

Herder was certainly not original in all his biological thought. Buffon for one deeply influenced him as Rouché has abundantly shown.[79] Goethe's possible influence must not be forgotten either, though I have felt all the more justified to omit Goethe from the present discussion since his ideas on evolution form the subject of a recent paper by Riese.[80] If I have chosen Herder as my main witness for the connection of biological and historical thought, it is because this connection in his own mind certainly existed (as Rouché[81] has pointed out), because his direct and indirect influence on Schelling as well as on many biologists[82] is well attested, and, above all, because he was the chief protagonist of an organic concept of history with its emphasis on the individuality of each culture.

5

In 1774, when epigenesis had not yet gained recognition,[83] there appeared Herder's essay, *Auch eine Philosophie der Geschichte zur Bildung der Menschheit.*[84] This essay gives a new turn to the old analogy between historical epochs and the ages of man.[85] Herder thinks of mankind as a person

---

1847, p. 492: "Animals are only the persistent foetal stages or conditions of man." See also Russell, *op. cit.*, p. 90 f.

[77]Döllinger, *Von den Fortschritten* etc., p. 3: "So wie der Mensch an der Spitze der irdischen Schöpfung steht, und alle Naturproducte als Versuche gelten können, welche vorangehen mussten, ehe sich in einem Vollendeten das Bild der Gottheit würdig abspielen konnte. . . ."

[78]See Lovejoy, *The Great Chain of Being*, p. 279 f.

[79]Rouché, *La philosophie de l'histoire chez Herder*, p. 207. Arthur O. Lovejoy, Buffon and the problem of species, *The Popular Science Monthly*, 1911, vol. 79, pp. 464–73 and 554–67, see p. 566.

[80]Walther Riese, Goethe's conception of evolution and its survival in medical thought, *Bull. Hist. Med.*, 1949, vol. 23, pp. 546–53.

[81]Rouché, *loc. cit.*, pp. 226 and 231; see also Carl Siegel, *Herder als Philosoph*, Stuttgart und Berlin, 1907, p. 156 ff.

[82]Herder is quoted by Joh. Christ. Reil, *Von der Lebenskraft* (Klassiker der Medizin, herausgegeben von Karl Sudhoff, Leipzig, 1910, pp. 12 and 32). J. F. Meckel, *Handbuch der menschlichen Anatomie*, 1. Band, 1815, p. 71 (see also Beneke, *op. cit.*, pp. 66 and 112). F. Joseph Gall and G. Spurzheim, *Anatomie et physiologie du système nerveux en général, et du cerveau en particulier*, 4 vols., Paris 1810–1819, *passim*. For Carl Ernst von Baer see further below. See also Walzel, *loc. cit.*, Ernst Hirschfeld, Romantische Medizin, *Kyklos*, 1930, vol. 3, pp. 1–89, *passim*, and Walter Pagel, *Virchow und die Grundlagen der Medizin des XIX. Jahrhunderts*, Jena, 1931, p. 8 ff. (Jenaer medizin-historische Beiträge, 14).

[83]In the same year the second Latin edition of Wolff's *Theoria generationis*, edited by one of his friends, was published.

[84]Herder, Auch eine Philosophie der Geschichte zur Bildung der Menschheit, in *Herders sämmtliche Werke*, herausgegeben von Bernhard Suphan, fünfter Band, Berlin, 1891, pp. 475–594.

[85]Friedrich Meinecke, *Die Entstehung des Historismus*, 2 vols., München und Berlin, 1936; see vol. 1, pp. 60 and 260; vol. 2, pp. 314 and 423. John Arnold Kleinsorge, *Beiträge zur Geschichte der Lehre vom Parallelismus der Individual- und der Gesamtentwicklung*, Diss. Jena, 1900, has traced the history of the analogy from earliest Christian times with special regard for its pedagogic significance. In particular he has shown how this analogy implied a law of recapitulation that was made explicit in the late 18th century. Thus he quotes (p. 30) Gedike as writing in 1779: "Die Entwicklung einzelner Menschen geht eben den Gang, wie die des ganzen Menschengeschlechts."

that, in course of historical time, has passed through infancy, childhood and manhood. But each civilization of the past, just as each age of man, has its own individuality.

Youth is not happier than innocent contented childhood: nor is quiet old age more unhappy than fervently striving manhood. . . . Nobody is in his age only; he builds upon the preceding one which becomes nothing but the basis of the future, does not want to be anything else—thus speaks the analogy in nature, the telling model of God in all works! manifestly so in the human race! The Egyptian could not be without the Oriental, the Greek built upon both of them, the Roman arose upon the back of the whole world—truly progress, progressive development even if no single unit gained by it.[86]

It is not difficult to perceive the similarity between this concept of history and Döllinger's concept of "historical" physiology as outlined above.[87]

In the *Ideen,* which began to appear ten years later, the comparison between epochs of history and ages of man no longer stands in the foreground. Instead, Herder elaborates his genetic concept of ontogeny and emphasizes the parallel between biological species and national civilizations. All animal organization is fundamentally of one type, but this type shows innumerable adaptations to the different circumstances of life.[88] All mankind is fundamentally one, but there are many historical adaptations to different time, climate, political, and other circumstances. And just as in embryology and the successive creation of species, it is an inner force that accounts for historical development too. "Living human forces are the spring of human history, and since man takes his origin from and in one race, his formation, education, and way of thinking hereby become genetic."[89] In the last analysis then, there is a threefold parallelism between (1) ontogeny and the ages of man, (2) successive creation of species, and (3) the history of mankind through successive civilizations.

We can thus perceive a peculiar relationship between the concepts of history and ontogeny in German romanticism. As Herder's works indicate, the "genetic modes of thought"[90] are elaborated in regard to human history, and, with Wolff and Blumenbach, conquer embryology. In turn, embryology loans its concrete image of the ontogeny of an individual to the other realms.[91] Schelling, as we have seen, views the succession of animal species as if it were the ontogeny of one ideal organism. Herder traces the history of the one mankind. Still later, Hegel will construct all human history as the development of the all comprehensive "spirit." And this

[86]Herder, Auch eine Philosophie, *loc. cit.,* p. 512 f.
[87]See above p. 379.
[88]Herder, *Ideen,* book 10. V. See Rouché, *La philosophie de l'histoire chez Herder,* pp. 213–28; Lovejoy, *The Great Chain of Being,* p. 279 f.
[89]Herder, *Ideen,* book 12, VI, 1.
[90]Arthur O. Lovejoy, Buffon and the problem of species, *loc. cit.,* p. 567: ". . . the strong impulse towards genetic modes of thought which was already active in the mid-eighteenth century."
[91]See Morris Cohen, *loc. cit.,*

whole pattern of romantic thought is kept together by an idealistic philosophy with a strongly religious note.

In writing his *Ideen,* Herder believed to trace God's thoughts and to find in nature and history the answer as to man's destiny. Schelling's philosophy of nature had a pantheistic bias; in her highest product, man, nature became conscious of herself, so that nature and mind were united in the knowledge of the absolute. For the pious Albrecht von Haller the span of mortal life was determined by God, but aging and death were conceivable as mechanical processes.[92] The romantic biologists, on the other hand, read a metaphysical meaning into biology. For Döllinger the whole of human life, from conception to death, was a struggle for individual freedom achieved by the rebirth of death. Likewise, his pupil, Carl Ernst von Baer, a great admirer of Herder,[93] believed that the development of organisms was "a maturing towards death."[94] He solved the riddle of death by making the species appear "the abiding thoughts of creation" and the individuals "passing manifestations of these thoughts."[95] And these "thoughts" themselves form a successive series at the end of which stands man in whom matter has come under the rule of an ever progressing mind.[96]

Sentiments like these were echoed by Thomas Huxley when, in 1852, he wrote:

The individual animal is one beat of the pendulum of life, birth and death are the two points of rest, and the vital force is like the velocity of the pendulum, a constantly varying quantity between these two zero points. The different forms which an animal may assume correspond with the successive places of the pendulum.

In man himself, the individual, zoologically speaking, is not a state of man at any particular moment as infant, child, youth, or man; but the sum of all these, with the implied fact of their definite succession."[97]

When this was written, Huxley did not yet believe in the theory of descent. His revered master was Carl Ernst von Baer of whose creed we are reminded by Huxley's later phrase, "the mind of which the universe is but a thought and an expression."[98]

Life, thus conceived, is of course a mere idea, comparable to the "spirit" of Hegel's philosophy of history. The analogy seems indeed striking

[92]For the dualism of Haller's religious and biological views see Stephen d'Irsay, *Albrecht von Haller,* Leipzig, 1930, pp. 17–33.

[93]Karl Ernst v. Baer, *Reden gehalten in wissenschaftlichen Versammlungen und kleinere Aufsätze vermischten Inhalts,* erster Theil, St. Petersburg, 1864, pp. V and 61 f.

[94]*Ibid.,* p. 39.

[95]*Ibid.,* p. 41 f. "Die Organisationsformen, diese durch Zeugung zusammenhängenden Reihen, scheinen bleibende Gedanken der Schöpfung; die Individuen sind vorübergehende Darstellungen dieser Gedanken." However, as defunct species prove, the "thoughts" too can pass so that "the passing thoughts" become but expressions of a "fundamental thought (Grundgedanke)," p. 61.

[96]*Ibid.,* pp. 57 and 72.

[97]*The Scientific Memoirs of Thomas Henry Huxley,* ed. M. Foster and Ray Lankester, vol. 1, London, 1898, p. 147 f.

[98]*Ibid.,* p. 307. See also Owsei Temkin, Metaphors of human biology, *Science and Civilization,* ed. by Robert C. Stauffer, Madison, 1949, p. 174 f. [Essay 20, p. 273 f.].

enough. To the biologist, individual life represents the species. To Hegel, the individual finds its proper place in his national culture and his state. The biologist admits the destruction of species and the emergence of new ones. To Hegel, world history is represented by a succession of national civilizations.[99] Finally, life or a genetic force is made the somewhat mysterious substratum behind nature's history, just as "the world spirit" calls forth the various nationalities whenever they are needed for its progress. This analogy may also help to explain how a generation that accepted such a view of world history, could be relatively little concerned about the question as to how new species had come into existence if not by descent. If evolution, in nature as well as in history, depended on its own inner creativeness,[100] then the mystery of man's origin was not solved by making him emerge from an ape.[101]

We started out with a discussion of the physiology of man's course of life. We found that in Germany, around 1800, a concept was formulated in which the ages of man were reviewed as a "historical" sequence from conception to death. In the formation of this concept, embryology on the one hand and true history on the other played a decisive role, both influencing each other on the basis of a common idealistic philosophy with religious undercurrents.

---

[99]Hegel, Vorlesungen über die Philosophie der Geschichte, *loc. cit.,* vol. 11, p. 112 f., where the "spirit" is said to reappear in new forms for which the old ones present the material. This is reminiscent of Herder's creation of new species from the material of those destroyed.

[100]I use this expression as a reminder of the connection of thought between romanticism and Bergson. See Arthur O. Lovejoy, Bergson and romantic evolutionism, *University of California Chronicle,* 1914, vol. 15, no. 4.

[101]Carl Ernst v. Baer, *Reden,* p. 56; see also S. J. Holmes, *op. cit.* Arthur O. Lovejoy, The argument for organic evolution before "The Origin of Species," *The Popular Science Monthly,* 1909, vol. 75, pp. 499–514 and 537–49, as well as in other publications, cited above, has shown how frequently the problem of evolution had been discussed before Darwin. As long as natural processes were conceivable as external manifestations of thought, the theory of descent need not have had the same irresistible appeal it has to us for whom an uninterrupted chain of material causes and effects is a main metaphysical postulate. The turn towards a mechanistic biology which, in Germany, took place in the late 'thirties thus appears as a prerequisite for the ready acceptance of Darwinism.

28

The Idea of Descent
in Post-Romantic German
Biology: 1848–1858*

I

So GREAT WAS the effect of Darwin's book on German scientists, philosophers, and educated laymen, that, in retrospect, the very doctrine of evolution seemed to have come as something new. Towards the end of his life, the philosopher Eduard von Hartmann (1842–1906) wrote:

The time from 1830 to 1860 was a period of pure observation in biology. The students of the '50's had no idea that French scientists and German philosophers had envisaged such a thing as the evolution of nature, because at that time, a professor would have thought it unscientific even to mention such fantasies.

Darwin's work "On the Origin of Species" (1858 English, 1859 German) struck this dull narrow-mindedness like lightning from a blue sky and brought about a veritable mental revolution.[1]

This picture is certainly wrong. The mere fact that Chambers' *Vestiges of Creation,* as Lovejoy has shown,[2] influenced a man like Schopenhauer and was translated into German in 1851,[3] is sufficient evidence that even in Germany the silence cannot have been complete. Darwin himself, in a later edition of the *Origin,* could cite a considerable number of those who had believed in descent before him. As early as 1862, A. Braun stated that the theory of descent did not reach an unprepared science.[4] By 1875 controversies were under way as to whether de Maillet, Robinet, and Buffon could be called "forerunners" of Darwin,[5] and Potonié, in 1890, cited about a dozen names of German evolutionists during the period with which we

*From *Forerunners of Darwin, 1745–1859,* edited by Bentley Glass, Owsei Temkin, and William L. Straus, Jr., Baltimore: The Johns Hopkins University Press, 1959, pp. 323–55.

[1]Eduard von Hartmann, *Das Problem des Lebens;* Biologische Studien. Bad Sachsa im Harz: Haacke, 1906, p. 1 f. The importance of this reference evinces from its being cited in *Ueberwegs Grundriss der Geschichte der Philosophie,* vierter Teil, p. 315 f. (12th ed. Berlin, 1923).

[2]A. O. Lovejoy, "Schopenhauer as an Evolutionist," *The Monist,* 1911, *21*: 195–222. See this volume, p. 415.

[3]See below.

[4]H. Potonié, "Aufzählung von Gelehrten, die in der Zeit von Lamarck bis Darwin sich im Sinne der Descendenz-Theorie geäussert haben," *Naturwissenschaftliche Wochenschrift,* November 9, 1890, 5: 441–45; see p. 442. Braun's own attitude to transformism seems ambiguous; cf. Potonié, ibid., p. 444, and Walter Zimmermann, *Evolution.* Freiburg-München: Alber, 1953 (*Orbis Academicus* 11/3), p. 380 ff.

[5]Georg Seidlitz, *Die Darwin'sche Theorie.* Zweite vermehrte Auflage, Leipzig: Engelmann, 1875, p. 31 ff.

are concerned here.[6] Because many of the publications are hard to obtain even in Europe, I have not been able to analyze all of the works. On the other hand, I have taken the word German in the broad linguistic sense of German writing authors, thereby including the Austrian, Unger, and the Swiss, Nägeli. Though incomplete as far as coverage is concerned the following analysis may yet throw some light on the question: What was the relationship of German biologists towards the doctrine of evolution in the post-romantic decade before the appearance of the *Origin?*

The pertinency of this question is evident if we remember the role Darwinism was to play in German biology. It offered a solution to two problems: that of the origin of species and that of the correlation between structure and function. It was no longer necessary to believe in the creation of species, and it became possible to explain the apparent finality of the organism and its parts by adaptation without recourse to plan or purpose. Both answers bolstered greatly the mechanistic and materialistic tendencies in German biology. Darwinism became the symbol of materialistic thought. Thus it seems worth while asking what role notions of biological descent played in the period before the appearance of the *Origin of Species* when materialistic tendencies were rising.

The materialistic tendencies of German biologists fell into two categories. The first aimed at a mechanistic explanation of life and denied the existence of a vital force. A decisive attack in this direction was made by Schwann in his *Microscopical Researches* of 1839. There followed Lotze's famous article on vital force of 1842. Shortly afterwards, three pupils of the great Johannes Müller (1801–1858) banded together in their fight against vitalism: Helmholtz, Brücke, du Bois-Reymond. They were joined by Carl Ludwig. The program of the school was formulated in 1848 by du Bois-Reymond in the preface to the first volume of his *Untersuchungen über thierische Elektricität.* Physiology was to be reduced to analytical mechanics. Ludwig's textbook of physiology was written in the spirit of this mechanistic philosophy which viewed even the cellular theory with some suspicion.[7]

The materialism of the second category was directed against the belief in

[6]Potonié, *op. cit.* (ftn. 4). Of the subsequent books and articles listing German forerunners of Darwin I mention here E. Rádl, *Geschichte der biologischen Theorien.* II. Teil, Leipzig: Engelmann, 1909, *passim;* J. H. F. Kohlbrugge, "J. B. de Lamarck und der Einfluss seiner Descendenztheorie von 1809–1859," *Zeitschrift für Morphologie und Anthropologie,* 1914, *18*: 191–206; J. H. F. Kohlbrugge, "War Darwin ein originelles Genie?" *Biologisches Zentralblatt,* 1915, *35*: 93–111; J. F. Pompeckj, "J. C. M. Reinecke, ein deutscher Vorkämpfer der Deszendenzlehre aus dem Anfange des neunzehnten Jahrhunderts," *Palaeontologische Zeitschrift,* 1927, *8*: 39–42; Otto H. Schindewolf, "Einhundert Jahre Paläontologie (Paläozoologie). Ein Rückblick auf ihre Entwicklung in Deutschland." *Zeitschrift der Deutschen geologischen Gesellschaft,* 1948, *100*: 67–93 (Dr. Bentley Glass kindly drew my attention to this article); Schindewolf, "Einige vergessene deutsche Vertreter des Abstammungsgedankens aus dem Anfange des 19. Jahrhunderts, *Palaeontologische Zeitschrift,* 1941, *22*: 139–68. Eduard Uhlmann, "Entwicklungsgedanke und Artbegriff in ihrer geschichtlichen Entstehung und sachlichen Beziehung," *Jenaische Zeitschrift für Naturwissenschaft,* 1923, *59*: 1–116, is particularly important because it contains lengthy quotations from originals, including some not available to me.

[7]See Owsei Temkin, "Materialism in French and German physiology of the early nineteenth

the existence of an immaterial human soul or of any realities outside of "matter and force." The leaders of this faction were Carl Vogt, Moleschott, and Louis Büchner.[8] The biological mechanists, as we may characterize the former group, were not necessarily metaphysical materialists in the sense of the latter. Schwann held a Cartesian position and was a devout Catholic.[9] But materialism of a metaphysical shade was spreading among the German biologists of the fifties, and the controversy, which had a strong anti-clerical undertone, came to a head at the thirty-first meeting of the Society of German Scientists and Physicians at Goettingen, in 1854, when Rudolph Wagner presented "an anthropological address" (as the subtitle called it) on "Human Creation and the Substance of the Soul."[10] The paper defended the belief in the descent of man from one pair (as against a multiple origin) and denied science the right to interfere in matters concerning religion. Although Wagner was not directly discussing animal descent, a passage in his published speech characterizes his attitude:

As a matter of fact, only animals of one and the same species mix fruitfully. Animals of different, closely related species mix under special, mostly artificial, conditions. But the hybrids are sterile and die out. This fundamental law exists for the protection of the historical existence of species.[11]

The ensuing debate was stormy, with the materialists having the upper hand,[12] and the following years witnessed a literary feud between Carl Vogt (who was an old opponent of Rudolph Wagner) on the one hand,[13] and Rudolph Wagner and Andreas Wagner[14] on the other, in which both sides excelled in tactless invective. In the midst of this controversy appeared the popular book on "Force and Matter" by Louis Büchner, which became one of the basic works of German philosophical materialism and was reprinted again and again in subsequent years.[15]

---

century," *Bull. Hist. Med.,* 1946, *20*: 322–27 [Essay 25], and "Metaphors of human biology," in Robert C. Stauffer (ed.), *Science and Civilization.* Madison: University of Wisconsin Press, 1949, p. 173 [Essay 20, p. 273].

[8]On this and the following see Erik Nordenskiöld, *The History of Biology.* New York: Tudor, 1942, pp. 448–52.

[9]Temkin, "Materialism in French and German physiology," *op. cit.,* (ftn. 7) p. 324 [p. 342].

[10]Rudolph Wagner, *Menschenschöpfung und Seelensubstanz.* Ein anthropologischer Vortrag, gehalten in der ersten öffentlichen Sitzung der 31. Versammlung deutscher Naturforscher und Aerzte in Goettingen am 18. September 1854. Goettingen: Wigand, 1854.

[11]*Ibid.,* p. 13.

[12]For a description of the events see *Ueberweg's Grundriss,* (ftn. 1) p. 287 and Nordenskiöld, *loc. cit.* (ftn. 8).

[13]Carl Vogt, *Köhlerglaube und Wissenschaft.* Eine Streitschrift gegen Hofrath Rudolph Wagner in Göttingen. I have used the second printing of the fourth edition which appeared in Giessen: Ricker, 1856. In this pamphlet Vogt relates his earlier controversies with Wagner.

[14]Andreas Wagner, *Naturwissenschaft und Bibel* im Gegensatz zu dem Köhlerglauben des Herrn Carl Vogt, als des wiedererstandenen und aus dem Französischen ins Deutsche übersetzten Bory. Stuttgart: Liesching, 1855. The allusion is to Bory de St. Vincent (1780–1846), on whom see Henry Fairfield Osborn, *From the Greeks to Darwin,* second edition, New York: Scribner's, 1929, pp. 291–93.

[15]Louis Büchner, *Kraft und Stoff.* Empirisch-naturphilosophische Studien. In allgemeinverständlicher Darstellung. Frankfurt a. M.: Meidinger, 1855. He was a practicing physician who, for a short time, had taught at the University of Tübingen.

The biological mechanists had one thing in common with the metaphysical materialists: both were opposed to the *Naturphilosophie* of the preceding era. Naturphilosophie in the spirit of Schelling was no longer a scientific power in the 1840's. But it was remembered as a destructive influence in German science. And it was still remembered that Naturphilosophie had encouraged the idea of descent. There is no doubt that evolutionary ideas had been rife among German romantics since the end of the eighteenth century. Yet in the individual case it is hard to ascertain whether the notion of evolution implied actual descent. Romantic thinkers were inclined to envisage all creation as an ever-ascending evolution of things from inanimate matter to man. But this concept of evolution did not imply that every higher species actually descended from lower ones. Many, if not the majority, believed that in creating higher species nature improved upon herself, but that, nevertheless, each species had to be created anew. They could, therefore, easily accept the doctrine of the destruction of prehistoric animals by catastrophes. Yet some among the German romantic biologists definitely believed that there was a transmutation of lower forms into higher ones.[16]

Both rightly and wrongly, Naturphilosophie, which had dominated German science during the romantic era, was tainted with the suspicion of upholding ideas of descent. The botanist, E. Meyer, in an article of 1854, wrote: "Among the deplorable [influences of Naturphilosophie] I reckon the deep shaking of the belief in the constancy of species...."[17] Admittedly, a shaken belief in the constancy of species is not yet a positive belief in their historical transformation.[18] Isolated remarks which sound as if their authors affirmed descent must not be taken at their face value without careful investigation.

This holds equally true of the period under discussion. Thus the zoologist, Julius Victor Carus, is usually referred to as a forerunner of Darwin, and this reference is based on a passage from his *System der thierischen Morphologie* of 1853. The passage in question reads:

... on the other hand, I may hope not to be misunderstood if, with regard to the present form of our classificatory endeavors and the *relationship* [*Verwandtschaft*] of certain forms of organic beings, I call attention to the fact that the first created forms, which from the admittedly oldest geological strata confront us as witnesses for an earlier creation which was closer at least to the first,—that these forms, apart from their organic character show the general character only of the group in which we place them. Consequently, in a sense limited of course by the absolute lack of

[16]See Jane Oppenheimer's contribution in this volume; also Owsei Temkin, "German concepts of ontogeny and history around 1800," *Bull. Hist. Med.*, 1950, *24*: 227–46 [Essay 27], and the literature cited above, footnote 6.

[17]Quoted from Potonié, *op. cit.*, (ftn. 4) p. 442 f. (E. Meyer's article is said to have appeared in the *Königsberger naturwissenschaftliche Unterhaltungen*, vol. 3, under the title: "Ueber die Beständigkeit der Arten, besonders im Pflanzenreich.")

[18]Walter Baron, "Die idealistische Morphologie Al. Brauns und A. P. de Candolles und ihr Verhältnis zur Deszendenzlehre," *Beihefte zum Botanischen Centralblatt*, 1931, *48*: 314–34; see p. 317. This article provides an excellent comparison between the different points of view and aims of the "idealistic morphologists" and the followers of Darwin.

possible demonstration, we can consider them the ancestors from which through perpetual generation and accommodation to progressively very different conditions of life, there originated the wealth of forms of the present creation.[19]

Taken by itself, this passage seems, if not clear, to be at least a clear reference to descent of present forms from earlier ones. But as far as I see, the bulk of the book leaves it undecided whether Carus has in mind concrete, or ideal, "evolutionary series in the animal world."[20] Towards the end of the book he expresses himself in a manner which seems to contradict the idea of descent. Morphology, he says, "not only demonstrates to us the immutable quality of the laws [i.e., of "formation"] but also their perfection from the very beginning. Often as the formative activity of the Creator manifested itself in the production of new animal worlds, still no forms proceeded from his hand which did not follow the same uniform plan."[21]

Seidlitz, in 1875, introduced the quotation of Carus' statement by the following remark: "The reserve with which this investigator, now an unconditional follower of Darwin, vents his transformistic thought in one single passage of the introduction is very significant for the public opinion of science at that time."[22] Seidlitz may have been right, but it must not be overlooked that, as the example of Virchow will show, ideas held before 1859 were sometimes given a new interpretation afterwards. It is for this reason that I have omitted a discussion of authors whose publications were not accessible to me, even where excerpts from their writings were available.[23]

[19]J. Victor Carus, *System der thierischen Morphologie.* Leipzig: Engelmann, 1853, p. 5: " . . . darf aber auf der andern Seite wol hoffen nicht misverstanden zu werden, wenn ich mit Rücksicht auf die gegenwärtige Form unserer classificatorischen Bemühungen und auf die *Verwandtschaft* gewisser Formen der organisierten Wesen daran erinnere, dass die erstgeschaffenen Formen, welche uns aus den anerkannt ältesten geologischen Lagern als Zeugen einer früheren, der ersten wenigstens näher stehenden Schöpfung entgegentreten, ausser ihrem organischen Charakter nur den allgemeinen der Gruppe zeigen, zu welcher wir sie stellen, dass wir sie also, natürlich nur in einem durch den absoluten Mangel eines möglichen Beweises beschränkten Sinne, als die Urahnen betrachten können, aus denen durch fortgesetzte Zeugung und Accomodation an progressiv sehr verschiedene Lebensverhältnisse der Formenreichthum der jetzigen Schöpfung entstand." Part of that passage is quoted by Uhlmann, op. cit., (ftn. 6) p. 69 and misquoted by Ernst Haeckel, *Natürliche Schöpfungsgeschichte,* Sechste verbesserte Auflage. Berlin: Reimer, 1875, p. 98.
[20]"Entwickelungsreihe in der Thierwelt," discussed by Carus, *op. cit.,* on pp. 275–78.
[21]*Ibid.,* p. 505 f.
[22]Seidlitz, *op. cit.,* (ftn. 5) p. 52.
[23]As far as I can see, this omission includes:
W. Hofmeister (1849–1851), see Potonié, op. cit., (ftn. 4) p. 444 who refers to Sachs, *Geschichte der Botanik,* pp. 214–17. But in the English translation of this work (second impression, Oxford: Clarendon, 1906) Hofmeister is not cited as holding transformist views, although it is emphasized that his results were incompatible with the idea of constant species.
H. P. D. Reichenbach, who, according to Seidlitz, *op. cit.,* (ftn. 5) presented a paper at the twenty-eighth meeting (at Gotha) of German Scientists and Physicians, published in 1854 at his own expense in Altona (where he practiced medicine) under the title *Ein kleiner Beitrag zur Anthropologie und Philosophie.*
Oswald Heer, who in his *Tertiäre Flora der Schweiz* of 1855, according to Seidlitz, op. cit., (ftn. 5) p. 53, spoke of " 'Umprägung der Arten' . . . wie er die in relativ kurzer Zeit erfolgende Umänderung der Arten nennt."
F. T. Kützing, from whose "Historisch-kritische Untersuchungen über den Artbegriff bei

To be sure, scientific opinion was preponderantly against the idea of transmutation. But there was no unity in the camp as to the alternatives. In view of the geological record, the eternity of all species could no longer seriously be defended, as Virchow made clear in his attack upon Czolbe.[24] Those who upheld a belief in creation in accordance with the biblical account may well have found their leader in the Swiss zoologist Louis Agassiz (1807–1873), who, in 1846, had emigrated to the United States.[25] In matters of descent, his views were uncompromising. Admitting that the fossil record showed "a manifest progress in the succession of beings," he insisted:

But this connection is not the consequence of a direct lineage between the faunas of different ages. There is nothing like parental descent connecting them. The fishes of the Paleozoic age are in no respect the ancestors of the reptiles of the Secondary age, nor does Man descend from the mammals which preceded him in the Tertiary age. The link by which they are connected is of a higher and immaterial nature; and their connection is to be sought in the view of the Creator himself, whose aim, in forming the earth, in allowing it to undergo the successive changes which geology has pointed out, and in creating successively all the different types of animals which have passed away, was to introduce Man upon its surface.

Agassiz' thought was summed up as follows:

To study, in this view, the succession of animals in time, and their distribution in space, is therefore to become acquainted with the ideas of God himself.[26]

The ease with which a fundamentally pious biologist like Schleiden who was opposed to materialistic tendencies of a philosophical kind could gloss over the Mosaic account of creation, demonstrates the tenuous hold of

---

den Organismen und dessen wissenschaftlichen Wert," *Programm der Realschule zu Nordhausen,* 1856, Uhlmann, *op. cit.,* (ftn. 6) p. 71 ff. gives several excerpts.

Gustav Jaeger, who is credited by Seidlitz, *op. cit.,* p. 53 with having "developed the theory of descent to its last consequences" in 1857 before a select group of young scientists. Its late publication in 1864 in the *Zoologische Briefe* is attributed to the reluctance to flaunt the opinion of scholars before 1859.

Although Schopenhauer's evolutionary ideas fall within our period, I have not referred to them in view of Professor Lovejoy's article.

[24]Rudolf Virchow, "Alter und neuer Vitalismus," *Archiv für pathologische Anatomie* etc., 1856, 9: 3–56; see below, p. 410.

[25]Louis Agassiz and A. A. Gould, *Outlines of Comparative Physiology,* Touching the Structure and Development of the Races of Animals, Living and Extinct. For the Use of Schools and Colleges. Edited from the Revised Edition, and greatly enlarged, by Thomas Wright, M.D. London: Bohn, 1851. Agassiz' erstwhile student, Carl Vogt, in *Altes und Neues aus Thier-und Menschenleben.* 2 vols., Frankfort a. M.: Literarische Anstalt, 1859 (the preface is dated March 31), vol. 1, p. 353 quotes Agassiz's work on fossil fish, vol. 1, p. 171, for the belief in a personal creator who, twenty times or more, destroyed all life to replace it by better forms.

[26]Agassiz-Gould, ibid., pp. 417–18. There is a good deal of an older tradition in this whole line of thought. Walter Baron. "Zu Louis Agassiz's Beurteilung des Darwinismus," *Sudhoffs Archiv für Geschichte der Medizin und der Naturwissenschaften,* 1956, 40: 259–77, has pointed out that Agassiz was motivated by ideas of natural theology rather than of Naturphilosophie or sentimental religiosity. But it has to be added that the concept of "ideas of creation" is to be found in Herder and von Baer as well; see Temkin, "German concepts of ontogeny," *op. cit.* (ftn. 16).

biblical orthodoxy on the minds of German scientists. It cannot be taken for granted that all those who neglected to express themselves on the origin of species, unquestioningly accepted their supernatural creation. Unless they dismissed the whole problem from their minds, another possibility was left to them, viz., a series of spontaneous generations. In their *Grundzüge der Botanik,* Endlicher and Unger, in 1843, wrote:

The genesis of the present vegetation, like that of all earlier vegetations, can, however, only be conceived as a spontaneous generation in accordance with the idea of the plant organism eternally progressing towards perfection. It probably emerged, if a conclusion based on present experiences is admissible, from a slimy carbonaceous substratum [*Matrix*], out of which cells developed into shoots, and these into complete plants.

In these acts of spontaneous generation of which the earth does not seem constantly capable, but only after longer or shorter intervals, and only after previous violent changes on its surface and in the medium surrounding it, plant species were created in large numbers and according to certain contrasts. . . .[27]

This quotation reflects the status of the cellular theory in the 'forties, when the principle of *omnis cellula a cellula* had not yet been developed by Remak (1852)[28] and formulated by Virchow (1855). In 1859, Carl Ernst von Baer tried to limit the need for such spontaneous generations to a minimum. Like many other scientists, he felt uneasy about them, admitting that spontaneous generation was merely another word for creation minus the stigma of supernatural intervention.[29] But it is well to remember that Pasteur's first publication on the subject appeared in 1860, after Darwin's *Origin.* And even then spontaneous generation was not eliminated as a postulate, least of all by speculating Darwinists like Haeckel and Huxley. The difference was that after 1859 spontaneous generation was banished to a semi-mythical time at the beginning of evolution. Before 1859, many nontransformists as well as transformists assumed that it might have initiated every new "creation." This, I think, explains why, to the mechanistically minded biologist, spontaneous generation was more important as a principle than was descent. "Lest we take refuge in miracles and the incomprehensible, we must admit the origin of the first organized creatures on the earth by the free creative power of matter itself . . ." wrote Hermann Burmeister (1807–1892),[30] who dismissed the notion of descent, although he was not unsympathetic to it. And Rudolf Virchow, in 1856, insisted on

[27]Stephan Endlicher und Franz Unger, *Grundzüge der Botanik.* Wien: Gerold, 1843, p. 461.
[28]Bruno Kisch, *Forgotten Leaders in Modern Medicine:* Valentin, Gruby, Remak, Auerbach. Philadelphia: The American Philosophical Society, 1954 (*Transactions of the American Philosophical Society,* New Series, vol. 44, part 2, 1954), p. 258.
[29]See Seidlitz, *op. cit.,* (ftn. 5) p. 55 f. Zimmermann, *op. cit.,* (ftn. 4) p. 503: "Bis zur Mitte des vergangenen Jahrhunderts nahmen auch namhafte Biologen, wie H. G. Bronn (1800–1862), K. E. v. Baer, K. v. Nägeli (für Pilze) plötzliche, sich in unseren Tagen abspielende Urzeugungen als erwiesen an."
[30]Hermann Burmeister, *Geschichte der Schöpfung.* Eine Darstellung des Entwicklungsganges der Erde und ihrer Bewohner. Für die Gebildeten aller Stände. Fünfte verbesserte Auflage, Leipzig: Wigand, 1854, p. 325.

the need of admitting spontaneous generation. Though he is not clear as to details, his way of expressing himself does not point to the limitation of spontaneous generation to a single event at the dawn of organic life.[31] He needed a principle that avoided eternity of species and supernatural intervention, yet upheld the idea of progress.[32] Against this background the various arguments for transformism have now to be viewed.

II

The beginning might well be made with the geologist Bernhard Cotta's (1808–1879) "Letters on Alexander von Humboldt's Kosmos." The first volume appeared in 1848, and the dedication, dated April 2 of that year, shows the author under the perturbing influence of the revolution; the occupation with the book has helped to quiet his mind, and he hopes "that the result of this occupation may affect others similarly."[33] As is to be expected from his desire for equanimity, the tone of the book is not polemical, although Cotta declares his antagonism to the speculative philosophy in Germany. The true scientist, he says, does not believe the world to be a result of his thought, but rather he believes his thought to be the end-product of the world, of his observation of the world. A few lines later Cotta offers a hypothetical explanation: "Indeed, from our limited earthly point of view we might even be tempted to assert that man with his intelligence is the final result of a long evolutionary series [*Entwicklungsreihe*] of organic beings, a series which, through all its generations, has absorbed an immeasurable sum of external impressions (unconscious observations of nature and of its laws) and has thereby worked its way up to a thinking, rational being."[34] A rash interpretation of the sentence as referring to descent will be checked by the realization that it is the "evolutionary series" that works its way up.

Cotta offers a good example of how important it is to distinguish between evolution and transmutation (or descent). "In the 24th letter I wrote to you something about the sequence in which the organic forms originated one after the other on the earth. In this we recognized a *gradual evolution* [*Entwicklung*] *from the lower to the higher.*"[35] Cotta's italicization enhances the

[31]Virchow, *op. cit.*, (ftn. 24) p. 25: "Aber selbst wenn wir die Erfolglosigkeit aller Versuche, einzelne Zellen zu erzeugen, in unserer Zeit zugestehen müssen, so können wir darin keinen Grund für ihre Ewigkeit finden. Das Gesetz, nach dem ihre Bildung erfolgte, muss nothwendig ein ewiges sein, so dass jedesmal, wenn im Laufe der natürlichen Vorgänge die Bedingungen für seine Offenbarung günstig werden, die organische Gestaltung sich verwirklicht." See also below, p. 409.

[32]*Ibid.* "Die Zeiträume, welche der Mensch überblickt, sind, selbst wenn wir den grössten Rahmen ausspannen, indem wir die Jahrtausende nach Millionen rechnen, immerhin sehr beschränkt, und doch gestatten sie uns, die befriedigende Ueberzeugung zu gewinnen, dass ein freilich sehr langsamer und häufig unterbrochener Fortschritt in der Welt ist."

[33]Bernhard Cotta, *Briefe über Alexander von Humboldt's Kosmos.* Erster Theil, Leipzig: Weigel, 1848, p. III.

[34]*Ibid.*, p. VI. This idea is taken up again at the end of the volume, p. 340, and given a rather clear materialistic sense.

[35]*Ibid.*, p. 262.

impression that he has evolution in the modern sense in mind, i.e., transmutation. But the immediately following sentence shows that evolution is used in a broader sense: "Yet how the single organisms, i.e. the first individuals of each species originated is still veiled in deep obscurity."[36]

Nevertheless, in the 24th letter as well as later he discusses transmutation in unmistakable terms. He presents it as a hypothesis advanced by others, even though his own inclination towards it is obvious. "Here I must point out to you right away," he writes in the 24th letter, "that much esteemed scientists have made the assertion that the diversity and the change of organic forms on the earth are altogether not caused by the origin of entirely new species, but only by an ever more diverse and higher evolution [*Entwicklung*] of the originally formed. According to this opinion, in the course of immeasurable periods, and corresponding to the respective external conditions there arose from one organic form all others. Accordingly we must consider man too as the highest evolutionary step of a first organic seed [*Keim*]. This explanation of the diversity in organic nature has a good deal for it. . . ."[37]

Even in his main discussion of organic life on earth Cotta does not forget to emphasize the hypothetical character of an explanation by descent.

The opinion *that the different organic forms developed gradually from one another* has already often been expressed, and defended by argument, by true natural philosophers. Quite recently an anonymous Englishman sought ingeniously to prove this view in the book *Vestiges of the Natural History of Creation*, and indeed, there is much to be said for it even though it will, in the very nature of the matter, long remain a mere hypothesis. The law of the organization of matter is as yet completely undiscovered; its results have, as already stated, not yet been drawn into the sphere of the inevitable. If, however, for the moment we assume that such a law governing matter exists, that certain substances in certain circumstances unite and become organic forms, then the special diversity of these substances and circumstances will determine the diversity of the forms and be reflected in them. In the simplest external circumstances, the simplest, most suitable, organic forms will have arisen; and as the circumstances changed and became diversified, the organic forms gradually changed and became diversified also.[38]

From the above and a few other passages it is possible to form an impression as to why Cotta hesitated to associate himself frankly with transformism, why, nevertheless, he defended the idea, and along what line he looked for a possible explanation. Apart from our general ignorance of the laws of organization, he sees a main obstacle in the sharp separation of species. Never has an actual transition been observed between really different species. They differ, down to their minutest parts, "though *perhaps* we must assume that they developed historically from one another."[39] On what can he base the latter possibility? Cotta has great faith in the effect of

[36]*Ibid.*, pp. 262–63.
[37]*Ibid.*, p. 140.
[38]*Ibid.*, p. 263.
[39]*Ibid.*, p. 262. Italics mine.

long periods of time. While in the shortness of historical time we have not observed the formation of truly new species, yet table fruits and domestic animals can be considered as "almost" new formations of species.[40] Unbounded time could achieve what cannot be observed in relatively short periods. But this is at best a defense of transformism. What is Cotta's argument *for* it? In the first place, aversion to the acceptance of divine acts of creation: "If for every special form you refer to the creator of the world, that means cutting through the knot rather than untying it. You put an *assumption* instead of an *explanation* just because you lack the latter."[41] Apart from suggesting an explanation of the variety of species, the idea of transmutation also avoids a multiplicity of spontaneous generations and supports a progressive view of man. As we shall see, Cotta, in these points, meets with the botanist Unger.

Since Cotta does not expressly make the idea of descent his own, it is not surprising to find relatively little thought given to its possible mechanism. Nevertheless, though he does not mention the name as far as I see, enough is said to characterize his attitude as Lamarckian. Greatly impressed by the harmony between structure and environment, Cotta cites as an especially impressive instance Charles Darwin's account of *Birgus latro,* a large crab living on the Keeling islands, that eats coconuts. "Had a species of crab previously living in the sea found pleasure in living on land and enjoying coconuts and had, therefore, through thousands of generations gradually changed its whole organization so as to become able to eat the nuts with relative ease? Or, was an animal, adapted for this special end, produced by a special act of creation?" Such questions cannot be answered directly; however, there are "the thousands of less conspicuous yet analogous cases in which the organization of animals manifestly changes gradually for a definite purpose through exercise, as the greyhound has taken on a form quite different from the dachshund or butcher's dog, and the race horse a form different from the draught-horse."[42]

In the same year, 1848, the botanist Schleiden too published a popular work, *The Plant.*[43] Schleiden argued for transformism but, in contrast to Cotta he did so unreservedly. Schleiden has no doubt that the world is God's creation, but to him that does not imply accepting the Mosaic story. He tries to fit the origin and development of plant life into the history of the earth, which makes him think that

In some period of this gradual shaping of the earth, the first of organic existence originated, through forces, which may indeed still be in action, but under conditions and co-operation of those various forces such as now appear no longer possi-

---

[40]*Ibid.,* p. 264.
[41]*Ibid.,* p. 263.
[42]*Ibid.,* p. 266.
[43]M. J. Schleiden, *The Plant;* a Biography. Translated by Arthur Henfrey. Second edition, with additions. London: Baillière, 1853. However, judging from the quotations given by Uhlmann, *op. cit.* (ftn. 6), ideas of descent were already expressed in the first German edition of 1848.

ble upon our earth. The ocean was probably the birth-place of these organisms. . . .[44]

A little later, Schleiden adds: "In subsequent periods, organisms also originated upon the dry land . . ,"[45] which sounds as if he too believed in repeated spontaneous generations. But then he seems to deny such an interpretation because he ascribes the whole subsequent process to gradual descent from a single cell.

This view, that the whole fulness of the vegetable world has been gradually developed out of a single cell and its descendants, by gradual formation of varieties, which became stereotyped into species, and then, in like manner, became the producers of new forms, is at least quite as possible as any other, and is perhaps more probable and correspondent than any other, since it carries back the Absolutely Inexplicable, namely, the production of an Organic Being, into the very narrowest limits which can be imagined.[46]

This summary shows Schleiden's reason for believing in transmutation. As to the "how," he first proposed a hypothesis for the formation of varieties by referring to tropical conditions:

The principal causes producing a luxuriant and varied world of forms in the tropics, are moisture and warmth, the causes of their multiformity appear to lie in the richness of the soil in readily soluble inorganic matters, which in the first place give rise to a variation in the chemical processes of the plant, and thus to a greater or less deviation in the form. These two conditions *meet* in the tropics, because they are dependent one upon the other, since the more luxuriant vegetation called forth by the moist, warm atmosphere, prepares by its death and rapid decay, a soil richer in soluble inorganic matters, for the succeeding generation.[47]

Once formed, varieties "when they have continued to vegetate under the same conditions for several generations, pass into subspecies, that is into varieties which may be propagated with certainty by their seeds. . . ." Assuming now that the same influences continue to act for a very long period,

will not, at last, as the variety thus becomes a sub-species, so also this become so permanent, that we shall and must describe it as a species [?] Then, if the first cell be given, the foregoing points out how the whole wealth of the vegetable kingdom may have been formed by a gradual passage from it through varieties, subspecies and species, and thus onward, beginning anew from each species—in a space of time, indeed, of which we have no conception, for which, however, since there is nothing *real* wanting, we may provide at pleasure in our dreams; for it may be mentioned here that all the recent distinguished Geologists come ever more and more to the opinion, that very much, in the formation of the crust of our earth, which was formerly ascribed to violent, convulsive and sudden revolutions, has rather been the product of forces acting slowly through the course of enormous periods of time.[48]

[44]*The Plant*, p. 277 f.
[45]*Ibid.*
[46]*Ibid.*, p. 293.
[47]*Ibid.*, p. 289 f.
[48]*Ibid.*

Schleiden presupposes a very long geological time (which would have easily been granted to him by German scientists of the period); he also presupposes the principle of "actuality" in geology as defended by von Hoff in Germany and Lyell in England, and a modifying influence of the environment upon plant form. It should be noted that the environmental factors which he cites do not necessarily require adaptational tendencies on the part of the plant. They work through chemical and physical forces. Schleiden was opposed to any "vital force," though he was equally opposed to metaphysical materialism. Indeed, in 1863 he published a severe attack upon the materialistic tendencies in modern science.[49]

Environmental changes, though of a very different nature, are also invoked by Karl Heinrich Baumgärtner (1798–1886), from 1824–1862 professor of clinical medicine in Freiburg i.B.[50] In his younger years he had worked on the segmentation of the ovum, and to this work he referred again in the "Textbook of Physiology" of 1853, where he enunciated his theory of transmutation through influences upon surviving ova of creatures destroyed in earlier phases of geological history.[51] Two years later, in 1855, he issued in short theses the ideas prepared in the "Textbook" and subsequently elaborated.[52] They may here be sketched in the presentation he gave them in his *Schöpfungsgedanken*, "Physiological Studies for the Educated," as Baumgärtner called the book he published in 1859.[53] The first part, giving his evolutionary thought, had appeared before;[54] so that any suspicion of an early influence by Darwin's *Origin* may be dismissed.

Baumgärtner had discovered—or believed to have discovered—what he called "the law of the ascending germ-metamorphosis in the periods of creation."[55] He argues that the chicken must have existed before the egg and the cock before the semen. Neither they nor their seed can have originated by spontaneous generation. Nor can they have originated from free organic substances. Likewise, the transformation of a complete organism into a different animal is very unlikely. Therefore, animals must have developed from germs; i.e., the higher animals must have developed from the germs of lower organisms.[56]

In particular, evolution took the following course. "Through organizing influences," as Baumgärtner calls them, in the first creative process, the simplest organism originated from nitrogen, carbon, hydrogen, and oxy-

---

[49]See Temkin, "Materialism," (ftn. 7) p. 324 [p. 342].

[50]E. Th. Nauck, "Die ersten Jahrzehnte des psychiatrischen und neurologischen Unterrichts in Freiburg i. Br.," *Ber. Naturf. Ges. Freiburg i. Br.*, 1956, *46*: 63–84; see p. 64 f.

[51]Karl Heinrich Baumgärtner, *Lehrbuch der Physiologie mit Nutzanwendungen auf die ärztliche Praxis*. Stuttgart: Rieger, 1853, pp. 71 ff. and 190.

[52]K. H. Baumgärtner, *Anfänge zu einer physiologischen Schöpfungsgeschichte der Pflanzen- und der Thierwelt, und Mittel zur weiteren Durchführung derselben*. Stuttgart: Rieger, 1855.

[53]K. H. Baumgärtner, *Schöpfungsgedanken. Physiologische Studien für Gebildete*. Freiburg: Wagner, 1859.

[54]*Ibid.*, p. iii–iv.

[55]*Ibid.*, p. 307.

[56]*Ibid.*, pp. 310–16.

gen.[57] The original cell formed through spontaneous generation and became differentiated in analogy to the differentiation of animal and vegetal poles in the egg. A separation into primitive animals and plants may have been the direct result. The succeeding creative period began with a destruction of all the existing adult creatures and a change in their surviving seed. General cosmic phenomena accompanied by electrical polarizing forces were responsible for the catastrophe as well as the evolutionary step.[58] The new polarizations in the surviving seed brought about cleavages in new directions and therewith possibilities for the development of new, higher species. Baumgärtner does not assume that all the animals of the new creation were immediately available. They might start out as particles of the dividing ovum, gradually changing into the final forms. In particular, Baumgärtner depicted the evolution of man during the last period of creation as a transformation of low embryonic forms into the adult form. Evolution proceeded in many series, the various races of men might well have been the results of different evolutionary series. Spontaneous generation was not limited to the very first creation, but occurred again in each new period.[59] All this assured to evolution a great variety of possibilities and to the author an opportunity of indulging in peculiar speculations. For instance, beasts of prey and their victims are thought to be adapted to one another because they originally formed from the same egg. Again, some men were still leading a larval existence in the water while others more perfect watched them as they walked along the shore.[60]

Baumgärtner's arguments for descent are not convincing. If, as he believes, spontaneous generation can take place at the beginnings of all creative periods and if new species of animals lead a long life in a larval state, why then is it necessary to assume a mutation of earlier germs at all? One cannot help suspecting that Baumgärtner's motives for favoring descent were in part metaphysical ones. In his *Schöpfungsgedanken,* at least, the metaphysical element is obvious. All the changing organizations lead to the idea of a cosmic organism which, in turn, presupposes a directive power. "Thus," he writes, "physiological research leads us to the idea of God, viz. to the conviction that there is a thinking power to which the natural laws themselves and the final reason of all things must be traced back.[61] Moreover, the "law of transformation of germs and of the progressive evolution of mental life shows us that at any rate the movement marches on and that, therefore, our hopes for a higher destination are no empty illusion."[62]

In contrast to the popular books of Cotta, Schleiden, and Baumgärtner, Unger's "Attempt at a History of the Vegetable Realm" of 1852 is a work of a vastly different character. Himself professor of botany at the University

[57]*Ibid.*, p. 318.
[58]*Ibid.*, p. 326 ff.
[59]*Ibid.*, p. 336 f.
[60]*Ibid.*, p. 346.
[61]*Ibid.*, p. 373.
[62]*Ibid.*, p. 370 f.

of Vienna, Unger presents a solid paleontological investigation. And while we could quote a passage of 1843 where he (and Endlicher) clearly asserted repeated spontaneous generations, Unger has now changed his mind.[63] The assumption of spontaneous generation contradicts contemporary experience and the idea of descent recommends itself just because it helps to avoid such an awkward hypothesis. Going back in time, Unger finds algae as the most primitive of all later forms. In theory, at least, he dares to go even further and assume the previous existence of an "Urpflanze" (we are immediately reminded of Goethe), or even a primary cell, "which is at the bottom of all vegetal existence."[64] Comparing the flora of past ages with that of more recent ones, he finds that the number of new species increases with the periods. If, therefore, all species originated spontaneously, spontaneous generation should have occurred more and more often, and most frequently in our own period. This is contrary to all experience. Accordingly, descent is the alternative—descent, however, which is due to inner forces. External conditions may have played a minor role, but they could not have been decisive because of the regularity noted in the development of new plant forms. "Nothing has been added in this regulated evolutionary process of the vegetal world that had not been previously prepared and indicated, so to speak. Neither genus, nor family, nor class of plants has manifested itself without having become necessary in time."[65] This allows Unger to consider the totality of plants a "truly coherent organism."[66] But how does this agree with the alleged stability of species? Unger avoids a clear-cut answer. He says that uniformity does not exclude variations. Old species did not simply change into new ones. Rather, some individuals metamorphosed while the old type still remained existent for some time.

His idea of an "inner development" allows Unger to avoid the question as to the origin of the *Urpflanze* and, at the same time to place this development into a grandiose cosmic frame. The unity of plant life stands in contrast to inanimate nature. Though we do not know how the first cell originated, we can at least accept it as "the origin of all organic life and, therefore, the true bearer of all higher evolution."[67] There is no reason to believe that the productive activity will stop. Our present period is still young, our world is full of imperfections and thus man strives after accomplishment of the ideal he has in his mind. The same is true of animals and plants. The formation of new races is but the urge to perfection, the attempt to be ready for entry into the next cosmic period.[68]

In opposing transmutation to spontaneous generation Unger did not

---

[63]Among the German followers of the theory of transmutation during the period under discussion, Unger and Schaaffhausen (with the exception of Schopenhauer) are probably best known. Both are mentioned in Darwin's "Historical Sketch," and their writings are discussed by Zimmermann, *op. cit.*, (ftn. 4).

[64]F. Unger, *Versuch einer Geschichte der Pflanzenwelt*. Wien: Braumüller, 1852, p. 340.

[65]*Ibid.*, p. 344.

[66]*Ibid.*, p. 345.

[67]*Ibid.*, p. 340.

[68]*Ibid.*, p. 349.

stand alone. Cotta had advanced the argument that the occurrence of spontaneous generation could not be decided by direct observation. Anyhow, Cotta thought, "if it is true that the single organic forms developed from one another through the influence of changed external circumstances of life, this is again a reason against the spontaneous generation of single individuals."[69] Likewise, in Cotta's opinion gradual development points to further progress. At present, man is the highest stage of organization, "but we cannot know what more gifted being will result from many thousands of years of further development."[70] Humanity as a whole advances in abilities, knowledge, and morality. Indeed the dependence of morality on development is the great justification for the scientist's endeavor "to replace the personal activity of a creator by evolution through scientific law."[71]

Here is the place to point out the role which the optimistic belief in progress played in biology before Darwin. Virchow, in the above mentioned essay of 1856, frankly stated his preference for a view that recognized progress in the history of living forms as against a view that considered species eternal and immutable.[72] I believe that at that time, Virchow, temporarily at least, acquiesced in the assumption of repeated occurrences of spontaneous generation. But the underlying sentiment was the same as Unger's, though Unger expressed it in terms of a theory of descent and an idealistic philosophy.

In the face of such views it is hard to decide whether even Unger was led to accept descent as a purely logical consequence of his paleontological and geographical research, or postulated it under the influence of metaphysical predilections. The form he gave to it indicates that his general views on man, the world, and their progress played a considerable part. It is, therefore, all the more interesting that Schaaffhausen's famous article "On the Constancy and Transformation of Species," which appeared but one year later, in 1853, is an acceptance as well as a rejection of Unger's evolutionary ideas. Schaaffhausen states that not only von Baer, but even Vogt and Burmeister recoiled from the idea that man originated from the orangutan.[73] Opinions vary, from Agassiz who believed in twenty renewals of creation, to Unger who propounded that "the evolution of the vegetal realm began with an *Urpflanze* and that the various types appeared gradually in ever-increasing number, having emanated due to an inner formative urge of the plant itself."[74] In the main, Schaaffhausen is concerned with the problem of the constancy of species. He combats this idea with all the material and arguments at his disposal. At the head of his

[69]Cotta, *op. cit.*, (ftn. 33) p. 267.
[70]*Ibid.*
[71]*Ibid.*, p. 268.
[72]Virchow, *op. cit.*, (ftn. 24) p. 24 f. Erwin H. Ackerknecht, *Rudolf Virchow: Doctor, Statesman, Anthropologist.* Madison: University of Wisconsin Press, 1953, p. 200.
[73]Hermann Schaaffhausen, "Ueber Beständigkeit und Umwandlung der Arten," *Anthropologische Studien*, Bonn: Marcus, 1885, pp. 134–64; see p. 135.
[74]*Ibid.*, p. 136.

summary there stands the sentence: "The immutability of species which most scientists regard as a natural law is not proved, for there are no definite and unchangeable characteristics of species, and the borderline between species and subspecies [*Art* and *Abart*] is wavering and uncertain." [75] Schaaffhausen stresses the need for more and more exact observation, expecially regarding variations. This is a very sober attitude, though more is involved than is at first apparent. Beside expecting an ever-increasing discovery of missing links, he also confronts the opponents of evolution with the alternative "that the oak or horse originated from the elements." [76] And in contrast to Unger's inner urge, he puts his belief in the influence of, and adaptation to, external influences. [77] But he does not explain the mechanism of such influences and adaptations. Moreover, his subsequent attitude shows that his work on species was not quite free from general ideas. In a paper of 1860, he opens a short polemic against Büchner and Virchow with the words: "In our days, when a new materialistic school even denies the order in the world at large because it leads to the assumption of the concept of God, when one admires the chaos rather than the cosmos, it is all the more necessary to call to mind the doctrine of the unity of life and to show how well founded it is." [78] And he closes the polemic by saying: "But if we see the organic forms emanating one from the other and life obtaining its vigor from the sources of telluric nature only, and the earth receiving air and warmth from another star whose course again follows a higher law, then with this insight we approach the eternal mind whose creative thought also was creative deed, by which he made and at every moment makes anew, the world and its wonders." [79]

At this point one may wonder why strictly scientific arguments were not allowed to stand by themselves. Unfortunately, scientific results were sometimes more confusing than enlightening. In 1851, Johannes Müller had observed snails developing within echinoderms. This alleged discovery threw him and many others into utter confusion. [80] Snails and echinoderms belong not only to different species, but to different phyla! If such a metamorphosis were possible, then anything was possible!

Among the effects of the puzzling phenomena of *Generationswechsel* and parasitism seems to have been a predilection to view descent as a series of mutations rather than continuous changes. Such a predilection was noticeable in Baumgärtner, we shall find it again in Büchner, and it looms large in the evolutionary thought of the botanist Carl Nägeli (1817–91), which we analyze on the basis of his paper on "Individuality in Nature" presented in 1856. [81]

[75]*Ibid.*, p. 163.
[76]*Ibid.*, p. 161.
[77]*Ibid.*, p. 138.
[78]"Ueber die Gesetze der organischen Bildung," *op. cit.*, (ftn. 73) pp. 294–326; see p. 325.
[79]*Ibid.*, p. 326.
[80]Emil du Bois-Reymond, "Gedächtnisrede auf Johannes Müller," *Reden.* 2 vols., Leipzig: Veit, 1886–87; vol. 2, p. 262 ff.
[81]Carl Nägeli, "Die Individualität in der Natur mit vorzüglicher Berücksichtigung des

The paper starts out with a reference to the dispute between materialists and spiritualists. It soon becomes clear that Nägeli, though a biological mechanist, occupies, philosophically, an idealistic position. Scientific empiricism, he insists, moves within the narrow bounderies marked by imperfections of our sensory perceptions, by the eternity of space and time, and by their infinite divisibility. It cannot transcend the threshold to the world of the spirit.[82] This agnostic criticism is balanced by an idealistic evaluation of progress. As he himself says, the main part of the paper attempts to show that "material nature, through individual formations which come into being and pass away, rises to the highest point of development in a continual evolutionary urge and necessary gradation."[83] All this is similar to the tendency of mankind towards perfection through a change of individuals. The organic species, as he writes at the end of the paper, "itself is an individual which develops through continuous change, which finds a limitation through this change, and in this limitation creates new species." Material forms perish, the idea remains, " . . . for the material phenomena are but the transitory points, empty of content, of a movement which ceaselessly strives towards a better goal."[84]

Within this idealistic framework, Nägeli discusses the reasons for giving preference to the hypothesis of transmutation of species over that of new creations. Even in the short interval of historical time, hereditary tendencies combined with external influences lead to the formation of new races. The parents bequeath to the offspring a tendency to resemblance, as well as divergence. The artificial cultivation of plants illustrates how the tendency to change in a certain direction can be utilized. If such a tendency went on and on over long periods of time, it would lead to new species. If in reality species appear constant, this does not mean that they do not undergo internal change. Their chemical condition is modified up to the point where it leads to a sudden change in the offspring, as illustrated by the alternation of generations.[85] Thus Nägeli believes in a saltatory evolutionary change rather than a gradual one, although he admits the existence of both.

Nägeli does not ascribe apodictic certainty to his views. "The way in which they [i.e., species] originated, remains a matter of surmise."[86] Nevertheless there are reasons for assuming descent. Since the history of the earth is the result of "natural laws acting by necessity," we like to assume the same for the changes of organic nature. "But it is more natural that plant originated from plant and animal from animal than that they were created

---

Pflanzenreiches," *Monatsschrift des wissenschaftlichen Vereins in Zürich*, 1856, *1*: 171–212. I was led to this publication by Uhlmann, *op. cit.* (ftn. 6). The paper is a semi-popular presentation and it is possible that other works by Nägeli prior to 1859 deal with transformism from a different point of view.

[82]Nägeli, *op. cit.*, (ftn. 81) p. 176.
[83]*Ibid.*, p. 171.
[84]*Ibid.*, pp. 211 and 212.
[85]*Ibid.*, p. 209, footnote.
[86]*Ibid.*, p. 203.

anew from inorganic substances." Nägeli adds an argument that sounds very modern:

To be sure it appears as if thereby the difficulty is only moved back, since organic life must have begun at some time. However, the difficulty is also diminished; for it is more probable that out of inorganic compounds organic substances originated, that from the latter the simplest unicellular plants became organized, and that out of these the higher plants developed in a gradual sequence.[87]

It is surprising to find that in spite of this argument Nägeli still believed in the actual spontaneous generation of certain fungi.[88]

Nägeli does not doubt that evolution proceeds from the lower to the higher, his illustration being the old one of the ladder with higher rungs above those below. The law of recapitulation is cited in support of this belief.[89] But when we consider that the idea of progress was an integral part of the evolutionary thought of the time, we may also agree that the assumption of a transformation from "lower to higher" was not merely thoughtless anthropomorphism, which took it for granted that man stands at the top of creation. Rather it appears as a projection into the realm of nature of the general idea of progressive perfection.

In view of the place that the notion of "progress" occupied in the evolutionary thought of men like Cotta, Baumgärtner, Unger, and Nägeli, one may well inquire more closely into the attitude of such "progressive" biologists as Vogt and Virchow towards transformism.

This question leads to the German translation of Chambers' *Vestiges of the Natural History of Creation*. The English original when published anonymously in 1844 had created a scandal. The author had affirmed his belief in the spontaneous generation of organisms and the transmutation of species. This belief was part of his radical deistic position. God had created nature and her laws, which then did the rest without His active intervention. The German translation of the book of 1851 became well known. Baumgärtner and Schaaffhausen both cite it.[90] However, we are here concerned less with Chambers' work than with the translator, who was none other than Carl Vogt, "monkey Vogt," as he was to be popularly known later when he had started preaching the gospel of Darwinism. But in 1851 Vogt was as yet a confirmed opponent of descent. Why then did he translate the work and what did he have to say about it?

Although Vogt had studied medicine, he turned to zoology and for some time was a co-worker of Agassiz. In 1847, he was appointed professor in Giessen, and at the beginning of the next year the translation was finished and printing had begun. Then Vogt, a radical republican, became involved in the revolution, lost his position in Giessen, and the preface of his transla-

[87]*Ibid.*, p. 206.
[88]*Ibid.*, p. 207. However it is in line with this belief that Nägeli still clings to the formation of cells from amorphous matter, ibid., p. 188, footnote 2.
[89]*Ibid.*, p. 207.
[90]Cotta, as we have seen above, p. 398, depended on the English original.

tion is dated from Bern, October 1849. Vogt, as we have already seen, was one of the most militant free-thinkers of the time. His "Physiological Letters," published in 1845–1847, was one of the starting points of German philosophical materialism.

But why did Vogt translate Chambers' work at a time when he was still opposed to descent? In his preface, written after the unsuccessful revolution of 1848, he makes the following remark:

> To the Constitutional Party of Germany, whose influence should soon be limited to the innocent reading of innocent books, I recommend this book in all good will. It will find here a constitutional Englishman who constructed a constitutional God, who at first made laws as an autocrat but then of His own accord gave up autocracy and, without direct influence on the governed, allowed law to rule in His stead. A splendid example for princes![91]

Vogt, an extremely sarcastic person, must have written this with his tongue in his cheek. It can hardly have been the whole reason for undertaking the translation. However that may be, he takes up the same thought in a footnote stating his objection to Chambers.

> The dispute between the theory of succession which presumes a gradual transformation of creatures, as does our author, and the theory of revolution which continually allows new fauna to appear on the earth, is as old as the study of petrifactions itself; and from the theoretical point of view, no solution is possible. It is a question of judging the most detailed facts and particulars of the delimitation of the variations which a species may undergo, and the decision will only be known when we have shown to what extent the specific characteristics of every shellfish can be modified.

Thus far he is the objective scientist who postpones the decision until every detail is known, which means a postponement *ad Kalendas Graecas*. But then he continues in a different vein:

> In a more general discussion of the question from the theoretical point of view we must, however, take into consideration that the assumption of successive, different creations does not, as our author believes, in any way imply the concept of a Creator and opposes that of a natural law. Similarly, on the other hand, the assumption of a gradual modification does not necessarily postulate the assumption of a natural law without creative intervention. We believe also that no species passed from one formation into another, but that with every geological revolution there was a complete destruction of organisms and a renewal of them; yet we do not on this account assume a Creator, either at the beginning or in the course of earth history, and find that a self-conscious Being existing apart from the world and creating the world is just as ridiculous if it changes the world and its organisms twenty-five times or still oftener till it hits on the right arrangement, as when, after the creating the world and making the natural laws, it pensions itself off and retires, as our author would have it do.[92]

[91]*Natürliche Geschichte der Schöpfung des Weltalls, der Erde und der auf ihr befindlichen Organismen, begründet auf die durch die Wissenschaft errungenen Thatsachen.* Aus dem Englischen nach der sechsten Auflage von Carl Vogt. Braunschweig: Vieweg, 1851.
[92]*Ibid.,* p. 124, footnote.

In other words, Vogt objects to reference to any divine agency, conceived theistically or deistically. But he does not tell us how he envisaged the origin of species, though it would be intriguing to know, in view of the fact that he is highly sceptical of spontaneous generation.[93] In most of the footnotes he limits himself to factual corrections—which Chamber's work certainly needed. But one remark at least we cite because it confirms what we said at the beginning about the contemporary attitude to evolutionary ideas: "The opinion of the author [i.e., Chambers] resulting from Naturphilosophie, that the species in the course of the geological epochs gradually trans-formed into others. . . ."[94] Whether Chambers received his evolutionary bias directly or indirectly from German Naturphilosophie need not concern us here. But it is pertinent to state that to a German around 1850, transformation was immediately related to Naturphilosophie. It does not sound convincing that Vogt, who improved upon Cabanis by likening the production of thought by the brain to the secretion of urine by the kid-ney,[95] rejected descent because he recoiled from the idea of descent of man from the orangutan, as Schaaffhausen claimed.

It seems more likely to assume that Vogt had an ambivalent attitude towards transmutation. He was in sympathy with it and yet rejected it, because acceptance seemed to conflict with his ideal of scientific method. The following remark in a work that appeared in 1859 seems to bear this out.

Stripped of the comical trimmings which the natural philosophers and their conscious and unconscious hangers on managed to give this theory, it still retains something which seems to us to be of great importance. As far as that is possible in the limited scope, namely, it brings the history of earlier creations into harmony with the prevailing general, physical, and organic laws and banishes completely the fiat of the rational personality, a creator, assumed by many other scientists. This theory of the transition of one species into another and of the gradual evolution of the organic form-type under the influence of external agents, would undoubtedly offer much greater inner credibility, if the hitherto known facts did not thwart and hinder. To these, however, we must defer until perhaps the faulty observations contained in them are discovered, and thereby the fact itself is rectified.[96]

To put it pointedly, Vogt regrets that he cannot accept the theory of descent. A scientist has to bow to facts, but he is allowed to hope that some day the facts will be corrected.

I do not know whether in the preceding years, too, Vogt had secretly hoped for a removal of the obstacles to the theory of descent. But it seems very probable that Rudolf Virchow had had this hope from at least 1856. At that time, as we have seen, Virchow emphasized the necessity for assum-ing spontaneous generation, and left open the possibility of a series of such

---

[93]*Ibid.*, p. 132 ff. and Vogt's comments.
[94]*Ibid.*, p. 98, footnote.
[95]Temkin, "Materialism," (ftn. 7) p. 324 [p. 342].
[96]Karl Vogt, *Altes und Neues aus Thier- und Menschenleben*. 2 vols. Frankfurt a. M.: Literarische Anstalt, 1859; see vol. 1, p. 351.

events to explain the formation of progressively higher species. He did not declare himself a transformist, but he did not hide his sympathy either:

As long as it is still not possible in the sense of the school of natural philosophers to show a continuous development of plants and animals from the simplest form to the most highly developed organisms in such a way that genus is transformed into genus....[97]

As Ackerknecht has pointed out, Virchow was not an anti-Darwinist, although he warned against uncritical acceptance and generalization of Darwinistic ideas.[98] In an essay "On the Mechanistic Concept of Life" that appeared in 1862, he claimed to have insisted on transmutation as a necessary link in a mechanistic view of life, even before the appearance of Darwin's book. This essay purported to be the speech he had made at the 1858 meeting of German Scientists and Physicians.[99] In the published essay we read:

But life must have had a beginning, for geology leads us into epochs of the earth's development in which no life was possible, where no trace, no remnant, of life is extant. But if there was a beginning to life, then it must also be possible for science to fathom the conditions for this beginning. As yet this is an unsolved problem. Indeed, our experiences do not even give us the right to consider the invariability of species which at the moment seems to be so assured, as a fixed rule for all time. For geology teaches us to recognize a certain series of steps by which the species succeeded one another, higher ones succeeding lower ones, and however much the experience of our own time conflicts with it, I am bound nevertheless to confess that rather it seems to me to be a necessity for science to return to the possibility of transition from species to species. Only then does the mechanical theory of life attain real security in this respect.[100]

Virchow apparently felt that his readers might suspect him of having written under the influence of the *Origin* which had appeared in the meantime. Thus he added the following footnote:

Charles Darwin's book (*On the origin of species by means of natural selection*, London, 1859) which became famous so quickly, had not yet appeared when the foregoing was written.[101]

---

[97]Virchow, *op. cit.*, (ftn. 24) p. 24: "So lange es noch nicht möglich ist, im Sinne der naturphilosophischen Schule eine fortschreitende Entwickelung der Pflanzen und Thiere von der einfachsten Form zu den höchst entwickelten Organisationen in der Art zu zeigen, dass Gattung sich in Gattung umbildet; so lange man, wie Czolbe selbst anführt, mit Linné schliessen muss, dass alle Gattungen schon von (ihrem) Anfang an als solche existirten: so würde es nothwendig sein, um den Gedanken einer Epigenese der Gattungen, einer 'Schöpfung' zurückzuweisen, dass man die Ewigkeit aller organischen Gattungen aufstellte."

[98]Erwin H. Ackerknecht, *op. cit.*, (ftn. 72) p. 199 ff.

[99]Rudolf Virchow "Ueber die mechanische Auffassung des Lebens. Nach einem frei gehaltenen Vortrag aus der dritten allgemeinen Sitzung der 34. Versammlung deutscher Naturforscher und Aerzte. (Carlsruhe, am 22. September 1858)," in *Vier Reden über Leben und Kranksein*. Berlin: Reimer, 1862, pp. 1–33. Note that the speech was not read from a manuscript!

[100]*Ibid.*, p. 31.

[101]*Ibid.*, p. 31, footnote.

Since Virchow emphasized that the speech was not read from a manuscript, it is quite likely that no manuscript existed in 1858. However, there appeared a short official report which included the following passage:

For it is already very difficult to decide whether there are rigid differences between plant and animal cells. For the sequence of organic development from the simpler to the higher forms, as taught by Naturphilosophie, no proofs have as yet been found, and one is inclined to constancy of form. There seems to be a limited, preestablished route by which the principal characteristics of organisms are reproduced by inheritance and remain constant. Always the same form arises from earlier form without particular development. However ingratiatingly the indicated sequence of development may present itself to us, however desirable its proof may be to the individual investigator, the natural scientist who sacrifices himself and his pet inclinations to calm knowledge is obliged to designate this view as a fantasy. We are bound to assume the immutability of genera and species as a necessary consequence of organic laws. This compulsion is valid, however, only for the present, for the state of our knowledge today, and permits us to hope that more information will be found later.[102]

The two versions differ not only in letter, which is to be expected, but also in emphasis. According to the official report, transmutation is an unproved idea of Naturphilosophie; the true scientist views it with scepticism; he must admit the immutability of genera and species at the present time, though he reserves judgement as to what future research may reveal.[103]

These notions agree reasonably well with the article of 1856, and they also agree with a remark Virchow made in 1877 when, in the face of the great success of Darwin, he wrote in a reminiscent vein:

For those of us who were still acquainted with the old Nature-philosophy, it was certainly somewhat surprising to see how the genius of a single man restored to its rightful place, after its long and, alas, not entirely unjustified banishment, an idea already given official status as an *a priori* necessity by the Nature-philosophers, not only reactivating it but making it the basis of a general conception of the history of the organic world.[104]

It thus seems likely that both Vogt and Virchow, before the appearance

[102]The report is reprinted in Karl Sudhoff, *Rudolf Virchow und die Deutschen Naturforscherversammlungen.* Leipzig: Akademische Verlagsgesellschaft, 1922, pp. 5–7; see p. 6 f. The report continues: "Der Redner rechnete es sich als ein gewisses Verdienst an, dieses ihm widerstrebende Gesetz auch in Krankheiten nachgewiesen zu haben, indem er zeigte, der Körper tue nichts, wozu ihn nicht seine Bildung im voraus berechtigt; hieraus folgt, dass man die generatio aequivoca ablehnen muss. Der Naturforscher vermag auf die drängenden Fragen keine bestimmte Antwort zu erteilen."
Comparison with the printed version of 1862 indicates that Virchow thought above all of present conditions. In the version of 1862, he goes so far as to postulate the origin of life at some time in the geological past, allowing transmutation to take over from that event. The official excerpt is not clear as to Virchow's attitude to spontaneous generation in the past.
[103]In view of our uncertainty regarding the authorship of the official report and its denial of spontaneous generation, I hesitate to take it as manifest contradiction of the version of 1862. But it seems fair to say that the report throws doubt on Virchow's unequivocal support of transformism at the meeting.
[104]Rudolf Virchow, "Standpoints in scientific medicine [1877]," translated by L. J. Rather, *Bull. Hist. Med.,* 1956, *30*: 537–43; see p. 540.

of the *Origin,* realized that a theory of transmutation would fit better than any other into a mechanistic biology. Both, however, believed that the true scientist must sacrifice "pet inclinations" to facts. It would, moreover, seem that, after 1859, Virchow persuaded himself that he had insisted on this theory with greater emphasis than may actually have been the case.[105]

Vogt and Virchow were professional scientists of repute and, therefore, supposed to put facts before theory whenever the two disagreed. Louis Büchner, on the other hand, was hardly more than a scientifically trained popularizer of materialistic metaphysics, and in his *Kraft und Stoff* of 1855 we find indeed an outright proclamation of the belief in descent as an almost scientific fact. To Büchner it appears "scarcely understandable how some scientists can object to the assumption of a law of gradual transmutation—for no other reason than that as a rule, under our present-day conditions, such a separation of the individual species of animals is observed, that like parents always create only like offspring."[106]

Admitting that recent research left little room for spontaneous generation, Büchner nevertheless deemed it "not unlikely that it is still possible for the smallest and most imperfect organisms."[107] Johannes Müller's alleged discovery of snails developing in echinoderms is proclaimed as incontrovertible proof "that conditions must once have been possible where such a process could take place in higher animals or in which a monkey, nay any other animal gave birth to a human being!"[108] We have no right to draw inferences from the short period of our experience and from prevailing conditions to the endlessly long prehistoric times and to those states of the earth "in which nature undoubtedly was younger and stronger and more powerful in producing organic forms."[109] There is a law of transmutation according to which the transmutation was not, as the old school of natural philosophy demanded, a very gradual one, but rather saltatory and vested in the embryonic development. Thus he summarizes:

> From the most improbable beginning, the simplest element of organic form produced by a union of inorganic materials in involuntary generation, from the sorriest plant or animal cell, it was possible, with the help of extraordinary natural forces and endless periods of time, for that whole, rich world to develop which, infinitely varied in its ramifications, we find surrounding us.[110]

III

The foregoing survey lacks completeness as to authors as well as works covered. However, none of the great biologists claimed as adherents of the

---

[105]In the following paragraph (*ibid.,* p. 540), Virchow says that in the Karlsruhe lecture of 1858, he expressed "the variability of species as a necessary presupposition of the mechanical theory of life ... in the most clear-cut manner."
[106]Louis Büchner, *op. cit.,* (ftn. 15) p. 82.
[107]*Ibid.,* p. 73.
[108]*Ibid.,* p. 87.
[109]*Ibid.,* p. 82 f.
[110]*Ibid.,* p. 87 f.

idea of descent has been completely disregarded. It seems, therefore, permissible to attempt some general statements.

Our initial question related to the role of the idea of transmutation in German biology during a decade of rising materialism. The idea did not agree with the biblical account, but was otherwise philosophically neutral. If we use the terms "idealist" and "materialist" in the broad sense of the preceding pages, we find more numerous support among the idealists:[111] Schleiden, Baumgärtner, Unger, Schaaffhausen, and Nägeli. Among the materialists, only Büchner supported it outright. Cotta favored it without committing himself. Vogt, though sympathetic, opposed it, and however much it may have appealed to Virchow, his open acceptance is unproven.

This result serves first of all as a renewed reminder of the importance of distinguishing between the idea of transmutation and Darwinism as a particular mode of it. It is not our task to inquire into the reasons for the great success of Darwinism. But we shall try to find reasons for the weakness of the idea of transmutation before 1859. Whether the idea was intrinsically weak, i.e., whether it lacked logical compulsion and factual evidence, shall not occupy us here, since Professor Lovejoy has examined this question in a much broader framework. Rather, we shall see whether the arguments offered were weak *qua* arguments and lacking in persuasive power.

Such weakness is demonstrated first of all in the failure of winning a large number of followers. I mention this obvious phenomenon only in order to emphasize my doubt that suppression by the prevailing scientific opinion is largely to blame. In the case of Vogt and Virchow this could scarcely be the case; their aggressive temperament would have induced them to fight for the principle of transmutation had they felt sufficiently sure of it. Conversely, their reserve towards a theory which had their sympathy indicates that, rightly or wrongly, German biologists before 1859 considered the evidence against transmutation to be too strong.

The weakness is further documented by the multiplicity of arguments and explanations among those upholding transformism. Remarkably enough, none of the authors, except Cotta, was satisfied with accepting the views of any contemporary or previous champion, and of Cotta it would not be strictly correct to speak in terms of acceptance. However much they were influenced by Lamarck, Naturphilosophie, the *Vestiges of Creation,* or any other of Darwin's forerunners, such influence was not considered decisive.[112] Instead, most of them elaborated explanations of their own, or, like Unger and Schaaffhausen, avoided entering into details. In particular, Cotta, Schleiden, Unger, and Schaaffhausen seem to have thought of gradual changes, whereas Baumgärtner, Nägeli, and Büchner thought rather of sudden mutations.

[111]Rádl, *op. cit.* (ftn. 6), has indicated that evolutionary ideas were favored by a number of men who subsequently to 1859 became anti-Darwinists. In this connection the article by S. J. Holmes, "K. E. von Baer's perplexities over evolution," *Isis,* 1947, *37*: 7–14 is instructive.

[112]The only exception is Cotta who, however, went to the other extreme of not adopting openly the views which he reported.

Moreover, of the explanations adduced, some were ingenious, some were vague, and others (like Baumgärtner's and Büchner's) were fantastic. None of them, however, carried Darwin's great gift to the physiologist, viz., freedom from the embarrassment of teleology. In view of the fact that some of the explanations offered, like those of Schleiden and Baumgärtner, might also be called "mechanistic," this seems significant. It suggests that a theory of descent that failed to explain the mutual adaptation between body structure and environment lacked a good deal of the appeal which Darwinism exerted for physiologists like Helmholtz and du Bois-Reymond, to whom the question of the origin of species was of secondary importance.[113]

There was agreement that supernatural influences had to be excluded. There was, moreover, a more or less strongly pronounced desire to exclude, or reduce to a minimum, the frequency of spontaneous generations. Nägeli stated the case most distinctly—but vitiated it by admitting spontaneous generation even in his own day. Unger was most consistent, but then carried over old concepts of *Urpflanze* and idealistic morphology. Most difficult is the evaluation of the relative weight of scientific and speculative arguments. With Baumgärtner and Büchner the impression prevails that they believed in descent and thus found arguments for it, while Schaaffhausen went perhaps furthest in postulating transmutation because the case for the constancy of species seemed very doubtful to him. Taking our authors in the aggregate, all we can say is that nowhere do we find a theory of descent defended in isolation from a *Weltanschauung*, even if exclusion of supernatural creative acts is classed as a premise of scientific reasoning.

On the other hand, it is manifest that the idea of descent was not shrouded in complete silence. Even if weak, it was alive and found outspoken supporters. Thus one cannot help wondering why it did not exert a larger appeal in a time and region which was so favorably inclined to historical thinking. The appeal of an idea does not, after all, necessarily rest on its logical strength and supporting facts. *Entwickelungsgeschichte* was fashionable among German historians and biologists. Why was there no stronger temptation to applying it to species, especially since the concept of progress spoke in favor of transformism? It cannot even be said that another idea of great psychological force, such as biblical orthodoxy, opposed it. Remarkably enough, the Mosaic account of creation plays a negligible role in the argumentation as compared with the constancy of species. The latter of course was the main argument opposed to transmutation. But, whatever its merits, its psychological power is open to doubt.

---

[113]Helmholtz, in a paper of 1853 (*Popular Lectures on Scientific Subjects*, translated by E. Atkinson, New York: 1873, p. 48) mentions the view "that during the geological periods that have passed over the earth, one species has been developed from another, so that, for example, the breast-fin of the fish has gradually changed into an arm or a wing." Without committing himself he adds that probably the majority of observers do not incline to this view. For du Bois-Reymond see John Theodore Merz, *A History of European Thought in the Nineteenth Century.* Vol. II, 3rd ed. Edinburgh–London: Blackwood, 1928, p. 435.

I think that a psychological explanation has to take account of the fact that, far from being forgotten, the idea of transmutation was only too well remembered from the days of Naturphilosophie and speculative science.[114] To the post-romantic generation of German biologists, transformism lacked the appeal of newness. This generation prided itself on its rigorously scientific attitude which implied resistance to mere speculation. A comparison with the parallel fate of the idea of a microorganismic etiology of infectious diseases may help our understanding of the situation. Both ideas, that of transmutation and that of the bacterial cause of disease, were widely accepted after 1859: the former suddenly and dramatically with the appearance of Darwin's book, the latter more slowly in the wake of the work of Pasteur. Both ideas were not only well known before 1859, but suffered the fate of being too well known.[115] Nothing essentially new had been added to them, and they might profitably be disregarded by progressive scientists, intent upon the discovery of concrete facts. Whether in either case supporting facts were so conspicuously lacking as to justify that attitude is a different question which cannot be answered within the narrow limits of the period under discussion.

[114]J. H. F. Kohlbrugge, "War Darwin ein originelles Genie?" *op. cit.* (ftn. 6), has emphasized the widespread interest in theories of transmutation before Darwin and has pointed out several of the factors that account for it. His arguments are, however, influenced by the desire to belittle Darwin's claims, which gives them a one-sided tendency.

[115]As Henry E. Sigerist, *The Great Doctors* (Translated by Eden and Cedar Paul, New York: Norton, 1933), p. 352, pointed out, Henle's *Pathologische Untersuchungen* of 1840, in which he cogently argued for the microorganismic etiology of infectious diseases, found little recognition because "people were willing to believe the evidence of their own eyes. But they were weary of speculation." Erwin H. Ackerknecht, "Anticontagionism between 1821 and 1867," *Bull. Hist. Med.*, 1938, 22: 562–93, with reference to Henle, says "that what to us appears a vanguard action, impressed Henle's contemporaries rather as a rearguard action...." Yet even before Pasteur, the arguments for the *contagium animatum* were supported not only by speculation but by observable facts as well!

VI

Health and Disease

29

Health and Disease*

HEALTH AND DISEASE are familiar notions, commonly used in a comple-
mentary sense, viz., health as absence of disease and disease as a
lack of health. But any attempt at a precise definition of these two concepts
meets with considerable difficulties and throws doubt on the validity of the
popular usage.

A person suffering from an ordinary cold may declare himself ill,
whereas the same person laid up with a broken leg may claim to be in
perfect health. These common examples indicate the complexity behind
the concepts of health and disease, a complexity apparent throughout the
history of mankind. Health and disease have been experienced by almost
every human being, and the emotional as well as rational reactions have
differed and have manifested themselves differently. The history of these
two ideas must, therefore, take into account definitions and explanations
by philosophers and physicians, as well as the reactions and usage of others.
Within this vast history, any order can be achieved only by neglecting
innumerable details, by paradigmatic use of relatively few opinions and
practices, and by admitting that a different point of view may show a
different panorama.

The myths of many ancient civilizations tell of a golden age, free from
ills, then followed by troubled and disease-ridden times. Before Pandora's
box was opened, men lived on earth "without evils, hard toil, and grievous
disease." But now that the lid is off, "thousands of miseries roam among
men, the land is full of evils and full is the sea. Of themselves, diseases come
upon men, some by day and some by night, and they bring evils to the
mortals" (Hesiod, *Works and Days,* 90–103). Sickness here is just one among
the many forms of suffering to which man has been subjected at all times.
When and where he began to separate illness from other kinds of suffering
we do not know, and down to our own days the demarcation has remained
uncertain.

In the *Atharva-Veda* of ancient India there is a prayer for a mad person,
that the gods might "uncraze" him, as the translator has it. "Crazed from
sin against the gods, crazed from a demon—I, knowing, made a remedy,
when he shall be uncrazed." It seems impossible to tell whether the crazy
person is believed "sick" or whether he falls into a different category. The
Atharva-Veda is not a medical work; it contains prayers against many ills and
sings the praise of many things. In this case it is not easy to maintain a sharp
distinction between disease and other kinds of suffering.

*From the *Dictionary of the History of Ideas,* edited by Philip P. Wiener, 4 vols. New York:
Charles Scribner's Sons, 1973, vol. 2, pp. 395–407.

Evidence of very early specialization in ancient Egypt suggests, on the other hand, that some groups of people learned how to remedy certain painful or incapacitating conditions and bequeathed such limited knowledge without any theories or even clear notions of disease.

The manner in which illness was approached in the archaic civilizations of Egypt and Mesopotamia shows considerable similarities. Disease is described as a complex of symptoms; often the localization in a special part of the body is stated. There are many different complexes of symptoms, of what may "befall" the person (the meaning of the Greek word *sumptoma*), and there are consequently many diseases, which may be given names or may be connected with actions of demons and deities. The disease pictures can offer indications for the outcome, for death or recovery; they also offer a basis for action.

Most of the types of disease are described as symptoms or syndromes presenting themselves at a certain moment. For instance, the surgical Edwin Smith Papyrus, whose original composition probably goes back to the Old Kingdom, tells what the physician will find when he examines injured men. The descriptions vary with the kind of injury and its location, and there is something approaching a diagnosis, and a prognosis, and there is, of course, therapy. Examination of the patient has led to a recognition of the nature of the case. The text then adds that the ailment is one "which I will treat," or "with which I will contend," or "not to be treated," verdicts connected with a forecast of the disease as curable, uncertain, or incurable. Analogy with the development of prognosis in the times of Hippocrates (ca. 400 B.C.) suggests the possibility of a social motive for such forecasts. The physician may have felt the need to protect himself against possible later reproach, especially if he undertook the cure of a patient who then died.

While an injury invited examination and an immediate decision, internal ailments also were described in both Egypt and Mesopotamia as pictures presenting themselves at the height of the illness. However, such a static view was not the only one. In Mesopotamia, where the reading of omens was developed into an art, the symptoms of the disease were understood as omens too, just as a potsherd found by the exorciser on his way to the sick man could be of ominous portent. The symptoms need not all appear at once; they could be observed over a length of time or could change. "If, at the beginning of the disease, the temples show heat and if, afterwards, heat and transpiration disappear, (it is) an affection due to dryness; after suffering from it for two or three days, he will recover" (Labat, 1951). The reference to dryness points to the realm of observation and to reasoning in terms of natural phenomena. But in a subsequent case, the demon "râbisu" is accused of having attached himself to the sick man, feeding on his food and drinking his water.

Disease in Mesopotamian medical texts often was connected with "the hand" of some deity, and "the hand" of such a god was also recognized in nonmedical contexts (Labat, 1951). Similarly, Leviticus 13 describes a skin condition diagnosed as *Zara 'ath*, which is usually translated as leprosy. Not only is this identification medically doubtful, but *Zara 'ath* was more than a human disease; it could be found in houses and garments as well. It was a term denoting ritual impurity, sometimes inflicted as punishment by God, as in the case of Miriam (Numbers 12:10) and of Gehazi, the servant of Elisha (II Kings 5:27).

Disease receives meaning when placed in man's moral universe, when its occurrence within a scheme of creation and right and wrong actions, is accounted for. In the archaic civilizations of Egypt, India, Israel, and Mesopotamia, this universe was comprised of everyday life, as well as of magic and religion. Disease was punishment for trespass or sin, ranging from involuntary infraction of some taboo to wilful crime against gods or men. Disease could also be due to the evil machinations of sorcery. Gods or demons could cause disease without taking possession, or they could represent the disease within the body. The magic and religious interpretations of disease did not necessarily exclude naturalistic explanations. Archaic civilizations were not logical systems rejecting what did not fit into the dominant scheme of things. Mesopotamian medical works have been characterized as mere literary fixation of old medical lore (Oppenheim, 1962). For ancient Egypt it has been contended (Grapow, 1956) that no single concept could be found to cover the different approaches to disease. Yet there were beginnings toward a speculative rather than magical view of disease. The connection of heart beat with pulse beat was recognized, and systems of blood vessels were invented, thought to carry disease to various parts of the body. Possibly a noxious agent (*Wḥdw*) was assumed, which spread putrefaction and indeed forced the body or its parts to undergo the very process against which embalming was to protect the corpse (Steuer, 1948). *Wḥdw* could also be a demon, and this has suggested the transfer from an originally demonistic to a more physiological principle. If this interpretation (Steuer, 1948) is correct, we see here the beginning of the metamorphosis of archaic into the rationalized and systematic thought of the medical and philosophical works of classical India, China, and Greece. But no arbitrary end can be assigned to the archaic ways of looking upon health and disease; many features even survive in the superstitions and the unconscious motivations of modern man.

II

In the Indian *Caraka Samhitā* the emergence of diseases prompts the great sages, compassionate doers of good, to acknowledge that "Health is the supreme foundation of virtue, wealth and enjoyment, and salvation," and that "diseases are the destroyers of health, of the good of life, and even of life itself." They send a messenger to Indra to ask him how to remedy diseases, whereupon the god teaches the messenger the science of life, which begins with general speculations on the world, on causality, on man and his components, viz., mind, spirit, and body. Body and mind are the dwelling places of health, as well as of disease. Wind, bile, and phlegm are the three "dosa" responsible for disease in the body, while passion and delusion cause disease of the mind. Somatic and spiritual remedies help in the former, whereas the latter must be approached through "religion, philosophy, fortitude, remembrance and concentration" (Sutrasthana, Ch. I). Both health and disease thus have their place in a religious, philosophical, and medical sphere. Diseases originate from a wide range of external or internal causes of a somatic or psychological nature; but demons are still one of the possibilities.

In India, medicine, *ayurveda*, is the veda of longevity. Similarly, in China, health and disease are incorporated into the philosophy of the Tao and the two polar principles, the yin and the yang. Health and disease are now states of the human microcosm, which has its parallel in the macrocosm. In accordance with the role played in Tao philosophy and practice by the notion of prolonging life, health and longevity tend to be identified. However, there is a gulf between the natural association of good health and long life on the one hand, and the association of health and potential immortality on the other. Western religions and, until the eighteenth century at least, prevailing Western philosophy too, thought of death as man's unavoidable fate (Gruman, 1966). The same is true of Buddhism. "So this is life! Youth into old age, health into disease" (*Dhammapada*). This was the insight that started Prince Siddhartha on the long journey leading to his illumination as Buddha. His four noble truths have been compared with the questions an Indian physician would ask himself when confronted with a patient: Is he ill, what is the nature and cause of his illness, is the disease curable, what treatment is indicated? (Zimmer, 1948). But Buddha's goal of treatment was not immortality; it was Nirvana, eventual extinction.

For the Greeks, too, health was one of the greatest goods. To be healthy, said Theognis (frag. 225), is the "most desirable" thing. The high level of Greek medicine is, in itself, a sign that disease was abhorred. Hygiene, the maintenance of health, played a very great role, above all for the well-to-do, who were expected to devote much of their time to it. For the philosopher, health had its value as the necessary basis for the practice of virtue. But since health does not altogether depend on man's actions, the Stoic philosophers did not declare health an absolute value. The sage was superior to all disease, of body as well as of soul (Cicero, *Tusculan Disputations*, III, xxxiv, 82), but this did not prevent Stoic philosophers from taking great interest in the minute classification and subdivisions of disturbances (*perturbationes; ibid.*, IV, x, 23 ff.). They thought of disturbances of the mind, discussing them in analogy to bodily diseases. For since early times, disease, to the Greeks, was a somatic disturbance with manifestations that could be somatic or psychic. The causes of disease could be many; gods, too, could send diseases and could cure them, as they could cause or alleviate any disaster. But Greek physicians and philosophers agreed that disease was a natural process, so that the secularization of the concept of disease was limited only by the divinity of nature herself. A Greek physician of about 400 B.C. could, therefore, say that all diseases were divine and all were human (Hippocrates, *On the Sacred Disease,* Ch. XXI), thereby meaning that all diseases had their roots in the body and in human actions and were influenced by external agencies which, like cold, sun, and winds, were divine. Epidemic diseases were attributed to pollutions (*miasmata*) in the air inhaled by all the people of an afflicted region. The *miasmata* might be caused by the action of the sun, which replaced the sun god Apollo, who, according to the myth, had inflicted a plague upon Thebes which was polluted by the deeds of Oedipus (Sophocles, *Oedipus the King,* 96–98).

Medical speculations on the origin of disease paid little attention to divine or magic interference, but all the more to mistakes in the way of life, above all in diet (Hippocrates, *On Ancient Medicine,* Ch. III). Some four hundred years later, the Latin author Celsus believed that in Homeric times health had been generally good. Indolence and luxury had later spoiled man and led to much disease. Therapy fell into the hands of physicians who treated by means of diet, and who became interested in natural philosophy (*De medicina,* prooemium, 1–5 and 9).

On the practical side, dietetic treatment paralleled practices of the athletic trainers. On the theoretical side, it went together with a view of health as balance, harmony, symmetry, and of disease as their disturbance. Using political metaphors, Alcmaeon of Croton (fifth century B.C.) taught that health was maintained by the balance (*isonomia*) of such powers as moist, dry, cold, hot, bitter, sweet, whereas disease was caused by single rule (*monarchia*) (frag. 4). Other explanations were offered in terms of elements, body fluids (humors), or atoms. In the second century A.D. Galen, in the tradition of Hippocratic, Platonic, Aristotelian, and Stoic ideas, elaborated a doctrine which was schematically systematized in late antiquity and then remained dominant till the seventeenth century. Four basic qualities in binary combinations characterized four elements which had their analogues in the four principal humors of the body. Hot and dry corresponded to fire and yellow bile, hot and moist to air and blood, cold and dry to earth and black bile, cold and moist to water and phlegm. These analogues could be extended to the ages of man, the seasons, and winds, so that man in health and disease was explicable in terms of natural philosophy. The humors were products of digested food and of metabolism, and man's functions were regulated from the anatomical centers of liver, heart, and brain, from which veins, arteries, and nerves originated, and in which the natural soul, the vital soul, and the rational soul, respectively, had their seats. The soul had somatic, as well as psychological, functions: the natural soul represented man's appetites and regulated his nutrition; the vital soul represented the passions, especially anger, and regulated the body heat through the *pneuma* of the arteries; the rational soul accounted for thinking, feeling, and willing, receiving messages and imparting its commands via the nerves.

Man was in good health if his body, its parts and humors, had the temperament proper to them, and when the structure and functions of the organs were intact. Otherwise there was disease, as a consequence of which all possible symptoms could befall the patient. In view of the labile condition of the body, ideal health was rarely attained. But only when there was pain, and when a man was impeded in the functions of his personal and civic life, was actual disease considered to be present. There existed a borderland of relative health between perfection and actual disease.

Such a concept of health and disease rests on a teleologically conceived biology. All parts of the body are built and function so as to allow man to lead a good life and to preserve his kind. Health is a state according to Nature; disease is contrary to Nature. It is thus possible to speak of disease as a disturbance, and of health as good, as deteriorating, or as improving.

In its medical aspect the Galenic doctrine grew out of a particular set of ideas found in the works of Hippocrates, whose name was given to some seventy Greek medical writings of about 400 B.C. Many of these writings, allegedly associated with the island of Cos, the birthplace of Hippocrates, reveal a strongly individualizing approach to disease. It is left to the physician to combine the many physical and mental symptoms into a diagnosis of the particular case.

But that did not exclude recognition of diseases as entities. The Hippocratics spoke of consumption, pneumonia, pleurisy, the sacred disease, i.e., epilepsy, On the last there even exists a monograph which discusses causes, development, course, and major symptoms; it illustrates that a disease was thought of as a process developing in time. On the other hand, rather than arrange symptoms into disease pictures, Hippocratic physicians often associated symptoms with the constitution of their patients, usually expressed in humoral terms. The four temperaments, phlegmatic, sanguine, choleric, and melancholic, still spoken of today, echo a psychosomatic classification of human constitutions according to the Hippocratic–Galenic tradition.

In some books of the Hippocratic collection, ascribed to the medical center of Cnidos, disease entities stand in the foreground. Four "diseases" are connected with the kidneys; there is a dropsy coming from the spleen; the disease "hepatitis" is attributed to the black bile flowing into the liver. In short, diseases are classified, ascribed to organs, and, together with their symptoms, explained in humoral terms. After the advances made in anatomy from the early third century B.C., anatomical considerations were given increased space, for instance in Galen, Rufus of Ephesus, and Aretaeus.

Not all ancient physicians thought it necessary to give anatomical and physiological explanations for disease. The "empiricist" sect, relying on experience only, tried to assemble the syndromes of diseases but refrained from dealing with any causes other than such evident ones as cold, hunger, fatigue. The "methodist" sect, though it had developed from the atomistic speculations of Asclepiades (first century B.C.), according to which the pores of the body could become too wide or too narrow, was satisfied with acknowledging the existence of three conditions: constriction, relaxation, and a mixture of both, conditions recognizable from the symptoms without recourse to speculation (Edelstein, 1967).

At the end of antiquity, these sects all but disappeared in the Greek-speaking East. The Galenic system predominated and was inherited by Syrians, Arabs, Persians, and Jews, to make its entrance into the West from the eleventh century on. The biological basis of the Galenic system was little changed. But it was transferred into a world that looked upon health and disease otherwise than did the pagans.

III

To the Greeks, the preservation of health through temperance in eating, drinking, and other activities was a model for healthy thinking (Snell, 1953), *sōphrosynē*, soundness of mind. With it were connected well-being and deliverance from ills, as the etymological roots of the allied Greek words *sōs, sōtēria,* suggest. For Aeschylus (*Eumenides,* 535–37) "much desired happiness, beloved by all, [comes] from a healthy mind." To the Stoic philosopher, happiness lay in virtue; a person was healthy if his contentment relied on the things in his power (Seneca, *Epistulae morales,* lxxii, 7). The wisdom of the sage thus coincided with his attainment of true health.

Here was a transition from the classical ideal of health as symmetry and beauty (Plato, *Timaeus* 87E–88A) to the ideal of spiritual beauty and spiritual health, acquired, if necessary, at the expense of the body, "the flesh," as the Gospel has it.

Suffering in general and disease in particular had long been seen as consequences of sin. With the spread of Christianity, they could appear as chastisement of those whom the Lord loved. Disease could be a portal through which man acquired eternal salvation. Jesus told the sufferer from a palsy that his sins were forgiven. To show "that the Son of man hath power on earth to forgive sins," he bade the sick man: "Arise, take up thy bed, and go unto thine house" (Matthew 9:2–7). Again, Jesus justified his eating "with publicans and sinners" by saying that "They that be whole need not a physician, but they that are sick" (*ibid.,* 10–13). Thus sickness was not only a consequence of sin, sin itself was a disease which needed healing. This has found expression in endless allegories from Origen to authors of modern times. When Matthew (17:14 ff.) speaks of a lunatic boy whom Mark (9:14 ff.) describes as deaf and dumb, Bede interprets this as a reference to persons waxing and waning in sundry vices as the moon changes, deaf to the sermon of faith and dumb because not expressing faith.

The ascetic life regarded disease not only with indifference but even with pride, as mortification of the flesh. To care for the lepers and thereby to expose oneself to infection was a sign of sanctity. It has to be admitted that the positive evaluation of disease had also another, secular, root. In the pseudo-Aristotelian *Problems* (xxx,i) the question was raised why all men outstanding in philosophy, politics, poetry, or the arts appeared to be of melancholic temperament, even to the extent of being afflicted with the sicknesses arising from the black bile. This was to lead to the notion of melancholy as a disease of superior intellects, a notion that achieved its best-known artistic expression in Dürer's engraving *Melencolia I* (Klibansky et al., 1964) and its most learned treatment in Burton's *Anatomy of Melancholy* (1621).

The concept of disease at a given period is not altogether independent of the nature of the prevailing ailments. The Middle Ages and the Renaissance suffered much from infections that appeared in massive epidemic waves or were endemic, i.e., native to the population. Arabic and Latin authors of the time elaborated the ancient concept of infections and contagious disease. As a dye or a poison (*virus*) could stain a large amount of water or kill a large animal; as putrescent material, marked by an evil smell, corrupted what had been sound, so an infection polluted the body and could spread among a population. Virus, stain, evil smell, putrescence, and miasma were the notions associated with infection and contagion.

The concept of infection was broad and unclear: infection could develop in the body with the disease, it could be due to the influence of the stars (hence "influenza"), and it could take on different forms (the word "pestilence" designated any severe epidemic). If the disease spread by personal contact, it was contagious. Of all epidemics, the plague, which manifested itself in bubonic and pulmonary forms, was the most severe. It appeared during the reign of the emperor Justinian (A.D. 527–65), then in the fourteenth century ("the black death"), and in many subsequent outbreaks, of which those of London (1665) and Marseilles (1720) were among the last in Western Europe. The plague, dreaded as contagious, provoked public health measures, quarantine and isolation, to counteract the danger. In *Romeo and Juliet* (Act V, Scene ii) the searchers of the town, suspecting that Friar Laurence and his brother monk " . . . both were in a house/ where the infectious pestilence did reign/ seal'd up the doors . . ." and did not let them leave.

The most serious endemic contagion was leprosy; then from about 1495, syphilis assumed first place. Whether syphilis was imported from the new world by the crew of Columbus or had existed in Europe before is a moot question. The disease became widely known as the French disease (the French, in turn, calling it *mal de Naples*). The name syphilis was given to the disease in a Latin poem *Syphilis sive morbus gallicus* (1530), by Girolamo Fracastoro, who also elaborated a theory of contagious disease which in its fundamentals survived till the mid-nineteenth century. Imperceptibly small particles, *seminaria,* capable of propagating themselves, transferred contagious diseases by direct contact, through an object (*fomes*), or at a short distance. It is not likely that he thought of the *seminaria* as microorganisms; rather he anticipated something of the notion of a leaven (Greek: *zumē*). A contagious disease was specific: it retained its character in the transmission from man to man. The ontological view of diseases, i.e., thinking of them as real, distinct entities, was nothing new. Even the comparison of a disease with an animal was old—Plato (*Timaeus* 89B) had used it, and Varro (116–27 B.C.) had actually spoken of animals, too small to be seen by the eye, "which by mouth and nose through the air enter the body and cause severe diseases" (*Rerum rusticarum* 1, 2). But in the sixteenth to seventeenth centuries the ontological concept of disease was considerably strengthened. The Paracelsists, including their master Paracelsus (1493–1541) and their rebellious member van Helmont (1577–1644), contributed by endowing disease with a body, thinking of it as a parasite, attributing its causes to external factors independent of man. Van Helmont, in particular, opposed the old theory of diseases as catarrhs, as fluxes from the brain to which vapors had ascended. He spoke of the *spina*, the thorn, i.e., irritations, the form in which diseases acted in the body. Outside the circle of Paracelsists, William Harvey (1578–1657) in his embryological work (Exercise 27) thought of tumors as leading a life of their own, and of diseases from poison or contagion as having their own vitality (Pagel, 1968).

The most impressive presentation of the ontological point of view came from Thomas Sydenham (1624–89). He took up the Hippocratic notion of the "constitution" of a year, associated with the diseases prevalent during the period. According to Sydenham, epidemics had different constitutions depending upon "an occult and inexplicable alteration in the very bowels of the earth, whence the air becomes contaminated by the kind of effluvia which deliver and determine the human bodies to this or that disease" (*Opera,* 1844). Diseases should be observed and their species studied as plants were studied by the botanists, and though he could not explain the formation of the species, Sydenham, nevertheless, hinted at their origin. When the humors of the body could not be concocted, or when they contracted "a morbific blemish from this or that atmospheric constitution" (*ibid.*), or when they turned poisonous because of a contagion, then they were "exalted into a substantial form of species" (*Works,* 1848). The disease itself was Nature's struggle to restore health by elimination of the morbific matter. With great praise, Sydenham quoted the Hippocratic saying, "Nature is the healer of disease." Nature needed simple help from the physician; sometimes not even that.

Sydenham was one of the founders of nosology, the science of classifying diseases, which came into its own at the time of the great systematist Linné (1707–78). Boissier de Sauvages (1706–67), Cullen (1710–90), Pinel (1745–1826), and Schoenlein (1793–1864) created nosological systems which, on the basis of clinical symptoms, classified diseases into orders, families, genera, and species. This was the practitioner's science: if, by its symptoms, he could diagnose the disease and find its place in the scheme, he could then also prescribe the remedies recommended for it. If he wished, he could go further and instruct himself about the scientific explanation of the disease, but he need not do so if he distrusted the various theories offered.

IV

With the decline of Aristotelian science, the challenge to the Galenic doctrines by the revolutionary Paracelsus, the reform of anatomy by Vesalius, and the discovery of the circulation of the blood by William Harvey, pathology had undergone decisive changes. The humors did not disappear at once, but the new physics and chemistry replaced the Galenic doctrine of health and disease as a balance or imbalance, respectively, of the qualities. Descartes thought of the animal body as a soulless machine; even in man only the conscious mental processes involved the soul. To overcome the difficulty regarding acts which were seemingly purposeful yet independent of, or even contrary to, man's will, Descartes introduced the idea of reflex action. The Cartesian philosophy favored a physiology and pathology on strictly mechanical principles with the help of a corpuscular theory which permitted the inclusion of chemical explanations.

If the body is a machine, health will be represented by a well-functioning machine, disease by a defective one. A machine can have some self-regulatory mechanisms built in, but it does not create new ones when the situation so demands. It was, therefore, logical for Robert Boyle to refuse to see all diseases as healing processes. His theological bias was against the pagan view of nature as a benevolent being. Natural processes were blind and could be destructive. A dropsical person might be plagued by thirst, yet drinking would aggravate the disease (Boyle, 1725). The radical Cartesian dichotomy of body and soul also entailed a basic difficulty concerning mental diseases. It was logically absurd to think of the soul, a *res cogitans,* as being prone to sickness in the manner of the body; this could only be done metaphorically in the manner in which crime, sin, heresy had long been called diseases of the soul.

Revolutionary as the new mechanical orientation was, it did not sweep everything before it. Even those physicians who were inclined towards mechanistic theories admitted their ineffectiveness at the bedside. They recommended a Hippocratic attitude and patient observation of the disease. Many physicians were unwilling to follow the new mechanistic trend, and to some of them theories altogether meant little.

Generally speaking, in the seventeenth century mechanization was less successful in biology than in the world of physics. Harvey himself, van Helmont, Glisson, Wepfer, Stahl are outstanding among those who, in one form or another, did not believe that life, health, and disease could be understood without assuming the participation of the soul or of vital principles immanent in the body. They spoke of *anima,* of the Archeus, of a "president," or they endowed all fibres with irritability. It all meant that the human organism was actively engaged in preserving or restoring health.

Before the middle of the eighteenth century, discussions about the respective roles of mechanism and vitalism were mainly carried on by doctors of medicine, who devoted their attention and practice to internal diseases. Apothecaries were interested in chemical medicine, and it fell to them to prepare the chemical drugs that had come into vogue with Paracelsus. In England they gradually assumed the role of general practitioners. Here the apothecary, who sold the medicine, dispensed medical advice together with his medicines. For this kind of practice nosological orientation was particularly valuable. Another class of medical man, the surgeon, also looked upon disease differently from the doctor of medicine. In the Middle Ages the surgeons had become separated from the physicians and were organized in guilds, usually together with the barbers. They looked after wounds, ulcers, abscesses, fractures, dislocations, diseases of the skin and venereal diseases, tumors, possibly also cataracts, herniae, and stones of the bladder. Moreover, they bled patients if the doctor so prescribed. Their domain was external disorders in contrast to internal illness. In most cases, these disorders were localized, and in judging them and treating them the surgeon had to know something of the anatomy of the human body. Anatomy became the surgeon's preferred science, as chemistry was that of the apothecary.

With the exception of relatively few well-trained men, the guild surgeon was not educated enough and his social status was too low to allow him a decisive influence on medical thought. Nevertheless, it is not by chance that, though a doctor of medicine, Vesalius, the reformer of human anatomy, was professor of surgery at the University of Padua. With the appearance of his *Fabrica,* in 1543, normal human anatomy became firmly based on dissections of human cadavers. Pathological anatomy, which studied morbid changes, developed more slowly, in spite of the fact that postmortem dissections to establish the cause of death had been performed prior to anatomies intended to teach the structure of man's body. Postmortem dissections concerned cases where the disease showed unusual features or where legal questions arose. With G. B. Morgagni's *De sedibus et causis morborum* ("On the Seats and Causes of Diseases," 1761) pathological anatomy became a science in its own right. Its practical aim was to correlate the course of the disease and its symptoms with the changes noticed after death.

As the title of his book indicates, Morgagni traced the symptoms back to lesions in the organs, something surgeons had usually done. But in surgical disorders, the lesions were mostly visible or palpable, which in internal diseases they were not. Pathological anatomy, therefore, was of little use to the physician as long as it was not possible to explore the condition of internal organs during life. Two steps helped realize this goal. Auenbrugger taught (1761) that changes in sound elicited by percussion of the chest yielded information about changes in the consistency of the organs of the chest. Auenbrugger's work was popularized by Napoleon's physician, Corvisart, after the French Revolution had led to a union of medicine and surgery. The second step, made by Laennec, consisted in the introduction of the stethoscope (1819). With its aid Laennec was able to compare more effectively than before the sounds heard over the heart and the lungs under normal conditions with sounds heard when these organs were ill. Percussion and auscultation helped the physician to obtain an objective view of the patient's illness; he was less dependent on subjective complaints. The Paris school, leading in the new anatomical concept of disease, found followers in London, Dublin, Vienna, and elsewhere. The new insight into disease through the combination of clinical and anatomical pictures led to the elimination of old disease entities and the solid establishment of others, like typhoid fever, gastric ulcer, multiple sclerosis, and diphtheria.

The new objectivity found its place in the hospitals, which housed a large number of patients, many of them suffering from the same disease. Apart from wards, hospitals also included dissection rooms and then laboratories. Down to the later nineteenth century, the hospital was predominantly a place for indigent patients, who were not under the personal care of a particular physician but became "material" for observation and charitable treatment. Thereby the large hospitals invited a statistical approach to sickness and to therapy. In the eighteen-twenties Louis, in Paris, investigated the influence of bleeding in the early stages of pneumonia upon the course of the disease. Some patients were bled early, as was the custom, others were not. The results showed that early bleeding did not improve the chances for recovery. A very important insight into the unreliability of time-hallowed therapeutics had been gained, and the numerical method had been well illustrated.

The objective view of illness found in the large hospitals had not origi-nated there alone. The rise of the modern state developed statistical methods which covered the nation's health. In England, bills of mortality stating the number of deaths from various causes had come into use some-time in the sixteenth century. Originally designed as intelligence about the spread of epidemic disease, these bills, in the seventeenth century, were used by John Graunt as a basis for vital statistics. Mercantilism, with its advocacy of national industries in the interest of a positive balance of trade, calculated the economic advantages of health and the loss incurred to the national economy through sickness and untimely death. Bellers, in 1714, suggested that Parliament make provisions for the improvement of medicine so that the population

... may, once in Sixty or Seventy Years, be Reprieved from Destruction; and con-sequently, the Number of the People in the Kingdom, in that time, may be doubled, and many Millions of the Sick may be recovered from their *Beds* and *Couches*, in Half the time that they usually are now.

Every Able Industrious Labourer, that is capable to have Children, who so Un-timely Dies, may be accounted Two Hundred Pound Loss to the *Kingdom* (p. 3).

The lack of sentimentality which permitted estimating human life and suffering in terms of shillings and pence presupposed the existence of a large anonymous population in urban centers. It expressed the develop-ment of a rationalized way of life.

With beginnings less clearly defined, the medical application of scales, clocks, and thermometers also promoted objective study of disease. These instruments and a few simple chemical reactions were the forerunners of the powerful array of the diagnostic laboratory. Greek physicians had al-ready used clocks to measure the pulse rate and had proposed scales to determine metabolic processes. Moreover, both these instruments, and the thermometer for measuring the temperature of the body, had been explored for medical use by Santorio Santorio (1561–1636). But their wide-spread acceptance was very slow. As late as 1860 Wunderlich found it necessary to argue that the use of the clinical thermometer was neither too expensive, neither too time consuming for the practitioner, nor too bothersome nor altogether superfluous (Ebstein, 1928). A common principle underlying these instruments and their much more complicated successors is the need to establish numerical data. In the Galenic tradition, normalcy had been viewed as an optimal natural state. Vesalius described the human body in its theoretical perfection. But the numerical limits of normal pulse rate or body temperature must be based on measurements in many individuals. The elaboration of tables of numerical values gave health and disease a statistical aspect, and the physiognomy of diseases could be expressed on graphs. The typical fever curves of many infectious diseases, worked out by Wunderlich, enabled the physician to make a tentative diagnosis from the chart.

To be sure, all these aspects of modern "laboratory medicine" (Ackerknecht, 1955) were far ahead of the eighteenth century, when even scales, clocks, and thermometers were used only by a few relatively audacious minds. Yet it is not without significance that De Haen (1704–76), whose hospital reports were a major contribution to the practical medical literature of the century, also urged the use of the thermometer and tried to establish the normal temperatures for various age groups (Ebstein, 1928). Essentially, the use of numerical data in the diagnosis of disease presupposes that the latter is a physiological process. The activities of the body can increase and diminish and still remain within the range of the "normal." There is a transition from undoubted health to manifest disease.

This notion was elaborated in the system of John Brown (1735–88). He assumed that the interaction between the excitability with which the body was endowed and the stimuli, external and internal, which it encountered during life determined health and the contrasting conditions of asthenia and sthenia. Health was the territory between these two conditions. In a few countries the direct impact of this system was dramatic, in others it was slight. But its indirect influence on the development of physiological medicine in the nineteenth century was very great. Both health and disease represented life, and disease differed only in representing life under changed circumstances.

v

To look upon disease as detrimental to the national interest, as a natural process under changed but yet natural conditions, as a process to be studied objectively at the bedside, in the dissecting room, and in the laboratory, was part of the "Enlightenment" of the Western world after about 1700. But the Enlightenment, notably in the teachings of Jean Jacques Rousseau, had its own sentimentality, which it also bequeathed to the nineteenth century.

Rousseau and his followers looked upon health as a gift of man's natural state, which luxury and civilization had spoiled. Mothers should breast-feed their babies, children should wear clothes that do not restrict their bodies as fashionable dress does. It was bad to expose the mind, especially the feminine mind, to the incessant reading of novels. In the eyes of middle-class society vices led to disease, and some diseases, notably alcoholism and venereal disease, were shameful because rooted in an immoral life. The fight which Tissot (1728–97) and generations of physicians after him led against masturbation, warning against its alleged baneful effects upon health, was a secular version of a biblical taboo (onanism). On the other hand, Tissot gave advice in matters of health to the people who had no access to medical help, and Johann Peter Frank's great work, *System einer vollständigen medicinischen Polizey* (1779 ff.), was to serve the absolute, yet enlightened authorities in ruling their subjects for the latter's own good.

That health was seen as such a good was in itself significant. The more the promises of another world receded, the more desirable health appeared, not only as a state to which all people at all times had aspired, but as an ideal toward which society might actively work. The practice of variolation was a step in this direction. Paradoxically enough, in the United States it found an early advocate in Cotton Mather, who had played so notorious a role in the Salem witchcraft trials of 1692. Variolation, since it transferred real smallpox, though by means of dried matter from a light case, still was a risky procedure. The risk was eliminated by Edward Jenner's introduction of vaccination with cowpox in 1798. In this case at least it was now proven that man need not be helpless but could remove the very threat of epidemics.

Vaccination was introduced during the English industrial revolution, which created health problems of its own and, like wars, illustrated the dependence of health not only on nature but on social conditions as well. Enlightenment and, to some extent, the industrial revolution brought about a revaluation of the significance of disease. Epidemics and the appearance of new diseases had often been viewed as signs of the wrath of God punishing sinful mankind. The 1495 mandate of Emperor Maximilian, which mentioned syphilis as the punishment for man's blasphemous life, was as typical of this concept as were the sermons preached in New York in 1832, when Asiatic cholera made its appearance (Rosenberg, 1962). But medical disasters could be averted. Edwin Chadwick, a pupil of Jeremy Bentham and secretary of the Poor Law Commission, was responsible for the report on *The Sanitary Condition of the Labouring Population of Great Britain* (1842). The report urged the prevention of illness to save expense and pointed out the sanitary factors responsible for widespread sickness and early death. Moreover, industrialization had led to new hazards in the occupational life of the workers, and these should be prevented.

The attention of the student of public health was forcibly drawn to the social conditions of the times. It was against this background that Virchow, in 1848, claimed for the history of epidemics a place in the cultural history of mankind: "Epidemics resemble large warning tables in which the states-man of great style can read that a disturbance has appeared in the de-velopment of his people which even indifferent politics must no longer be allowed to overlook." This meant that social factors superimposed them-selves upon biological ones to the extent that certain diseases really were social phenomena (Ackerknecht, 1953). Such ideas, evoked in the revo-lutionary period of 1848, were largely dormant in the following decades, only to reappear in the twentieth century.

Few movements might be expected to show less affinity than industrial revolution and romanticism. Yet while pulmonary tuberculosis was pre-dominant among industrial workers, it also numbered among its victims John Keats, Novalis, Chopin, Schiller, and two of the great medical ex-plorers of tuberculosis, Gaspard Bayle and Laennec. If periods have dis-eases fitting their style (Sigerist, 1928), pulmonary consumption was a romantic disease just as syphilis had belonged to the late Renaissance, gout and melancholia or love-sickness to the baroque. But apart from the high incidence of tuberculosis during the time (1760–1850) covering both the industrial revolution and the romantic movement, disease, somatic as well as mental, received almost loving care by romantically inclined authors and opera librettists. This is not only true of tuberculosis, but also of chlorosis, the anemia of the young girl, and of morbid mentality ranging from mad-ness in the gothic novels to somnambulism and the bizarre characters of E. T. A. Hoffmann and Edgar Allan Poe. The neurotic character as hero made its debut with Goethe's Werther (Feise, 1926). The romantic move-ment thus reaccentuated the concept of disease as a contributor to cultural life.

Equally romantic, however, was the frequent glorification of healthy primitive life. "Beneath the rustic garb of the plowman and not beneath the gildings of the courtier will strength and vigor of the body be found," exclaimed Rousseau (*Discours . . .* , p. 104), and "Healthy as a Shepherd-boy," sang Wordsworth. Nature, the country, the wilderness were the anti-dotes to the cities, the foci of human degeneracy. Disease was caused by an infringement of the laws of nature, and these laws, so the phrenologists claimed, included mental life too, since the mind had its organs in areas of the cerebral cortex. An infringement of Nature's laws was an infringement of God's laws. Health was not only desirable; in Anglo-Saxon countries its preservation was propagated as something like a moral duty, a glorification of God. This combination of enlightened thought and romantic mood gave a religious overtone to the sanitary movement in its broadest sense.

The medical profession was strongly represented among the phrenologists and various kinds of sanitary reformers. Skepticism of tra-ditional curative methods led many physicians to believe that the healing power of nature was superior to any medication, especially since the homeopaths with their unbelievably weak solutions of drugs showed at least as good results as did regular practitioners. Some expected progress from

433

prevention rather than from therapy. The so-called therapeutic nihilists, e.g., Josef Dietl, thought that medicine should exert all its efforts towards becoming a science; until then, it would be best to abstain from all healing and merely help nature by providing hygienic conditions for the sick. There was, moreover, no uniform understanding of disease and its causes. The anatomico-clinical trend, which led to the recognition of new disease entities, seemed to favor an ontological concept of disease. But upon reflection, this appeared doubtful. It could be argued that while an ulcer of the stomach explained some of the concomitant symptoms, the presence of the ulcer itself remained unexplained. Anatomy did not provide an understanding of the causes of disease, which could only be obtained from physiology, an experimental science.

It was the stress on experiment that distinguished the new physiological concept of health and disease from the earlier one of John Brown and Broussais. Claude Bernard's *Introduction à l'étude de la médecine expérimentale* (1865; *Introduction to the Study of Experimental Medicine*, 1926) became the classical philosophical exposition of the new concept. "The words, life, death, health, disease, have no objective reality," wrote Claude Bernard. Life referred to a number of functions which could proceed normally or abnormally. The task of physiology was to find out how the body worked, and this could only be done experimentally. The supremacy of the physiological concept of disease had been recognized by Claude Bernard's teacher Magendie and by the German school of physiologists, pathologists, and clinicians, who, in the 1840's, were aligning German medicine with the progress made abroad. It was also recognized by Virchow, though his epoch-making contribution, *Die Cellularpathologie in ihrer Begründung auf physiologische und pathologische Gewebelehre* (1858), was in some respects a culmination of older trends.

After Morgagni had looked to the organs as the seat of diseases, after Bichat (1771–1802) had pointed to the tissues, Virchow declared the cells responsible for the body's health and disease. To Virchow, the body was a social organism dependent on the functioning of its elements, just as the state depended on the activities of its elements, the citizens. Virchow tried to explain changes visible in the cells physiologically, by recourse to the concepts of irritation (for active processes) and degeneration (for passive ones). But these physiological explanations were not the direct outcome of experimental work, and cellular pathology impressed the medical world as anatomical in character. Nor was it free from vitalistic features displeasing to a group of physiologists around Carl Ludwig, Du Bois-Reymond, Brücke, Helmholtz. They, too, had their own revolutionary program, which Du Bois-Reymond proclaimed in 1848: eventually physiology would be dissolved into biophysics and biochemistry, with analytical mechanics as the ideal form of all science. This was radical reductionism in its classical form.

The physiological concept of disease, whether reductionist or not, did not well agree with ontological systems. There was no reason why nature should be bound to rigid types. Since every individual differed from another, and since life could be subjected to an infinite variety of changed conditions, every sick person really represented his own disease. Claude Bernard did not overlook this. Ordinary causes, such as cold, hunger, thirst, fatigue, and mental suffering, were modified by idiosyncrasy, which was partly congenital and partly accidental. The pathological predispositions were nothing but special physiological conditions: a starved and a satiated organism reacted differently.

In disease, nature played the role of the experimenter; the observable changes could be viewed as experiments of nature and analyzed accordingly. Nosology, it was argued, was no more than a practical makeshift to be disregarded by the medical scientist. The existence of a clear demarcation between health and disease was altogether doubtful. Virchow, who had followed Henle in defining disease as life under changed circumstances, later came to realize the inadequacy of this definition. Circumstances might change drastically; a man could find himself in jail and yet remain healthy. Disease began at the moment when the regulatory equipment of the body no longer sufficed to remove the disturbances. "Not life under abnormal conditions, not the disturbance as such, engenders a disease, rather disease begins with the insufficiency of the regulatory apparatuses" (Virchow [1869], p. 93).

In this respect, Virchow and Claude Bernard were not very far apart. The latter placed increasing emphasis upon the internal milieu, i.e., blood and tissue fluids, which provided a steady environment for the cells composing the body and made it independent of the vagaries of the external environment. The constancy of the internal milieu was largely maintained through the regulatory functions of the nervous system. Later (1928) Walter Cannon introduced the term "homeostasis" to designate the condition of actively sustained equilibrium prevailing in the organism. By then, the significance of endocrine glands in the regulatory mechanisms of the body had been recognized.

VI

Both Claude Bernard and Virchow had expressed their respective ideas before Robert Koch's discovery of the tubercle bacillus in 1882 won the decisive victory for the germ theory of disease. Many reasons militated against easy acceptance, one of these being the clash with the anti-ontological tendencies of many medical scientists. Louis Pasteur, Koch, and their followers had demonstrated that specific microorganisms were responsible for specific diseases. Diseases could even be defined bacteriologically. Thus the argument about the relationship of pulmonary consumption and the disease in which tubercles appeared was now solved: tuberculosis was a disease characterized by the presence of the tubercle bacillus,

435

just as diphtheria was "caused" by the diphtheria bacillus; the formation of a membrane which originally had given its name to the disease was no more than an anatomical symptom.

Although bacteriology concerned infectious diseases only, its influence on the general concept of disease was great. Presumably, diseases could be bound to definite causes; hence the knowledge of the cause was needed to elevate a clinical entity or a syndrome to the rank of a disease. Moreover, an infection had a beginning and it ended after the annihilation of the invading microbe. Between these two points in time the person in question was sick; before and afterwards he was healthy; consequently, health was absence of disease. What really mattered was the invasion by the microbe, hence the study of the microbes and of the circumstances of their transmission appeared of primary importance. The consideration of social and nonscientific environmental factors, which were so important to the older sanitarians, receded into the background (Galdston, 1940). Bacteriology and the science of immunology, which developed in its wake, had their home in the laboratory, where experiments were performed on animals, sera obtained from them, and vaccines produced out of attenuated or dead cultures of bacteria and out of sera obtained from animals. To the die-hard sanitarian this was the negation of the holy campaign against filth; the new science did not lead to real health, which was to be freedom from suffering for man and beast alike (Stevenson, 1955).

Actually, of course, bacteriology was far from proving so simple in its concepts of health and disease as at first appeared. The microorganism was not just a demon which possessed man once it had entered. It remained true that during epidemics some people became ill, others did not. Cases became known of persons harboring pathogenic microorganisms without themselves falling ill. Obviously then, the microorganism was not the sole cause; generally speaking, bacteria were just one form of external cause of disease. Traditionally, antecedent, predisposing causes of disease were distinguished from proximate causes, which, under the name of *aitiai prokatarktikai,* the Greeks had identified with external causes. Julius Cohnheim, an early sponsor of Robert Koch, declared in his famous lectures on general pathology (1877) "that the causes of disease are not and cannot be anything else but conditions of life or, expressed differently, they are *outside the organism* itself" (p. 8). In the general field of pathology, this paralleled what Pasteur and other early bacteriologists claimed for infectious diseases. At the same time, Cohnheim's argument was a logical extension of the view of disease as life under changed circumstances. The body's regulatory mechanisms enabled it to function normally, i.e., as observed in the majority of people. Disease was a deviation from the normal process of life caused by a reciprocal action between external conditions and the internal regulatory abilities of the organism. It seemed logical to argue that "the normal process of life" could be "disturbed" only by an overpowering change in external conditions.

Cohnheim, like many others before and after him, believed that the concept of health and disease could be derived from a statistical definition of what was "normal." But statistical deviations only separate the frequent from the rare. If disease was to be defined as deviation from the regular, i.e., the healthy process of life, then deviation must imply a more than statistical evaluation.

Cohnheim and many physicians, then and now, unconsciously adhered to the old biological idea of "normal" as successfully self-preserving and self-propagating, and of "abnormal" or morbid as an impediment of, or danger to, these potentialities. Thus Virchow, in 1885, could even go so far as to say that disease was "life under dangerous conditions" (p. 221). From the reductionist point of view such a definition was hardly tenable, for what does "dangerous" mean in physical and chemical terms? Indeed, Ricker (1951), a German pathologist of the twentieth century, denied that health and disease were truly scientific concepts. They belonged to the realms of applied sciences, "health and its preservation to that of theoretical *hygiene,* disease to that of medicine as the doctrine of the healing of diseases."

VII

Modern concepts of disease are the result of a linking of scientific thought, practical achievements, and social factors. Bacteriology developed at a time when Western countries were entering a new phase of the industrial revolution, marked by the association of technology and science. Antiseptic surgery offered an immediate practical application of the germ theory. From the mid-seventies an increasing number of diseases were made accessible to surgical treatment; more important perhaps, surgical treatment could increasingly count on a successful outcome. Here was one branch of medicine where medical help promised results rather than mere hope. Health began to take on the nature of a purchasable good, but at the same time, the purchase of health began to become more costly. Major surgical operations now were more easily performed in the hospital than at home, and the replacement of antiseptic surgery by aseptic methods reinforced this trend. The pattern that surgery established by utilizing scientific methods was followed by internal medicine, which also relied more and more on the laboratory and on hospital facilities. Application of the principles of bacteriological sterilization led to obvious results in decreasing infant mortality. Bacteriology and immunology offered scientific tools for the sanitation of disease-ridden districts and the prevention of many infectious diseases. DDT proved a successful contact poison against the insect vectors of pathogenic microbes. The sulfonamides (1935) and, by the end of World War II, the antibiotics, presented "miracle drugs" in the treatment of infectious diseases.

Helped by these scientific achievements, the disease picture since the middle of the twentieth century differs from that of around 1900. The infectious diseases have yielded their place in the table of mortality to degenerative diseases, to tumors, and to accidents, and life expectancy

437

(particularly at birth) in Western nations has continued to rise. The more possible it has become to avoid diseases, or to be cured of them and to enjoy health, the more health appears as a desirable good to which everybody has a "right." Such a right did not extend to other purchasable goods, but the special status that Christianity once granted to the sick prepared the way for this special claim. Social developments during the nineteenth century moved the matter from the realm of religion and philanthropy to that of politics. Compulsory sickness insurance was introduced in Germany in 1883 as a strategic measure in Bismarck's fight against the social democrats. In the twentieth century, other countries followed. In the United States, voluntary insurance and medicare and medicaid programs all serve the idea of making medical care available to an increasing number of people. Western achievements look no less desirable elsewhere, including the so-called underdeveloped countries. Even in the League of Nations the health activities continued after the decay of the political body. Its UN successor, the World Health Organization, has accepted a program geared to the definition of health as "a state of complete physical, mental, and social well-being and not merely the absence of disease or infirmity."

The history of the ideas of health and disease begins with the crystallization of these ideas out of human suffering. Of the stages through which these ideas have gone, some belong to the past, others have merely seen a metamorphosis. Disease as a physiological process and disease as an entity are recurrent themes which have been likened to the struggle between nominalism and realism. Disease has been seen as nothing but a form of misery, and health as part of man's salvation. But there are also those, like Thomas Mann (*The Magic Mountain*), who see a positive value in disease as the price at which a higher form of health must be bought. The prevailing tendency at the present moment seems to merge disease once more with much that formerly was considered distinct from it and to take so broad a view of health as to make it all but indistinguishable from happiness.

The history of the ideas of health and disease cannot decide these issues; it can only present them. In doing so it can, however, point out that health and disease have not shown themselves to be immutable objects of natural history. Health and disease are medical concepts in the broadest sense. This means that man's life in its inseparable union of body and mind is seen under the aspects of possible preservation and cure. Thus they are distinguished from purely scientific concepts on the one hand and from purely social ones on the other.

BIBLIOGRAPHY

The literature on the history of the concept of disease is very great, and the items listed below are but a very small selection. The books of Berghoff, Riese, Sigerist, Edelstein (for Greco-Roman antiquity) deserve particular attention.

Erwin H. Ackerknecht, *Rudolf Virchow: Doctor, Statesman, Anthropologist* (Madison, 1953), p. 127; *idem, A Short History of Medicine* (New York, 1955). *Atharva-Veda*

Samhitā, trans. William Dwight Whitney, rev. ed. Charles Rockwell Lanman, Harvard Oriental Series, Vols. VII, VIII (Cambridge, 1905), VII, 361. John Bellers, *An Essay Towards the Improvement of Physick. In Twelve Proposals. By which the Lives of many Thousands of the Rich, as well as of the Poor, may be Saved Yearly* (London, 1714), p. 3. Emanuel Berghoff, *Entwicklungsgeschichte des Krankheitsbegriffes*, 2nd ed. (Vienna, 1947). Claude Bernard, *An Introduction to the Study of Experimental Medicine*, trans. Henry Copley Greene (New York, 1927), p. 67. Robert Boyle, "A Free Inquiry into the Vulgar Notion of Nature," *The Philosophical Works*, 3 vols. abridged, ed. Peter Shaw (London, 1725), II, 106–49, esp. 143. *The Caraka Samhitā* (Jamnager, India, 1949), II, 4, 13. Julius Cohnheim, *Vorlesungen über allgemeine Pathologie* (Berlin, 1877), I, 8, 12. Erich Ebstein, "Die Entwicklung der klinischen Thermometrie," *Ergebnisse der inneren Medizin und Kinderheilkunde*, 33 (1928), 407–505, esp. 462, 482. Ludwig Edelstein, *Ancient Medicine: Selected Essays*, ed. Owsei Temkin and C. Lilian Temkin (Baltimore, 1967). *The Edwin Smith Surgical Papyrus*, with translation and commentary by James Henry Breasted, 2 vols. (Chicago, 1930). Ernst Feise, "Goethes Werther als nervöser Charakter" (1926), reprinted in *Xenion: Themes, Forms, and Ideas in German Literature* (Baltimore, 1950), pp. 1–65. Iago Galdston, "Humanism and Public Health," *Bulletin of the History of Medicine*, 8 (1940), 1032–39. Hermann Grapow, *Kranker, Krankheiten und Arzt. Grundriss der Medizin der alten Ägypter*, III (Berlin, 1956). Gerald J. Gruman, *A History of Ideas About the Prolongation of Life*, Transactions of the American Philosophical Society, 56, 9, new series (Philadelphia, 1966). Raymond Klibansky, Fritz Saxl, and Erwin Panofsky, *Saturn and Melancholy* (London, 1964). *The Dhammapada*, translated from the Pali by P. Lal (New York, 1967). René Labat, *Traité akkadien de diagnostics et pronostics médicaux* (Paris and Leiden, 1951), pp. 157, xxiii. Claudius Mayer, "Metaphysical Trends in Modern Pathology," *Bulletin of the History of Medicine*, 26 (1952), 71–81. A. Leo Oppenheim, "Mesopotamian Medicine," *Bulletin of the History of Medicine*, 36 (1962), 97–108. Walter Pagel and Marianne Winder, "Harvey and the 'Modern' Concept of Disease," *Bulletin of the History of Medicine*, 42 (1968), 496–509; this article contains references to Dr. Pagel's important works on Paracelsus and van Helmont. Gustav Ricker, *Wissenschaftstheoretische Aufsätze für Ärzte*, 2nd ed. (Stuttgart, 1951), p. 48. Walther Riese, *The Conception of Disease, its History, its Versions and its Nature* (New York, 1953). George Rosen, *A History of Public Health* (New York, 1958). Charles E. Rosenberg, *The Cholera Years* (Chicago, 1962). Jean Jacques Rousseau, *Discours sur les sciences et les arts*, ed. George R. Havens (New York, 1946), p. 104. Henry E. Sigerist, *Civilization and Disease* (Ithaca, N.Y., 1943); *idem, A History of Medicine*, 2 vols. (New York, 1951–61); *idem*, "Kultur und Krankheit," *Kyklos*, 1 (1928), 60–63; *idem, On the Sociology of Medicine*, ed. Milton I. Roemer (New York, 1960). Bruno Snell, *The Discovery of the Mind*, trans. T. G. Rosenmeyer (Cambridge, Mass., 1953), p. 162. Robert O. Steuer, "Whdw, Aetiological Principle of Pyaemia in Ancient Egyptian Medicine," *Supplements to the Bulletin of the History of Medicine*, no. 10 (Baltimore, 1948). Lloyd G. Stevenson, "Science Down the Drain," *Bulletin of the History of Medicine*, 29 (1955), 1–26. Edward A. Suchman, *Sociology and the Field of Public Health* (New York, 1963). M. W. Susser and W. Watson, *Sociology in Medicine* (London, 1962). Thomas Sydenham, *Opera omnia*, ed. G. A. Greenhill, Sydenham Society (London, 1844), pp. 30, 16; *idem, The Works*, trans. R. G. Latham, 2 vols. (London, 1848), I, 19. Owsei Temkin, "The Scientific Approach to Disease: Specific Entity and Individual Sickness," *Scientific Change*, ed. A. C. Crombie (New York, 1963), pp. 629–47 [Essay 30]. Rudolf Virchow, in *Medicinische Reform*, No. 8 (25 August 1848),

439

reprinted in *Gesammelte Abhandlungen aus dem Gebiete der öffentlichen Medicin und der Seuchenlehre* (Berlin, 1879), I, 22. Rudolf Virchow, "Über Akklimatisation," (1885) and "Über die heutige Stellung der Pathologie," (1869), in Karl Sudhoff, *Rudolf Virchow und die deutschen Naturforscherversammlungen* (Leipzig, 1922), pp. 221, 93. Henry R. Zimmer, *Hindu Medicine* (Baltimore, 1948), pp. 33 f.

30

The Scientific Approach
to Disease: Specific Entity
and Individual Sickness*

THIS PAPER should perhaps be described as the thoughts of an historian of medicine on a subject that is not, in itself, historical. We are not dealing here with the historical development of the concept, or of the typology, of disease, for which we can refer to a series of competent publications.[1] Nor shall we try to evaluate the interplay of external and internal factors, since this has been done by Mr. Shryock[2] whose comments appear below. Rather we shall discuss some historical illustrations of the role which the notions of specific entity and individual sickness have played in the scientific approach to disease.

The basic situation involved is a perennial one. When a man is ill, that is when he feels dis-ease, he has experiences which are partly his own, partly open to others. This is his individual sickness which in exactly this particular form with all its details will never repeat itself in others or even in himself. But the sick man, his family, and neighbours, the physician (if there is one), all will try to understand what is happening to him. When Job was smitten by Satan he complained:

... wearisome nights are appointed to me. When I lie down, I say, When shall I arise, and the night be gone? and I am full of tossings to and from unto the dawning of the day. My flesh is clothed with worms and clods of dust; my skin is broken, and become loathsome. ... When I say, My bed shall comfort me, my couch shall ease my complaint; Then thou scarest me with dreams, and terrifiest me through visions: So that my soul chooseth strangling and death rather than my life. I would not live alway: let me alone; for my days are vanity.[3]

*From *Scientific Change: Historical Studies in the Intellectual, Social and Technical Conditions for Scientific Discovery and Technical Invention from Antiquity to the Present,* edited by A. C. Crombie, New York: Basic Books, 1963, pp. 629–47.

[1]Of the very large literature dealing with, or related to, this subject, I name here Emanuel Berghoff, *Entwicklungsgeschichte des Krankheitsbegriffes* (2nd ed., Vienna, 1947); Friedrich Curtius, *Individuum und Krankheit, Grundzüge einer Individualpathologie* (Berlin, 1959); Lester S. King, "What is Disease?", *Philosophy of Science,* XXI (1954) 193–203; Richard Koch, *Die ärztliche Diagnose* (Wiesbaden, 1917); L. J. Rather, "Towards a Philosophical Study of the Idea of Disease", *The Historical Development of Physiological Thought,* ed. Chandler McC. Brooks and Paul F. Cranefield (New York, 1959) 351–73; Walther Riese, *The Conception of Disease, its History, its Versions and its Nature* (New York, 1953). A few additional items will be cited below, with my apologies to the very numerous authors whose publications I am unable to mention.

[2]Richard H. Shryock, "The interplay of social and internal factors in the history of modern medicine", *The Scientific Monthly,* LXXVI (1953) 221–30. [My paper was followed by commentaries by Sir George Pickering and Richard H. Shryock.]

[3]Job, vii, 3–5 and 13–16.

This is part of the way in which Job, the sick man, tries to express what he feels, sees, and thinks when being diseased. The narrator of the book puts it more briefly: "Satan . . . smote Job with sore boils from the sole of his foot unto his crown."[4] This is the diagnosis of a disease: generalized sore boils caused by Satan.

Speaking of 'sickness', or 'illness', or 'disease', we have introduced a conceptual denominator uniting many such individual events. The individual may not think of himself as being ill or dis-eased. By thus labelling him, his friends, physician, or society, have classified his experience. From here on it becomes possible to approach the matter scientifically. But the introduction of the label has also determined the reply. The person's experience has become the sickness of X. Use of the term disease raises the question of the nature of disease. Here we may avail ourselves of the observation of Lord Cohen of Birkenhead that two main ideas have been dominant: disease as an entity that befalls a healthy person, and "disease as a deviation from the normal," where a number of factors have influenced a man so as to make him suffer. To this observation Lord Cohen adds:

> Many terms are used to cover these two concepts—e.g., *ontological*—indicating the independent self-sufficiency of diseases running a regular course and with a natural history of their own, as opposed to the *biographical* or *historical* which records the history of the patient. Other names arise from the founders of the schools of thought which appear to have given these concepts birth—e.g., *Platonic* and *Hippocratic;* from the philosophies from which they are primarily derived—the contrasting *realist* and *nominalist*, *rationalist* and *empirical*, *conventional* and *naturalistic* schools. The names are of little importance. The two notions varying a little in content and occasionally overlapping have persisted, the dominance of the one or the other at different epochs reflecting either the philosophy of the time or the influence and teaching of outstanding personalities.[5]

Without inquiring into the historical emergence of these two ideas which, for brevity's sake, we shall here refer to as the 'ontological' and the 'physiológical', I shall make a few comments on their interplay, and this will also lead us to other aspects.

II

Ontologists find themselves hard pressed when asked what exactly they mean by the existence of specific diseases. In the case of 'demoniac possession' the answer is reasonably clear. The demon which has entered a person struggles with his personality: it speaks out of the mouth of the possessed; it makes him commit unusual acts, it inflicts pain which causes the possessed to cry or to wrestle with the demon.[6] Ontologists have, therefore, been

[4]*Ibid.* ii, 7.

[5]Henry Cohen, "The evolution of the concept of disease," in *Concepts of Medicine*, ed. Brandon Lush (Oxford, 1960) 160.

[6]T. K. Oesterreich, *Possession, Demoniacal and Other* (London, 1930).

suspected of clinging to a demoniac aetiology of disease, even if the demon was replaced by a bacterium. Indeed there are analogies between the demonistic and bacteriological interpretation, at least where bacteriology appears in the crude assumption of a specific micro-organism as *the* cause of the specific disease. In both cases the entrance of a certain living being is made responsible for the disease, and the expulsion or killing of this being is considered the essential part of therapy. In both cases there is a clear-cut difference between health and disease.

But even the extreme bacteriologist of the nineteenth century had to deviate from this ideal of medical ontology. The bacterium might be made responsible for all the symptoms of the disease, yet it could cause the symptoms only by damaging parts or organs of the body or otherwise interfering with their normal functions. The disease was represented by the injured organism which the bacterium had poisoned. With the elimination of crude and one-sided modes of thinking, the bacteriologist had to visualize the relationship between parasite and host as an interaction, and it was this interaction which manifested itself as the disease.

In the history of medical ontology, specific aetiology is not a constitutive element. The ancient Empiricists, a sect founded in the third century B.C., did not believe that nature could be understood, and they rejected aetiological research beyond such evident causes as hunger and cold. They concentrated on "pathognomonic syndromes" as Galen tells us.[7] A Greek author of the sixth century indicates that the Empiricists thought of diseases as species. "Of symptoms," he writes,

some constitute species of the diseases and definitely appear together with them. The Empiricists call them 'pathognomonic' as characterizing the nature of the species (*idea*) of the diseases: for instance, cough, fever, dyspnea, and stabbing pain in pleurisy. Other symptoms, foreign [to the idea of the disease] appear later. . . .[8]

Since the scepticism of the Empiricists regarding the comprehensibility of nature reflects the scepticism of the Academy, as Edelstein has shown,[9] their belief in species of disease as Platonic ideas would not be improbable.

Sydenham, the arch-ontologist of modern times, also disparaged the search for the remote causes of diseases. He claimed that "Nature, in the production of disease, is uniform and consistent; so much so, that for the same disease in different persons the symptoms are for the most part the same. . . ."[10] On the other hand,

---

[7]The passages are conveniently available in Karl Deichgräber, *Die griechische Empirikerschule* (Berlin, 1930), see Index *s.v. syndrome*.

[8]Stephanus, "Commentarii in priorem Galeni librum therapeuticum ad Glauconem", *Apollonii Citiensis, Stephani, Palladii, Theophili, Meletii, Damascii, Ioannis, aliorum scholia in Hippocratem et Galenum*, ed. F. R. Dietz (Regimontii Prussorum, 1834) I, 233–344 (p. 267).

[9]Ludwig Edelstein "Empirie und Skepsis in der griechischen Empirikerschule", *Quellen und Studien zur Geschichte der Naturwissenschaften und der Medizin*, III, 4 (1933) 45–53.

[10]*The Works of Thomas Sydenham, M. D.*, trans. R. G. Latham (London, 1848) I, 18.

a disease, however much its cause may be adverse to the human body, is nothing more than an effort of Nature, who strives with might and main to restore the health of the patient by the elimination of the morbific matter.[11]

Put together, this amounts to the definition of diseases as uniform patterns of the organism's attempt to restore its health. The "concentration of symptoms"[12] is nature's method for the elimination of the peccant matter. This is not very far removed from a very recent statement that "physicians now consider most diseases to be distinct from one another insofar as they represent patterned responses or adaptations to noxious forces in the environment."[13]

The difficulty inherent in the ontological idea of the separate existence of diseases is matched by the difficulty of making the diseases or patterned responses conform to the variety of individual sickness. Sub-divisions that made the distinction between disease and symptom illusory had to be assigned in the nosological schemes of Boissier de Sauvages, Cullen, and Pinel. In the first half of the nineteenth century, pathological anatomy helped to weed out a number of diseases and to secure the position of others. But many contemporary investigators recognized that the anatomical changes, though they might account for a number of clinical symptoms, were products of the disease rather than the disease itself.[14] This led to a discussion of the nature of the disease behind anatomical and clinical symptoms. In this discussion ontologists fared badly until bacteriologists were believed to have discovered the source of disease outside the body and geneticists inside it.

The hope that bacteriology would allow a reliable classification on the basis of specific causes, at least in the realm of infectious diseases, also proved doubtful. If this principle were pushed to the logical extreme, there should be as many specific diseases as there are pathogenic organisms, or even strains.

The weakness of a bacteriological definition of specific diseases is shared by the definitions based on other aetiological classifications. There should be as many specific deficiency diseases as there are substances whose absence can affect the body adversely. Finally, there should also be as many hereditary diseases as there are different genes representing abnormal submolecular chemical structures. A person with haemoglobin-C genes, we are informed, will suffer from so-called homozygous haemoglobin-C disease. If he has one haemoglobin-C gene only, while the other is a haemoglobin-S gene (sickle-cell-anemia gene) "he suffers from a disease that has been given the name haemoglobin-C: sickle-cell anemia."[15] Since

---

[11]*Ibid.* p. 29.

[12]*Ibid.*

[13]Stewart Wolf, "Disease as a way of life: neural integration in systemic pathology," *Perspectives in Biology and Medicine,* IV (1961) 288–305 (p. 288).

[14]Knud Faber, *Nosography* (2nd ed., New York, 1930) 53.

[15]Linus Pauling in *Disease and the Advancement of Basic Science,* ed. Henry K. Beecher (Cambridge, Mass., 1960) 3.

about twenty kinds of abnormal human haemoglobin are said to exist, the number of combinations and possible 'specific diseases' in this one province seems very large. In short, if based on causative principles such as micro-organisms, absence of nutritive substances, or inherited genes, danger arises lest specific diseases be postulated which have no clinical reality, or, vice versa, that clinically important entities like appendicitis have no logical place in the nosological scheme.

III

The weaknesses of ontology are avoided by the physiological idea of disease. This has been cultivated by Hippocrates and his scientific (in contrast to the purely empirical) successors from Galen to our own times. When we turn to the Hippocratic *Epidemics*, it is true, disease entities are accepted as a matter of course and referred to by names, such as "phthisis," which had probably been in common popular usage. Hippocrates, or whoever the physicians were whom this name connotes, is outstanding for having seen disease as a process in time, not as a mere stationary picture.[16] The book *On the Sacred Disease,* that is epilepsy, is probably the earliest monograph on a disease, describing its pathogenesis, symptoms, pathological physiology, and prognosis. Diseases have their nature; but they are seen as rooted in the general nature of man. There is neither a studious exclusion of disease entities nor a one-sided concentration on them. In judging diseases we are told to take into account "the peculiar nature of each individual".[17] Most of the patient's activities, mental and physical, are considered, from thoughts and dreams to eructation and flatulence. The list of things to be observed included diseases and symptoms as well as functions and discharges such as respiration and urine. This allows the gathering of a very large number of data in each case. Since the totality of these data will vary from patient to patient, each will have a description of symptoms fitting him only.

But the ancient followers of Hippocrates did not believe that Hippocrates had given them a science of the individual. Galen, the last of the ancient Hippocratics, and Galen's Byzantine successors ended on a sceptical note.[18] They thought Hippocrates right in demanding that the nature of the disease as well as of the individual be studied. The nature of disease was to be found in man's temperament, the structure of his parts, his physiological and his psychological dynamism. Thus the nature of disease was grounded in the nature of man. All men have humours and divers parts and organs; they all digest and possess sensation and mobility. Con-

[16]Owsei Temkin, "Greek Medicine as science and art," *Isis,* XLIV (1953) 213–25 (p. 223). [Essay 8, p. 149 f.].
[17]Hippocrates, "Epidemics," I, 10, *The Genuine Works of Hippocrates,* trans. Francis Adams (London, 1849) I, 367.
[18]For the following see Galen, *Ad Glauconem de medendi methodo* I, 1, *Opera,* ed. C. G. Kühn (Leipzig, 1821 ff.) XI, 1 ff., and the commentary on this work by Stephanus, *op. cit.*

sequently, they also have diseases in common. But no two men will be completely alike. The individual differences are "ineffable and cannot be subjected to concepts."[19] Therefore, it was concluded, there is no science of the individual, and medicine suffers from a fundamental contradiction: its practice deals with the individual while its theory grasps universals only.[20]

Ancient medicine had a particular reason for this scepticism.[21] The physician possessed an approximate picture of the behaviour and appearance of healthy individuals.[22] He could compare his patient to this picture of the normal and decide what was "according to nature" (*kata physin*) and what "against nature" (*para physin*). But just because of the physician's strongly individualizing inclination, such a comparison was considered insufficient. For instance, his patient's face might indicate a morbid discolouration. If the patient's colour always had been like this, the finding was meaningless, while in a new patient, the physician had nothing to refer to. It was advisable that the doctor be his patient's friend and know him intimately.[23] Such intimate knowledge was possible in private practice only, and, according to Celsus, where it was impossible, medicine of an inferior kind was practised because it relied on the features common to many diseases:

> For in like manner those who treat cattle and horses, since it is impossible to learn from dumb animals particulars of their complaints, depend only upon common characteristics; so also do foreigners, as they are ignorant of reasoning subtleties, look rather to common characteristics of disease. Again, those who take charge of large hospitals, because they cannot pay full attention to individuals, resort to these common characteristics.[24]

Celsus made this remark in discussing the ancient sect of the Methodists who judged disease according to whether it exhibited a *status strictus, laxus,* or *mixtus.* Thessalus, a Methodist of the time of Nero, boasted of teaching medicine to anybody within six months.[25] Methodism was popular in the Roman Empire, and it would be of interest to find out whether it had its social roots among military surgeons and in the latifundia, since such hospitals (*valetudinaria*) as existed in Antiquity were for soldiers and slaves.

Few things mark the chasm between ancient and modern medicine as impressively as does the different character of the hospitals. The ancient hospital, just because it housed many patients, was looked down upon as neglecting individual sickness. The modern hospital, just because it houses

[19]Stephanus, *op. cit.* p. 235.

[20]*Ibid.*

[21]The nature of the medical scepticism of the Hippocratic authors as rooted in their individualistic approach has been brought out by Edelstein, *op. cit.*

[22]Celsus, *De medicina,* I, 2, 4.

[23]*Ibid.*, Prooem., 73.

[24]Ibid., 65; Celsus, *De medicina,* with an English translation by W. G. Spencer (London, 1935 ff.) I, 35.

[25]Galen, *De sectis ad eos qui introducentur,* VI, refers to Methodists in general, but seems to have Thessalus in mind.

many patients, has developed into an institution where individual sickness can be described with some degree of precision.

In the hospitals of the nineteenth century it became possible to observe many cases of the same disease, clinically as well as anatomically, and thus to strengthen the diagnosis of 'diseases'. At the same time, it became possible to establish standards of what was normal, and to elaborate tests which expressed numerical agreement with, or deviation from the norm. The norm here was a value found in a smaller or greater number of healthy persons. Without this norm, measurements were of little avail. The ever lengthening chart of data accumulating in the course of medical examinations, from pulse rate and temperature curve, to X-ray pictures, chemical, physical, bacteriological and immunological tests, mirrors this development which has been traced admirably by Knud Faber for the nineteenth and early twentieth centuries. A modern physician has at his disposal infinitely more objective data concerning a particular patient than the Greek doctor could ever dream of. Ophthalmoscope, bronchoscope, etc. allow him a direct view of the conditions of many parts. Experimental medicine enables the physician to interpret his findings so as to translate the language of symptoms and tests into the language of physiological processes. Here then is a scientific approach to individual sickness.

Thus it might appear that modern medicine has succeeded where ancient medicine failed. This success is due to giving statistical attention to what is normal and abnormal. The Ancients did not evaluate statistically what was "according to nature" and "contrary" to it. Still, there is a significant parallel between their attempt to explain certain diseases as an imbalance of qualities or humours and our numerical occupation with the normal and abnormal. The parallel can be formulated in the question: what deviation constitutes sickness? We know that 'the normal individual' is a construct, not to be found in nature. Likewise, the Galenists realized that a complete balance of the four humours and their qualities represented an ideal temperament. We allow variations within the normal;[26] the Ancients conceived of temperaments where the predominance of one or the other humour characterized the still healthy organism. But where exactly was, and is, the line to be drawn where imbalance or variation becomes disease?

Galen defined health as a condition "in which we neither suffer pain nor are hindered in the functions of daily life."[27] In as far as this definition is concerned with impeded function, it leads to the equation of disease with *functio laesa*, popular among the academic physiologists of modern times. "The condition of the living body whereby the ability of exercising any one function is abolished, is called disease," writes Boerhaave in his *Institutions*, and he adds the following comment to the word disease: "we correctly define it as 'functio laesa'...."[28] In speaking of the functions, Boerhaave

---

[26]John A. Ryle, "The meaning of normal," *Concepts of Medicine, op. cit.* pp. 137–49.
[27]Galen, *De sanitate tuenda*, I, 5.
[28]Hermann Boerhaave, *Praelectiones academicae in proprias institutiones rei medicae*, ed. Albertus Haller (Turin, 1742 ff.) V, 4 and 10.

had in mind the traditional natural, vital, and psychic functions, all of which could be diminished to the point of disappearance.

But, if the ontologist was rightly challenged by the demand that disease must be understandable as a process of life, the physiologist was challenged to show cause why the endless variations of form and gradations of function should somewhere admit classification as healthy and diseased.[29] It is a truism to designate 'health' and 'disease' as medical categories. It is not easy to decide whether these categories themselves, though relating to biological phenomena, still belong in biology. Following in the footsteps of Broussais,[30] the young Virchow referred to disease as life under changed circumstances. But Virchow himself later admitted that a man in prison also lived under changed circumstances without therefore necessarily being ill.[31] The answer may depend on the biologist's philosophical orientation. If he excludes all teleology, he may, with Ricker, believe that health and disease are not scientific terms.[32] If he does not mind using teleological notions, he may find it pertinent to pay attention to those states where nature fails in two of its main aims, as Galen had them, assurance of the life of the individual and of the species.[33]

But disease does not necessarily threaten life. To supplement his teleological biology, Galen added nature's aim of assuring a "good life."[34] A blind man might be able to live and to have progeny, yet he would not live well. But there are no limits to the "good life." For man, the good life extends far into his mental and social well-being. This is best illustrated by Galen's reference to pain in his definition of health and in his explanation of the functions of daily life as our ability "to take part in government, to bathe, drink, and eat, and do the other things we want."[35] Participation in government and frequenting the bath were activities of the member of the ancient city state. In another civilization, different functions might be required for health, or, if absent, mark disease.

Examples for this are most easily adduced from the field of mental abnormalities. Theologians of the Renaissance persecuted witches as confederates of the devil, and the worldly authorities executed them because of their alleged danger to society. The defence of witches could claim that the devil was powerless to bring about the evil deeds ascribed to witches, themselves victims of the devil who caused their illusions. This argument

---

[29]This problem has been dealt with very lucidly by G. W. Pickering, "The concept of essential hypertension," *Concepts of Medicine, op. cit.* pp. 170–6.

[30]Erwin H. Ackerknecht, *Rudolf Virchow* (Madison, 1953) 50–1.

[31]Virchow, "Über die heutige Stellung der Pathologie," in Karl Sudhoff, *Rudolf Virchow und die Deutschen Naturforscherversammlungen* (Leipzig, 1922) 77–97 (p. 91); see also Paul Diepgen, "Die Universalität von Rudolf Virchows Lebenswerk," *Virchows Archiv.,* CCCXXII (1952) 221–32 (p. 228).

[32]Ricker distinguishes between medical and scientific thinking; cf. also Claudius F. Mayer, "Metaphysical trends in modern pathology," *Bulletin of the History of Medicine,* XXVI (1952) 70–81.

[33]Galen, *De usu partium,* VI, 7; ed. G. Helmreich (Leipzig, 1907) I, 318.

[34]*Ibid.:* τὸ καλῶς ζῆν.

[35]Galen, *De sanitate tuenda,* I, 5.

was a theological one,[36] which explains the accusation made against Weyer, the defender of witches, that he meddled in things which were none of his, the physician's, concern. Instead of being victims of Satan, witches could be declared to suffer from a natural disease, preferably hysteria. Similarly, convulsions, often taken as demonstrations of demoniac possession or of divine enthusiasm, were diagnosed as *grande hystérie* by the school of Charcot.[37]

In contrast, Charcot's own time tended to refuse recognition to disease where it existed. It is not so very long ago that people who felt ill, or who suspected illness, would consult a physician to be told after a thorough physical examination that there was nothing wrong with them, and that they could go home. Thomas Huxley who suffered from "the blue devils and funk" could not make out what it was and suggested "liver."[38] Disease in the second half of the nineteenth century meant somatic disease, if one disregarded the frank psychoses. This attitude reflected the prevailing materialistic philosophy which Huxley himself had helped to shape. It also reflected the conviction that there is a science of disease separable from medicine as the art of healing. Men of this persuasion might have much human sympathy for the sick, but they were not easily influenced in their scientific work by vague subjective complaints. A whole realm of disease was in danger of losing the right to existence because of the dissociation between the sick person's complaint and the physician's philosophical outlook.

Functio laesa is not a self-explanatory definition of disease in man. The ontologist avoids this difficulty by accepting entities which are set apart from health or 'normal' functioning. However he may define disease, it is something strange to man in his ordinary life: it enters or befalls him. In this respect, the ontologist's weakness is also his strength. There is a tendency in ontology to consider disease entities as persistent and to corroborate the specific nature of a disease by tracing its existence through the ages. Bretonneau said of diphtheria, "because during a long series of centuries it remained so constantly the same that in each of the epochs where it appeared it was recognized in the admirable description of Aretaeus,"[39] giving this among the arguments for diphtheria as a specific affection. Since, according to Charcot, *grande hystérie* was "a perfectly well characterized morbid entity," his school tried to prove its existence long before its scientific discovery.[40]

The ontological bias of the perennial existence of the specific diseases can express itself moreover in a reluctance to admit the appearance of new

[36]Gregory Zilboorg, *The Medical Man and the Witch During the Renaissance* (Baltimore, 1935) 117.
[37]Owsei Temkin, *The Falling Sickness* (Baltimore, 1945) 321.
[38]Leonard Huxley, *Life and Letters of Thomas Henry Huxley* (New York, 1901) II, 112–13.
[39]Pierre-Fidèle Bretonneau, *Traités de la dothinentérie et de la spécificité,* publiés, etc. par le Dr. Louis Dubreuil-Chambardel (Paris, 1922) 309.
[40]Cf. above, ftn. 37.

diseases or the existence of specific diseases during a short period of time. The plague of Thucydides has challenged diagnostic acumen and has been variously interpreted as plague, smallpox, typhus, measles. Without denying the possiblity of identifying it with some disease of our modern nosological catalogue, I still fail to see proof of the necessity. Similarly, the "sweating sickness" which appeared in epidemic waves, chiefly in England, between 1485 and 1551, is but reluctantly acknowledged as a disease unknown to modern nosology.

The ontologist thus avoids a difficulty which the radical physiologist must face. The difference in attitude between the two is expressed in the encounter between Michel Peter and Pasteur as told by René Dubos. Peter claimed that "Disease is in us, of us, by us", whereas

Pasteur emphasized that contagion and disease could be the expression of the living processes of foreign microbial parasites, introduced from the outside, descending from parents identical to themselves, and incapable of being generated *de novo*.[41]

Pasteur made it clear that contagious disease was the expression of a foreign life. But if disease has to be looked for in our own nature it has to be accounted for differently. If we attribute it to genes we still have recourse to ontology, as I indicated previously, an 'internal' ontological orientation in contrast to the external of the bacteriologist. It is probably neither possible nor advisable to renounce ontology completely. The wisdom of Hippocrates documents itself in accepting such popular disease entities as were known, rather than denouncing them. The danger which the physiologist faces, as well as the consequences which may ensue, are illustrated by Freud's work—if it is permissible to broaden the term physiology so as to admit his psychological method.

In the meaning of our context, Freud offered a physiological explanation of neuroses by explaining them as the result of a reaction between psychic urges and restriction imposed upon them. He believed himself to be dealing with psychological phenomena like the one symbolized as the Oedipus complex, necessarily engendered in all civilized human beings. This being the case, everybody was fundamentally neurotic, the intensity and particular turn of the neurosis depending on the experiences of the individual's life. Psycho-analysis thus succumbed to the danger of what the Greeks called *aeipatheia,* perpetual illness.

Psycho-analysis insisted upon a minute scrutiny of the patient's life in order to find, and to make conscious, those experiences with which the patient had been unable to cope successfully. This meant that the disease was not due to some accident. More than others, Freud and his followers leaned on the biographical approach, on the detailed case history of the patient. Finally, as the name indicates, psycho-analysis originated from Freud's therapeutic activity. Freud gained his insight into neuroses while treating patients. Since the contact between patient and psycho-analyst in-

[41]René J. Dubos, *Louis Pasteur, Free Lance of Science* (Boston, 1950) 246.

variably involved an emotional engagement (on the patient's side at least), the psycho-analysis had to affect the patient. Thereby Freud ran counter to one of the scientific ideals of his time: the study of an object without interfering with it.

Whatever the merits of psycho-analysis may be, I believe that it was consistent (though possibly wrong) in imputing neurosis to everybody, looking for the vicissitudes of man's neurosis in his biography, making the judgment of manifest disease dependent on the patient's inability to cope with the aims of society or of himself, and avoiding a gulf between the diagnostic and therapeutic activity of the physician who deals with individual sickness.

Consistency is not necessarily a virtue, but it has the advantage of laying bare what may otherwise pass unnoticed. I believe that Freud elucidated the part played by the case history and therapy in the comprehension of individual sickness.[42]

IV

Case histories form one of the glories of Hippocratic medicine; they mark the appearance of the form by which the physician tries to deal with an individual illness. The Hippocratic case histories are remarkable for what they contain, a passionless description of the symptoms and outcome of the case, and for what they largely lack, details as to the patient's diet and therapy.

In course of time, the case history changed, especially with the introduction of the new clinical teaching methods in Leyden. The diagnosis, usually meaning a disease entity, was incorporated, the treatment was registered, and, if available, a post mortem report was added in cases with fatal outcome. Detailed case histories emanated from the hospitals of the Old Vienna School of the eighteenth century. In the nineteenth century, a separation between the subjective history of the patient and the objective examination by the physician became noticeable. The objective signs of percussion and auscultation were the early core of the examination; temperature curves, and the results of the ever increasing tests and special examinations, followed. Thus the case history has come to incorporate all the data obtained through the scientific progress of medicine.[43]

As the member of a profession, the physician has used case histories to contribute to the spread or advance of medical knowledge. This, probably, was already the function of the Hippocratic case histories. All cases that are unusual because of the patient's illness, or its outcome, or the treatment employed, reveal new possibilities regarding human disease. The case his-

[42] In thus summarily dealing with Freud and psycho-analysis, I am conscious of some degree of historical and material oversimplification for the sake of brevity.

[43] On the history of the case history see: Pedro Lain Entralgo, *La historia clínica* (Madrid, 1950); Walther Riese, "The structure of the clinical history," *Bull. Hist. Med.* XVI (1944) 437–49; O. Temkin, "Studien zum 'Sinn'—Begriff in der Medizin," *Kyklos*, II (1929) 43–59.

tory therefore has played a great role in the history of medicine. As casuistic material in combination with the post mortem protocol, it led to the rise of pathological anatomy for reasons which become clearer when this development is compared with the rise of normal anatomy.

The study of anatomy as based on dissection did not derive from the opening of many bodies. Both Galen and Vesalius described the structure of *the* body (of animal or man). They were aware of variations which, it is true, could be established as such by repeated autopsies only. Yet it is fair to say that both expected an immediate insight into the body, as God or nature had willed it, that is into the norm. This insight was then cleared by discounting individual variations or morbid changes.[44]

Although some of the ancient physicians had the idea of a pathological anatomy, pathological anatomy, as we know it, began with the medieval *anatomia privata*. This was a dissection performed in an individual case to establish the cause of death, especially if foul play was suspected. It differed from the *anatomia publica* where the fabric of man's body was demonstrated to a large audience. Benivieni's little book of 1507 from which we conventionally date the literary beginning of pathological anatomy, was named significantly: "On Some Hidden and Singular (*mirandis*) Causes of Diseases and Cures," the causes being revealed by the autopsy. Bonet's *Sepulchretum* of 1679 was a huge collection of casuistic material culled from the literature. Morgagni's *De sedibus et causis morborum* was to be a revised edition of Bonet's *Sepulchretum,* and the work as it finally emerged in 1761 still shows its descent. Its backbone is the hundreds of case histories elucidated by post mortem findings. It differs from its predecessors by having overcome the limitation of the singular and remarkable. It systematically applies the method to diseases in all parts of the body, *a capite ad calcem,* and tries to draw generally valid inferences. Thereby it marked the beginning of something new. After Morgagni, it became more convenient to envisage the pathological anatomy of disease processes, a trend that culminated in Rokitansky's *Manual* of the 1840's. Here too a huge casuistic material was utilized, yet it was integrated into a work which dealt with disease entities.[45]

It is not immediately clear why the anatomical interpretation of disease had to follow the road from case histories to disease entities. The idea of an anatomical substratum of disease was not unheard of. Pneumonia and pleurisy, as their names indicate, were differentiated by ancient authors according to the organs involved.[46] Dysentery was described by Aretaeus as due to ulcers of the intestine.[47] Medieval textbooks named quite a number of diseases. Conceivably, one might have started out by describing the anatomy of disease after disease, following the example of normal anatomy. One or a very few cases should have sufficed to give an insight

[44]William L. Straus, jr. and O. Temkin, "Vesalius and the problem of variability," *Bull. Hist. Med.* XIV (1943) 609–33.

[45]Strictly speaking it deals with the pathological anatomy of tissues and organs.

[46]Cf. Galen, *Opera,* ed. Kühn, *op. cit.* XI, 77.

[47]Aretaeus, *The Extant Works,* ed. and trans. Francis Adams (London, 1856) 353.

into the particular disease; nor is it likely that such private anatomies would have met with external obstacles. The obstacles were of a different nature. It was assumed that diseases were sufficiently known, so that only the unusual was worth investigating. Moreover, the traditional disease entities were not sufficiently suited to such an anatomical analysis.

The role of the case history in a particular phase of medical development elucidates further the notion of the abnormal in medicine. Even if expressed in numerical values it retains the character of something that is not as nature or man would have it. To bring a person back to normal, therefore, means to bring him back to where he should be. But where should he be?

To this query the old formula of complete curative success gave a superb answer: *in integrum restitutus est,* he has been restored to his former condition. The formula leaves it undecided whether this connotes health or simply the state before the physician was called in. In either case the answer is a doubtful one; treatment may have made the patient 'a changed person' as the saying goes. The sickness which brought the patient to the doctor may even reveal a lack of previous health, and the cure of a neurotic patient may consist in not restoring him *in integrum.* Each patient's sickness is truly individual in the role it plays in his life; it has a meaning for him. But here where disease melts into the patient's whole life, science finds its limits. In bringing a patient back to health the physician will take as his frame of reference what is commonly considered as health. The patient is cured when he feels well, when his life is not in danger, and when he can safely do what healthy people generally do. This will often require far-reaching adaptations. If a person who was close to death undergoes a religious conversion, this in itself is outside the physician's concern. The physician traditionally is not supposed to judge his patient's morality or to influence his religion.[48] The case history is the form in which the physician links the science, which does not deal with the unique directly, and the patient, who requires attention as an individual. Replete with scientific data and possibly utilized to serve the advance of medical science, the case history documents the physician's art. It is the closest approach to an individual's sickness, yet it does not become the whole life story of a person while sick. Job fell ill and was restored to health and wealth. But the *Book of Job* is not a case history: the 'meaning' of Job's illness is not of medical concern.[49]

V

Nevertheless, the interdependence of treatment and of the idea of disease is a very real one. It is by no means true that treatment is always

---

[48]O. Temkin, "Medicine and the problem of moral responsibility," *Bull. Hist. Med.* XXIII (1949) 1–20 [Essay 3].

[49]For arguments against the metaphysical interpretation of sickness by the physician see Curtius, *op. cit.* and his "Hippokrates und die moderne Medizin," *Tägliche Praxis,* II (1961) 1–9.

adapted to the nature of the disease. Treatment can determine how disease should be considered. The rise of pathological anatomy at the turn of the eighteenth to the nineteenth century was stimulated by the growing influence of the surgeons and of their localistic point of view.[50] Ontologists have been inclined to favour the treatment of diseases and to look for possible specifics. Sydenham hoped for plants with specific actions on specific diseases, such as cinchona upon malaria.[51] While localized pathology was favoured by surgeons, specifics were favoured by the apothecaries who liked to sell drugs that promised cures of symptoms, syndromes, or diseases. By contrast, the physician of the physiological school opposed the routine use of standard treatments. At the end of the fifteenth century, Leoniceno warned doctors against trying to cure the French disease with the same medicine in all cases, in imitation of "a bad cobbler who tries to fit everybody with the same shoe."[52]

Similar notions are at the bottom of the maxim to treat the patient, not the disease. This is reinforced by the declaration that only sick individuals exist, that diseases are mere abstractions. Most physicians are likely to subscribe to this declaration, even if they find the abstractions useful. It is not altogether by chance that Hippocrates figures as the author of the case histories of the *Epidemics* and of the Hippocratic *Oath*. There is reason to doubt this authorship, especially that of the *Oath*.[53] But the fact remains that the *Oath* formulates classically the ethics of the doctor-patient relationship. Until not so very long ago, 'medicine' was the domain of the physician who treated patients, privately or in the hospital. The medical sciences too were cultivated by men nearly all of whom were engaged in medical practice. Somewhat over a hundred years ago, a change took place: medical scientists, chiefly professors at German universities, began to separate themselves from practical medical work and to devote themselves 'full time' to anatomy, physiology, or pathology. The change set in at about the same time as the abandonment of the traditional therapy. Therapeutic nihilism and autonomy of the full-time medical scientist are, in my opinion, but two aspects of the same movement.[54] Therapeutic nihilism was a passing phase, while the growth of the basic sciences was accelerated with the development of bacteriology, immunology, and experimental pharmacology, and the increasing alliance with industry. As a result, medicine ceased to be the exclusive domain of the physician who treated patients. The contributions of the chemist Pasteur were fundamental, as well as symbolic, for the things to come.

Pasteur invented an anti-rabies vaccine the effectiveness of which he tested in dogs. In the scientific part of this discovery the rabies virus and

[50]O. Temkin, "The role of surgery in the rise of modern medical thought," *Bull. Hist. Med.* XXV (1951) 248–59 [Essay 33].

[51]Sydenham, *op. cit.* I, 23.

[52]Karl Sudhoff, *The Earliest Printed Literature on Syphilis,* adapted by Charles Singer (Florence, 1925) 172.

[53]Ludwig Edelstein, *The Hippocratic Oath* (Baltimore, 1943).

[54]I have dealt with this matter in more detail in my Josiah Trent Lecture at Duke University, 1960, which now awaits publication.

the possiblity of counter-acting it were under consideration. But from the practical point of view it was the disease embodying a well-known course with fatal outcome that was to be combated. In the background there was Jenner's discovery of the prevention of smallpox by vaccination with cowpox. In contrast to Jenner, who was a physician, Pasteur was not qualified to vaccinate; the boy Joseph Meister, who had been bitten by a mad dog, was vaccinated by physicians associated with Pasteur. Although the actual treatment, preventive or therapeutic, may still be applied or supervised by the physician, there is behind him a growing organization of persons and institutions who are screened from individual patients, yet work towards the cure and prevention of disease. In the scientific part of their work, 'the disease' may play no role at all; their minds may be occupied with bacteriological, immunological, and chemical details. Yet the work is directed against diseases as the public health officer, rather than the practitioner, sees them. There are laws aimed at preventing smallpox, and Jenner discovered a means of preventing it. Thousands of children are vaccinated against a disease which, at the time, may not show a single sufferer in the country. In all this work and in campaigns to eradicate this or that disease, the picture of the disease as an entity devoid of individual features has a very real existence, though we must leave it to the metaphysician to determine the nature of this particular form of existence.

We began with a denunciation of ontology and end with its reassertion. In between we discussed the strength and weakness of the physiological approach and the case history in which the physician's art comes closest to individual sickness. We would like to draw the inference that in the scientific approach to disease the notions of both specific entity and individual sickness play their roles. The question: does disease exist or are there only sick persons? is an abstract one and, in that form, does not allow a meaningful answer. Disease is not simply either the one or the other. Rather it will be thought of as the circumstances require. The circumstances are represented by the patient, the physician, the public health man, the medical scientist, the pharmaceutical industry, society at large, and last but not least the disease itself. For our thinking about disease is not only influenced by internal and external factors, it is also determined by the disease situation in which we find ourselves. Sydenham, the ontologist, lived at the time of the great plague of London, and the plague, I understand, has little concern with individual variations. In contrast, the practitioner of our time, who has to deal with degenerative disorders and neuroses demanding much individual attention, may have little use for disease entities. He may be inclined to leave them to the laboratory or the public health man for prevention.[55] With the changing disease situation our thoughts about disease change too. As Hippocrates said, "The art consists in three things—the disease, the patient, and the physician."[56] To the historian's mind, the histories of all three are bound up in the history of the art itself.

[55]For concepts of disease in social medicine see Iago Galdston, *The Meaning of Social Medicine* (Cambridge, Mass., 1954) 73 and *passim*.
[56]Hippocrates, *Epidemics* I, Sect. 2, 5, in *Works, op. cit.* I, 360.

31

An Historical Analysis of the
Concept of Infection*

THE MOST RECENT edition of one of our standard medical dictionaries
defines "infection" as follows: "Invasion of the tissues of the body by
pathogenic organisms in such a way that injury followed by reactive
phenomena results."[1] This definition shows the earmarks of modern medical research. It is only since about 1800, the days of Bichat, that we have
become accustomed to speak of the tissues of the body. The words
"pathogenic organisms" remind us of the rise of bacteriology. Obviously, a
definition of infection like the above could hardly have been formulated
before the days of Pasteur, Koch, and Lister. And the qualification that the
presence of pathogenic organisms, though necessary, is not sufficient, that
injury followed by reactive phenomena must have resulted, points to an
even more recent date. In short, the above definition of infection seems to
be scientifically accurate, consisting, as it does, mainly of terms which bear a
well defined connotation verifiable by observation. I say *mainly*, because
here, as elsewhere in medicine, there remains an element of more doubtful
character. What exactly is an "injury," and what is an "invasion?" We shall
come back to these disturbing elements in the definition. For the moment
let us be content with the fact that the modern concept of infection is
reasonably clear and that it is couched in the language of modern science.

This being the case, we may be all the more permitted to wonder at the
incongruity between the definition and the term defined. The word "infection," as well as its counterparts in other languages, is much older than the
nineteenth century. I need hardly point out that infection is derived from
the Latin *infectio*. Now, one may easily say that there is nothing unusual in
an old term receiving a more precise explanation with the advance of
science. People talked about "fever" long before they knew how to measure

---

*From *Studies in Intellectual History* [by various authors]. Baltimore: The Johns Hopkins
University Press, 1953, pp. 123–47.

In partly different form and under different title, this article was originally presented as a
paper before the Sigma Xi Society, in Ithaca, N. Y., in 1952. Because of the great role of
infection in medicine, the article is, by necessity, incomplete as to historical details and literature quoted. The following works may be cited as supplementing some of its omissions: C. E.
A. Winslow, *The Conquest of Epidemic Disease*, Princeton University Press, 1943, Richard H.
Shryock, *The Development of Modern Medicine*, New York, Knopf, 1947; John E. Gordon, Evolution of an Epidemiology of Health, in *The Epidemiology of Health*, Iago Galdston, editor, New
York-Minneapolis, Health Education Council, 1953; also Vilmos Manninger, *Der Entwic-
kelungsgang der Antiseptik und Aseptik*, Breslau, 1904 (Abhandlungen zur Geschichte der Medicin, Heft XII).

[1]*The American Illustrated Medical Dictionary*. Twenty-second edition, Philadelphia, W. B.
Saunders Co., 1951, p. 738.

the temperature of the body, and of "pneumonia" before any post mortem dissections had been performed on human bodies. Infection must have occurred at all times; the word expresses a phenomenon that has remained the same, although its scientific explanation was reserved for a more advanced age. Encouraged by this thought, we turn to ancient medical literature and we find indeed that Theodorus Priscianus, a physician of the fifth century A.D., devotes a whole chapter to *"infectio"* in his textbook of medicine. However, the chapter is entitled: *De infectionibus capillorum,*[2] i.e., "On the dyeing of hair." We shall have to admit, I think, that the matter is not quite as simple as we assumed. The word included a connotation which it no longer possesses today.

There is no other way but to inquire more closely into the meaning of those words which have come to be used for the concept of infection. The Latin *"infectio,"* as we just heard, means staining or dyeing. And to stain or to color is one of the principal connotations of the verb *"inficere."* The root meaning of this word is to put or dip into something, and the something may be a dye; or to mix with something, especially a poison; or to stain something in the sense that it becomes tainted, spoiled, or corrupted. Indeed, the English word "to stain" can still be used in the double sense of dyeing as well as polluting. Let us remember, then, that an infection is basically a pollution. And the same is true of the term "contagion" which indicates a pollution, especially by direct contact. Peculiarly enough, the Greek verb *miaino* presents a counterpart to the Latin *inficere.* Here too the mere staining can be included together with physical or moral defiling. And the corresponding noun *"miasma"* originally meant any pollution or polluting agent.

This brief linguistic excursion will suffice to bring out a basic element in the concept of infection: impurity. If we look for examples we have only to turn to chapter 13 of Leviticus which deals with Zara'ath, the disease commonly translated as leprosy. "And the leper in whom the plague is, his clothes shall be rent, and his head bare, and he shall put a covering upon his upper lip, and shall cry, Unclean, unclean. All the days wherein the plague shall be in him he shall be defiled; he is unclean; he shall dwell alone; without the camp shall his habitation be" (ch. 13, vs. 45 and 46). The leper is obviously isolated so that he may not communicate his uncleanness; for persons, animals, and things unclean make those who come in contact with them unclean too. This, according to the Bible, holds true of men suffering from gonorrhea, and of men and women in the sphere of sexual functions; it holds true of the beasts that are unclean and forbidden food; and it also holds true of dead objects.

The chapter dealing with Zara'ath greatly influenced the medieval attitude towards leprosy and the segregation of lepers. The contagiousness of leprosy was dreaded beyond the real danger of infection. Nevertheless, this attitude may have helped to make those countries where regulations were

---

[2]Theodorus Priscianus *Euporiston libri III,* ed. Valentine Rose, Lipsiae, 1894, I, c. 2, p. 5 ff.

rigorously enforced almost free of leprosy around 1600. No wonder that the sanitary significance of Leviticus has been greatly praised, especially since washing of clothes and bathing in water were mandatory in the process of purification![3] It is not necessary to deny that, as far as leprosy, gonorrhea, and the eating of carrion flesh are concerned, an empirical insight into the real danger existed. But the guiding thought was that of a ritualistic religious taboo. "Thus shall ye separate the children of Israel from their uncleanness; that they die not in their uncleanness, when they defile my tabernacle that is among them."[4] The diseases mentioned as unclean in Leviticus are but one type of pollution among others.[5] We are not even quite certain exactly what disease Zara 'ath was. Even if it included what we now call leprosy,[6] it must have included other conditions as well. The sufferer from Zara 'ath might recover and be cleansed from his impurity. On the other hand, even garments and houses could be affected by Zara 'ath.

According to an age-old belief, disease could be sent by the gods as punishment for a crime with which men had defiled themselves. The Bible mentions leprosy as well as plague as instances. According to the Greeks, Apollo shot his plague arrows upon the Greek host before Troy because their leader, Agamemnon, had abducted the daughter of his priest. The girl had to be returned. "And," as Homer tells us, "they purified themselves, and cast the defilement into the sea, and offered to Apollo acceptable hecatombs of bulls and goats by the shore of the unresting sea."[7] Likewise, Apollo sent the plague upon Thebes because Oedipus, the King, had killed his father and married his mother, so that a pollution, a miasma, infested the land.[8] The ideas of a disease caused by a foul deed, and of a disease defiling the sufferer, were almost interchangeable.

Around 400 B.C., a Greek physician wrote a book "On the Sacred Disease," the popular name for epilepsy, in which he attacked the popular healers. "For the sufferers from the disease they purify with blood and such like, as though they were polluted, bloodguilty, bewitched by men, or had committed some unholy act." But to the belief that gods or demons might cause the disease, our author opposes his own enlightened view: "However, I hold that a man's body is not defiled by a god, the one being utterly corrupt the other perfectly holy. Nay, even should it have been defiled or in any way injured through some different agency, a god is more likely to purify and sanctify it than he is to cause defilement."[9] This opposi-

---

[3]Leviticus, ch. 14, v. 8.

[4]Leviticus, ch. 15, v. 31.

[5]Wolf von Siebenthal, *Krankheit als Folge der Sünde,* Hannover, 1950, passim, has shown a similar relationship in other civilizations between disease and pollution.

[6]This has been doubted by F. C. Lendrum, *J. A. M. A.,* 1952, vol. 148, p. 222.

[7]Homer, *Iliad,* I, 314–16. Translation by A. T. Murray, Loeb Classical Library, I, p. 27. E. R. Dodds, *The Greeks and the Irrational,* Berkeley, 1951, p. 36, claims that the belief in pollution as infectious was post-Homeric; see, however, my review in *Isis,* 1952, vol. 43, p. 375 f.

[8]Sophocles, *Oedipus the King,* 96–98.

[9]*Hippocrates,* with an English translation by H. W. S. Jones, Loeb Classical Library, II, p. 149.

tion of a natural explanation of disease to the religious or magic one which is expressed in the so-called Hippocratic writings is of great import for the concept of infection. Speculating on the significance of air, another Hippocratic author reasons that pestilences or epidemic fevers must be due to the air that all men inhale at the same time. "So whenever the air has been tainted with such pollutions (*miasmasin*) as are hostile to the human race, then men fall sick. . . ."[10] Keeping within the old terminology of miasma, a secularization has been achieved. The plague is no longer considered a punishment for religious or moral defilement; instead it has become the result of a defilement of the air, due to some mysterious agents suspended in it. The transmutation is not even so startling as we might think at first. In the myths it is the sun god Apollo that sends pestilences, now it is still the sky—especially the sun—that acts upon the air. "Why is it that when considerable vapor arises under the action of the sun, the year is inclined to plague?" asks a somewhat later philosopher.[11] We have it on good ancient authority that the forecasting of "droughts and rainstorms and plagues and earthquakes and other changes in the surrounding vault of a similar character" was considered a serious part of astronomy not on a par with the casting of nativities.[12]

Medicine from Antiquity to the Renaissance is replete with references to planets and conjunctions that breed pestilences and new diseases. The name for "influenza" is derived from the influence of the stars. But there is also intermingled a good deal of climatology that may be wrong but not dependent upon ideas of universal sympathy and astral spirits. At any rate the notion that epidemic diseases were connected with weather and winds, seasons, floods, and earthquakes remained firmly established until the second half of the nineteenth century. Here again it is hard to say where actual experience of the seasonal prevalence of such diseases as infantile paralysis, malarial fevers, upper respiratory infections, diarrhea of infants, and others ended and where meteorological speculation, which saw in epidemics a telluric event of divine or cosmic origin, began.

II

Although all diseases could conceivably be judged as punishment for crime, it appears that there existed a popular classification of diseases into clean and unclean, the latter being "infections" par excellence. Of these latter, we mentioned leprosy, gonorrhea, plague, and epilepsy, to which

---

[10]*Ibid.*, p. 235. I have substituted "tainted" where Jones has "infected."

[11]Pseudo-Aristotle, *Problems*, I, 21. Translation by W. S. Hett, Loeb Classical Library, I, p. 19. According to a late Greek source (Clemens Alexandrinus) the Egyptians too derived epidemics from the sun; see Theodor Puschmann, *Die Geschichte der Lehre von der Ansteckung*, Wien, 1895, p. 4.

[12]Sextus Empiricus, *Against the Professors*, V, 2. Translation by R. G. Bury, Loeb Classical Library, IV, p. 323. On Aristotle's theory, e.g., to explain evaporations and earthquakes by action of the sun, cf. Otto Gilbert, *Die meteorologischen Theorien des griechischen Altertums*, Leipzig, 1907, p. 307.

insanity might be added. In the popular mind these types of diseases had and have a moral or religious stigma. The plague as God's wrath at a sinful people, leprosy and venereal disease as filthy, mental disease as a disgrace, are notions very much alive even today. In former times these diseases were popularly considered not only as pollutions but also as possibly catching. The superstitious Greek or Roman spit when he met insane or epileptic persons, and people were afraid to eat or drink from a dish an epileptic had used. The pressure of opinion seems to have induced medieval physicians to uphold this belief, at the same time rationalizing it by a natural explanation. The breath of the epileptic was now accused of carrying the contagion. This explanation was ready-made since the ancients had ascribed such a role to the breath in other diseases, e.g., consumption. Only in the sixteenth century was the fable of the contagiousness of epilepsy definitely eliminated from the medical literature.[13]

Although the occurrence of contagion among men and animals was known to the ancients, they did not elaborate the concept systematically.[14] It is still one of the great puzzles of historical pathology that such infections as measles, scarlet fever, and smallpox are not recorded in classical literature. Did they not exist, or were they not conceived as specific diseases? Whatever the answer may be, the fact remains that the first systematic enumeration of contagious diseases is to be found in the so-called *Book of Treasure,* an Arabic textbook of medicine, compiled not later than about 900 A.D. The author enumerates the following contagious diseases: "Leprosy, scabies, small-pox, measles, ozaena, ophthalmia and the pestilential diseases."[15] To this list we may add a Latin one, dating from the thirteenth century, naming acute fever, consumption, epilepsy, scabies, ignis sacer, anthrax, ophthalmia, and leprosy.[16] These lists show a considerable knowledge of "contagious diseases, that is those which infect others," as they were called,[17] although their nosological interpretation is not easy. Karl Sudhoff explained the "acute fever" as plague or typhus, and "ignis sacer" as erysipelas, although ergotism is just as likely an interpretation. Sudhoff was obviously guided by the idea that these diseases should be infectious from our point of view. The naming of ozaena in the Arabic list, together with epilepsy in the Latin one, shows how misleading this may be. Ozaena is a condition characterized by a foul discharge from the nose. Quite possibly it was the evil smell that led to the belief of contagiousness. Nevertheless, we

[13]See O. Temkin, *The Falling Sickness,* Baltimore, The Johns Hopkins Press, 1945, pp. 7 and 114 ff.

[14]See Puschmann, *Die Geschichte der Lehre von der Ansteckung,* Wien, 1895; Karl Sudhoff, Infektionsverhütung im Wandel der Zeiten und Anschauungen. Reprinted in *Arch. Gesch. Med.,* 1929, vol. 21, pp. 207–18. The concept of medical infection is clearly expressed in Thucydides' account of the plague, especially II, 51 where he uses the same verb *"anapimplemi"* that also carries the notion of "defiling."

[15]Max Meyerhof, The "Book of Treasure," an Early Arabic Treatise on Medicine, *Isis,* vol. 14, 1930, pp. 53–76, see p. 61.

[16]Karl Sudhoff, Die acht ansteckenden Krankheiten einer angeblichen Baseler Ratsverordnung vom Jahre 1400. Reprinted in *Arch. Gesch. Med.,* vol. 21, 1929, pp. 219–27, see p. 224 f.

[17]*Ibid.,* p. 227: *"Hii sunt morbi contagiosi, id est inficientes alios. . . ."*

may say that the clinical study of infectious diseases was well under way. By the middle of the sixteenth century, the nervous diseases had been eliminated from serious medical consideration, while syphilis, typhus, scarlet fever, and influenza had been added. The further development of this clinical knowledge is outside our theme. Instead we have to return to the theory of infection as pollution and the associations it evoked of something bad, to be avoided and if possible removed.

III

The statement that epidemic disease is caused by miasms, i.e., pollution of the air, in itself seems to have given the illusion of an explanation. This illusion was supported by the meaning of infection as staining. The analogy with a tincture where a small drop of dye-stuff suffices to color a large amount of fluid played an important role in medieval alchemy and medicine. It helped to explain how the whole body could become sick from mere contact or inhaled breath.[18] Finally, and perhaps most important, there was the decay and putrescence of organic bodies, *"sepsis,"* to cite the Greek word which we still use. Putrescence became the pattern of pollution and the evil smell it propagated was taken as an indication and guide. To quote an old English version of a medieval poem, the so-called School of Salerno:

> Though all ill savours do not breed infection,
> Yet sure infection commeth most by smelling[19]

The evil smell from the refuse of slaughter houses and from a sick person was supposed to cause infection, as was the unpleasant odor hovering over marshes, the malaria, bad air, of later days. The latter in particular was called *"virus,"* a word that could also designate the poisonous secretion of snakes. A chain of associated words and images thus provided a theory of infection, and it is remarkable how our modern terminology has remained within the orbit of ancient and medieval imagery. Indeed, the fight against epidemic diseases was guided by very similar notions in the fourteenth century and in the middle of the nineteenth. In 1347 bubonic plague, the black death, began its devastating reign and stimulated the creation of public health measures in medieval towns in times of pestilence. The streets were cleaned, the keeping of pigs and the emptying of cesspools were forbidden. In England the first general statute against nuisances was enacted in 1388.[20] To cleanse the air, pyres were lighted in the streets, the rooms and beds were scented with vinegar and perfumes. Since

---

[18]Aretaeus, VIII, 131, speaking of the communicability of elephantiasis (leprosy) refers at once to the *"baphe"* (in the sense of the Latin "infectio") and its transmission (*"metadosis"*) by the breath.

[19]*The School of Salernum,* New York, Hoeber, 1920, p. 87.

[20]John Simon, *English Sanitary Institutions,* London, 1890, p. 41, note.

461

evil smell caused sickness, a pleasant one would remove it.[21] Here we witness the fallacy of ascribing physical effects to what was pleasant, a confusion of science and aesthetics. Pyres disappeared in the eighteenth century when better means of ventilation were invented, but in many respects the great sanitary movement of the nineteenth century followed in the old medieval footsteps. It started in England in the 1830's under the impact of the asiatic cholera that had invaded Europe in 1831 and of the appalling morbidity and death rate of the working population herded into the cities by the industrial revolution. These people lived in squalor and filth, and the sanitarians directed their efforts against these conditions. This is what John Simon, one of the medical protagonists of public health, in 1874, had to say of the fatal influence of uncleanliness:

... I do not refer to it in its minor degrees, as compared with high standards of cleanliness or chemical purity, but refer chiefly to such degrees of it as fall, or ought to fall, within the designation of FILTH:—to degrees, namely, which in most cases obviously, and in other cases under but slight mask, are such as any average man or woman should be disgusted at: such as, eminently, the presence of putrescent refuse-matter, solid and fluid, causing nuisance by its effluvia and soakage. Also in imputing to Filth, as thus illustrated, that its effluvia are largely productive of disease, I do not ignore that disease is also abundantly caused by air which is fouled in other ways.[22]

More briefly and poetically the same thought had been expressed in the following verses:

> In houses where you mind to make your dwelling,
> That neere the same there be no evill sents
> Of puddle-waters, or of excrements,
> Let aire be cleere and light, and free from faults,
> That come of secret passages and vaults.[23]

Today we distinguish between disinfectant and deodorant. But as long as pollution of the air was a guiding concept, including any impurity noticeable to the senses or by its alleged results, such a distinction was almost impossible to make. In 1881, Littré's dictionary still defines "désinfection" as: "Action d'enlever à l'air, à un appartement, aux vêtements, aux divers tissus organiques, ou à un corps quelconque, les miasmes dangereux ou les odeurs désagréables qui les infectent."[24] It is, therefore, not astonishing to see that physicians and surgeons in using disinfectants or antiseptics largely relied on their deodorant effect. Thus Semmelweis, who in 1847 discovered that childbed fever was caused by "disintegrating organic material"

---

[21]The idea of fire and good odors combating the plague goes back to antiquity. Ps.-Galen, *Ad Pisonem de theriaca liber,* c. 16 (ed. Kühn, vol. 14, p. 281) tells the story of Hippocrates who ordered the Athenians to have fires lighted throughout their city and to use the best smelling substances as fuel.

[22]John Simon, *Public Health Reports,* vol. 2, London, 1887, p. 450.

[23]*The School of Salernum, op. cit.,* p. 87.

[24]E. Littré, *Dictionnaire de la Langue Française,* T. 2, Paris, 1881, p. 1105.

carried by the attending obstetricians, prescribed disinfection of hands with chlorinated lime, guided by the deodorant action of this substance.[25]

As regards the scientific explanations of infection originating between the late Middle Ages and about 1850, they did not contribute much to a better understanding either, ingenious and interesting, nay even prophetic, as many isolated contributions were.

Limiting ourselves to a very brief survey, we find Fracastoro, in the sixteenth century, elaborating a theory of contagion that summarizes ancient and medieval experience; while Sydenham in the seventeenth century reformulates epidemiological doctrines.[26] According to Fracastoro, contagious diseases spread by a transfer of imperceptible particles (*seminaria*)[27] from an infected body to another by direct contact, via an intermediate object (*fomes*), or at a distance.[28] While infection can originate in a sick body spontaneously, contagion accounts for the transmittal of the same disease to other bodies. Infection, primary as well as induced, is a form of putrescence.[29] The most original feature in Fracastoro's work, apart from his clinical differentiation of typhus and other diseases, is his insistence that the seeds of contagion are particles which can even propagate themselves in neighboring parts, and his differentiation of two kinds of putrefaction, one accompanied by "a stench and a disgusting taste"[30] and the other which may proceed without it like the change of wine into vinegar. These views are interesting regardless of whether Fracastoro really anticipated the fermentative, or enzymatic, action involved in infectious processes or merely realized that there are different ways for things to get spoiled.

Sydenham's interest, conforming with his intention to imitate Hippocrates and to describe diseases as they appeared and disappeared, centered on the epidemic constitution of years and seasons. It is not too great an exaggeration to say that the medical theory of infection around 1850 had not progressed considerably beyond these two men. For one thing it was very much confused. Infection was used synonymously with, or differently from, contagion. If distinguished, infection was attributed to agents consisting "almost entirely of decayed or diseased organized substances, and of animal emanations or secretions . . . found to exist most abundantly in marshy and alluvial soils, in slaughterhouses, common-sewers, dissecting rooms, graveyards, and in those places where a large number of living

[25]Ignaz Philipp Semmelweis, Die Aetiologie, der Begriff und die Prophylaxis des Kindbettfiebers, in *Gesammelte Werke,* ed. Tiberius von Györy, Jena, G. Fischer, 1905, p. 130: "Dass nach der gewöhnlichen Art des Waschens der Hände mit Seife die an der Hand klebenden Cadavertheile nicht sämmtlich entfernt werden, beweist der cadaveröse Geruch, welchen die Hand für längere oder kürzere Zeit behält."

[26]For details cf. C. E. A. Winslow, *op. cit.*

[27]Hieronymus Fracastorius, *De contagione et contagiosis morbis et eorum curatione, libri III.* Translation and notes by C. Wright, New York, Putnam, 1930, book I, ch. 3, p. 10.

[28]*Ibid.,* ch. 2 ff.

[29]*Ibid.,* especially chs. 1, 3, and 9.

[30]*Ibid.,* ch. 9, p. 41. Although Fracastoro hardly believed in the organismic nature of these particles, such a view became widespread towards the end of the seventeenth century, see Manninger, *op. cit.,* p. 26 ff.

persons are crowded together, particularly if the effluvia of their excretions taint the atmosphere. Such places are called centres or foci of infection, because from the morbid influence there concentrated, disease spreads in every direction."[31] The infectious agents or miasms were usually supposed to enter the system through the lungs. Contagious diseases "strictly so called" were those "which cannot be traced to any other source than communication mediate or immediate with persons already attacked by them, and which cannot be referred to any atmospheric or other external cause, or combination of causes, but only to pre-existent causes of the same kind. . . ."[32]

The existing confusion can best be documented by another quotation from the same author, Stillé of Philadelphia.

A cargo of rags from the Levant arrives at one of our ports, and on being discharged, creates disease in all the neighbourhood of the vessel; if the disease thus originating is like one which was prevalent at the place whence the cargo came, the rags are a source of *contagion*. If there is no such similarity, or there was no prevalent disease at the Eastern port, then the newly-arisen malady must be attributed to the filth of the cargo, which is, in that case, a source of infection.[33]

No wonder that there was violent disagreement over the infectious or contagious character of such diseases as plague, cholera, and yellow fever![34] This controversy was embittered by the practical consequences that if these diseases were contagious, ships from suspected countries had to be quarantined for a lengthy period of time. The confusion was further heightened by the assumption of "septic poisons, or those which are generated by putrefaction," and were believed to enter the body with the food, through the air, or "through a wound as so frequently happens to those engaged in anatomical studies."[35] But whether infection or contagion, the question remained how the virus acted in the body from the moment of its introduction to the outbreak of the disease. Stillé cites Liebig as believing in a fermentative action comparable to that of yeast. "Other observers," he adds, "upon the ground of an alleged discovery, that leaven acts by propagating vegetable germs, suppose the different sorts of virus to contain animal ova, or vegetable germs, which, by rapid generation, fill the body with parasitic insects or invisible plants, whose presence constitutes the disease." Stillé recommends waiting till the microscope has "revealed the existence of either of these sorts of bodies."[36]

We have cited Stillé's work at some length as a representative example of generally accepted medical theory. The book appeared in 1848 when the great sanitary movement was under way in England and when demands for

[31] Alfred Stillé, *Elements of General Pathology*, Philadelphia, 1848, p. 95.
[32] *Ibid.*, p. 100.
[33] *Ibid.*, p. 101.
[34] See Erwin H. Ackerknecht, Anticontagionism between 1821 and 1867, *Bull. Hist. Med.*, 1948, vol. 22, pp. 562–93.
[35] Stillé, *op. cit.*, p. 93.
[36] *Ibid.*, p. 104 f.

public health reform were heard on the Continent as well. If it is true that the insight into the nature of infectious disease had not changed much between 1550 and 1850, then the intensification of the fight against infection must be due to other factors which had relatively little to do with an understanding of its mechanism.

IV

Viewed in long-range perspective, the intensification of the fight against "filth" that animated the sanitarians can be seen as a stage in the process of civilization, a consequence of the ever increasing interdependence of men since the Middle Ages.[37] It can also be seen as specifically conditioned by industrialization, urbanization, and outbreaks of cholera,[38] and facilitated by the use of statistical methods. In addition, however, it can be understood as a changing attitude towards cleanliness.

Looking backwards we have difficulties in gauging the degree of cleanliness of past ages as judged by modern standards.[39] We are too easily misled by superficial analogies with our customs and their allegedly rational motives. For instance, the medieval custom of frequenting a bathhouse has been hailed as an important chapter in the history of hygiene. Undoubtedly persons bathing regularly will acquire a certain degree of cleanliness, although bathing is of little avail if the clothes are not kept clean too.[40] There are even medieval pictures showing groups of people using a tub and otherwise cleaning themselves. But other pictures, showing men and women bathing together, eating, drinking, and listening to music, indicate that the main attraction was not cleanliness but pleasure or the medicinal effect of water.[41]

As late as 1752, a passage in Smollett's *Essay on the External Use of Water,* one of the few medical writings of the novelist, expresses the traditional evaluation. "Indeed," he writes, "the warm Bath is so well understood in its Anodyne capacity, that every body (almost) after the fatigue of a journey, or other hard exercise, has recourse to the Bagnio for refreshment: and so agreeable is the operation of this medicine, that in ancient times, as well as in these days, it has been considered as a point of *luxury* and *pleasure...*"[42]

[37]Norbert Elias, *Über den Prozess der Zivilisation,* 2 vols., Basel, Haus zum Falken, 1939.
[38]See above, p. 462.
[39]Material bearing on this and related questions will be found in Cabanès, *Mœurs intimes du passé,* Paris, Albert Michel; Norbert Elias, *op. cit.,* and Reginald Reynolds, *Cleanliness and Godliness,* New York, Doubleday and Company, 1946.
[40]This has been emphasized by J. F. D. Shrewsbury, The Plague of Athens, *Bull. Hist. Med.,* 1950, vol. 24, p. 11.
[41]The medicinal effect of bathing has to be clearly separated from its hygienic one. According to Meuli, Scythica, *Hermes,* 1935, vol. 70, pp. 121–76, there is also a relationship between the Finnish bath and shamanism. For pictorial material see Alfred Martin, *Deutsches Badewesen in vergangenen Tagen,* Jena, Diederichs, 1906.
[42]Tobias Smollett, *An Essay on the External Use of Water,* edited with introduction and notes by Claude E. Jones, Baltimore, The Johns Hopkins Press, 1935, p. 61 (italics mine). Praise and blame of bathing can be found in Martial's epigrams and is succinctly expressed in the *School of*

At the same time, the religious and ceremonial meaning of purity or cleanliness still stands very much in the foreground. Thus the large German encyclopedia published by Zedler around 1750 contains detailed discussions of the meaning of purity in the Bible, while the same entries have nothing to say about worldly cleanliness. A book by the famous Dr. Friedrich Hoffmann, that appeared in 1722 and described how to enjoy health and long life in conformity with the teachings of Holy Writ, is a popular text on personal hygiene.[43] It mentions food, drink, the use of wine, baths, and tobacco—with hardly a word about cleanliness.

All this goes to show that as late as the eighteenth century the avoidance or removal of substances because of their potentially harmful physiological action has not yet become the leading concept of the idea of cleanliness. This "physiological concept" of cleanliness is however gaining ground, especially, it would appear, in the Anglo-Saxon countries, concomitant with sanitary reforms in the army, navy, and jails.

It has been stated that cleanliness used to be a matter of aesthetics.[44] The truth of this is confirmed by Francis Bacon's dictum: "For cleanness, and the *civil beauty* of the Body was ever esteemed to proceed from a modesty of behaviour, and a due reverence *in the first place* towards God, whose creatures we are, then towards society, wherein we live; and then our selves, whom we ought no less, nay, much more to revere, than we do any others."[45] These lines occur under "Cosmetic" which, according to Bacon, relates to the beauty of the body rather than to its health. Shortly afterwards, the theme is taken up by George Herbert who demands of the country parson that "his apparrell [be] plaine, but reverend and clean, without spots, or dust, or smell; the purity of his mind breaking out and dilating it selfe even to his body, cloaths, and habitation."[46] Elsewhere Herbert generalizes this sentiment in the following verses:

> Affect in things about thee cleanlinesse,
>   That all may gladly board thee, as a flowre.
> Slovens take up their stock of noisomnesse
>   Beforehand, and anticipate their last houre.
> Let thy minde's sweetnesse have his operation
> Upon thy body, clothes, and habitation.[47]

Salernum, loc. cit., p. 84:

> "*Wine, women, Baths, by Art or Nature warme,*
>   *Us'd or abus'd do men much good or harme.*"

[43]Herrn Friederich Hoffmanns *Gruendlicher Unterricht* etc., Ulm, Daniel Bartholomäi, 1722.

[44]Henry E. Sigerist, *Civilization and Disease*, Cornell University Press, 1943, p. 26.

[45]Francis Bacon, *Of the Advancement and Proficiencie of Learning*, Interpreted by Gilbert Wats, London, 1674, Book 4, ch. 2, p. 130.

[46]The Country Parson, ch. 3, in: *The English Works of George Herbert*, ed. G. H. Palmer, 3 vols., Boston and New York, Houghton Mifflin and Company, 1905; vol. 1, p. 214. The parson is also to teach that "after religion ... three things make a compleate servant: Truth, and Diligence, and Neatnesse or Cleanlinesse" (*ibid.*, p. 237).

[47]The Church Porch, LXII, *ibid.*, vol. 2, p. 57.

The last two lines are used by John Wesley in 1791 in his sermon "On Dress," in which he argues that "slovenliness is no part of religion" and that Scripture nowhere "condemns neatness of apparel. Certainly this is a duty, not a sin. 'Cleanliness is, indeed, next to godliness.' Agreeably to this, good Mr. Herbert advises every one that fears God:—

> Let thy mind's sweetness have its operation
> Upon thy person, clothes, and habitation.

And surely every one should attend to this, if he would not have the good that is in him evil spoken of."[48]

It has been noticed long ago that Wesley refers to "Cleanliness is next to godliness" as to a proverb.[49] However that may be, the significance of the quotation does not lie in the expression of a new truth; rather it lies in the religious fervor with which "the lower and middle ranks of life," i.e., those whom scripture forbids "to be adorned with gold, or pearls, or costly apparel,"[50] are admonished to keep themselves clean in appearance. Wesley wanted the dress of the Methodist to be plain as well as cheap. This meant that he could not easily hide dirt under perfumes and fashionable clothes. To the Methodist—as probably to the Quaker and others before him—cleanliness becomes a sign of respectability, and that means that even the respectable poor are now expected to avoid dirt.

Significantly enough, the stress on the religious meaning of cleanliness is paralleled by increasing emphasis upon its medical meaning. As a preacher, John Wesley quoted Herbert; as a lay medical adviser he quoted the physician George Cheyne. The latter, in his *Essay of Health and Long Life,* had said: "Every one, in order to preserve their Health, ought to observe all the Cleanness and Sweetness in their Houses, Cloaths, and Furniture, suitable to their Condition."[51] With slight changes, these lines reappear in the preface to John Wesley's *Primitive Physic,* dated 1747.[52]

There are other voices, apart from Wesley's, praising the medical and

---

[48]John Wesley, "Sermon 88, On Dress," in *Works,* vol. 7, fifth edition, London, 1860, p. 16. For the date, 1791, see *N. E. D. s. v.* "Cleanliness."

[49]W. Davenport Adams, *Dictionary of English Literature,* new and revised edition, London, Paris and New York, Cassell Potter and Galpin, p. 138.

[50]John Wesley, *loc. cit.,* p. 17.

[51]George Cheyne, *An Essay of Health and Long Life,* London, 1724, p. 18. The particular meaning of these words evinces from p. 12: "Nor shall I add any pressing instances, to avoid *wet* Rooms, *damp* Beds, and *foul* Linen, or to remove *Ordure* and *Nusances;* the Luxury of *England* having run all these rather into a *Vice.*"

[52]John Wesley, *Primitive Physic:* or, An Essay and Natural Method of Curing most Diseases. Twenty-first edition, London, 1785, p. xiii: "Every one that would preserve health, should be as clean and sweet as possible in their houses, clothes and furniture." The date of the preface is given on p. xvi. The role of John Wesley in the spread of a "health" movement has probably been over-emphasized by Sir George Newman, *Health and Social Evolution,* London, Allen and Unwin, 1931, p. 61; cf. Shryock, *op. cit.,* p. 90. Moreover, Sir MacFarlane Burnet, in the *Lancet* of Jan. 17, 1953, p. 103, has drawn attention to the efforts made in the nineteenth century to impart the relatively high standards of cleanliness of upper class society to its lower strata. But it seems nevertheless important to note the currents among other than aristocratic and well-to-do circles.

moral virtues of cleanliness. Dr. William Buchan, in his famous *Domestic Medicine,* a popular medical handbook, has a chapter "Of Cleanliness" in which it is recommended "as necessary for supporting the honour and dignity of human nature, as agreeable and useful to society, and as highly conducive to the preservation of health."[53] Reversing the order, John Pringle, the British army physician, says: "Cleanliness is conducive to health, but is it not obvious, that it also tends to good order and other virtues?"[54] And Benjamin Rush, who quotes these lines with approval, states that "too much cannot be said in favour of cleanliness, as a physical means of promoting virtue."[55]

The insistence on cleanliness is vague as long as it is not accompanied by definite requirements. In 1794, Dr. Hufeland, in his treatise on long life, suggested not only daily washing but even, if possible, a daily change of linen.[56] For the majority of the population, the latter was as yet a utopian demand. However, the introduction of the Leblanc process, in 1791, for the manufacture of soda, and the contemporary revolution in the cotton industry laid the preconditions for an eventual realization of this utopia. At any event, by the end of the eighteenth century, the physiological concept of cleanliness had not only been greatly advanced over previous times but had also become imbued with a moral and religious force. Cleanliness was transferred from the domain of cosmetics to that of health, and with the Enlightenment, the appeal to health became an ever more powerful motive for action. Guided by their own rationalization of life, men also rationalized the past. The laws of the Bible imposing the ritualistic stamp of clean and unclean were now explained as wise sanitary prescriptions by a shrewd law giver.[57] This change in the mentality of modern man also brought about a change in his concept of infection.

[53]William Buchan, *Domestic Medicine:* or, A Treatise on the Prevention and Cure of Diseases by Regimen and Simple Medicines. Second edition, London, 1772, p. 131. The whole chapter (VIII) is worth attention because of the inferences it allows to the widespread prejudice against cleanliness in the case of sick people.

[54]Quoted from Benjamin Rush, *An Inquiry into the Influence of Physical Causes upon the Moral Faculty* (1786), Philadelphia, 1839, p. 15. Rush refers to Pringle's "oration upon Captain Cook's Voyage, delivered before the Royal Society in London" as his source (*ibid.*). In his *Observations on the Diseases of the Army,* seventh edition, London, 1775, p. 92. Pringle writes that "officers judge rightly with respect to the health of the men, as well as to their appearance, when they require cleanness both in their persons and clothes." Remarkably enough, he believes that "plague, pestilential fevers, putrid scurvies, and dysenteries, have abated in Europe within this last century; a blessing which we can attribute to no other second cause, than to our improvement in every thing relating to cleanliness, and to the more general use of antiseptics" (p. 332). Regarding London, he admits that there is room for hygienic improvement, but adds that "some of the main points have been well attended to; such as regard the privies, the common sewers, and the supplies of fresh water; and the people in general are very cleanly" (p. 335).

[55]Rush, *loc. cit.*

[56]Christopher William Hufeland, *The Art of Prolonging Life.* Translated from the German, 2 vols., London, 1797; see vol. 2, p. 236.

[57]See e.g. Rush, *loc. cit.*

The nineteenth century completed what we may call the secularization of the concept of infection by redirecting the basic meaning of the term, by giving it a new scientific content and a new moral force. If we look up the words "infection" and "to infect" in the New English Dictionary, we find that the medical meaning is emerging as the most concrete one. The notion of immersing or staining an object has become obsolete and so has the notion of impurity in the chemical sense of an alloy or the adulteration of a substance. The medical meaning, in various shades, stands in the foreground and overshadows the other broader meanings of corruption and defilement. The latter still exist but seem relegated to the status of similes and metaphors. Such a semantic circle was made possible by the purge to which the Enlightenment of the eighteenth century had subjected everything "superstitious." But the semantic change could not have been achieved without filling the notion of infection with a more strictly scientific content than it had had before. This was done by the rising science of bacteriology which substituted pathogenic microorganisms for the miasmata, contagia, effluvia, and corruptions of old. It would be repetitious to recount the well-known tales of Schwann who proved that putrefaction needed an external agent; of his colleague Henle, at the Berlin laboratory of Müller, who postulated the identity of contagions and miasms, believing in the organic nature of both; of Josiah Nott's animalcular theory of the transmission of yellow fever; and of John Snow's theory of cholera propounded a few years later. The endeavors of these and many others prepared the way for Pasteur's investigations and the work of Robert Koch and Joseph Lister. Much resistance had to be overcome, yet by 1900 the victory was complete. To dwell upon the progress which has since been made would be to repeat another often told tale. Instead we had better sum up what we have said so far.

We started out with the observation that our modern medical concept of infection emerged from the notion of ritualistic or religious pollution of which disease was but one type. The Greek physicians accepted this older terminology, at the same time giving it a naturalistic turn. This was the first secularization of the concept. I must leave it to those better trained psychologically to decide how successful this turn was. I expect that they will claim that a good deal of the dread of higher powers and of feelings of guilt still are hidden in our minds. During the Middle Ages and Renaissance we found a progressive recognition of what, today, we call infectious diseases. The belief in disease entities of a specific character was strengthened in the nineteenth century by the discovery of bacteria as specific etiologic agents. The interpretation of infection as resulting from filth guided public health measures in the medieval cities as well as in the industrial centers of the early nineteenth century. The notion proved insufficient and was replaced by deepened scientific insight. But the emergence of nineteenth century hygiene and bacteriology and asepsis were themselves conditioned upon willingness to rationalize the conduct of life in accordance with medical rules. This process, initiated in the eighteenth century by a widening regard for individual cleanliness, led to the second secularization of the concept of infection. The medical meaning of the word, backed throughout by the sciences of bacteriology and immunology, has become the prime meaning.

These are the structural elements of the concept of infection which our historical analysis has revealed to us. To check its completeness we turn once more to the definition from which we started. Infection, we read, is an "invasion of the tissues of the body by pathogenic organisms. . . ." We may stop here and wonder again about the use of the curious word "invasion," reminiscent of hostile armies whose onslaught ought to be resisted. If we had looked up another dictionary we might have found another word instead of "invasion." Yet some image seems necessary to explain the encounter between the human being and his enemies, the pathogenic organisms.

In its early enthusiasm of some seventy years ago, the bacteriological school believed that man plus germ equalled disease. It was then realized that the matter was not so simple and that natural or acquired immunity and somatic as well as psychic disposition had to be taken into account in order to explain why some people fall ill, while others remain healthy; and why the same person may long harbor germs before the germs suddenly produce disease. It was during that period that Dr. Ottmar Rosenbach, in an essay still worth reading, pointed out the similarity between the old protective measures against evil spirits defiling man's soul and the extreme bacteriologist's endeavor to protect the welfare of the body.[58] Far from accepting Dr. Rosenbach's analysis as criticism, I believe that he really laid bare a necessary desideratum. As long as infection was held to be a pollution, it was understandable in human terms. It was punishment for a trespass, a sin, or a crime, or merely the danger threatening from a supernatural power. At any rate, man thought he knew why he had become infected.

The nineteenth century tried to break radically with this anthropomorphic heritage. It succeeded as far as the explanation of the mechanism of infection is concerned. The bacteriologist's job was to find out what happened after man and germ had met. Why had they met? As far as the bacteriologist was concerned, this question was irrelevant. "By accident," he might say, if an answer was insisted upon. But as a physician, or public health officer, or citizen, the same bacteriologist took quite a different attitude. The more he came to know about the mechanics of infection, the more he believed that he knew how infection could and should be avoided. Responsibility for the prevention and cure of infection has now become a moral and even political force which it never was before. This being the

---

[58]O. Rosenbach, *Physician versus Bacteriologist,* New York and London, 1904, p. 247.

case, our attitude has to be acknowledged as part of our concept of infection. In defining infection as an injury caused by an invasion by pathogenic microorganisms, we indicate our readiness to resist them. Modern physics boastfully or plaintively speaks of the meaningless universe. But there is no meaningless universe in medicine. Human beings are not satisfied with viewing health and disease as matters of mere chance separable from their lives. Health, diseases, recovery, and other medical categories mark biological conditions as desirable or undesirable. The latter characteristic accounts for the medical nature of the concept of infection and for its persistence under different cultural conditions with different notions about the fight against pollution.

32

On the History of
"Morality and Syphilis"*

ANY ATTEMPT to write about the history of syphilis immediately encounters the difficulty of dating the beginning of syphilis in Europe.
Here, however, this controversial question can be disregarded, for a moral
judgment of syphilis can only begin with the recognition of lues as a disease
entity—and this is hardly the case before 1493–94. A history of the moral
assessment of syphilis thus dates only from this point, and it is therefore
from this point that our investigation must begin.

It is certain that from the beginning a stigma was attached to this disease.
But in the course of history the nature of this stigma has changed repeatedly, and it is our task here to extricate its various forms and to discover their roots in the morals of the time. From this point of view we can
divide the years from 1493 to our own day into four big periods, and,
although this inevitably involves a certain schematization, the broad outlines of the picture will become clear.

The first period runs from 1493 until the recognition of syphilis as a
venereal disease, the second from this recognition to the emancipation of
the bourgeoisie, the third until social currents gained strength in the
nineteenth century, while the fourth and last comprises our own time since
around 1880. This division will be justified in some detail in the following
paragraphs.

Clearly, a tremendous difference is bound to exist between the moral
judgment of syphilis in a period in which it is recognized as a venereal
disease and one in which such was not yet the case. The great syphilis
epidemic of 1493 to around 1520 occurred at a time when the connection
between lues and sexual intercourse was not yet clear. To be sure, the
suspicion was voiced in the most varied quarters, but there was as yet
certainly no general acceptance of the view. Syphilis was a new, unheard-of
pestilence with dreadful consequences. It was feared like a plague, and
hated like the plague. One tried to put the blame for its spread on one's
neighbors; to this the well-known nomenclature of the time bears
witness—mal de Naples, French pox (Franzosenblattern), etc. But just as
with plague, the single individual was not responsible for contracting
syphilis: syphilis was a pestilence. The mandates against blasphemers[1] is-

---

*"Zur Geschichte von Moral und Syphilis," *Archiv für Geschichte der Medizin* [now *Sudhoffs
Archiv* (Wiesbaden: Franz Steiner Verlag)], 1927, vol. 19, pp. 331–48. Translation by C.
Lilian Temkin.
[1]Karl Sudhoff, "Das Gotteslästerermandat, Berthold von Henneberg und die Syphilis,"
Mitteilungen z. Gesch. d. Medizin, vol. 12 (1913).

sued under Maximilian show clearly that it was thought that the general godlessness was to be blamed for the infliction of this new scourge on humanity. We know that at this time it was not thought shameful to suffer from lues.[2] Patron saints of syphilis were chosen. Men like Ulrich von Hutten wrote openly of their illness, described exactly all the sufferings they had endured, without boasting and without shame. One was of the opinion also that exhalations, the proximity of the sick, and so on, could also spread the pestilence. Thus, we must first bear in mind that the sickness was not considered a disgrace and must determine what character the times gave it.

The years 1493 to about 1520 are those of the fading Middle Ages, the height of the Renaissance, and the beginning Reformation. All these can a priori be expected to find expression in the way syphilis was judged.

The mandates against blasphemers manifestly breathe the spirit of the Middle Ages. Swearing, gambling, etc., are forbidden because God then punishes the general public and inflicts scourges upon them—and one of these scourges is syphilis, just as in times gone by it was the plague. And in some places the sufferer from lues was treated just as the leper had been treated, the city gates being shut in his face. Here one need only to think of the famous Paris ordinances.

If here we have a medieval element, we distinctly encounter the spirit of the Renaissance in the *"Ballade sur la grosse vérole"* of 1512.[3] This ballad, quite in the style of a François Villon, speaks of the malady with amazing objectivity. The author, who already acknowledges a venereal cause, alerts the reader to the dangers involved in order to admonish him to be cautious—but with no hint of condemnation or of taint. Although of a somewhat later date, I would be inclined to place Fracastoro's didactic poem here too, imbued as it is with an entirely humanistic spirit. This connection with the Renaissance also seems to me to indicate an explanation for the curious nomenclature that we already noted. The period in which Machiavelli's *Prince* appeared evinces a certain nationalistic movement that was assuredly fundamentally different from the nationalism of the nineteenth century, but which nevertheless is expressed also, for example, in the Reformation. Now, syphilis was not the only disease to be named after neighboring lands, but with no other did this occur to such a pronounced degree. And this, I think, is no accident. These names express a national hatred unthinkable in a time without national consciousness. The fact that astrology was in its heyday in the Renaissance would harmonize well with the attempts to attribute the origin of syphilis to a constellation of the stars. Ulrich von Hutten, whose treatise is written in perfect Latin and who ranks with the most eminent German humanists, embodies at the same time a transition to the Reformation. On the one hand, the Reformation marks the new; it overcomes the Middle Ages; but in its strong revival of

[2] A. Martin, "The patron saints of syphilis and the pilgrimage of syphilitics," *The Urologic and Cutaneous Review*, vol. 27 (1923).

[3] Hernaut, *Le mal français à l'époque de l'expédition de Charles VIII en Italie* (Paris, 1886), p. 162.

the spirit of religion and theology there is an element that is more akin to the Middle Ages than to the Renaissance. And this paradox is to be found also in Hutten's views of syphilis. Whereas the mandates against the blasphemers had seen the cause of syphilis in God's punishment of man's corruption, Hutten disagrees, asserting that humanity had been visited by pestilences in other times also, even in the time of the Emperor Augustus, when Christ walked the earth.[4] On the other hand, he contends that one should remain chaste and continent during treatment, for God grants a cure only to those who lead a worthy life.[5]—Thus we have, on the one hand, a rejection of medieval leanings and, on the other, an emphasis on the necessity for the individual to be pure and moral in order to partake of God's mercy.

Let us now take a look at what the physicians of the period thought about syphilis. At the beginning of the epidemic they preferred to ignore it. It struck them as shocking and dreadful, and they refused to treat the victims. The malady fitted no Galenic or Arabic system. Therapy was left to barbers, surgeons, charlatans, and the like, and we know that these used mercury from the very beginning and that they employed it in horrible fashion. Ulrich von Hutten gives a gruesome picture of the sufferings that this treatment occasioned. He informs us that more patients died of it than were cured by it, and that many chose to die of the disease itself rather than to be anointed to death in the sweating chambers. And it was Ulrich von Hutten who at the same time sang the praises of guaiacum, the guaiacum that triumphed in the sixteenth and seventeenth centuries, along with other drinks derived from wood. It seems justified to ask how the dreadful salve therapy of the period could be possible at all. How did it happen that, when guaiacum was recognized by almost everyone as an excellent remedy, it did not completely oust mercury and its tortures? But to solve this question, we must try to clarify who prescribed guaiacum and who allowed himself to be treated with it, and who with mercury. We shall find the answer to this when we look at the transition from the first period to the second, the time when an understanding of syphilis as a venereal disease began to make headway.

This view seems to have become general in the years between 1520 and 1530. As has been seen, there were earlier sponsors of the idea, but they were only isolated voices, and only now did the knowledge become common property. This was a significant development, for the moment syphilis is connected to sexual life its moral assessment is subjected to the sexual and marriage morals of the time and inextricably bound up with them. Henceforward we need only inquire into the attitude of society toward marriage and sexual life to obtain a lead to its attitude toward, and its judgment of, syphilis.

---

[4]*Ulrichi de Hutten de guaiaci medicina et morbo gallico liber unus.* In *Ulrich von Huttens Schriften* (Leipzig, 1861), pp. 401–02.

[5]*Ibid.*, p. 446. Cf. also Joseph Grünpeck, *Von dem Ursprung des bösen Franzos* (Augsburg, 1496).

J. de Béthencourt seems to have been one of the first, perhaps the very first, to use the name "mal vénérien," venereal disease. He was joined by Paracelsus and many others, and the way in which this physician justified the therapy is significant. He says: "It is never resolved except under the influence of a medication which imposes on the body the chastisement of its impurity and on the soul the punishment of its errors."[6] Pignot raises the question of the justification of this therapy, citing Béthencourt's dictum in explanation: "The patient was a sinner, a culprit whom it was necessary at once to cure and to chasten; hence the prolonged fasting, the lenten penitence, the purgatories of expiation invented by our fathers as if to render arbitrarily painful and dangerous the use of the most useless of remedies."[7] I certainly accept this interpretation. The torture of mercury was at the same time the atonement for sin. Guaiacum therapy began to flourish around this time, but it was unable to oust mercury, because the latter seemed to be in keeping with the character of the disease. If mercury came into use in the first period because no better therapy was shown, if ignorance of the right dosage was at first the cause of its tormenting employment, from now on at least the agony had also the profounder motivation expressed in the words of de Béthencourt. And who were the main employers of mercury from now on? As already indicated, it was the surgeons, barbers, and the like. And whom did they treat? The common people—and I believe J. de Béthencourt's view was primarily that of the common people. Among them, medieval-theological trends were to live on for a long time, and it is through these that we can grasp the attitude toward syphilis and its treatment.

Among the nobility matters were quite different. Erasmus of Rotterdam tells us that a nobleman who had not contracted the new disease was considered "ignoble and a rustic."[8] Francis I, and probably also Henry III and Charles V, suffered from lues, to mention only ruling princes and to pass over in silence the host of members of the high nobility and church dignitaries who were infected. Were Béthencourt's words applicable here? Therapy may furnish the answer. Ulrich von Hutten, who sang the praises of guaiacum, was a member of the nobility. After experiencing several cures with mercury, he turned to the holy wood and all of his rank with him. Francis I is known to have preferred to use drinks derived from wood. But who cured the nobility? The rich aristocracy could afford to call upon learned physicians to treat them,[9] and it was the medical men who were the most ardent advocates and supporters of guaiacum, leaving mercury in the hands of the barber-surgeons, who used it eagerly on their patients from

---

[6]J. de Béthencourt, *Nouveau carême de pénitence.* French trans. by A. Fournier (Paris, 1871), p. 55.

[7]Pignot, *L'hôpital du midi et ses origines* (1885), pp. 34–35.

[8]*Utilissima consultatio de bello Turcis inferendo,* in Erasmus of Rotterdam, *Opera omnia* (Leyden, 1704 ff.), vol. 5, col. 346: "Nam eo res devenisse videtur, ut inter aulicos bellos ac festivos quemadmodum sibi videntur homines, ignobilis et rusticanus habeatur, qui sit ab hoc immunis malo." See also Martin, *op cit.*

[9]Pignot, *op. cit.*

among the people. Pignot writes (p. 59): "For the majority of the public, for the burghers and the little people, mercury, in spite of its numerous detractors, remains the great antidote, and the preferred method of application is still firm or gentle inunction. When Master Antoine Le Cocq, a learned and expert man though a mediocre courtier, receives an invitation to give his opinion on the pox of King Francis I, 'He must be rubbed,' he cries, 'he's a villein who has contracted the pox; he must be rubbed like anyone else, like the humblest in his kingdom, for he has defiled himself in the same manner.'" This may be only an anecdote, "but it shows that the School considered mercurial inunction a violent and brutal treatment employed above all by villeins" (note, pp. 59–60). One conclusion at any rate may be drawn: the humblest in the kingdom was anointed, the "villein," the non-noble, the common man. We know, on the other hand, that learned physicians practiced the much gentler guaiacum therapy on their patients, who came largely from the richer strata of society, from the nobility, and used mercury with great caution. This time of transition between the two periods, when the boundaries are vague, has alerted us to the beginning of a change in the point of view concerning syphilis, for lues becomes, on the one hand, a venereal disease; it encounters, on the other hand, different interpretations among the nobility and the common folk. In the first period it was a pestilence that befell all alike; its origin was rather obscure, and it was treated more or less skilfully in all ranks of society by more or less ignorant people, for the physicians declined to concern themselves with it. It was, however, not yet considered shameful, at least not generally. But now a change is in the offing: its venereal etiology is recognized, nobility and common people are divided in its treatment and also in moral assessment. We shall now analyze this last element exactly by first clarifying our picture of the structure of this second period.

Here we are concerned with a time in which society was gradually beginning to divide into aristocracy and nonaristocracy, a process which culminated in the eighteenth century in the deprivation of the bourgeoisie of their political rights, in the enslavement of the peasantry, and the supremacy of aristocratic privilege. The aristocracy, however, had changed in character since the Middle Ages. The knight had succumbed; Maximilian, the "last knight," had been succeeded by the cavalier, and the cavalier had become the aristocratic ideal. But what of the cavalier's morals, and above all his sexual morals, with which we are particularly concerned? Amorous adventure is as much a part of his make-up as is a certain chivalry—we need only think of the court of Elizabeth of England in the sixteenth century, of Louis XIV and Louis XV! It is, in fact, in amorous conquest that the cavalier proves himself!—but the consequences too presented themselves, including syphilis, which, since it is the badge of the cavalier life, becomes the cavalier's disease. This is the key-word with which its moral assessment among the aristocracy may be characterized. The guaiacum therapy of the sixteenth and seventeenth centuries corroborates this, for clearly the cavalier was desirous of ridding himself of his disease in the pleasantest manner possible. His moral code had nothing to do with ideas of atonement and retribution. He did not favor being treated with mercury. His physicians prescribed some convenient guaiacum, combined perhaps with sweating procedures, such as those Boerhaave still ardently recommended. The common folk, on the other hand, fared quite differently! In sixteenth-century Paris, syphilitics in the hospitals were scourged and treated by barbarous methods.[10] An aristocrat, however, was scarcely ever hospitalized and did not have to submit to the scourging of syphilitics, which did not scandalize the world of the period; indeed, the very idea of such submission would have been absurd.

Some examples from the literature of the seventeenth and eighteenth centuries will serve to document our thesis further and make clearer the light in which syphilis was seen. Such a lengthy period is bound to vary within itself, even though some one idea may predominate.

In the seventeenth century, in the Thirty Years' War, a soldier's morality is manifest, and it is of interest to investigate its attitude toward syphilis. The soldier—and here I do not mean the officer, who usually belonged to the aristocracy—takes up a special position between nobility and common folk, belonging, as he does, by descent to the latter but feeling closer by profession to the aristocracy. He not only lives together with his aristocratic officers but is also the mainstay and defender of the aristocratic state. His profession, which causes him daily to scorn death and raises him above the bourgeois prejudices from which he perhaps stems, leads him toward a less serious concept of life's worth, of disease, and of death. The "pious" trooper (*Landsknecht,*) has his own religion, which does not prevent him from drinking, murdering, raping, and thieving. In the songs of the German *Landsknecht,* we see the spirit of men who know that they are in God's hands, who commend their souls to God and confess their sinfulness, yet find this sinfulness fully in keeping with their profession and play with death and the devil. As a well-known *Landsknecht* song has it, "Not for us are prayers and fasting; That we leave to priests and monks; They derive from it their benefice; While pious troopers wander begging."[11] What then is the soldier's attitude toward syphilis?

It was a soldier's disease from the very beginning, and troopers and mercenaries were probably most responsible for spreading it. Here the agreement of morals and profession in a given period with its view of syphilis is particularly clear. When the mercenary system reaches its height in the Germany of the Thirty Years War, Grimmelshausen[12] has a camp

---

[10]*Ibid.,* p. 49.

[11]"Das Fasten und das Beten lassen wir wohl bleiben und meinen, Pfarrer und Mönch mögen es treiben, die haben dafür ihren Stift, dass mancher Landsknecht frumme im Gartsegel umbschifft." According to Jacob and Wilhelm Grimm, *Deutsches Wörterbuch,* vol. 4,1,1 (Leipzig: Hirzel, 1878), col. 1425, "Gartsegel" refers to their homeless wandering, like that of the sailor. To "garten" as "begging," cf. *Hans Sachs,* ausgewählt und erläutert von Karl Kinzel (13th and 14th ed., Halle: Buchhandlung des Waisenhauses, 1927) (Denkmäler der älteren deutschen Literatur, 3.1). Page 91, footnote.

[12]*Simplicius Simplicissimus,* chap. 24 of the "Buch von der Landstörtzerin Courage."

follower say: "Amongst these, most officers were greatly inclined towards that which I was glad to give them for a fee; but then when, for great craving for the money thereby gained and because of my own insatiable nature, I went too far and went indiscriminately with almost anyone who wished, behold I got what by rights I should have got twelve or fifteen years before, namely the dear French pox did me the favor! It broke out and began to adorn me with rubies, as the gay and merry spring garnished the whole ground, decorating it with all manner of beautiful flowers." Somewhat later we read: "In consequence thereof I provided myself with a fine coach, two horses, a man and a maidservant, cut from the same cloth as myself except that she was not yet plagued with the above-mentioned merry disease." Thus, "merry disease," "began to adorn me with rubies," etc.—does one need to read between the lines to detect a moral code that deals lightly with all troubles? And yet, in the phrase, "what by rights I should have got twelve or fifteen years before," there seems to be another note too, namely, a knowledge of the justice of all punishment, such as was certainly alive among the people in the sixteenth and seventeenth centuries. Here again is the same trait as we found in the attitude toward therapy by mercury.

Let us proceed to the eighteenth century, the time of the Rococo, the acme of aristocratic dominance and of the "cavalier." If the aristocratic attitude described above remains true for this time also, the Rococo gives it a racy twist of its own. For how else should one understand Voltaire's saying about an actress infected with lues:

> "Belle Duclos,
> Vous charmez toute la nature!
>   Belle Duclos,
> Vous avez les dieux pour rivaux
> Et Mars tentrait l'aventure,
> S'il ne craignait le dieu Mercure,
>   Belle Duclos!" [13]

Mars, the cavalier's symbol, would dare to attempt the amorous adventure, were he not afraid of the consequences, of syphilis, the disagreeable result of an incautious cavalier's life. Or take Voltaire's poem on Francis I:

> Quelques lauriers sur sa personne,
> Deux brins de myrte dans ses mains
> Etaient ses atours les plus vains,
> Et de vérole quelques grains
> Composaient toute sa couronne. [14]

---

[13] "Fair Duclos, you charm all nature! Fair Duclos, you make rivals of the gods, and Mars would try his luck, if he did not fear the god Mercury, fair Duclos!" Quoted after Brandes, *Voltaire* (Berlin, 1923).

[14] "His person bedecked with laurel, two sprigs of myrtle in his hands, these were his vainest adornments; and a few beads of the pox were his whole crown." After Brandes, *op. cit.*

Casanova expresses himself even more clearly, giving, as it were, the password for his contemporaries. He tells of repeated intimacies with a beautiful Greek in return for sponsoring the promotion of her husband: "But on the second day after the exploit, instead of recompensed, I found myself punished and obliged to put myself in the hands of a spagyrist, who in six weeks restored me to perfect health. This woman, when I was stupid enough to reproach her for her mean trick, replied with a laugh that she had only given me what she had herself, and that it was up to me to be on my guard. But the reader cannot imagine how chagrined I felt, nor the shame this misfortune caused me. I considered myself a man disgraced."[15]

This last remark is not to be taken too tragically. When one reads Casanova, one gets the impression that he was ashamed rather because of the unpleasant results—his six weeks of abstinence—than from any real feeling of shame. Why, otherwise, would he write so openly about it? It is true, one could raise the objection that this was not a matter of syphilis but of gonorrhea, but it should not be forgotten that these were the days of the theory of identity, and that the two diseases were considered essentially the same. So no rose without thorns—the rose is the sexual life of the cavalier, the thorns its unpleasant result, venereal disease.

But here, in the eighteenth century, the cavalier's conception of syphilis reaches its climax. We already suggested that a new period begins with the emancipation of the bourgeoisie, which gave rise to entirely new points of view.

Casanova's memoirs originating in the late decades of the eighteenth century, breathe a spirit of lechery which is palliated only by its wit. If we accept it as the expression of the period of gallantry, we are faced with an unbroken chain of seduction, adultery, incest, prostitution, and so on. Yet no-one seems to be scandalized by it; it is taken as a matter of course, and one rejoices in one's own perversity. And no European country of the time forms an exception to the rule. We need only think of the petticoat government in the small courts, of Catherine II of Russia, of Madame Pompadour and Madame Dubarry in France. Mozart composes his "Don Juan" in which, it is true, the hero finally goes down to hell, but after a life that assuredly delighted the public more than the edifying end satisfied them. Don Juan and Casanova become symbols of their age.

But in the same years in which Casanova was writing, we see something quite different, indeed the opposite. Richardson writes his *Clarissa*, Lessing his *Miss Sara Sampson*, and here a new world is revealed. Lengthy novels, five-act tragedies are written about young girls who have gone astray, and the public sheds copious tears over them. The contrasts are such that we

---

[15]Jacques Casanova de Seingalt, *Histoire de ma vie* 1.7; p. 140 (Wiesbaden: Brockhaus, and Paris: Plon, 1960). Originally a German translation was used which deviates considerably from the French text and which made Casanova say, "Unfortunately, there are no roses without thorns," which explains the allusion in the next paragraph.

immediately feel that a new people, a new philosophy have come to the fore. One cannot reconcile the complacent reading, perhaps even with approval, about hundreds of seductions, on the one hand, with leaving the theater in a deluge of tears because a young girl once fell from grace.

Here we encounter the new morality of the rising bourgeoisie, which bases its morals on the family and its sanctity. In the aristocratic eighteenth century, the husband who is in love with his own wife is the prototype of the ridiculous. One enquires about another's mistress rather than about his wife, and virtue is a prejudice. The bourgeoisie heralds virtue and it becomes its ideal. In its enthusiasm for the classical, the French Revolution glorifies "Roman virtue"; Schiller's "Vershwoerung des Fiesko" contrasts the wicked young Doria with the virtuous Verrina; Beethoven's Leonore is a glorification of marital fidelity. The bourgeoisie admires the virtuous young girl, the modest and respectable wife, as Schiller's "The Bell" delineates them. And the opposite of virtue is vice. He who offends against the strict bourgeois morality is wicked. Virtue and good repute belong together, as do vice and disgrace. How must the syphilitic appear in this setting?

Syphilis is a venereal disease that is acquired above all through extramarital intercourse, *coitus impurus*. Acquisition of lues is proof of offence against morality, of an alliance with vice. Syphilis and vice are linked together, and the reward of vice is disgrace. Thus syphilis is inevitably stigmatized as disgraceful. This is its new moral assessment, or, to put it more exactly, condemnation.

This new character is at first not easy to recognize, for the rise of the bourgeoisie is accomplished under circumstances that are bound to obscure the picture. The French Revolution, and Storm and Stress in Germany, bring conditions in their wake that apparently contradict our thesis. But the contradiction is only apparent and is caused by the voicing of a demand for individual freedom and equality.

These two trends are of vital importance for us too. The bourgeoisie is oriented toward individualism, as is evident if we consider its classical economic theory, as constructed by Smith, Ricardo, and so on. The best way to serve the community is found in the competition between individuals. All interference by the state is rejected, for the individual must be allowed every freedom, and all are equal before the law. In the equality of human reason, as the Enlightenment expressed it and as Kant perfected the concept, is to be found the basis from which the equality of man before a moral tribunal is inevitably inferred. Thus we must keep three factors in mind: the emphasis on individuality, the democratic trend, and the family as the foundation of bourgeois life.

At first, admittedly, we find in the Storm and Stress such a preponderance of individual freedom that its consequences veil the broad outlines. To the Storm and Stress the vigorous fellow who loves life to the full is an ideal, and the brothel is a stage for its dramas. But once the first wave has ebbed away, once Storm and Stress and the French Revolution have roared past, the picture comes into clearer focus.

Lichtenberg writes: "Dr. Girtanner writes of nothing but French disorders—first he wrote about venereal diseases, then about the Revolution, and now about French chemistry."[16] But this witty remark already characterizes syphilis as a "disorder," one which conflicts with bourgeois orderliness. In Ebstein's essay (from which the above quotation is taken), it is worth noting that with the rise of the *Burschenschaft,* which as the champion of the bourgeoisie was also more rigid in its moral precepts, the incidence of venereal infections among students dwindled sharply. Moreover, the words of a luetic student, apparently writing in bodily and spiritual agony, furnish a good example of the connection between the concept of virtue and syphilis: "Virtue is its own reward."[17]

Having just mentioned the name of Girtanner, let us compare the serious introduction to his book with the work of a Frenchman who supplies the recipe for a "chocolate aphrodisiac" and boasts that it does no harm to the healthy and can be drunk in the morning by the whole family, without the other members suspecting that they are drinking the chocolate with which the father, for instance, is curing his syphilis.[18] Of course, one should be very cautious in evaluating such comparisons, for differences may be involved which are conditioned by disparate national character.

A passage from A. H. Niemeyer's *Principles of Pedagogy and Instruction for Parents, Private Tutors and School Teachers*[19] (Vienna, 8th ed. 1829), seems to offer a particularly good testimony to the position of syphilis in this period: I quote here from Proksch:

The spitirual and moral aspect of sexual life, the longing for union with a being adorned with moral grace, must be nourished rather than suppressed in adolescence. One should not forbid the youth and young girl to love, nor make it a sin. Rather, virtuous love must be portrayed as the foundation of family happiness and as the most worthy object of desire, an object, however, that must be earned by one's own virtue and useful activity. This end is served, particularly in youths, by: a) Filling their minds with profound abhorrence of animal lust. One should therefore beware of all levity in speaking of the violation of innocence or of marital infidelity and should call vice and the vicious by their true ancient names, not by milder ones which debased morality has affected; one should speak of wantons and whores, not of paramours and lady-loves, and so on. One must also contrive to show the misery, in hospitals and charity wards, to which vice leads and let youths see the often more dreadful despair of seduced innocence with which a seducer burdens his conscience. b) Inspiring in them an ideal to be pursued in real life. c) Cautious association

---

[16]Quoted from E. Epstein, "Zur Geschichte der venerischen Krankheiten in Göttingen," *Janus* (1905): 186.

[17]Epstein, *op. cit.,* pp. 186–87.

[18]Le Febure de St. Ildephont. Paris, 1775, p. x.

[19]*Grundsätze der Erziehung und des Unterrichts für Eltern. Hauslehrer und Schulmänner,* 3 vols. (8th ed., Vienna, 1829), quoted after Proksch, *Die Vorbauung der venerischen Krankheiten* (Vienna, 1872).

with educated, unspoiled young females.—True family life is an excellent preserver of pure morals.

Here it stands in juxtaposition: virtue—and syphilis, the punishment for vice, the opposite of virtue. The disgrace redounds upon the individual; it is no longer the scourge that God inflicts on the human race because of its general depravity, nor is it any longer the sin of the flesh that is being punished, as the common people believed in the second period. Now it is a sign of the moral degeneracy of the single individual who has transgressed the laws of the moral world. Thus it is no longer primarily a religious offence, but a moral offence, even unrelated to religious belief.

If society was stratified according to social standing in the second period, bourgeois society was dominated by a democratic spirit, as we have already emphasized. And this principle of bourgeois equality is expressed also in the attitude toward syphilis. Formerly we found different judgments, according to whether it was a matter of the nobility or of the common people: predominance of a cavalier's morality among the aristocracy, strong religious elements among the people. But as inequality of social standing disappeared, so too did the double moral code. Moral obligations were incumbent on all, and for all trangression of the rules meant disgrace. Disease was now forgiven no-one, whether aristocrat, bourgeois, or peasant. For one and all it spelled disgrace.

It is remarkable, incidentally, that in such a religiously liberal epoch the church expressed itself sharply and along strict theological lines. As is known, in 1826, Pope Leo XII condemned the condome, "because it hinders the dispositions of Providence, which intended to punish the creature in the member with which it had sinned."[20] But this is no contradiction of the foregoing. Rather, it is self-evident that at a time when marriage was again sacred, the church too should express its opinion and, understandably in its case, in theological terms.

We stated that the period just characterized began in the second half of the eighteenth century with the rise of the bourgeoisie. It lasts about a hundred years, until the last decades of the nineteenth century. Then begins the fourth period, which continues down to our own times. But just here we must proceed with great caution, for in dealing with our own time the lack of distance makes it easy to go wrong.

It is in the influence of evolving social trends on the assessment of syphilis that I see the principal justification for allowing a new period to begin at this point. The bourgeois age was, it is true, democratic in orientation, but it had proclaimed the freedom of the individual, which ought not to be curtailed by the state. Free competition was a principal factor in the life of bourgeois society, and it demanded that the state not interfere in the life of the individual. But now new demands arise. The individual's unlimited freedom to live life to the full leads in the first place to untenable

---

[20]G. Vorberg, *Zur Geschichte der persönlichen Syphilisverhütung* (Munich, 1911), p. 21.

conditions in the economic sphere. Impoverishment of great masses of workers spurs the enactment of social legislation in Germany, France, and England, and ideas that first gained ground in the economy slowly penetrate other areas also. The development of society is no longer left to the interplay of free forces; rather, the state now plays an active part. Education, for instance, is now encouraged much more than formerly. The talented individual must no longer fight for his education against the opposition of others. The state supports him with every means. People's universities, libraries, etc. testify to this.

What is now the attitude toward syphilis? To the previous epoch the family was sacred. The syphilitic had broken this sacrament and was branded. Now, however, syphilis is seen to be not only immoral, but dangerous. Moreover, the danger threatens not only the individual but society, which must defend itself: the state interferes.

Hereditary syphilis was known early—in the sixteenth century—and Paracelsus speaks of it. It was known, the symptoms were described, and it was perhaps thought that God was meting out punishment for the sins of the fathers unto the third and fourth generation. But attention was chiefly directed to the sickness of the individual, whether the malady was acquired or transmitted through heredity. Although toward the end of the nineteenth century paralysis and tabes were recognized as consequences of syphilis, investing it with new horrors for the syphilitic, the danger to his environment and to posterity which he presented was now quite differently evaluated.

Ibsen writes "Ghosts," but it is quite significant that the main point is not the fact that the young hero suffers from syphilis, but that he has inherited the disease. The 'nineties saw the publication of Fournier's book, *Syphilis and Marriage*. Dramas like "The Shipwrecked" crop up like mushrooms, down to our own educational films. Here too the problem begins with the family, but syphilis is no longer a stigma signifying violation of the sanctity of the family; now attention is directed to it as the ruin of family and progeny, thus as the danger threatening the development of society.

Until now syphilis had been the concern of the individual. He might be deemed a sinner, considered despicable, but he was looked upon mainly as a sick individual. Now lues is no longer a private matter, but the concern of society, of the community. "The health of the nation is being undermined" is now the slogan in the fight against the pestilence.

This shifting of the interest taken in the disease leads also to an alteration in its moral evaluation. The syphilitic endangers the community, and therefore the community has the right to defend itself against him. But those who evade society's regulations and defensive measures, and consciously bring harm, they are guilty of crimes against the body politic, and against them the state moves with force and retribution. Thus, unless all measures have been taken to counteract its menace, syphilis now appears in the final analysis as a crime.

For these statements evidence abounds. The state shuns no expense in meeting the danger prophylactically. Large exhibitions are organized with the object of fighting venereal diseases, and lectures are arranged to enlighten the public. In the armies and navies of some countries prophylactic measures are taken on a compulsory basis, and other citizens are offered free preventive treatment. If all possible prophylaxis is unavailing and infection ensues, the state tries to implement as rapid and complete a cure as possible. Health insurance agencies are obliged to cover the treatment of venereal diseases, arrangements are made for giving advice and for examination, and people with modest incomes are cured without cost. But society goes much farther. The patient not only has the right to be freed of his disease; rather, it is also his duty to do everything in his power to accomplish this. Here the state ruthlessly disregards the interests of the individual and does not shrink from using compulsion and force. The physician's code concerning confidential information is suspended at the demand of more important considerations. The new law to combat venereal disease speaks unequivocally: the patient is forced to undergo treatment, and if he refuses and continues to spread the disease, he is a criminal and should be in prison. This expresses quite clearly the present concept of syphilis. It has a paragraph to itself in the code of criminal law: it is a crime against the nation and the state.

Let us now summarize once more the characteristics of the four periods. In the first, syphilis, like the earlier plague and other scourges, is a pestilence visited by heaven upon depraved humanity. Later it is seen, according to social standing, as the cavalier's disease by the nobility, as sin and divine punishment of the individual among the populace. Bourgeois society considers it a disgrace with which the individual has polluted himself, while for the modern state it finally becomes a threat to the nation and a crime.

I am, of course, aware that this sketchy outline is brief and schematic. There is, to be sure, no such clear demarcation between the characteristics of the various periods; indeed, they are organically interwoven by tradition and gradual development, and the spirit of each period is still alive today. Today syphilis is still called the "scourge" of the world, the nomenclature "cavalier's disease" is still current, and many people still consider it a sin or disgrace. This is obviously true of the individual periods too, but we were concerned with making a survey in broad outline of the differences between epochs and their moral attitudes to syphilis, and with contributing thereby to the recognition of the close connection between the general culture of a time and its diseases.

VII

Surgery and Drug
Therapy

33

The Role of Surgery
in the Rise of Modern Medical
Thought*

Sir CLIFFORD ALLBUTT in an address on *The Historical Relation of Medicine and Surgery to the End of the Sixteenth Century,* delivered at St. Louis in 1904, tried to show the benefit medicine had derived from its connection with surgery. In writing this paper he was motivated by the professional separation of the two branches of the healing art then still existing in England. The essay gives the impression that the surgeon from antiquity to the renaissance was much closer to modern medical thought than his contemporary medical colleague who indulged in unverifiable speculations.

There is a good deal of persuasiveness in Allbutt's book. The great surgical works of the past, beginning with the Smith papyrus, speak a language which is more familiar to us than that of the philosopher physicians. Even in the Hippocratic collection, the surgical chapters can, on the whole, more easily be translated into our diagnostic schemes than the clinical descriptions of other diseases. Now if modern medicine really is more akin to older surgery than to older internal medicine, the question may well be raised whether this kinship can possibly be explained, in part at least, by the role of surgery in the rise of modern medical thought. I trust that you will allow a medical historian to take the word "modern" in a broad sense, for I intend to limit my discussion to the period from about 1700 to 1830, from the time of the great Dutch clinician, Boerhaave, to the height of the so-called Paris school. And since this school, in some respects, was leading at the turn of the century, I shall largely dwell on French developments.

That surgeons were of influence will easily be conceded: the name of John Hunter alone would suffice. But it is not so easy to imagine that men like Corvisart and Laennec could be indebted to the rough sawbones of the wars of the Spanish succession, or even that the latter had much in common with the elegant Paris surgeons of around 1830. To weaken these objections we must remove two misunderstandings, viz. that the domain of surgery, in the eighteenth century, was the exclusive possession of the guild-surgeons and that operations with the knife accounted for all surgical activity.

In Germany, until the last third of the 18th century, the old distinction prevailed between "medical surgery," represented by university graduates,

*Bull. Hist. Med., 1951, vol. 25, pp. 248–59.
Read at a meeting of the Johns Hopkins Medical History Club on March 5, 1951.

without practical experience of their own, and "practical surgery," as represented by uneducated barbers and feldschers who practised surgery with little insight into their art.[1] Lorenz Heister who mastered both medicine and surgery was an exception. Only toward 1770 did the distinction begin to disappear and practical surgery become an academic discipline. In England conditions were different. The doctor of medicine, as in Germany, usually refrained from surgery which was exercised by the barber-surgeon, who might be an apothecary at the same time, thus engaging in general practice. From this group there emerged the great hospital surgeons, consultants of a high professional rank who dominated the Surgeons' Company, founded in 1745,[2] and, for some time, also its successor, the College of Surgeons.[3] Though in 1745 the association with the barbers had come to an end, the majority of the members of the Company or College continued to represent the general practitioner. The surgeon Lydgate in George Eliot's *Middlemarch* is a good example of this type of a somewhat later period.

In Italy, on the other hand, the home of the great surgeon-anatomists of the Renaissance, medicine and surgery had long lived in close proximity. Outside of Italy, it was mainly the Netherlands where not only the new clinical teaching was developed in the 17th century, but where anatomy, both normal and pathological, and surgery were closely drawn into the orbit of the medical sciences. Although Holland too had its surgical guilds, quite a number of graduated doctors of medicine devoted themselves to anatomy and surgery. Rau, Albinus, Peter Camper, Sandifort may here be mentioned in the first place. Ruysch designated himself as a professor of anatomy and surgery.[4] In his practice he seems to have been helped by master surgeons although he was not above lending a hand himself.[5] At any rate, his knowledge of surgery was such that only a formal distinction could exclude him from this field.

Most interesting, however, is the situation in France. Largely under the influence of such works as Quesnay's *Recherches critiques,*[6] our attention has centered upon the struggle between the Paris faculty of medicine and the Paris surgeons, who, in 1731, founded the Académie Royale de Chirurgie. Granted that the gulf between surgeons and physicians was wide and that among the latter many were woefully ignorant of anatomy and surgery, the fact remains that here—as in the Netherlands—some doctors overcame the

---

[1]Lorenz Heister, *A general system of surgery,* translated into English from the Latin of Dr. Lawrence Heister, London, 1743, p. 2 f.

[2]Cecil Wall, *The history of the Surgeons' Company,* 1745–1800, London, 1937, pp. 88 ff. and 73 ff.

[3]S. Squire Sprigge, *The life and time of Thomas Wakley,* London, New York and Bombay, 1897, see especially ch. 18.

[4]"Observationum anatomico-chirurgicarum centuria," Dedication, p. 2 r.: "... jam ab Annis viginti et ultra exerceo Anatomes et Chirurgiae Professionem...." In *Frederici Ruyschii opera omnia anatomico-medico-chirurgica,* vol. 1, Amsterdam, 1721.

[5]See, e.g., *ibid.,* "Observatio XLII," p. 41.

[6]François Quesnay, *Recherches critiques et historiques sur l'origine, sur les divers états et sur les progrès de la chirurgie en France,* Paris, 1744.

separation. Littre,[7] Poupart,[8] Pourfour du Petit,[9] and Antoine Petit[10] were skilled in both domains. Du Verney and Winslow were above all anatomists, but both taught surgery and Du Verney's *Diseases of the Bones* is a surgical work devoting much space to the setting of fractures and reducing of dislocations. Even among some of the French physicians who had no official connection with surgery, the interest in this branch documented itself in their writing. Senac, for instance, body physician of Louis XV and author of a classical treatise on the heart, is said to have brought out in his young years a French edition of Heister's anatomy and an essay on lithotomy.[11] Small wonder, then, that Brocklesby, an English army physician, in 1764 could write:

> For as no nation of this age have pretended to superior knowledge in surgery so much as the French, so they are known to be generally the most ignorant and worst Physicians in Europe, ever since their Surgeons came to impose and obtrude their pretenses, in the knowledge of anatomy, upon the world, as the perfection of medical science.[12]

The French revolution in abolishing different schools for doctors and surgeons, abolished outworn external distinctions. But medicine and surgery had been in contact before the revolution, and the surgical specialist existed afterwards too. There remained the necessity for the great surgical operator to have special training and there remained the lack of necessity for the internist to learn techniques he did not use. This had been so before the revolution[13] and remained true afterwards, in France as well as elsewhere, even in the United States where a professional distinction had never taken deep roots.

Long before the 18th century, surgery as a discipline had not been limited to the guild surgeon and in the course of the 18th century the contacts of physicians with surgery increased in many countries. The interest of the doctor, even if he did not himself operate, must not be underrated. The growth of surgery is not understandable if the work of Monro, Haller and others who kept in close touch with the discipline of surgery is disregarded. This remains true in spite of the fact that the guild surgeons usually in-

[7]"Eloge de M. Littre," *Histoire de l'Académie Royale des Sciences, année MDCCXXV,* Paris, 1727, p. 133.

[8]"Eloge de M. Poupart," *ibid., année MDCCIX,* Paris 1733, p. 126.

[9]"Eloge de M. Petit, Médecin," *ibid., année MDCCXLI,* Paris, 1744, p. 171.

[10]Article "Petit (Antoine)" in *Dictionnaire encyclopédique des sciences médicales,* deuxième série, t. 23, Paris, 1887, p. 759: "Quoi qu'il se fût livré spécialement à la médecine, cependant on le vit aussi faire plusieurs opérations chirurgicales avec beaucoup d'habileté."

[11]Article "Senac (Jean-Baptise)" in *Nouvelle biographie générale,* t. 23, Paris, 1864, col. 740 f. Where my information on the surgical activities of the Dutch and French doctors named is derived from general reference works, verification through source material not at my disposal remains a desideratum.

[12]Richard Brocklesby, *Oeconomical and medical observations,* London, 1764, p. 88.

[13]According to Paul Delaunay, *Le monde médical parisien au dix-huitième siècle,* Paris, 1905, p. 199 f., even Antoine Petit, in 1757, stated that one could not properly practice medicine or surgery without specializing in one or the other, although he considered both as branches of the one healing art.

cluded in their ranks the great surgical operators. Amongst them, of course, the French excelled. In the diaries of his travels in Holland, England, France, and Germany, between 1725 and 1728, Albrecht von Haller has left us interesting accounts of their work. Under the date of September 21, 1727 (Paris), Haller writes:

Saw the excision of a cancer of the lip. A great deperdition was needed and, since two sutures had to be made, I was bored. They also opened an abscess behind the ear, cut away the callosities etc. yet found hardly any pus, only had a bloody wound. O wonders of man.[14]

The patient with cancer of the lip died. A great many operations were followed by death, and post-mortem reports seem to fill much space. The entries sound depressive enough and it is said that these experiences restrained Haller from ever practising surgery[15] so that he limited himself to teaching it.

This agrees with the picture we usually have of surgery of the preantiseptic era. The most ingenious operations come to naught because the patient succumbed to infection or shock. There is a good deal of truth in this view. But the marvellous progress of surgery since Lister has also tempted us to an unjust disparagement of older surgery—unjust, if only because surgery never was identical with major operative surgery. Let us not forget the everyday cure of wounds, inflammations, ulcers, dislocations, and fractures; the removal of foreign bodies; catheterization, as well as scurvy, diseases of the eyes and ears, skin diseases, and venereal diseases, the treatment of which the surgeon shared with the physician. Of course, surgical infections occurred frequently, though not as often as is commonly assumed, provided that the treatment took place outside the large hospitals. I even venture to say that, in the period under discussion, the treatment of external disorders, as surgical diseases were sometimes called, was therapeutically more effective than the treatment of internal diseases.

Having thus dealt with preliminaries, we have to consider the possible role surgery as a discipline played in the formation of medical thought. We shall begin with a few brief remarks on the progress of practical surgery between 1700 and 1830.

Considerable improvements were made in the technique of such major operations as amputations and herniotomy, in the diagnosis and treatment of fractures, diseases of the joints and urinary apparatus, of the eye, ear and the teeth. Some disorders became better understood and could be attacked surgically, to mention but Dupuytren's contracture. An almost new field was opened by Delpech with orthopedic surgery and the technique of subcutaneous tenotomy and myotomy. But, above all, the second

---

[14]Albrecht Haller, *Tagebuch der Studienreise nach London, Paris, Strassburg und Basel 1727 bis 1728*, mit Ammerkungen herausgegeben von E. Hintzsche, Bern, 1942, p. 26 (Berner Beiträge zur Geschichte der Medizin und der Naturwissenschaften, Nr. 1).
[15]*Ibid.*, p. 44.

half of the eighteenth century witnessed an increased determination of surgeons to save organs and their functions and to limit mutilating or cruel operations. The history of heroic ligatures of major blood vessels in severe hemorrhage or arterial aneurysm is too well known to need recounting here. It begins before Hunter and extends far into the nineteenth century. Conservative bone surgery originated with attempts to amputate as near the affected part as possible. It culminated in 1768 in the work of Charles White in Manchester who, in a case of osteomyelitis of the proximal end of the humerus, sawed off this part, preserving the arm; and Park in Liverpool who, in 1781, followed a similar course in resecting the knee joint of a sailor. In addition we might here mention the preference for lithotrity as against lithotomy, and the revival of plastic surgery by Carpue in London in 1814 and Karl von Gräfe in Berlin two years later. On the other hand, the development of operative procedures in conservative surgery was paralleled by the tendency to limit operations altogether. The book of the Prussian army surgeon, Bilguer, *On the inutility of the amputation of limbs,* published in 1761, inveighed against the innumerable amputations on the battlefield and created a sensation. Some surgeons came to feel that operations should be an ultima ratio. In his surgical lectures, John Hunter said:

> This last part of surgery, namely, operations, is a reflection on the healing art; it is a tacit acknowledgement of the insufficiency of surgery. It is like an armed savage who attempts to get that by force which a civilized man would get by stratagem.[16]

The stratagem consisted mainly in closer attention to the causes of disease and the constitution of the patient. For while the internist, through lack of training, could not easily compete with the surgeon where operations were involved, the surgeons, on the other hand, were not averse to prescribing both regimen and drugs for their patients.[17]

To what factors then can we attribute this manysided development? In the first place, to the ambition, inventiveness, and courage of individual surgeons. Second, to the general progress of civilization which revolted against cruelty in law as well as in medicine and, at the same time, agitated for a higher educational standard for surgeons and a more practical training for physicians. And, above all, to the advance of anatomy, both normal and pathological, and experimental physiology.

It is a fact, generally acknowledged, that "many of the best anatomists of the 18th century . . . were so-called surgeon-anatomists."[18] This is true of Albinus of Leyden to whom his pupil, Haller, gave high praise, noting also his neatness and that he always worked with cuffs on his hands. "This cleanliness," Haller added, "is of greater necessity than one might think, as anybody experiences who, at Paris, has helped the French pigs in their

---

[16]*The works of John Hunter,* edited by James F. Palmer, vol. 1, London, 1835, p. 210.

[17]This holds especially true of Great Britain, see Wall, *op. cit.,* p. 89.

[18]Fielding H. Garrison, *An introduction to the history of medicine,* fourth edition, Philadelphia and London, 1929, p. 332. See also above, p. 488.

work."[19] This uncharitable remark probably referred to Le Dran[20] and possibly also to Winslow who was teaching anatomy at the Jardin des Plantes where Du Verney and Pierre Dionis had also been active. Paris was the main seat of anatomical research in the first half of the century. Much of the work of its early surgeon-anatomists is published in the volumes of the Académie Royale des Sciences which, like its English sister body, was interested in useful science rather than the social provenience of its members. Here Littre described a case of primary thrombosis in the pulmonary vein or left atrium of the heart, later quoted by Virchow;[21] here, in 1710, he also mentioned the possibility of making an artificial anus.[22] Incidentally, this suggestion was put into practice in 1776 by Pillore of Rouen and perfected by Amussat in Paris in 1839,[23] another example of continuity, even in intestinal surgery. We also find in the publications of the Académie the beautiful experimental work of Pourfour du Petit on the sympathetic innervation of the eye,[24] and a host of anatomical and physiological contributions by Méry who, until his death in 1722, had worked at the Hôtel Dieu. Many of these reports appeared under the section of "Anatomy," the common scientific denominator for surgery, obstetrics, anatomy, experimental physiology, and pathological anatomy.

The remark has been made that "even long after the publication of Morgagni's great work (1761) surgical pathology had no real existence."[25] This statement seems to overlook a basic fact. Long before Morgagni, surgeons had to rely on physical signs in their diagnosis and had to correlate the clinical picture to structural changes. In other words, they did exactly what the schools of Paris and Vienna were to achieve with regard to internal diseases. Wounds, ulcers, abscesses, gangrene, and tumors on the surface of the body presented themselves to the eye or to the palpating finger and the probe. The ends of broken bones could be felt, crepitation could be heard, the transparency of a scrotal tumor in case of hydrocele could be seen. The surgeon could hardly operate for hernia, aneurysm, cataract, or lacrimal fistula without visualizing a localized structural change. He engaged in anatomical work not just because he was fond of dissecting but because the knowledge of structure, both normal and morbid, was essential

---

[19]*Albrecht Hallers Tagebücher seiner Reisen nach Deutschland, Holland und England (1723–1727)*. Herausgegeben von E. Hintzsche. St. Gallen, 1948, p. 44. Regarding the cleanliness of the Dutch medical men see also H. Haeser, *Lehrbuch der Geschichte der Medicin*, 3. Bearbeitung, vol. 2, Jena, 1881, p. 653.

[20]Haller, *ibid.*, footnote 63.

[21]"Sur une mort subite," *Histoire de l'Académie Royale des Sciences, année MDCCI*, Paris, 1743, p. 25 ff. Rudolf Virchow, *Thrombose und Embolie*, eingeleitet von Rudolf Beneke, Leipzig, 1910, p. 66, footnote (Klassiker der Medizin, Band 7–8).

[22]*Historie* etc. *année MDCCX*, Paris 1732, p. 36 f.

[23]J. Z. Amussat, *Mémoire sur la possibilité d'établir un anus artificiel*, etc., Paris, 1839. See also Zachary Cope, *Pioneers in acute abdominal surgery*, London, 1939, pp. 29–46.

[24]"Mémoire dans lequel il est démontré que les nerfs intercostaux fournissent des rameaux qui portent des esprits dans les yeux," *Histoire de l'Académie Royale des Sciences, année MDCCXXVII*, Paris, 1729; Section "Mémoires," pp. 1–19.

[25]Garrison, *op. cit.*, p. 344.

to him. This becomes apparent from the writings of men like Jean Louis Petit, the great surgeon of the College of St. Côme, no less than from those of Cheselden and Pott. Even physicians who were skeptical of the value of anatomy for internal medicine readily admitted its necessity for the surgeon. Barchusen, in 1723, agreed that anatomy demonstrated the "obstructions of the viscera as well as any part of the body that is ulcerated, suppurating or filled with stone, polyp, worms or similar bodily vices," and that such knowledge was necessary to the surgeons "for the restitution of dislocated limbs or broken bones and for the cure of the wounds of viscera and other parts of the body. For if ignorant of anatomy, the surgeon will by no means be fit for trephining of the skull, laryngotomy, paracentesis and the performance of similar operations full of danger."[26] This was but stating the obvious. It might be added that even the law, for centuries past, required the surgeon to testify in court.[27] Heister sounded a note only too familiar to us when he printed a form which the young surgeon could follow in writing his post-mortem report for the authorities.[28]

It will then be agreed that the surgeons studied anatomy and that they enriched medical literature with their discoveries and observations of use to every medical man. But it will be asked whether their contributions, with the exception of Hunter's, really were so great as to merit comparison with such works as Morgagni's *De sedibus et causis morborum*. And Morgagni was not a practising surgeon.[29] The answer is that the surgical point of view more perhaps than the contributions of individual surgeons played the decisive role. Here too we can refer to a physician, the great Boerhaave, who in his *Aphorisms* first discussed the surgical diseases and before turning to internal diseases remarked:

> Whoever therefore has so thoroughly understood the diseases already described, and laid before his eyes, as to be well acquainted with their several causes, nature, effects, and method of cure; and has applied all these particulars to the internal and unseen parts of the body; and compared them with the actions of the sound parts, and afterwards with the several appearances of internal diseases, will find that what is internal corresponds exactly with what is external; that external diseases, which fall under the surgeon's care, ought first to be treated of; and that otherwise nothing regular or just could be performed or advanced in the practice of physick.[30]

[26]Joh. Conr. Barchusen, *De medicinae origine et progressu dissertationes*, Trajecti ad Rhenum, 1723, p. 131.

[27]See Erwin H. Ackerknecht in *Ciba Symposia*, vol. 11, no. 7, 1950, pp. 1287, 1290.

[28]Heister, *op. cit.*, p. 33. Heister had, of course, a much older forerunner in Ambroise Paré (*Oeuvres complètes*, ed. J.-F. Malgaigne, vol. 3, Paris, 1841, p. 655 ff.).

[29]J. B. Morgagni, *The seats and causes of diseases investigated by anatomy*, translated by Benjamin Alexander, vol. 3, London, 1769, p. 34: "And as you know very well, how much this profession (i.e., surgery) was lov'd and cultivated by Valsalva, you perhaps expect a great number of observations; if not from me, whom you know not to be form'd, by nature, for the cutting of living bodies, as I am for that of dead bodies, yet at least from him" (book IV, letter 50). Morgagni is here referring to "tumours, wounds, ulcers, and others that relate to surgery" (*ibid.*).

[30]Gerard van Swieten, *The commentaries upon the Aphorisms of Dr. Herman Boerhaave*, vol. 4, London, 1745, p. 436. In beginning with surgical disorders Boerhaave was no innovator.

These words of Boerhaave's need little elaboration. The internist dealt with symptoms which he wished to explain. This he could do by reference to humors, acrimonies, increased irritability or other concepts of a largely speculative general pathology. Or, with Morgagni and his followers, he could look for the proximate causes of disease in the body. These causes, upon dissection, revealed themselves as effusions, hemorrhages, tumors, abscesses, ulcers, inflammations—in short he found within the body what the surgeon found on its surface.

Fortunately we possess the testimony of Laennec himself to substantiate our claim for the role of surgery in the rise of modern medical thought. In the second edition of his *Traité de l'auscultation médiate,* Laennec summed up the aim of his research: "In one word, I have tried, with regard to diagnosis, to put the internal organic lesions on the same level as the surgical diseases."[31] And Bouillaud seconded Laennec's words by saying: " . . . in heart and lung diseases, the ear, if I may so express myself, *seeing* and *touching* these organs, by means of an attentive examination picks up signs which, as Laennec said, render the diagnosis of most of the diseases in question as certain as that of some surgical diseases such as fractures and dislocations."[32]

What we call the Paris school came into being after the French revolution had united medicine and surgery in the medical schools. Bichat, one of the leaders of the new generation, had come to Paris as a pupil of the surgeon Desault. After Desault's death he edited the latter's works and gave courses in anatomy, physiology, and surgery. Only around 1797 did he turn to medicine[33] and to "medical anatomy,"[34] as he characterized his general anatomy which offered a basis for a new general pathology. Corvisart, although doctor of medicine of Paris, had been stimulated to the study of medicine by an anatomical lecture of Antoine Petit. One of his main teachers and protectors was Desault, and under the latter's direction he is said to have given courses in physiology, obstetrics, and surgical oper-

---

Galen too had started the detailed discussion of diseases in his "Methodus medendi" with wounds and ulcers, as the "simplest" (*Opera,* ed. Kühn, vol. 10, Leipzig, 1825, p. 162). Here again we have to emphasize that the eighteenth century did not mark a revolutionary beginning in pathology. But whereas ancient and medieval physicians had usually been satisfied with postulating inflammations, ulcerations, abscesses, etc. of internal organs, medical men from the Renaissance on began more and more to rely on autopsy.

[31]R.-T.-H.-Laennec, *Traité de l'auscultation médiate,* seconde édition, t. 1, Paris, 1826, p. xxv: " . . . en un mot, j'ai tâché de mettre, sous le rapport du diagnostic, les lésions organiques internes sur la même ligne que les maladies chirurgicales. . . ."

[32]J. Bouillaud, *Essai sur la philosophie médicale et sur les généralités de la clinique médicale,* Paris, 1836, p. 86: "C'est ainsi, par exemple, que, dans les maladies des poumons et du coeur, l'oreille, s'il m'est permis de parler de la sorte, *voyant* et *touchant* ces organes, recueille, au moyen d'un examen attentif, des signes qui, comme l'a dit Laennec, rendent le diagnostic de la plupart des maladies dont il s'agit, aussi sûr que celui de certaines maladies chirurgicales, telles que les fractures et les luxations entre autres."

[33]Maurice Genty, "Bichat et son temps," ch. 4, III, *La médecine internationale illustrée* (July 1934–September 1935).

[34]Xav. Bichat, *Traité d'anatomie descriptive,* t. 1, Paris, 1801, p. viii: "Je présume qu'on trouvera que mon Anatomie générale est une vraie anatomie médicale."

ations before he definitely decided in favor of internal medicine.[35] Through his pupils and through the example of his clinical teaching, Desault emerges as the man from whom the Paris school derived perhaps more inspiration than from anyone else. The situation has been summed up by Wunderlich in these words:

Indeed, the whole trend of recent French medicine comes from the surgical school. Desault has without doubt exercised the greatest influence as a paragon of exact observation and in relating surgery to its anatomical basis.[36]

Soon the reputation of the school came to rest on the physicians Corvisart, Pinel, Laennec, Broussais, Andral, Louis, Chomel, and on the surgeons Larrey, Dupuytren, Richerand, Alibert, Roux—just to mention some of the best-known names. It is hardly possible to claim that the medical reform came first, the stimulus of surgery afterwards. And if we turn from France to other countries, the picture changes even more in favor of surgery. The leading medical figures in Britain between 1800 and 1830 were the surgeons Abernethy, William Lawrence, Sir Astley Cooper, Everard Home, Benjamin Brodie, Charles Bell. Even several of the outstanding British physicians of this period had been under the surgeon's tutelage: Matthew Baillie was a nephew and disciple of the Hunters; his work on pathological anatomy was largely based on William Hunter's collection. Jenner had been a pupil of John Hunter, and only in 1792 with the acquisition of a medical degree from St. Andrew's had he given up the surgical side of his practice.[37] Richard Bright owed his taste for morbid anatomy to Astley Cooper under whom he had worked at Guy's Hospital in 1811.[38] In Germany, medicine was largely under the sway of the Romantic philosophy of nature, stimulating to certain branches of biology, but retarding on the whole to internal medicine. Yet surgery, even in these years, progressed in Germany. Gräfe revived plastic surgery, Stromeyer developed tenotomy and myotomy, and it was the surgeon Dieffenbach who agitated for the call of Schönlein to Berlin, thereby helping to introduce the new French methods of diagnosis in the Prussian capital.

A brief survey like the present leads easily to overemphasis and misunderstanding. It is, therefore, necessary to stress the limitations of the role of surgery and to define more precisely the aim of this presentation. Assuredly, the model of surgery was not the only determining factor in the reorientation of medicine. Quite apart from their connection with the healing art, anatomy and physiology had a scientific tradition of their own. Even among surgeons many were antagonistic to physiological research, as

---

[35]Louis Héchmann, *Corvisart et la percussion*, Thèse de Paris, 1906, p. 25.

[36]C. A. Wunderlich, *Geschichte der Medicin*, Stuttgart, 1859, p. 244. Ch. Daremberg, *Histoire des sciences médicales*, t. 2, Paris, 1870, p. 1295, praises Desault above all "parce qu'il a le premier constitué une École clinique pour les étudiants, à l'Hôtel-Dieu, et qu'il a suggéré à son élève et ami, Corvisart, l'idée d'une même institution pour la médecine, à la Charité."

[37]John Baron, *The life of Edward Jenner, M. D.*, vol. 1, London, 1838, p. 105.

[38]Article "Bright, Richard" in *Dictionary of national biography*, vol. 2, New York, 1908, p. 1242.

the example of John Hunter's adversaries proves.[39] Chemistry, which played an increasingly important part, stood closer to medicine than to surgery. Above all, even a localized pathology was in need of a general pathology, a desideratum for both medicine and surgery. It is, perhaps, significant that here decisive steps in a new direction were claimed simultaneously, about 1804, by the physician Laennec and the surgeon Dupuytren.[40] But when all this has been said, the following thesis can still be maintained.

Surgery, for many centuries, had relied on an objective anatomical diagnosis. In turning to a localized pathology, medicine adopted a point of view prevalent among surgeons. In part at least, the reorientation of medicine was due to an increasing approximation between medicine and surgery during the 18th century, with pathological anatomy and experimental physiology as a common ground cultivated by both disciplines. Because the reorientation of medicine took place within a relatively short period and led to dramatic results in diagnosis and nosology, it has impressed us more than the steady advance of surgery. And since surgery, in its practical possibilities, was still restricted until the advent of anesthesia and antisepsis, medicine has appeared as the progressive branch while surgery has seemed to lag behind. No doubt, surgery benefited greatly from the reform of medicine. But it was not in need of a diagnostic and pathological revolution (if we except bacteriology), and as to treatment, it still had the advantage. Medicine ran into the cul de sac of therapeutic nihilism, while surgery, with all its imperfections before 1846, could and did cure with some confidence.

[39]I intend to discuss the connection between surgery and experimental physiology in another context.

[40]R. T. H. Laennec, "Note sur l'anatomie pathologique," *Journal de médecine, chirurgie, pharmacie*, etc., t. IX, an XIII, pp. 360–78, see especially p. 368, footnote. G. Dupuytren, "Observations sur la note relative aux altérations organiques, publiée par M. Laennec" etc., *ibid.*, pp. 441–46; also "Anatomie pathologique" in *Bulletin de l'école de médecine de Paris*, an 13, no. II. See also Léon Delhoume, *Dupuytren*, 3e édition, Paris, 1935, p. 45 ff.

34

Merrem's Youthful Dream:
The Early History of Experimental
Pylorectomy*

IN 1810, Daniel Karl Theodor Merrem, born in Duisburg, Germany, on April 19, 1790,[1] published a booklet of 46 pages entitled *Animadversiones quaedam chirurgicae experimentis in animalibus factis illustratae*[2] which, among other things, contains an account of experimental pylorectomy. The significance of that account was recognized by Gussenbauer, an assistant of Billroth, who himself had started a series of similar experiments. Gussenbauer and von Winiwarter's publication of 1876 included an analysis of Merrem's work.[3] This study of his assistants, seconded by similar work at Czerny's clinic in 1881, led Billroth to perform a successful pylorectomy on a patient, after attempts in a similar direction had been made by Péan.

While Merrem's role in the history of pylorectomy is receiving full recognition in the surgical literature,[4,5] some details regarding his contribution and its antecedents do not seem equally well known. I shall, therefore, present an account of his experiments on excision of the pylorus based mainly on translations of the more important passages from the chapter dealing with the subject. Secondly, I shall inquire into the background of the experiments and shall finally try to evaluate their place within the *Animadversiones* as well as contemporary surgery.

Bull. Hist. Med., 1957, vol. 31, pp. 29–43.

Based on a lecture before the Johns Hopkins Medical History Club, March 16, 1953. I am indebted to my wife for assistance in the English phrasing of my Latin translations.

[1]For a short biographical sketch see the obituary in *Allgemeine medicinische Central-Zeitung*, Nov. 2, 1859, *28*: 695–96, and Gurlt-Hirsch, *Biographisches Lexikon der hervorragenden Aerzte aller Zeiten und Völker*. Second ed., vol. 4, Wien und Leipzig, Schwarzenberg, 1932, p. 176.

[2]"Some surgical observations illustrated by experiments made on animals." The book appeared at Giessen with Tasché and Müller. A copy of the book is in the National Library of Medicine to which I am indebted for a microfilm copy.

[3]Carl Gussenbauer and Alexander von Winiwarter, "Die partielle Magenresection," *Archiv für klinische Chirurgie*, 1876, *19*: 347–80.

[4]See e.g. the following American publications: J. M. T. Finney and W. R. Rienhoff, Jr., "Gastrectomy," *Archives of Surgery*, 1929, *18*: 140–62.—J. M. T. Finney, Jr., "Pyloroplasty and gastroduodenostomy," *Surgery*, 1937, 2: 738–58.—Julius L. Spivak, *The Surgical Technic of Abdominal Operations*. Fifth ed., Springfield, Ill., Charles C Thomas, 1955, p. 538.—H. G. Moore, Jr. and H. N. Harkins, *The Billroth I Gastric Resection with Particular Reference to the Surgery of Peptic Ulcer*. Boston, Little, Brown and Co., 1954, p. 3 f.

[5]Of other recent works I mention here W. v. Brunn, *Kurze Geschichte der Chirurgie*. Berlin, J. Springer, 1928, p. 285. Garrison and Morton, *Medical Bibliography*. Second ed., New York, Argosy Bookstore, 1954, p. 300. Cesare Menini, "Spunti storici sulla resezione gastrica," *Minerva Chirurgica*, 1955, *10* (reprint).

Merrem's experiments on pylorectomy are related in the third chapter of his book, headed "Extirpation of the pylorus."[6] He attempted to remove the pylorus in three dogs. The first operation is described as follows:

Experiment I

On November 15, 1809, in the presence of my fellow students and friends Beyerle, de Beauclair, and Claus, Doctors of Medicine, I made an incision into the skin on the right side below the false ribs where the stomach passes into the duodenum. This was done on a black Pomeranian dog after the hair had been shaved. The dog was small, of uncertain age—perhaps two years old; on the preceding evening I had offered him a little bread and water, but today I had offered him nothing but water until 10 o'clock when I performed the extirpation. After the muscles had been cautiously dissected and the peritoneum opened, I inserted the index finger of my left hand and over it enlarged the upper and lower ends of the wound to the length of three inches. A prolapsed part of the duodenum and jejunum, together with the smaller omentum, was immediately placed back in the natural position. Then I separated the pylorus from the small omentum and a part of the duodenum from the mesentery. While this was being done, the pyloric artery[7] was torn—which hardly seems avoidable. I checked the rather large effusion of blood with a sea sponge soaked in spiritus vini rectificatus. Afterwards I extirpated the pylorus by twice applying the scissors so that I removed a part approximately three lines long from the stomach and duodenum. At the same moment both injured parts contracted with such force that with their edges turned backwards they formed two sphincters impeding all access. Therefore I drove in three needles, equidistant from one another, half an inch from the ventricular edge, and, at the same distance, I pushed them through the internal surface of the duodenum to its external surface. Nevertheless I was not able to complete the invagination by pulling the ends of the threads, nor could I effect anything except the accurate connection of the edges. The suturing of the abdomen was difficult; the omentum constantly prolapsed and became entangled with the threads. Finally, however, after the omentum had been carefully put back, the suture was completed with five threads. As to the threads of the enterorrhaphy, I affixed them to the external integument of the abdomen by means of adhesive plaster.

Upon the suture I put a triple compress moistened in spiritus vini, secured around the body by several turns of a simple bandage. For the sake of greater firmness and to prevent the access of air, I used, in addition, another bandage four inches wide which I fastened with pins on the back of the dog.

The animal was completely exhausted by the effusion of blood that equaled about two ounces. The weakness of the hind legs appeared very great so that the animal could hardly stand on them. A few drops of spiritus vini seemed to bring back the exhausted strength. The heart beats were slow and weak. The dog lay quietly until 5 o'clock at which time it drank one ounce of milk. However, when 8 o'clock had passed, it vomited with great difficulty, disgorging this milk together with some potatoes and bread which it had previously consumed.[8]

---

[6]*Animadversiones,* p. 21: "Exstirpatio pylori."
[7]*Arteria pylorica,* i.e., the right gastric artery.
[8]*Ibid.,* p. 23 f.

The detailed postoperative record shows that Merrem did all he could to keep the dog alive by means of nutritive enemas, and he succeeded in doing so until December 8, 1809, when the dog died, 23 days after the operation. During the interval, the animal had a leakage of bile through the wound, vomited frequently, and finally suffered from convulsions. The post mortem account reads:

In the internal abdominal scar and next to it to the extent of an inch many fleshy abnormal fibres had grown extending from the peritoneum to the pylorus. The pylorus itself, or to speak more truly, the end of the stomach, was nearly three eighths of an inch distant from the peritoneum, indeed its posterior part had coalesced very tightly with the transverse colon, and its lateral parts with the omentum and mesentery. From this and the induration the place of the extirpation was recognized. All vestiges of the gastro-duodenal suture had disappeared. The stomach was much contracted, having the width of only one inch, like the small intestine which, in conformity with nature, contained a mild, whitish juice. The colon and caecum were so swollen with much green fecal fluids that they were wider than the stomach. The rectum was so narrowed that I could hardly introduce a thin probe at the distance of one hand from the intestine. In the internal part of the liver lobe that covers the stomach I found a scirrhous whitish spot. The gall bladder together with the bile ducts was very much expanded, to the size of a Bergamotte pear, and contained much green bile. Pancreas and spleen were normal. The urinary bladder was of the size of an infant's head, darkish-black, surrounded by large vessels, and was so far from being blocked up that, on the contrary, a coffee-like urine to the weight of nearly one pound easily flowed out. The glans penis was denuded, the testicles swollen.[9]

The second experiment was the most successful and also the most disappointing. The operation itself is described briefly:

On the eighth of December, I extirpated the pylorus of a small, deaf, black *fricator*(?) dog of advanced age that had devoured a great quantity of lentil soup some minutes before. With only Dr. Claus assisting, an incision of two inches in length was made, whereupon a large part of the intestine prolapsed and was put back with great difficulty. For the rest I proceeded in the same manner as in the first experiment, so that I cut off three-eighths of an inch from the stomach and one from the duodenum. Since the apertures of the stomach and duodenum were not much contracted, I introduced the former into the latter for about half an inch with the help of three threads. The abdominal suture was completed with two threads. I estimate the loss of blood at between an ounce and an ounce and a half. In this dog too I observed a weakness of the hind legs immediately after the operation.[10]

There follows the detailed history of an uneventful recovery until December 18, when the entry reads: "December 18. The scar becomes more and more contracted. The color of stool and urine is natural. Normal strength has been regained."[11] For more than five weeks afterwards the

[9]*Ibid.*, p. 29 f.
[10]*Ibid.*, p. 30 f.
[11]*Ibid.*, p. 32.

dog seems to have led a normal life, for there are no more entries until January 24, 1810, when Merrem writes: "The dog which until this time had enjoyed the best of health, was stolen."[12]

The third experiment, performed March 5, 1810, on a small, blind mongrel dog, did not differ much from the preceding one. Here too the stomach was invaginated into the duodenum.[13] However, the animal died on the following morning. The dissection of the cadaver revealed this picture:

> The external integuments already cohered. In the region of the pylorus I found a small quantity of whitish pus. The stomach and duodenum had not yet coalesced. I noticed no signs of inflammation, not even in the actual site of the operation.[14]

Of the three animals, the last succumbed soon after the operation, the first apparently died from inanition, while the second regained perfect health and survived for a period long enough to allow Merrem to state: "Thus it seems confirmed by these experiments that the extirpation of the pylorus can be successfully performed; but experience has also taught that this operation is very difficult."[15]

2

What stimulated Merrem to the experimental extirpation of the pylorus? Gussenbauer writes: "According to Merrem, a Philadelphia physician had already made an unsuccessful attempt to resect the pylorus in a dog and a rabbit. This physician too was inspired to do so by observing a cancer of the pylorus in a medical friend."[16]

In a footnote, Gussenbauer remarks that Merrem did not give the source for his statement regarding the "Philadelphia physician."[17] Subsequent research has led to the opinion that John Jones was the physician concerned.[18] I believe that this is improbable[19] and that Gussenbauer's incomplete rendering is responsible for a search in the wrong direction. Merrem's account, for which I propose the following translation, is more explicit. It easily leads to the identification of the man and explains why it was unnecessary for Merrem to give any further reference.

---

[12]*Ibid.*

[13]*Ibid.*, p. 32 f.

[14]*Ibid.*, p. 33.

[15]*Ibid.*, p. 33 f. See also Finney and Rienhoff, *op. cit.* (ftn. 4) p. 141.

[16]Gussenbauer and Winiwarter, *op. cit.* (ftn. 3) p. 368: "Nach Merrem hat bereits früher ein Arzt in Philadelphia [footnote: "Quellenangabe fehlt"] die Pylorusresection am Hund und Kaninchen erfolglos versucht. Auch diesem wurde der Gedanke daran durch die Beobachtung eines Pyloruscarcinoms an einem befreundeten Arzte besonders nahe gelegt."

[17]*Ibid.* See ftn. 16.

[18]See the literature quoted above in footnote 4.

[19]Being a Tory, Middleton at the outbreak of the Revolutionary War went to Bermuda and returned to New York after the British occupation of the city (*Dictionary of American Biography*, ed. Dumas Malone. Vol. 12, New York, Scribner's, 1933, p. 603.) John Jones, on the other hand, went to Philadelphia when the British occupied New York (*ibid.*, vol. 10, 1933, p. 181). Similar reasons also argue against John Morgan mentioned by Menini, *op. cit.* (ftn. 5).

A certain very distinguished teacher, a man highly to be respected, who rendered great service in restoring people to health in Philadelphia, where he once held the position of first physician to the Hessian auxiliaries, was very much shaken by the premature death of Doctor Middleton from an indurated and contracted inferior orifice of the ventricle. He pondered on the most efficacious remedy whereby this very dangerous disease might be conquered. The great and horrible tortures of his most beloved friend could not only not be removed, but could scarcely even be mitigated by all the remedies thus far recommended. Thus nothing was left but to remove the cause of the disease and to extirpate the pylorus itself. However, this operation seemed to be accompanied by such great and serious difficulties that the friend did not wish to perform it at that time. Two years ago he finally had experiments made on several dogs, some of them very sturdy ones, and on a rabbit. But all these experiments had unfavorable results, the blame for which I attribute to the difficulty of the operation itself, and to the inexperience of the surgeon.[20]

From this account the following conclusions can be drawn. The patient was Dr. Peter Middleton, a Tory at the time of the Revolutionary War, who is known to have died of cancer of the pylorus in New York on January 9, 1781.[21] Dr. Middleton's friend, the "distinguished teacher," was a physician with the Hessian auxiliaries. He thought of the possibility of curing Dr. Middleton by pylorectomy, an idea that he did not dare to translate into practice. However, he did not forget the matter and finally had some experiments performed about two years before Merrem wrote his book.

We are thus confronted with two unidentified men: the "teacher" who was a Hessian army doctor during the Revolutionary War, and the "surgeon" who performed some actual experiments about 1808. As to the physician with the Hessian troops, the quest leads to Christian Friedrich Michaelis (1754–1814) who in 1779 had become physician to the general staff of the Hessian troops in America.[22] While in New York, he apparently became very friendly with Drs. Bard and Bailley whom he frequently mentions in his letters to Germany, published in Richter's *Chirurgische Bibliothek*.[23] We find Michaelis in Charleston too, which had surrendered

[20]Merrem, *Animadversiones*, p. 21 f. "Praeceptor quidam perillustris, vir summe devenerandus et de reddenda hominibus sanitate meritissimus Philadelphiae, ubi medici primarii auxiliorum Hassiacorum vices quondam gerebat, morte praematura Doctoris Midleton (sic!), ex ventriculi orificio inferiori indurato coarctatoque orta commotus, de remedio eoque efficacissimo cogitabat, quo periculosissimus hicce morbus vinci posset. Amici dilectissimi tormenta magna et horribilia, omnibus hucusque commendatis remediis non solum non tolli, sed etiam vix mitigari poterant. Nihil ergo reliquum erat, quam morbi causam evertere, ideoque pylorum ipsum exstirpare; quae autem operatio cum tantis tamque gravibus difficultatibus conjuncta videbatur, ut tunc temporis eam perficere nollet amicus. Ante duos annos tandem experimenta in canibus compluribus, ex parte valde robustis, et in cuniculo fieri curavit, quae omnia tamen exitum habuerunt iniquum, cujus culpam et ipsius operationis difficultati et chirurgi imperitiae adtribuo." See also below, footnote 25.
[21]See article in *Dictionary of National Biography*, *op. cit.* (ftn. 19) p. 602, and Kelly and Burrage, *Dictionary of American Medical Biography*. New York, Appleton, 1928, p. 841 f.
[22]L. Pierce Clark, "Biographical sketch of Michaelis, the pioneer worker on nerve-regeneration," *Medical Record*, 1906, 69: 425–26.—Franz Gundlach, *Die akademischen Lehrer der Philipps-Universität in Marburg von 1527 bis 1910*. Marburg, 1927, p. 193.
[23]Cf. D. August Gottlieb Richter's *Chirurgische Bibliothek*, Göttingen. Vol. 5, erstes Stück, 1779, pp. 111–32 (from London); *ibid.* drittes Stück, 1780, pp. 534–55 (from New York); *ibid.*

to the British in 1780.[24] I do not know whether he was ever able to visit Philadelphia and am, therefore, unable to explain the reference to Philadelphia in Merrem's account.[25] It may of course be a mere mistake, Philadelphia having slipped in for New York thirty years after the event. On the other hand, Michaelis not only counted Benjamin Rush among his friends, but also, in his writings, referred to some personal contacts with "Dr. Redmann in Philadelphia."[26] Michaelis is best remembered through his work on croup and on nerve regeneration. In connection with the latter subject, Dr. Pierce Clark, in 1906, published an article on Michaelis which contains some interesting biographical detail,[27] but there is still space for further research.

After his return to Germany, Michaelis first went to Cassel; then, in 1786, to the University of Marburg where he held the chair of surgery until his death in 1814.[28] It was at this university that the young Merrem received his M. D. degree.[29] In other words, Merrem must have been a pupil of Michaelis. I suggest, therefore, that it is Michaelis whom Merrem calls "a certain very distinguished teacher."

Doubts about the identity of Dr. Michaelis with Dr. Middleton's friend are dispelled by other references in Merrem's *Animadversiones* (to which we

---

viertes Stück, 1780, pp. 734–46 (from New York); vol. 6; erstes Stück, 1782, pp. 113–68: "Auszug aus verschiedenen Briefen des Herrn General-Staabsmedicus, Doctor Michaelis, zu Newyork" (mentions his experiences in the Charleston campaign); *ibid.* viertes Stück, 1783, pp. 722–41; vol. 7, drittes Stück, 1784, pp. 579–80 (see also vol. 8, erstes Stück, 1785, p. 122 ff.) "Ueber die Regeneration der Nerven," refers to him as "Liebmedicus," by this time he held the position at Cassel (see below). See also Clark, *op. cit.* (ftn. 22). On Michaelis' friendship with Dr. Bard see John Brett Langstaff, *Doctor Bard of Hyde Park.* New York, Dutton, 1942, p. 134 f. and *passim.*

[24]See preceding footnote.

[25]The reference remains puzzling regardless of whether we translate as we did above or understand the passage to read: "In Philadelphia, where he once held the position of first physician to the Hessian auxiliaries, a certain very distinguished teacher, a man highly to be respected who has rendered great service in restoring people to health, was very much shaken by the premature death of Dr. Middleton" etc. This reading would be the correct one were it not for the absence of a comma before "Philadelphia."

[26]*Medicinisch-praktische Bibliothek* von C. F. Michaelis, Leibarzt und Professor zu Cassel. Ersten Bandes, erstes Stück, zweites Stück, Göttingen, J. Ch. Dieterich, 1785–86, p. 238: "Mein Freund Dr. Rush . . .", p. 112: "Auch Dr. Redmann zu Philadelphia versicherte mich . . ." In Richter's *Chirurgische Bibliothek,* vol. 7, drittes Stück, 1784, p. 581 (see above, ftn. 23), Michaelis mentions "a certain Dr. Schiel" who had imported salt as a remedy for internal bleeding from Ireland to Philadelphia and continues: "Es ward bald unter den dortigen Aerzten bekannt; sie versuchten es, und fanden ihre Erwartungen übertroffen. D. Rusch (sic!), Schippen, Kühn u.s.w. lobten es ausserordentlich; und durch diese habe ich es zuerst kennen lernen." All this points to a visit by Michaelis to Philadelphia towards the end of his stay in America.

[27]See above, ftn. 22.

[28]In addition to the publications cited above, ftn. 22, see H. Hermelink und S. A. Kaehler, *Die Philipps-Universität zu Marburg 1527–1927.* Marburg, Elwert (Braun), 1927, p. 447 and *passim.* See also E. Ebstein, "Zur intravenösen Behandlung von inneren Blutungen mit Kochsalz-Chlorkalzium-Injektionen," *Münchener medizinische Wochenschrift,* 1917, *64*: 801–03; p. 801.

[29]Gurlt-Hirsch, *op. cit.* (ftn. 1) states that the *Animadversiones* served as his M.D. thesis. However, Merrem's own words (see below) contradict this. From A. C. P. Callisen, *Medicinisches Schrifsteller-Lexicon,* vol. 12, Copenhagen, 1832, p. 478, I gather that the title of Merrem's thesis was *Observationes in Authenritii methodum tussi convulsivae medendi* (Marburg 1810).

shall return later) and the fact that the contemporaries were well aware of Michaelis' role. This evinces from one of the reviews of the book that appeared in 1811. A review in the *Allgemeine medicinische Annalen* limited itself to a short summary.[30] A review in the *Bibliothek für die Chirurgie* edited by Langenbeck included some scathing remarks on pylorectomy. "It is inconceivable to me how one could even hit upon the idea of extirpating the pylorus in man, and it should not even be necessary to give reasons why the operation can never succeed in man. . . ." And again: "I consider this operation a means of expediting from this world, more quickly but in an excruciating manner, a man who is past saving."[31]

The last of the three reviews which I have been able to trace appeared in the *Medizinisch-chirurgische Zeitung;* it was much more friendly, and contained the following interesting summary of the pre-history of Merrem's experiments. "In America, Professor Michaelis had the misfortune of seeing Dr. Midleton [sic] die of an induration of the lower orifice of the stomach. Some years ago, he therefore performed experiments regarding extirpation—all of which ended fatally. The author [i.e., Merrem] here relates his experiments in dogs" etc.[32] This reviewer credits Michaelis not only with the idea of curing the disease by pylorectomy, but makes him perform the early experiments. It is doubtful whether Merrem would have given such a detailed and unsparing account of the bungling manner in which the previous experiments had been performed[33] if the actual experimenter had been his revered teacher. However that may be, I am unable to throw any further light upon the experimenter of c. 1808.[34]

Michaelis' connection was still remembered in 1841 in the paragraph on "Extirpation of the pylorus" in the second edition of Blasius' textbook of surgery, where we read:

In scirrhus of the pylorus, when cure by drugs is impossible, Merrem has proposed to extirpate it after laparotomy and then to fasten together stomach and

[30]*Allgemeine medicinische Annalen,* Supplement Bd. 1801–10, Heft 2, 1811, col. 180. Regarding the experiments on pylorectomy, the entry states correctly that of the three dogs "one at least escaped with his life."

[31]*Bibliothek für die Chirurgie,* hrsg. von C. J. M. Langenbeck. Vierter Bd., erstes Stück, Göttingen, 1811, pp. 120–39; see pp. 135 and 138. Omodei in the *Annali di Medicina Straniera,* 1814 (quoted by Menini, *op. cit.* above ftn. 5) also expressed doubts about the practical applicability of the experiments.

[32]*Medicinisch-chirurgische Zeitung.* Zweyter Band, Salzburg, 1811, pp. 177–80; p. 178. The three reviews I discuss here are mentioned in Callisen, *loc. cit.* (ftn. 29).

[33]The detailed description continues directly upon the passage quoted above, footnote 20. "Sectione cruciformi, cujus pars perpendicularis a cartilagine xyphoidea ossis sterni ad regionem umbilicalem usque tendebat, usus est. Intestina prolapsa post horam dimidiam demum reposita, duodenum in ventriculum invaginatum, hepar saepe laesum etc. etc.; imo in cuniculo extremam partem alterius cujusdam intestini non nominati in alterum pollicis latitudine invaginavit, ita ut ductum felleum et pancreaticum rumpi, vel tamen obturari necesse esset. Quibus de animalibus tam male affectis nullum per horas XXIV vixit, cuniculus autem jam duodecim horis post obiit."

[34]Menini, *op. cit.* (ftn. 5), referring to F. Freschi, *Storia della medicina in aggiunta a quella di Curzio Sprengel,* Milano, 1851, writes: "Primo di lui [i.e., Merrem], però F. G. Michaelis (1754–1814), l'anatomico di Marburgo, aveva proposto tale intervento, eseguendolo anche sui cadaveri . . ."

duodenum. The animal experiments made by him and Michaelis were insufficient and could not be decisive anyhow. Langenbeck is right in his judgment that the operation would only cause a faster and more excruciating death to the patient who is past saving.[35]

Since it was this entry that drew Gussenbauer's attention to Merrem and his work,[36] Gussenbauer's reference to "a physician in Philadelphia" is all the more remarkable and must be attributed to Merrem's indirect way of referring to Michaelis as "a certain very distinguished teacher." The last reference to Merrem's experiments on pylorectomy—before Gussenbauer's rediscovery—apparently is the short entry in 1861 in Günther's voluminous work on surgical operations. The paragraph reads:

Exstirpatio pylori

The proposal made by Daniel Carl Theodor Merrem (c. 1811) to extirpate the carcinomatous pylorus in man, we mention only as a curiosity. He bases his proposal on his experiments on three dogs in which he had extirpated the pylorus and which, however, all had succumbed.[37]

The inaccuracy of this report indicates that it was written without direct acquaintance with the *Animadversiones.* Pylorectomy had become an all but forgotten idea.

3

Michaelis must have discussed the pros and cons of pylorectomy in man at some length. As Merrem tells us, his "most illustrious teacher in his academic lectures" was cautious in recommending the operation and raised a number of doubts. "I shall set forth here," Merrem writes, "the doubts and counterarguments of this man, to whom I owe the highest respect and reverence, and shall add my own comments, be they as they may."[38] The first doubt referred to the uncertainty of the diagnosis. Michaelis believed that the operation might be indicated if:

(a) the patient appeared a certain prey of death, all other remedies having proved of no value after prolonged trial;

(b) upon palpation "an indubitable induration in the right region of the stomach" was found;

(c) the patient suffered "from obstruction of the bowel and chronic vomiting shortly after meals."[39]

Throughout the discussion, Merrem appears more sceptical than his teacher. In particular he points out that "when an induration is perceived

---

[35]Ernst Blasius, *Handbuch der Akiurgie.* Dritten Bandes erster Theil, 2. Aufl., Halle, Anton, 1841, p. 133.

[36]Gussenbauer and Winiwarter, *op. cit.* (ftn. 3) p. 367. The other reference they mention (p. 368) is Günther, on whom see below.

[37]G. B. Günther und B. Schmidt, *Lehre von den Operationen am Bauche des menschlichen Körpers,* Leipzig-Heidelberg, Winter, 1861, p. 31. (*Lehre von den blutigen Operationen,* IV, 2).

[38]Merrem, *Animadversiones,* p. 34.

[39]*Ibid.* See also Finney and Rienhoff, *op. cit.* (ftn. 4) p. 141.

in the right region of the stomach, it is by no means necessary that it always originate from the pylorus since it could hail from an induration of the abdominal integuments or of the pancreas in the place where it is attached to the duodenum, or from some other tumor." To this he adds the following story:

That such an induration of the pancreas can present all the symptoms of a compressed and indurated pylorus, nobody will deny. A singular and memorable example of such a doubtful diagnosis was once presented by a man in the medical clinic who vainly took much and manifold medication over a long period of time and who is still alive today. The very distinguished teacher believed this disease to be an induration of the pylorus. On the other hand, Sternberg, the prematurely deceased erstwhile professor of medicine,[40] tried with many arguments to prove that the patient suffered from an indurated pancreas. Thus, the two men, steeped in knowledge and experience, went quite different ways, nor is it possible to doubt the disastrous outcome of the operation if the patient had consented to the extirpation of the pylorus and Sternberg's opinion had been confirmed by the experience, granted that examples are not lacking of the successful removal of the pancreas in dogs.[41]

Briefly summarized, the other "doubts" involve the very dangerous nature of wounds of the stomach, the digestive difficulties necessarily resulting from the operation, the occasional healing of the disease through suppuration by the healing power of nature, the uselessness of the operation "if the induration originated from a true scirrhus of the pylorus,"[42] the possibility that the ductus choledochus and the ductus pancreaticus might close, and, finally, that bile would enter the stomach without impediment. To the discussion of these doubts, Merrem adds the following remark:

To these doubts, proffered by the inventor of this operation himself, one might add the very great debility of the patient weakened by the indurated pylorus and by hunger, the fact that this disease mostly affects persons of advanced age, in their sixties and seventies, whose nature is rarely strong enough to support the art, and the great difference between those persons and healthy and lively dogs.[43]

The discussion of the doubts throws some light upon the state of contemporary surgery. In the first place, we obtain a picture of the difficulty of diagnosis and of the uncertain status of pathology. "True scirrhus" meant cancer; its distinction from induration was not clear.[44] But it is remarkable

---

[40]According to Gundlach, *op. cit.* (ftn. 22) p. 212 f., Johann Heinrich Sternberg (1772–1809) was Professor of Pathology and Therapy at Marburg from 1804 to 1809.

[41]*Animadversiones,* p. 35 f.

[42]*Ibid.* p. 39: "*Dubium V. Induratione pylori ex scirrho vero orta exstirpatio nil proficit.* Hic casus ex sententia perillustris praeceptoris perquam raro occurrit. Mihi hac de re judicium non competit."

[43]*Ibid.* p. 40.

[44]The word *scirrhus* denoted either merely a hardened swelling or the initial stage of cancer (see Meissner und Schmidt [editors] *Encyclopädie der medicinischen Wissenschaften,* vol. 11, Leipzig, 1833, p. 110); it is probably in the latter sense that Michaelis speaks of "true scirrhus." The contemporary vagueness is well illustrated by the remark of F. G. Voigtel, *Handbuch der pathologischen Anatomie,* 2. Bd., Halle, Hemmerde und Schwetschke, 1804, p. 519: "Die

that Michaelis apparently believed cancer of the pylorus a rare disease, admitting at the same time that pylorectomy might be of no avail for its cure. Here Merrem merely stated his teacher's opinion, declaring himself incompetent to judge.[45] Gussenbauer and v. Winiwarter, reviewing Vienna post-mortem protocols from 1817 to October 1873, among a total of 61,287 dissections found 903 cases of cancer of the stomach, a large number of which were localized in the pylorus.[46] The article of these authors has been credited with drawing attention to the frequency of cancer of the pylorus as well as the chances of cure by pylorectomy.[47]

Of interest too is the attitude towards animal experimentation. Merrem distinguishes between the physiological results and the medical inferences. Although he knows of successful removal of the pancreas in dogs (probably a reference to J. C. Brunner's experiments[48]), he does not even mention the possibility of removing a diseased pancreas in man. His own experiments prove to him that theoretically pylorectomy is a possibility, practically a more than doubtful hazard.

But Merrem's qualified scepticism regarding pylorectomy in man must not overshadow the fact that this chapter of the book, like all the others, has a surgical outlook. The first chapter of the *Animadversiones* received sufficient attention to be translated into French.[49] It deals with "A speedier method for the treatment of wounds of the skull made by the trepan."[50] In a dog and a cat Merrem showed that the bone removed in trephining could be used to cover the defect. He proposed the use of the same procedure in man, or, if the removed piece were too badly injured, substitution by "a piece of bone of the same size from a sheep, dog, cat, or other animal."[51] Von Walther in 1821 is said to have employed the method successfully in a patient,[52] and Merrem is thus assigned an important place in the history of cranioplasty.[53]

Incidentally, this chapter also shows that Merrem did not perform animal experiments lightly. He tried out a perforating instrument of his invention on animal and human cadavers, but not in living animals, because

---

wichtigste Krankheit des Pförtners ist dessen Ausartung in eine knorpelartige und scirrhöse Verhärtung, wodurch er verengert und zum Durchgange der Speisen ungeschickt gemacht, oft gänzlich verschlossen wird."

[45]See above, footnote 42.

[46]*Op. cit.* (ftn. 3) p. 373 ff.

[47]Ludwik Rydygier, "Ueber Magen-Resection, mit Demonstration von Praeparaten," *Archiv für klinische Chirurgie*, 1881, 26: 731–43; see p. 732.

[48]R. H. Major, "Johann Conrad Brunner and his experiments on the pancreas," *Annals of Medical History*, 1941, ser. 3, *3*: 91–100.

[49]According to Callisen, *op. cit.* (ftn. 29) the translation was made by Laroche and appeared in *Journ. complém. du Dict. des Sc. méd.*, t. 7, 1820, cahier 25. Juil. pp. 54–62.

[50]*Animadversiones*, p. 7: "Vulneribus cranii modiolo factis celerior medendi methodus."

[51]*Ibid.* p. 17.

[52]See Burkard Eble in his continuation of Sprengel's *Versuch einer pragmatischen Geschichte der Arzneikunde*, VI, 1, Vienna, Gerold, 1837, p. 424, who, however, gives priority for the idea to Maunoir. I have not been able to verify this claim.

[53]A. Earl Walker, *A History of Neurological Surgery*. Baltimore, Williams and Wilkins, 1951, p. 242.

the matter was self evident and "because torments inflicted on animals go against humane feeling if they serve to illustrate a matter that needs no explanation rather than the explanation of important things."[54]

The title of the second chapter maintained the thesis that "Tracheotomy may yet be undertaken for the removal of bodies which have been carried through the trachea as far as the lungs."[55] The case of a girl in whom a kidney bean had entered the lung gave rise to the question whether a foreign body could be removed through an opening by tracheotomy. In two cats, Merrem introduced a wax ball the size of a pea through a tracheotomy wound. The ball could be recovered through the aperture, and the wound healed.

Next in order comes the chapter on pylorectomy, while the fourth (concluding) chapter of the book deals with "The varying effect of the extracts of narcotics upon the eyes."[56] The experiments, in a dog and cat, were made in the hope of obtaining useful leads for the cure of blindness. The following drugs were instilled into the eye: extractum hyoscyami, extractum stramonii, extractum aconiti, extractum belladonnae, extractum cicutae, extractum opii, aqua Laurocerasi. The strong mydriatic effect which he obtained with extractum stramonii induced Merrem to try it on a patient (the nature of whose eye trouble is not quite clear) with some encouraging initial results.

Garrison thus appears right in classing Merrem among the early representatives of "physiological surgery."[57] From the preface of the *Animadversiones* we learn that Merrem had planned to use his research as part of his doctoral thesis. There were, however, as he says, some obstacles which made this impossible at the time.[58] Thus he was already a full-fledged doctor of medicine when the *Animadversiones* appeared.[59] Yet he was still conscious of his status as a beginner; he ends the preface with the wish not to appear to the reader "wholly unsuited to be admitted to the practice of surgery."[60] As the opening lines of the first chapter show, he has a very high opinion of the status of surgery in his days. "Surgery, in our times, has made such great progress as hardly any other science. Diseases, which once were hardly cured in the course of many years, are now cured perfectly in the space of a few days. Diseases once incurable are now, in some cases, removed within minutes."[61]

We may ascribe this statement to youthful enthusiasm—but I believe that

---

[54]*Animadversiones*, p. 15.

[55]*Animadversiones*, p. 19: "Tracheotomia pro eliciendis corporibus per tracheam ad pulmones usque delatis, adhuc institui potest."

[56]*Ibid.* p. 41: "Extractorum narcoticorum vis varia in oculos."

[57]Fielding H. Garrison, *An Introduction to the History of Medicine.* Fourth ed., Philadelphia, Saunders, 1929, p. 728.

[58]*Animadversiones*, p. 3. See above, footnote 29.

[59]The title page carries "Med. Doct." after his name. According to the obituary of 1859 (see ftn. 1) he was graduated on February 3, 1810.

[60]*Ibid.* p. 4.

[61]*Ibid.* p. 7.

it echoes a sentiment of the times. Strange as it may seem to us who are inclined to think of surgical progress as beginning with the discovery of inhalation anesthesia and antisepsis, surgeons before 1846 did not lack self assurance. In 1826, only sixteen years after Merrem, A. Lembert described the results of his experimental intestinal resections with subsequent enterorrhaphy by the suture named after him.

This operation (he wrote) is so simple in dogs that I have seen several of them begin to eat, digest, and defecate two days after the enterorrhaphy. Subsequent to the operation one noticed in these animals only a slight sadness and lack of appetite. But hardly had 48 hours passed when they regained their customary vivacity and vigor. Five dogs were operated upon, and all five survived.[62]

Anatomically and physiologically speaking, the fundamental technique of pylorectomy had thus been established some fifty years before its successful application in man. To be sure, it was not a planned project. As far as I can see, Lembert did not refer to Merrem or Michaelis.[63] Yet I believe it permissible to see a connection between the grasp of the idea of pylorectomy c. 1780 by Michaelis, its experimental pursuance by Merrem, and Lembert's experiments. The connection lies in the perspective which, as I have had occasion to point out elsewhere,[64] presents the history of modern surgery as a pace-maker of medical thought—especially with regard to "the anatomical idea." Seen in this perspective, some of the most daring surgical exploits of the time, e.g., Ephraim McDowell's ovariotomy of 1809, and the ligating of major arteries, do not appear quite the isolated deeds they are sometimes described. Such a view does not detract from the greatness of the individual surgeon. On the contrary, it adds to his stature by allowing us to distinguish between the professional self assurance of the time and the individual's insight and boldness to attempt the possible. With regard to pylorectomy, the situation was summed up somewhat quizzically by the surgeon Dieffenbach. Dieffenbach himself, as early as 1836, successfully used Lembert's suture in resection of the intestine in a case of incarcerated hernia.[65] Three years later, Amussat brought out his memoir on lumbar colostomy,[66] and in 1846 Sédillot proposed gastrostomy for artificial feeding. Writing in 1848, Dieffenbach said:

If a patient with incurable obstruction of the oesophagus cannot get any food down and if tubes for feeding him will not pass through, an incision should be made

[62]A. Lembert, "Mémoire sur l'entéroraphie, avec la description d'un procédé nouveau pour pratiquer cette opération chirurgicale," *Répertoire Général d'Anatomie et de Physiologie Pathologiques* etc. Paris 1826, 2: 100–07; see p. 106. For this and the following see V. Zachary Cope, *Pioneers in Acute Abdominal Surgery.* London, Oxford University Press, 1939.

[63]Jacob Wolff, *Die Lehre von der Krebskrankheit,* vol. 4, Jena, G. Fischer, 1928, p. 158, claimed that "Antoine L. Lembert [in the above article] richtete die Aufmerksamkeit der Chirurgen wieder auf Merrem's Versuche."

[64]Owsei Temkin, "The role of surgery in the rise of modern medical thought," *Bull. Hist. Med.,* 1951, 25: 248–59 [Essay 33].

[65]Dieffenbach, "Glückliche Heilung nach Ausschneidung eines Theiles des Darms und Netzes," *Wochenschrift für die gesammte Heilkunde,* 1836, pp. 401–13.

[66]J.-Z. Amussat, *Mémoire sur la possibilité d'établir un anus artificiel dans la région lombaire sans pénétrer dans le péritoine.* Paris, Germer Baillière, 1839.

through the abdominal wall, the stomach opened and the edges of the wound sewed to the external skin. Now if the same man were also suffering from an obstruction of the large bowel, so that the faeces could not pass out behind, and if according to Amussat the establishment of an artificial anus were indicated, then mouth and anus would be so close together that one might truly say human life is but a span!— In such operations, however, there is no salvation and they are no more practical than the ingenious Merrem's youthful dream of the diseased pylorus.[67]

Considering the circumstances, Dieffenbach's criticism of pylorectomy as a dream was probably justified. But the dream, or rather the vision, belonged to Michaelis, while Merrem had the ability to perform some difficult experiments where another man had failed and the insight to distinguish between positive results, theoretical possibilities, and doubtful applications. This contention is documented by the paragraph with which he concludes the chapter on pylorectomy:

From the doubts brought forward against the extirpation of the pylorus, from the arguments with which they may be answered, and from the additional observations, it appears quite clear that this operation which bears testimony to the very great ingenuity of its famous inventor, is undoubtedly the only means of removing this grave disease. And the operation is clearly not fraught with such great danger as to inspire the fear of death as a certain consequence, or such injury to the functions that the life to which a man is restored must forthwith be spent in sickness and misery. Indeed, the second experiment teaches both physiologists and physicians something most worthy of remembrance, viz. that an animal can live and feel well without a pylorus and its valve. The extirpation of the pylorus can, therefore, not be rejected entirely for anatomical and physiological reasons. At the same time, however, we are taught that the diagnosis is extremely doubtful. This fact, together with the condition of the patients and the effect to be expected from the extirpation of the pylorus, is such that a cautious physician can scarcely ever be audacious enough to have recourse to it.[68]

Far from being "youthful" (except in the biographical sense), Merrem's attitude was that of the practical man he proved himself to be by his subsequent career. Participating in the campaigns of the late Napoleonic wars he soon attained high administrative and teaching positions and died, in 1859, as a "Geheimrat" in Cologne.[69]

---

[67]Johann Friedrich Dieffenbach, *Die operative Chirurgie,* vol. 2, Leipzig, Brockhaus, p. 445 f. Dieffenbach, *ibid.* p. 443 says: "Von der Estirpation des Pylorus sagt der geistreiche Sprengel: Ein Traum von Merrem." F. Helfreich, "Geschichte der Chirurgie" in Neuburger-Pagel's *Handbuch der Geschichte der Medizin,* vol. 3, Jena, G. Fischer, 1905, p. 209, states that Merrem in 1780 (sic!) had first raised the question as to the possible removal of the diseased pylorus, but that his experiments on animals had been unsuccessful. He adds: "Schreger (1825) hatte diesen Gedanken als einen Traum bezeichnet." In the absence of more exact references, I have been unable to trace either of these two alleged sources. In his "Critical review of the state of medicine during the last ten years," Sprengel wrote: "D. K. J. Merrem's proposal to extirpate the pylorus in incurable indurations of it, shows how little the surgeon dreads the most difficult operations" (quoted from the English translation, *Edinburgh Medical and Surgical Journal,* 1816, *12*: 385–411; 1817, *13*: 137–65. See p. 153).

[68]Merrem, *Animadversiones,* p. 40 f.

[69]See articles cited above, footnote 1.

35

A Postscript
to "Merrem's Youthful
Dream"*

IN A PREVIOUS article,[1] I suggested that the idea of pylorectomy as a cure
for stenosis of the pylorus was conceived by Dr. Christian Friedrich
Michaelis (1754–1814), physician with the Hessian troops during the Revolutionary War and eventually professor of surgery at the University of
Marburg. I claimed that this idea had occurred to Michaelis while attending
his friend, Dr. Peter Middleton, and that it was Michaelis who subsequently
inspired his pupil, D. K. Th. Merrem, to perform the experiments on dogs
for which the latter is justly remembered.

There were, however, some gaps in the evidence for this thesis. In the
first place, it seemed puzzling that a Hessian army doctor should be the
friend of a notorious Tory who died in New York and also have connections
with Philadelphia and with men like Redman, Rush, Shippen, and Kuhn.[2]
Moreover, there was no proof that Michaelis actually had attended Dr.
Peter Middleton in his last and fatal sickness.

I have now found that the latter point is definitely attested to by Dr.
Middleton's will.[3] The abstract, printed in the *Collections* of the New York
Historical Society,[4] shows the testament as dated "this First day of
November, 1780."[5] A "Codicil," dated December 14, 1780, contains the
following passage:

And I leave mourning rings to Dr. [Jonathan] Mallet, and to Dr. Samuel Bard, and
to Dr. Michalis [!] and Dr. Bayley, for their kind attentions during my painful and
lingering illness.[6]

This makes it clear that Dr. Michaelis really was the "friend" of Dr.
Middleton to whom Merrem refers.[7] As to Dr. Michaelis' relationship to
Philadelphia, I had previously overlooked an article by Whitfield Bell, Jr.,[8]

---

*Bull. Hist. Med., 1960, vol. 34, pp. 74–75.
[1]Owsei Temkin, "Merrem's youthful dream; the early history of experimental pylorectomy," *Bull. Hist. Med.*, 1957, *31*: 29–43 [Essay 34].
[2]*Ibid.*, p. 34 f. [p. 501 f.].
[3]My attention was drawn to Middleton's will by the article in the *Dictionary of American
Biography*, Vol. 12, New York, Scribner's, 1933 pp. 602–03.
[4]The New York Historical Society, *Collections for the Year 1901*. New York: Printed for the
Society, 1902. The abstract of the will of Peter Middleton is to be found on pp. 20–22.
[5]*Ibid.*, p. 20.
[6]*Ibid.*, p. 21.
[7]Temkin, *op. cit.*, p. 33 f. [p. 501 f.].
[8]Whitfield J. Bell, Jr., "A box of old bones: a note on the identification of the mastodon,
1766–1896," *Proceedings of the American Philosophical Society*, 1949, *93*: 169–77.

which leaves no doubt about Dr. Michaelis' Philadelphia contacts. Michaelis is said to have approached General Washington as early as 1782 to obtain help for excavations in search of old bones.[9] At any rate, in 1783, Michaelis was in Philadelphia where he visited Dr. John Morgan who showed him his collection of mastodon bones.[10] It was his palaeontological work, I assume, which led to his subsequent election, on January 22, 1785, as a foreign member of the American Philosophical Society.[11]

Michaelis may be visualized as a German surgeon and scientist without deep personal involvement in the political events of the times. Thus he was able to befriend a Tory like Peter Middleton and to establish scientific contacts with men on the revolutionary side as soon as conditions permitted.

[9]*Ibid.*, p. 172.

[10]*Ibid.*, p. 171 ff.

[11]*Ibid.*, p. 172, ftn. 15; see also *Year Book 1958* of the American Philosophical Society Philadelphia, 1959, p. 99, where Chr. F. Michaelis is listed among the former foreign members.

36

Fernel, Joubert,
and Erastus on the Specificity
of Cathartic Drugs*

IN HIS ATTEMPT to prove the four humors, blood, phlegm, yellow bile, and black bile, to be the constituents of the human body, the author of the Hippocratic work *On the Nature of Man* referred to the action of cathartic drugs. Every one of the humors could be evacuated by a drug which by nature was closest to it, and, therefore, moved it first, just as seed drew from the earth what corresponded to its nature. If the purging was excessive, all humors would be evacuated one after another, until death ensued.[1] This notion was elaborated by Galen into the doctrine of specific cathartics which, "by similitude of the whole substance" attracted a specific humor.[2] Only in the cases of hypercatharsis would another mechanism come into play: the drug would irritate the body and thus cause discharge.[3]

As long as classical humoral pathology was basic to medicine, the doctrine of specific cathartics remained fundamental too. The existence of specific cathartics, though not accepted by all physicians at all times, yet represented something of a dogma in the sixteenth century, and certain drugs were well-known for their alleged specific action. Thus Antonius Ludovicus wrote: "For agaric purges phlegm, scammony carries off yellow bile, fidicula (?) moves and expels black bile, and from old times comes the tale of Proetus' mad daughters having been cured by hellebore."[4]

But the recognition of specific action did not necessarily imply acceptance of its explanation as attraction by similitude of the whole substance, which Galen himself had pleaded in analogy to the attraction of the magnet for iron. Among the dissenters, who yet did not leave the orthodox fold, at least three physicians of the sixteenth century were outstanding: Jean Fernel (1497–1558), Laurent Joubert (1529–83), and Thomas Erastus (1527–83). Their views on this topic will be reviewed in outline. Of the

---

*From *Science Medicine and Society in the Renaissance: Essays to Honor Walter Pagel*, ed. by Allen G. Debus, 2 vols., New York: Neale Watson Academic Publications (© Science History Publications 1972), 1972, vol. 1, pp. 61–68.

[1] Hippocrates, *On the Nature of Man*, ch. 6.

[2] Galen, *De simplicium medicamentorum temperamentis ac facultatibus*, book III, chapters 25–26, ed. Kühn, XI, Leipzig, 611–15, and book V, ch. 17, 760 f.

[3] *Ibid.*, book III, chs. 27–28, 615–18, also Galen, *On the Natural Faculties*, book III, ch. 13, The Loeb Classical Library, London, 1916, 300, where the relationship of specific attraction and irritation is less clear. Cf. Temkin, Owsei, "The classical roots of Glisson's doctrine of irritation, *Bull. Hist. Med.*, XXXVIII (1964), 310 [Essay 23, p. 301].

[4] Ludovicus, Antonius, *De occultis proprietatibus libri quinque*, Lisbon, 1540, book I, prooemium, fol. 3r. "agaricum enim pituitatem expurgat, scammonium flavam bilem excernit, fidicula atram movet et expellit, et veratro furentes Proeti filias sanatas iam olim proditum est."

three, Fernel stood closest to the traditional line.[5] He defended not only the existence of specific cathartics against those who had believed that their specificity was a function of their strength;[6] he also upheld similitude of substance as a cause. But this to him meant the specific form, that shibboleth of the Aristotelian scholastics. In detail, Fernel suggested the following mode of action.[7]

In contrast to the magnet which was active whenever in the vicinity of iron, a specific cathartic was activated during its digestion with the help of the internal heat.[8] While its substance remained in the stomach or intestines, the drug gave rise to an acrimonious vapor which, through invisible ducts, spread to all parts of the body and thus reached the noxious humor. By its acrimony, the vapor cut up the humor, and by its adverse quality it strongly stimulated (*stimulat*) the containing part and provoked (*proritat*) it to discharge. The local action of the vapor was supplemented by the attractive action on the part of the substance of the drug, so that the humor was forced to descend to the stomach. The double stimulus of drug and humor was more than the stomach could bear. "It throws out both with all its force, until it gets rid of them, and expels them through appropriate places."[9] Indeed, every cathartic drug, apart from its specific action, also possessed a purgative potency.[10]

Obviously, Fernel did not preserve the theory of specific attraction in its purity, but combined it with the theory of irritation originally reserved for hypercatharsis. Joubert and Erastus did away with attraction altogether, and Joubert replaced attraction, i.e. some form of sympathy between specific drug and specific humor, by antipathy between the two. The title of the "paradox" in which he expounded his theory clearly states his thesis: "Cathartic medicaments do not attract humors from our bodies, but rout and expel them. And they accomplish their work by antipathy rather than by sympathy. Most antidotes, which are falsely said to draw forth poisons, act in the same manner, nor is there anything capable of extracting splinters or other things stuck in the body."[11] We shall here limit ourselves to Joubert's discussion of cathartics.[12]

---

[5]Fernelius, Methodus medendi III, chs. 4–6, in *Universa medicina*, Paris, 1567, 390–94; also De abditis rerum causis, chs. 17–18, *ibid.*, 123–30.

[6]For this and the following cf. Methodus medendi, ch. 4; *Universa medicina*, 390–92.

[7]For the following cf. *ibid.*, ch. 6, 393–94.

[8]The attractive power of innate heat was discussed by Galen, *De simplicium*, book III, ch. 18, ed. Kühn, XI, 596.

[9]Fernelius, *Universa medicina*, 394; he also refers to Aristotle, *Problems*, I, 42, and adds a theory of expulsion through appropriate places, but into this we need not enter here.

[10]Fernelius explained that in *ibid.*, ch. 5, 392 f.

[11]Joubert, Laurent, *Laur. Iouberti Delphinatis, apud Monspelienses artis medicae professoris, Paradoxorum decas, prima atque altera*, Lyons, 1566. The second *Decas*, carries *Paradoxum IX* (493–514), with the following heading: "Medicamenta cathartica humores e corporibus nostris minime attrahere, sed potius fugare et expellere, atque *antipatheia* verius quam *sumpatheia* opus suum perficere: eodem modo et pleraque alexiteriorum, quae venena extrahere falso dicuntur: nec esse quae surculos, aliave corporibus infixa extrahere possint: Ad D. Hieronymum Chambonem, Medicum, et Philosophum perspicacissimum."

[12]Galen, *De simplicium*, book V, ch. 17, had linked cathartic drugs and protective ones (*alexeteria*).

Among the arguments Joubert, and Erastus after him, mustered against the attractive faculty of drugs was its alleged parallel to the attractive faculty of the living parts of the body, whereby they selected their appropriate food.[13] If this parallel were true, the drugs should exert attraction for their own benefit—which indeed would be hard to imagine. Drugs, Joubert maintained, held a middle position between the body (or its nourishment) and a poison. The closer they were to our own nature the weaker was their action, and the more distant they were from us the more harmful they were.

Joubert argued "that the expelling faculty was the cause of the removal of noxious things."[14] How then did purgative drugs assist expulsion? The answer was divided into five modes, according to the region of the body that was to be purged. First, there were the cathartics taken by mouth and acting upon the excrementitious humors deposited in the abdomen or constituting the refuse of the food. When the drug reached the stomach it drove the humors into the intestines. This action was performed by a vapor or a force otherwise communicated to the major branches of the vena portae in whose region the humors were assembled, but it was antipathy alone that was involved. Above all, recognition had to be given "to the discharging power of the parts, helped and excited by the medicament. While this power had formerly stayed asleep, it now joins forces with the medicament and, making a major effort, rises to expel the humor."[15]

The second mode concerned the action of enemas. Their fluid dissolves thick faeces and the drug contained in them may "titillate, may even torment the small openings of the mesenteric veins, so that the upper parts [of the body] are thereby irritated and, not long afterwards, belch forth and vomit, so to speak, the noxious humors (which they hold with difficulty) into the intestines, just as the stomach gives up what is contained in its fundus, when the upper part of the esophagus is provoked by a feather or by the finger."[16]

The third mode concerns the general purge of the whole body; in addition to the abdomen, the vena cava and the parts it reaches are now involved. Here Joubert admittedly follows Galen's *On the Natural Faculties*, book 3, ch. 13[17] and relies entirely on the irritation exercised by the drug on the discharging faculty. Once the belly has been emptied, a free place has been provided to which all parts begin to send their excrements. Yet this explanation meets with a major objection. Obviously, if a drug merely irritates, its action is no longer selective, i.e. specific. Joubert meets this objection by several arguments. Once Nature has been given some help (by

---

[13]The attractive faculty, as well as the expelling and retentive faculties (mentioned further below), belongs to the natural faculties with which, according to Galen, all parts of the body are endowed; cf. Temkin, *op. cit.*

[14]Joubert, *op. cit.*, 498.

[15]*Ibid.*, 500.

[16]*Loc. cit.*

[17]Joubert, *op. cit.*, 502.

emptying the intestinal tract), she is free to remove from the other parts of the body what most needs removal, i.e. the noxious humors. Besides, the antipathy of the drug to excrement in the lower belly also extends to the impurities in the blood above the liver.

This does not exhaust the subtle reasoning regarding this mode and the two remaining ones, which deal with the humors in the legs and in the most distal parts of the body respectively. But since nothing fundamentally new is added, it may be disregarded here, except for Joubert's explanatory remarks on action by antipathy. Though, on the whole, Joubert has relied much more on irritation of the expellent faculty, he makes a point of the contributory action of antipathy and appeals to the kind of innate extrasensory vision animals seem to possess. An infant must have an imaginative vision which directs it to move its lips to the breast, although it has no previous knowledge of the breast or of the milk. The grazing horse avoids a poisonous plant without even having tasted it. The newly hatched chick shudders at the flight of a hawk. Thus the living organism has a vision of the enmity between the drug and the humor, and this vision induces its discharging faculty to action.[18] Today, Joubert's innate vision would be called instinctive knowledge.

Compared with both Fernel and Joubert, Erastus' reasoning in his disputation of 1574, *On the Power of Purgative Medicines,* was more sober;[19] it had no place for either attraction or antipathy, and, though he admitted occult forces, he interpreted them in a way to be expected from this enemy of Paracelsus, of natural magic, and of astrology.[20] To Galen's dogma of the attractive faculty of drugs Erastus opposed his own thesis: "We, on the contrary, believe them to purge, because they are troublesome to Nature, either because of their quality or quantity, or their whole nature: and thus excite Her to expel whatever is fit to be purged."[21]

Erastus did not believe that the substantial form, which was destroyed during digestion, could be held responsible,[22] nor did he refer to similitude of substance, for this "was neither approved in time past by the learned, nor does it find a place with persons of some erudition today."[23] We are not capable of explaining exactly how the expelling force, when irritated, ejects

[18]*Ibid.* 507: "Ex his tandem perspicuum fieri arbitror, quorundam generum contrarias esse differentias, ex quibus inimicae species oriantur, quae licet contrariae species non habeantur, sunt tamen principia individuorum ad contrarias actiones perpetrandas. Iam eius generis differentiam aliquam inter *pharmakon* et humorem, formae animantis esse perspectam, utpote sibi connatam, quid obstat"?

[19]Erastus, Thomas, *De occultis pharmacorum potestatibus . . . Accessit huic tractatui disputatio alia eiusdem fere argumenti, De medicamentorum purgantium facultate, tribus absoluta quaestionibus, in qua tota prope horum pharmacorum natura declaratur,* Basel, 1574. Our analysis covers pp. 148–194.

[20]On Erastus cf. Thorndike, Lynn, *A History of Magic and Experimental Science,* V, New York, 1941, 652–67, especially 661–64, and Pagel, Walter, *Paracelsus, An Introduction to Philosophical Medicine in the Era of the Renaissance,* Basel—New York, 1958, 311 ff.

[21]Erastus, *op. cit.,* 148. A marginal note shortens this to: "Quae purgant ideo purgant, quia molestiam creant naturae."

[22]*Ibid.,* 151.

[23]*Ibid.,* 170.

the noxious humor from the body, but there are at least examples pointing to an explanation. Something mordant and pungent in our nose, capable of arousing the expelling force of the brain, makes us sneeze. Hiccup and vomiting are other possible examples.[24]

As long as no recourse was taken to selective attraction or to the specific form, Erastus was tolerant toward those who spoke of an occult force of cathartics.[25] His tolerance, it would seem, was prompted by the belief that these forces were *as yet* occult and might eventually be amenable to rational explanation.

However this may be, Erastus, as Joubert before him, had to explain how an irritating drug could lead to selective results. As long as the body was healthy, he thought, the retaining power of the parts did not desert its duty; its effort to retain what was useful was all the greater, the harder the expelling force was engaged in removing something. As a result "only the useless may be ejected while the useful is preserved."[26]

The literature of the sixteenth century on purgative drugs was large; Erastus himself recommended to his readers a book by Puteanus, physician in Grenoble.[27] Much of what Fernel, Joubert, and Erastus said had been said or hinted at before.[28] Yet their presentation is justified, because Fernel was the most influential clinical author of the period, and because Joubert's and Erastus' discussions were deemed important enough to be reported by Daniel Sennert (1572–1637),[29] who admitted: "Indeed there is probability in Erastus' arguments, and by means of them he even succeeded in making very learned physicians concur in his opinion."[30]

William Gilbert, for instance, the famous investigator of magnetism, wrote in the vein of Erastus, when he argued against the common assumption that the purging drugs attracted specific humors.[31] The vicious smells and vapors of such drugs by their badness "irritate the faculty of the sentient parts, and nature makes an effort to shake them off and to drive them

[24]*Loc. cit.*

[25]Erastus, *op. cit.*, 191 f.: "Quod si quis malit causam, cur alia medicamenta bilem flavam, alia nigram, alia pituitam alia aquam vel serum educere videantur, ad occultam potestatem referre, haud me praebebo difficilem, modo non adscribat potentiae per electionem tractrici;" similarly p. 183. As Pagel, *op. cit.* 312 f. has pointed out, Erastus "was not altogether opposed to the use of sound observation and reasoning. This is shown for example in his treatise on the 'Occult Virtues of Pharmaca'...."

[26]Erastus, *op. cit.*, 170: "ut sola inutilia ejiciantur, servatis utilibus."

[27]*Ibid.*, 184: "velim te legere, quae de hac ipsa re scripsit D. Guilielmus Puteanus Medicus Gratianopolitanus libro, de medicamentorum purgant. facult. 2. cap. penultimo: ubi multa recte monet huc spectantia." The title of the book is: *De medicamentorum quomodocunque purgantium facultatibus, nusquam antea neque dictis, neque per ordinem digestis libri duo*, Lyons, 1552.

[28]This will be considered in a history of irritability on which I am engaged.

[29]Sennert, Daniel, Institutiones medicinae, lib. V, pars 1, sect. 1, c. XI: "De purgantibus per alvum." In *Opera*, 1, Paris, 1641, 622–28; see 622.

[30]*Ibid.*, 622: "Et sane probabilia sunt argumenta Erasti, quibus etiam tantum effecit, ut doctissimos Medicos in suam sententiam pertraxerit."

[31]Gilbert, William, *Gulielmi Gilberti De mundo nostro sublunari philosophia nova. Opus posthumum ed. ex museio Gulielmi Boswelli*, Amsterdam, 1651 [facsimile reprint Menno Hertzberger]. Book 1, ch. 35: "De attractione a dolore." (99–106).

out."[32] Attraction had nothing to do with it. Since Gilbert, himself a physician, was acquainted with some of Erastus' medical work,[33] direct influence is not improbable.

It cannot be said that the notion of specific attraction by cathartics was supplanted by that of mere irritation at the beginning of the seventeenth century. Neither Fernel, nor Joubert, nor Erastus denied the alleged evacuation of specific humors; only their explanations differed. It seems that as long as the effect remained undoubted, the old explanation remained alive too. This, at least, is what Sennert's statement implies, which he added to his remarks on Erastus:

> But, though we do not deny that purging drugs are endowed with the power of stimulating the discharging faculty, we still cannot concede that this confluence [of the bad humor] takes place solely because the discharging faculty, irritated and provoked, expels what is useless. For if irritation alone were the cause, there would be no need to choose among the drugs. Different humors would not be evacuated by different drugs; rather any medicament could purge any humor, if only it provoked and stimulated nature to expel what is useless and molesting.[34]

The successful undermining of such beliefs needed a more radical attack, such as was to be offered by van Helmont.[35] The preceding discussion shows the rising divergence from traditional views, without a revolutionary upheaval. This divergence was part of a development which, via Harvey and van Helmont, culminated in Glisson's concept of biological irritability.

[32]Gilbert, "De attractione . . . ," 101. In *On the Magnet,* London, 1900, book II, chap. 2, 51, Gilbert says: "Concerning the action and potency of purgatives we shall speak elsewhere."

[33]*Ibid.,* 3: "Guilielmus Puteanus in his *Ratio Purgantium Medicamentorum* discusses the loadstone briefly and learnedly. Thomas Erastus, knowing little of magnetic nature, finds in the loadstone weak arguments against Paracelsus."

[34]Sennert, *op. cit.,* 622.

[35]Cf. Haeser, Heinrich, *Lehrbuch der Geschichte der Medicin,* 2. Bd., 3. Bearbeitung, Jena, 1881, 361. The passage (for which I am indebted to Dr. Pagel) is in van Helmont's De Febribus, ch. 5 (*Ortus medicinae,* ed. F. M. van Helmont, editio nova, Amsterdam, 1652, 755–58).

37

Therapeutic Trends
and the Treatment of Syphilis
before 1900*

In Memory of Max Neuburger†

AT ABOUT 1495, a disease became known which the army of the French king, Charles VIII, retreating from Italy, spread in other countries. Whether the *Mal de Naples, Malafranczos, Morbus Gallicus, French Pox* had existed in Europe long before, or whether it had recently been imported from America by the crew of Columbus, has not yet been decided. It seems certain, however, that in a relatively short time large numbers of people were infected, and that the contemporaries thought of the disease as epidemic.[1]

Whether old or new, the disease was recognized as a special entity. How, then, does one find a treatment for a new disease? It is most remarkable that almost as soon as we hear of syphilis we also hear of its treatment by mercury. Yet there is nothing mysterious about this coincidence. The old sources tell us how it happened. Mercury was used in ointments for scabies and leprosy long before the appearance or recognition of syphilis.[2] The new disease, too, manifested itself upon the skin, and what was more natural than to apply the same remedy? Treatment by analogy has no rational basis; Paracelsus already had remarked: "Should this be a reason for such treatment of the disease because the pox resembles leprosy more than fever?"[3] Yet I wonder how many treatments then and now have been tried because of some resemblance between two diseases. Potassium bromide was introduced into the treatment of epilepsy after its success in hysterical fits.[4] And the history of syphilis itself offers another example:

Bull. Hist. Med., 1955, vol. 29, pp. 309–16.
†This paper, read (in slightly different form) before the Johns Hopkins Medical History Club, December 17, 1947, had been intended for publication in the Festschrift in honor of Professor Max Neuburger's eightieth birthday.
[1] Hans Haustein, Die Frühgeschichte der Syphilis 1495–1498. *Archiv für Dermatologie und Syphilis*, 1930, vol. 161, pp. 255–388, has adduced good evidence that syphilis, in the early years really spread in epidemic proportions.
[2] Cf. Karl Sudhoff, *Aus der Frühgeschichte der Syphilis*, Leipzig, Barth, 1912 [Studien zur Geschichte der Medizin, 9] pp. 55 and 120.
[3] Paracelsus, Von der französischen Krankheit drei Bücher, *Medizinische, naturwissensch. u. philosophische Schriften*, ed. Sudhoff, vol. 7, München, 1923, p. 76.
[4] Cf. Owsei Temkin, *The falling sickness*, Baltimore, The Johns Hopkins Press, 1945, p. 286.

potassium iodide came into use after it had been applied to goiter and scrofula.[5]

A remedy may have many degrees of usefulness. Some suppress or alleviate symptoms; others are expected to eradicate the disease. We are very much conscious of these distinctions which, for instance, play such a great role in the discussions of malaria therapy. In former centuries, this distinction was not as sharply drawn. Disappearance of symptoms was often taken for a cure. We must not forget that thinking in long-range terms is a habit which even scientists have acquired relatively late. In the eighteenth century a man could be pronounced cured of syphilis according to the ruling by Boerhaave, the greatest clinician of that century: "If anyone is cured of the disease, and remains free for a week or fortnight, and is nevertheless doubtful whether he is well or not... let him take the most stimulating medicines, and then if anything remains, it will immediately show itself; and if nothing appears, there is the greater reason to believe the patient is cured."[6]

Here it has to be added that our knowledge of the effectiveness of a treatment depends on our knowledge of the disease itself. We should make a serious mistake if we forgot how uncertain the diagnosis even of well recognized disease entities was in former centuries. Tabes and general paresis, for instance, were not definitely connected with syphilis before the late nineteenth century. Before that time, then, anti-syphilitic treatment, to be approved, did not have to prevent the occurrence of these late forms. Or, to take another example, Ricord, the greatest syphilologist of the nineteenth century, who finally separated gonorrhoea from syphilis, in 1851 firmly believed in the abortive cure of syphilis by cauterization or excision of the chancre. He only stipulated that this must be done not later than five days after infection.[7] This suggests that Ricord did not yet differentiate between syphilitic chancre and chancroid,[8] and that the treatment seemed to be effective where in reality the patient had never suffered from the disease. On the other hand, since the diagnosis of so many diseases was difficult, the suspicion of syphilis was ever present as a *refugium ignorantiae*.

Under these circumstances, the question as to the most effective and radical form of treatment was bound to remain open to widely different answers and no consensus was reached whether syphilis was curable at all. In the early sixteenth century Vigo doubted the curability of an infection that had passed beyond the early symptoms.[9] These doubts were soon

[5]Cf. Jules Rochard, *Histoire de la chirurgie française au XIXᵉ siècle*, Paris, 1875, p. 127 f.

[6]*Boerhaave's academical lectures on the lues venerea*, transl. Jonathan Wathen, London, 1763, p. 42 f.

[7]Ph. Ricord, *Lettres sur la syphilis*, Paris, 1851, p. 180.

[8]Cf. Alfred Fournier, *Traitement de la syphilis*, Paris, 1893, p. 53.

[9]Joannes de Vigo, *Pars prima practicae copiosae dictae*, lib. V, c. 3; 1521, fol. 184 v. Cf. also Proksch (see note 20) p. 45.

transferred to the therapeutic power of mercury. In the late fifteenth and early sixteenth centuries the mercurial treatment of syphilis usually was very intensive, extending over periods from about five to thirty and more days. During this time the patient was kept in an extremely hot room, carefully secured from any fresh air. The inunction was performed close to an open fire once or several times daily, and the patient was made to sweat copiously afterwards. If a relapse occurred, the treatment was repeated. In the case of the famous humanist, Ulrich von Hutten, eleven such cures were performed in nine years. But they did not free Hutton from his crippling tertiary osseous lesions, nor were other remedies like arsenic and vitriol of any avail.[10] Then, in 1518,[11] he was persuaded to undergo a cure with guaiacum, the wood from the West Indies that was being imported by the firm of the Fuggers and was just then much talked about and publicized by the doctors Poll and Schmaus. The new remedy had a marvellous effect upon Hutten, and in 1519 appeared his poem in praise of the wood. Hutten's book exerted a great influence. Paracelsus in 1529 stated that "the first clamor about the wood was raised by an inexperienced and worldly man in Germany with no other ascendent in him than having his mouth resound with the latest craze. This man has been the schoolteacher and professor of the doctors and masters. What good he taught them, can daily be heard from the sick."[12] But in his criticism of contemporary therapy of syphilis, Paracelsus was far ahead of his time. Hutten had proclaimed his cure prematurely; only a few years after the publication he died of syphilis. This was ignored; the earlier claim lived on. No less a doctor than Jean Fernel copied long passages extolling guaiacum over mercury. Mercury, Fernel contended, cured the disease in few people, and then only in those who were strong and where the evil was in its very beginning.[13] Fernel, and many physicians of the sixteenth century, replaced mercury altogether by guaiacum. But even where no such radicalism prevailed, guaiacum, sarsaparilla and other "sudorific woods" remained in use because something more than mercury was needed, especially in tertiary syphilis.[14] I have the impression that the popularization of potassium iodide through Wallace and Ricord since 1836 made these decoctions fade into near oblivion. However, the question of the curability of syphilis was not solved. When Fournier, in 1893, published his work on the treatment of syphilis, the toxic effects of mercury were well known and avoided as far as possible. Treatment by mercury and iodide took the form of well regulated and repeated courses. But what answer had Fournier to give to a patient who finally

[10]Cf. Ernest L. Zimmermann, The French Pox of that great clerke of Almayne, Ulrich Hutten, Knyght, *Janus*, 1932, vol. 36, p. 248.

[11]Cf. Zimmermann, *loc. cit.*, p. 249.

[12]Paracelsus, Vom Holz Guajaco gründlicher Heilung (ed. Sudhoff, vol. 7, A II, verso); cf. also Georg Sticker, Entwickelungsgeschichte der spezifischen Therapie, *Janus*, 1929, vol. 33, p. 229.

[13]Jean Fernel, *Le meilleur traitement du mal vénérien*, transl. L. Le Pileur, Paris, 1879, p. 88.

[14]Cf. Boerhaave, *op. cit.*, pp. 317 and 345.

asked him whether he was absolutely cured? Couched in more encouraging words, the answer essentially followed Ricord's dictum: "There is neither a dose nor a pharmaceutic form, nor any length of treatment which confers immunity with certainty, which carries the guarantee of the complete, absolute and radical extinction of the pox." [15]

I have tried, so far, to emphasize the role of empirical factors in our treatment of disease: knowledge of the disease itself, knowledge of the therapeutic and toxic effects of the drugs in man. But, however large a place we may allow to non-prejudiced clinical observation and accumulating experience, we shall hardly believe that these alone mould our concepts of treatment. Down to the eighteenth century, for instance, physicians quite generally believed in the occult powers of human blood, and of animal excrements. Then in the course of a few decades, much too short for experimental trial, most of this was relegated to superstition because the philosophy of the Enlightenment did not admit the occult. We cannot always establish direct connections between the particular treatment of a disease and philosophical movements. Yet in between the two we have theory which links detailed facts and general ideas. And the concept of treatment and the pathological theories of the time are quite definitely interdependent. During the Renaissance and long afterwards, pathology rested on the theory of the humors which had become deranged in sickness and had to be purged by bleeding, cathartics, and emetics. Nature in her attempts to free the body from the morbific matter tried to eliminate it through the urine, feces, sweat, or through pustules, abscesses, ulcers, and other discharges and cutaneous eruptions. In many ways this theory influenced the treatment of cutaneous and venereal diseases. The venereal poison, having entered the body, was compelled towards its exterior. Fortunate those in whom it was discharged in form of a gonorrhoea, for they might escape the true lues! This discharge should not be prevented by astringent remedies, since the poison would, thereby, be prevented from leaving the body altogether. I do not believe that the humoral theory was chiefly responsible for the doctrine that gonorrhoea and syphilis were due to the same cause. Rather their common characteristic of venereal diseases and, possibly, the occurrence of mixed infections engendered this confusion. But the humoral theory encouraged it, and the same theory exerted, moreover, a profound influence upon the therapy of syphilis since it regarded an elimination of the morbid humors through salivation or sweating as essential for the cure. Fracastoro, who in his poem of 1530 coined the name syphilis, wrote: "You will see the excrements of the evil continuously flow through the mouth in unclean spittle." [16] And for about 200 years or more, to treat syphilis by mercury or "to salivate" became synonymous expressions. There were those who, like Sydenham, insisted upon a dis-

[15]Fournier, *op. cit.*, p. 587.
[16]Fracastoro, Syphilidis lib. II; *Opera omnia*, sec. ed. Venetiis, 1574, fol. 180 r.

charge of "about four pints in the twenty-four hours" until the symptoms had disappeared.[17] Boerhaave advised a similar amount of salivation and, since he stands between the older humoral pathology and the more recent solidary one, his theory of the proper treatment of syphilis deserves some notice. According to Boerhaave, the disorder resides in the fat and bone marrow, which, therefore, must be dissolved.[18] This aim he tried to achieve by emaciation, i.e. by putting the patient on a starvation diet, by purgatives, by sudorifics (guaiacum) or by salivation. He calculated that a minimum of twenty-eight to thirty days of salivation would produce 112 pounds Troy of spittle, and assuming one half of our humors to be oil "it is evident the whole fat must have been dissolved and expelled; and that if a very corpulent man was to be thus cured, not the least vestige of his fat would remain."[19]

In course of the eighteenth and nineteenth centuries, the humoral pathology gave way to a solidary one which located diseases in organs, tissues and finally cells. This change in pathology was also accompanied by changes in medical treatment. For one thing, I believe that the spread of a milder mercurial treatment without salivation, the so-called Montpellier method,[20] was facilitated as soon as physicians did not expect to see the discharge of the vicious humors. Besides, a solidary pathology is much more likely to consider disease as localized in certain parts without affecting the whole body. John Hunter as well as Ricord and others considered the syphilitic chancre as a localized disease which if extirpated might not spread over the body. Then with the advance of bacteriology this view gained renewed impetus. Though the causative agent of syphilis was not known, it was postulated by analogy with the bacteria found in other infectious diseases. The question of an abortive treatment merely consisted in finding the best way of preventing the syphilitic virus from wandering into the regions next to the colony it had first formed.[21]

In many cases it is easy to see how theory was responsible for a therapeutic concept and how the two changed together. Yet I do not believe that it is always possible to tell what accounted for a trend: theory or experience. I should like to mention one example, if only in order to pose a question. Reading the early literature on syphilis, I have become impressed by the emphasis placed on heat and sweating, be it in course of the mercurial treatment, be it in course of the guaiacum cure. I wonder all the more whether this treatment was in the direction of the modern idea of hyperpyrexia, since in Boerhaave I also read the following passage: "In the history of cures, it is evident that this contagion was never removed, except by a fever, by mercury, by antivenereal decoctions, or violent sudorifics."[22]

[17]*The works of Thomas Sydenham*, transl. by R. G. Latham, vol. 2, p. 44, London, Sydenham Society, 1850.
[18]Boerhaave, *op. cit.*, p. 305.
[19]*Ibid.*, p. 341.
[20]Cf. J. K. Proksch, *Die Geschichte der venerischen Krankheiten*, 2. Theil, Bonn, 1895, p. 381.
[21]Cf. Fournier, *op. cit.*, p. 45 f.
[22]Boerhaave, *op. cit.*, p. 43.

At any rate Boerhaave believed that something like a fever arose during the sweating procedure[23] and I wonder whether he and the empirics before him had been on the right track or whether they had just been carried away by mere fancy.

There is still another aspect of the relationship between empiricism and theory, which the early history of syphilotherapy also helps to illustrate. Mercury, as was said before, owed its introduction to the empirical discovery that it was helpful in syphilis just as it had been helpful in some diseases of the skin. Some early prescriptions are recipes against the French Pox with little or no attempt at individualization. As early as 1497 Leoniceno in Ferrara held forth just against this very procedure. "Let doctors beware, lest after the fashion of a bad cobbler who tries to fit everybody with the same shoe, they also endeavour to cure the French disease in everybody with the same medicine."[24] This warning revealed two different attitudes, often represented by two professions. The barbers, pox doctors and low surgeons declared mercury an antidote, or specific as we should say, against syphilis, and contented that it *had* to be used since the disease would not yield to anything else. The learned physicians, on the other hand, whether they used mercury or not, insisted that each case had to be considered individually and that only a doctor who could judge the temperament of his patient really knew how to manage the case on a rational basis. For the one the remedy was everything, for the other it was but a good or bad instrument. If formulated generally and without restriction to syphilis, this problem is not without interest today. I have the impression that our treatment of infectious diseases has become more standardized than that of organic and functional disease because in the first category we have had to deal with masses of people rather than individuals. In the prevention or treatment of epidemics or crippling endemics, the general denominator, i.e., the disease, is of greater importance than the individual variations which in cases of essential hypertension or of neurosis may mean everything.

Most of us, when engaged in the solution of a problem, have the feeling that the value of the work of our predecessors depends on their good or bad observation, collection of sufficient data, right or false reasoning and similar factors inherent in the method of the science in which we are engaged. I have just now touched upon the possibility that concepts of medical treatment may have been influenced by extraneous factors. Of this I wish to give a few more examples. I may start with a very crude one of the influence of economic motives. In the sixteenth century Hutten mentions a doctor who originally stood rather aloof from guaiacum, but when he saw

---

[23]Cf. *ibid.*, p. 317. The word "fever" which occurs in the English translation at my disposal should not be taken in its modern connotation as used in the expression "fever therapy."

[24]Nicolaus Leonicenus, Libellus de epidemia, quam vulgo morbum gallicum vocant, in: Karl Sudhoff, *The earliest printed literature on syphilis* (adapted by Charles Singer), Florence; Lier, 1925, p. 172. The context indicates that Leoniceno probably has treatment by mercurial inunction in mind.

how well it sold, he quickly changed his attitude and arrogated to himself the right of prescribing it.[25] It has also been stated by medical historians that the whole story of the American origin of syphilis was used—if not invented—to bolster the sale of guaiacum, the wood that was imported from America. There may be a grain of truth in this last story, but I doubt its significance for shaping a long term trend. Nevertheless, I believe that the therapeutic controversy of the sixteenth century had its social background. Mercury, as indicated, was used by the surgeons who traditionally had to deal with injuries and external diseases. Even much later, when medicine and surgery had ceased to be different professions, this medieval heritage in continental Europe accounted for grouping skin and venereal diseases together into the same specialty, with the result that the visceral and nervous manifestations of syphilis were relegated to medicine and psychiatry. Even in modern times this dichotomy may not have been without influence upon the therapeutic point of view. But 400 years ago the cleavage was socially significant. The barber-surgeon treated the common man; whereas the doctor of medicine had his main clientele among the rich and the nobility. These two social strata had a somewhat different point of view towards venereal diseases. The common people accepted the terror of the mercurial cure as a punishment for their sins. The nobility were less inclined to seek moral improvement from their physicians and preferred a treatment that was less severe.[26]

At a first glimpse such a motivation may seem far-fetched. But I think that Paracelsus' books on guaiacum and on syphilis will convince everybody of the powerful religious motives exerted even upon details of therapy. Nor do I believe that the influence of religious and moral ideas was limited to the sixteenth century. Whoever reads the "History of Venereal Diseases" by Proksch will notice the fact that the author praises the replacement of salivation by less severe treatments from the eighteenth century on as a victory of humaneness. We may well ask whether the humaneness of a treatment has any more to do with its effectiveness in purely scientific terms than has the question of sin and penitence. Probably not. But neither as scientists nor physicians can we live outside the world of culture and morality. Medical therapy as a branch of our civilization necessarily is sensitive to all concepts which make up this civilization. This sensitivity goes far beyond mere legal matters and etiquette. It permeates our thoughts, and if we do not realize this, then history can make us conscious of it.

[25]Cf. Zimmerman, *op. cit.*, p. 278.
[26]Cf. O. Temkin, Zur Geschichte von Moral und Syphilis, *Archiv für Geschichte der Medizin*, 1927, vol. 19, pp. 335–37 [Essay 32].

Index

THE JOHNS HOPKINS UNIVERSITY PRESS

This book was composed in Baskerville type
by the Composing Room of Michigan, from a design
by Susan Bishop. It was printed on 50-lb. Warren 66
paper and bound in Joanna Arrestox cloth
by Universal Lithographers, Inc.

LIBRARY OF CONGRESS CATALOGING IN PUBLICATION DATA

Temkin, Owsei, 1902–
    The double face of Janus and other essays in the
history of medicine.

    Includes bibliographical references and index.
    1. Medicine—History—Collected works. I. Title.
[DNLM: 1. History of medicine—Essays. WZ9 T279d]
R131.T4 610'.9 76–47380
ISBN 0–8018–1859–1